third edition

Administrative and Clinical Procedures for the Canadian Health Professional

third edition

Administrative and Clinical Procedures for the Canadian Health Professional

valerie d. thompson

Conestoga Institute of Technology and Advanced Learning

Pearson Canada
Toronto

Vice-President, Editorial Director: Gary Bennett
Acquisitions Editor: Don Thompson
Marketing Manager: Jenna Wulff
Supervising Developmental Editor: Madhu Ranadive
Developmental Editor: Allison McDonald
Project Manager: Ashley Patterson
Production Editor: Katie Ostler (Element)
Copy Editor: Lesley Saffrey
Proofreader: Jennifer McIntyre
Compositor: Element
Photo Researcher: Kerri Wilson
Permissions Researcher: Tom Wilcox
Manufacturing Specialist: Jane Schell
Art Director: Julia Hall
Cover and Interior Designer: Miguel Acevedo
Cover Image: George Doyle/Getty Images

Credits and acknowledgments for material borrowed from other sources and reproduced, with permission, in this textbook appear on the appropriate page within the text on page 648.

If you purchased this book outside the United States or Canada, you should be aware that it has been imported without the approval of the publisher or the author.

Library and Archives Canada Cataloguing in Publication

Thompson, Valerie D., 1948–
Administrative and clinical procedures for the Canadian health professional / Valerie D. Thompson.—[3rd ed.]

First ed. published under title: Administrative and clinical procedures for the health office professional
Includes bibliographical references and index.
ISBN 978-0-13-289255-1

1. Medical offices—Canada—Management—Textbooks.   2. Medical assistants—Canada.   I. Title.

R728.8.T53 2013   651'.961   C2012-905434-8

10 9 8 7 6 5 4 3

ISBN 978-0-13-289255-1

To my husband, Doug, whose continued medical advice has been invaluable. To the memory of Samantha Scully, without whom this book would not have been possible. Her enthusiasm and invaluable support, and the confidence she had in me during the initial writing, will be forever remembered and treasured. To Pearson Education Canada, for providing me with unwavering direction and support in preparing this edition.

Contents

Preface

The health-care system in Canada is close to the hearts of all Canadians. It has undergone tremendous changes in the last decade and continues to face numerous challenges. The very principles of health care as outlined in the *Canada Health Act* are in question. Although the principles appear ideal, problems exist, compounded by the demands of delivering high-quality, comprehensive, cost-effective health care in the 21st century. Over the past five years the federal and provincial governments have strategized to improve the accessibility to and quality of health care available to Canadians with some degree of success. The long waiting lists for surgery and diagnostic tests have been reduced, but waits for access to many procedures still exist. The number of doctors in Canada, particularly family physicians, has increased, but there are still millions of Canadians without a family doctor. Nurse practitioners and a team approach to primary care have been adopted in most jurisdictions, which has improved access. Still, there are increasing demands being placed on our health-care system, one of which is addressing the needs of an aging population. Still, Canadians in general are proud of the health-care system we call "medicare" and overwhelmingly want to preserve it.

More and more responsibility has been transferred to administrative professionals in all sectors of health care. Doctors' offices, hospitals, and other health-care facilities need skilled and knowledgeable graduates from postsecondary health administration programs who are prepared to meet the challenges offered in this dynamic field. This book will help health professionals in all sectors of health administration meet these challenges. The third edition of this book, *Administrative and Clinical Procedures for the Canadian Health Professional*, continues to fill the void for a comprehensive and current resource that deals with the complexities of the Canadian health-care system, including the unique and diverse entities of provincial/territorial billing and primary care reform.

Administrative and Clinical Procedures for the Canadian Health Professional is designed for use in Canadian postsecondary schools, such as community and private colleges, as well as for health offices, hospitals, and other health-care facilities for related in-service programs. It can also be used as a resource text by persons employed in health administration.

ABOUT THE BOOK

This book is divided into five parts. Part I introduces the reader to the concept, roles, and responsibilities of the health professional. It provides an overview of the characteristics, practices, and skills that combine to contribute to the student's success and professional development in health administration.

Part II, Health in Context, looks at health and the individual, health and culture, and health in the context of the Canadian health-care system. These chapters combine to explain how health affects individuals in a multicultural society as they interface with the Canadian health-care system. Chapter 2 discusses how illness can alter the communication and response of clients, their families, and loved ones in the face of illness. It provides the student with both insight into and strategies for dealing effectively with clients and their families in sickness and in health. It stresses that response to illness is both individual and varied and emphasizes the need for patience, empathy, and understanding. The chapter updates and expands on current health issues, including discussions on leading causes of death; obesity and diabetes; and the movement in Canadian schools to remove unhealthy foods from cafeterias.

Chapter 3 is not intended to replace any courses that students may take on culture and health; it does provide the student with a cursory knowledge of how culture can affect a person's health beliefs, practices, understanding, and compliance with treatment modalities. Basic strategies for communicating effectively in a multicultural society are discussed. Respect for different beliefs and practices and suggestions for "bridging the gap" between these beliefs and practices, and traditional Western approaches to health, illness, diagnosis, and treatment are introduced. The chapter has been further updated with a new section on ageism. Chapter 4 focuses on the principles and practices of the Canadian health-care system. It provides the student with an understanding of the structure and function of health care in Canada. This chapter discusses the increasing role of the consumer in health care, and explains the move to a more team-oriented approach to care as a result of primary care reform initiatives, with a focus on the implications of these changes for the health professional. For this edition, recent changes to primary care in several provinces are investigated.

Part III, Health-Care Basics, provides an overview of the knowledge essential for the Canadian health office professional in all health-care settings. Chapter 5 addresses the essential standards and safety in the health-care setting. Emphasis is placed on quality assurance, the concept of asepsis, standard precautions, and infection control. This is increasingly important with the current challenges facing health providers; for example, the rise in the numbers and variety of nosocomial infections such as VRE, MRSA, and C. *difficile*. Strategies for preventing injury to clients in various age groups and with disabilities in the health office are also highlighted. The chapter also updates the vaccination protocols for specific provinces. Chapter 6 is designed to provide students with information about laboratory and diagnostic tests levelled to their need, role function responsibilities, and scope of practice. This includes basic health teaching information and information on the administrative responsibilities related to filling out requisitions and booking tests for clients in both office and hospital settings. The increased use of electronic requisitions is highlighted in this chapter.

Chapter 7 deals with current trends in pharmacology and provides up-to-date information about the most frequently prescribed medications. As well, this chapter discusses the role of the health professional in client education, handling requests for prescription refills, handling and safely storing drugs in the health office, drugs and the law, and how to effectively communicate with members of the pharmacy team. Tips for recognizing drug-seeking behaviour in clients are included. This edition places more emphasis on electronic prescriptions and how they are initiated and kept secure.

Part IV, Office Procedures, examines the basic administrative needs of the health office: communications, scheduling appointments, provincial/territorial billing, and maintenance of the medical record. Chapter 8 addresses techniques and strategies to promote effective communication skills ranging from telephone triage and interacting with clients in person, to techniques for effective inter-professional communication. A new section on human relations within the workplace setting rounds out the discussion on effective communication skills. Strategies for the proper use and management of email are included. Chapter 9 emphasizes the increasing use of medical software in the computerized office environment, particularly as it pertains to new scheduling procedures, including an expansion of the section on triage. Chapter 10 summarizes the concept of insured services in

Canada. This chapter includes recent changes in regulations affecting health-care plans and policies across the country. The chapter reflects a national focus, reviewing generic insured physician and hospital services in Canada, the use of billing codes, interprovincial/territorial billing through the Reciprocal Agreement, and private insurance. Chapter 11 provides the student with an overview of provincial/territorial health coverage, and explains the principles of provincial/territorial billing and billing for primary care organizations. The material presented in this chapter is general in nature, stressing elements that are common across the country; for example, claims review and health-card validation.

Chapter 12 discusses the actual process of claims submission and the technologies available to facilitate it, as well as outlining approaches to billing payers other than provincial/territorial health plans. Chapter 13 focuses on health information management with a focus on electronic medical records and electronic health records. It explains the data entry capabilities of an EMR/EHR system and includes detailed information on the role of the health professional in the conversion process from paper charts to the electronic format. EMR/EHR is updated to include details about how to use them effectively and how the system is evolving.

Part V, Hospital Procedures, addresses the needs of graduates from postgraduate programs in health office administration seeking employment in the hospital setting. It focuses on the skills required for employment (primarily as a clinical secretary) within the hospital. Chapters 14 and 15 introduce the student to the hospital setting, discussing a range of topics including the structure and function of hospital departments, hospital charts and documents (in both the computerized and non-computerized environments), and the roles and responsibilities of various health professionals found in the hospital setting.

In many parts of Canada, transcribing doctors' orders (order entry) is a complex responsibility that the clinical secretary (or ward clerk/communications coordinator) has assumed. Chapters 16 to 21 explain the order entry process and other responsibilities of the clinical secretary, including orders related to patient entry, IV therapy, nutrition, digestion, respiration, and patient rest and activity. This section of the book reflects the increasing use of a variety of computerized modules in the order entry process. That aside, many hospitals across Canada are still adapting to a computerized environment; even within facilities, some units are more prone to using paper-based charts than others. Therefore, the order entry process as covered in Part V also explains the administrative process for order entry in the manual environment for selected procedures. The overview of Vital Signs included in the appendix has been removed, but will be available in the Instructor's Manual.

LEARNING FEATURES

The following features of this book aim to help students understand, apply, and retain core concepts and ideas:

- **Learning Objectives.** Each chapter begins with a list of learning objectives related to key concepts contained within the chapter.
- **Illustrations, Figures, and Charts.** Each chapter contains illustrations, figures, and charts to supplement related text.
- **Key Terms.** Key terms are highlighted in the text and defined in the margins for quick reference. These terms and definitions are also consolidated in a glossary at the end of the book.

- **Websites of Interest.** For further exploration of chapter topics, we have identified pertinent websites at the end of each chapter.
- **Chapter Summaries.** At the end of each chapter, key points from the chapter are summarized.
- **Future Trends.** At the end of each chapter, a new feature entitled Future Trends summarizes developing technologies, practices, and innovations that relate to specific chapter content.
- **Review Questions.** At the end of each chapter, you will find extensive questions designed to review the content of that chapter.
- **Application Exercises.** End-of-chapter application exercises assist the student to apply skills and knowledge learned in the chapter either through group discussion or independent activities.

Supplements

The following instructor supplements are available for downloading from a password-protected section of Pearson Education Canada's online catalogue (www.pearsoned.ca/highered). Navigate to your book's catalogue page to view a list of those supplements that are available. See your local sales representative for details and access.

Instructor's Manual (0133219691)
The Instructor's Manual offers guidance to instructors using the text, including teaching suggestions, solutions to end-of-chapter problems and exercises, and chapter test questions.

Power Point Slides (0133129659)
The PowerPoint slides are new to this edition. They provide a comprehensive selection of slides highlighting key concepts featured in the text to assist instructors.

CourseSmart for Instructors (ISBN 0133129667)

CourseSmart goes beyond traditional expectations—providing instant, online access to the textbooks and course materials you need at a lower cost for students. And even as students save money, you can save time and hassle with a digital eTextbook that allows you to search for the most relevant content at the very moment you need it. Whether it's evaluating textbooks or creating lecture notes to help students with difficult concepts, CourseSmart can make life a little easier. See how when you visit **www.coursesmart.com/instructors**.

CourseSmart for Students (ISBN 0133129667)

CourseSmart goes beyond traditional expectations—providing instant, online access to the textbooks and course materials you need at an average savings of 60%. With instant access from any computer and the ability to search your text, you'll find the content you need quickly, no matter where you are. And with online tools like highlighting and note-taking, you can save time and study efficiently. See all the benefits at **www.coursesmart.com/students**.

Technology Specialists

Pearson's Technology Specialists work with faculty and campus course designers to ensure that Pearson technology products, assessment tools, and online course materials are tailored to meet your specific needs. This highly qualified team is dedicated to helping schools take full advantage of a wide range of educational resources, by assisting in the integration of a variety of instructional materials and media formats. Your local Pearson Education sales representative can provide you with more details on this service program.

Pearson Custom Library

For enrolments of at least 25 students, you can create your own textbook by choosing the chapters that best suit your own course needs. To begin building your custom text, visit www.pearsoncustomlibrary.com. You may also work with a dedicated Pearson Custom editor to create your ideal text—publishing your own original content or mixing and matching Pearson content. Contact your local Pearson Representative to get started.

ACKNOWLEDGMENTS

Publication of a textbook is a collective effort, and this text is no exception. I would like to acknowledge those who have contributed along the way.

I am grateful to Susan D. Milne, BA, MA, Plain Language Consultant, who contributed a section to Chapter 8. A debt of gratitude is owed to Joanne Polkiewicz, Pharmacist, for her continuous support. Joanne has done a substantive review of Chapter 7 (Pharmacology) for each edition of this text. Her valuable suggestions for improvement and updates are very much appreciated. Thanks also to Janice Hong, M.O.A., clinical secretary at Women's College Hospital in Toronto and Cambridge Memorial Hospital in Cambridge, Ontario, for her valuable contributions to Chapters 14 to 21.

Thanks to Marnie Fletcher, BA CCHRA(C), Director of Health Information Services at St. Joseph's Healthcare, Hamilton, who contributed significantly to the initial content preparation and organization of Chapter 13. This chapter has been kept current and relevant with the assistance of Gail F. Crook, CHE, CHIM CEO and Registrar, CHIMA. Thank you, Gail, for your expert assistance and guidance.

Thank you to Brenda Moffatt, CDAII, CDR, ATM(S), who worked tirelessly to provide me with the information related to administrative management in the dental office. Special thanks to Sherry Czekus for validating information in Part V, and designing the PI screen used in that section. I am grateful also to Jennifer Purych, Instructor for the Nursing Unit Clerk Program, Vancouver Community College, British Columbia, for taking me on a guided tour of various hospitals in B.C., and to Rachel Mann, Maxine Lloyd, and Betty Furtad for updating me on the scope of practice of clinical coordinators in that province. I am also indebted to Heather Geerdink, President of the Medical Office Assistant Association of British Columbia, for the assistance she provided to me with respect to medical billing in that province. Linda A. Smith, PID, AED, M.Ed. Instructor, HealthCare Communications Mgt. Dept., Vancouver Community College, and Paula Castling, HealthCare Communications Management Professor, Nursing Unit Clerk—thanks for your valuable advice regarding the role and responsibilities of the unit clerk in British Columbia.

Finally, thanks to P&P Data Systems, especially Jo Tadros, Executive Assistant to the president and CEO, who spent significant time organizing and preparing screen captures for print, and to Moshe Pinas, President, CEO for his time and technical assistance, and for allowing us to use P&P screen captures in this edition.

The comments and suggestions by the following instructors who reviewed the manuscript prior to publication were invaluable:

Nancy Weatherhead, Conestoga College

Nancy Camacho, Everest College, Scarborough

Judith Rance, Everest College, Ottawa

Linda Welsby, Medix School, London Campus

Jacqueline Hingley, Georgian College

Amy Greene, triOS College

Debbie Gamracy, Fanshawe College

Michelle Naugle, MTI Community College

Cheryl Russell-Julien, Everest College

I owe a debt of gratitude to the following friends, colleagues, and institutions that have contributed their time, knowledge, and other resources to the development of this book.

Jennifer Beavis, Workplace Safety and Insurance Board, Ontario

Glenn Budgell, Regional Director, Medical Care Plan, Newfoundland and Labrador

Lynn Strugnell, Director Clinical Programs, Huron Perth Healthcare Alliance–Stratford General Hospital

Huron Perth Enterprise Information Technology Services

Nancy White, BScN, Clinical Educator, Maternal/Child, Stratford General Hospital

Gail Williams, Accreditation Product Development Specialist (Accreditation Canada)

Rachel Brown, MA, MLIS, Senior Advisor, Knowledge Management/Conseillère principale, gestion des connaissances, Canadian Health Services Research Foundation

Brenda Hancock, Manager of Medical Affairs and Training, MCP, Department of Health and Community Services, Newfoundland and Labrador

Bill Kocmarek, Charge Technologist Hematology/Transfusion Medicine, Stratford General Hospital

Ontario Ministry of Health and Long-Term Care

Jay Patterson, Vice-President of Technology, Advanced Computer Systems Limited

Rose Ann Kreps, RN, BScN

Doug Pinder, RN, BScN, MBA, Ontario Home Health

Valerie Pinder, RN, BScN, MEd, Professor, Conestoga College

Sheila Knectal, RN, Information Technology, Stratford General Hospital

Elizabeth Barker, RN, BScN, Stratford General Hospital

College of Physicians and Surgeons of Ontario

Dr. Douglas Thompson, MD, FRCP, Stratford, Ontario

Dr. Marcie McEwan, General Surgeon, Stratford General Hospital

Dr. Grace Langford, MD, FRCP, Stratford, Ontario

Christy Beavis, Clinical Secretary, Grand River Hospital, Kitchener, Ontario

Jennifer Wamil, Clinical Secretary, St. Mary's Hospital, Kitchener, Ontario

Sandra Frisker, Clinical Secretary, St. Mary's Hospital, Kitchener, Ontario

Heather Anne Berry, CCHRA(C), BA, HCA(Cert.), Manager, Health Records, South Bruce Grey Health Centre

Sandra McKenzie, CMS, Medical Office Manager

Medical Office Assistants' Association of British Columbia

Ontario Medical Secretaries Association—Health Care Associates

Sherry Czekus, Clinical Secretary, St. Mary's Hospital, Waterloo, Ontario

Maureen McCandless, Director, Communications, The Canadian Chiropractic Association

Katherine Kelly, Federal/Provincial/Territorial Relations, PEI Department of Health

Gaylene MacDonald, Health Website Project, Corporate Relations and Evaluation, Corporate, PEI Department of Health

Rachel Mann, Nursing Unit Coordinator, St. Paul's Hospital, BC

Maxine Lloyd, Nursing Unit Clerk, Royal Columbian Hospital, BC

Betty Furtad, Nursing Unit Clerk, Royal Columbian Hospital, BC

I would also like to thank several people at Pearson Education Canada for their professional support, including Don Thompson, Acquisitions Editor; Allison McDonald, Developmental Editor; Ashley Patterson, Project Manager; and Katie Ostler, Production Editor.

Valerie Thompson

Part I
Introduction

Part I of this textbook briefly discusses the history of the roles and responsibilities of individuals working in a variety of health administration positions. Qualities and skills that promote success in this occupation are outlined, along with the importance of professionalism. You will learn about the roles and responsibilities of the modern administrative health professional (AHP) and how your previous work and volunteer experiences can help you.

Chapter 1   The Administrative Health Professional (AHP)

Appendix 1A Sample Résumé

Chapter 1
The Administrative Health Professional (AHP)

Learning Objectives

On completing this chapter, you will be able to:

1. Discuss the AHP workplace environment including benefits, responsibilities, and professional associations.

2. List six potential employers of administrative health professionals.

3. List five personal qualities that an AHP should possess.

4. Identify the core competencies required by an AHP.

5. Discuss the importance of professional appearance and attitude in the health office.

6. Explain four ethical principles related to the health-care environment.

7. Describe the five steps to ethical decision making.

8. Outline the administrative and clinical responsibilities of the AHP in the medical and dental office setting.

9. Demonstrate how to construct an effective résumé.

10. Understand how to conduct a job search.

11. Define the respective rights and obligations of employer and employee involved in a cooperative work placement.

12. Discuss the importance of continuing professional development.

The health-care profession is dynamic, complex, and challenging. You are entering it during a time of both change and opportunity. A career path in health-services administration offers you varied and stimulating job opportunities. The health office includes a wide variety of settings, ranging from a physician's office to dental offices and clinics. The first four parts of this text, although primarily devoted to the medical office, include information on working in a dental office.

❶ WHAT'S IN A NAME?

THE TERM **ADMINISTRATIVE HEALTH PROFESSIONAL (AHP)** IS USED IN THIS BOOK TO cover the diverse roles of graduates from health office/services administration and similar programs. People in this profession work in a wide variety of health-care settings and perform a mix of duties, which are becoming more and more complex. Each health-care facility may have its own job title and unique job description. What is common, however, is the knowledge, level of competence, and the degree of professionalism required to perform competently as a health office professional. The role of the administrative health professional is critical in providing efficient, organized health care. Wherever you work, you will be a valued member of a health-care team; you will make a significant contribution toward delivering excellent, compassionate, client-centred health care.

In the occupational setting, a graduate may be assigned a job title such as *medical secretary* or *medical office assistant*. In the hospital setting, titles include *nursing unit coordinator, communications coordinator, communications clerk, ward clerk,* and *clinical secretary*. In community nursing the term *nursing coordinator* may be used as the position that often involves arranging a schedule for nurses to visit clients in the community. Dental offices use the titles *dental practice receptionist, dental office manager, dental treatment coordinator,* and *dental administrative assistant*. Such terms as *clinical secretary* may be used in this book if relevant to the specific occupational setting being discussed.

In this text, we call people seeking health-care services *clients*—a term that has recently replaced *patients* in many areas of health care, though *patient* is still used by many doctors and most hospitals. **Client** suggests a consumer who purchases health-care services and who actively participates in her own care and in decisions regarding this care, while *patient* has historically been used to describe a submissive, passive recipient of medical care. The term *client* has been slow to catch on—and realistically, will probably never replace the term 'patient'. Client is rarely if ever, used in the hospital setting, or by physicians. Physicians may be uncomfortable with the implications of the term client, use 'patient' out of habit, or simply do not see the need for change. Many think the use of the term client has taken political correctness one step too far. In recent years patients/clients and physicians almost always collaborate on the individual's plan of care—thus the patient is viewed in terms of being participatory in his care, making decisions that are congruent with his lifestyle, beliefs and values (and he is still called a patient).

administrative health professional (AHP) a graduate from an accredited health office administration program who assumes administrative, communication, and/or clinical responsibilities in a health-care setting.

client a person seeking or receiving health care; synonymous with *patient*, but suggests a more active role.

1955

Busy medical office requires secretary. Needs good telephone skills. Good with people. Will train. Start immediately.

1965

Busy doctor's office requires medical secretary to start immediately. Commercial course required. Typing skills, good with people, organized. Knowledge of medical terminology an asset. Duties include booking appointments, answering the telephone, billing, general office duties.

1970

Medical secretary urgently sought by Cardiologist. Successful candidate must have secretarial training: typing, dicta typing, medical terminology, bookkeeping skills required. Previous experience an asset. Duties include filing, billing, telephone management, processing mail, and maintaining inventory. Salary commensurate with experience.

1980

Medical secretary required by group practice. Certificate in related program an asset. Must know medical terminology, medical transcription, typing, and accounts receivable/payroll. Good telephone and communication skills. Pleasant manner. Duties include general office management, provincial billing, maintaining medical records, and referrals. Apply with résumé to Dr. M. Black, 222 Brunswick Street, Burnaby.

1990

Medical secretary for busy solo practice. Graduate of a health administration course an asset. Excellent communication skills a must. Previous experience an asset. Duties include booking appointments, provincial billing, medical transcription. Health-care terminology a must. Must be a team player, multi-tasker, organized, with a pleasant, outgoing personality. Apply with résumé to Dr. R. Collins. 111 Chester Ave., Sheffield. Ph 306-233-2222.

2009

Medical assistant required immediately. Looking for a dynamic, outgoing, and progressive individual to join our Family Health Organization. Duties include provincial billing, scheduling for four family doctors, assisting physicians and nurse practitioner with patient care, EMR chart management and patient flow in the Division of Primary Care. Familiarity with voice-recognition software and editing of voice-recognition documents an asset. Successful applicant should have a knowledge of X-Wave Medical Software, and be proficient with Microsoft Office Applications. Other duties include obtaining vital statistics on client; under instruction record medical information in EMR chart; coordinate prescription refills and referrals; maintain logs and educational materials. Must have outstanding communication skills and keyboarding speed of 50 wpm. Three years' previous experience or a diploma from a two-year college program in Health Office Administration required. Must be CPR certified—health professionals level. Excellent remuneration for successful applicant. Fax résumé to 519-433-3333 Attn: Dr. Decker.

2012

CENTRAL CLINIC ALBERTA HEALTH SERVICES

ADMINISTRATIVE HEALTH PROFESSIONAL—PRIMARY CARE

START DATE: IMMEDIATE

JOB NUMBER 45323

Multidisciplinary team implements primary health and dental care to the surrounding community. Our services include counselling, harm reduction, advocacy, and community development. We interface with multiple community agencies.

GENERAL RESPONSIBILITIES:

You will provide initial and ongoing personal and telephone contact for the professional staff, clients, and visitors. As a member of our primary care health team, you will help facilitate the smooth operation of the clinic's administrative function, perform administrative and selected clinical duties assisting a variety of health providers (intake interviews, blood pressures, urine and blood sugar testing). You will be the front-line person in triaging clients in accordance with clinic protocol and ensuring that scheduling of clients is done in an efficient, client-oriented manner.

ACCOUNTABILITY:

The medical secretary reports to the director of primary care.

QUALIFICATIONS:

Diploma from a community college medical secretary's program or the equivalent, keyboarding speed of 50 wpm or greater, demonstrated computer literacy and the ability to easily adapt to new software, previous experience in health/social services an asset, ability to work well under stress and maintain a calm demeanour, proficient use of proper English in oral and written (also spelling) communication, outstanding communication, conflict management, and interpersonal skills.

Salary Range: $3450–$4350 /month plus benefits

Figure 1.1 Advertisements for a medical secretary as they would have appeared over the past 60 years show the growing complexity and breadth of skills required from the 1950s to today

Administrative Health Professional: The Medical Secretary

The role of the administrative health professional has shifted over the years, becoming more responsible and complex (see Figure 1.1). Today, a high level of education and skills is necessary to meet the demands placed on this responsible position. You can see this reflected in the ads illustrated in Figure 1.1.

Today, administrative health professionals must be computer literate and knowledgeable about provincial or territorial billing, pharmacology, laboratory and diagnostic tests, ethics, and human relations. Many community colleges and independent business colleges offer AHP programs, which vary from a one-year certificate program to a two- or three-year diploma program. Some programs are accelerated, offering, for example, a two-year diploma program in a shorter time frame. Many colleges integrate simulated office experiences or co-op or workplace experiences, either throughout the program or at the end.

In the hospital setting, the responsibilities of the **ward clerk** or clinical secretary have also dramatically increased in both scope and volume. Initially, the ward clerk was not allowed to process doctor's orders, take laboratory or diagnostic reports over the telephone, or respond to most physician requests. These tasks were primarily the responsibility of the head nurse. In the past few years, the term *ward clerk* has been replaced in many settings by *clinical secretary*, *clerical associate*, or *communications coordinator* to better reflect increased responsibilities, notably, transcribing physicians' orders. The clinical secretary coordinates written and oral communication and plays key administrative roles. These positions are usually filled by AHP graduates or by long-standing employees who have gained a wealth of knowledge on the job. The duties and responsibilities of the clinical secretary are discussed in more detail in Chapter 15.

ward clerk an individual who manages the administrative and communication needs of a client-care unit. The title is being replaced with *clinical secretary* or *communications coordinator.*

The Dental Office

Dental administrative assistants are usually graduates of health administration programs or specialty programs for dental administration. Sometimes other members of the dental team (e.g., dental assistant) assume additional administrative responsibilities. However, in most offices operating with a variety of dental health professionals, administrative duties are assumed by a person trained in the administrative field. Conversely, to increase office efficiency, some dental offices will cross-train their administrative staff to assume limited chair-side duties, thus multitasking. Additional responsibilities may include sorting, sanitizing, and sterilizing instruments. Some colleges integrate the specific knowledge and skills needed to work in a dental office into an administrative health professional program; others may offer a specialized program in dental administration, such as Vancouver Career College in Kelowna, BC, and the KLC College in Kingston, Ontario.

❶❷ EMPLOYMENT OPPORTUNITIES

Positions

Administrative health professionals work in a variety of positions with different titles and duties. The following summary outlines some of the more common ones.

Medical Office Assistant   The role of **medical assistant** is more clearly defined in the United States than in Canada. In the United States, the medical assistant primarily

medical assistant (U.S.) a person who is trained to assist a physician with various clinical tests, examinations, and procedures.

assists the physician with clinical tasks but may also handle some administrative responsibilities. This term is often used in British Columbia as well. More closely aligned to the medical assistant in Canada is a recent addition to the health-care team of a physician assistant whose responsibilities are primarily clinical in nature. In most of Canada, however, the more common term is **medical office assistant** or office manager, and this job description generally includes more administrative than clinical responsibilities. Medical assistants in the United States are trained to take blood specimens, administer injections, give oral medications, administer electrocardiograms and other laboratory tests, and perform other specialized tasks—tasks generally performed by nurses in Canada. Medical assistants also take vital signs, prepare clients for procedures, take health histories, prepare the examination or treatment room, assess client need when scheduling appointments, and determine when clients need to be seen urgently. Canadian administrative health professionals assume many of these responsibilities in some health-care settings.

Integrating some nursing duties into the AHP's job is not new but is becoming more common as the changing face of health care demands multi-skilled, versatile, and cost-effective workers. In some offices, the AHP assumes expanded duties, such as giving allergy shots and assisting with procedures. The AHP must be trained by the physician or other qualified health practitioner to carry out these tasks, some of which are legally considered "delegated acts," meaning that the health practitioner involved takes responsibility for the employee's actions.

Administrative Nursing Coordinator An increasing number of community agencies supply a range of in-home medical services, especially home-based nursing care to clients discharged from hospital with conditions requiring ongoing care and assessment. Community nurses start and maintain intravenous (IV) therapy in the home, apply dressings, and maintain and monitor clients on respirators. These clients may have chest tubes and other complex medical devices. Clients are routinely admitted to the agency's services and discharged when their need for care terminates. Each agency needs someone in an administrative role, often called a *nursing coordinator*, to coordinate the agency's needs and activities. This person is aware of the caseloads of various nurses, assigns new admissions on the basis of caseload and priority, conveys vital information about clients' medical needs, and keeps track of admissions and discharges. To take on this role, you must be aware of the responsibilities of the various types of nurses within the organization and the related scope of practice for each group (discussed in detail in Chapter 15). You must be able to prioritize information and be familiar with medications, critical lab values, and other components of community care.

Clinic Administrator/Manager Over the past few years, more clinics have appeared—for example, central clinics associated with primary care groups, or those privately owned and operated by independent practitioners such as physiotherapists. At medical clinics, services include a complete range of care from family medicine to day surgery. Clinics such as the Preventous Collaborative Health clinic in Calgary provide a range of preventive health-care services (these services are not covered by provincial/territorial plans). A clinic may offer one service or a variety of services by more than one health professional. Managing the administrative needs of a clinic requires excellent organizational skills and the ability to make sound decisions, while working harmoniously with a variety of professionals (and personalities). You must be able to multitask, think quickly, and take responsibility. Specific skills range from triaging and scheduling clients, solving problems, and maintaining a client-oriented environment to managing the busi-

medical office assistant (Canada) a person who handles primarily administrative responsibilities, but also some clinical duties, in a health office. The title varies (e.g., medical secretary, medical office manager).

ness aspects of the clinic. In addition, you may be responsible for staff scheduling and recruitment. If the clinic is privately operated you must work toward cost effectiveness while maintaining a high standard of client care.

Medical Transcriptionist   A medical transcriptionist produces medical reports, correspondence, records, client-care information, statistics, medical research, and administrative material. In a hospital, transcriptionists are members of a larger team in the Medical Records or the Information Health Department. The transcriptionist listens to recorded reports or reads rough notes and produces formal reports in document form. In highly computerized environments, the transcriptionist edits and formats documents that have been transcribed by voice-recognition technology. Documents transcribed include discharge summaries, referral letters, and reports on health histories, physical examinations, operations, consultations, autopsies, radiology examinations, and obstetrics. As well as specific training in transcription, the medical transcriptionist must have general medical knowledge, sound judgment, and logical and problem-solving abilities. A good transcriptionist can spot mistakes in a report and check, when necessary, with the doctor to get the right information.

Dental Administrative Assistant   A dental administrative assistant performs many of the same tasks as an administrative health professional; however, the job usually entails more extensive work with insurance forms and billing to various insurance providers. It also requires a sound knowledge of tooth identification systems and tooth anatomy. Dental administrative assistants are also responsible for client education, accounts payable and receivable, referral systems, and the management and analysis of practice reports. Many scheduling procedures may also differ; it is often necessary to schedule clients for other members of the dental team, such as dental assistants or dental hygienists, as well as for the dentist. In some occupational settings, the dental administrative assistant may be trained to assist the dentist with basic procedures.

Occupational Settings

A wide variety of positions are available for the administrative health professional. The health-care field is diverse, and opportunities continue to broaden as the industry restructures and the roles of health-care professionals change. Occupational settings range from the fast-paced challenge of the emergency room to the less hectic environment of a specialist's office, and from a busy walk-in clinic with a lot of client contact to a Medical Records department with limited public contact. Many positions are also available in sectors of the allied health-care and alternative health-care fields. The administrative health professional is considered to be part of the allied health-care field, along with other professions more centred on direct client care. **Allied health care** includes any duty or function that supports primary health-care professionals, such as physicians, in the delivery of health-care services. Allied health-care professions include physiotherapists, osteopaths, midwives, and nurses. Many of these professionals are in independent practice while working collaboratively with other health-care professionals. For example, with the current move to community-based care, there has been an increase in the number of independent nursing service organizations. Some sectors of the allied health-care industry offer valuable employment opportunities for the AHP.

    Alternative health care, also referred to as **complementary health care**, is considered by most to be the natural approach to treating the causes of illness and disease. Alternative health care includes non-traditional methods and practices such as chiropractic, acupuncture, massage, and aromatherapy. These professions offer the consumer a replacement or

allied health care   any duty or profession that supports primary health-care providers, such as physicians, nurse practitioners, or midwives, in delivering health-care services.

alternative health care or **complementary health care**   nontraditional methods and practices based on a natural approach, including chiropractic, acupuncture, massage, and aromatherapy.

an adjunct to traditional health care. Alternative health-care professions are growing in number and popularity as Canadians face (and become fed up with) increasingly long waits for medical care. Many allied, alternative, and mainstream health-care professionals work independently and/or in facilities that offer the client collaborative care, as well as a range of health-care choices. Alternative and allied health-care professionals provide employment opportunities for administrative health professionals with duties and responsibilities similar to those in traditional health-care offices. Throughout this book, we focus primarily on physicians' offices and hospitals, the two settings most covered in health administration courses, as it would be impossible to do justice to the whole range of possibilities in a single textbook. But keep in mind that your basic skills and knowledge can take you in many directions.

You might find a job in any of the following workplaces—and even this list is not complete.

Office and Community

- Doctor's office (group or solo practice), generalist or specialist
- Health-care agencies
- Regional health authorities
- Ambulatory care or walk-in clinics (also may be called urgent-care clinics or centres)
- Primary care group **clinic** (for rostered clients)
- Dental offices
- Optometry offices
- Community agencies, such as Public Health
- Victorian Order of Nurses (VON)
- Canadian Red Cross
- Canadian Cancer Society
- CCAC (Community Care Access Centre) or equivalent
- Independent community authorities

clinic a facility providing medical care on an outpatient basis. It may be free-standing or associated with a hospital. Many clinics have a specialty, such as ongoing care for diabetes, orthopedics, or cancer. The term is currently also applied to primary care groups that offer outof-office services where rostered clients can seek medical care when their physician is unavailable.

Clinics (often connected with hospitals or community-based health services)

- Orthopedics
- Prenatal/postpartum/birthing centres
- Diabetic
- Mental health
- Systemic therapy
- Renal dialysis
- Oncology
- Palliative care
- Laser surgery

Alternative/Allied Health-Care Facilities

- Acupuncture
- Reflexology

- Massage therapy
- Aromatherapy
- Chiropractor
- Osteopath

Hospital Departments

- Admitting/client registration
- Medical Records/Information Health
- Emergency room
- Laboratory (various departments within the laboratory)
- Maternal/child
- Pediatrics
- Medicine
- Surgery
- Operating room
- Social Services
- Radiology

Hospital Departments: Choosing the Right Unit for You

Working in a hospital as a clinical secretary is an exciting vocation offering numerous options (as listed above). You can choose a unit with a slower pace, or one that is fast moving and exciting. Choosing the unit that suits your abilities is most important. Additionally, selecting an area that meshes with your own preferences is a bonus—for example, palliative care if you are comfortable dealing with individuals suffering from terminal illnesses, or a geriatric unit if you are at home dealing with older people. Whatever the specific unit, you will be responsible for coordinating a client-care unit. You will manage almost all aspects of the unit's communication, and be accountable for the execution of doctor's orders (called order entry) via the unit's computer software system. A commonly used system is called Meditech; another is Med-Connect. You will work closely with the nurses, doctors, and other members of the health-care team. In addition, you will be a vital link to health care for clients and their loved ones and families. If this interests you, please see a more detailed description of this important vocational choice in Chapter 14.

Other Health-Care Facilities

- Long-term care facilities (nursing homes)/residential care facilities
- Seniors' residences/assisted-living facilities
- Rehabilitative centres

Other

- Insurance companies
- Community college schools of health sciences or health unit
- Provincial or territorial health plan offices
- Health Canada
- Local public health departments

- Industrial health departments
- Medical supply companies
- Private laboratories and diagnostic clinics
- Medical transcription facilities
- Pharmaceutical firms
- Medical software companies
- Veterinary practices
- Canadian Armed Forces

Occupational Settings for the Dental Office Administrator

- General dentist
- Orthodontist
- Pedodontist
- Periodontist
- Prosthodontist
- Oral and maxillofacial surgeon
- Dental hygienist (practising independently)
- Dental distribution or dental manufacturing company
- Dental department of a hospital
- Dental laboratory
- Public health department
- Dental insurance organizations

❸❹❺ ATTRIBUTES AND SKILLS OF THE ADMINISTRATIVE HEALTH PROFESSIONAL

To be a member of any profession demands academic preparation as well as a distinctive set of attributes and skills. A shy person might not suit a marketing position. A person who thrives on artistic creativity and dislikes math (even if good at it) would be poorly suited to a position in accounting. Those who truly succeed in their chosen field usually have a natural affinity for it as well as qualities and skills that enhance their work.

attribute an inborn personal quality or characteristic.

Attributes and skills are not the same thing, though they overlap. A skill is learned. We think of attributes as inherent traits, although certainly some qualities can be developed purposefully. Consider loyalty and honesty. Although you may have a natural propensity for one or the other, you are not born loyal or disloyal, honest or dishonest. These attributes develop as you grow and experience the world around you.

Personal attributes, therefore, are a combination of inborn individual traits and development. Some people just seem to be naturally organized—a desirable trait for anyone working in an office—but organizational ability can be improved through practice; thus, some aspects of organization can be regarded as skills. Skills are more tangible than assets. You learn to type, you learn health-care terminology, you learn how to communicate effectively—although, here again, some people are just naturally effective communicators. Skills may be divided into soft and hard skills. Hard skills are specific and measurable: for example, keyboarding at 50 words per minute. Soft skills are more general: for example, communicating in difficult situations or projecting an image of trust and competency.

Each profession or vocation calls for a certain set of attributes and skills. A good police officer, for example, should have the attributes of courage and the ability to remain calm under stress, and the skills of marksmanship and negotiation.

Because job opportunities for health office professionals vary, a variety of qualities and skills may be suited to different positions. Some, however, are essential for all positions.

Attributes

Professionalism   One of the most important attributes of an administrative health professional is professionalism. The person must recognize his career as the important, vital profession it is and one that carries tremendous responsibility. The roots of professionalism lie in the term *profession*. A profession is a grouping of tasks, duties, and responsibilities requiring specialized knowledge and specialized preparation. Some professions, such as nursing, medicine, and law, are formally recognized; others are not. Administering a health office is a profession but currently has no legal boundaries or regulating body. A professional (noun) is an individual who has prepared to work in a profession, and, by implication, is one who practises and upholds its standards, rules, and policies. The adjective *professional* describes conduct appropriate to a given profession; more generally, it refers to a courteous, businesslike, respectful attitude, manner, and appearance.

Professional Appearance   Professionalism is conveyed by both appearance and manner. An appropriate professional appearance is imperative for an administrative health professional. You will frequently be the first person that the client meets. Your appearance will create a lasting impression and may well set the tone for how that person feels about you and your place of employment. If you are negligent in your personal appearance, people may assume that you will be negligent in your work; this impression will reflect badly on both your employer and your occupational setting. Think about how some of the health professionals you have seen dress. You may have seen, for example, nurses wearing shorts and socks with running shoes, jogging suits, or scrubs with less-than-clean sweaters and sporting long, unrestrained hair; dangling earrings; long, painted fingernails; and numerous rings. You may have encountered an administrative assistant in a health office who was dressed conservatively, with a neat lab coat, contained hair, light make-up, and minimal jewellery. Which made a good impression?

There is a time and a place for everything—a fact that seems to be difficult to convey to some health professionals. Many seem to think that the more glamorous they look—or, conversely, the more casual—the more appealing they are. Many students also seem to think that the lessons of decorum they learn become irrelevant after graduation. It cannot be emphasized enough that the health-care setting requires professional, appropriate attire.

What is considered professional will vary, within limits, with places of employment. Dress in health care is usually conservative. In the health office or hospital, dress codes may vary from scrubs or uniforms to "dressing casual." Jeans of any description, jogging apparel, shorts, and T-shirts are rarely acceptable. Scrubs are cost effective, convenient to launder, and comfortable. They should be changed daily and kept clean and wrinkle free. If a sweater is worn over scrubs or a uniform, ensure that it is clean, neat, and a neutral colour. Alternatively, a lab coat is also easily laundered and looks crisp and clean. It should be worn only within the health-care facility or office. Uniforms/scrubs should be worn only in the facility—most provide change rooms and lockers. This is often an infection-control requirement.

A name tag is always appropriate in the office. Health-care facilities usually require that photo ID be worn, for security as well as identification. As in many professions, dress codes in health care are becoming more casual. You need to find the appropriate balance for your work environment: neither too strict and sterile nor too casual. Certain elements, however, transcend setting:

- Neatness
- Cleanliness
- Sensible, discreet use of make-up
- No fragrance (e.g., perfume, aftershave) because of increasing allergies among the public
- Subtle jewellery, if any. Most facilities allow jewellery worn for religious purposes. Body piercings and multiple earrings are discouraged or banned.
- Comfortable, clean shoes

A word about shoes: shoes must look appropriate, be comfortable, and meet any workplace safety requirements (e.g., no high-heels or strappy sandals) and safety standards in such settings as hospitals (which usually require closed-toe shoes). Good foot support is still important if you stand for long periods or do a lot of walking. Choose shoes in neutral colours (e.g., no bright greens or pinks) and materials that can be easily cleaned. Whatever style you choose, keep the shoes clean and in good repair. Keep your laces, if you have them, spotless. Some facilities do not allow employees to wear their work shoes outside.

Many offices and clinics have a dress code, and uniforms are sometimes part of this dress code. Hospitals often prefer the clinical secretary to wear scrubs or appropriate business attire with a clean lab coat over top.

Professional Manner   A professional appearance is ineffective unless it is accompanied by a professional manner, behaviour, and attitude. A professional manner is reflected by treating people with respect and kindness; recognizing your professional boundaries and staying within them; and being positive, honest, and trustworthy. Treat each person as unique and important, and even during a brief exchange, give him or her your undivided attention. Greet people with a smile and be pleasant. Convey a warm and attentive attitude toward your clients. Address their concerns promptly, follow through with promises, and try to keep a sense of humour while maintaining a caring and friendly environment.

Professionalism also means being proud of yourself and confident in who you are and what you do. Refrain from making personal calls at work or using the workplace telephone. Use the internet at work for work purposes only, and turn your smartphone off when at work (an anticipated emergency is an exception). Adhere to agency rules. It is normally fine to use your cellphone or smartphone on breaks if in a private area. In addition, do not become involved in the personal issues among other members of the health-care team. Refrain from taking sides in discussions and issues, work-related or otherwise. If there is a serious problem, there will be a proper agency protocol to follow for those affected. Becoming involved will create "sides," bitterness, and even hostilities. This could negatively affect everyone in your workplace. Individuals have been disciplined and even fired for these types of infractions. Preserve workplace relationships if at all possible.

Analytical Thinking   The administrative health professional must be able to grasp and apply concepts and analyze and synthesize facts and information. This ability is partly a matter of natural intelligence, partly the result of consciously developing cognitive skills, and partly the result of a solid knowledge base and familiarity with your job, your roles, and your responsibilities. Good analytical skills are the first step in making good judgments:

- Prioritize and perform multiple tasks, often at the same time.
- Make knowledge-based decisions.
- Solve problems and take action.
- Respond appropriately to emergency situations.

Good Judgment   Good judgment is essential and is required in almost every task or duty that you perform. Good judgment relies not only on a strong knowledge base but also on the ability to weigh consequences and outcomes and make effective decisions. In the health office, you use judgment every time you make an appointment for a client. You decide how long the appointment should be and how soon the client needs to see the doctor. You screen the physician's phone calls, deciding which ones to put through to the doctor, which to refer to the nurse, and which to handle yourself. **Triage**—assessing clients' need for treatment and the urgency of that need—is an important function in most office or clinic settings. You will sometimes have to decide whether a client needs to be urgently seen by the physician or sooner than someone else who may be waiting. Judgment is also applied to clients who call the office with health complaints. You must be able to recognize a potential emergency and refer the client appropriately.

Some decisions will make you unpopular. It can be difficult to face criticism of your decisions. To make sound decisions,

- carefully evaluate and assess facts before making the decision,
- remember that compromise is sometimes necessary, and
- if you are convinced that your decision is the right one, stick to it and accept disapproval with as much equanimity as you can.

triage   assessing the seriousness of a client's presenting problem to determine who needs to have medical help first. For example, someone coming to the emergency department with chest pain would be brought in to see the doctor immediately, whereas someone with a sore throat would be considered a non-urgent case and able to wait.

Approachable Manner and Friendly Personality   An open, approachable manner and friendly personality are among the most important qualities for dealing with the public—all the more so when interacting with people who are anxious or under stress, such as those who are concerned about their own or their relatives' health. You need to speak pleasantly, show empathy and caring, and use diplomacy. Clients should be made to feel that they and their concerns are important. A pleasant, friendly AHP will put clients at ease, create a positive and caring atmosphere, promote trust, and, in many cases, invite a pleasant, friendly response. Clients are more apt to return if you are welcoming. For some providers, this is critical to client recruitment and retention and the success of their business.

Getting Along with Others   Also called adaptive interpersonal skills, the ability to get along with those you work with, manage conflict, and promote a pleasant, accommodating and productive work environment may well be a combination of natural ability and learned skills. A workplace that fosters tolerance and respect for others contributes to an occupational setting that is a pleasure to work in. There is nothing worse from a professional and personal perspective than dreading going to work, or dreading having to work with a particular individual. It affects you, those you work with, and the workplace setting in general. There is a higher staff turnover rate in health-care facilities that are ruled by tension and stress. Often this is generated by one person. Do not let that person be you. Strategies for effective communication are discussed in more detail in Chapter 8.

Sense of Responsibility   To be successful in the health-office setting, you must be accountable for your actions, take responsibility for yourself, and be honest. Clients and employers alike rely and depend on you. You must keep promises, and you must be able to accept and deal with the consequences of your actions. For example, if you are supposed to notify a client about an abnormal laboratory result, the physician is counting on you to carry through with that action. If you forget, you need to admit your error and take responsibility. Trying to find excuses or blame someone else would be dishonest and unprofessional. Know your limitations, and seek help when appropriate. You may sometimes be asked to do something that you do not feel qualified to do. It is far better to say so openly than to do a substandard job, or, worse, make a mistake that affects client care. One graduate commented of her hospital placement: "There is no forgiveness for mistakes in health care, but it is even worse if you do not admit your mistake, correct it, and take steps to ensure that the same mistake does not happen again." When people know they can rely on you, you gain their trust—one of the most valuable things you can establish with employers, peers, and clients.

Flexibility   To be flexible is to have the ability to easily adapt to new or changing requirements. Any given day may start out in a reasonably organized manner, but invariably there will be many days that do not end that way. Clients may not show up for appointments; you may have several who need to see the doctor urgently when there are no openings; or the physician may be called away to the delivery room or the Emergency Department, necessitating cancellation of appointments. A report you expected to have for a client may be delayed. In the hospital setting, you may get several admissions at the same time, preventing you from tackling your "to do" list. The surgeons may be grumpy and make you bear the brunt of their anger. Being able to reorganize schedules, priorities, and clients and adapt mentally to such changes will reduce your frustration and ultimately help things run more smoothly.

It is important also to be flexible with respect to your working relationships. You need to be able to work independently and as a member of a team. This involves sharing responsibilities at some times and assuming them at others, changing your way of doing things when a better suggestion comes along, or letting go of something you feel you have ownership of. It may involve changing a procedure rather than clinging rigidly to a policy. Recognize that no rule will fit every person or situation all the time. Flexibility allows for personal and professional growth and opens the door to new opportunities.

Calm Demeanour   The health office, and the client-care setting in particular, can be hectic and stressful. A high stress level often interferes with a person's ability to remain calm. Yet, a calm demeanour in all situations is important. Becoming flustered and anxious can interfere with effective action and communication and may cause you to say or do something you regret. A calm, methodical response is essential in a crisis. For example, suppose you witness a cardiac arrest in a hospital. You must remain calm and focused and remember the steps you are to follow to notify switchboard to announce the code over the hospital public address system. An administrative health professional must be able to control impulsive behaviour, to respond to a variety of situations, and to think clearly and apply knowledge before taking efficient and effective action.

Initiative   Initiative is one of the first qualities an employer looks for. It implies the ability to assess when something needs to be done and to do it: to act without clear guidance. If you have initiative, you can complete tasks independently and seek out new learning opportunities. You go the extra distance to accomplish more than you must.

Tolerance   Tolerance means allowing people to have their own beliefs, opinions, and ways of doing things. It means accepting people for who they are whether you agree or disagree with their lifestyle, personal decisions, or personal beliefs. Sometimes, you bite your tongue rather than saying something critical. You listen to and support clients, even when you feel tired or fed up.

Empathy   Being empathetic means being able to put yourself in others' shoes and imagine their thoughts and feelings. It gives you an emotional connection that makes the client feel understood, accepted, and respected regardless of the situation. Do not confuse *empathy* with *sympathy*, the ability to commiserate or share another's feelings. Sympathy is emotional, while empathy involves sensitivity or comprehension.

Ethical Attitude   A person who does not behave ethically has no place in the health profession. Your position is one of trust that demands respect for the client's rights and beliefs. You must recognize and respect a client's health-care opinions and decisions. *You must be fully aware of confidentiality guidelines* outlined in provincial/territorial and federal legislation and abide by them. Ethical responsibilities are addressed later in this chapter.

Skills

Although your skill set as an administrative health professional will continually grow, upon graduation you will have established **core competencies**, both cognitive and performance based, in the following areas.

core competency   the basic or essential skills that one needs to succeed in a particular profession.

Organizational Skills   As previously noted, being organized can be a natural attribute. However, even the most naturally organized person will have to work to develop organizational skills to manage a busy office or client-care unit efficiently. To get the necessary things done, you will need to prioritize, establish procedures, and follow through with a well-thought-out, methodical approach. Attention to detail is also important. Remember to ask colleagues for ideas and suggestions and to work together. Good organization applies to every area of your job, from filing, to scheduling appointments, to arranging things in the office. Organization is not something you do before you start: it is an ongoing process you must engage in every day. It pays off, however, in an efficient use of time and saves a great deal of frustration.

Effective Communication   Communication skills are essential in any job involving personal interaction. A person may have the important qualities of empathy and tolerance, but it is communication that conveys these to others. You need to be able to communicate effectively in structured settings with clients, families, significant others, and all members of the health-care team. Communication involves both receiving and conveying information accurately and effectively. Communication can be written, oral, and non-verbal (involving facial expressions, gestures, posture, and tone of voice). You need to be proficient at all three.

Your speech must be clear and articulate. Correct grammar, in both speech and writing, reflects professionalism. If, for example, you say, "her and I" or "it don't," you will sound uneducated and careless. At a deeper level, you must be able to impart and elicit a sense of trust and warmth, and listen for the emotional as well as the literal message from clients. You need to be able to control a conversation, when necessary, and to communicate effectively with people from many different cultures. The latter requires the skill and patience to understand the message when the speaker's English is flawed. Knowledge of effective communication skills allows you to assess situations and respond appropriately.

Keyboarding Skills   Health office professionals must keyboard accurately and quickly. Many facilities use a minimum typing speed of 55–60 words per minute or higher as a hiring criterion. Most colleges require a minimum speed (perhaps 30 words per minute) as a *prerequisite* for admission to the administrative health professional program, with the expectation that speed will increase by graduation. Computer and medical transcription courses can help increase accuracy and speed. There are also excellent websites for testing and practising your keyboarding skills.

Computer Literacy   Competencies in this field are essential for the AHP. Health offices and hospitals are moving steadily toward a paperless system of administration and practice. Computerized environments are constantly being upgraded and improved. You will need a general knowledge of computers and proficiency in word-processing programs, accounting software, data-management programs, and even presentation software. More importantly, you need to be able to transfer these skills to the customized computer programs that may be used in your workplace. It is important that you be able to embrace new technology and actively work toward staying current. This is especially challenging in physicians' offices and clinics, with ever-changing software systems and the move to electronic medical and health records. As well, there are hundreds of new billing codes, incentive codes, and blended forms of remuneration that you must be able to manage electronically.

Knowledge of Health-Care Terminology   No one can function competently in the health-care environment without knowing the language of medicine and dentistry. Special health-care terminology is used daily in health-care settings. You need to be able to use medical and dental terms properly, both in speech and writing.

Background Knowledge   You need an in-depth grasp of anatomy and physiology, pharmacology, and laboratory and diagnostic tests, including designated critical values.

Medical Transcription   Straight medical transcription skills are still required in many occupational settings. You must be able to transcribe accurately and to interpret, type, and format various medical reports and documents.

Editing Documents/Voice-Recognition Software   Voice-recognition software such as Dragon is used by many medical practitioners. Even the best software is not perfect—the resulting documents invariably contain mistakes related to the inability of the voice-recognition software to accurately record what was said. This is caused by a variety of things ranging from accents to the way the speaker pronounces certain words. Successful use of voice or word recognition software improves with length of use, the amount of "training" the user has done with it, and how well it recognizes the user's voice. Documents produced using such software must be carefully reviewed and mistakes corrected. One missed word can have dire consequences. In one extreme example, a doctor recorded "the baby cried," but the software recorded "the baby died." The mistake was overlooked and the flawed document was sent out, causing serious problems. In addition, these documents must be scanned for correct use of commas, parentheses, apostrophes, and other punctuation.

⑥⑦ ETHICS AND THE ADMINISTRATIVE HEALTH PROFESSIONAL (AHP)

AS PREVIOUSLY MENTIONED, ETHICAL BEHAVIOUR IS ESSENTIAL FOR THE AHP. ETHICS IS the study of standards of right and wrong in human behaviour. Ethical perspectives are shaped by culture, ethnicity, religion, upbringing, and social influences. Ethics deals with values and morals. **Values** are the principles, standards, or qualities that a person holds dear. For example, you might value honesty in your friendships or efficiency at work. **Morals** are what a person believes to be right and wrong. For example, you may have a moral belief that one should always keep promises.

Few professions demand a higher **code of ethics** than health care. As a member of a health-care team, you have moral obligations to the following:

- Your profession: to uphold excellence in clinical and administrative practice, work within your scope of practice, and have a sense of **duty** to all stakeholders

- The public: to practise in a competent, responsible, and honest manner, maintain public trust, and treat each person with respect. You have a moral obligation to adhere to the rules and laws that govern confidentiality.

- Your employer: to be faithful and accountable, and to adhere to the principles and policies of your workplace

- Your colleagues: to recognize their rights and treat them as you would want to be treated

Ethical Principles

Ethical principles provide guidance for moral action and ethical decision making. Ethical principles are applicable to any profession. They provide the foundation from which many professions adopt a code of ethics. The five principles discussed below are widely accepted in the health-care profession and should serve as guides for conduct and decision making.

1. *Autonomy.* **Autonomy** recognizes the **right** of a mentally competent individual to make independent decisions without coercion, once given the facts. Health professionals

ethics the philosophical study of standards accepted by society that determine what is right and wrong in human behaviour.

values the beliefs a person holds dear and that guide that person's decisions and behaviour or conduct.

morals what a person believes to be right and wrong pertaining to how to act, treat others, and get along in an organized society.

code of ethics a set of guidelines for ethical conduct.

duty a moral obligation.

autonomy a person's right to self-determination. In health care it refers to a client's right to make his own decisions without coercion—decisions for treatment for example, based on fact and being fully informed of all treatment options.

right a moral, legal, cultural, or traditional claim.

Tip

Remember that understanding and accepting someone else's ethical stand does not mean you are compromising your own ethical principles.

often try to influence the client's decisions, thinking they know what is best. Health professionals have a duty to respect the decisions of informed, autonomous adults. Consider this example: Yoko is dying of cancer and refuses to sign a consent form for chemotherapy. Dr. Berfeltz urges her to do so because he believes that chemotherapy treatments would prolong her life. Yoko believes that the treatments would make her sick and diminish the quality of life she has left. Dr. Berfeltz has a duty to respect Yoko's right to autonomy, and thus to respect her decision. You may not always agree with decisions clients make, but you must respect their right to make them. Consider also a high-profile case that began in 2011 in BC. Gloria Taylor, who suffers from **ALS** challenged the Supreme Court for the right to die, saying, "I'm dying piece by piece and I'm asking the court to let me die with dignity." Euthanasia and assisted suicide areillegal in Canada; thus she has taken her case before the courts—thus, Taylor has taken her case before the courts. The issue at stake is the right to die at a time of one's own choosing (in the face of a debilitating and ultimately fatal disease) versus the illegality of the act (considered euthanasia).

ALS Also known as amyotrophic lateral sclerosis or Lou Gehrig's disease. This is a progressive disease affecting the nerves that are responsible for muscle stimulation. There is no known cure.

2. *Veracity.* Veracity, or honesty and truthfulness, is the second universal ethical principle. Not many things are as personal or valued as one's own health, and clients expect honesty from health professionals. Rarely can withholding the truth be justified—even under the guise of sparing the client bad news. Deceit and dishonesty can rarely be justified at any point in your professional career. Honesty builds trust, which is a critical component of the health professional–client relationship. This principle includes keeping health information confidential, not disclosing information given to you in confidence by a patient (unless contraindicated by the law), keeping promises, and avoiding conflicts of interest.

3. *Faithfulness.* Also referred to as fidelity, faithfulness means meeting the reasonable expectations of others. In health care, it refers to carrying out obligations and duties to employers, clients, and peers. For example, your employer has the right to expect that you do your job well, honour commitments and contracts, and be respectful of him or her and the organization both at and away from your place of employment. It is important to realize that there may be situations where you feel you have a moral obligation to deviate from the principle of faithfulness because of conflicting moral principles. The situation could involve legal issues as well as moral principles.

4. *Beneficence.* The principle of beneficence requires that we benefit others and act in the person's best interests. The principle holds that we must do no harm, remove harm when it is being inflicted, and when possible, act to prevent harm from occurring.

5. *Justice.* The principle of justice in health care considers concepts of fairness and entitlements, and can involve moral or legal issues. For example, a client may be denied access to a treatment option because of long waits, or be harmed as a result of an incompetent act on the part of a health-care professional.

Under the *Personal Information Protection and Electronic Documents Act* (PIPEDA) you are legally bound to follow legislation protecting the public's health information. The Act provides guidelines for the collection, storage, use, and disclosure of all personal information. This legislation will be discussed in Chapter 13.

Ethical Decision Making

Ethical decision making in health care is complex. Health professionals deal with a wide range of facts, concepts, contexts, principles, and people. Ideally, decision making is organized, includes all affected parties, and considers all the facts and the feelings of people involved. It results in action (or inaction) that brings about the best results for the greatest number of people. Decision making typically follows these five sequential steps:

1. *Identify the problem.* First, determine whether there is a problem. Ethical problems can start off as something as small as an uncomfortable feeling, or they can be significant and easily identified.

2. *Gather information.* Next, gather relevant information from all available resources. Consider who is involved, what principles are involved, and the context of the situation.

3. *Determine the ethical approach.* Examine the possible solutions by using the most reasonable approach. In the process, ask yourself what benefit or harm each course of action will produce for each person involved. Consider the moral rights of those involved. Think about what course of action ensures equal treatment for everyone unless there is a justifiable reason not to do so.

4. *Make a decision.* Explore all practical alternatives before you finalize your decision. Even an action that seems ridiculous might have some valuable ideas hidden in it. You may decide on a blend of alternatives as the best solution.

5. *Take action.* Depending on the situation, you may find it beneficial to analyze the results of your action, and modify your actions if necessary.

Practising your profession in an ethically responsible manner, remaining objective, applying the five universal principles, and making informed decisions are important components of professional and personal success. Rarely will you have to make independent ethical decisions involving a client; however, you may be asked for input by other members of your health-care team when ethical situations arise. If this happens, stay calm, stay focused, and keep an open mind. Careless decisions are made in a hurry; adequate decisions are made with some thought; good decisions are made by applying ethical principles.

❽ DUTIES AND RESPONSIBILITIES

ALTHOUGH THE ADMINISTRATIVE HEALTH PROFESSIONAL'S PRIMARY ROLE IS ADMINISTRATIVE, in many offices, duties and responsibilities are a blend of clinical and administrative functions. Sometimes there is a fine line between these functions, and sometimes they overlap. In the health office, you may be the providers' main source of support. In the words of one physician: "My staff run the practice. I could not function without them. They keep me organized and the office organized. The clients depend on them too." In a solo dental or medical practice, the office professional may run the office alone, handling clinical as well as administrative responsibilities. In clinics and larger practices, the duties will likely be divided. In some occupational settings, you may have the opportunity to select duties or rotate through different administrative areas, such as reception/booking appointments, filing, communication/telephone, showing clients to examination rooms, and/or obtaining brief histories. The more common duties and responsibilities are listed below. Specific elements of some of these duties and responsibilities are discussed in appropriate chapters.

Administrative Responsibilities

- Greeting clients
- Managing incoming and outgoing telephone calls
- Managing other forms of communication, such as fax and email
- Scheduling and confirming appointments
- Maintaining the appointment book in an organized and confidential manner
- Reviewing and validating all health cards
- Coordinating consultations, lab procedures, diagnostic tests, and OR bookings
- Following referral procedures
- Triaging clients
- Entering data
- Reviewing incoming lab results; flagging abnormal results for the physician's attention
- Screening and processing office correspondence
- Initiating and maintaining client health records in electronic or paper format
- Billing the provincial or territorial system
- Following dental insurance billing procedures
- Keeping oneself informed of all changes in the billing process and maintaining currency
- Maintaining confidentiality
- Maintaining accounting and bookkeeping procedures unique to the office setting (may range from payroll to simple management of petty cash)
- Organizing business trips/meetings for the physician
- Acting as a liaison between the physician and other health-care professionals
- Arranging hospital admissions; looking after billing issues related to hospitalized clients
- Managing the physician's schedule (on-call time, time at ER, walk-in or urgent-care clinic, meetings, speaking engagements)
- Speaking with drug reps; arranging meetings with the physician; receiving and signing for pharmacy samples
- Transcribing and editing documents, including those created from voice-recognition software
- Preloading charts (includes converting paper-based charts to electronic format and managing EMR and EHR)
- Ordering supplies; maintaining inventory
- Managing capital expenditure
- Maintaining office equipment
- Arranging office cleaning
- Keeping the office/reception area neat and appropriately stocked with reading material
- Setting up examination rooms
- Completing components of insurance and claims forms

- Maintaining office security
- Ensuring the phone message is appropriate and current, or informing the answering service of schedule changes
- Updating the office procedure manual
- Managing staff

Clinical Responsibilities

Administrative health professionals are not trained or expected to perform clinical procedures or any activities within the domain of the nurse or other regulated professionals. Certain activities are regulated and may be performed only by health professionals qualified to do so. Many of these activities are considered controlled acts. For example, prescribing a medication is traditionally within the scope or practice of a physician, nurse practitioner, midwife, or—in some jurisdictions—a pharmacist. Other activities, such as taking vital signs, are not considered controlled acts and may be carried out by anyone trained to do so. Unregulated personnel may perform other procedures in a medical or dental office, if the physician or dentist takes responsibility for the personnel's actions ("delegated" acts).

Administrative health professionals may sometimes carry out the following duties:

- Interviewing clients to complete insurance forms, filling in history forms for new clients, or updating charts
- Escorting the client into the examination room and taking a brief statement regarding the reason for the visit
- Entering history of the present illness onto the EHR
- Preparing the examination room between clients
- Sanitizing and disinfecting instruments
- Taking weight and vital signs
- Testing urine with a dipstick
- Preparing infants for well-baby examinations (weighing and measuring length and head circumference)
- Preparing clients for examinations (giving them a gown and/or having them disrobe appropriately)
- Assisting, as required, with examinations (e.g., being present for a Pap smear or pelvic examination)[1]
- Supporting nervous clients during examinations
- Educating clients
- Explaining tests and procedures to clients or directing them to the appropriate resource
- Ensuring that clients who have had allergy shots remain in the office for approximately 20 minutes in case they develop a serious reaction
- Giving non-urgent, non-diagnostic telephone advice, as directed by the physician

---

[1] Although there is no legal requirement to do so, many physicians request a female staff member to be present during examinations involving vaginal contact. Some clients feel more comfortable with another person present, and having a witness protects both the client and the physician if accusations of improper conduct arise.

The Workplace Environment

For the most part, health offices are well equipped. Workspaces vary in size and design, from a small, relatively contained office area with a reception room to a large, more open area suitable for several employees. Client charts are usually accessible to the adminis-trative staff. In smaller offices, a half-glass partition often separates the office from the reception area, providing security and confidentiality for business and conversations. If you work in a hospital, you will primarily sit at the nurses' station, with a computer and telephone as your main tools.

Most health offices are open from 9 a.m. to 5 p.m., but some clinics and offices have evening and, occasionally, weekend hours. A number of physicians' offices close on Wednesday afternoons. Some providers want the office administrator in the office dur-ing that time to answer the telephone and attend to office business. Other offices close entirely, reducing the work week to 4½ days. The dental office usually operates five days a week and does not close for an afternoon. Dental offices and clinics may provide even-ing or weekend hours.

In a hospital client-care unit, shifts may be eight to 12 hours long. Twelve-hour shifts may be from 7 a.m. to 7 p.m. and 7 p.m. to 7 a.m. In some hospital departments, however, there is no clinical secretary on overnight duty; there may be a day shift from 7 a.m. to 7 p.m. and an evening shift from 4 p.m. until midnight, with a three-hour overlap. Most hospital positions require that you work your share of weekends. Such departments as Day Surgery and Outpatient Clinics may offer Monday-to-Friday daytime hours.

Most health offices close for an hour for lunch. Coffee breaks may be integrated into your working day, especially if you are the only person in the office. In the hospital, the charge nurse, clinical manager, or team leader usually assigns coffee and lunch breaks, which are staggered to ensure that staff are always available. Some facilities start coffee breaks as early as 9 a.m. and lunches around 11:30 a.m. Lunch breaks are most often half an hour, and coffee breaks average 20 minutes. Supper breaks in the hospital start at approximately 4:30 p.m. and are finished by 6 p.m. (1800 hours—see Figure 1.2 for the 24-hour clock used in most hospitals). Often, your break will depend on how busy you

Figure 1.2 The 24-hour clock, used in most hospitals and other health-care facilities

are. Smaller hospitals may not have a cafeteria open during the evening and night shifts, although there may be a coffee bar available.

Job Prospects

Across Canada, employment in the medical environment is expected to grow at least as fast as other occupations over the next several years. Jobs will be created both by growth in health-services industries and by retirement. Obviously, some regions offer more job opportunities than do others. Smaller communities can support only so many individuals in any given occupation. Thus, chances are that not all graduates from programs in smaller communities will find suitable employment locally.

Health office administration is not a **regulated profession**, such as nursing, medicine, or respiratory therapy. There is no legal requirement that an office assistant or clinical secretary have any particular education or qualification. Nevertheless, education and skills are expected in an increasingly responsible job, and graduates of medical/health office administration programs will have the best employment opportunities.

> **regulated profession** a field legally restricted to practitioners with a specific professional qualification and/or provincial or territorial registration.

Salaries and Benefits

What salary can you expect as a graduate once you do find a job? Salaries vary; though the pattern is not consistent, experience, location, setting, and the type of job and duties are factors. Typically, hospitals and similar facilities offer somewhat higher wages than do some health offices, but that gap is closing. With increased responsibilities in all sectors of administrative practice, the need for formal education is, in most cases, mandatory; thus, salaries have risen over the past three or four years.

Physicians' offices offer an average starting wages from $18 to $20 per hour or more (a new graduate might be offered $15–$18 with increases in salary after a period of probation). For candidates with more experience, the hourly wage would range between $25 and $30 per hour. In the hospital setting, the hourly wage usually starts around $22/hour. Some industries, such as insurance, will start a new graduate off at $32 000 to $35 000 a year, with full benefits. Hospital unit clerk or clinical secretary positions have various levels which will also reflect the hourly wage. Hospitals offer benefits to full-time employees and usually provide remuneration in lieu of benefits to part-time employees. Physicians' offices do not usually offer benefits. However, if the physician works for a primary care reform group, benefits may be included. In some jurisdictions, primary health groups have a CEO and separate board that, among other things, assumes responsibility for hiring administrative staff for their own needs (they may include such services as a central clinic, diabetic counselling, smoking cessation programs, diabetic clinics, and hypertension management) as well as for the physicians involved. Primary care groups typically offer competitive wages plus full benefits and paid holidays. Because wages and the inclusion of paid vacation and benefits vary across the country (amoung individual practitioners as well as groups and clinics), you should research the current wage and benefit packages offered by facilities in your area. A website listed at the end of this chapter includes a chart reflecting wages for medical secretaries in Canada.

⑪⑫ PROFESSIONAL GROWTH

GRADUATION FROM A HEALTH ADMINISTRATION PROGRAM IS ONLY THE FIRST STEP IN YOUR career. You will continue to grow through workplace experience, continuing education, membership in a professional association, and interaction with colleagues and other health

Tip

Check to see whether there is a professional association or an association chapter in the community in which you work. Despite the absence of a provincial/territorial organization, there may be independent chapters of a related association within that community.

professionals. Current and past employment and volunteer experiences, even if they seem unrelated, also help build general, transferable skills, such as reliability, organizational and communication skills, leadership ability, and teamwork. Workplace experience, if offered by your college program, will also consolidate your skills in a practical setting.

Professional Associations

Membership in a professional organization or association has many benefits. Associations support the purpose, mission, and goals of the profession. They help members become involved in the profession; keep them abreast of trends and changes within the field; offer resources, learning materials, and continuing education; and promote cohesiveness and professional pride. Many of these organizations offer student memberships to students in their last year of a college administrative program.

licensure a legal document, obtained after passing written and clinical examinations, that is required for health-care practitioners in regulated fields.

Some professional associations offer a certification program for the membership, achieved by passing an examination or series of examinations. Unlike **licensure**, which is mandatory for regulated professions, certification is usually voluntary. However, the status and tangible proof of meeting standards of practice are assets when seeking employment.

Associations may be provincial or territorial, national, or international. Some of the major organizations are profiled below.

The Medical Office Assistants' Association of British Columbia (founded in 1961) is available to individuals working in physicians' offices, hospitals, and other health-care facilities who are performing administrative or a blend of administrative and clinical duties. Benefits of membership are similar to those offered by other such organizations. Continuing education is cited as their main objective, with workshops and seminars available through local chapters. As with similar organizations, student membership is available and does offer a number of benefits, including networking within the province and across Canada. The website provided at the end of this chapter offers contact information for chapters throughout BC.

The Association of Administrative Assistants, a Canada-wide organization founded in 1951, originally grew from evening classes at the University of Toronto. The association strives to develop members' skills, knowledge, and professional growth in order to enhance employment opportunities and establish the value of its certified professional designation. Being a Qualified Administrative Assistant (QAA) is an important criterion in hiring and promotion. More information can be obtained from the organization's website listed at the end of this chapter.

International Association of Administrative Professionals (IAAP) The IAAP is the world's largest association for administrative support staff, with more than 600 chapters and 28 000 members and affiliates worldwide. There are chapters across

Canada from St. John's, Newfoundland, to Victoria, British Columbia. Founded in 1942 and headquartered in Kansas City, Missouri, IAAP provides up-to-date research on office trends, cutting-edge publications, seminars and conferences, and resources to help administrative professionals enhance their skills and become more effective contributors to their employers. The association works to educate employers and the public about the value of administrative professionals and the advantages of an administrative career. Most chapters offer professional development and networking at monthly meetings, seminars, and conferences. IAAP administers two certification programs—the Certified Professional Secretary (CPS) rating and the Certified Administrative Professional (CAP) rating. Detailed information about these designations and how to contact the organization can be obtained from the website listed at the end of this chapter.

Canadian Dental Assistant Association (CDAA)   The CDAA is a voluntary Canadian association for dental administrative assistants. Dental assisting is a health-care profession with all of the responsibilities that the title implies. The evolution of the profession is a reflection of the changing nature of dentistry, regulatory structures, new technologies, and Canadian society. In facing this change, the CDAA remains committed to its mission to provide the best possible programs and services to promote the professional growth and recognition of its members.

Membership opportunities for administrative assistants vary across the country. For example, in Ontario any dental business assistant can join the ODAA and take the required coursework to become a CDR or CTC (Certified Dental Receptionist or Certified Treatment Coordinator). If you have been approved for a post-secondary health administration program, the ODAA will allow direct writing of the CDR exam instead of having to take the required courses online. Information on contacting the CDAA and the ODAA can be obtained from the websites listed at the end of this chapter. The ODAA website Links page provides links to the websites of other provincial dental assistant association.

National Association of Health Unit Coordinators   NAHUC is a professional association for health unit coordinators. Its mission is to promote health unit coordinating as a profession through education and certification. Any individual working as a hospital unit coordinator/clerk can apply for membership. Despite the term "National" in the title, the NAHUC claims to be more of an international organization. The NAHUC currently has members in British Columbia, Ontario, and Prince Edward Island. The NAHUC offers certification exams across the U.S. and Canada. They are in the process of reviewing this textbook for purposes of studying for this exam. More information can be obtained from the organization's website listed at the end of this chapter.

Workplace Experience

Almost any workplace experience is a valuable opportunity for learning, growth, and a line on your résumé. Often, students underestimate the value of current and past employment experiences. For example, when asked what kind of a part-time job she had, Susan replied, "Nothing much. I work as a supervisor at McDonald's. It's a nothing job, but I need the money." What Susan did not see was that she had developed a sense of accountability and responsibility as well as leadership and management skills that were transferable to any position.

The more closely linked your work experience is to your future career, the more direct the benefits are in terms of specific skills. However, remember that any position will help you develop essential general attributes, such as communication and interpersonal skills and the ability to assume responsibility to handle multiple tasks and to work as a team member. Workplace experience also develops confidence and contributes to your personal development and maturity. Employment experience will make you aware of areas in which you may need to improve. For example, you may find that your organizational skills or your communication skills are lacking. Most employers will ask you about your weaknesses. If you say, "I don't know"—or even worse, "I don't think I have any"—the employer may think you lack insight. Rare is the person who has nothing to improve upon.

You can demonstrate self-awareness, honesty, and the desire for growth by acknowledging the areas in need of improvement in a positive manner. For example, "I have been working to improve my organizational skills and feel that they have improved significantly." Or, "I have sometimes found it difficult to maintain a conversation with a customer, particularly when I am busy, but I have learned some excellent strategies to help me with this." Or, "Computers have always been something that I have shied away from. However, I realize that computer literacy is essential in almost any position, so I have taken several courses, and I am feeling much more comfortable in the computerized environment than I did six months ago. I am looking forward to another course that starts next week." or, "Computer literacy is a huge part of my current college program, and I am doing well."

Résumés

If you have not already done so, composing a résumé in your first semester is a good idea, especially if you are looking for a part-time job or a volunteer position. It will also give you something to add to as you progress through your program. Keep your résumé in a folder, and add course outlines, assignments you are proud of, and any special student activities or positions you hold, such as peer tutor, class representative on student council, or mentor to a first-year or international student. Update your résumé periodically so that it reflects newly developed skills and attributes.

A résumé must be complete, concise, and properly written. There are several common formats. You may benefit from expert assistance. Student Services in most colleges can provide advice and guidance, as can the websites at the end of this chapter.

Writing a Résumé   A résumé is a summary of your current education, work experience, and relevant aspects of your community and personal life. It should be no more than one or two single-sided pages in length. When writing your résumé, use single spacing, 10- or 12-point font (Times New Roman or Arial), and print on 8.5×11 white or off-white paper. If you are a new graduate with little relevant experience, make your résumé one page. If you have considerable relevant experience, such as summer jobs, extracurricular leadership, and volunteer experience, two pages are justified. Remember that résumés containing too much detail crammed into a small space are often discarded because they are untidy looking and difficult to read.

An effective résumé will grab an employer's attention within several seconds and motivate him or her to read it all the way through. To achieve this, the résumé should be organized, clear, and concise, and should address the skills and knowledge base the employer is looking for. Most employers scan a résumé quickly to determine if the candidate seems to meet the majority of requirements; if so, a more detailed look at the résumé, and perhaps an invitation to an interview, will follow. Remember, the résumé will get you an interview; the interview will get you the job.

As a new graduate, it is best to focus on the quality of skills you have gained in college and through workplace experience. Remember that your résumé should highlight the relevance of your skills and knowledge to the job to which you are applying. You can give more detail in the covering letter and at your interview. You can emphasize assignments that you have done during your program that demonstrate a specific skill. For example,

- Demonstrated skills with medical office scheduling and billing [and bring the assignment with you to the interview if you get one]. Proven, accurate keyboarding skills (60 wpm).

There are numerous formats for constructing a résumé and many helpful books on the market to give you ideas, two of which are listed at the end of this chapter. Choose the headings, the content, and the layout that will showcase your skills and experience in a manner that will appeal to the employer. Each time you apply for a job, review your résumé to make sure the format and content are suitable for that particular job.

In the header, include your name, address, a contact telephone number (home and/or cell), and an email address. Ensure that the phone number is current and that it has a voice mail option. Your email address should be professional looking. If possible, get an email address that uses your name and your server, or something suitably neutral, such as yourname@getmail.ca. If your contact information changes after you have sent your résumé, contact any employer who may still be considering your application.

Electronic Résumés   Electronic résumés are popular, particularly with larger organizations such as insurance companies and large medical centres. Many jobs found on Workopolis require you to send in an electronic résumé (often referred to as an e-résumé). It can be constructed in much the same way as a paper résumé. Some organizations scan résumés for key words. Use words from the job description in your résumé as these are the key words that the computer has likely been programmed to look for.

Job Search

Approach your job search with an organized plan and with a goal in mind. Focus your search on employment opportunities in the area of health care that most interests you. Use available resources. Most colleges offer job banks through Student Services (or an equivalent), and they are usually free of charge. Student Services will ask you to provide

Tip

Have someone review your résumé and cover letter—preferably a person familiar with the type of job you are seeking. If you are asked for a "working interview," dress neatly, be prompt, and research the facility. Anticipate what needs to be done, and ask if you can help—even if it differs from the role you are applying for. (e.g., a veterinarian on a working interview saw the technicians were very busy and pitched in to assist them). Be cheerful, professional, and approachable. Often staff members are asked for input as to who should be hired (from the short list of candidates). A friendly, sunny demeanour and the willingness to pitch in could make a difference in who they choose.

the department with a current résumé and a summary of the type of job you are looking for. Student Services will then automatically send your résumé to prospective employers. The process may vary with different colleges.

Your professional organization may also offer access to lists of employment opportunities, more commonly in offices or clinics. The IAAP and the Medical Office Assistants' Association of B.C., for example, have job banks members can access.

Most hospitals keep a current list of job opportunities posted on their websites. Jobs are also posted internally, usually in designated areas. Insurance companies also post available positions and require that you submit your résumé online in most instances.

Online job sites, such as Workopolis, can be useful search tools. You can often select the region you want to concentrate your job search in and the type of job you are seeking.

If you want to work for government—for example, Health Canada—you can access the Careers section of the relevant website. Provincial and territorial websites—ministries or departments of health—also have links to current employment opportunities. If there are government offices in your region, visit them and submit a résumé. These include regional health authorities, public health centres, or provincial or territorial billing offices (most provinces and territories have regional resource offices). Your local employment office will likely have listings. Government departments at the federal, provincial or territorial, and municipal levels usually list their employment opportunities with public employment offices.

Networking and cold calling are other choices that may help you find a position. Many jobs are secured by personal recommendation and word of mouth, or because an employer has your résumé on hand and met you when you dropped it off. Employers save time and money when they do not have to advertise a position (this can be done in most non-unionized organizations). Network by telling people about your qualifications, your skills, and the type of employment you are looking for. Tell your family doctor, your dentist, or a nurse at the hospital. If you have completed a work placement with your college program, keep your eyes open for opportunities within the organization or with similar organizations. If you are competent and professional, chances are they will seek you out or request that you leave a résumé with them in case a position becomes available.

Cold calling involves making contact with people you have not met before, but who you think may have a job you're interested in. Don't underestimate the value of checking with your local employment agencies either. Agencies in your area are in the telephone book under *Employment*.

Finding a job takes time and effort. It can be discouraging if you do not get immediate results. Keep your résumé current and tailored to the job you are applying for. Be choosy but flexible. Accepting a job that is not exactly what you want may lead to something more suitable. For example, accepting a position as a switchboard operator in a hospital may lead to a position as a clinical secretary. Volunteering to help with filing at a doctor's office can also lead to employment. Stay positive and unrelenting in your search.

An **externship**, or job placement experience, is part of many college programs and provides you with an excellent opportunity for application of theory to practice, often in the workplace setting of your choice.

externship a cooperative or workplace experience or period of training for a student that is provided by the student's educational facility.

Volunteer Work

If you do not have a job or a co-op placement through your college, volunteering is another way to obtain a variety of experiences and develop transferable skills. Volunteers are both needed and welcomed in almost every area. Everyone admires and respects the commitment of individuals who volunteer their time to community organizations. Volunteering not only develops skills but also is a rewarding personal experience and contributes to the organization and the people it serves. Volunteer work illustrates a commitment to others, concern, initiative, and selflessness—all character traits that can only enhance an individual personally and professionally. You will gain concrete experience to show employers, as well as character references for such things as punctuality, commitment, and initiative.

Before applying for a volunteer post, consider how much time you have to commit. Many volunteer positions require commitment to a certain number of hours on a regular schedule. If school does not leave you enough time for a regular position, you could volunteer for special functions, such as food drives, especially during the holiday season.

Volunteer opportunities may be found in hospitals, nursing homes, community organizations such as Meals on Wheels, mental health organizations, the Canadian Cancer Society, the Red Cross, medical offices, or hospices. You will get the most direct benefit from volunteering in an area related to your career path. You gain relevant experience in that area, are exposed to the general duties and responsibilities of other health-care professionals with whom you may be working, and augment what you are learning at college.

If you are interested in working in a client-care unit in a particular hospital, for example, apply to be a volunteer in the clinical setting at that hospital. If you think you would like to work in the Medical Records department, ask if they could use some help with filing or other general duties. If you want to work in a doctor's office, contact one (perhaps one that you have been referred to), and ask if you can help out for a few hours a week. Suggest something that you feel prepared to handle, such as filing.

List volunteer experiences in your résumé, noting why you chose to volunteer, your specific experiences, how you managed any difficult situations, and what you gained from the experience.

Applying for most volunteer positions is much like applying for a job: a formal process that may require a résumé, personal and educational references, an application form, an interview, and a police background check. This is because the organization has an obligation to its clients to ensure that anyone working with them is suitable, safe, knowledgeable, honest, and trustworthy. Usually, a large organization such as a hospital has a volunteer coordinator who serves as a contact with applicants. An applicant would typically have an interview, much like a job interview, that covers interests and experience. Once accepted, a second interview is common to discuss specific placement. Training may also be required before assuming volunteer duties.

Simulated Office Experience

Medical office simulations are integrated into medical office administration programs in many colleges. The simulations not only provide practical exposure to activities that might be encountered on the job in a medical office but also reinforce many of the topics covered in a medical office procedures subject.

Cooperative Work Experience

Some college programs have a workplace experience component, which may either be integrated into the program or placed at the end just prior to graduation. A workplace experience component may also be called a co-op (cooperative experience), practicum (practical application of skills), consolidation (an experience wherein the student consolidates acquired skills and theory), or externship (getting experience outside the college environment). The workplace experience involves a contractual agreement among the employer, the student, and the college. The time frame varies with the length and structure of the program. The purpose of this experience is to provide the student with the chance to put theory into practice—to apply the skills learned in college to the workplace setting. The student is able to assume some job responsibilities while still under the guidance of a **preceptor** or someone the student can turn to for guidance and advice.

preceptor   a mentor who guides and supervises a student throughout a workplace experience.

In most co-op programs, students can seek placement in an area of interest, assuming suitable opportunities are available and the experience offered matches program requirements. Most facilities require the student to apply for the experience in the same manner as one would for a job. Students thus gain experience with résumés and interviews. If more than one student applies for the same opening, the selection should be based on suitability, just as in any job competition. Do not take it personally if you are not selected—and make sure to apply for more than one position. Some programs do not use an application process; instead, the employer asks the program coordinator or a placement officer to select the best-suited student. Usually, student requests are an important part of any decisions made.

Cooperative Work Experiences Offer

- the opportunity to apply what you have learned in college to a practical setting;
- general work experience;
- personal insight into your own abilities, strengths, and needs for improvement, and
- the opportunity to develop a level of professionalism and professional ethics.

Expectations and Responsibilities   The employer has the right to expect that the student involved in the experience is qualified (at an entry level) and will abide by the workplace's rules. In health-care settings, for example, where health office professionals frequently have access to confidential client records, students may be required to sign a confidentiality statement.

The college and the student have the right to expect that the employer will provide an experience that reflects the objectives and expectations outlined by the initial agreement. On occasion, an employer will view the student as merely an extra set of hands, forgetting that the student is there to complete a set of learning outcomes. Students should discuss such problems with their preceptors or employers and, if they remain unresolved, with their faculty advisors.

Student Preparation   Before entering a workplace experience, you must be prepared and organized. To ensure that you start off on the right foot, before accepting a position you should meet with the employer and/or preceptor to review your own and the employer's expectations and to determine the duties and responsibilities of the position. Review all relevant materials such as evaluation criteria with the appropriate persons. Discuss the evaluation tool itself and how often evaluations will take place. Most health-care facilities require a visible liaison between the facility and the faculty advisor for the duration of the student's experience. Find out what type of contact will occur and how often; if possible, set up appointments in advance. Review your responsibilities to the college to ensure that there are no mix-ups or misunderstandings. Some colleges will expect you to send your faculty advisor weekly summaries or to submit a final paper on completion of the workplace experience.

Evaluation   Evaluations should be done at regular intervals during any cooperative experience—every two weeks is not unreasonable—to provide continuous feedback and allow the student and the employer to discuss any problems as they arise. Positive feedback is equally important. Knowing that you are doing a good job provides you with confidence and a sense of accomplishment. If you feel that you are not getting positive feedback, tactfully ask for it. "What do you see as my strengths during these past two weeks?" "In what areas do you feel I am best suited to this experience?" Self-evaluations are also helpful and should normally resemble the employer's evaluation. If the two are very different, the reasons need to be investigated.

Employment Expectations   Any workplace or co-op experience should be viewed as if it were an actual job. Approach the experience with a positive attitude and a sense of commitment. Act like a professional in dress, manner, and attitude. Be punctual, and notify the employer if you are ill. Seek out new learning opportunities, complete tasks in a timely manner, demonstrate organizational skills, and try to work harmoniously with other team members. Although it is important to work as independently as possible, it is equally important to recognize your limitations, seek help appropriately, and work within your designated **scope of practice**. Not adhering to this can cause difficulties for you, your preceptor or employer, and perhaps others.

> **scope of practice**   the parameters of duties and responsibilities outlined by one's professional training and skill set.

A cooperative experience may lead to employment, but there is no guarantee, and you should not enter into it with that expectation. A positive cooperative experience will, however, provide you with a good reference to add to your résumé.

Continuing Education

Graduating from an accredited program as a health-care professional is only the first step in the educational process. Most community colleges and independent educational centres across Canada offer courses in a wide range of clinical and administrative skills. You may be required to take courses to keep abreast of technological and communication advances within the administrative setting or to prepare you to assume a wider range of responsibilities in your current job setting.

Many colleges articulate with universities, offering advanced standing to college graduates wanting to pursue a degree in Health Administration. Athabasca University in Alberta is one such facility. The trend to expect multiple skills will continue to grow. Continued learning is not only a professional responsibility—a duty to yourself as well as your employer—but is an effective way to broaden your career opportunities. Employers value self-motivation and the combination of experience and additional educational qualifications. Keeping abreast of the latest administrative procedures and technological advances makes you a valuable asset to any health-care setting.

Future Trends

The scope of practice and level of responsibility in health administration are rapidly expanding and becoming more complex for three main reasons: increasing demands, the electronic environment, and primary care reform.

Increasing Demands

First, increasing demands on all health providers are limiting the time they have for administrative responsibilities. Physicians are busier than ever, responding to increased client loads because of physician shortages and treating individuals who have complex illnesses that demand more time. Health providers will thus rely on the administrative professional to assume duties the health providers previously took responsibility for.

Electronic Information Management

Second, establishing a Canada-wide system for electronic health records is a priority of the federal, provincial, and territorial health ministries. This is a complicated process that will continue to evolve over the next several years and will affect every office, hospital, clinic, and health organization in the country.

Although most health practitioners are comfortable with electronic environments, they rely heavily on administrative staff to manage large components of this technology. Physicians, for example, access different components of an electronic system than their medical administrator does. You would be more involved with the scheduling, electronic billing, electronic report filing, and tracking such things as immunizations and specified medical procedures.

In addition, administrative professionals must be knowledgeable about federal, provincial, and territorial privacy legislation to guarantee the confidentiality and security of electronic information. Maintaining security of information will be a continual challenge.

Primary Care Reform

Third, the solo practice in medicine has all but disappeared in favour of numerous primary care reform models. This affects the role of the administrative professional. She will be required to work with a variety of health professionals within one organization—a physician, pharmacist, dietitian, social worker, and chiropractor, for example. The administrative professional will also be required to keep abreast of changes in how providers are paid, including capitation-based funding formulas, incentive fees, and a battery of billing codes that are constantly changing.

Lifelong Learning

The number of jobs in health office administration will continue to grow. Many will be management positions. Thus, health office administration programs must assume more responsibility for educating students about their responsibility for lifelong learning and prepare them for leadership roles. Opportunities are there. For instance, more universities are offering people with diplomas entry to degree programs in health office administration. At the same time, employers will be looking for employees with demonstrated ability to communicate, solve problems, manage organizations and human resources, apply the principles of health-care planning to electronic health systems, and work effectively with community partnerships to support those systems.

SUMMARY

1. Health office professionals have many different job titles, depending on the areas in which they work. Advancing technology and the changing Canadian health-care system have created a need for knowledgeable, multi-skilled people in administrative positions. Most employers now seek graduates of certificate or diploma programs.

2. Health office professionals find work in many settings, including medical and other health-care offices, specialty clinics, alternative and allied health-care facilities,

hospital departments, long-term care facilities, seniors' residences, government offices, and companies. Employment is expected to grow.

3. Desirable attributes of the administrative health professional include a friendly, approachable personality, a sense of responsibility, flexibility, good judgment, and the ability to remain calm in stressful situations. Although these attributes are often inherent, some people have to work to develop them.

4. Professionalism is reflected in dress, thought, speech, and action. As the administrative health professional is usually the client's first contact, a positive first impression is important. Although dress codes vary, cleanliness, neatness, and appropriateness always apply.

5. Skills, while they may overlap with attributes, are generally learned. Communication skills are essential, including clear enunciation, excellent spoken and written grammar, sensitive listening, and the ability to express empathy and to understand and convey information clearly. Keyboarding, computer literacy, and the ability to understand, use, and write medical terms are also indispensable.

6. Typical administrative responsibilities include greeting clients, managing communications, scheduling appointments, triaging clients, and billing. Clinical responsibilities may include doing client interviews, assisting with medical examinations, taking vital signs, and educating clients.

7. As a health-care professional, you enter into a social contract with the public, your employer, and your colleagues. Given the nature of health care, expectations are high that you will perform your professional responsibilities with honesty, integrity, impartiality, and competence. Following a code of ethics based on the universal principles of autonomy, truthfulness, faithfulness, beneficence, and justice will promote trust, respect, and ethical practice.

8. Membership in a professional organization offers a wealth of benefits, including opportunities for ongoing education, links to employment opportunities, and networking with other members of the profession.

9. All work experience is valuable in developing transferable skills. Volunteering is an excellent way to develop skills and build your résumé while contributing to the community and showing your personal commitment.

10. Some colleges have a simulated medical office component integrated into the medical office administration program and some colleges have a cooperative or workplace experience that allows students to apply their learning in a controlled environment. The college, employer, and student all have rights and obligations.

Key Terms

administrative health professional 3
allied health care 7
ALS (amyotrophic lateral sclerosis) 18
alternative health care (complementary health care) 7
attribute 10
autonomy 17

client 3
clinic 8
code of ethics 17
core competency 15
duty 17
ethics 17
externship 29
licensure 24
medical assistant 5

medical office assistant 5
morals 17
preceptor 30
regulated profession 23
right 17
scope of practice 31
triage 13
values 17
ward clerk 5

Review Questions

1. How have the duties and responsibilities of the administrative health professional changed over the past 10 or 20 years, both in the hospital and in the health office setting?

2. Differentiate between attributes and skills. Identify and discuss three attributes and three skills that are important in health office administration.

3. Define professionalism and discuss what it means for the health-care professional.

4. What is meant by the term *triage*? How does effective triage relate to good judgment?

5. What are the main benefits of remaining calm in an emergency?

6. What are the main advantages of belonging to a professional organization?

7. What is the purpose of a medical office simulation component, an externship, or cooperative placement experience?

8. What is the recommended font, spacing, and size and colour of paper when writing a résumé?

9. What is the advantage of networking with respect to a job search?

10. Compare and contrast the responsibilities and expectations of the student and the employer during a co-op or workplace experience.

11. What does working within your scope of practice mean?

12. List the benefits of ongoing education for the administrative health professional.

Application Exercises

1. Review the list of possible employment opportunities for the administrative health professional. Add any others you can think of or that are available in your community. Select two or three that interest you. Either individually or in a small group, list the duties and responsibilities you think would apply to each. Over the next week, interview individuals who work in these or similar settings, or research the jobs on the internet or at the library. Add any new information to your original list. Share your findings with the class.

2. Identify volunteer opportunities available in your community in the following settings (or in settings in which you would like to work). For each, describe the types of volunteer placement you would seek.

   a. A pediatrician's office

   b. A Medical Records Department

   c. An active client-care unit in a hospital

3. Read the following scenario:

   Irum works in a busy medical office. A colleague, Molly, makes life miserable for her and the other staff members. She is uncommunicative, abrasive, and abrupt. She works in isolation, does not pass on messages, and refuses to work collaboratively. Information often is not passed on, appointments are mixed up, reports are not read or passed on to the doctor, and clients blame everyone in the office. What steps could you take to deal with this issue?

4. Construct a résumé suitable for applying for a part-time job, an externship, or a volunteer position. Ask the resource people available at your college to critique your résumé and suggest improvements. Keep this résumé in a file folder. Add all of your course outlines (learning outcomes) to this folder along with assignments that you are proud of. Using tips from the websites provided at the end of this chapter, format your résumé to suit an electronic format.

5. The following exercise is designed to help you identify the attributes you can bring to a job. This will help you set goals, present your strengths in a job interview, and develop a plan to build new strengths.

   a. In small groups, or as a class, discuss each professional quality identified in this chapter as important for administrative health professionals. Add others that you feel are relevant. Analyze each quality, and list specific examples/situations where you feel that quality would be an asset.

   b. From the above list, select some personal qualities that you think you possess. Under each quality, write a brief summary of ways in which you demonstrate that quality, including examples. Consider achievements you are proud of, in school, volunteer work, family life, or hobbies. What personal qualities, strengths, and motivators were instrumental in helping you achieve? Now, ask a classmate or friend to select from the list qualities that she thinks you possess. How do the two descriptions differ? Can you explain these differences? Do you feel you are looking at yourself realistically? Do you come across differently to others from the way you see yourself?

   c. Compare your list and your friend's list with the list of qualities from Part a. Are there qualities you need to improve? Prepare a list of strategies.

   d. Identify three people you admire, whether they are people you know personally or public figures. Why do you admire these people? List the qualities you admire in them. Are they qualities you feel you have or ones you would like to develop?

   e. Design the perfect job for yourself, specifying setting, employer, and responsibilities. What qualities do you think you would require for this job? How closely do they match the qualities you identified in Part b? If you chose a fast-paced, hectic Emergency Department, do you feel that you work well under pressure? Do you have excellent critical thinking skills? If you chose an area such as medical transcription, do you pay attention to detail? Are there any areas where you think you need improvement? Make developing these a personal goal. You may choose a dental office—why? What aspects of the dental office environment do you think would better suit your skills and attributes compared with a doctor's office?

6. Using the ethical principles listed in this chapter as a foundation, develop a 10-point code of ethics for your profession. Work in groups of four or five. Discuss the rationale for each point. Have someone in your group record your final list. Identify a leader in your group to display your code of ethics, and as a class compare and discuss each list. Form a code of ethics for health office professionals by combining the best points from each group.

7. Independently or with a partner, conduct internet research for a recent story involving one of the five ethical principles discussed in this chapter, for example, the principle of autonomy and the court challenge for the right to physician-assisted suicide by Gloria Taylor, who has amyotrophic lateral sclerosis (also known as ALS or Lou Gehrig's disease).

   a. Discuss the significant principles you feel are involved in the case you chose.

   b. What, if any, legal barriers exist? Consider the conflict between moral principles and the law.

   c. Describe what you would do in a similar situation, outlining your personal feelings and rationale. Use the steps of problem solving to reach your conclusion.

8. Hassan Rasouli, a 59-year-old, had surgery at Sunnybrook Health Sciences Centre in Toronto in October 2010, to treat a benign brain tumour. He developed complications, ending up in a coma; doctors claim he is in a futile and vegetative state. Since then, he has been kept alive by a ventilator and a feeding tube. Doctors want to remove the man from life support without the family's consent. As doctors moved more aggressively to

remove life support, in April 2012 the family asked the Supreme Court of Canada to intervene. The family feels that Mr. Rasouli has improved and responded appropriately to verbal stimuli. What do you think? Should doctors have the right to make such decisions? What do *you* feel are the rights of the family? Research this ongoing case, gather pertinent details, and come to a conclusion. You can do this in small groups and conduct a debate on the subject. How does morality clash with legal issues? What ethical principles are important in the stand both sides have taken?

Books about Résumé Writing

Kennedy, Joyce L. *Résumés for Dummies*. John Wiley & Sons (2006).

Whitcom, Susan Britton. *Résumé Magic: Trade Secrets of a Professional Résumé Writer*. JIST Works (2006).

Brown, Lola M. *Résumé Writing Made Easy*. Pearson Education (2006).

Websites of Interest

Immanuel Kant and the Ethics of Duty
http://ethics.sandiego.edu/presentations/Theory/Kant/Duty/Kant,%20Duty%20and%20Universality.ppt
This site provides a slide presentation on the ethics of duty.

Job Searching

http://jobsearch.about.com/od/findajob/Job_Search_Advice.htm
This site offers advice on beginning a job search.

Health Careers Interaction
www.healthcareersinteraction.com?gclid=CNvWrM2WlJACFRGCGgodbjTSAQ
This is a job search website for health professionals. Click on Job Search in the left column.

Public Service Commission of Canada
www.psc-cfp.gc.ca
This site offers a federal government job search, including Health Canada employment opportunities.

Canada Jobs
www.canadajobs.com/articles/category.cfm?Category=Job%20Search
This site has job search tips and advice, plus links to employment opportunities.

Monster job search
www.monster.ca
This site provides links to jobs across the country.

Find Private Clinics
findprivateclinics.ca
This is a resource for private clinics in Canada.

Canada Prospects
www.canadaprospects.com/products/cp_nav/home.cfm?yearid=10&sectionid=4&art_number=3&l=e
This site provides excellent advice on job searches and résumé writing, including some advice on adapting your résumé to an electronic format.

Volunteer Canada
www.volunteer.ca
This site gives general information, lists special events, and allows you to register as a potential volunteer and browse a database of organizations.

Résumé Writing

Each of the following sites offers a slightly different approach and different information that may be useful in constructing your résumé.

http://jobstar.org/tools/resume/index.cfm

www.rockportinstitute.com/resumes.html

http://careerplanning.about.com/cs/resumewriting/

www.sass.uottawa.ca/careers/resources/resumes/eresume.php

Medical Jobs Canada

www.jobcanada.org/medical.html

This job referral site lists jobs available, open sites, and general information for job seekers.

Professional Associations

International Association of Administrative Professionals

www.iaap-hq.org/index.htm

This site provides information on membership and certification programs, as well as a newsletter and a research and trends section.

Association of Administrative Assistants

www.aaa.ca

This site provides information on membership, certification programs, courses, and career development and technology.

Medical Office Assistants' Association of British Columbia

www.medicalofficeassistantsofbc.com

National Association of Health Unit Coordinators

http://www.nahuc.org/

The international test sites for the Health Unit Coordinators Examination, including Canada, are listed at:

http://www.goamp.com/displayTCList.aspx?pExamID=21014

Canadian Dental Assistant Association

http://www.cdaa.ca/

Ontario Dental Assistants Association

http://www.odaa.org/

This site will link you to the Ontario Dental Assistants Association. The Links page provides links to other provincial dental assistant association websites.

Medical Secretaries—Canada Salary and Wage Guide

http://www.livingin-canada.com/salaries-for-medical-secretaries-canada.html

APPENDIX 1A Sample Résumé

JINATO LIAN

234 Anywhere Street ♦ Vancouver, BC V4Z W4T ♦ (604)-433-4444
♦ ljinato@donet.ca

KEY QUALIFICATIONS

- Detail oriented
- Proficient MS Word, Meditec, and Visual Practice
- Medical Office Assistants of B.C. member
- Excellent communication skills
- Demonstrated ability in order entry
- Proven knowledge base in terminology
- Proficient with medical dictatyping

RELATED SKILLS

ADMINISTRATIVE AND ORGANIZATIONAL

- Demonstrated proficiency with order entry
- Ability to prioritize and schedule laboratory and diagnostic tests
- Error-free dicta typing with a keyboarding speed of 55 wpm
- Proven ability to edit documents—hard copy and computer generated from voice-recognition software
- Experience in organizing nursing schedules, finding replacements for ill staff members
- Solid knowledge of medical terminology, anatomy and physiology, pharmacology, laboratory and diagnostic tests
- Experience using various medical databases and managing electronic health records
- Familiar with ICD 10 coding strategies

COMMUNICATION AND INTERPERSONAL

- Ability to interact professionally and effectively with clients and clients' family members
- Highly ethical, professional in dress and manner
- Knowledge of privacy legislation and my related responsibilities
- Ambitious, seek new learning opportunities
- Work well independently and as a team member
- Work within my scope of practice, seek assistance when needed
- Reliable, honest, and trustworthy

EDUCATION

Health Office Administration Program, 2008–present, Douglas College, New Westminster, BC
General Arts and Science, 2002–2004, University of Waterloo, Waterloo, ON

EMPLOYMENT HISTORY

Customer Service Representative, Maben Marketing, Calgary, AB, 2000–2002
Receptionist, Ribera Chiropractic, Saskatoon, SK, 2002–2004

VOLUNTEER EXPERIENCE

New Westminster Memorial Hospital, pediatric unit, 2002–present

Part II
Health in Context

Part II will give you the background that will serve as a common thread throughout the rest of the textbook. It discusses health and illness from the perspective of the individual in Canada's multicultural society. It then introduces you to Canada's health-care system. Chapter 2 discusses health, health beliefs, and current concepts of health and illness, using the health–illness continuum. It explains how altered health and changes in role function affect clients and their families. You will learn how to respond constructively to clients and their families in sickness and in health and how to establish a trusting and supportive relationship with them. Chapter 3 builds on what you have learned in Chapter 2, with the introduction of cultural variation. Cultural barriers to health care are discussed, as well as the importance of accepting and understanding people from other cultures. This chapter will provide you with guidelines for effective cross-cultural communication, including using an interpreter. Chapter 4 will provide you with an overview of the structure and function of health care in Canada, including the principles and conditions of the *Canada Health Act* and primary care reform initiatives.

Chapter 2
Health and the Individual

Learning Objectives

On completing this chapter, you will be able to:

1. Explain the relationship between health beliefs and health behaviour.

2. Discuss the concepts of health and wellness.

3. List and discuss the five dimensions of wellness.

4. Describe the health–illness continuum.

5. Explain the typical responses to the stages of illness.

6. Discuss how roles change with sickness and how this affects clients and their families.

7. Discuss the effects of hospitalization.

8. Summarize the implications of altered health behaviours for the health office professional.

Altered health has subtle and profound effects on a person and the person's family, friends, and social and work-related contacts. This chapter is designed to help you understand and recognize the behaviour patterns that altered health generates in those who are affected both directly and indirectly. Understanding why your clients act as they do can help you communicate more effectively and offer stronger support to them. If this chapter is not included in your curriculum, you will find it valuable supplemental reading to Chapter 8 on communication.

Behaviour is defined as a person's discernible responses and actions. It includes actions and reactions to people, situations, and emotions. Most people's behaviour is fairly consistent throughout their daily lives. Behaviour, however, changes in response to various stimuli. When upset, stressed, or angry, a person may react in an uncharacteristic manner. A stressful day at work can cause someone who is normally easygoing and friendly to become cross and snippy. Under excessive stress, a normally competent, organized person may become unable to focus or to function efficiently. Over time, most of us get to know how we respond to various stimuli. We develop coping strategies to modify and control ineffective behaviour or we simply avoid unpleasant or stressful situations.

Illness is a stressor for most people. Illness affects people emotionally as well as physically, changing their behaviour patterns. An ill person may feel vulnerable, fearful, uncertain, and worried about the stress the illness is placing on others. The person may respond by becoming passive and dependent, withdrawn and uncommunicative, or short-tempered, outwardly angry, and critical.

Illness affects the behaviour not only of the ill person but also of those close to him. Others' responses depend on a number of factors, including their relationship to the ill person (e.g., wife, husband, parent, friend), the nature of the illness, the treatment plan, the prognosis and recovery time, and the person's professional, social, and family roles.

Most of us value support and understanding in times of illness, especially from those who know us and understand how to offer reassurance. You cannot expect to know clients well enough to know how they respond under stress or how to support them as individuals. It is important, however, to have a general understanding of how people react and to know some helpful response patterns. You will often be the first point of contact for clients when they seek medical assistance. In the face of prolonged illness or investigations, you may have ongoing contact with the client and the client's family. When they call the office for information or to make appointments, or call the hospital for updates, a supportive and empathetic response will do much to comfort them. Responding effectively to clients and their families and offering empathy and appropriate support will help them feel valued and cared for and will contribute to their well-being and sense of security. It makes the experience of illness less stressful.

behaviour a person's discernible responses and actions.

❶ HEALTH BELIEFS

HEALTH BELIEFS ARE THINGS A PERSON BELIEVES TO BE TRUE ABOUT HEALTH, ILLNESS, prevention, treatment, and cure. A person's health beliefs are influenced by many factors, including culture and life experiences. Among health beliefs are people's understanding of their own susceptibility to illness and the effect of lifestyle on disease prevention and health promotion—for example, their estimate of self-imposed risks, such as smoking. A person may not believe that smoking causes lung cancer. Even if he does, he may convince himself that he is immune or that it will not happen to him. "I won die of lung cancer. Grandpa Smith smoked two packs a day and lived to be 90." One factor is something called *locus of control*: people's beliefs about whether their lives are shaped primarily by their own actions or by external forces. People with an internal locus of control believe they are responsible for what happens to them. People with an external locus of control believe they are victims or beneficiaries of luck, fate, or other people. A person with an internal locus of control is more likely to take responsibility for her own health: "I need to eat well and avoid smoking to maintain my health." Someone with an external locus of control tends to discount the effects of her own behaviour: "So I smoke. It's the only enjoyment I have. If I am going to get lung cancer, I will get it anyway. I might as well enjoy myself while I can." As this comment shows, beliefs also reflect how a person weighs immediate enjoyment against long-term effects.

Health beliefs also include attitudes to treatment options. Some people, for example, believe that doctors are powerful and generally have the answers. Others have lower expectations of the health-care system and may be suspicious of doctors' recommendations. ("Oh, that doctor, she just likes to put everybody on pills. She doesn't really know what's wrong with me.") People also hold beliefs about the relative effectiveness of conservative and holistic approaches to medicine. Some view alternative therapies as an adjunct to the medical model of treatment, some view all forms of alternative medicine as quackery, and still others believe that alternative modalities can cure or prevent all diseases. Health beliefs also influence attitudes toward decisions on end-of-life issues, such as whether to use life support and how aggressively to pursue treatment in the face of a terminal illness.

Health beliefs influence perceptions of health and health behaviour. Health beliefs can determine whether people actively seek to maintain health, how often they seek medical care, what treatment options they choose, and how they respond to illness.

❶ HEALTH BEHAVIOUR

Health behaviour includes all the things a person does to stay healthy, physically and psychologically. For example, some people watch their diets, take vitamin supplements, try to exercise regularly, and avoid second-hand smoke. They may consciously avoid overwork and make a point of relaxing. Other people do such things sporadically. Still others may ignore diet and exercise but carefully avoid exposure to sick people. An individual's health behaviour is determined by her health beliefs, personality, health experiences, culture, and ethnicity, and the nature of an illness and the degree of understanding and support she receives when ill.

One aspect of health behaviour is illness behaviour, also called sick role behaviour (discussed in more detail later). Illness behaviour refers to people's activities and behaviours in response to illness. It includes those behaviours from the point of believing that an illness exists through to recovery or death.

Many people take good health for granted. They may never have experienced serious illness and have no idea how they would respond.

❷❸ CONCEPTS OF HEALTH AND WELLNESS[1]

Health

Health, according to one definition, is "a relative state in which one is able to function well physically, mentally, socially, and spiritually in order to express the full range of one's unique potentialities within the environment in which one is living."

A more recent definition[2] of **health** goes further to include spirituality as having an impact on our health. It considers each person unique with specific abilities and capabilities. The inclusion of the phrase "relative state" indicates that health is individualistic and not constant. What Bob may consider to be good health, Maria may not. Today, concepts of health vary from person to person, but most people include such things as quality of life, happiness, and spiritual and intellectual components.

Wellness

Wellness is another word frequently associated with health. Generally, **wellness** refers to a state of physical and emotional well-being, as well as the practices that promote and maintain this state. Wellness, like health, is often defined personally. Usually, it includes physical health but also embraces lifestyle, enjoyment of life, and intangible things such as happiness, contentment, and an overall quality of life. Some people may consider that they have achieved wellness even though they are not physically healthy. For example, a person with a chronic disease or disability may accept her limitations and be emotionally well. The disability or illness is then integrated into the person's concept of wellness. A person with multiple sclerosis (MS) may accept the disease and consider herself healthy. If her health continues to deteriorate, she might no longer define herself as being well; if, however, she accepts the degenerative nature of the disease, her sense of wellness might remain constant.

The concept of wellness includes five dimensions that combine to shape our lives. Each dimension plays a different but important role. Consider a machine with five components: Take out one part, and the machine still runs. Take out two or three parts, and the machine may still run, but not efficiently. Take out four parts, and the machine stops. In a holistic understanding of wellness, all components must be working properly for a person to be happy and healthy. If one or two components need "adjusting," the person can still function but may seek assistance. Clients may seek health care because of physical problems or problems related to stress, anxiety, and depression. Always remember that people have many dimensions. Try to look at the whole person and not just the illness. Seeing your clients as whole beings will help you understand the many levels on which they respond to their problems. Your understanding and tolerance will help you interact more effectively.

Wellness is thought of in five dimensions: physical, emotional, social, intellectual, and spiritual.

Physical   The physical dimension refers to the body's health and functioning. Promoting physical wellness requires us to make intelligent choices relating to diet, exercise, risk-taking behaviours, and lifestyle.

health   according to one definition, "a relative state in which one is able to function well physically, mentally, socially, and spiritually in order to express the full range of one's unique potentialities within the environment in which one is living."

wellness: a state of physical and emotional well-being, broadly considered.

---

[1] World Health Organization, 1943.

[2] *Miller-Keene Encyclopedia and Dictionary of Medicine, Nursing and Allied Health*, 6th ed. Philadelphia: WB Saunders, 1993.

Emotional Emotional wellness involves recognizing one's own strengths and weaknesses, being able to analyze and deal with problems, and recognizing when one needs help. Emotional wellness means a person can manage stress appropriately and adjust to change. In today's world, stress is a part of daily life for most people. Stress can immobilize a person. The ability to manage stress, conversely, promotes both physical and emotional wellness. A positive outlook on life reduces stress, tension, and the risk of developing depression. Part of this is self-acceptance, self-confidence, and an inner feeling of well-being. It involves knowing who you are, striving to achieve your personal goals, and believing in yourself.

The link between physical and emotional wellness works both ways. On the one hand, such emotions as anxiety contribute to diseases, such as rheumatoid arthritis, hypertension, and stomach ulcers, and aggravate many chronic illnesses. Depression and stress can cause a wide range of physical symptoms. On the other hand, physical illness can result in emotional distress. For example, a thyroid imbalance can cause low or fluctuating moods. Illness can be saddening or deeply frightening. Ill clients' emotional reactions may cause them to make decisions that are not well thought out or analyzed.

Social Relationships and interactions are an integral part of everyday life. Our ability to connect with others contributes to our adaptive functioning. Most people strongly value healthy relationships involving trust and intimacy. Moreover, relationships provide a matrix of support in times of need. Research shows that people with partners and strong social networks are more likely to be physically healthy, and individuals with chronic terminal diseases live longer if they have a supportive social network. One reason women live longer than men (although the gap is closing) is that women are more likely to seek support in times of illness and stress.

People working in health care must interact in a positive manner and establish a trusting bond with clients. Clients who feel cared for, and who trust and are at ease with the health professionals they interact with, are more likely to have a positive attitude toward their health care. This attitude increases compliance with treatment, reduces stress, and promotes recovery.

Intellectual The intellectual dimension of wellness involves our cognitive ability to determine what is right and good for us and what is not. It involves assessment and analysis of what goes on around us and allows us to make choices to improve and educate ourselves.

People with physical limitations may compensate by using their intellectual abilities. Similarly, people with intellectual limitations can be helped to develop and achieve intellectual wellness to the level they are able.

Spiritual For some people, spirituality means a belief in, and dedication to, a higher power. Others experience spirituality as a personal, interior quality, tied to emotions, values, morals, and an ethical philosophy that guides them in their daily lives. In either sense, spirituality can give our lives purpose, direction, meaning, and structure. For many, it provides a sense of inner peace and harmony, and gives hope and strength in the face of adversity.

The spiritual needs of ill people are all too frequently ignored, which can increase their stress and undermine their ability to cope. Many of us look for something higher to believe in and seek comfort from when we are ill. Clients with a strong sense of spirituality tend to respond more calmly, more philosophically, and more positively to their illness, treatment, and potential recovery.

CURRENT HEALTH CONCERNS

PERCEPTIONS OF HEALTH AND ILLNESS HAVE CHANGED OVER THE YEARS, AS HAVE THE TYPES of illnesses people are coping with. Infectious diseases used to be the most common, many of them untreatable until the discovery of antibiotics and other curative measures. As well, people have assumed much more responsibility for their own health care than they did even 15 years ago.

In April, 2003 the previously unknown coronal virus that causes SARS (Severe Acute Respiratory Syndrome) resulted in 44 deaths out of 251 confirmed cases in Canada. SARS made the health-care community more acutely aware of the need to practise strict infection-control measures. There is continued emphasis on containing such communicable diseases as those caused by MRSA (methicillin-resistant *Staphylococcus aureus*), VRE, (vancomycin-resistant *Enterococci*) and C. *difficile* (*Clostridium difficile*) which are almost always found in hospitals, nursing homes, and other long-term care facilities. C. *difficile* is the most common cause of hospital-acquired diarrhea in the developed world. After a brief decline, in recent years it has reappeared as a hypervirulent strain. The result is increased morbidity and mortality rates. It is usually transmitted through the fecal–oral route, and there has been evidence of airborne transmission. Washing hands with soap and water has proven more effective than alcohol-based solutions in preventing transmission of this organism (see Chapter 5 for more detail).

MRSA and VRE are pathogens that, in many cases, have become resistant to the most effective antibiotics used to treat them (methicillin and vancomycin respectively). These organisms usually cause symptoms in persons who have other diseases and/or weakened immune systems (such as older people, and those in hospital). See Chapter 5 for more detail. As for C. *difficile*, according to the Public Health Agency of Canada, it is the leading cause of infectious diarrhea in our hospitals and long-term facilities. See Chapter 5 for more details on infectious diseases. In addition, you can obtain more information from the Related Websites at the end of this chapter.

For other infectious diseases, including the human immunodeficiency virus (HIV), and the human papilloma virus (HPV), major inroads have occurred in their treatment. HIV is now regarded more as a chronic disease than an acute disease where death is imminent.

Post-traumatic stress disorder (PTSD) has become an important health concern. It has been more readily recognized (or perhaps acknowledged) since Canada and the United States have engaged in combat initiatives in Iraq and Afghanistan. Hundreds of soldiers suffer from PTSD and are coming forward seeking medical help and, where possible, applying for disability related to PTSD. This disorder also affects many Canadians who have endured other types of trauma and emotional stress.

Two-thirds of the deaths in Canada annually are attributed to chronic disease. These are a major health threat, especially for seniors. Partly because of our aging population, the majority of clients seen in a general practice present with more than one disease, usually with at least one chronic disease. It takes more time for the physician to assess and treat these individuals. There may be little time left for the other important elements of client care—support, reassurance, and encouragement. This situation is complicated by the shortage of physicians and the large numbers of Canadians relying on walk-in or ambulatory-care clinics for their health care. Continuity of care is lost and the quality of care is compromised.

The administrative health professional can help to fill this void by communicating effectively with the client in an empathetic, patient, and supportive manner. Clients who are coping with multiple ailments are often overwhelmed with their treatments, are discouraged by the limitations their health problems place on their lifestyle, and are uncertain about their future.

Millions of Canadians still have no family doctor despite recent initiatives to solve this problem (increased enrolment in medical schools, enhanced measures to license foreign doctors, and incentives for graduating doctors to choose family medicine as a specialty). Others endure long waits for diagnostic tests, to see specialists, and to receive surgery. Between 2007 and 2011, wait times in some areas have improved, for example, for cardiac bypass surgery, cataract surgery, and hip replacements. There has not been much improvement in the wait for knee surgery. Wait times for diagnostic tests, although improved, vary throughout the country—indeed, even within provinces. A website listed at the end of the chapter illustrates wait times for various diagnostic tests across Canada.

Leading Causes of Mortality and Morbidity in Canada

According to Statistics Canada (2012), cancer has passed cardiovascular disease as the leading cause of death in Canada in almost every province and territory. Cardiovascular disease, which includes both heart disease and stroke, is second everywhere except in Nunavut, where suicide ranked second. Diseases of the respiratory system, accidents, diabetes, and Alzheimer's disease follow closely behind. Diabetes is also a major concern and is a disease that affects other body systems. The Canadian Diabetes Association (CDA) reports that, in 2011, in excess of 9 million Canadians live with diabetes, or pre-diabetes. Of these, approximately 80 percent will die of related complications such as heart disease and/or stroke. The CDA predicts that diabetes will cost the Canadian health-care system $16.9 billion, including diagnosis, treatment, medications, and treating related diseases. Influenza is an annual concern, with Health Canada striving to encourage Canadians to get the seasonal flu shot. Individuals who do not get the flu vaccine pose the risk of transmission to others.

Impact on Canadians

A 1980s Angus Reid poll asked Canadians what they considered the most important national issue. So few people named health care that it did not even register as a response. By 2000, more than half of the respondents listed health care as the most important. In 2008, more Canadians were worried about the economy, but health care remained a concern. This remains true today. The problems facing our health-care system are caused largely by financial constraints, management of health-care resources, a shortage of physicians and nurses, limited access to modern medical technology, and long waiting lists. The product of health care is less available, even while the demand for it grows.

In many ways, Canadians are less able to cope effectively with illness, especially serious illness, than they were a generation or two ago. The length of hospital stays has been drastically reduced, primarily because of financing concerns. Community-based care programs (sometimes referred to as "hospitals without walls") have been implemented to care for individuals at home. For example, many primary reform groups and community health services offer clinics to follow and treat people with hypertension or diabetes. In addition, there is an emphasis on prevention, such as enhanced access to prenatal care and screening programs for breast cancer. Some provinces have introduced incentives for family doctors to closely follow clients to ensure that their clients (as appropriate) are up to date on immunizations, Pap smears, screening for colorectal cancer, and so on.

Thus, much of the onus for the care of the client has again fallen on the family. Community support, such as home care, can provide only so much assistance. In the average Canadian family, both parents are working, making child care a challenge. When middle-aged adults must take on the responsibility for aging parents as well, it takes a toll on the family. Illness threatens not only an individual but also the economic and structural well-being of the family unit.

Responsibilities of each family member change. If a child becomes ill, the parents—especially the mother—are forced to spend more time on care, which often disrupts their working lives and the lives of other children. Siblings may have to take on extra responsibilities or give up certain activities. A parent becoming ill can be even more disruptive and disturbing. It may mean a substantial loss of income—sometimes even a loss of two incomes if one spouse must care for the other. Again, children may have to take on extra responsibilities or may find themselves suddenly in new child-care arrangements. Children may also find it distressing to see a parent, who is supposed to be in charge, being incapacitated or dependent.

All jurisdictions except Alberta have developed minimum standards for family care leave rights. Most provinces and territories also have short-term leave allowing Canadians to care for health-compromised family members. British Columbia allows a five-day Family Responsibility Leave.[3] Nova Scotia, Manitoba, New Brunswick, and Prince Edward Island offer up to three days; Newfoundland offers up to 12 days short-term leave. In Ontario in late 2011, an amendment to the *Employment Standards Act, 2000* was introduced to create Family Caregiver Leave, for individuals meeting certain criteria. The initiative will provide eligible employees with up to eight weeks of job-protected unpaid leave. Moreover, the Ontario government is urging the federal government to extend employment insurance benefits for approved individuals.[4]

❹ THE HEALTH–ILLNESS CONTINUUM

A CONTINUUM IS A SCALE ON WHICH SOMETHING CAN BE MEASURED. A CONTINUUM to measure health illustrates how a person's health status is constantly changing. Poor health moves towards death at one end, and optimum health is at the other end. An area in the centre is called compensation—most of us move between optimum health and compensation. Where a person places himself on the continuum is highly personal. Someone with a chronic illness or debilitating injury might still consider herself to be in good health, while another would place himself in compensation closer to poor health. One's outlook and acceptance of one's health state (even death) has a great deal to do with where one places oneself on the continuum. (The continuum itself is simply a measurement tool.) There are various health–illness continuum models, each with somewhat different interpretation and evaluation criteria. Figure 2.1 illustrates the continuum as

---

[3] British Columbia Law Institute and the Canadian Centre for Elder Law, "Care/Work: Law Reform to Support Family Caregivers to Balance Paid Work and Unpaid Caregiving," February 2010, http://www.bcli.org/sites/default/files/FamilyCaregivingReport.pdf.

[4] Hicks Morley Human Resources Law and Advocacy, "Ontario Introduces Family Caregiver Leave," December 8, 2011, http://www.humanresourceslegislativeupdate.com/general-employment/ontario-to-introduce-family-caregiver-leave/.

Optimal Health	Good Health	Compensation	Poor Health	Serious Health	Premature Death/Death

Probable direction of movement · Probable direction of movement

Figure 2.1 The health–illness continuum with optimal health at one end and death at the other

a straight line with optimal health and good health on the left, compensation near the centre, and movement toward poor health and eventually death on the right.

Optimum or good health, to the left on this continuum, is defined as the height of physical, emotional, spiritual, and intellectual health. Compensation is an area in the middle of the continuum representing a person who may be experiencing altered health but is able to cope independently. People experiencing serious health problems (actual or perceived) usually move to the right end of the continuum. It depends, of course, on the person's response to a serious illness and how he adapts.

Death is viewed by some theorists as a natural part of the life cycle and therefore adaptive when it occurs in an older person, especially when the person accepts death. The death of a younger person, referred to as premature death, is not considered adaptive. In either case, a dying person who has accepted his plight would usually be placed at the extreme end of the continuum.

❺ THE STAGES OF ILLNESS RESPONSE

Everyone responds differently to illness. The stages of illness response describes the process individuals go through when they face a potential or actual health problem.

Our state of health affects every aspect of our lives: how we feel, our level of energy, what we do and how we do it, our judgment and perception of people and things around us, and our interactions with others. A client's response will affect how he adapts to an illness, choice of treatment, and ease of recovery. The client's response also affects everyone close to him. Response to altered health depends not only on the nature and severity of the illness, but also on the client's culture, social, and family influences, beliefs, perception of health and illness, and personality. Responses vary from mild to extreme and from adaptive to ineffective. An understanding of these stages will help you understand, anticipate, and deal with your clients' reactions. Although individual responses will vary in sequence and intensity, typical stages include the following:

1. Preliminary phase: the appearance of clinical signs

2. Acknowledgment phase: sustained clinical signs

3. Action phase: seeking medical intervention

4. Transitional phase: diagnosis and treatment

5. Resolution phase: recovery/rehabilitation or death

1. Preliminary Phase

Physical signs, although they may be vague, are the first indication a person has that something is wrong. Many people consciously note the signs but attach no particular significance to them and carry on with their activities. Others may immediately begin to analyze the sign or behaviour and be concerned that it signals a change in their health pattern. Regardless of the response, at this stage, most people keep the information to themselves.

If the clinical signs persist, the individual will give them increasing attention. Some people attempt to correlate the signs to an existing or previous condition or speculate on a cause, usually perceived as not serious. They may or may not mention these signs in an offhand manner to someone else but are still thinking, "It's probably nothing." Others will think of a list of possibly serious conditions and may research possible causes. They may be thinking, "This could be serious. I am probably coming down with . . ." or, "I'll give it a bit more time." At this point, an element of denial remains.

2. Acknowledgment Phase

If signs of the illness persist, people will become more concerned. They may want someone to reassure them that nothing is wrong, or to validate that there is a problem. They often confide in someone close to them and whom they trust. If the perceived condition is potentially serious, an element of denial is more likely to persist. The person may attempt to rationalize symptoms: "I have stomach cramps because of all the Aspirin I took last week." "I was at the cottage and probably picked up something from the water there." "This chest pain is probably just indigestion. I should avoid those hamburgers." The client may attempt self-treatment, perhaps with alternative remedies or over-the-counter (OTC) medications. The short-term response is to wait and see. If clinical signs continue, the person will proceed to the next phase.

3. Action Phase

The next step is to contact a primary health-care provider, usually the family doctor or a nurse practitioner. At this point, the person has most likely admitted that something is wrong but has little idea of what is wrong or how serious it is. At this stage, people may be unwilling to face the possibility of a major change in their health because they cannot cope with having to change their daily routines and roles.

Through the process of describing clinical signs and history to the provider, the person acknowledges the altered health pattern and is prepared to investigate probable causes. She becomes actively involved, cognitively and otherwise, in seeking a diagnosis.

4. Transitional Phase

Response to a diagnosis varies. If it is a simple problem, easily and quickly treated, the person will typically accept the diagnosis and begin the recommended treatment. If the diagnosis is more serious, resulting in protracted treatment with an undesirable or unpredictable prognosis, acceptance may be delayed. The person may seek a second opinion and experience denial, anger, and bargaining before coming to accept it. Some people never accept a really frightening diagnosis. This refusal often has a devastating effect on the family.

Once having accepted the diagnosis, the client considers treatment options, makes a choice, and starts treatment. Most providers will invite the individual to participate in any necessary decision making. Often, the provider will explain treatment options and will make recommendations, but will let the client make the final decision. More decisions may be needed as treatment continues: for example, if the condition does not respond to the initial treatment, the client and doctor may need to reassess and decide whether to try a different treatment. Decisions are rarely purely medical. Other factors come into play, such as pain or inconvenience, cost, time (how long a client has to wait for treatment and how long treatment may take the client away from normal activities), emotional factors (such as fear or distaste), and the effects of treatment on family members. Thus, family members may also be involved in making decisions.

5. Resolution Phase

Once treatment is initiated, the individual's focus shifts to recovery. If the problem is transient, treatment is usually short term, and the client quickly returns to his former position on the health–illness continuum. If the problem is more protracted, the client will continue to focus on recovery. Recovery does not always mean a return to the former health state. For example, a client facing a chronic illness may reach a resolution that involves some limitations and a change in lifestyle. Dealing with this new state takes some adjustment. Over time, most people do come to accept their altered health state. Others fluctuate between acceptance and denial and perhaps may never come to terms with what has happened to them. In the most serious cases, despite treatment, the final resolution may be death. This, too, often involves a series of stages, from learning the prognosis, through denial and anger or bargaining, to acceptance. When the client faces long-term disability or death, family members, too, need to go through a process of assimilating the information and learning to accept it and rebuild their lives.

Implications for the Health Office Professional

By the time clients call the doctor's office for an appointment, they have acknowledged that a health issue exists, and most will be feeling some level of stress about their health state. A cheerful, positive, and caring manner will go a long way to comfort the client. If you sense that the client's condition warrants prompt attention or that the client is very anxious, try to schedule an early appointment (see Chapter 9). In prioritizing appointments, a client's emotional state can be as important as the physical complaint.

Clients who are diagnosed with a serious illness understandably experience prolonged stress and display different coping mechanisms. Some clients are initially in complete denial. "It's a mistake. Those test results can't be accurate. We should repeat them." Or, "This can't really be happening. I can't believe it's happened to me. I've done nothing to deserve this." The information they have been given may not register. Other clients may know intellectually that what the doctor has told them is true but may not believe it on an emotional level. Some clients may want a second opinion. If they ask you to make an appointment with another physician, gently refer them back to the doctor. Explain that this is something they must discuss with the doctor and that they must have a doctor's

Tip

Remember that illness affects everyone differently—including loved ones of the sick person. If a client seems stressed, irritated or angry, give them the benefit of the doubt. Be patient, remain calm and empathic. MOST of the time, a client will respond in a positive manner, and leave the office feeling valued and cared for.

referral to see another physician. Though a second opinion is sometimes a good idea (and doctors themselves will sometimes ask for one), most territorial and provincial health plans will pay for a visit to a specialist for a second opinion only if the primary care provider requests a consultation.

Be sensitive to the client's mood and emotional state. The range of responses is wide. A client may not respond at all. She may pick up her belongings, smile, and leave the office. Another client, usually pleasant and talkative, may become just the opposite. A client may appear preoccupied, inattentive, or angry and resentful. Don't take such responses personally. Do your best to remain pleasant, empathetic, and helpful.

❻ THE SICK ROLE AND ILLNESS BEHAVIOUR

PEOPLE ASSUME SOCIAL **ROLES** IN LIFE: POSITIONS THAT CARRY EXPECTATIONS OF responsibilities and of appropriate behaviour. We have jobs and tasks we must perform, obligations to fulfill, and people who rely on us. Occupational roles determine how a manager and an employee should act; family roles determine how a mother, father, child, or sibling should act. Each of us plays more than one role in life. For example, Bob has roles as a father, a husband, and a teacher. As a father, he has responsibilities to his children. As a husband, he has responsibilities to his wife. As a teacher, he has responsibilities to his colleagues, his employer, and his students. Bob has also taken on roles as a member of the board of his local library and as a scout leader, each of which involves certain obligations.

role a position in life that carries expectations of responsibilities and of appropriate behaviour.

When people become sick, they are, to varying degrees, excused from their normal roles. When ill, it is acceptable for Bob not to go to work, not to play ball with his children, not to lead his scout troop on a hike. In fact, being sick itself may be considered a role.[5] A person taking on this role, while exempt from normal responsibilities, is expected to behave in certain ways: to rest, to seek professional assistance, and to follow doctor's advice. So far, this behaviour is adaptive.

However, the **sick role** can become ineffective. Some people, more commonly those facing a more serious illness, develop a passive, submissive pattern of behaviour that may be quite unlike their normal attitude. Some people, often those with an external locus of control, seem to have continuous ailments and expect others to wait on and care for them. Others take on a passive role in the face of serious health problems perhaps because of stress, fear, or uncertainty. They may prefer a physician or other health professional to make decisions for them because they trust that person's knowledge and experience or because the loss of their own familiar roles has undermined their sense of autonomy.

sick role a particular social role that an ill person adopts, which involves giving up normal responsibilities and accepting care. May sometimes involve uncharacteristically passive behaviour.

This abdication of responsibility is most common when a client is hospitalized, perhaps because of the unfamiliar and highly controlled environment. When you are dependent on others for your food, your mobility, and even your toileting, it can be hard to feel in control of your own life. A client who, to all appearances, becomes immobilized by illness is difficult to deal with for both health professionals and family. The expectations placed on family members are overwhelming. The client may become so passive that she will not participate in her treatment, which impedes recovery. Health professionals

---

[5] The concept of the sick role was first developed by sociologist Talcott Parsons as part of an attempt to define health and illness within a general theory of social action. T. Parsons. *The Social System*. Glencoe, IL: Free Press, 1951. Cited in Soma Hewa, "Physicians, the Medical Profession, and Medical Practice," in B. Singh Bolaria and Harley D. Dickinson, eds., *Health, Illness, and Health Care in Canada*, 3rd ed. Scarborough: Nelson Thomson Learning, 2002.

must be careful not to cultivate client dependence and should encourage the client to be actively involved in disease prevention, health maintenance, and the treatment of their own illnesses.

Always be sensitive to clients' responses to illness. Recognize that they may need support and encouragement. If a client is cranky or whiny, be patient. If a client seems angry and wants to blame others, be tolerant (within reason). Try to relate the behaviour to the nature, stage, and severity of the client's illness.

Effects on Others

Response to illness is not confined to the person who is ill. Everyone who is closely associated with the sick person will be affected to some extent, spouses and children especially. How much the family is affected will depend on which family member is ill, how serious and how long the illness is, and what cultural and social customs that family has.

A sick person's role starts a chain reaction, affecting everyone who depends in any way on him. The severity of the effects depends on the nature and seriousness of the illness, as well as on the relationship to the sick person.

Consider Katya, a 35-year-old mother of three children. Her husband, Greg, is an electrician. Katya works part-time for a busy obstetrician. She is a Girl Guide leader. She accompanies the church choir and is on the board of the library. Each of Katya's roles carries with it responsibilities, and there are people in each of those areas who depend on Katya to carry out those responsibilities.

Let us suppose that Katya comes down with bronchitis. The doctor prescribes an antibiotic and advises Katya to take a few days off. She calls her office to say she will not be in. She has to miss a library board meeting, which she was to chair. She has to cancel choir practice because they have no other pianist. She has to miss a Girl Guide field trip, which means the troop will be short one chaperone and must cancel the event. She is unable take the kids to school or to pick them up.

Greg has to get the kids their breakfast and drive them to school, making him an hour late for work. Greg must also pick up the kids from school and put them to bed. He therefore must cancel an important meeting and miss his weekly golf game the next evening.

The kids are whiny because they miss their mother's attention. Dad does not know that Jamie likes porridge for breakfast, and he does not read the right kind of bedtime stories. Katya is not only in discomfort, but she also feels helpless and frustrated because she is bereft of her normal roles and guilty that she is letting everyone down. Greg is frustrated and feeling inadequate because the kids are not satisfied with the way he does things. He feels somewhat resentful that he has to miss his meeting and golf game. His supervisor is not happy that he came in late, which delayed an important job. The choir members feel under-rehearsed for their next performance. The library board is concerned because it postpones voting on an important matter until the next month. . . . And on it goes.

These examples show how illness affects not just the ill person, but everyone in that person's circle, especially the family. Effects on the family may include

- changes in a person's duties and responsibilities,
- increased stress because of anxiety related to the illness,
- conflict over unaccustomed responsibilities,
- financial problems,

- change in social patterns,
- loneliness (if the family member is hospitalized), and
- pending loss (if the illness is serious).

Implications for the Administrative Health Professional

It is important to recognize that the whole family is affected when one family member becomes ill. You and other members of your team may have to support not only the client but also family members during interactions. They may call or come into the office seeming angry, resentful, or just plain worried. Understanding what they are going through will help you put any unpleasant behaviour in perspective and maintain your calm and empathetic manner. It is helpful also to consider personality types.

ILLNESS AND PERSONALITY TYPES

Clients You Rarely See

Some clients deal with their health responsibly and rarely seek medical assistance. They are straightforward about their concerns, they know when to seek attention, and they follow the recommended advice. They are pleasant, easy to deal with, matter-of-fact, and accountable. Another group of clients puts off making appointments even when they should because they are shy and "hate to bother anyone." Other clients may avoid seeking medical attention because of nervousness about interacting with hospitals and physicians. Denial may be the motivating factor that keeps them from seeking help. These individuals can be their own worst enemies because their delays result in more protracted and serious illnesses.

Shy clients and nervous clients should be encouraged to seek medical help when necessary and to keep annual appointments for check-ups. Sometimes, encouraging them to call the office when they feel unwell keeps them in touch and provides a communication link.

Clients You See Frequently

Many doctors will tell you that 20 percent of their practice takes up 80 percent of their time.

These clients are often the ones you and the provider may become impatient with. They are often sensitive to even the slightest alterations in their health. They may worry excessively, use home remedies, and call for medical advice or come to see the doctor frequently. They are demanding of the physician's time and apt to be critical when they think they are not getting enough time. This is not to trivialize the client's condition or complaints. For the most part, their concerns are very real to them.

It is important to remain polite to these clients and to be as accommodating as you can. It is up to the physician to speak to the client about visits that are too frequent and to ask the client to limit the discussion to what is causing the most distress. (Often, the client will come in with one complaint and then expect the doctor to address several, most of which are ongoing. Usually, they become perceptive enough to assure you that they are only "coming in to see about the swelling in my ankles," for example, saving the rest of the list for the doctor.) Unfortunately, if the client cries wolf often enough, a valid complaint may not immediately be taken seriously. When this type of client calls the office, never ignore a complaint. Be especially aware of a new complaint or significant change to an established complaint. Listen to the tone of the client's voice; is there an element of stress that is not usually there?

There is no real solution for the client who wants more time and attention than the physician and administrative staff have to give. Seeking another physician these days is not a viable option for most clients, given the current shortage of doctors. Remain courteous and as supportive as you can be.

❼❽ THE EFFECTS OF HOSPITALIZATION

HOSPITALIZATION IS A MAJOR SOURCE OF STRESS TO THE CLIENT AND FAMILY MEMBERS, particularly now that hospital stays are reserved for the very ill. By the time a person is hospitalized, he has reached the treatment phase of the health response sequence. Usually, the client has already accepted the illness and the treatment regimen. However, in the face of more serious illnesses, the client may go through a second stage of rejecting the diagnosis and choice of treatment. Some people accept their situation with a positive attitude; others may become overly passive and refuse to work toward recovery.

Hospitalization disrupts

- privacy,
- autonomy and independence,
- lifestyle,
- role function, and
- financial security.

Privacy

Privacy is important to everyone, in or out of hospital. Most people find comfort and security in having a space to themselves, especially introverts. Time to be alone to think and reflect provides a chance to regroup and renew. In the hospital, likewise, people need time to be quiet, to rest, and to think. They also need and have the right to physical privacy. Though some people can change or shower comfortably in the presence of others, some are very private about disrobing and doing personal hygiene. Their need for privacy does not disappear because they're in a hospital.

Privacy also relates to how close we let others get to us emotionally and physically. We all have emotional and physical comfort zones that others should not enter without permission. Culture, personality, gender, and religion influence the boundaries we set.

There is an old saying that when you enter a hospital, you leave your privacy at the front door. Often, the crowded state of hospital wards makes privacy difficult to ensure, but sometimes it is just a matter of busy nurses and other health professionals taking a moment to think about it. It is difficult, especially in semi-private or standard accommodation, to maintain privacy in the presence of other clients and their visitors, hospital personnel with tasks to do, and the noise of the paging system. The nurses usually do their best to preserve clients' privacy by closing doors or pulling curtains when giving treatments and nursing care.

Sometimes you can help. If a client requests quiet time, let the nurses know, or pull the curtains around the bed or close the door. This simple measure will at least give the client a visual break.

If you know that a client is going to have a meeting with a doctor, family member, or clergy, try to arrange for a quiet, private environment. You can book a conference room (if the unit has one) or suggest an empty room. If the client cannot move out of the room, perhaps other clients in the room can.

If you need information from the client—about insurance coverage, for example, or discharge arrangements—ask quietly. Never ask a client to disclose potentially sensitive information within the hearing range of other people.

Autonomy

Autonomy is a person's independence, or ability to operate without outside control. Unfortunately, autonomy diminishes in the hospital environment. Clients are told when and what to eat, when to get up, when to go to bed, when to take their pills, and when they can have visitors. Many people find it difficult to adjust to this loss of control. Some struggle to retain what control they can. Others become almost dependent, allowing others to make decisions for them and take care of them. A family member may say, "I can't understand it. Fred is usually such an independent person." It could be that Fred is relinquishing control because he is simply too sick or discouraged to cope. It could be that he has given up. He may feel intimidated by the authority of hospital staff, or he may be enjoying the opportunity for a good rest!

The clinical secretary can help by allowing clients to do as much for themselves as possible. For example, offer a client meal choices rather than suggesting something. If there is an insurance form to fill out, give it to the client and let her do as much as she can by herself. If you need to help, ask the client if you may sit down, offer to draw the curtains, and proceed to obtain the information, allowing the client as much opportunity for expression as possible. Too many closed questions can make a client feel like a robot, spurting our short "yes" or "no" answers with no opportunity to discuss anything.

Lifestyle

Hospitalization changes almost every detail of a client's daily life—getting up, bathing, working, eating, socializing. He may miss simple things he took for granted at home, such as a portable phone or electric razor. Clients with disabilities may miss their own assistive devices if these are not permitted in the hospital. A different walker, cane, or wheelchair can upset a client and alter mobility. All this change makes many people uneasy: some may become withdrawn and uncommunicative, others may be openly resentful, and some others downright angry.

Role Function

Though someone who is ill at home may be able to continue with some routine activities and function in some roles, the hospitalized client experiences an almost total change in role function. Responsibilities are either taken over by someone else or put on the back burner. This creates stress and anxiety for the client and family members. Some clients will push for discharge from the hospital before they are ready, which can result in complications and delayed recovery. On occasion, a client will actually leave the hospital without the physician's permission.

Financial Security

The longer a client is in the hospital, the more likely finances will become a problem, especially if the client is the primary wage earner. Many people have some type of disability insurance or other coverage in the event of illness. For those who do not, the loss of wages can be a major blow. Families may also face additional expenses, ranging from child care to transportation.

Implications for the Administrative Health Professional

Although clinical secretaries do not give client care, they do frequently communicate with the client, friends, and family members. If you understand the stressors for both the hospitalized client and the family members, you can help ease them a little and communicate more effectively. You need to keep communication clear, accurate, and professional, while at the same time being supportive, understanding, and empathetic—not an easy task. It takes skill and patience to read the mood of the client and to respond appropriately to the anxious husband, wife, brother, or sister. Trying to direct questions to the appropriate source or withholding confidential information from an inappropriate person can evoke angry, sometimes explosive, responses from individuals who feel that they are entitled to the information on the spot. Do not take it personally; it can help you stay calm and deal effectively with these individuals if you realize that most of them would not behave this way under less stressful circumstances.

HEALTH STATUS

HEALTH PROFESSIONALS, ESPECIALLY THOSE WORKING IN HOSPITALS, OFTEN FIELD INQUIRIES from family, friends, and acquaintances about a client's health status. Family and friends will often call the hospital asking how a client is doing on a particular day. Carefully follow federal and hospital guidelines for the release of such information. Usually, it is prudent to allow callers to speak to the client's nurse, especially family members who are entitled to the details of the client's condition. Otherwise, most facilities allow only general information to be released and sometimes not even that.

If you are allowed to give information, make sure it is up to date—an individual's health status can change from moment to moment. This information may be kept updated on the client's chart or Kardex (see Chapter 14). If you are asked to give general information, you will probably use the following standard terms:

> *Critical:* The client is hanging in the balance between life and death and is receiving active, intense intervention. The client is often in the emergency room, the operating room, intensive care unit (ICU), critical care unit (CCU), or recovery room.
> *Poor:* The client is near death but not receiving active intervention.
> *Guarded:* The client has moved from critical toward the wellness end of the continuum—but only just. The client's condition is still volatile and easily subject to change.
> *Stable:* The client's condition has steadied, usually after a period of fluctuation, usually on the side of being critical. This is usually good news but does not necessarily indicate a sure recovery.

Satisfactory: The client continues to improve and, usually, is out of danger. Although the position is optimistic, fluctuation or regression is still possible.

Good: The client is believed to be on a firm footing and is expected to recover. Note, however, that it does not always mean the client will return to the previous level of functioning. A stroke victim's condition, for example, may be described as "good" when she is not in danger of dying, although function may still be limited.

Future Trends

Along with the economy, unemployment, the national debt and the environment, health care remains a significant worry for Canadians. This includes wondering whether the system is sustainable, and long wait times for access to specialists, tests, and medical and surgical procedures.

Although Canadians have become somewhat more responsible for their own health, obesity and diabetes are a growing concern among the population. This is especially so among Canada's Aboriginal people. Continued efforts are required on the part of Canadians to engage in prevention, for example, exercise, maintaining a healthy weight, and eating a healthy diet. Government intervention is necessary to assist Aboriginal Canadians move towards achieving these goals—and it will take time.

Clients must continue to be proactive in pursuing the health services they need. Many feel that long waits for treatment have threatened their health and violated their rights. To obtain sometimes life-saving health care, some Canadians continue to seek the necessary diagnostic tests and surgery from private clinics inside and out of the country and pay for these services themselves. Some reapproved medical and surgical services are covered by health insurance, but others are not. For example, angioplasty, an endovascular procedure, is not covered by insurance to treat chronic cerebrospinal venous insufficiency in individuals with multiple sclerosis. The procedure is generally consider to be experimental. There have been several court challenges regarding timely access to health care. The Chaouilli case (*Chaouilli vs. Attorney General (Quebec)*, 2005) was a landmark constitutional case that forced the Quebec government to remove its ban on private insurance for services covered under the provincial health plan, and to acknowledge that the Quebec health-care system violated the Quebec Charter of Rights and Freedoms. Many believe it is only a matter of time before a similar case will overturn the Canadian Charter in favour of allowing Canadians access to more insured private services.

Long wait times take a toll on the health of clients, their families, and the economy.

The good news is that, according to the Canadian Institute of Health Information, wait times are improving with many procedures being performed in accordance with benchmark time frames. A website listed at the end of the chapter shows wait times for various procedures across Canada.

Millions of Canadians still do not have family doctors despite increasing enrolment in medical schools and allowing foreign physicians to qualify more easily to practise in Canada. Still, increasing physician numbers is proving to be an uphill battle. According to Nadeem Esmail of the Fraser Institute, approximately 38 percent of Canada's physicians were aged 55 or older in 2010. Mr. Esmail calculates that Canada requires about 2300 medical school graduates each year between 2011 and 2020 to maintain the current physician-to-population ratio. He also recommends continued strategies to help foreign doctors qualify sooner to practise in Canada.[6]

A significant number of medical students avoid specializing in family medicine. The other specialties remain more appealing because of higher income and better hours. Some medical schools are taking steps to encourage medical students to choose family medicine. Most provincial and territorial governments offer incentives for graduates in family medicine to practise in more remote areas. As well, more women are graduating from medical schools and choosing to work limited hours in order to raise a family.

People with multiple medical conditions are living longer; thus the stress of caring for an older population will continue. Caring for older adults and people with unhealthy lifestyles is time-consuming and a tremendous

---

[6] Nadeem Esmail, quoted in "Doctor Shortage Getting Worse," *The Big Wait* website, http://www.thebigwait.com/doctor-shortage-canada/doctor-shortage-getting-worse/#more-1567.

cost to the health-care system. Obesity and diabetes are reaching epidemic proportions, according to author Dr. Mark J. Eisenberg, Jewish General Hospital, Divisions of Cardiology and Clinical Epidemiology. "Obesity is expected to surpass smoking as the leading cause of preventable morbidity and mortality."[7] These entities add billions to the cost of health care in Canada when combined with treating related complications such as generalized vascular disease, high cholesterol, high blood pressure, and heart problems.

In December 2011, the federal government announced its plans for health-care spending, which will extend to 2024 (12 years as opposed to the usual 10 for funding plans). The current federal health transfers allow an increase of 6 percent per year. This accord expires in 2014. The government will maintain annual transfers increasing at 6 percent per year until 2019. After that the dollar value of transfer payments will be tied to Canada's economic growth.

This has important implications for how health-care services are managed, and whether our "medicare" can be sustained in its present form. Former Bank of Canada governor David Dodge is quoted as saying "the status quo simply isn't working anymore—we need fundamental reform of how Medicare is delivered to Canadians. And Canadians are going to have to pay more whether in the form of higher taxes or user fees or perhaps through health savings plans."[8]

[7] Mark J. Eisenberg, Renée Atallah, Sonia M. Grandi, Sarah B. Windle, and Elliot M. Berry, "Legislative Approaches to Tackling the Obesity Epidemic," *Canadian Medical Association Journal,* April 2011 DOI: 10.1503/cmaj.101522

[8] CTV News, "Flaherty Sketches Out Health Spending until 2024," December 19, 2011, http://www.ctvnews.ca/flaherty-sketches-out-health-spending-until-2024-1.742394.

SUMMARY

1. Behaviour is a person's observable responses and actions. Behaviour changes in response to stress, including illness.

2. Health beliefs affect our lifestyles and how we care for ourselves. Some people adopt self-imposed risks, such as smoking, sedentary habits, and poor diet, because they do not believe that they affect health or because they rationalize that nothing will happen to them. Others consciously work to improve and maintain their health.

3. Definitions of health and wellness are individual. At one time, health was thought of as the simple absence of physical disease. Today, health is understood in broader terms. *Wellness* refers to the well-being of the entire person, embracing physical, emotional, social, intellectual, and spiritual components. All five elements interact: for example, anxiety can cause physical illness, and physiological disorders can also cause anxiety. At one time, health care was seen as a response to sickness, and people expected medical science to take care of them. Many people have now adopted a more preventive approach that emphasizes individual responsibility and healthier lifestyles. Recognition of the influence of social and economic factors has also grown.

4. The *health–illness continuum* is a scale on which to measure a person's perception of their health state. Optimal health is at one end of the scale, and death is at the other. Two individuals with the same symptoms may place themselves at different points on the continuum. Most people, most of the time, place themselves somewhere in the area of optimal health or compensation, meaning they are experiencing some health problem but are coping on their own.

5. Although individuals respond differently to illness, there is a typical pattern of response. In the preliminary phase, people often ignore the first appearance of signs or come up with their own explanations. In the action phase, people respond to sustained clinical signs by contacting a health-care provider and seeking a diagnosis. In the transitional phase, people accept or reject a diagnosis and then accept treatment offered or seek alternatives. The resolution phase may be brief or may involve adjustment to permanent changes.

6. People have many roles in life—as workers, family members, and members of a community—each involving responsibilities. Illness affects their ability to play these roles. It also affects the roles of others in their lives.

7. Personality affects response to illness. Some clients rarely contact the health office, either because they can handle their health on their own or because they are denying or ignoring health problems. The latter need to be encouraged to come in more regularly. Others are overly concerned with their health and demand a great deal of the physician's time. It is important to handle them firmly but tactfully and to recognize when they do report a new and serious problem.

8. Hospitalization is stressful for clients and their families because it disrupts privacy, autonomy, lifestyle, role function, and financial security. Try as much as possible to preserve the client's privacy and independence.

9. When asked about a client's health status, follow institutional policy on confidentiality, and make sure any information you give is up to date.

Key Terms

behaviour 41
health 43

role 51
sick role 51

wellness 43

Review Questions

1. Define the following:
   a. Health behaviour
   b. Health
   c. Wellness
   d. Health beliefs
   e. Self-imposed risk
   f. Role function
2. State the World Health Organization's definition of health.
3. List the five dimensions of wellness, and give an example of each.
4. Compare and contrast the perceptions of health that Canadians have today to those held in the early part of the 20th century.
5. List the top three causes of morbidity and mortality in Canada today.
6. What is a chronic illness? What impact do chronic illnesses have on our society today?
7. Discuss the structure and purpose of the health–illness continuum.
8. Identify the five stages of illness and the typical responses at each stage.

9. Discuss the effects of illness on family members, considering changing role functions.

10. Identify and discuss the effects of hospitalization on clients and their families.

Application Exercises

1. Look up the definitions of *health* and *wellness* in two other health books or dictionaries. Think about what health means to you personally. List the components that you think relate to good health and to wellness. Now, develop your own personal definitions of health and wellness. Compare your definitions with those of other students in the class, as well as the dictionary definitions and the World Health Organization's definition. Discuss similarities and differences.

2. List any self-imposed risks or risk-taking behaviours that you personally engage in. Research the health effects of one of these risks. Now, develop strategies to stop or reduce your risk-taking behaviours. Set goals for yourself. For example, if you smoke, you might decide that you want to quit or cut down to a specific number of cigarettes by a particular date. If you do not exercise, you might decide that you want to walk for 20 minutes, three times a week. Set a short-term goal (e.g., "By next Friday, I will reduce smoking by four cigarettes a day") and a long-term goal. List realistic steps you can take to achieve those goals. It may be helpful to brainstorm strategies with classmates with the same risk-taking behaviours.

Keep a daily log of your progress. If you have not met your goals, document why. Modify your plan accordingly. Each week for a month, take a few minutes at the beginning of the class to discuss your progress with your small group or partner. At the end of the month, review your goals. If you have made progress, you may want to continue. If not, you may decide to start over, modifying your goals or developing new strategies based on the information in your log.

3. Omar, a client in your busy medical practice, has been diagnosed with terminal cancer of the bowel. The doctor has strongly recommended a course of chemotherapy for Omar as well as surgery. Omar has refused. "I believe I can have a higher quality of life with the time I have left," he told the doctor. You, as the office manager, have come to know Omar well. You know how committed he is to his family and that he values life and health immensely. You believe that Omar is making the right decision. The doctor, however, has asked you to speak with Omar to try and persuade him to consent to treatment. The doctor feels that accepting treatment will prolong Omar's life by several months.

a. How would you respond in a similar situation?

b. Do you think Omar has the right to make his decision without undue interference on the part of the doctor?

c. What do you think Omar means when he says he would rather enjoy a higher quality of life without the treatment as opposed to a few more months of life that treatment may be able to offer?

4. Janet is a 34-year-old mother of two. She is separated from her husband and sends Susan, 5, and Matthew, 3, to daycare. She has no child support as her separation is still before the courts. Janet is a sales consultant at a local department store. She is on an anti-depressant. Janet volunteers at a local food bank but otherwise is not involved in community activities. She is new to the area and has only one casual friend. Janet smokes a pack of cigarettes daily. She belongs to a gym but does not go. Her favourite foods are hamburgers, fries, and wings, and she prefers Coca-Cola to milk. Janet has noticed some blood in her stools for the past three months. She feels it is unimportant, likely due to hemorrhoids.

One night, she notices a substantial amount of blood in the toilet. She calls the office for an appointment, reluctant to come in that week. Tests reveal that Janet has a tumour of the ascending colon. She is hospitalized for a bowel resection. She is terrified of both the hospital and the impending surgery. She arrives on the floor tearful and frightened. As the clinical secretary, you are asked to take Janet to her room and give her a brief orientation to the patient care unit. Janet asks you to send down the nurse to help her get undressed and into bed. She asks you to bring her some water and to telephone her babysitter to see how the children are doing.

a. What is Janet's primary role?

b. Identify three other roles Janet plays.

c. What are Janet's attitudes toward health maintenance and disease prevention?

d. List three self-imposed risks that Janet takes.

e. Discuss Janet's behaviour up to and including her first physician's appointment in terms of the altered health response scale.

f. Describe Janet's behaviour on arriving at the hospital in terms of the sick role.

g. How should you deal with Janet? How can you calm her down?

h. What problems will Janet face regarding her children over the next few weeks?

Websites of Interest

Health and Wellness in Canada
www.windfall.ca/healthwellness.html

Public Health Agency of Canada: Information on VRE, *C. Difficile*, and MRSA
http://www.phac-aspc.gc.ca/nois-sinp/vre-erv-eng.php

Information on Vancomycin-resistant *Enterococci* (VRE)
http://www.phac-aspc.gc.ca/id-mi/cdiff-eng.php

Fact sheet on *Clostridium difficile* (*C. difficile*)
http://www.phac-aspc.gc.ca/id-mi/mrsa-eng.php

Fact sheet on Methicillin-resistant *Staphylococcus aureus* (MRSA)
Public Health Agency of Canada: Healthy Living
http://www.phac-aspc.gc.ca/hp-ps/hl-mvs/index-eng.php

Canadian Alliance of Community Health Centre Associations
http://www.cachca.ca/index.html

Wait Times for Health Care in Canada
http://canadaonline.about.com/od/healthcarewaittimes/Wait_Times_for_Health_Care_in_Canada.htm

Wait Times in Canada—A Comparison by Province, 2011
http://secure.cihi.ca/cihiweb/products/Wait_times_tables_2011_en.pdf

Chapter 3
Culture and Health

Learning Objectives

On completing this chapter, you will be able to:

1. Define culture.
2. Explain the elements that have increased intercultural exposure, and the need for cultural tolerance and understanding.
3. Discuss barriers to good cross-cultural health care and measures to overcome them.
4. Identify the problems that result from language barriers.
5. Explain how to effectively select and use an interpreter.
6. Summarize techniques and practices to deliver high-quality, culturally sensitive health care to an ethnically diverse population.

Canada is one of the most culturally diverse countries in the world. Every province and territory, indeed, every community, has a unique blend of cultural and social influences. Within each community, there is great cultural variation, especially in large cities such as Toronto, Vancouver, and Montreal. Knowing about different cultures promotes understanding and acceptance and encourages adaptive, rather than antagonistic, relationships. As an administrative health professional, you can communicate with clients and support them if you understand something about their culture and how it shapes their health beliefs, behaviours, and expectations.

Canada has accepted immigrants from almost every nation of the world. In 2006, according to Statistics Canada the combined visible minorities by the end of 2012 will form a majority in both Toronto and Vancouver. Statistics from 2011 show that there has been a recent rush of immigrants to western Canada, particularly to Manitoba, Saskatchewan, and Alberta. This is due to the robust economies in these regions—mostly in the mining and natural resource sectors. Previously, Ontario received most immigrants.

Currently the focus for immigration is to keep Canada's economy strong, particularly after the recent recession. Statistics Canada shows that 60 percent of new immigrants came through the economic stream. This stream allows admission to the country based on the individual's ability to contribute to the economic development of the country (e.g., skilled workers, investors, entrepreneurs, and those with the high potential for self-employment). According to Statistics Canada, the immigration plan for the next few years will also include more admissions for spouses and children in the family category. These individuals will bring specific cultural needs with respect to health care, as well requiring access to family doctors and other health-care services.

In 1971, Canada became the first country in the world to adopt a multiculturalism policy, illustrating a commitment to ethnic diversity. In 1986, the federal government passed the *Employment Equity Act*, and in 1988, it passed the *Canadian Multiculturalism Act*. The *Canadian Multiculturalism Act* directs the federal government to work toward equality in the economic, social, cultural, and political life of the country. It is commonly said that while the United States is a melting pot, Canada is a mosaic. People are encouraged to join in Canadian life while retaining their own customs and cultural identity. And indeed this happens—sometimes. Walking along certain city streets, one has the sense of being in an international bazaar. Saris, babushkas, and dreadlocks mingle with business suits and faded denim; the cadences of many languages greet the ear; every imaginable food from every corner of the world seems to be on offer. Yet, the mosaic is not without problems. Members of ethnic and cultural minorities report very different experiences: some feel welcome and cherished; others meet with discrimination and rebuffs. Some feel that multiculturalism is merely a tourist gloss on profound social division. Although governments can formulate policies, only people can make them work.

❶ WHAT IS CULTURE?

THE TERM *CULTURE* MEANS DIFFERENT THINGS TO DIFFERENT PEOPLE, AS DO MANY OF THE terms connected with it. Let us start by reviewing a few.

Culture may be defined as "the languages, beliefs, values, norms, behaviours, and even material objects that are passed from one generation to the next."[1] More broadly,

culture the languages, beliefs, values, norms, behaviours, and even material objects that are passed from one generation to the next.

---

[1] James M. Henslin and Adie Nelson. *Essentials of Sociology: A Down-to-Earth Approach.* Scarborough: Allyn and Bacon Canada, 1997.

culture refers to a collection of beliefs, rules, and practices that are shared by a group of people,[2] whether or not they are passed from generation to generation. These beliefs and norms are so basic to our lives that we are often unaware of them until we see people from other cultures following different norms. Our own culture becomes, in a sense, invisible to us. To people who have grown up that way, it simply feels natural to brush their teeth in the morning, eat three meals a day (rather than two or six), go to school, wear jeans, stand in line for movie tickets, say thank you when given something, and listen to music on the radio. Yet none of these behaviours are natural; they are all learned as part of a culture. We often become aware of culture only when we see someone from another culture behaving differently. We may observe this behaviour as simply different or regard it as something we do not understand. Canadians often accept certain cultural variations, such as those in clothing and cuisine, and enjoy them as part of our rich, multicultural landscape. Yet, it may be harder to recognize some of the subtler variations in culture. Seeing someone stand closer and speak louder than the Canadian norm or haggle over prices may make one dismiss the person as simply vulgar, loud, or cheap, without recognizing that he is simply following a different set of cultural rules.

Generally, culture is learned through imitation and observation rather than direct instruction. Culture affects people on personal, social, economic, environmental, and political levels. It may define appropriate behaviours for men and women: for example, when and whom a person marries. Culture influences attitudes toward older adults, family planning and parenting styles, social expectations and commitment, sexual practices, nutrition, and medical practices.

Though culture tends to be associated with a national or ethnic group, there are many variations. For example, the culture of a rural Maritimer will be a little different from the culture of an Ontario city dweller. A person who was born in Jamaica but grew up in Canada may share some cultural characteristics with Jamaicans but others with Canadians. Within a society can also be found many **subcultures**: groups that share many cultural aspects with the general society but have their own distinct cultural practices as well. There is, for example, a gay subculture, a biker gang subculture, a rap subculture. Often, young people have a somewhat different culture from that of their parents, despite being part of the same broader culture.

subculture the values and practices of a group that distinguish it from the larger culture.

Ethnicity

ethnic relating to groups of people with a common racial, religious, linguistic, or cultural heritage.

The word **ethnic** comes from the Greek term *ethnos*, "people." The dictionary defines *ethnic* as "relating to groups of people with a common racial, religious, linguistic, or cultural heritage." In this sense, we all have an ethnic origin. A fifth-generation Canadian of British ancestry is no more or less "ethnic" than an immigrant from Vietnam. Yet, in another usage, the term is used only for ethnic minorities and is sometimes used interchangeably with the terms *race* or *minority group*. Social scientists use the term, however, to refer to cultural characteristics. In this sense, a person's ancestry and physical characteristics are not necessarily the same as their ethnicity. A black person who grew up in France will probably have a different ethnic identity from one who grew up in Trinidad, even if their physical characteristics are similar.

---

[2] Athena du Pre. *Communication about Health*. Mountain View (California), Toronto, London: Mayfield Publishing Company, 2000.

Race is often used to refer to groups of people with similar physical characteristics and a common ancestry. Some divide humanity into three races, others into four or more. However, most anthropologists have now rejected the categories as unscientific. Though human beings obviously have marked differences in physical characteristics, such as skin tone and facial features, there is no strong rationale for any particular lines of division among these variations. *Caucasian*, for example, is sometimes used as a synonym for *White* or *European*. Yet, as once used by anthropologists, the term denoted a race including not only white Europeans but also dark-skinned South and West Asians. Despite the inexactness of racial divisions, there are times when it is important in health care to note genetic and metabolic characteristics common to groups of people. For example: sickle-cell anemia is found mostly among blacks; Tay-Sachs disease is found mostly among people of European-Jewish ancestry (regardless of their ethnic identity or religion).

Ethnic identity is not the same as nationality. *Nationality* is manifested when a person belongs to a country, with all its legal benefits (such as the right to participate in elections) and social benefits (such as the right to health care and education). The person may gain citizenship by birth or may apply for citizenship in a new country. Many countries allow dual citizenship.

Ethnicity refers to the cultural characteristics of a particular ethnic group. It includes such things as traits, background, allegiances, and self-identification. Many minority groups find that their sense of ethnic identity fades over time as each generation becomes more immersed in the culture and practices of the country in which they live. For example, a family may move from India to Canada and faithfully practise their religion and related traditions. The children may retain their traditions and sense of identity while becoming more integrated into Canadian culture. When they have children of their own, who are born in Canada and exposed to Western culture from birth, adherence to traditional practices may be more difficult. Some people feel torn between two worlds; others quite comfortably establish their own cultural identity, blending elements of the new country and the old. In the case of mixed marriages and groups that have migrated, identity can be complex: "I am a Canadian Muslim from Uganda, of Gujarati background," or, "I am a Canadian, part Ukrainian and part Chinese."

Quebec is an example of a society that is actively trying to preserve its uniqueness and ethnicity. Laws in Quebec restrict the use of English in signage, business, and education. In France, too, such bodies as the Académie Française try to root out English colloquialisms, such as "le weekend."

Canada's Aboriginal peoples are also trying to preserve their ethnicity by keeping their traditions, practices, and laws alive, which is often a struggle. Some languages, for example, are on the verge of extinction. Again, attitudes vary. Some Aboriginal people feel that preserving old customs is essential to their identity. Many feel free to pick and choose which aspects of traditional culture to embrace and resent the implication that they are less "authentic" if their lives resemble those of other Canadians in many ways. Aboriginal cultures vary widely, and a person is less likely to identify with the broad category "Indian" or "First Nations" than with a specific cultural group, such as Cree, Inuit, or Ojibwa.

Multiculturalism or Cultural Diversity

Multiculturalism refers to people of various cultures living together in relative harmony and mutual respect. *Cultural diversity* implies maintaining distinct cultures within a broader society. The ideal is to celebrate differences without dwelling on them, in an atmosphere of understanding, respect, and tolerance.

Prejudice and Ethnocentrism

Prejudice means "prejudging" or coming to conclusions about a person or group on the basis of untested assumptions, without regard for the facts. Prejudice can be a negative or hostile attitude or thought based on intolerance and ignorance. It may just be felt internally or may be expressed. Prejudice may be expressed against any group, minority or not, and it may be found among any group. A common form of prejudice is *stereotyping*: assuming that all members of a group will be alike. Stereotyping may be applied to cultures and subcultures, age and gender groups, and occupations. For example, teenagers in groups may be viewed as a source of trouble; accountants may be stereotyped as interested only in figures. We have all heard blonde jokes, based on the notion that fair-haired women are not intelligent. Although prejudice is usually thought of as negative, positive prejudices are also possible: for example, assuming that a black person will be athletic or a Welshman will be a good singer. There indeed may be behaviours that are more common among certain groups of people, but assuming that everyone in a perceived category has the same characteristics is inaccurate and harmful. An example from a health-care perspective is the assumption that Asian women do not complain during childbirth, while Italian women are very vocal.

Do not confuse prejudice with *discrimination*. Usually, discrimination follows prejudice, but prejudice can occur without discrimination. Discrimination occurs when people are denied justice or treated unfairly because of their membership in a group.

More broadly, **ethnocentrism** is the tendency to use our own culture's standards as the yardstick to judge everyone. To some degree, this is inevitable. All people look at the world from the point of view of their own culture, and most of us naturally believe that the values and beliefs with which we have been raised are right. But ethnocentrism can act like blinders, preventing us from seeing the big picture or from understanding another's point of view. At its worst, ethnocentrism leads us to view our own group and culture as superior to all others and leads to intolerance or condescension.

ethnocentrism the tendency to use one's own culture's standards as the yardstick to judge everyone; the belief in the superiority of one's own group or culture.

❷ THE NEED FOR INTERCULTURAL UNDERSTANDING

NEVER HAS IT BEEN MORE IMPORTANT TO RESPECT AND LEARN TO COMMUNICATE AND LIVE in harmony with people from different cultures. Understanding is necessary from a social and humanitarian perspective, and to ensure our economic and political well-being.

Populations have become increasingly mobile. The beginning of this chapter discussed how varied the Canadian population is. Tourists and businesspeople from around the world visit Canada and sometimes need health care here. Educational exchanges have increased in recent years. Students from other countries undergo the culture shock of dealing with a new country, culture, educational system, and language. Trying to understand their individual health beliefs, expectations, and how they interface with health care in their own country is important. Canadians, too, travel frequently to visit friends and family and to do business. International trade agreements lead to job relocations. We often converse with people from other cultures and may not always understand the things they say, why they say them, or what they mean. For example, in an international chat group, a Swede was discussing his grandfather's peaceful end through euthanasia. A Canadian responded that euthanasia was nothing short of murder. Each was viewing the matter through the lenses of his own culture. In Sweden, euthanasia is legal and seen as an act of kindness when it respects the dying person's autonomy and wishes. In Canada, euthanasia is still illegal and is highly controversial. Understanding and respecting another's point of view does not mean that you must agree with it, but it does allow fruitful discussion and enhances tolerance.

Recent global conflict has intensified intercultural intolerance. The first few years of the 21st century saw the September 11, 2001 attack on the World Trade Center in New York; wars in Afghanistan, the Congo, and Iraq; and escalated conflict in the Middle East. The past decade has seen ethnically motivated mass killings in Europe, Southeast Asia, and Africa, as well as internal unrest in Syria and the slaughter of thousands of Syrian citizens. Internationally, mistrust and tension among peoples and nations have been rising, particularly in the Middle East (e.g., Israel and Iran). These tensions spill over to Canada's diverse society. It is unrealistic to expect that all Canadians—new and established—will embrace every culture enthusiastically. People may find themselves living next door to someone from a group or culture they grew up learning to regard as a bitter enemy. Such feelings do not simply evaporate by virtue of being in a new country. Friends and adversaries alike immigrate to Canada seeking business opportunities, proximity to family, and peace and freedom. In spite of these common goals, where prejudice exists, it takes time for wounds to heal and for attitudes ingrained over generations to change. Long-time Canadians, too, can find it difficult to accept change and may regard newcomers as interlopers. Despite official goals of equality and acceptance, racial and ethnic prejudices are not uncommon among some groups in Canada.

In health care, cultural acceptance is a gateway to positive relationships that enhance effective care and client health and wellness. As a administrative health professional, you will play an important role in the delivery of this health care. You will, in many cases, act as advocate for the client. You can help break down cultural barriers and make the client's health-care experience more positive from both medical and personal perspectives. You may be the first person an individual comes into contact with when seeking health care. A positive interaction is the first step toward establishing an adaptive and trusting relationship. The most important thing you can do is to help your client feel valued and respected. This, however, is not always as simple as it sounds. It may involve looking inward and coming to terms with your own thoughts, feelings, values, and attitudes. Make it a personal goal to understand your own attitudes toward various cultures and to work toward tolerance, understanding, and acceptance. Try to see people for who they are, to understand where they are coming from, and to develop a positive and caring attitude.

If you feel that a client fears prejudice, you must do your best to reassure her by being consistently professional, warm, and friendly. Conversely, if you feel that a client is prejudiced against you, for whatever reason, you must set aside your natural resentment and be patient. As you continue to behave in a professional and friendly manner, you will be helping to break down that prejudice.

❸ BARRIERS TO CROSS-CULTURAL HEALTH CARE

CULTURE PLAYS A ROLE IN SHAPING PEOPLE'S HEALTH BELIEFS—WHAT HEALTH, WELLNESS, and illness mean to them, who assumes responsibility for their health, their perception of illness and disease, and how they respond to medical intervention and care. Even the values attached to life and death are influenced by culture.

Dealing effectively with health-care issues in an ethnically diverse population is difficult, even under ideal conditions. Problems within the health-care system magnify these challenges.

Changes in Health-Care Delivery

As recently as 10 years ago, most primary-care physicians had more time to establish a relationship of trust and understanding with their clients. This allowed the physician more opportunities to discuss medical issues and personal concerns in detail with each client, to answer questions, and to offer support. Most people had a family doctor they felt comfortable with and trusted. Today, a shortage of physicians means that many people receive primary health care in walk-in or urgent-care clinics and in Emergency Departments. Newcomers to Canada may be unable to find a family physician, let alone one with whom they can establish an adaptive client–physician relationship. At a clinic, the doctor barely has time to deal with the illness, treatment, and prognosis, let alone develop an understanding of the patient's personality, beliefs, and culture. Continuity of care is also a problem, in that clients may see a different physician each time they go to a clinic. Resulting care can be incomplete and fragmented.

Although current statistics (2012) indicate that the number of doctors in Canada has risen, there is still a shortage of family doctors, so finding one is difficult for most new immigrants to Canada. Family doctors are taking care of larger practices and treating clients with more complex health problems, resulting in less time to get to know their clients. Clients may feel frustrated, angry, and helpless. When cultural differences and language barriers further complicate the relationship, clients may feel that the provider does not view them as important or is giving them substandard care because of lack of cultural knowledge and understanding or prejudice. In desperation, they may go to a clinic to seek other providers, perpetuating the cycle. Frustrations related to the long waits to see specialists and to access diagnostic services also compound health problems for those dealing with cultural adjustments.

Advances in Medical Technology

For some newcomers to Canada, modern Western technology may seem daunting. This will depend on what level of technology and medical services the person has been exposed to in her country of origin.

Some may find the equipment disconcerting and the choices of treatment options overwhelming, especially when none of them seem to relate to the person's own experiences, beliefs, and values. This happens even within Canada when individuals from areas that have fewer services require care in large centres—for example, Aboriginals who have led healthy lives in the far North and have not required much in the way of medical services.

Canada's Aboriginal population continues to struggle with the poorest health among identified populations.[3] This is, in part, due to loss of culture and identity, and to racism. Aboriginal life expectancy is seven to eight years shorter than that of the average

---

[3] Section 35 of the *Constitution Act of 1982* recognizes First Nations and Métis as aboriginal populations. *Aboriginal* more recently also includes Canada's Inuit population. Metis are people of mixed First Nations and European ancestry.

Canadian. Social and health issues remain the highest in the country. Inadequacies in the technology and health infrastructure in most northern communities remain, although every attempt is made to deliver health care within Aboriginal communities. In smaller communities, health care is given at nursing stations, often by nurses or nurse practitioners, with support online, by telephone, or from visiting physicians. Clients with health problems that cannot be managed locally are transported, mostly by air ambulance, to distant medical centres offering a wider range of medical services. People from remote communities may find this sudden transfer to a busy hospital intimidating. They also face the stress of being away from their own familiar environment and the support of family and friends.

The Hospital Environment

To most of us, hospitals, nursing homes, and other client-care facilities are a familiar part of the health-care landscape. Admission to an acute-care hospital is fairly common, depending on the nature of the illness. Moving to a nursing home is becoming the norm for older adults who can no longer care for themselves and whose families cannot provide for them.

To some cultures, however, health-care agencies, whether acute care or long term, are frightening and unwelcome. Koreans, for example, may view admission to hospital as an imminent sign of death and a disharmony with the life forces of yin and yang. Many ethnic minorities will avoid hospitals at all costs, preferring to manage their illnesses at home.

Continued nursing care in a health-care facility poses even greater problems. The thought of entering a nursing home, particularly for cultures where the norm is to care for seniors at home, is often repugnant. Asian cultures, such as the Vietnamese and Chinese, typically have a tradition of caring for senior family members at home, with hospitalization being a last resort. An older adult may avoid or refuse hospitalization, fearing separation from family. Yet, in Canada, attempts to keep an older or ill family member at home may become problematic. Family members, despite their cultural norms, may be struggling with full-time jobs and raising a family as well as the stress of bridging two cultures. If they cannot manage with home care and other community support initiatives, the feeling of failure is two-fold: family members may feel they have not fulfilled their responsibilities, and the client admitted to care may feel abandoned.

The pace of the hospital routine in itself may upset the client. Latin Americans, for instance, take a more relaxed approach to life in general. They like to take their time, to have things explained, and to consider alternatives. The hectic pace of the hospital may so intimidate and confuse them that they may find it difficult to participate in their own health care. Likewise, in the health office, they may not accept the urgency of a test and may try to fit it into their schedule, rather than rearrange their schedule.

Professionals' Attitudes and Lack of Knowledge

For the health-care system to be fully effective, professionals must understand and adapt to the varied mix of cultural, racial, socioeconomic, and generational differences within their practices. This is a complex undertaking that can't be achieved overnight. Lack of understanding may lead professionals to be condescending to clients or to otherwise treat them in a way they find disrespectful. Someone with a history of being discriminated against will be quick to perceive any slight and will be hurt. Even a simple error or misunderstanding can lose the client's trust. At worst, the relationship is so impaired that even clients' simple needs are not met.

Cross-cultural understanding has recently been identified as needing significant improvement for health professionals dealing with Aboriginal people. There is a need to recognize the importance of both family roles and community responsibilities within a community when rendering health care. As well, health professionals need to respect traditional Aboriginal medicine and the role of elders in the community.[4]

❹ DIFFERENCES IN BELIEFS AND PRACTICES

CLIENTS COME TO A HEALTH OFFICE BRINGING VARIED EXPECTATIONS, SHAPED BY A BLEND of their culture and their experiences. A person who grew up with a very different health-care system may be surprised at how things are done and may not understand much of what is done and why. People's culturally based beliefs also influence both their decision to seek treatment and their expectations of treatment. This section outlines a few culturally based attitudes that may affect health care. Keep in mind that these are very general. You should never assume that all members of cultural minorities share the same beliefs, practices, and attitudes. This approach is stereotyping and likely to lead to misunderstandings. Not only do cultures vary, but individuals vary too. Your own attitudes toward health might be quite different from your sister's or your best friend's, and they may change over the course of your lifetime as a result of your own life experiences. Be alert to differences in how individuals approach health care; be aware of their expectations, their compliance with medical treatment, and their understanding of issues affecting their health and treatment.

Recent newcomers (especially younger people) may adopt typical Western health beliefs, values, and expectations quickly. Others may incorporate a blend of Western beliefs and behaviours with those of their country of origin, while still others do not embrace Western culture at all. First- and second-generation Canadians are often at odds with their parents and grandparents regarding health beliefs and behaviours. This may promote disharmony within the family. You may at times feel that you are caught in the middle, attempting to honour the rights of the client as well as those of the parents.

Confidentiality

The issue of confidentiality can be complicated by cultural expectations. It is not unusual for a parent to come into the office and demand confidential information about her teenage child or demand that a plan of care for a son or daughter be withdrawn or changed. In some cultures, it is expected that a parent will have access to this type of information, whereas in Canada the matter is usually between the teenage client and the provider. Conversely, a grown child may come in demanding information about a parent. In some cultures, it is expected that the eldest son, for example, will assume responsibility for care of the parent and therefore have the right to all medical information. In Canada, the exchange of this type of information is not permitted without the client's expressed permission. In such circumstances, it is best to remain neutral and to discuss the issue with the doctor.

The Philosophy of Prevention

As we discussed in Chapter 2, a preventive model of health care currently predominates in Western culture. Individuals are encouraged to take responsibility for their own wellness.

---

[4] Janet Smylie, B.A., M.D., C.C.F.P. *A Guide for Health Professionals Working With Aboriginal People*. Society of Obstetricians and Gynecologists of Canada, December, 2000.

Virtually every community, in partnership with various levels of government, has agencies that promote health education and adaptive lifestyles. Doctors and other health-care professionals have also assumed responsibility for health teaching related to health promotion. Members of some minorities may resist or may not understand this approach. Some cultures, such as those of some First Nations, see health and illness as matters of the "here and now." Visiting the doctor's office for an annual physical examination (as is recommended in many jurisdictions) is not a standard practice. This is not deliberate noncompliance or disregard for one's health, just a different perspective. Carefully explain to the client the reasons for the examination. If this does not change the client's attitude and behaviour, you may simply have to respect her perspective. Remember that you can accept and respect a person's point of view without agreeing with it.

The Concept of Illness and Treatment

Many cultures do not accept the concept of chronic illness. When people in these cultures feel better, they consider that the illness has been cured; if they feel poorly again, they consider that a new illness. To someone with this attitude, it is difficult to explain the cycle of **remission** and **exacerbation** that characterizes such illnesses as multiple sclerosis (MS). With MS, there are usually periods when the client feels better (remission) and may be completely symptom free. This is usually the result of a well-established treatment regime. Even with treatment, clinical signs or symptoms will generally reappear (exacerbation). Treatment is adjusted, and perhaps the client will enjoy another remission. Clients who do not see this cycle as part of a chronic illness often stop taking their medication as soon as they feel well, which interferes with effective management of the disease. Consider a client, Ana, with a urinary tract infection for which the physician has prescribed an antibiotic four times a day for 10 days. The doctor assumes she will take the medication as prescribed. As expected, the clinical signs disappear in a day or two. Four days later, Ana calls with complaints that should have been managed by the medication. As soon as Ana felt better, she assumed that she was cured and stopped taking the medication. The way to prevent this problem is to give clients a careful, detailed explanation of the importance of taking the medication until it is finished, even when they no longer experience the signs, and to invite questions to make sure the clients understand.

remission the phase of a chronic disease characterized by a relief or absence of clinical signs or symptoms.

exacerbation the phase of a chronic disease characterized by a return of clinical signs or symptoms.

Explanatory Systems

Some cultures have systems of traditional or folk medicine that explain health and illness according to principles different from those of modern Western medicine. Some link health and illness with the supernatural or spiritual world. Some African Canadians, for example, believe in a direct connection between the body and the forces of nature. They may consider propitious dates, stars, and numbers in booking appointments or making decisions about their health care. Traditional Chinese medicine explains health and illness largely in terms of opposing principles. The causes of diseases originate from two sources, those operating from the outside and those operating inside. External causes relate to hot and cold. For example, some foods and some conditions are considered "hot" and others "cold." These terms do not refer to temperature but to inherent qualities of substances. People with a "hot" condition are advised to eat "cold" foods and vice versa. First Nations and Inuit Canadians have a holistic view of health. They consider health to include a range of mental, physical, and emotional factors. Good health requires a balance among these aspects. Healing can involve the use of herbal medicines, talking circles, sweat lodges, and teaching from elders.

You cannot ask clients whether they believe in magic or in folk medicine, but you can find out about their beliefs by asking what they think is the cause of their symptoms. Such beliefs may influence anything from the food they eat to their level of activity and when they bathe. Respect where they are coming from. Remember that Western medicine does not know everything. Whether or not health beliefs have any basis in fact, people are more likely to do well if they are confident in and comfortable with their treatment. Comply with their requests whenever possible. In some cases, you may need to accept that the client will not choose the treatment the health-care provider deems best. There is no universal formula that will allow you to resolve the difference, but remember that the foundation of good health care is respect for the individual. Ultimately, it is the client's health and the client's decision.

Attitudes toward Mental Illness

According to Health Canada, mental illness affects one in five Canadians at some point during their lifetime. Those with mental-health issues, disabilities, and addictions face multiple discriminatory barriers, from individuals as well as from institutions. This includes health care and law enforcement. In 2012 more emphasis was placed on police being better trained to deal effectively with mentally ill individuals and to work with social workers and mental-health-care professionals.

Discrimination compounds the effects of living with mental-health disabilities. It makes it harder for the individual to seek appropriate treatment for her problems. Recovery is difficult because of limited support systems. Despite awareness campaigns and increasing acceptance, mental illness still carries a certain stigma in Western society. For example, although depression is a widespread diagnosis, and anti-depressants are commonly used, many people are reluctant to admit the diagnosis or the use of medication even to friends and family. In 2012 Bell Canada launched a campaign to initiate discussion about mental-health issues; Olympic athlete Clara Hughes, who has suffered from depression, participated in the campaign.

The stigma of mental-health problems is even stronger among people, such as Vietnamese Canadians, whose culture believes mental illness is governed by spiritual entities. Chinese and Hispanics also will often avoid seeking treatment for psychiatric illnesses, feeling that such issues are personal and should be discussed only with family members. Followers of Scientology believe there is no such thing as mental illness and that treating perceived mental illness with therapy or drugs is useless, if not unethical.

Be tolerant, understanding, and discreet with these clients and their family members when discussing related tests and treatment times, and when booking referral appointments.

End-of-Life Issues

Advanced technology makes it possible to prolong life for terminally ill clients. Some individuals want every measure possible used to sustain life; others advocate little or no intervention. These decisions reflect cultural, religious, and experientially acquired beliefs and practices. Muslims, for example, generally find it unacceptable to prolong life with machinery unless the individual will be able to lead a satisfactory life.

The death of a member affects families of different cultures in various ways. The Vietnamese may mourn a loved one for up to three years. They do not usually allow autopsies, believing that the body should remain intact. They may also be reluctant to register as organ donors.

In 2012 the CBC brought two cases to light regarding the termination of "extraordinary" life support measures at Sunnybrook Health Sciences Centre in Toronto. Two physicians are required to concur on the withdrawal of life support and/or other measures deemed extraordinary if they feel that these measures are futile. The decision of the physicians overrides the family's desire to continue these measures for whatever reason, whether cultural or the personal belief that their loved one will or can recover, even in part.

Child Care

In contemporary Western society, mothers often work full time outside the home, relegating child care to a hired nanny or a daycare centre. Although many women make this choice for financial reasons, the practice is generally accepted. In some other cultures, however, such as many African and Indian cultures, mothers are more likely to seek work where they can take the child with them or to have extended family members take care of the child. Although these arrangements can be more difficult in Canada, it is not unusual to have grandmothers, aunts, or sisters care for children. When the child comes into the office, it is not uncommon for the mother as well as the child's other caregiver(s) to come for support. They may all want to be in the examination room with the child. Accommodate this wish if space allows and if there is no medical reason not to. You may want to ask who is coming in with the child so that you can use a larger examination room if one is available.

Modesty

In Western society, most people are only mildly uncomfortable about setting aside modesty for a physical examination. However, for people from some cultures, such as many Asian and Middle Eastern cultures, it is difficult and stressful to expose one's body to a stranger, even a physician. It is especially distressing for a woman to expose her body to a man because of the strong norm of modesty in these male-dominated cultures. For this reason, many South Asian women prefer a female provider. If you are aware that modesty is a concern, try to do what you can to make the client more comfortable. If you are using the standard examination gowns that open at the back, give the client two gowns, with the second facing the front. Let the doctor know that the client is modest so that he can be careful to expose only one area at a time. In most Canadian offices, it is typical for a nurse or office professional to be present during the examination, particularly for a pelvic examination and Pap smear. If the physician wants you to be present but you feel that your presence is uncomfortable for the client, keep a distance, and busy yourself with other work while being available to assist the doctor when required. If the client wants to have a family member present, allow this.

Religious Constraints

People's religious beliefs may make certain medical treatments or procedures unacceptable to them. For example, Jehovah's Witnesses will refuse organ transplants or transfusion with blood or blood products. This decision must be respected when the client is an adult. The issue becomes more complicated for children, and courts have considered cases in which parents have refused treatment that doctors felt was necessary for the children's survival. Hindus, Buddhists, or Jains may object to medical products that use animal products, as may Orthodox Jews (who do eat meat, but only if it meets the rules of *kashrut*). In general, see if an alternative is available when a client is uncomfortable with any proposed treatment.

Number of Visitors

Many hospitals have strict rules regarding the number of visitors a client may have in the hospital room, partly to avoid disturbing other clients. However, in some East Asian and South Asian cultures, the prolonged presence of family and friends is considered essential to an ill person's comfort, security, and well-being. The challenge here is how to adapt the rules to meet the needs of the client. If you work in a client-care unit, carefully explain the hospital policies regarding visitors to a family member, and at the same time, try to find a compromise. One might be to move the client to a private room. Another solution, if clients are ambulatory, is to ask them to visit in the reception area. If these options are not feasible and other clients are being disturbed, you might suggest a compromise: reducing the number of visitors, asking them to be as quiet as possible, and placing limits on visiting time, while allowing a little more than the standard hours. If clients and their families see that you are trying to make compromises, they will feel valued and respected and will often be willing to meet you half way. However, rules created for public health reasons, particularly related to the spread of infectious diseases, place much tighter restrictions on visitors—including visiting times and the number of visitors allowed into a room (these may vary with situations). If your hospital has such rules, there is probably little you can do beyond explaining the rules and being sympathetic.

Childbirth

Cultures have different approaches to childbirth and parenting. For example, some South Asian and East Asian women are quite stoic when in labour. If such a woman calls the office to report that she is in labour, asking her if she is having much pain may not reveal much about how advanced the labour is. You may get a more accurate impression by asking how far apart her contractions are and how long she has had them.

Health professionals may get the wrong impression about a couple's relationship if the father seems to wish no involvement in the birth. It has become common recently in Western culture for fathers or significant others to be present for the entire birthing process. A Western man who shows no interest in the pregnancy and does not wish to be present for the birth *may* be indicating a lack of commitment to fatherhood. (Or he may just be uncomfortable with first-hand exposure to childbirth.) In some cultures, this disinclination simply reflects a cultural norm and says nothing about the man's love for his wife or his excitement about the coming baby.

It has also recently become common in the West for mothers to be sent home very soon after delivery, usually from four to 24 hours **postpartum**. The mother who is up and about and back to a reasonable level of activity quickly is admired for her quick recovery and tenacity. Some cultures, however, such as those in parts of India, encourage new mothers to recuperate for 40 days. During this period, a time for rest and spiritual and physical renewal, they are cared for by family members. Health professionals may worry needlessly about an Indian woman who spends a lot of time in bed after giving birth.

postpartum   after delivery.

She may not be a disinterested mother or suffering from postpartum depression; she may simply be following a cultural norm that calls for her to rest.

5 6 LANGUAGE DIFFICULTIES

COMMUNICATION IS A SIGNIFICANT CROSS-CULTURAL BARRIER. MANY CANADIAN immigrants do not speak English or French fluently, and some not at all. Some start learning rapidly as soon as they arrive, but others may live in Canada for years and never learn. Access to English- or French-as-a-second-language courses is limited in some communities, and some people find getting to classes difficult, perhaps because they lack time or child care. Often, older adults do not even attempt to learn English because it is difficult and because they do not feel the need to do so. If they live with their family in an ethnic enclave, they can continue to speak their native language and manage quite well. Difficulties arise, however, when they interface with the health-care system. Furthermore, even people with good second-language skills may revert to their mother tongue in times of stress or may lose some of their fluency and comprehension skills.

Language difficulties may cause a person to put off making an appointment, leading to worsening health problems and possibly a more stressful intervention. Although you cannot entirely remove this barrier, you can be consistently patient and friendly on the phone so that at least the client need not fear embarrassment or rejection. Listen for halting speech or errors in usage or vocabulary; if the person's English appears to be limited, take a little extra time to speak clearly and slightly more slowly than usual. Make any instructions as uncomplicated as you can. Pause from time to time to allow the client to ask for clarification. Avoid both medical jargon and idioms that may be obscure to someone with limited English. For example, if a client asks you which of two laboratories to go to, don't say, "It's a toss-up," or "It's six of one, half-dozen of the other." The client may just wonder, "What is being thrown?" "Six of what?" Instead, you could say, "You may go to either lab." If in doubt, have the client repeat information for you. In fact, it is a good idea with any client to have the client repeat the appointment time for you. Calling the client the day before the appointment can also clarify information that may not have been understood.

The same principles of clear communication apply in the office. For example, if you are explaining a diagnostic test to a client, include details about the preparation, how the test will be done, how long it will take, and whether or not someone can come with the client. Encourage the client to ask questions, and answer her as accurately as you can.

Speaking clearly does not mean lapsing into pidgin English. Nor does it mean raising your voice. Stick to correct, complete sentences in your normal tone. Some people try to make instructions clearer by omitting words. For example: "You go there for appointment. Girl meet you at door." This can actually be more confusing as well as demeaning. Keep in mind that some people understand better than they can speak and will be bitterly insulted at baby talk. Say, instead: "Your appointment is on the third floor of the hospital. I will ask the receptionist to meet you at the door." When efforts at telephone communication appear too difficult, arrange for a family member or friend to act as an interpreter.

Using an Interpreter

In Canada there is a requirement that medical practitioners provide their deaf clients with interpretation services. There is no such requirement for individuals with other language barriers. In some cases, language barriers (perhaps coupled with a profound sense of modesty or a belief that illness is an admission of weakness) will stop a person from seeking needed health care. Even if the client does come, she will not understand anything about her condition or the treatment if you do not have a language in common. In many communities, access to interpreters is limited. Most hospitals keep a list of staff members who speak various languages. Of course, a second language is also an asset in the health office, but, more often, you will rely on family or friends as interpreters. If you feel an interpreter is needed, ask an appropriate person to come for each office visit. Some clients will be insulted, feeling that they are considered incompetent. Try to explain that you just want to make sure you understand each other clearly and that having an interpreter will benefit both parties. When the client understands the reason for certain things and recognizes that you care enough about her to take the time to explain, she will feel respected and cared for and will usually be more compliant. The friend or family member can also speak on the client's behalf and can help the client feel supported.

If you have a choice of interpreter, the client will usually feel most at ease with someone of the same gender and approximately the same age. In Indian cultures, it is sometimes expected that the provider give any information about the client to a male member of the family, such as the father, the brother, or the son. A sibling or adult child may be a good choice, or may not, if the client wants to keep certain things private. Usually, a child or teenager is not the best choice; not only may young people lack the maturity to understand everything, but discussion may also expose them to matters they are not prepared to handle or that parents would rather keep from them.

Book a longer appointment for a client who will be using an interpreter. Information will have to be repeated by the interpreter and perhaps restated by the provider for clarification. The interpreter should be at the same physical level as the client—if the client is lying in bed, offer the interpreter a chair beside the bed. Always face the client, not the interpreter, and make eye contact, even though the client will have to look to the interpreter for the information. The inability to effectively communicate affects the health professional as well as the client. Be patient. While you may be getting frustrated, keep in mind that the client is equally frustrated and may also be anxious and may feel inadequate, which undermines self-esteem. The importance of effective communication cannot be overemphasized. See the following Tips box for suggestions on cross-cultural communication in the health office.

Tips

Try to be culturally sensitive to ethnic minorities, regardless of your own culture.

Do not assume anything. One person from a certain country may have adopted Western attitudes; another may not have.

If a language barrier exists, speak slowly and clearly. Use simple words, and avoid medical jargon. Watch for nonverbal cues: facial expressions, body language, and gestures.

Do not assume that a nod or smile means the client understands or accepts what you say. Sometimes, a client is confused but is trying to be polite.

Always greet a client you do not know by surname. Switch to first names only at the client's invitation. Though many North Americans like the informality of first names, it can be considered intrusive in many cultures. Even in North American culture, many seniors consider uninvited use of the first name a sign of disrespect.

Keep in mind that some languages such as Chinese and Arabic place the family name first. Some people retain this format; others switch to the English style. If you are not sure, ask: "Excuse me, I'm not sure how to pronounce your name." Use the same approach if you do not know how to

>

pronounce the name, rather than guessing. Some people will not correct you.

Observe carefully how the client looks at you. Most North Americans consider direct eye contact a sign of self-confidence and forthrightness. Many cultures, including some Asian and some First Nations cultures, consider direct eye contact domineering and disrespectful. If you notice that the client avoids eye contact with you, stop looking directly. Looking at the client quickly and then away is usually acceptable. Sustained eye contact is more likely to offend.

Smile, especially while greeting someone. Almost all cultures appreciate smiles, as long as they are appropriate to the situation.

Speak softly, but loudly enough to be heard. A loud voice may be perceived as aggressive. Remember that speakers of other languages are not deaf and will not understand better if you speak louder.

Try not to appear impatient or rushed. This is difficult when you are responsible for a busy office. However, being rushed will increase clients' anxiety and stress and can interfere with their ability to communicate.

Be aware that different cultures have different comfort zones that regulate how close you can stand next to someone in conversation. If you feel that a client is intruding in your personal space, try to decide whether he is being confrontational or simply following his culture's rules. If it is the latter, try to ignore it. Conversely, if a client takes a step back from you, do not take it personally; you may have entered her personal space.

If a client extends his hand, take it. Although shaking hands is not usual in Canadian health offices, refusing an offer to shake hands may be taken as a slight and as evidence of prejudice.

Show genuine interest in the client, and always demonstrate a friendly, warm attitude.

Be receptive to any culturally based requests. Do what you can to honour requests. If appropriate, tell the client you will discuss it with the doctor. Even if the client's request does not seem feasible, do not reject it outright. Compromise is much easier if the client feels you have made an effort.

Involve the client in any decision making when you can. This affords a feeling of control, which is particularly important when a client is feeling otherwise overwhelmed.

When booking tests, ask clients when the best time is. This may hinge on when a family member and/or interpreter is free to accompany them.

Write down instructions. Printing is usually easier to understand. If possible, have the interpreter write the instructions down in the client's first language. Many laboratories have client instructions in different languages. Highlighting the area that the client will be referring to will help avoid confusion.

Remember the SMILE Principle

Sensitivity	Be sensitive to the needs of the client.
Mutual respect	The client who feels respected feels valued and will respect you in turn. Mutual respect enhances communication and promotes trust.
Interest	Showing interest in the client keeps the lines of communication open and helps make the health-care experience positive.
Language	Assess language barriers and adapt accordingly. Are you communicating clearly with the client, or do you need an interpreter?
Explanation	Explain clearly to the client and family.

Future Trends

Ten years ago the bulk of immigrants to Canada came to Ontario, half of those individuals settling in and around Toronto. By 2010 only 42 percent settled in Ontario. Currently, western Canada—Alberta in particular—has seen a dramatic rise in immigration.

The 2006 census showed a surprising growth in Canada's Aboriginal population figures—an increase of 45 percent since 1996. This is partially due to more people completing the census and acknowledging their ethnicity. This "stepping forward to claim one's heritage" is called

>

a population shift. Nearly 54 percent of Aboriginals live in urban centres such as Winnipeg, Regina, and Toronto. These cities have established health centres that support traditional Aboriginal medical practices along with conventional medical services. The Aboriginal population has continued to grow, with Aboriginal youth being the fastest-growing segment of the Canadian population.

The overall health of immigrants to Canada is reported as "good." Those who do not speak English at home are less apt to report their health as good. They are also less likely to seek health care, particularly if they don't have a family physician and if there is a language barrier. Immigrants on the whole still tend not to seek health care as readily as first-generation Canadians.

Cross-cultural and generational differences in health care beliefs will continue to pose problems, particularly in the areas of mental and reproductive health. As well, communication patterns will continue to differ (for example, between first-generation immigrants and their children), as will outlooks on preventative health care and lifestyle. The January, 2012 trial in Kingston, Ontario of the Shafia family resulted in first-degree murder convictions for three members of the Afghan family after they arranged the "honour killings" of four other family members. The murdered daughters did not comply with the family's perception of cultural behaviour.

Serious cultural and social problems persist for Aboriginal Canadians. Isolation, poor living conditions, and poor or absent infrastructure have contributed to altered health (e.g., diabetes, hypertension, and addiction problems. These matters must be addressed—but how to do this effectively while respecting the culture and autonomy of Aboriginal populations is an ongoing challenge. Consider the housing crisis in Attawapiskat in Northern Ontario that surfaced in January 2012. Many of the 1800 people on the reserve were living in unsafe structures, tents, and unheated trailers—many without power, sanitation, or clean water.

SUMMARY

1. Canada is an increasingly multicultural country. Being responsive to the differing needs and expectations of people from different cultures is essential to effective health care.

2. Culture affects our attitudes and behaviours and almost every aspect of our lives. It is so ingrained that we are often unaware of its influence. Ethnocentrism can cause us to fail to see another's point of view and can impede understanding.

3. Cultural understanding is more important than ever in a shrinking world, but international conflict has exacerbated tensions. Cultural acceptance in the health office is essential to a trusting, positive client relationship.

4. A shortage of doctors means less time with patients, making it more difficult to establish relationships and overcome cultural barriers. Many immigrants to Canada are unable to find doctors. Immigrants may also be daunted by medical technology and hospitals, and may meet with disrespect or condescension from some health professionals.

5. People from some cultures may not accept prevention, considering health in the "here and now." Some do not accept the concept of chronic illness, viewing each exacerbation as a new illness. Some have explanations of health and illness that differ from those of modern Western medicine, and some attach a strong stigma to mental illness. Though it is important to be alert for these differences, it is equally important not to make assumptions about a client's attitudes. Treat each client as an individual.

6. Differing attitudes toward child care, childbirth, schedules, modesty, and visiting practices can require flexibility from the health-care professional. Try to accommodate clients' requests whenever possible.

7. Language often poses a barrier. If the client's English is limited, speak clearly and slowly, avoid medical jargon and colloquialisms, check for comprehension, and encourage questions. If you are unable to communicate clearly, try to arrange for an interpreter, who may be a hospital staff member or a friend or relative of the client.

Key Terms

culture 63	**exacerbation** 71	**subculture** 64
ethnic 64	**postpartum** 74	
ethnocentrism 66	**remission** 71	

Review Questions

1. Define *culture*, and explain the various components of culture.

2. Explain the relationships among culture, ethnicity, race, and nationality.

3. Explain how changes in the Canadian health-care system have adversely affected immigrants and their access to health care.

4. Outline some of the problems related to hospitalization that are experienced by ethnic minorities.

5. How can the administrative health professional protect the privacy of a very modest client?

6. Explain some steps the administrative health professional can take to overcome language barriers.

7. Describe three techniques that will enhance communication with a client who has limited English language skills.

Application Exercises

1. (a) In groups of two or three, select and interview someone from a different culture about his experiences with health care in Canada. Develop a picture of what health care was like in that person's country of origin, and compare it with that in Canada. Ask the person to identify problems he has encountered and what steps could be taken to resolve those problems. (b) Prepare a short oral presentation on the basis of the information gathered from your interview. Research health care in that person's country of origin to create a more complete picture of the differences from and similarities to the health-care system in Canada. Make a list of the person's recommendations for change, adding any that your group can think of.

2. In small groups, create a scenario to illustrate difficulties with language barriers, for example, trying to explain the importance of medication to a client or trying to schedule a test. Role-play an ineffective way to manage the problem and then an effective way. Ask the class for suggestions.

3. Identify the two prevalent cultures in your area. Summarize key cultural expectations related to health and health care of these groups. In small groups, create a scenario in which clients and health professionals have different expectations. (Use your research summary to identify these expectations.) For example, a client refuses a physical examination or a client in hospital refuses to ask her eight family members to leave after visiting hours are over. One student should role-play the client and one the administrative health professional. Ask the class for suggestions on how to resolve the disagreement.

4. Panaji Singh is a 13-year-old female born in Canada who has come to see the doctor wanting birth control pills. She has a boyfriend and is sexually active. Her parents resent the relationship, and do not know Panaji is sexually active. Panaji's parents are traditional and believe their daughter should follow cultural and family rules—sex before marriage is not one of them. They also believe that that any health concerns their daughter has must be shared with them, thus client–physician confidentiality (as it is understood in Canada) is an issue. A week later, Mrs. Singh calls the office wanting to know why her daughter came in. She wants to make an appointment with the doctor to discuss her daughter's visit and subsequent treatment—without Panaji present.

   a. How would you respond to her on the phone?

   b. How do you feel about client–physician confidentiality and Panaji's rights when culture is involved?

   c. Outline what you believe to be the rights of the parents and Panaji's rights.

   d. What kind of a dilemma does this put the doctor in?

5. In groups of two or three, choose a province or territory, and explore the status of its Aboriginal population. Consider cultural details demographics such as population distribution, access to health care, overall health, and social issues.

6. Using the internet, research the problems of the First Nations community of Attawapiskat. List the main problems; identify the strategies laid out to address the problems, and by whom; and describe the progress to date. What solutions would you suggest?

Web Sites of Interest

Evaluation of the Provincial Nominee Programme
http://www.cic.gc.ca/english/resources/evaluation/pnp/section1.asp

Cultural Diversity in Health Policy
http://www.hhsc.ca/body.cfm?id=1783

Population Information
www.canadalegal.info/ref-canada-population/canada-stats-occupations.html
www.statcan.ca/start.html
Click on "population and demography" on the lower right side.
Current State of Multiculturalism in Canada
http://www.cic.gc.ca/english/pdf/pub/multi-state.pdf

Diversity in Health Care
http://www.rnao.org/Page.asp?PageID=924&ContentID=1200

Chapter 4

The Canadian Health-Care System

Learning Objectives

On completing this chapter, you will be able to:

1. Summarize the history of the health-care system in Canada.
2. Explain the five principles and two conditions of the *Canada Health Act*.
3. Recognize the structure of health-care administration and services in the provinces and territories.
4. Discuss how health care is financed in Canada.
5. Define primary health care.
6. Explain the concept of primary care reform.
7. Examine how health providers are remunerated in Canada.

Health care in Canada is provided to all eligible residents under provincial and territorial health insurance plans, regardless of income, employment, or health. Although our health-care system has had its share of problems, most Canadians want it to be preserved. Most agree that continued initiatives to promote and maintain cost-effective, high-quality care are essential if our health-care system is to survive. This chapter includes a brief overview of significant events in the history and development of health care in Canada to help you understand the basic structure of the system, how it functions, and some of the challenges it faces. Table 4.1 contains a chronological summary of significant events in the evolution of legislation and regulations that have led to the public health care system we have today.

❶❷ THE *CANADA HEALTH ACT*

THE CANADA HEALTH ACT (1984) IS THE CURRENT FEDERAL INSURANCE LEGISLATION. It replaced previous legislation and consolidated all components of health insurance. Each province and territory is responsible for the delivery and administration of its own health services. The federal government contributes a designated amount of money to health care. The provinces and territories pay the balance of what is required to deliver health care within their own jurisdictions.

The *Canada Health Act* is composed of five principles and two conditions that all provinces and territories must meet in order to receive the health-related transfer payments from the federal government. Under the Act, the federal government can impose various other penalties if these conditions are not met. These conditions and principles provide the foundation for health-care delivery in Canada.

Principles

1. Public Administration
Health care in each province or territory must be

- managed by a public authority (may not be privately operated),
- managed on a non-profit basis, and
- subject to federal inspections and financial audits.

2. Comprehensiveness

- Each province and territory must ensure that those who are eligible receive all services designated medically necessary by doctors and hospitals.
- This includes coverage of any surgical dental procedure that is considered necessary from a medical/dental perspective and that must be carried out in hospital.
- Where the law permits, the plan must cover the insured person for additional insured services rendered by other health-care **providers**.

provider any person or group of persons who delivers a health-care service.

3. Universality

- Every resident of each province and territory is entitled to fair and equitable public health insurance coverage.

Table 4.1 Chronology of Legislation and Regulations Affecting Health-Care Coverage in Canada

Year	Event
1946	Citizens of Swift Current, Sask. establish the first public health insurance program in North America, making health services available to all residents.
1947	Saskatchewan's CCF government, led by Tommy Douglas, introduces the first provincial hospital insurance program in Canada.
1948	The Liberals introduce a *National Health Grants Program* to assist provinces and territories with construction of new hospitals, keeping their promise to introduce cost-shared social programs.
1957	The federal government introduces the *Hospital Insurance and Diagnostic Services Act* to encourage the development of hospital insurance plans.
1961	All provinces and territories have public insurance plans in place for in-hospital care.
1962	Saskatchewan extends health insurance to include out-of-hospital coverage for physician services.
1965	A Royal Commission, headed by Emmett Hall, calls for a universal, comprehensive national health insurance program, with minimum standards set across the country.
1966	Under the *National Medical Care Insurance Act*, Ottawa agrees to pay 50 percent of provincial and territorial health costs.
1972	All provincial and territorial insurance plans cover physician services.
1977	Trudeau's Liberals replace 50/50 cost-sharing with five-year block funding that gives provinces and territories more control over health spending. *Established Programs Financing* combines health-care transfers with educational transfers.
1984	The *Canada Health Act* is passed unanimously by the House of Commons, allowing Ottawa to withhold funds if provinces and territories do not comply with the five principles. This bill bans extra-billing and charging for insured services.
1985–93	Federal share of spending on health under the Mulroney government drops from 30.8 percent in 1985 to 23.5 percent in 1993.
1995	Canada Health and Social Transfer (CHST) brings massive cuts in transfer payments to health and social programs.
1995–99	Federal-to-provincial/territorial transfer payments continue to drop, and provincial and territorial expenses continue to grow. Hospitals are closed and services are slashed.
2000	Bill C-45 makes new funding available for health-care services and for updating technology and health information systems.
2002	The federally commissioned Romanow Report recommends increased federal health spending and sets out guidelines.
2002	The Kirby Report recommends a dedicated health-care tax and guaranteed limits to waiting times for medical services.
2003	The premiers reach an accord to implement a new health plan. The federal government agrees to provide $34.8 billion over five years to go toward a Primary Health Reform Fund, drug coverage, and updated diagnostic and medical equipment.
2004	In January 2004, Prime Minister Paul Martin pledges $2 billion in health-care funding to the provinces and territories and participation in continued discussions for a long-term action plan for health care. The provincial and territorial leaders also agree to establish a new public health agency that will be similar to the Centers for Disease Control in Atlanta, Georgia, to deal with infectious diseases.

Table 4.1	(continued)
2004	Introduction of *PIPEDA*—federal legislation protecting personal information. This affects some health-care organizations. In the 2004–05 fiscal year the CHST was split into the Canada Health Transfer (CHT) and Canada Social Transfer (CST).
2006	The Public Health Agency of Canada receives royal assent on December 12, 2006. This establishes the agency as a separate organization within the health portfolio. The agency's directive is to assist the federal minister of health to complete his or her duties.
2011	The Canadian government unilaterally put forth a new accord for the funding and management of health care for the provinces and territories. According to the new agreement, the federal government will guarantee the provinces and territories 6 percent health-care funding increases until the 2016–17 fiscal year. After that time, the annual finding will be tied to the gross domestic product (GDP). Unlike previous accords, the new accord does not contain the federal government's parameters for spending. The provinces and territories are free to use the money at their own discretion. The ministers of health hope to stimulate negotiations with respect to this accord. The federal government estimates that health-care spending will rise to from $30 billion in 2013 to $38 billion in 2018. The accord contains a "no strings attached" policy, in that the federal government will not interfere with any province that experiments with or expands private delivery of publicly funded care. However the core principles of the *Canada Health Act* are maintained in that user fees, fully private care or other major violations of the Act will still result in clawbacks.

4. Portability

- The province or territory must grant insurance coverage to an eligible person within three months.

- The plan must provide coverage for insured persons who are travelling outside their resident province or territory. Host-province rates apply to health care provided in other provinces or territories. The persons must be covered by their province of origin during any waiting period imposed by any other province or territory.

- Out-of-country coverage must be provided according to established guidelines.

5. Accessibility

- Each province and territory must provide fair and reasonable access to all insured health services through uniform terms and conditions. Residents of all regions are entitled to the same medical care and benefits.

- The plans must make reasonable compensation to all providers for insured health services.

Conditions

There are also two conditions that must be met under the *Canada Health Act*:

1. Each province and territory must provide information and statistics on insured health care to the federal government.

2. Each province and territory must formally recognize the financial contribution of the federal government.

❸❹ RESPONSIBILITIES AND FINANCING

THE FEDERAL GOVERNMENT WORKS IN PARTNERSHIP WITH PROVINCIAL AND TERRITORIAL governments to finance and deliver national health care. The provinces and territories themselves are constitutionally responsible for administering and delivering health-care services within their jurisdictions. They decide, among other things, how much money to spend on health-care systems, where to locate hospitals, how many physicians they will need, and which supplementary health services to cover. For example, although not required by the *Canada Health Act*, most provinces and territories cover the costs of medication and nursing care for seniors managing at home.

Federal Government Responsibilities

- Setting, administering, and monitoring all national standards for medicare
- Making payments to provinces and territories for health care under the *Canada Health and Social Transfer Act*
- Financing and delivering services to specific groups, including veterans, First Nations Canadians living on reserves, military personnel, inmates of federal penitentiaries, and the Royal Canadian Mounted Police (RCMP)
- Providing leadership in health promotion, protection, and disease prevention, including public education

Provincial and Territorial Responsibilities

- Delivering health services to eligible residents
- Funding and managing insured hospital, physician, and allied health services
- Managing and evaluating cost-effective delivery of health services
- Managing components of prescription care and public health services

Financing

Health care in Canada is funded, for the most part, by the federal, provincial and territorial, and municipal governments through a blend of personal and corporate taxes, and by Workers' Compensation Boards. Some provinces also use revenue from sales taxes and lotteries. British Columbia and Ontario require eligible residents to pay health-care premiums, although this is not a requirement mandated by the *Canada Health Act*. Moreover, it is estimated that about 30 percent of health-care costs are paid for by the private sector. This is primarily at the municipal level through volunteer and private organizations. Many of these groups contribute funding to the construction of new hospitals, diagnostic services, and other services deemed necessary within a community. They also support services to individuals within a community, such as Meals on Wheels and home care. Currently provinces and territories claim that the federal government contributes approximately 16 cents on the dollar for health care.

Federal government transfers funds to the provinces and territories in the form of both cash and tax points, which are calculated using a complex formula. There are four main transfer programs: the Canada Health Transfer (CHT), the Canada Social Transfer (CST),

Equalization, and Territorial Formula Financing (TFF). According to Canada's Department of Finance, in 2011–12, the provinces and territories collectively received $57.7 billion in major transfers from the federal government—an estimated $15.8 billion increase since 2005–2006. The CHT cash and tax transfers are currently allotted on a per-capita basis.

Equalization payments are unconditional payments made by the federal government to less prosperous jurisdictions to ensure they can deliver an acceptable level of health care. These payments are unconditional in that the provinces can spend the money they receive at their own discretion, as long as it relates to health care. In the 2012–2013 fiscal year, Quebec and Ontario received the most money, followed by Manitoba, Nova Scotia, New Brunswick, and Prince Edward Island.

Insured benefits vary slightly from one province or territory to another. In all jurisdictions certain benefits are available only to individuals with specific financial or health needs. Private health insurance covers many supplementary or uninsured health services. Many private and group health insurance policies are paid, at least in part, through employee benefit packages. See Chapter 10 for more detail on coverage.

In Canada, 95 percent of hospitals are non-profit and publicly funded. Some long-term care and specialized facilities are operated for profit. These facilities are regulated by provincial and territorial governments.

Some provinces and territories have a single authority responsible for all health care. Others have an overall responsible body but two administrative bodies, one to handle hospitals and health-care facilities and the other, medical care. These organizations negotiate remuneration and other policies with professional bodies, such as the College of Physicians and Surgeons in each province, the Canadian Association of Optometrists, the Ontario Medical Association, the Ontario Dental Association, the Medical Society of Nova Scotia, the Manitoba Medical Society, and the British Columbia Medical Society.

All provinces and territories with the exception of Prince Edward Island and Alberta have regional health authorities throughout the province/territory that assess the needs of a given community, then allocate funds accordingly (as outlined by their respective Ministry of Health). For example, in Ontario these organizations are called Local Health Integration Networks or LHINs. These LHINs have autonomy over the allocation of funds to various health services within their regions (in 2012 they were given the authority to fund primary health organizations). The Northwest Territories has eight health organizations called Health and Social Services Authorities. Health Prince Edward Island is that province's sole health authority, under its Department of Health and Wellness.

In 2008 Alberta eliminated its regional health authorities, as described on its website:

> Alberta Health Services (AHS) is the provincial health authority responsible for overseeing both the planning and delivery of health supports and services to the more than 3.7 million adults and children living in the province of Alberta. . . . The AHS Board governs all health services in the province, working in partnership with Alberta Health and Wellness The Board reports directly to the Minister of Health and Wellness.
>
> AHS was established on May 15, 2008, and became fully operational on April 1, 2009, incorporating the former 9 regional health authorities, the Alberta Mental Health Board, the Alberta Cancer Board and the Alberta Alcohol and Drug Abuse Commission (AADAC). Since 2009, there are 5 health zones.[1]

---

[1] http://www.health.alberta.ca/services/Alberta-Health-Services.html.

The structure of other provincial health services can be found on websites given at the end of this chapter.

Payment of Premiums

In Canada, there are two models for paying provincial and territorial premiums: (1) residents pay insurance premiums; and (2) the government covers health-care costs through blended taxation.

British Columbia and Ontario residents pay insurance premiums. In all other provinces and territories, health care is paid for by tax money from the federal, provincial or territorial, and municipal governments, including sales taxes, employer levies, and property taxes. Coverage is universal for legal residents, regardless of employment status.

British Columbia In BC starting January 1, 2012, monthly premium rates were $64 for one person, $116 for a family of two and $128 for a family of three or more. There are two premium assistance programs available to those requiring financial support.

Ontario The Ontario Health Premium is income based. Those with taxable income of $20 000 or less are exempt. Above that, premium levels rise with taxable income. The premium is deducted from employee pay and pension cheques through Ontario's personal income tax system.

Health-Care Delivery

Several models of health-care delivery and remuneration are used in Canada. Over the past three to four years, the number of physicians in solo (private) practices has diminished. Primary care reform initiatives across Canada are moving to a multidisciplinary team approach to health care. Thus, family doctors are increasingly working in groups or family health organizations with other providers, such as nurse practitioners, pharmacists, dietitians, and social workers. Some providers work in educational facilities, hospitals, clinics, community health centres, or public health facilities. Although several methods of payment are used, many physicians in Canada are still paid on a fee-for-service basis.

Health-care structures and settings are quite similar across Canada, both in and out of hospitals. Experimentation with various primary care reform initiatives continues across Canada. It has become evident that there is no "one model to fit all." Different physicians in different groups want different things. In most jurisdictions, the governments are flexible with respect to the models they fund. Other questions remain: What services should be covered? How are they best delivered? What can we do to improve access? What is the best approach to reducing wait times? Is private health care part of the answer? These issues are continually re-examined in the search for a balance between cost and quality.

❺ PRIMARY HEALTH CARE

PRIMARY HEALTH CARE IS THE PROVISION OF INTEGRATED HEALTH-CARE SERVICES by providers who address the majority of a client's health concerns. Primary health care also refers to treatment administered during the first medical contact for a particular health concern. Usually, family physicians (also called family practitioners) deliver primary care along with nurse practitioners and a team of health professionals, including pharmacists and physiotherapists. In some regions, other providers, such chiropractors

primary health care (1) integrated health care by a provider who addresses the majority of a client's health concerns; (2) treatment administered during the first medical contact for a health concern.

and naturopaths, are part of this team. In Canada, specialists are not considered primary care providers because a client must have a referral from a family doctor to be seen by one.

Physicians within a *family practice* provide *primary care*, and thus are primary care providers. However, family physicians provide a range of services well beyond the scope of what is defined as primary care services. Emergency Departments or urgent-care clinics provide primary care in emergencies but do not provide the full range of services offered in a family practice.

The family physician (also called a family doctor or general practitioner) is an MD (medical doctor) whose postgraduate specialty is in family medicine. Family physicians are generalists—they look after the general medical needs of clients from babies to seniors. Primary care includes health promotion, disease prevention, health maintenance, counselling, patient education, and diagnosis and treatment of acute and chronic illnesses in a variety of health-care settings (e.g., office, hospital, critical care, long-term care, home care, daycare). Primary care is performed and managed by a family physician, often collaborating with other health professionals and using consultation or referral as appropriate.

Primary care, in the sense of care at point of contact, is also provided by specialists in emergency medicine, or emergentologists.

locum tenens (locum) a doctor temporarily taking over another doctor's practice.

A **locum tenens**, often simply called a "locum," is a doctor temporarily taking over another doctor's practice, such as during vacations. If the practice is specialized, the locum must have the same specialty. Primary care physicians often use a locum when they travel.

Specialists and Primary Care

Specialists (also called consultants) are not considered primary care physicians, although some specialists do render some primary care services. (For example, obstetricians provide the same type of prenatal primary care assessments that family physicians do; clients are referred to them either because they are high risk or because their family physician does not deliver babies—which is the case with most family physicians.) Clients cannot go directly to a specialist but must be referred by a primary care physician. Most family practitioners quickly realize what conditions they are equipped to handle and when they should refer to a specialist for diagnosis or treatment. For example, Amina, who is 12 weeks pregnant, goes to see her family doctor for a routine prenatal check-up and follow-up on a glucose tolerance test the doctor had ordered. (Amina has a family history of diabetes.) The results of the test indicate that Amina has gestational diabetes. The family doctor then refers Amina to an obstetrician and an internist, both of whom will follow her through her pregnancy, labour, and delivery. The family doctor will be kept within the circle of care—all test reports and consultation reports will be sent to the family doctor to keep him informed about Amina's condition. The family doctor will provide care

Tip

if you are coordinating appointments among primary health providers, be sure that consultation reports are sent to the appropriate providers. This can be accomplished by listing the persons to whom copies should be sent with the original consultation request.

for her after her she has delivered and her condition has stabilized. He will also provide care for any unrelated health problems that occur in the meantime, such as an ear infection. Likely a pediatrician will look after the baby, at least for the first few days of life. As well, a midwife could be involved if the mother so chooses, at least at the beginning; but because Amina is considered a "high risk" pregnancy, the midwife would most likely turn care completely over to the specialists.

Primary Health-Care Settings in Canada

Solo Practice   Solo practice refers to a physician practising independently, with staff members who may include a health office professional, a nurse, or both. The physician in solo practice may share a call schedule with other doctors to provide extended coverage for clients. Physicians in solo practice are becoming few and far between.

Group Practice   A group practice involves several physicians who may or may not share office space, expenses, and support staff. Depending on the mix of providers, they may also share a call schedule. A group practice is usually, but not always, made up of providers within the same specialty, but the group may not be incorporated. The physicians may have a group number for provincial or territorial billing purposes. Often, the services of the group's physicians are provided through the group, are billed in the name of the group, and the resulting revenues are treated as receipts of the group.

Partnership   Strictly speaking, a partnership is a business formed by two or more individuals who are jointly and separately financially liable for the operation of the business. Some physicians form such legal partnerships. Although they submit fee-for-service claims individually and do not have a group billing number, their income, net of expenses, is considered by Revenue Canada to be personal taxable income of individual partners. Other physicians simply share certain expenses of the practice through an informal or formal agreement. Each physician has clearly defined responsibilities, rights, and obligations. Note that physicians will often speak loosely of colleagues with whom they share a call schedule as "partners," although they are not actually members of a partnership.

Professional Corporation   A professional corporation is a legally incorporated business that allows professionals to reap many of the benefits of a for-profit corporation. A medical professional corporation must be organized for the sole purpose of rendering medical services, and the shareholders must be licensed physicians. The corporation may simply handle expenses, with each physician otherwise practising independently. Alternatively, the physicians may be employees of the corporation, along with others, such as administrative staff. Services within a corporation vary. They may include physiotherapy, laboratory and diagnostic facilities, and alternative modalities, such as acupuncture and chiropractic. The main advantages are financial. Health maintenance organizations (discussed below) are one type of corporation.

Primary Care Groups   Corporations are becoming more popular as primary care reform models move to the team approach to health care, called FHOs or family health organizations in many jurisdictions.

Primary Health-Care Models   Names for primary health-care models include Family Health Teams or Family Health Networks (used in Ontario), Family Health Clinics and Primary Care Networks (used in Alberta), and primary health care cooperatives in

Saskatchewan. They differ slightly in structure and care delivery format. In such organizations, there is often a separate "corporate" component headed by one or two individuals who oversee and manage the business end of the enterprise—including components of human health resources. The providers function independently alongside or at arm's length from the corporation. This model is used for both legal and business purposes. In some jurisdictions the government provides significant funding to start and maintain primary care groups—most of which use a multidisciplinary team approach to care.

Many groups of this nature prefer a central setting—one building where the "team" resides, central management of administrative and support staff, and clinics related to the group. This model is appealing to clients as everything is close by, easily accessed, and details of their care readily available to team members. This model also attracts new doctors who are looking for a "turn-key" operation and coverage allowing them a more normal lifestyle.

Clinics   A clinic is a health-care setting that offers services to outpatients. A clinic can be managed by one physician or by a group of physicians and may offer services ranging from the simple diagnosis and treatment of complaints to therapeutic or preventive treatments. Some clinics offer a range of services under one roof, such as laboratory, physiotherapy, and consultations with specialists. There are also specialty clinics, such as prenatal, oncology, or orthopedic. Clinics may be privately owned, government sponsored, or organized by a group of doctors who share space and staff but bill separately. Clinics vary in name and in services offered. The following descriptions are general.

Some provinces have clinics (e.g., Alberta's Family Health Clinics), that provide a medical home for individuals without family doctors. The Mosaic Primary Care Clinic in Calgary is an example. The clinic provides both routine and complex care to its clients, including the management of chronic diseases such as diabetes.

■   *Walk-in clinics* (also called *after-hours clinics* or *ambulatory care clinics*) offer medical services to clients, usually without an appointment. Sometimes, a group of family physicians will offer after-hours care for **orphan patients** (clients who do not have a regular doctor) or for clients who, for whatever reason, could not see their own physician during office hours. A walk-in clinic may or may not treat urgent complaints, such as fractures and lacerations. Some facilities may combine services, such as the Coventry Hills Family Care Centre in Calgary which operates as both a walk-in clinic and a family practice centre.

■   *After-hours clinics*, most typically, are organized by physicians within a community to ease the stress on local Emergency Departments and are operated on a fee-for-service basis, with the physicians sharing office and administrative costs. As with walk-in clinics, they are likely to accept any client. This differs from Ontario after-hours clinics operated by formal groups, such as family health networks (FHNs), family health groups (FHGs), and family health organizations (FHOs), where services are restricted to clients who are rostered with the practice or who are clients of the physicians participating in the group. In Alberta most after-hours clinics clearly differentiate themselves from walk-in clinics, stressing that clients must first call the provincial HEALTHLink information service to be referred to a clinic.

■   *Urgent-care clinics* also offer services without an appointment. The main difference is the focus on immediate care of urgent but not life-threatening complaints, such as

orphan patient   a client who does not have a family physician and must get medical services from clinics and Emergency Departments.

lacerations or fractures. An urgent-care clinic may also offer diagnostic and perhaps pharmacy services.

■ *Outpatient clinics*, often located at or connected to a hospital, provide medical services to clients who have been discharged from the facility, as well as to others who need their often-specialized services. Clinics may or may not require appointments. Examples of types of outpatient clinics include oncology, diabetic, and orthopedic.

Emergency Department

Emergency departments (emergency rooms, ERs) do provide non-urgent primary care, but they are supposed to be reserved for clients in acute distress, such as chest pain, stroke symptoms (numbness or tingling in a limb, severe headache, visual disturbances), or breathing difficulties. Others are encouraged to see their family physician or seek medical care elsewhere. However, many clients go to ERs for health concerns that could easily be managed elsewhere, exacerbating overcrowding. Educating clients in a general practice setting about appropriate use of an ER is important. This overuse of ERs results partly from the large number of orphan patients across the country. If there are no available ambulatory care clinics, an orphan patient has nowhere else to go.

Not every hospital offers emergency services, and ERs in different hospitals may render different levels of care. Some ERs, for example, lack the capacity to deal with major trauma cases. All hospitals, however, will have procedures in place to direct emergencies, including evacuating clients to appropriate trauma centres. A fully active ER is open 24 hours a day, seven days a week, and is equipped to deal with almost all emergencies.

Managed Care

Managed care is a set of strategies, procedures, and policies designed to control the use of health-care services. Such strategies include a review of medically necessary services, enticement to use certain providers, and case management. The goal is to conserve health-care expenditure while maintaining quality by reorganizing health-care delivery within a community. Managed care techniques are most often practised by organizations and professionals who assume responsibility for the population of a geographic area. A health maintenance organization is an example of a managed care organization.

managed care a set of strategies, procedures, and policies designed to control the use of health-care services, sometimes by organizing doctors, hospitals, and other providers into groups in order to improve the quality and costeffectiveness of health care.

Health Maintenance Organizations (HMOs)

HMOs offer prepaid, comprehensive health coverage for hospital and physician services. Most commonly, HMOs combine a group practice with a payment or funding arrangement. Examples are community clinics in Saskatchewan and in Sault Ste. Marie, Ontario. Ontario offers such care in the form of health service organizations and community health centres. Community health centres are primarily small clinics on a **global budget**, with salaried physicians and a range of other health professionals offering centralized primary care. Quebec has *centres locales de services communautaires* throughout most of the province that provide an impressive range of health-care services.

global budget any arrangement in which a facility or provider receives a fixed amount of money for medical services, regardless of client volume, length of stay, or services rendered.

❻ PRIMARY CARE REFORM

Since the $800 million transition fund to implement Canadian primary care reform across Canada was established in 2000, as discussed above, different primary health-care delivery models have emerged. The process is ongoing.

In Alberta, family doctors in primary care networks (PCNs) work collaboratively with other health professionals to deliver primary health care. Under this model, clients can approach the clinic with a variety of complaints or questions and could be seen by a number of different providers, for example, a doctor, nurse, physiotherapist or even mental-health professional, depending on the nature of the problem. PCNs are physician led and are funded on a per-capita basis. Alberta also offers access to primary care services through family care clinics. These differ from PCNs in that individuals can access services such as lab tests, diagnostic services, and referrals to specialists without an initial physician appointment.

Ontario continues with its mix of primary health-care models, often referred to collectively as Patient Enrolment Models. These models require participating physicians to be part of a group practice or practice network. As of 2012, two-thirds of Ontario doctors worked within this type of framework, with 72 percent of Ontario's population enrolled.

Recently, most jurisdictions have been successfully introduced nurse practitioner–led clinics (NPLCs). Ontario opened the first one in Sudbury in 2007. Manitoba for example, has introduced what they call nurse practitioner quick-care clinics. These clinics offer extended hours and treatment for minor health complaints. This is part of the province's initiative to ensure that all Manitobans have a doctor by 2015.

The Particulars of Patient Enrolment Models

Most of these models require clients to enrol with a physician in the group. The models are commonly called Patient Enrolment Models, or PEMs. Family doctors moving to a PEM model must notify their clients of the process and explain the purpose and benefits of enrolment. The process itself is called rostering. This means the clients sign a form agreeing that they will seek all of their primary care services from that group, or from one physician within that group.

Clients who enrol with a group are entitled to extended services. Enrolment is based on the following principles:

- Clients are free to choose their physician.
- Clients agree to seek all care from that physician.
- Clients sign a contract with one primary care physician at a time.
- The signed contract outlines client–provider responsibilities and provides for enrolment termination.
- Enrolment is not automatic on conversion of a physician's practice. Physicians must invite clients to enrol in the group. Most of these reform models can have both enrolled and uninvolved clients. Thus clients who do not want to sign this agreement may continue to see their doctor under the fee-for-service system. For example, a university student living away from home would probably maintain a fee-for-service arrangement because, under the terms of most primary care reform contracts, the family physician would be penalized every time the student saw the campus doctor. This of course, would depend on the type of primary care reform group his family doctor belonged to—not all require rostering.
- Only eligible registrants of the provincial or territorial health plan will be accepted as enrolled members.

Clients agree to

- receive all primary health care from network providers, except in medical emergencies or when travelling;
- maintain valid health insurance and to obtain a photo health card, if necessary;

- advise the physician of any change in address or telephone number; and
- allow the release of certain information to the Ministry of Health, such as preventive care history (e.g., mammograms or screening colonoscopies).

The physician agrees to meet all the client's primary health-care needs.

Many primary care reform models/groups use blended funding. This includes a **capitation** model (also called **population-based funding**) in which the province or territory pays physicians a set amount per year for each patient enrolled, regardless of the type and number of services the physician provides for each client. Under this model, a physician receives more money for clients who are statistically more likely to require frequent services, such as older clients with multiple medical problems.

capitation or population-based funding a funding system that pays a physician a given amount per client enrolled, regardless of the number of services performed.

Advantages

Primary care reform models may offer clients a number of advantages. Offices hours may be extended depending on the needs of a particular practice and community. Continuity of care is enhanced because physicians involved share more information with one another, as well as with specialists, diagnostic and laboratory facilities, and other community services. Doctors are more actively involved with discharge planning, outpatient, and home-care services. The model may be able to offer both clients and providers access to a wide range of health educational materials. Also, a phone system can offer advice and triage for clients who are unsure about what kind of care to seek, especially outside of regular hours. For example, a client who calls with chest pains would be told to go to the nearest Emergency Department, perhaps by ambulance. A client with a sore throat might be advised to wait and see the doctor the next day. A mother with a feverish child might be advised to go to the nearest walk-in clinic or to see the physician on call. There is also a doctor available to advise the client if the nurse on the telephone needs more advice.

The funding for PEM models is complex, although capitation-based funding and fee-for-service (FFS) remain the primary methods of remuneration. In these models, certain services are bundled together in what is called a "basket" of services and included under the capitation payment plan. These services are primarily preventive in nature, such as mammograms, childhood immunizations, influenza immunizations, Pap smears, and screening for colorectal cancer (FTOB—fecal testing for occult blood).

Doctors are paid bonuses for achieving certain milestones related to these services. For example, for immunizations, the doctor would be paid one amount for immunizing 60 percent of those eligible in the practice, a higher amount for 70 percent, and so on. These bonus payments for most PEMs are paid annually. There are tracking codes that the doctor's office can use to tabulate how many services are rendered in each category. In Ontario these tracking codes are one group of "Q" codes. Doctors are also paid for "signing up" or enrolling clients. Other services they are paid for include diabetic management, smoking cessation, and mental health management. These are all billed using various "Q" codes. Premiums involve annual payment to the provider for goals met under the specific model guidelines and the completion of accurate records.

Implications for the Administrative Health Professional

Converting a practice from the fee-for-service model to a PEM model requires teamwork between the physicians and the administrative staff. If the model includes **rostering**,

rostering establishing a list of clients who agree to participate in a primary health network according to the rules of the province or territory.

initially all of the clients within a practice must be enrolled—that is, invited to sign a contract with the physician or group. In most jurisdictions, the Ministry of Health assists with the rostering process, at least initially. Clients must make an informed decision on the basis of an understanding of the rights and responsibilities of both parties. Clients should be given information sheets and the opportunity to discuss any concerns with either the physician or the office staff. You must keep track of all registered clients and the date on which their agreement was signed.

Running a primary care group also entails ongoing administrative responsibilities for the health office professional. Most provinces and territories require practices to continue to track services. (See *Shadow Billing* below.) You will also continue to submit claims for services excluded from the capitation agreement, such as house calls and hospital visits to clients. The services that the provider bills for vary with the specific framework of the model he practises within.

Working in a primary care reform model has a number of other challenges you might not encounter as frequently in a smaller office or clinic, particularly if it is newly formed or undergoing changes. This includes establishing one's job description and scope of practice. Any new environment suffers growing pains—a time when individuals involved grow and adjust to the environment's needs and required responsibilities. Not many such organizations (new or established) have formal job descriptions for administrative staff. Responsibilities are often left to staff members to sort out. This can foster discontentment and frustration among staff members, cause disorganization within the office or clinic, and lead to further frustration on the part of providers.

Tips for Working Within a Health Organization

- Try to define roles for each person working within your office or clinic setting, or on your team; this should be done collaboratively.

- Balance responsibilities fairly, taking into consideration an individual's expertise and preferences, if possible. This results in staff members feeling involved, valued, and respected.

- Address problems early, openly, and in a tactful and objective manner. Have the facts and, if possible, a solution to offer. Speaking out in a professional manner clears the air, brings problems to the forefront, and usually results in a satisfactory settlement.

- Collaborate with the physicians and other providers when problems arise and their input and/or direction would be beneficial. Remember that the providers are affected when problems occur in the administrative domain. This may cause them discontent and frustration as well, which could result in negative relationships with you and other administrative staff.

- Ensure that you have the proper training for tasks you are asked to assume. For example, if you are asked to summarize charts for conversion to the EMR/EHR format, you should have specific guidelines set out by the physician, and work through a number of charts with someone trained to do that.

- Be prepared to stand your ground—you are an educated, knowledgeable, and valuable member of the health-care team. At the same time, recognize that compromise is important as long as the solution is sound, fair, and workable—and one you are comfortable with.

- Do not form alliances with other members of the team that will result in a "we–they" situation. Treat every member of the team with respect, always. Remember that some personalities are more difficult to work with than others. This includes all of those with whom you work, from physicians and nurse practitioners to physiotherapists, pharmacists, and administrative staff. Try to build on their strengths.

- Do not underestimate the stress that a negative or uncomfortable work environment can cause—particularly on a continued basis. It is not uncommon for team members—from administrative staff to providers—to succumb to stress requiring time off. The stress can be that high.

❼ PAYMENT OPTIONS FOR PHYSICIANS

Fee-for-Service

There are a large number of physicians that still bill their provincial/territorial plans on a **fee-for-service** basis, either exclusively or as part of a blended remuneration system.[2] Each province and territory has its own fee schedule detailing insurable services and fees. (These schedules will be covered in more detail in Chapter 10.) In most jurisdictions, payment is based on the specific type and extent of service, including the complexity of the service. Other considerations may contribute to how much the provider is paid. For example, in British Columbia, the amount payable for a service also relates to the age of the client.

fee-for-service describes a system under which a provider is paid by public health insurance for each insured service rendered to an insured client. These providers are considered "opted-in" to the public payment system.

Example Dr. Harvey sees 25 clients on Monday. His health office professional submits claims to the provincial health plan for each encounter. On Tuesday, Dr. Harvey sees only 15 clients. He is paid for 15 services. In some provinces, the specific service rendered for each visit would determine how much the doctor is paid for each service. Suppose Mr. Jones has a sore throat, Mrs. Marchese has a skin rash, and Mr. Kirschen has abdominal pain. In Ontario, Dr. Harvey would be paid a different sum of money for each client on the basis of the complexity of each assessment. (See Chapter 12 for more detail.) In BC, Dr. Harvey would be paid a certain amount if Mr. Jones were 90 years old and a different amount if he were 35, regardless of the nature or complexity of the assessment.

Shadow Billing

Shadow billing is used in some primary care groups (PCGs) to allow direct comparison of the cost-effectiveness of capitation and fee-for-service. Claims are submitted as if the physician were billing fee-for-service but are marked with a special identifying code and a zero balance. Thus, a record is produced of how much would have been spent on rostered clients if each encounter had been billed fee-for-service.

Example Dr. Chen is working in a primary care reform group. In one calendar year, she was paid $300 000 under the capitation formula to take care of 2000 clients while providing extended hours and other health-care services to her clients. The shadow billing for her practice year showed that under the fee-for-service system, she would have billed the Ministry of Health $350 000. In this case, capitation saved the ministry $50 000.

---

[2] *The Medical Post*, January 22, 2008. The National Physician Survey is Canada's largest census survey of Canadian doctors.

Remuneration Options for Opted-In/Opted-Out Physicians

It is important to note that rules governing direct and extra-billing for **opted-in** and **opted-out** physicians vary—some jurisdictions allow opted-in providers to bill the client directly, some do not; some jurisdictions make extra-billing an offence, others indirectly deter extra-billing by eliminating any public insurance available for the services supplied by opted-out physicians and/or for the services supplied by opted-in physicians who try to extra-bill.

Direct Billing

As mentioned above, physicians who bill their provincial or territorial plan for services rendered are referred to as being opted-in to the provincial/territorial health plan. Opted-out physicians operate outside of the public plan and bill their clients directly for a service (this is also called direct billing). The client pays the physician, and the health plan reimburses the client. There are very few opted-out physicians, because provincial/territorial plans either disallow the practice or have implemented restrictions that render the practice unprofitable.

Extra-Billing and User Fees

Extra-billing occurs when a physician or other entity charges the client more for an insured service than the provincial or territorial plan will pay. The practice is not allowed under section 18 of the *Canada Health Act*. The federal government imposes penalties on any jurisdiction that allows **extra-billing**. It estimates how much money practitioners in a particular province or territory have extra-billed clients in each fiscal year. Then it withholds that amount dollar for dollar from its health transfer payments to that province or territory. This penalty is called a **clawback**. There are, however, some jurisdictions that allow extra-billing by doctors who are opted in or out of the public systems. For some individuals, private insurance will cover the additional costs incurred by extra-billing, but this coverage may be subject to legal restrictions depending on what province or territory they live in.

User fees are different than extra-billing fees. A user fee is any charge, other than extra-billing, for a health service: for example, a charge to use the Emergency Department of a hospital, or a charge to visit your family doctor. The person is charged to use a service, not for the service itself. Jurisdictions allowing user fees are subject to the same penalties as for allowing extra-billing. Charging clients reasonable fees for enhanced and uninsured services (discussed below) is *not* considered extra-billing or imposing user fees.

Be aware that you may be held liable for knowingly participating in extra-billing. Be careful not to inadvertently bill a client for any insured service. If you suspect that your provider is extra-billing, speak to your provider to clarify the issue, or seek legal counsel.

Salaries

A salaried doctor is paid a set fee for all services rendered during a designated time frame; thus hours, workload, and remuneration are clearly defined. Salaries are usually paid for a full-time position. Many physicians at universities are salaried to perform a mix of

opted-in (of a physician) billing the provincial or territorial plan for health services rendered.

opted-out (of a physician) billing clients for services rendered; clients pay the fee to the doctor and submit a claim to the health plan. Very few physicians chose to opt out. This may change, however, if private health care becomes more prevalent and clients can buy private insurance for medically necessary services.

extra-billing charging a client more than the amount paid by the provincial or territorial health plan for a medically necessary service.

clawback the amount, dollar for dollar, that the federal government cuts CHT payments to a province or territory that permits extra-billing.

research, teaching, and clinical work. Physicians in many community health centres are salaried but, to date, remain a small part of the population. Several provinces, such as Newfoundland and Labrador, have salaried district medical officers.

Global Budget

A global budget is a lump sum given to doctors in a group or corporation for services performed. Most academic health sciences centres receive a global budget from the provinces or territories and, out of that funding, may pay physicians in a number of ways. Physicians may be paid on a global budget to practise in a remote area; vacation time, professional development, and relocation fees may be offered as additional incentives.

Sessional Payment

Sessional payment is similar to a salary but is not usually for a permanent position. A physician on sessional payment is employed or contracted to perform designated services for a certain time frame. The contract may be renewed or renegotiated at the end of the term.

Capitation

Most provinces and territories use capitation to some degree. Capitation provides a fixed payment for all medical services a client may require in a given time frame. The physician may be paid more for individuals who are at higher risk for more health problems, such as seniors. A drawback of this payment plan is that it does not provide the **physician incentive** to extend the services he offers his clients. Many provinces have voiced a concern about the 2011 health accord proposed by the federal government in that federal-to-provincial/territorial payments will be capitation based. This will leave smaller provinces with less income.

physician incentive
Physicians are monetarily remunerated if they maximize services for their clients related to preventive medicine (e.g., immunizations, Pap smears, mammograms). This involves encouraging their clients to have screening tests.

Indirect Capitation

Indirect capitation occurs when an organization is given a set amount of money to manage health care for a designated population base: for example, a regional health authority or a managed care organization. With this funding, the organization must manage its health-care responsibilities (staff, services, administrative costs, capital expenditures, etc.) within the confines of its budget.

Blended Payment

There are numerous combinations of salary, fee-for-service, and capitation. Blended payment plans are increasingly popular among physicians, particularly those entering into primary care reform groups, in which capitation usually provides the funding base.

For example, a doctor could be employed by a university but charge fee-for-service in a private practice. Or a physician with a fee-for-service practice may also receive a part-time salary or sessional payment for seeing clients in a nursing home. Another example would be the coroner in a community. The coroner is paid a salary by the ministry or the local health authority but is often also a family physician in private practice.

Fees for Uninsured Services

Physicians may charge clients directly for services *not covered* under their provincial or territorial health insurance plan. Such services may include renewal of a prescription over the telephone, filling out insurance forms and documents associated with medical assessments, writing notes for someone who has been ill, filling out a passport form, or conducting certain client-related interviews. Some physicians offer an arrangement in which a client pays a lump sum of money (referred to as a block fee) for an individual or a family, for a range of uninsured services over a period of time—usually not more than 12 months. Some clients feel more comfortable with a block fee than with having to pay separately for uninsured services. Block fees are particularly appealing to older clients who often need telephone advice or to clients on numerous medications who frequently need one renewed. Some primary care reform groups include a basket of uninsured services for rostered clients, and thus block fees are unnecessary.

The College of Physicians and Surgeons in each province and territory has set out rules for the block fee model. You must ensure that these guidelines are posted in a prominent place in the health office. Similarly, fees for all uninsured services should be posted in the office or clinic. Clients must be aware of what the fee is before an uninsured service is rendered.

Other Uninsured Services

A large number of medical services in Canada are uninsured and privately paid for. Private services include most dental services (more than 20 percent), medical and diagnostic services provided at private clinics, drugs (more than 30 percent), and much of the cost of long-term care. Remember, only *medically necessary* services are covered under the *Canada Health Act*. That leaves gaping holes in the health service spectrum. According to Statistics Canada, private funds (including private insurance and out-of-pocket payment) represented more than 30 percent of Canada's overall health-care spending in 2007.

Clients may also pay for enhanced services. An example is for cataract surgery at a private facility. The surgery itself is covered by the provincial or territorial health plan, but the client may purchase a superior lens and pay for additional levels of postoperative care. The same is true of hip replacements. The client can pay for a superior-quality hip joint. Some provinces allow payment for an MRI (magnetic resonance imaging). The rationale is that although an MRI is deemed medically necessary within a "reasonable" time frame, an earlier MRI can be considered an "enhanced" service, and therefore a facility can legally charge anyone who is willing to pay for one. In many jurisdictions, a pregnant woman can pay for a 3-D ultrasound of her unborn child.

❼ PROVIDERS ELIGIBLE TO BILL FEE-FOR-SERVICE

IN ALL PROVINCES AND TERRITORIES, PHYSICIANS AND DENTISTS MAY BILL THE HEALTH plan if they meet that province's or territory's criteria. Other providers may also bill fee-for-service with specific limitations and restrictions.

Optometrists

Optometrists are graduates of a four-year degree program. There are two schools of optometry in Canada: one in Waterloo, Ontario, and one in Montreal. In most provinces and territories, optometrists may bill their provincial or territorial plans, with certain restrictions on fees and frequency of services. Most provinces and territories do not cover routine eye examinations for prescription lenses. The scope of practice of the optometrist and the ophthalmologist can be confusing. The optometrist renders much of the primary eye care required by clients but refers certain problems to an ophthalmologist (an MD specializing in the care of the eyes). For example, if an optometrist diagnoses a condition, such as macular degeneration, in a client, she will refer the client to an ophthalmologist for further investigation and staging of the disease. She might also provide the client with information about current treatments for the disease, such as vitamin therapy and the option of other treatments such as photobiomodulation therapy (not covered by provincial health insurance).

Dentists

Dentists are graduates of a four-year degree program also.

Across Canada, dentists and dental surgeons may bill their provincial or territorial plans for dental work that is both deemed medically necessary and carried out in a hospital. Other criteria vary across the country. No provincial or territorial plan covers the cost of all dental services for everyone, but many provinces and territories provide some dental care for individuals receiving social assistance. Newfoundland and Labrador provides basic dental services for children 12 and under, as well as for adolescents under 17 who are receiving income support. In most provinces and territories, dental associations have their own fee schedule and liaise with the Ministry of Health.

Chiropractors

Chiropractors complete a four-year postgraduate degree program at a chiropractic college. Provincial and territorial coverage for chiropractic care varies because of different interpretations of the *Canada Health Act* as to what is medically necessary. At present, only Manitoba, Saskatchewan, and Alberta offer limited health plan coverage. Such policies are subject to change; to confirm your province's or territory's coverage, consult the websites at the end of the chapter. Across the country, Workers' Compensation Boards and many insurance companies offer extensive coverage for chiropractic services. Chiropractic care is covered extensively by third-party players.

Physiotherapists

A physiotherapist is a graduate of a four-year degree program. (Soon a Master's degree will be the criteria for entry to practise.) Many physiotherapists are employed by hospitals and are therefore salaried. Some work in the community, primarily in physiotherapy clinics. Most provincial and territorial plans cover physiotherapy for in-hospital clients. Some provinces cover designated services outside the hospital.

Osteopaths

These providers diagnose and treat injuries and diseases of the musculoskeletal, circulatory, and nervous systems. Treatment modalities include manipulation, physiotherapy, medication, and/or surgery. Osteopaths train abroad and complete a one- to three-year internship before they are licensed to practise. Some provinces cover osteopaths' services.

Podiatrists

Podiatrists and chiropodists treat diseases and deformities of the foot. Treatment strategies include the use of braces, splints, shields, physiotherapy, medication, and surgery. Although many podiatrists train outside Canada, community colleges in some provinces offer three-year diploma programs.

Midwives

Midwifery is a rapidly growing profession in Canada. Legislation and models of midwifery care are diverse across the country. British Columbia, Manitoba, Ontario, and Quebec each have a publicly funded model of midwifery care; most recently, Alberta has begun funding for midwifery.

Midwives render antenatal, intrapartum, and postpartum care to their clients. They also help look after the baby for the first six weeks or so. Midwives can deliver babies in the hospital if they have admitting privileges, or at the client's home. They can order some laboratory tests and ultrasounds. If a midwife suspects that her client is at risk, she will send the client back to the family doctor or request a consultation. Note, however, that in terms of health plans, a *consultation* can be requested only by a physician. Thus, if you are working for a physician who confers with a midwife, you would submit the claim as an *assessment*.

Midwifery is recognized as an independent or regulated profession in Ontario, Alberta, British Columbia, Manitoba, and Quebec. The Saskatchewan College of Midwives was created in March 2008. There is no formal midwifery education available in Saskatchewan, but anyone who is accredited elsewhere in Canada may practice there, including a midwife from outside of Canada who has completed a bridging program (available in Ontario and BC). Midwifery is not currently regulated in PEI or in Yukon, but is under review in both jurisdictions. There is neither legislation nor public funding for midwifery in New Brunswick, Newfoundland and Labrador, Nova Scotia, and the Northwest Territories. Nunavut funds midwifery but has no regulatory system of its own; midwives must be qualified and registered in another province or country. Midwives are primarily government funded and work on contract.

Other Providers

Other providers are not yet allowed to bill fee-for-service but are, to a large extent, funded by the ministries through various payment plans.

Nurse Practitioners

Nurse practitioners (NPs) are practising in almost every jurisdiction across Canada. NPs have a scope of practice well beyond that of a registered nurse. They can conduct physical examinations, assess clients for routine problems, such as earaches, and write prescriptions for certain drugs. Nurse practitioners can specialize in such areas as primary care, cardiology, and pediatrics—the latter two working in hospitals. Nurse practitioners are primarily salaried with allocated funding coming from the federal or provincial/territorial governments, depending on where they work. Fee-for-service has not been deemed a viable model for remuneration. Some jurisdictions have initiated nurse practitioner–led clinics—a new primary care delivery model such as those established in Ontario (25 operational in 2012), as mentioned earlier. Care is collaborative with NPs, RNs, practical nurses, family doctors, and other health professionals.

Physician Assistants

Initially confined to the Armed Forces, physician assistants (PAs) are skilled health professionals who support physicians in a range of health-care settings, from doctor's offices (generalists as well as specialists) to emergency rooms. They work alongside physicians, nurses, nurse practitioners, and other members of the inter-professional health-care team. Enabling legislation for PAs as well as educational programs are increasing across the country. The Canadian Association of Physician Assistants website listed at the end of this chapter provides a current and more detailed look at role and scope of practice of the physician assistant. At this point, physician assistants are not allowed to bill their provincial or territorial plan for services rendered.

FINDING A FAMILY DOCTOR

ALMOST DAILY YOU WILL GET CALLS ASKING IF THE DOCTOR IS WILLING TO TAKE NEW clients. For the most part, the answer is no. However, some family doctors quietly accept new clients—for example, relatives or friends of current patients, or friends who have moved to town. It is a good idea to ask for guidelines regarding how to handle these requests. As a rule of thumb, suggest that the caller ask other health professionals—for example, their optometrist or dentist—if they know of anyone taking patients. Sometimes the ER in their local hospital will keep a list of "open" practices. A reliable resource is the provincial/territorial College of Physicians and Surgeons or College of Family Physicians. There should be a "find a doctor" link on the college's website. See the website of the College of Family Physicians of Canada listed at the end of the chapter.

Future Trends

The new health accord imposed by the federal government in late 2011 is controversial at best. How the provinces and territories deal with the accord over the coming years will be varied. It is anticipated that the cost of rendering health care will increase above the GDP. There could be more private health-care options introduced, or perhaps user fees. Provinces and territories are free to make their own decisions. Attempts to reduce the cost of health care will continue, and tough decisions will be made over the next few years. Ontario's Drummond Report has provided 105 cost-cutting recommendations to health care and related services which may provide a road map for other jurisdictions. The report's author, Don Drummond, advocates further streamlining of hospitals (amalgamating even further to reduce the number of boards) and providing more power to LHINs to allocate funds at a local level. He recommends expanded roles for other providers, such as allowing pharmacists to give immunizations, and improved use of computer technology. (For more on the Drummond Report, do an internet search to find a variety of news articles and documents that will provide you with a broader perspective than one weblink.)

The notion of a "medical home" is taking root in Canada. In many respects, only the term is new, as the model is prototypical of primary care models seen in varying forms across the country. The medical home is the central core for the person's health care services, and utilizes a team approach to client care. It consists of a personal family doctor who knows the client/family and provides comprehensive, continuous, and well-coordinated care. Quality improvement in client-care strategies, patient safety and the use of state-of-the-art technology and electronic medical records (EMRs) are principal objectives. The College of Family Physicians of Canada supports the medical home

>

concept—care that puts the patient first, and focuses less on the system per se. They recommend that every family practice across the country adopt the medical home principles ensuring that everyone has access to a family doctor and a medical home.

Between 1980 and 2010, the number of physicians in Canada increased by 87 percent.[3] Alberta has shown the largest increase (182.5 percent), and the NWT shows a decline (20.5 percent). The Alberta increase is consistent with the population growth and shift in immigration to that province (see Chapter 3). In 2010, approximately the same number of physicians were younger than 40 and older than 60. However, despite the fact that more doctors are choosing to stay in the workforce longer, it is difficult to predict how many will be retiring over the next few years. An aging population requiring more medical care, and a large number of physicians retiring will further impact physician availability.

In 2011 there were an estimated 36 199 family doctors in Canada (for a breakdown by location and specialty see the Canadian Medical Association statistics found via the weblink at the end of this chapter). According to Nadeem Esmail of the Fraser Institute, currently there are too few physicians in Canada to meet the demand for physician care under the present structure of medicare. The supply of physicians relative to population falls well short of that in other developed nations that also maintain universal approaches to health-care insurance. Esmail states that without a significant intake of foreign physicians, the physician-to-population ratio will fall in the coming years, despite the reported increase in physician graduates in Canada. Esmail's article is excellent, and you are encouraged to read it at the link provided in the footnote.[4]

Private health care is more prominent now than it was even five years ago. The principle of the *Canada Health Act* is maintained—medically necessary services are covered. Some medical treatments are approved by Health Canada but are not covered by public insurance; these are often new procedures that are being researched. For example, Dr. Graham Merry in Barrie, Ontario, has developed a new treatment for dry macular degeneration called photobiomodulation. Although the treatment is not covered by any provincial plan, this doctor is approved to treat individuals. Anyone paying for this treatment can submit receipts for it with their provincial/territorial tax returns. You can read more about this treatment at: www.photospectra.ca.

---

[3] "Supply, Distribution and Migration of Canadian Physicians, 2010," Canadian Institute for Health Information, https://secure.cihi.ca/estore/productFamily.htm?locale=en&pf=PFC1680.

[4] Nadeem Esmail, "Canada's physician supply," *Fraser Forum* March/April 2011, http://www.fraserinstitute.org/uploadedFiles/fraser-ca/Content/research-news/research/articles/canadas-physician-supply.pdf.

SUMMARY

1. In 1947, Saskatchewan was the first province in Canada to establish some form of provincial health insurance. The *Canada Health Act*, passed in 1984, was the beginning of a formalized national health-care plan.

2. The Canadian health-care system is built on the five principles of the *Canada Health Act*, which are meant to ensure that all Canadians have free access to all medically necessary health-care services. The act outlines conditions that the provinces and territories must meet to receive health funding from the federal government.

3. The federal and provincial or territorial governments share responsibility for health care. The federal government sets national standards and partially funds health care, but the provinces and territories deliver health care. In British Columbia and Ontario, residents pay premiums for health insurance; in all other provinces and territories, coverage is paid for by tax revenues.

4. Primary care settings in Canada include solo or group family practices, clinics, emergency departments, and managed care arrangements, including health management organizations.

5. Primary care reform aims to provide more comprehensive, high-quality, cost-effective health care. Because of this reform, family health networks or primary care networks are becoming common. Such arrangements, which are entered into voluntarily, involve a commitment from both providers and clients. Health office professionals are involved in rostering clients and making sure they understand the terms of the contract.

6. Fee-for-service is still the most common form of physician remuneration in Canada. The capitation model is used with primary care reform and other managed care models. Physicians may also be hired on salary or through a sessional contract. Some have blended sources of income.

7. Extra-billing and user fees are not commonly used in Canada. Extra-billing—billing the client for *insured* health services—violates the *Canada Health Act* and can lead to penalties. Billing for enhanced services is permitted. Regulations for billing for services outside of what is covered by the public plan varies across the country.

8. As well as physicians, providers who may bill health plans include (depending on the province or territory) optometrists, dentists, chiropractors, physiotherapists, osteopaths, podiatrists, nurse practitioners, and midwives.

Key Terms

capitation or population-
   based funding   93
clawback   96
extra-billing   96
fee-for-service   95

global budget   91
locum tenens   88
managed care   91
opted-in   96
opted-out   96

orphan patient   90
physician incentive   97
primary health care   87
provider   82
rostering   93

Review Questions

1. When was the first health-care legislation passed in Canada?
2. Which province had the first provincial health plan?
3. What is the purpose of the *Canada Health Act*, and when was it passed?
4. What are the five principles of the *Canada Health Act*, and what do they mean?
5. What are the responsibilities of the provincial or territorial and federal governments regarding health care?
6. What are the main recommendations of the Romanow Report?
7. What constitutes a primary care setting?
8. What is the purpose of primary care reform, and how do reform initiatives change the organization of primary care?
9. What is meant by rostering clients, and what is involved in the process?
10. What is meant by fee-for-service?

Application Exercises

1. In small groups, research primary care reform initiatives in your province or territory. How many primary care groups are operating? Describe how they were set up and how they operate. Try to interview clients who have been rostered (if applicable), asking them to compare their health care under the current model with their care under the fee-for-service model. What other primary care reforms are underway in your province or territory?

2. Research the types of providers in your province or territory who are allowed to bill the provincial or territorial plan. Choose three of these providers, and identify any billing restrictions placed on them.

3. Wait times in all provinces and territories differ, as do the number of orphan clients. Strategies for addressing these problems also vary. Investigate these issues in your own jurisdiction.

   a. What are the wait times for hip, knee, cataract, and cardiac bypass surgery, and MRIs?

   b. What is being done by your provincial or territorial government to rectify this?

   c. How many individuals in your jurisdiction are without family doctors? How are the province or territory and municipality trying to fix the problem?

4. Investigate the primary recommendations of the Romanow Report and the Kirby Report. Investigate progress made in health care since the recommendations were made public. Consider, in particular, home care, primary care, diagnostic services, and the implementation of a catastrophic drug plan. As of 2012, what still needs to be done? Summarize your findings in point form. How have these recommendations affected health care in your province or territory?

5. Divide into small groups. Research the types of private health-care services available in your province or territory. Suggested elements to address include opted-in/-out options, direct billing, extra-billing, and the legality of private insurance covering publicly insured services. As a class, compile a list of private services offered, including those that are financed in part by the public plan (e.g., private diagnostic clinics, physiotherapy clinics, corporate groups).

Websites of Interest

The *Canada Health Act*
www.hc-sc.gc.ca/hcs-sss/medi-assur/index-eng.php

Provincial Health-Care Plans and Systems

Newfoundland and Labrador
www.gov.nl.ca/health

Prince Edward Island
www.gov.pe.ca/health

Nova Scotia
www.gov.ns.ca/health/

New Brunswick
www.gnb.ca/0051/index-e.asp

Quebec
www.msss.gouv.qc.ca

Ontario
www.health.gov.on.ca

Manitoba
www.manitoba.ca/health

Saskatchewan
www.health.gov.sk.ca

Alberta
www.health.alberta.ca

British Columbia
www.gov.bc.ca/health

Yukon
www.hss.gov.yk.ca/

Northwest Territories
www.hlthss.gov.nt.ca

Nunavut
www.gov.nu.ca/health/

The Canadian Association of Physician Assistants
http://capa-acam.ca/

College of Family Physicians of Canada
http://toolkit.cfpc.ca/en/links.php

Provides links to provincial Colleges of Family Physicians, provincial medical associations, and primary care agencies within provincial ministries of health.

Canadian Medical Association: Number of Physicians by Province/Territory and Specialty, Canada, 2011
http://www.cma.ca/multimedia/CMA/Content_Images/Inside_cma/Statistics/01SpecProv.pdf

Part III
Health-Care Basics

Part III gets down to basic information about quality and standards, diagnostic testing, and pharmacology that applies to any health-related occupational setting. Chapter 5 introduces the principles of quality, standards, and safety in health care. Essential topics, such as occupational health and safety legislation, WHMIS, asepsis, infection control, and Standard Precautions are discussed in some detail. You will learn effective risk-management techniques appropriate to your role in health care. Environmental safety, both for health professionals and clients, is discussed. Chapter 6 will introduce you to diagnostic testing, including laboratory tests and diagnostic imaging, and to your role in the process. You will be instrumental in requisitioning these tests, accurately and responsibly reporting test results to the appropriate people, and booking appointments for clients. You will also inform clients about preparing for tests and about what to expect. Chapter 7 will provide you with a knowledge base about pharmacology suitable to your related responsibilities. You will gain an overview of types of drugs, drug effects and side effects, and routes of administration. You will learn how to deal with prescriptions in the health office and how to direct clients to appropriate resources when they have questions related to their medications

Chapter 5
Standards and Safety in Health Care

Learning Objectives

On completing this chapter, you will be able to:

1. Examine the role of quality assurance in health care.
2. Discuss the concept of infectious and communicable diseases, including patterns of infection.
3. Identify strategies to prevent and control the spread of infection.
4. Describe the three most common causes of nosocomial infections.
5. Summarize the principles of asepsis and sterilization applied in the health office.
6. Apply the principles of Standard Precautions.
7. Provide a safe health office environment for staff and clients.

When you go to a restaurant, you expect your food to be of high quality, prepared according to certain standards. When you purchase a shirt or a car, you likewise expect the product to reflect a certain quality. Even dealing with a bank, you expect that the individuals who manage your money will be appropriately trained and will know what they are doing. Health care is no different. It is a service; its scope and nature vary, and it is provided by individuals whom you expect to be appropriately trained and knowledgeable. You also expect the services you receive to be of a certain quality. As a health office professional, you must be aware of the standards of care and service that your facility and you yourself are expected to provide. You must participate in ongoing evaluation and ensure that you maintain a high standard of service.

❶ QUALITY ASSURANCE IN HEALTH CARE

quality assurance any systematic process of checking to see whether a product or service is meeting specified requirements. In health care, it is a systematic assessment to ensure that services are of the highest possible quality using existing resources.

QUALITY ASSURANCE IS ANY SYSTEMATIC PROCESS OF CHECKING TO SEE WHETHER A product or service is meeting requirements. Quality assurance also includes establishing, promoting, and maintaining a safe occupational environment. Industry and other occupational settings embody specific goals and criteria in their quality assurance initiatives. Industrial settings often have a full-time quality control officer.

Quality assurance in the health-care environment is an orchestrated and methodical approach of continuously scrutinizing, evaluating, and improving the quality of health services. Clients should expect nothing short of excellence in assessment, diagnosis, treatment, and ongoing care. They are entitled to prompt treatment, prompt reports on laboratory tests, accurate prescriptions, reasonable waiting times, direction regarding emergencies, and proper follow-up. Quality assurance is particularly critical when budgets are limited and resources scarce.

Quality assurance in health care is the responsibility of both employers and employees. Large facilities usually have a formal quality assurance committee. In small practices, you, as the health office professional, play a large role. To do so effectively, you must understand the principles of quality assurance and safety, including infection control. You must be conscious of both your own and the clients' safety in the office.

It is vital to maintain a safe environment in the health office—one that reduces risk of harm to both clients and staff. In the health office, you will encounter people from all age groups, with varied health problems, altered emotional and physical needs, and a wide range of abilities and disabilities. You have a special responsibility to protect those who cannot effectively protect themselves. You need to protect both yourself and them against injury, fire, and infection. A website at the end of the chapter gives a detailed summary of precautions essential to infection control in a doctor's office.

Hospitals

Hospitals and other health-care facilities participate in a process known as accreditation (discussed in Chapter 14), which demonstrates that they meet provincial or territorial standards. Health-care providers, such as doctors, nurse practitioners, and midwives, must go through a peer-review process of *credentialling* to establish and maintain privileges to admit and care for clients at a health-care facility. Health-care facilities conduct routine reviews of facility policies, procedures, and quality of care; this is usually the responsibility of the department called Risk Management or Quality Assurance (QA). The following are some of the problems frequently reviewed. Investigations into these areas cover policies, procedures, documentation, and actual client care:

- Clients who are readmitted to hospital within a certain number of days after discharge
- Deaths occurring within the hospital
- Unscheduled returns to surgery
- Infections contracted within the hospital
- Falls, medication errors, and other irregularities

Investigation will hopefully lead to improved client care.

Health Offices

Many smaller health offices do not have a formal quality assurance plan. If your office does not have such a plan, you may want to propose establishing one. However, quality assurance is addressed informally each time an action is taken to correct a problem or improve services to clients. Remember that a quality assurance plan can only be as good as the people who initiate and practise it. A quality assurance review should follow the following principles:

- In a large enough setting (for example, the health department of a large factory), a committee should be designated to oversee the process. This may require formal training of some or all of the committee members. In a smaller health office with few employees, it is most effective if everyone works as a team.
- Keep it positive. A review is not meant to punish those who make errors, but rather to find the causes of problems and correct them. Stress the goal of enhancing performance and client service.
- Actively involve all staff so that everyone "owns" the process. A collaborative effort generalizes problems, avoids pinpointing blame, and promotes working toward the common goal of improved service and care.

All services in the office should be open to review, with more thorough investigation of trouble spots, such as

- errors in writing prescriptions;
- mislabelling of test specimens;
- multiple needle-sticks by staff;
- frequent, long waiting periods for clients in the reception area;
- inadequate or delayed follow-up on abnormal test results;
- protracted delay in returning phone calls;
- not answering the telephone within a reasonable time frame;
- inaccurate or incomplete documentation and charting;
- errors in letters, reports, and so on;
- client concerns about involvement in selecting treatments; and
- client concern about the type and length of treatment offered.

Once areas of concern have been identified, measures to address each must be outlined and implemented. Periodic review is needed to assess progress. A suggestion box in the waiting room may help identify client concerns and generate valuable ideas.

The Incident Report

An incident report is formal documentation of any lapse in acceptable procedure, protocol, or policy that results in undesirable effects. Most large agencies, such as hospitals and busy clinics, design their own incident reports, containing generic information plus anything specific to the agency itself. All work-related injuries require completion of a workers' compensation board (WCB) accident form and perhaps an agency incident report as well. Some organizations have an employee incident form separate from the general incident report.

The incident report has long been dreaded as an instrument bringing blame and punishment to those perceived to be responsible. More recently, incident reports have taken on a more positive role, focusing not on assigning blame, but on identifying problems, determining why they occurred, and suggesting corrective steps. Often, incidents are not the fault of one person but are the result of a combination of events.

The format of an incident report will vary with the agency. However, most include

- a summary of the event;
- a detailed account of events leading up to the incident;
- date and time of the event;
- who was present initially, and anyone else involved in the incident;
- who was notified of the event (e.g., coordinator, clinical leader) and when;
- any untoward consequences;
- any action, medical or otherwise, taken as a result of the event (e.g., physician ordered an X-ray after a client's fall);
- an evaluation of the incident; and
- recommendations for preventing a similar occurrence.

The person discovering the incident should initiate the report. This may or not be the person responsible for the incident (if anyone is specifically responsible). The person immediately in charge of the area where the incident occurred must be promptly notified—a doctor, charge nurse, supervisor, for example. That person will likely assume responsibility to notify other individuals as required and oversee report completion.

Consider Mr. Dodhia, who fell out of bed because someone left the side rail down. He sustained a cut to the side of his forehead and complained of a sore arm. Nema, a unit clerk, found Mr. Dodhia on the floor beside his bed. Nema notified a nurse, who settled Mr. Dodhia back into bed. Nema also notified the charge nurse. An incident report was initiated. The doctor was called and, after examining Mr. Dodhia, determined there were no serious injuries. Preliminary investigation found that a nurse, Andrea, had taken Mr. Dodhia to the washroom and forgot to put up the side rail. Mr. Dodhia's family were glad his injuries were minor and left it at that. The completed report was signed by those involved and forwarded to the appropriate department (e.g., Risk Management or Quality Assurance). In such cases, further investigation, if required, would be conducted by Risk

Management or Quality Assurance. If appropriate, all findings, conclusions, and recommendations would be communicated to administration and perhaps the board of directors.

An incident report is not kept on the client's chart. In most cases, duplication of the report is prohibited, and those involved must refrain from discussing the incident inappropriately. An incident report can hold information that is potential ammunition for a lawsuit.

Workers' Compensation

Workers' compensation is a form of social insurance administered independently in each province or territory under provincial or territorial legislation. Federal legislation applies only to federally regulated workplaces, such as banks, and to federal government departments. Human Resources and Skills Development Canada is responsible for occupational health and safety in federally regulated workplaces. Employees of the federal government receive benefits and services, which are reimbursed by the federal government through provincial or territorial WCBs.

Employers pay premiums, which are gathered into a common fund out of which benefits are paid to workers injured as a result of their employment. In exchange, employees relinquish the right to sue employers for on-the-job injuries. Each province and territory has a workers' compensation board (WCB) or equivalent that administers funding and adjudicates cases.

The WCBs also promote workplace health and safety and consult with and educate employers and workers. Most WCBs also monitor compliance with Occupational Health and Safety regulations, but in Nova Scotia, this is the responsibility of the Department of Labour and Advanced Education. The Association of WCBs of Canada (AWCBC) coordinates the National Work Injury Statistics Program and provides statistical data on workplace-related injuries, diseases, and fatalities.

Across Canada, most businesses must register with their provincial or territorial WCB (called, for example, the Workplace Safety and Insurance Board in Ontario and the Workplace Health, Safety and Compensation Commission in Newfoundland and Labrador). Rules about who must register vary from one jurisdiction to another; criteria are often based on the size of the business, number of employees, and hours worked in a given time frame. A few examples: the Northwest Territories requires registration for all businesses regardless of size and status; even a one-person business, such as a family doctor with no support staff, must register. In British Columbia, a family that employs a nanny for more than 15 hours a week must register. In Nova Scotia, a business with three or more workers in an industry defined as "mandatory" must register; doctors' offices are not required to register. In Ontario, travel agencies, banks, private daycare centres, and private health-care practices—including physicians and chiropractors—are exempt (a situation that may change). Exempt businesses may apply voluntarily for WCB coverage for their employees. If you work in a hospital or large clinic, it is a safe assumption that you will be eligible for workers' compensation coverage. If you work in a small medical practice, it depends on the province or territory. Before starting a job, ask whether you are eligible for workers' compensation benefits or are otherwise insured against job-related injury.

Most provinces and territories have recently addressed situations involving West Nile virus and severe acute respiratory syndrome (SARS). In Ontario, for example, workers who are infected with West Nile virus in the course of their employment will be entitled to the usual benefits and services available under the *Workers' Compensation Act*. As in all disease claims, entitlement is decided on a case-by-case basis.

Workers' compensation boards or commissions work collaboratively with the Canadian Centre for Occupational Health and Safety (CCOHS), but focus on assisting the injured employee (wages, rehabilitation, training), whereas Occupational Health and Safety concentrates on providing a safe work environment. Workplace Hazardous Materials Information System (WHMIS) is federal legislation administered through Occupational Health and Safety that educates employers and employees about workplace hazards. You can learn more about CCOHS and WHMIS from the websites listed at the end of the chapter.

❷❸❹❺❻ MANAGING INFECTIOUS AND COMMUNICABLE DISEASES

infection a disease process that results from the entry and spread of a microorganism.

INFECTION CONTROL IS A MAJOR FOCUS IN ALL HEALTH-CARE FACILITIES. ANY SETTING that cares for ill people will naturally have increased risks of infection, which can result in serious illness and even death for both clients and health professionals, as the 2003 SARS outbreak in Toronto and Vancouver forcibly reminded everyone. Though we have a range of anti-bacterial and antiviral medications, the most effective way to deal with infectious diseases is to prevent the infection in the first place. It is the responsibility of every health professional, from physicians and nurses to administrative staff, to be knowledgeable about the infectious process and infection control strategies and to be diligent in preventing infections.

microorganism an organism so small that it can only be seen under a microscope.

contagious or communicable disease a disease that is spread from person to person.

An infectious disease is one that is caused by a **microorganism**—that is, an organism too small to be seen with the naked eye. Infectious diseases are generally, but not always, **contagious**, or **communicable**, meaning that they can be transmitted from one person to another (although some are much more easily transmitted than others). Communicable diseases range from the familiar common cold to more serious illnesses, such as "strep throat," tuberculosis, malaria, and acquired immune deficiency syndrome (AIDS). Some are serious enough to cause permanent disability or death. Some can be prevented through immunization, and many can be cured with medication. Most infections caused by bacteria, fungi, or parasites can be treated effectively with antimicrobial drugs, while most viral infections, like the common cold, are not effectively treated using current agents.

Infections may be classified in several ways. In terms of extent, they may be local (confined to a specific part of the body) or systemic (affecting the whole body). In terms of the pattern of development, they may be acute (immediate and time limited), chronic (persistent), latent (dormant between recurrences), or opportunistic (occurring in response to poor **immunity**). Of special concern for infection control are nosocomial infections, which are infections that clients pick up in the health-care setting.

immunity an individual's ability to fight off disease.

Patterns of Infection   An infection can occur anywhere in the human body, internally or externally. It can affect parts of the body or the body as a whole. An infection may be referred to as **local infection** if it is limited to a specific part or area of the body, usually external. An incision line, a scratch, or a cut can become infected. An eye can become infected. Local infections may be evidenced by redness, swelling, or increased warmth in the affected area. Local infections can be treated with **topical** antibiotic creams or with oral antibiotics. Some local infections can become systemic if not treated properly.

Systemic infections affect the entire body in some manner, although the source of the infection may be limited to one part of the body. For example, a kidney or bladder infection, although located in a particular organ, is likely to produce more generalized clinical signs, such as fever, increased pulse and/or respiratory rate, fatigue, loss of appetite, and generalized aches. Colds and "strep throat" are also considered systemic infections. Even **otitis media** (middle ear infection) can cause systemic responses, such as fever. Septicemia, or blood poisoning, is a disease caused by pathogens in the bloodstream that involves the whole body.

Acute and *chronic* refer to the onset and duration of the infection. Many familiar infections, such as bad colds and otitis media are usually **acute infections**. The course of the illness is usually short; the client may recover with or without treatment. Some acute infections, however, can be serious, leading to long-term damage or even death. A **chronic infection** occurs when the microorganism that causes it is present for a long period of time, sometimes persisting for life. The person may have signs or symptoms continuously or may have asymptomatic periods. Periods without symptoms are known as **remissions**; periods when symptoms occur again are called **exacerbations**. The organism may be transmitted even if the client is asymptomatic. An example of a chronic infection is hepatitis B. Although the person may show few symptoms or be completely **asymptomatic**, the person still carries the virus and can pass it to others. A **latent infection** is one in which the clinical signs disappear and recur, although some call any infection lasting more than two weeks a chronic infection. Most chronic infections show little change over their slow progression. For example, in herpes simplex virus 1 (HSV 1), after the initial infection, the virus can lie dormant for long periods until some stimulus, such as fatigue or stress, reactivates it. When clinical signs and symptoms reappear, the infection becomes an **active infection**.

A *primary infection* is the original or initial infection a client displays. It is not always the client's main medical problem. A *secondary infection* is one that occurs when a bacterial infection follows or complicates a condition already present. For example, Ms. Valdez develops viral pneumonia. This is the primary infection. Several days later, because of a build-up of mucus in her lungs, Ms. Valdez develops another infection caused by a bacterium. This is a secondary infection.

A **recurrent infection** is sometimes confused with a relapse or the reappearance of an initial infection. A recurrent infection is a repetition of an infection after recovery. It is a distinct episode; pathogens involved may be the same as or different from those responsible for the initial infection. A **relapse** involves a flare-up of the initial infection after it appears to have subsided. A relapse is caused by the same organism as the original infection.

A person does not get sick every time a microorganism enters his body. A healthy person with a fully functional immune system can resist many of these disease-causing agents. An **opportunistic infection** is one that occurs only under certain circumstances, such as when the person's immune system is compromised. For example, people whose immune

local infection   an infection that is confined to a specific region of the body, for example, a finger.

topical   applied to the skin or affected area.

systemic infection   an infection that has spread to more than one region of the body.

otitis media   infection of the middle ear.

acute infection   an infection that is time limited.

chronic infection   one that is persistent over a long period, perhaps for life.

remission   a period in which a chronic infection shows no symptoms.

exacerbation   a period in which a chronic infection shows symptoms.

asymptomatic   without clinical signs or symptoms.

latent infection   one in which the symptoms disappear and recur, while the disease-causing agent remains in the body.

active infection   an infection in which signs and symptoms are present.

recurrent infection   a distinct episode of an infection after recovery from the initial infection; may involve the same pathogens or different ones.

relapse   the re-emergence of an initial infection after it appears to have subsided but has not been cured.

opportunistic infection   an infection that does not ordinarily cause disease but does so under certain circumstances, for example, in compromised immune systems; so called because it takes advantage of an "opportunity."

system has been weakened by AIDS are susceptible to otherwise rare types of pneumonia and fungal infections that would not affect them if their immune system was healthy.

Clients come to health-care facilities to become well, and so, it is particularly distressing when the facility environment makes them ill. Yet **nosocomial infections**, those acquired in a health-care facility, are not surprising. Clients who are hospitalized are often ill, and their body's defences may be weakened. In addition, there are likely to be more infectious organisms in any client-care facility than in other places, and these organisms can be carried from one client to another by a variety of items or by health-care professionals. Nosocomial infections range from minor to life threatening.

Microorganisms

A microorganism is a microscopic life form too small to be seen by the naked eye, such as a bacterium, protozoan, or virus. A microorganism that can cause disease is called a **pathogen**. Some pathogens have the ability to produce toxins, which can cause an infectious process in the animal or person in which the microorganism is living. This infectious process may be local or systemic. The severity of an infection will depend on the nature and **virulence** of the infectious organism. This is determined by the strain of organism present, the number of these organisms present, and how potent these organisms are.

Normal Flora   Normal flora are microorganisms normally present in the human body that *do not* cause disease. Each body surface—including the skin and the lining of various organs and systems in the body, such as the respiratory tract, the gastrointestinal (GI) system, and the urinary tract—is home to microorganisms of some type. If a microorganism is a natural inhabitant of a body system, it is usually **nonpathogenic** as long as it remains within that body system. In fact, microorganisms are often beneficial. The normal flora in the GI tract, for example, may assist with the synthesis and uptake of vitamins, such as B and K, and may assist in breaking down food that would otherwise be difficult to digest. Normal flora can also help the body fight infection. However, a microorganism that is non-pathogenic to one body system may be pathogenic if it invades another body system. For example, *Escherichia coli*, a microorganism normally found in the GI system, is beneficial to that system. (Normal *E. coli* should not be confused with the particular strains of *E. coli* that have caused outbreaks of disease from contaminated food or water.) However, if this microorganism were to be transmitted to the person's urinary system, it could cause an infection.

Bacteria   Bacteria are single-celled organisms that multiply by cell division. Most bacteria are nonpathogenic, but some types of bacteria are the major causes of infectious diseases. They may be categorized by their demand for oxygen or their shape. **Aerobic** bacteria require oxygen to live and multiply. **Anaerobic** bacteria can live and multiply without oxygen. Both types thrive on moisture, darkness, warmth, and the presence of nutrients.

Viruses   A virus is a very small organism, much smaller than a bacterium, and cannot be seen with a regular microscope. Sometimes referred to as an "incomplete organism," a virus cannot live on its own, nor (unlike bacteria) can it reproduce itself outside of living tissue. A virus needs a host cell to multiply because it does not have a metabolism of its own. Viruses may cause such illnesses as the common cold, influenza, and infectious mononucleosis. Viruses are difficult to treat and do not respond to antibiotics. *This is why physicians will usually not prescribe an antibiotic for an infection (such as a sore throat) until they have confirmed, often through a laboratory test, that the cause is bacterial.* Vaccines are effective

---

nosocomial infection   a hospitalrelated infection; one that is not present or incubating when a patient is admitted to a hospital or a healthcare facility.

pathogen   a microorganism that causes disease.

virulence   the power of a microbe to produce disease in a particular host.

nonpathogenic   not causing disease.

aerobic bacteria   bacteria that require oxygen to grow.

anaerobic bacteria   bacteria that do not require oxygen to grow.

against some viral infections. Viral diseases are difficult to diagnose, and diagnosis is based on the client's symptoms and clinical signs or on a process of elimination. For example, if a client with a sore throat has a throat swab cultured with negative results, the doctor will usually assume that the infection is viral. *This client should not be given antibiotics.*

Fungi   A fungus grows mainly as a single-celled organism that uses spores to reproduce. Yeast is a type of fungus, and so are molds. Very few fungi cause diseases in humans. However, athlete's foot is a fungal infection, and moniliasis, a yeast infection, is common in women. Diagnosis of a fungal infection is usually made by examining samples of skin scrapings or hair, or sputum specimens and swabs from mucous membranes.

Protozoa   A protozoan is a single-celled organism, ranging in size from microscopic to visible to the naked eye, found mostly in contaminated water and sewage systems. Protozoa can cause Giardia, also known as "beaver fever," which is contracted by drinking contaminated water. It is manifested by diarrhea and cramping and is treated with a medication called Flagyl. Malaria is also caused by protozoa. Diagnosis of these diseases is based largely on the symptoms and clinical signs, as well as on stool specimens and blood samples.

The Chain of Infection

To understand the transition of an individual from a healthy state to an infectious state, one must examine a series of events known collectively as the infection cycle. The infection cycle has been compared to the links of a chain. All of the links in the chain must be present for infection to occur (see Figure 5.1). These steps include

- a causative organism;
- a host reservoir;

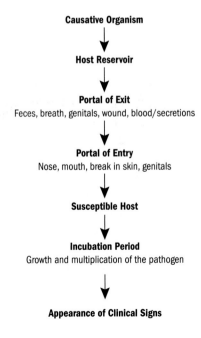

Causative Organism
↓
Host Reservoir
↓
Portal of Exit
Feces, breath, genitals, wound, blood/secretions
↓
Portal of Entry
Nose, mouth, break in skin, genitals
↓
Susceptible Host
↓
Incubation Period
Growth and multiplication of the pathogen
↓
Appearance of Clinical Signs

CYCLE BEGINS AGAIN

Figure 5.1   The chain of infection

- a portal of exit;
- a mode of transmission;
- a portal of entry; and
- a susceptible host.

Causative Organism To initiate an infection, the microorganism must be a pathogen.

Host A host (also referred to as a host reservoir) is where the pathogen is initially found. The host can be a person, an animal, or an environmental habitat, such as the soil, feces, water, food, and so on. The host must be capable of providing the microorganism with an environment in which it can live, grow, and multiply.

Portal of Exit The pathogen must have an exit from the host reservoir. In humans, this could be, for example, through the bowel, nose, or mouth, or in blood, semen, or saliva.

Mode of Transmission After the organism leaves the host reservoir, it needs transportation to the new host, or recipient host (the person receiving the organism). Methods of transmission include the following.

Direct contact: transmission from person to person. For example, Jenny has a pathogen in her throat and kisses Jake, transmitting the organism to Jake.

Indirect contact: transmission from a person to an object (such as a tissue) to a person. For example, a health office professional touches infected body fluid and accidentally transfers it to the new paper sheet on the examination bed. The pathogen in the fluid is transferred to the next client.

Droplet transmission: transmission by coughs or sneezes. Infections are commonly spread this way in the health office, especially during the cold and flu season. During influenza outbreaks, hospitals and nursing homes will often limit or ban visitors to reduce the spread of influenza.

Vehicle route: transmission via food, water, or blood and body fluids. Human immunodeficiency virus (HIV) and hepatitis can be transmitted via body fluids. This mode of transmission is similar to indirect contact, except that the object is the reservoir itself.

Airborne transmission: transmission through dust, evaporated droplets in the air, and airborne particles of hair and skin. Microorganisms carried in this manner can be dispersed widely by air currents, ventilation systems, and fans and may be inhaled by people at some distance. Transmission by evaporated droplets differs from droplet transmission in that the residue of the evaporated droplet remains suspended in the air for long periods. Dust from linens containing the infectious agent would be another example. The organisms are inhaled by or dropped on the recipient host.

Vector transmission: transmission in which a bird, animal, or insect (called the *vector*) carries the infectious agent. Malaria and West Nile virus are transmitted this way through mosquitoes.

Portal of Entry After the organism has left the host reservoir via some means of transmission, it must find a route into the recipient host. The common portals of entry are through the respiratory, the GI, or the genitourinary tract or by direct entry through an open wound, scratch, cut, or any other break in the skin. A wound infection usually results from the entry of a pathogenic organism through a break in the skin.

Susceptible Host The *recipient host* is the person to whom the organism is transferred. An infection does not occur every time a pathogenic organism invades a host. The susceptibility of the host depends largely on the person's immune system and defences.

Vaccines

There are numerous types of vaccines, differing in how they are made and how they are stored. They work because the body responds in the same manner to an **antigen** whether it is exposed to it naturally or via a vaccine. Vaccines are scientifically prepared, rigorously tested, and predominantly safe. A small percentage of immunized individuals suffer serious adverse effects—far less than those associated with the disease.

antigen a pathogen or any other substance that induces an antibody response.

In the health office, some of your clients may opt not to have themselves or their children vaccinated. This is a personal decision that must be respected. Some jurisdictions require certain vaccinations as a condition for school attendance. There may be exemptions for children with certain medical conditions.

Storing and Handling Immunizing Agents

Proper storing and handling of vaccines is essential to preserve product potency. Overseeing that immunizing agents are properly stored and handled may be your responsibility. Every office must follow the Public Health Agency of Canada's guidelines for storage and monitoring of vaccines. Each manufacturer will print storage guidelines on the package. Most recommendations specify that vaccines be stored at temperatures from +2°C to +8°C.

Most vaccines must be protected from light as well: for example, MMR, varicella, BCG, and flu vaccines. Keep them stored in the packages they come in. If a vaccine is reconstituted but not used, immediately return it to the fridge and dispose of it if it is not used within the manufacturer's recommended time frame. Your local public health authority will likely make routine checks on your office to ensure that vaccines are properly stored.

Pay attention to expiry dates, and adhere to the following procedures:

- Use a frost-free refrigerator.
- Have a designated person monitor the fridge temperature at the same time daily.
- Use a commercially available maximum–minimum thermometer, placed in the middle of the fridge. A large plastic bottle filled with water placed in the fridge will help maintain a stable temperature.
- Immediately place newly delivered vaccines in the fridge (even 20 minutes is too long to leave them sitting out).
- Store vaccines in the middle of the refrigerator to avoid extremes of temperature.

- Make sure the electrical cord is in a place where it will not easily become disconnected (you can use a safety lock plug).
- Keep vaccines with the earliest expiry date in front.
- Don't store lunches or other items (such as specimens) in this fridge.
- Remove vaccines right before use and refrigerate them as soon as the nurse/doctor has finished with them (they may do this themselves, but you can act as an extra check. It is easy for someone to leave a vaccine out, especially during busy times such as the influx of clients for their flu shots early in the flu season).
- Ensure the doctor uses an insulated carrier for vaccines equipped with a freezer pack (the vaccine should not be in direct contact with the freezer pack).
- If you discover your fridge is not working, transfer the vaccines to another fridge as soon as possible. If the time frame of the failure is unknown you may have to discard the vaccines.
- If there is a power failure, four hours is the accepted limit after which you must transfer the vaccines to another refrigerator.
- If you suspect the cold chain has been compromised, public health will assist you to make decisions regarding whether or not the vaccines are safe to use.

Recommended Vaccines for Clients You should know the recommended immunization schedules for clients (especially children) in your jurisdictions so that you can schedule the client's appointments appropriately. Some of these vaccinations are given in conjunction with a well-baby check-up. A child who is sick with a fever should have the immunization postponed until the child is better. Parents may be anxious (particularly new parents) when their baby receives an immunization, fearing the child will react or at the very least, be "out of sorts" for a day or two. Provide the parents with as much information and support as you can. The most common side effect from a childhood immunization is redness and tenderness at the injection site. A small child might also be cranky and fussy for a day or two. The PHAC website listed at the end of this chapter will provide you with detailed information on recommended vaccines as well as common questions clients may ask. It will provide you with a current list of childhood immunizations recommended by the Public Health Agency of Canada for your own jurisdiction.

Recommended Immunizations and Tests for Health Professionals In any health-care setting, you will naturally be exposed to more sick people than in most workplaces. Therefore, you should be immunized against the infections that present common threats. Many people object to vaccinations because they are too busy, they dislike shots, or they misinterpret minor local reactions as allergic reactions. However, immunizations not only protect you but also protect your clients: if you contract an infection, you are likely to pass it on to clients, some of whom are particularly vulnerable.

Tip

If you are entering completed vaccinations into the computer, for each entry you will be asked not only for the type of vaccine, but also its manufacturer and the expiry date. Have the package handy or write down the expiry date of each vial so you are not fishing for the information every time you make such an entry.

Check with your doctor to see that your routine immunizations are up to date. Some people believe that childhood vaccinations will protect them for life. Although this is true with some vaccines, many require boosters to maintain immunity. Many facilities have a specific list of immunizations required for employees and often for volunteers and students on externships. For some diseases, you may have the option of having **antibody** titres done, which would test for **immunity**. Some colleges may also require immunizations for health office administration students and will provide opportunities to receive all necessary shots.

antibody a protein specific to a certain antigen that weakens or destroys pathogens.

Influenza In most parts of the country, the influenza vaccine is readily available (usually in the fall), and it is generally recommended that everyone, including children, be immunized. Health-care professionals are at risk for contracting the flu and are potential host reservoirs for passing the infection to someone else. Health professionals are strongly urged to get the influenza vaccine. Otherwise they can easily pass on the virus to a population at risk.

In 2012 Health Canada recommended that children between 6 to 23 months of age should receive a full dose of influenza vaccine. Research shows that the full dose is both safe and more effective. Some jurisdictions may still give children in this age category two injections of 0.25 ml (half the adult dose) at least four weeks apart. (See the websites listed at the end of the chapter for a link to a Hospital for Sick Children webpage that discusses immunization for children.) As well, it has been ascertained that an allergy to eggs is no longer a reason for people to refrain from getting the influenza vaccine.

Hepatitis A and B Hepatitis A and B are serious, sometimes chronic or deadly, viral infections of the liver. Transmission of these viruses can occur in a health-care setting as a result of an accidental prick with a contaminated needle or other sharp instrument. Although there are separate vaccinations for hepatitis A and B, Twinrix is a popular vaccine that provides protection from both hepatitis A and hepatitis B together. There are rarely side effects for these immunizations; despite this, most practitioners recommend that clients stay in the office for at least 15 minutes in case of a reaction. The routine schedule for Twinrix is three doses—the second injection at least one month after the first, and the third six months after the first. However, an accelerated schedule of four doses is an option for those with time constraints. Some facilities make this immunization a condition of employment.

Measles, Mumps, Rubella Although most Canadians are immune to these diseases (older people because they had the diseases as children, and younger people from childhood immunizations), another dose may be recommended. The MMR vaccine is a combined preparation given in one needle. Contraindications include pregnancy, receipt of **immunoglobulins**, or a sensitivity to eggs or neomycin. There is controversy over individuals who have a sensitivity to eggs. Only life-threatening reactions are considered to be a firm contraindication; people with the potential for such reaction can be tested with a weaker version of the serum.

immunoglobulin a serum that contains antibodies that can help protect an exposed person from contracting the disease.

Pneumococcal Infections Although health-care professionals are not considered to be at higher risk than the general population, some facilities recommend this immunization for their employees' own protection. It is particularly recommended for health professionals with such chronic illnesses as diabetes, heart disease, or disorders of the immune system.

Diphtheria/Tetanus/Pertussis
Booster shots are recommended every 10 years after primary immunization has been given. Health-care professionals are not considered to be at higher risk than the general population.

Meningitis/Varicella/HPV
Other vaccines in current use include Menjugate (to prevent meningococcal infection) and Varivax (to prevent infection from the varicella-zoster virus, which causes chicken pox). A vaccine (Gardasil) for the HPV virus is currently being promoted by the Public Health Agency of Canada. A website listed at the end of the chapter will provide you with more information on this new and controversial vaccine.

Tuberculin Testing
Tuberculosis (TB) is a disease that is constantly being monitored. In Canada, after several decades of decline, the annual incidence rate of TB has remained about the same for the last 10 years, with an estimated 1700 to 2000 new cases reported annually. TB is not declining, primarily because of immigration and international travel to and from areas where it is prevalent, including East, Southeast, and South Asia; sub-Saharan Africa; parts of South and Central America; the Caribbean; Eastern Europe; and the former Soviet Union. Aboriginal people also have a higher incidence of TB, as do individuals with HIV and those living in poor economic circumstances. Recently a resistant form of TB emerged, causing global concern. The strain is resistant to both first- and second-line drugs. In 2007, several of these cases were reported in Toronto. These are called MDR-TB (multi-drug resistant) and account for an estimated one in four cases.

Preventing the Spread of Infection

Although hand washing is the most effective method of preventing the spread of infectious organisms, there are other steps you can take.

Even if you are not directly involved in client care, your actions can transmit pathogens or prevent their transmission. An understanding of **asepsis** is essential.

asepsis a state in which pathogens are absent or reduced. There are two principal types of asepsis: medical and surgical.

The first line of defence, in both the hospital and the health office, is personal cleanliness. You can easily carry microorganisms into the work setting or back home on your clothing and on your person. If you carry pathogens home, you can become ill or spread illness to your family. If you carry pathogens to the hospital or office, you may spread infection to vulnerable clients. For this reason, some health-care facilities ask direct-care staff members to leave their uniforms and shoes at work. Although this policy does not usually apply to administrative staff, it is a still good idea. Wearing a uniform or lab coat only at work limits the chance of transmitting harmful organisms both at work and outside. A uniform or lab coat also looks professional, is easy to launder, and protects your own clothes.

Medical Asepsis
Medical asepsis is killing germs *after they leave* the body. The purpose is to reduce or control the number of microorganisms; it does not completely eliminate them. We practise medical asepsis in our daily lives every time we wash our hands, use a tissue when we cough or sneeze, or clean countertops with a disinfectant after preparing food. Medical asepsis should be practised in every health-care setting.

The Health Office
The office and reception areas must be kept scrupulously clean at all times. You should provide the office cleaning service with guidelines for cleaning, including the use of disinfectants, as required. The more specific the guidelines, the better. A checklist for the cleaning staff to tick off will ensure that all required areas are cleaned and will document what has been done.

The reception area should be well ventilated, and seating should place clients at a comfortable distance from one another. If possible, have two or three groupings of chairs. Ask clients with known infectious conditions not to visit the office, or, if they must be seen, book them at the end of the day. Do not book clients who are susceptible to infections at the same time as someone who may have one, such as a person who thinks she might have the flu. There are times, however, when this information is simply not available. You can only do your best to keep infectious clients away from others, especially older clients and children. *Note*: Do not book a pregnant client at the same time as someone who might have rubella. The rubella virus can be **teratogenic** to the fetus in the first trimester of pregnancy.

Properly clean all instruments, such as stethoscopes, otoscopes, ophthalmoscopes, and thermometers. Some articles must be sterilized and others disinfected (discussed in more detail later in this chapter). Carefully clean the examination rooms between clients. Wipe down the examination bed and counters between clients if you suspect they have an infectious disease or if there has been contamination with any body fluid. Dispose of garbage frequently and properly.

Provide tissues and an adequate number of wastebaskets, and consider putting up a sign asking clients to use tissues when they cough or sneeze. If there are children's toys in the office, they should be the type that can be wiped down daily with a disinfectant. Books for small children are often available in materials that can be wiped clean.

Specimens, such as urine samples, left in the washroom should be handled with gloves. Wipe the counter and any visible spills after a specimen has been removed. Do not leave specimens (e.g., urine) sitting in the washroom where another client may spill them or come in contact with them.

Health-Care Facilities   Follow the principles outlined above, as well as facility guidelines on specific situations. Nosocomial infection is a serious problem in hospitals, leading to considerable morbidity and mortality, particularly among clients who are coping with other illnesses or recovering from surgery.

Hospital Infections

There are several infections that are currently of particular concern in the hospital setting. Infections occurring in the hospital (nosocomial infections) are troublesome; they can easily spread, causing longterm illness or death. Hospitalized clients are usually more susceptible to infection because of compromised immune systems, age, surgery, immobility, or the nature of their illness itself.

Containment and control of infectious outbreaks begins with adherence to strict hand-washing guidelines (discussed below) and other protocol on the part of *all staff* in the hospital. Some hospitals limit and/or track the transfer of clients from one facility to another and/or within one facility. Many hospitals across the country screen selected clients for the presence of these infections organisms on admission; this is particularly so for VRE, MRSA, and *Clostridium difficile*. Individuals with these infections are placed in isolation. Isolation is segregating the client in a private room. There are different levels of isolation dictating which precautions staff and visitors are required to take. The type of isolation depends on the seriousness of the infecting organism and how it is spread (e.g., droplet, airborne, direct contact). Details describing the specific isolation policy to follow will be in the hospital's procedures manual. Polices may involve wearing a mask, gown, and gloves when entering the client's room, for example.

MRSA *Staphylococcus aureus* is usually harmless bacteria found in healthy people. MRSA stands for "methicillin-resistant *Staphylococcus aureus*." It occurs when the staph organism is resistant to methicillin and vancomycin. These are the main antibiotics used to treat infections caused by this bacterium. Vancomycin is another antibiotic sometimes used to treat MRSA, but there has recently been evidence of the strains of *Staphylococcus* that are resistant to that (VRSA).

VRE Vancomycin-resistant *Enterococcus* is another bacterium that is cause for concern in health-care facilities. It occurs when *Enterococcus* mutates and becomes resistant to vancomycin, the primary antibiotic used against that organism. *Enterococcus* infections can occur in the urinary tract, in the blood, and in wounds, including surgical. Emerging strains that are resistant to previously effective antibiotics are very difficult to treat.

Clostridium Difficile Known more commonly as just C. *difficile*, this bacterium is one of the most common causes of often-deadly infections in hospitals and long-term care facilities. It is normally present in the gastrointestinal tract. It commonly emerges in the hospital setting as a pathogen in persons who have had the normal balance of flora in the GI tract altered. It can cause serious illness in immuno-compromised individuals and older adults.

General Precautions The janitorial staff clean most hospital areas thoroughly and regularly. They almost always wear gloves. Garbage cans are emptied frequently, and all areas, including clients' rooms, are dusted and wiped. A thorough *terminal cleaning* is done when a client is discharged.

Staff members who have potentially infectious diseases are encouraged not to come to work, and the general public with infectious conditions are asked not to visit hospitalized clients. Staff members in some facilities are required to receive the flu vaccine annually and keep other required immunizations current. This can be a contentious issue for employees who do not wish to have the flu vaccine, but most hospitals are firm about this policy.

When a facility imposes visiting restrictions, you may be required to inform visitors and to help enforce restrictions. It is not uncommon for long-term care facilities to be **quarantined** if there is an outbreak of the flu or other infectious disease. This may include a total ban on visitors to a single client-care unit or to the entire facility. Such events are stressful for everyone. Clients become anxious about illness and miss the contact with family and friends. They may become demanding and bad tempered. Family members may dismiss the need for quarantine and insist on visiting. They may be upset, argumentative, rude, and sometimes even aggressive. Staff are caught in the middle and may also be coping with increased workloads and longer workdays if some of the staff are ill. Infected clients may be isolated (see discussion later) in an attempt to contain the infection.

quarantine isolating or separating a client, client-care unit, or facility.

Hand Washing Hand washing is probably the single most important component of medical asepsis and the *single most effective method of protecting yourself and others from infection*. How often you wash your hands will depend on the scope of your non-administrative duties. Wash your hands after breaks and before and after preparing an examination room, assisting with a procedure, or assisting a client. Wash them before and after using gloves or handling specimens, waste, or potentially soiled instruments or other articles. Figure 5.2 illustrates the proper hand-washing technique.

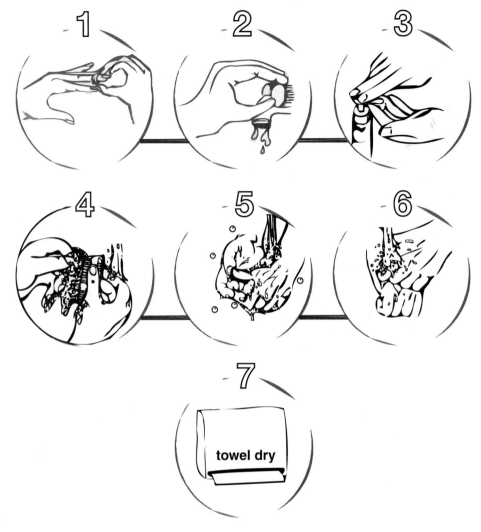

Figure 5.2 Sequence of hand washing

To wash your hands, properly, you need

- soap;
- running water;
- a clean towel; and
- a garbage can.

It really does not matter what type of soap you use. Soaps and detergents are not disinfectants. They emulsify, reducing surface tension to facilitate the removal of soil and organisms. Hands can be cleaned but never sterilized and will always harbour some organisms. Follow these steps:

1. Remove all jewellery, such as rings and watches, as these items can harbour bacteria and other organisms, preventing effective washing. Also, look for breaks in your skin, which provide a portal of entry/exit for organisms. If there are any, it is best to wear gloves.

2. Turn on water, and adjust to a comfortable temperature.

3. Add enough cleansing agent to your hands to create suds.

4. Wet hands, rubbing all areas vigorously. Ensure that you clean nails, fingers, between your fingers, and the front and back of the hands up to the wrist area. Nails need special attention, as do the areas between your fingers. Nail polish, especially if chipped, will also provide a hiding place for organisms. If you frequently touch clients, instruments, or other articles used in client care, it is a good idea not to wear nail polish in the office and to keep your nails reasonably short.

5. Scrub, using good friction, for one to two minutes.

6. Rinse off all soap, preferably by putting your hands under the running water fingers first and moving your hands up under the running water.

7. Dry your hands, again beginning at your fingertips and patting them dry up to the wrist.

8. Using the towel, turn off the taps.

9. Discard the soiled towel.

Remember: It is the friction and the running water that does the job.

The steps above describe a medical hand wash. A surgical scrub uses a slightly more effective cleansing agent, takes longer, and uses a more thorough technique.

Surgical Asepsis   *Surgical asepsis* is an extension of medical asepsis, otherwise known as sterilization. The goal is to destroy all pathogens before they can enter the body. An example is the sterilization of surgical instruments before an operation. No pathogens remain on the instruments, and so none are introduced into the body.

Sterilization uses physical or chemical procedures to destroy all microbial life, including highly resistant bacterial endospores. Sterilization of various objects and instruments is the primary method used in health care to protect clients from **contamination** with pathogens. Without this process, a client's risk of developing infection would be very high.

If you work in a hospital, you will not likely sterilize equipment, but you may be responsible for ordering sterile equipment and for maintaining stocks of sterile supplies. In some health-care offices, one person, often a nurse, is responsible for disinfecting and sterilizing instruments and equipment for reuse. In many practices, however, all staff share this responsibility. Some articles are sterilized, and others are disinfected. In either case, the first step is thorough cleansing.

Sterile Technique   All health procedures need to be carried out, and all sterile material must be handled, in such a way as to prevent contamination. This is called **sterile technique** (**sterile** means completely free from pathogens). For example, a nurse changing a surgical dressing would use sterile technique when opening the dressing tray, handling the instruments, and cleaning and redressing the wound. She might or might not wear sterile gloves, depending on the technique used, but would scrupulously avoid touching any part of the instruments or dressing considered sterile.

Sanitizing, Disinfecting, and Sterilizing

Three levels of hygiene are generally used in health-care facilities: **sanitization**, **disinfection**, and **sterilization**. These terms can be confusing because definitions overlap.

contamination   the presence of pathogens on an object.

sterile technique   methods to avoid contamination of sterile materials.

sterile   completely free of pathogens.

sanitization   removal of gross contaminants and some microorganisms from instruments, skin, and so on; the lowest level of medical hygiene.

disinfection   a more thorough removal of contaminants than sanitization but less thorough than sterilization.

sterilization   the process of destroying all microorganisms, including bacterial endospores and viruses. This is the highest level of cleanliness.

Sanitization and *disinfection*, for example, are sometimes used interchangeably. To disinfect, by definition, is to free an article or a substance from harmful organisms. Sanitization, disinfection, and sterilization all destroy microorganisms, but disinfection is more effective than sanitization in destroying a wider variety of more resistant organisms. Sterilization is a process that kills virtually all organisms and is the highest level or most effective cleansing process. Surgical instruments must be sterilized.

The specific health setting determines how many and what types of instruments require sanitization, disinfection, or sterilization and how often. In a dental office, for example, you may have to process instruments through all three levels of cleansing several times daily; a simple check-up may require treating a variety of instruments. A family physician's office, using fewer instruments, may sanitize and disinfect articles daily, but sterilize only certain instruments every couple of days. All offices using nondisposable equipment will have a protocol for cleaning, disinfecting, and sterilizing instruments, but protocols, solutions, and methods of sterilization will vary with the type of practice.

Disposable instruments and examination and dressing trays are popular and reduce the need for sterilization. For example, most health-care facilities use temperature-taking devices with disposable components. Offices and facilities using disposable tools must consider their effectiveness and convenience against the cost.

Sanitization

The word *sanitary* means "clean," and it comes from a Latin root meaning "health," showing the importance of cleanliness to maintaining health. Sanitizing is the first step in the cleansing process. It is necessary to sanitize instruments and other devices used in client procedures. As well as removing some pathogenic organisms, sanitizing articles removes blood, other fluids, tissue, and debris from surgical instruments and is crucial in preparing instruments to be sterilized. Articles that come in contact only with intact skin—with the exception of mucous membranes—may require only sanitization; however, that does not prevent a health office from using higher level disinfectant solutions. (If an article has been used on a client with an infectious condition, more thorough cleansing is needed.)

Sanitizers (solutions used for sanitizing) are specially formulated, nonabrasive, low-sudsing detergents with a neutral pH. These detergents are effective in removing fats and oils and help remove bacteria and other debris. Stronger detergents can damage instruments and other articles.

sanitizer a substance that significantly reduces the bacterial population in an inanimate environment but does not destroy all bacteria or other microorganisms.

Sanitize instruments as soon as possible after use to prevent fluids from crusting or drying. If you do not have time to sanitize immediately, rinse instruments under cold water (hot water may cause blood to solidify), and place them in an appropriate solution, such as an enzyme detergent with anti-rust properties. Always wear gloves when sanitizing instruments.

Start by rinsing articles thoroughly and carefully in cold water. To avoid injury, always check for sharp instruments (referred to as **sharps**), such as scissors, scalpel blades, and needles. Properly dispose of scalpel blades and needles in a special container (discussed below). Separate other sharp instruments, such as scissors, curettes, and pointed forceps. Clean each instrument separately. Make sure that you clean all surfaces of each instrument. (Any debris left on an article will impede sterilization because it blocks part of the instrument's surface area from the sterilizing agent.) Open movable instruments, such as forceps and scissors, and carefully check all surfaces. A small brush, such as a toothbrush, is helpful. The instruments may be slippery; so, concentrate on what you are

sharp any instrument with a sharp edge or point, such as a scalpel, scissors, or a needle.

doing and do not rush. Place each sanitized instrument carefully in a designated area, still separate from the other instruments, to dry.

Disinfection   As previously noted, disinfection is a term that can be broadly used in health care to refer to the removal of organisms from objects. Usually, it refers to the process of further removing pathogens from articles that have been sanitized. Disinfection uses stronger **disinfectant** solutions/chemicals than those used for sanitization. Become familiar with solutions used in your occupational setting, and follow office policy and manufacturers' directions when disinfecting items.

disinfectant   a chemical substance that destroys or eliminates specific species of infectious microorganisms. It is not usually effective against bacterial spores.

Chemical Disinfection   Chemical disinfection is used for heat-sensitive equipment that may be damaged by high temperatures. Chemical disinfection is not as reliable as boiling or sterilization. All instruments immersed in a chemical disinfectant must be absolutely clean and dry. Wet instruments will dilute the solution, and debris may impede complete exposure of the instrument to the chemical, thus rendering the disinfection process ineffective. Exposure to air can also interfere with the action of some solutions. Containers for soaking instruments should have a lid. It is easy to forget to replace the lid when you add an instrument, but an open container can mean ineffective disinfection. Pay particular attention to the disinfectant solution itself. It must be stored at the proper temperature and used and diluted accurately according to manufacturer's directions. All solutions have a shelf life, after which they begin to lose their disinfecting properties. Diluted solutions should be carefully dated and replaced appropriately.

Any instruments that have been chemically disinfected must be thoroughly rinsed before they come into contact with human tissue. If the level of disinfection must be maintained, sterile water is used to rinse them. After being properly disinfected, if an instrument, such as an oral thermometer, needs only to be clean for subsequent uses, it may be rinsed under tap water before each use.

There are disadvantages to chemical disinfection. There is no way to verify the level of disinfection achieved, and the solutions are often very hard on the instruments. However, it is effective for instruments that cannot withstand high-temperature methods of sterilization.

antiseptic   a cleansing agent that can be applied to living tissue to destroy pathogens.

Antiseptics and Disinfectants   *Disinfectant* and **antiseptic** are another pair of terms that can be confusing. Disinfectants and antiseptics both destroy microorganisms. A disinfectant solution, however, is usually considered more potent (that is, it can kill a wider variety of microorganisms) than an antiseptic and is not suitable for use on human tissue. An antiseptic destroys some microorganisms but is not too harsh to use on the skin. Hand washing removes microorganisms from our hands. There are solutions used in health care that are more effective for killing microorganisms than regular soap but are still suitable for use on human tissue. Antiseptic solutions are sometimes referred to as disinfectants, but unlike true disinfectants, they are suitable for use on skin and mucous membranes. (See Table 5.1.) Antiseptics are considered **bacteriostatic**, meaning they reduce or inhibit the number of microorganisms, while disinfectants are considered **bactericidal**, meaning they kill microorganisms. Isopropyl alcohol, for example, is an antiseptic frequently used to swab the skin before giving an injection. (*Note:* There is some controversy over the effectiveness of this practice, but most providers use some sort of cleansing agent. Some use normal saline.) Antiseptics are also used to prepare a client's skin before surgery. Betadine, povidone, and Savlon are other commercially used solutions.

bacteriostatic   reducing or inhibiting the number of microorganisms.

bactericidal   killing microorganisms.

Table 5.1	A Comparison of Antiseptics and Disinfectants
Antiseptic	**Disinfectant**
Bacteriostatic	Bactericidal
May be used on skin and mucous membranes	Not used on skin or mucous membranes
Weaker	Stronger
Examples: isopropyl alcohol, iodophors	Examples: hydrogen peroxide, bleach

In a health office, alcohol or another topical antiseptic is often kept in a dispenser with a retractable lid. Depressing the lid with a cotton ball saturates the ball with the solution. The container must be cleaned frequently and thoroughly and the solution replaced appropriately. Labelling the container with the date the solution was changed and when it should be changed will help you to remember when to change the solution. Other offices will use single use/packaged alcohol swabs, but these are more expensive.

Bleach remains a popular disinfectant and is known as the universal disinfectant. Javex is a familiar brand of bleach. Although most of us have come in contact with household bleach and suffered no skin damage, bleach is irritating, and repeated exposure can damage tissue. A 10 percent solution of bleach and water is very effective for a number of uses. It appears to be effective against most viruses, including HIV. Bleach solutions have a short shelf life when diluted and have corrosive properties.

Sterilization

Chemical Sterilization   Chemical sterilization is used for heat-sensitive equipment that may be damaged by high temperatures. A chemical classified as a **sterilant**, rather than a disinfectant, must be used. The sterilant must be used within its shelf life, usually one to four weeks. The solution must be carefully protected from contamination. Effective cold sterilization requires a thorough cleansing of instruments prior to processing because blood and organic debris may inactivate chemical germicides or shield microorganisms from the sterilization process. Examples of sterilants include chlorine (which requires a minimum of six hours), formaldehyde 6 percent solution (exposure time varies), and Cidex (which requires an exposure time of at least 10 hours). The effectiveness of chemical sterilization remains controversial.

sterilant   a substance that destroys or eliminates all forms of microbial life in an inanimate environment.

Moist Heat   Boiling instruments was previously thought to be a foolproof method. Indeed, most microorganisms are killed by exposure to boiling water (temperature 100°C) for 30 minutes. This is usually suitable for instruments that will not penetrate body tissue or be used on open wounds. However, some viruses and spores can survive at this temperature. Thus, moist heat is not a method of true sterilization.

Dry Heat   Dry-heat sterilization involves exposure to temperatures of 160°C to 170°C for at least two hours. The specific times and temperatures must be determined for each type of material being sterilized. This method, which can be used for substances and articles such as powders and glass, will penetrate parts of instruments that cannot be disassembled, and it does not corrode instruments. However, heat penetration is slow

Figure 5.3   The steam autoclave

and sometimes uneven. It is less efficient than moist heat and requires longer times and higher temperatures. It should be restricted to items that are unsuitable for exposure to moist heat.

The Steam Autoclave   Steam sterilization uses pressurized steam at 121°C to 132°C for 30 to 40 minutes. This type of heat kills all microbial cells, including spores, which are normally heat resistant.

autoclave   a device using steam for sterilization.

The **autoclave** (see Figure 5.3) is one of the most common sterilizers used in health care. There are many varieties and sizes available that are suitable for health offices and health-care facilities. The autoclave works on the principle of steam under pressure. Temperatures reach 124°C. This kills all pathogens, including spores. The autoclave is safe, convenient, dependable, and inexpensive to operate. The main disadvantage is that a number of instruments cannot withstand the high temperatures. Autoclaving also dulls instruments and causes deterioration of some rubbers and plastics.

Articles may be placed in the autoclave wrapped or unwrapped. Unwrapped articles are effectively sterilized in 20 minutes, while small bundles take 30 minutes, and larger bundles take up to 40 minutes.

You must carefully follow the directions that come with the particular autoclave you are using. Most autoclaves have automatic cycles, reducing the chances of mishaps such as superheated steam or wet steam. Wet steam can result from failure to preheat the auto-clave chamber. Bundles and articles remain wet even after completion of the drying cycle and are susceptible to picking up bacteria when they are removed from the autoclave. Putting cold instruments into the autoclave chamber also results in damp instruments and undermines sterilization. Condensation appears on the instrument, similar to the droplets that fog a person's glasses on coming in from the cold. Be careful not to open the door of the autoclave too widely during the drying cycle as this can also result in condensation.

If articles are to be kept for some time before use, they should be wrapped before autoclaving to keep out dust and pathogens. Wrapping materials vary and will affect how long the bundle may be considered sterile. Trays may be wrapped in disposable materials. Do not use torn or punctured wrapping material. In hospitals, however, wrappers are often repaired and then reused. Wrapping articles for the autoclave is as important as the autoclaving itself. All surfaces of all articles must be exposed to the steam. Therefore, the instruments, such as scissors, forceps, and needle-drivers, need to be in the open position inside their wrapping to allow the steam to penetrate the hinged portion. Make sure sharp instruments do not pierce the material they are wrapped in. If you are preparing a dressing tray for autoclaving, place a towel between the metal tray and the instruments. Most bundles or instruments are double wrapped, that is, wrapped in two different coverings or in one covering of double thickness. The procedure for wrapping trays and bundles may vary with the occupational setting. If you are required to prepare such trays, you should be given specific instructions.

Some models have indicators that verify sterilization, assuring providers of the validity of the process. Indicators work in different ways: they may respond to conditions indicating effective sterilization by melting or changing colour, for example. There are also processing indicators, which may be biological or chemical, that indicate that a batch of articles has been through a cycle. Other indicators specify that the correct time has elapsed or the correct temperature has been reached. Almost all facilities use autoclave tape, which contains a dye that changes colour in response to very high temperatures. This tape does not verify the sterility of a bundle, only that it has been subjected to a sterilization process.

Storage of Wrapped Supplies   Controversy remains about how long autoclaved articles remain sterile. Generally, double-wrapped bundles are considered sterile for up to four weeks. Mark each bundle with the expiry date, and store the oldest packs at the front to ensure that they will be used first. Keep them covered in a dry, dust-free area. An upper cupboard in an office or clinic is suitable. In the hospital, each floor will have a cart covered in plastic or canvas containing sterilized trays and so on. Any package that becomes wet is considered contaminated, as is any package with a broken seal. If there is any doubt at all, consider the bundle contaminated.

Standard Precautions

Standard Precautions protect both health professionals and clients from cross-contamination from a variety of pathogens, primarily those transmitted through blood and other body fluids. Standard Precautions, developed by the Centers for Disease Control and Prevention in the United States, are internationally implemented. These guidelines expand on similar standards developed in the 1980s, called Universal Precautions, and incorporate another system called Body Fluid Precautions.

Standard Precautions stress that it is virtually impossible to determine who is infected and who is not. Even clients who have tested negative for infections, such as HIV infection, may turn out to have the disease. Therefore, you should apply Standard Precautions *at all times regardless of the client's age, gender, diagnosis, or your level of familiarity with the client.* Consider blood and all body fluids, except sweat, as potentially infectious. Major concerns include HIV, hepatitis B (HBV), and other blood-borne infections, such as hepatitis A and C.

Standard Precautions involve the use of protective barriers, such as gloves, gowns, aprons, masks, or protective eyewear, to reduce your risk of exposure to infection. Not all measures are intended for all health professionals. As a health office professional with primarily administrative duties, you are at lower risk than are other health professionals. Your risk will vary, however, with your job setting and responsibilities. Specific sources of potential contamination for the health office professional are discussed later in this chapter. You must assess your own risk factors and follow the appropriate guidelines. Remember that a single exposure can result in serious consequences. It is better to be safe than sorry.

Use Standard Precautions (summarized in Table 5.2) when you expect to come in contact with one of the following:

- *Blood:* Be mindful of the presence of blood not only when it is visible (e.g., cleaning up spilled blood) but also when cleaning instruments and dressing trays or disposing of needles, linens, and gowns. Wear gloves whether or not you can see blood.

- *Body fluids:* Avoid contact with all body fluids, secretions, and excretions, with the exception of sweat. Urine, feces, nasal secretions, tears, sputum, saliva, and emesis (vomited material) can all be possible sources of infection. The risk is intensified if they are contaminated with blood.

- *Nonintact skin:* If you or a client has a cut, scratch, or any other break in the skin, the potential for contamination is greater. Any break in the skin is regarded as a breach in the body's first line of defence.

- *Mucous membranes:* Be aware of any possible situation where you might be exposed to a client's mucous membranes or to tissues, dressing materials, and so on that may have been contaminated with secretions from mucous membranes.

Gloves   When should you wear gloves? In some situations, it is your decision, based on your comfort level. Some health professionals wear gloves for nearly all client contact, others only when there is a more specific reason. Gloves may offend some clients who feel you are labelling them as unclean. However, as gloves have become more common in health care, people are getting used to them. You can explain that wearing gloves protects the client as well as yourself. There are a few guidelines about gloves:

- Wear gloves when touching body fluids, secretions, excretions, and contaminated items.

Table 5.2   Standard Precautions

Gloves: Wear gloves before coming in contact with blood, mucous membranes, nonintact skin, or body fluids. Change them after each procedure.

Hand Washing: Wash hands after glove removal, between clients, or after coming in contact with any body fluids or potentially contaminated surfaces.

Gown/Apron: Wear gowns or aprons during procedures in which you may be splashed with body fluids.

Mask/Eye Protection: Wear masks and eye protection during procedures in which you may be splashed with body fluids.

Scoop: Do not recap needles by hand. Recap needles by scooping the cap off the surface with the needle itself.

Sharps: Use designated sharps disposal containers to dispose of all needles, scalpel blades, or other sharp objects.

Wastes/Linens: Dispose of all wastes and linens in accordance with local policies and law.

Resuscitation: Keep mouthpieces and equipment on hand to use for emergency resuscitation to minimize direct contact.

- Change gloves between clients, between tasks and procedures on the same client, and after contact with material that may contain infectious organisms. *Never* simply wash your hands with your gloves on and proceed to another task or client.
- Remove gloves after use and before touching uncontaminated items and surfaces. Wear gloves for a specific task, not for a long time.
- Dispose of gloves appropriately, taking care to remove them without touching the outside surface (see Figure 5.4).

Wearing gloves may make picking up instruments, cleaning them, and disposing of sharps more difficult because the gloves may alter your sense of touch and reduce your dexterity. Work carefully and methodically when performing tasks with gloves on. Remember that even if you are wearing gloves, a puncture is a potential portal for infection.

> Be alert for latex allergy. Clinical signs include
> - skin rash;
> - hives;
> - flushing;
> - itching; and
> - symptoms of asthma, such as shortness of breath, itchy red eyes, and runny nose.
>
> If you or a client is allergic to latex, switch to nonlatex gloves.

Procedure for Removing Gloves   It is vital that you not touch the outside surface of the gloves you are wearing if there has been contact or even potential contact with a contaminated substance. Once you touch the outside of the glove, you are no more protected than if you had not worn gloves at all. It is important to wash your hands after removing your gloves. Do not rely on gloves alone to protect you from infectious contact.

1. Optional: If your gloves are soiled with blood or other secretions, some recommend rinsing them before removal. Others argue that wetting the gloves only makes it more likely that you will transfer contaminants to your hands during removal. It is your decision.

2. Grasp the glove on your right hand by the cuff. Slowly pull the glove down over your hand, turning it inside out. (The contaminated portion of the glove is now on the inside. The part of the glove that was against your uncontaminated hand is on the outside.)

3. Holding the removed glove in your left hand, grasp the inside of the other glove just below the cuff, taking care not to touch the outside.

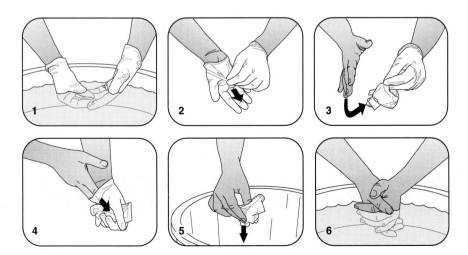

Figure 5.4   Removing gloves

4. Pull the glove off and over the first glove, which you are still holding in your left hand. Now, the second glove is covering the first glove. Only the outside portion of the second glove is visible.

5. Dispose of the gloves in an appropriate receptacle.

6. Always wash your hands after removing gloves.

Mask, Eye Protection, and Face Shield

You may require this type of protection if you work in a dental office and are cross trained to assist at the chair-side on occasion—otherwise use of this equipment is not likely to be needed. However, do wear them if you think you are at risk of being splashed or sprayed with blood, body fluids, secretions, or excretions. Conceivably, it could happen if you are washing contaminated materials or instruments.

Keep mouthpieces, resuscitation bags, or other devices with your emergency equipment in case you need to give mouth-to-mouth resuscitation.

Gowns or Aprons

Protect your skin and clothing if you are helping with any procedure that is likely to generate splashes or sprays of blood or other body fluids. Remove the soiled gown immediately after use, and as with gloves, dispose of it according to office/agency guidelines, again avoiding contact with the exposed surface. (Touch only the part that was against your body.)

Equipment Used for Client Care

Handle carefully any equipment that may have touched blood and other body fluids; remember that contamination might not be visible. Instruments commonly used in a physician's office include various types of scissors; suture equipment, such as a needle-driver; and a variety of forceps. Be especially careful when handling anything sharp, such as suture needles, injection needles, and scalpel blades. Always remove a scalpel blade with forceps, and *never* try to recap a contaminated needle by hand (holding the needle in one hand and the cap in the other). Dispose of the needle in the proper needle disposal unit without capping it. Most needles used today have a safety mechanism to protect the person disposing of the needle. Some models have a sheath over the needle, in other models the needle retracts into the barrel of the syringe. There should be a disposal unit in every examination room. When full, these must be properly disposed of following guidelines for biohazardous waste. Do not overfill sharps containers. If you must walk with a needle or other sharp instrument in your hand, point it away from your body and away from other people.

Specula, which are used for Pap smears, should be rinsed and cleaned only when wearing gloves and then put into an appropriate solution until they are sterilized.

If there is broken glass anywhere, wear gloves to sweep it up. *Never* pick it up with your hands.

Linen

Properly handle, transport, and process used linen soiled with blood and other body fluids, ensuring that you avoid contact with your clothing and other surfaces. When

Tip

It is the responsibility of the user to dispose of sharp instruments, such as lances and needles. However, do not assume that the provider has done so. Always look carefully for anything sharp, and isolate or dispose of it before you clean up a tray or anything else that has been used for a client procedure.

changing the linen or paper on an examination bed, wear gloves and roll the sheet up and away from you. Hold it at arm's length when carrying it to the nearest disposal area. Some offices double-bag linens in specially marked laundry bags.

The Health Environment Use the recommended disinfectant to wipe all potentially contaminated surfaces with the recommended disinfectant: for example, countertops, the examination bed, chairs (if soiled), the sink, and taps. Throw out all contaminated paper towels in the appropriate container, usually a plastic bag that is marked "biohazard."

Assisting with Examinations/Procedures Some physicians may ask you to assist with a variety of assessments, examinations, and procedures that are potential sources of infection. Assess each situation carefully, and use protective barriers, such as gloves, appropriately.

Well-baby assessments, for example, could involve weighing an infant and perhaps taking measurements, such as length, and head and chest circumferences. This could cause exposure to urine, feces, and other body substances. Another possible risk for contamination may occur if you are assisting with a procedure and are required to receive contaminated instruments from the physician.

Obtaining and labelling specimens is a potential source of contamination. Urine specimens left in the bathroom or in the examination room must be labelled, requisitioned, and prepared to be sent to a lab or tested in the health office. You may be asked to do routine dipstick testing for such things as sugar, protein, and ketones. In some offices, obtaining a finger prick for hemoglobin or blood sugar may be allocated to you as a designated task. You may be asked to assist in taking a Pap smear, throat swab, sputum specimen, or stool sample.

Cleaning up instrument trays may be a routine responsibility for you. One cannot overemphasize the importance of avoiding pricks from needles, scalpels, and other sharp instruments. Any needle or blade may have microscopic amounts of contaminated blood. Do not assume that the person using the instruments or needles has disposed of them properly. Be responsible for checking for forgotten or misplaced sharps. The following is a story of an actual occurrence in a health office:

> Lina worked for a busy pediatrician, Dr. Gonsalvez. Holly, a 16-year-old single mother, brought her five-day-old son in for a check-up and blood testing. Holly was staying at a women's shelter, had no fixed address, and was not known in the community. Lina was cleaning up after Holly and the baby left. In gathering up some cotton swabs left on the counter, she pricked her finger with a lance that had been accidentally left under the cotton swabs. The lance had been used to obtain blood from the baby's heel for a test. Lina's finger was bleeding. Although Holly was in a high-risk category because of her history of drug abuse, among other things, she had refused to be tested for HIV. Lina had little choice but to submit to a regimen of prophylactic treatment for potential exposure to hepatitis and HIV.

Tip

Be especially mindful of any contact with potentially infected sources if you have sores, open lesions, cuts, or chapped hands.

Infectious Diseases of Particular Concern

As mentioned earlier in the chapter, hepatitis A and B are infectious diseases that can be contracted by health professionals. The other disease to note is HIV.

HIV and AIDS are not the same thing. AIDS (acquired immune deficiency syndrome) is the advanced stage of the disease caused by HIV (human immunodeficiency virus). Not all HIV-infected persons go on to develop AIDS. HIV attacks the body's immune system and nerve cells. Eventually, the body's immune system deteriorates so that the body has no resistance to infection. The nervous system degenerates as well. When symptoms appear, the disease or syndrome is referred to as AIDS. Most clients with AIDS are burdened with numerous opportunistic infections, ranging from a variety of fungal and bacterial infections to cancer. HIV has a very long incubation period; some infected individuals do not develop full-blown AIDS for more than 10 years after they have been infected.

Modes of transmission include unprotected sexual intercourse; shared needles or other drug equipment; tattooing, skin piercing, and acupuncture with contaminated equipment; injury from a needle or sharp instrument contaminated by blood; renal dialysis or tissue transplantation; transfusion of blood or blood products; and transfer from an infected mother during pregnancy, delivery, or breastfeeding. Because HIV does not survive well outside the body, it cannot be transmitted through the more routine routes discussed earlier under The Chain of Infection. Normal daily contact with an infected person poses no risk.

Response to Exposure or Possible Exposure If you think you or someone else in your office may have been exposed to HIV, act promptly. Take the following steps immediately:

- Do not panic.
- If there is a cut or prick, allow it to bleed freely.
- Then wash the wound with soap and water.
- Some recommend swabbing the wound liberally with 70 percent alcohol.
- For splashes to the nose, mouth, or skin, liberally splash or rinse the area with water.
- If the eyes or other mucous membranes are exposed, flush clean with sterile water, saline, or a sterile irrigant.
- Notify your immediate supervisor promptly.

Fill out a WCB accident report form. The occurrence should be reported to the manager of the facility or office, the occupational health coordinator, and the employee health department, if these exist, and your Ministry of Health. If you are considered high risk for exposure to HIV your health-care provider will advise you about the risks and benefits of embarking on a postexposure prophylactic course of treatment. There is an excellent website at the end of this chapter that details living with HIV, how to interact with HIV-positive individuals and preventative measures.

Interacting with HIV-Positive Clients Some health professionals are uncomfortable interacting with people with HIV, let alone having physical contact. Knowledge may counteract fear. Remember that you cannot contract AIDS from casual, everyday contact, such as shaking hands or simple touching. Normally, you run no risk in, for example, assisting a client to prepare for an examination or taking blood pressure and vital signs.

Moral judgments and social stigma have also affected attitudes toward AIDS. You must be comfortable interacting with the client as a person before you can be comfortable interacting professionally. Remember that, like all your clients, individuals with HIV or AIDS are people first, not disease-carrying entities. They are coping not only with a frightening, potentially fatal disease but often with ostracism by friends and acquaintances. The best thing you can do for someone with either of these diagnoses is to treat them with respect, warmth, empathy, and acceptance.

❼ PREVENTING INJURY IN THE HEALTH OFFICE

To keep your clients safe, you need to make sure that the physical arrangement of the office is safe and also to plan safe practices, such as ensuring that children are properly supervised. The first step is to understand factors that put people at special risk.

Personal Risk Factors

Childhood   Every growth and development stage has certain typical characteristics. Understanding these patterns will help alert you to potential dangers.

Infants   Infants are helpless and depend on others to meet all of their needs, including safety. They are curious, like to explore their environment, and have no concept of danger. Infants love to touch and taste; they will grab anything they can reach and put it in their mouth. They are at risk of aspirating foreign objects, being poisoned, and falling.

- If you are weighing a baby, do not take your eyes off her. Even turning your back for a second can result in a fall.
- Never leave an infant unattended, even in an infant seat.
- If you notice a parent or caregiver turning her attention away from the baby, for example, when the baby is on the examination table, gently remind her of the dangers.
- Keep dangerous objects out of the baby's reach. An object is dangerous if it is
  - small enough to swallow;
  - sharp or pointed; or
  - toxic.

(Keep paper out of the baby's reach, too. It probably will not harm the baby, but it will do the paper no good.)

Young Children   As children learn to stand and walk, they greatly increase their mobility. But their sense of danger lags behind. They are curious and imitative and enjoy navigating new environments, including open doors and stairways. Their ability to climb puts them at risk of falling, and increasing problem-solving skills allow them to reach places you might have thought were secure. They love to investigate drawers and cupboards and will often find dangerous objects. Many will still put anything in their mouth, leading to choking or poisoning. They like to mimic others; for example, a child may find a soiled needle and use it to imitate the doctor.

Never allow a young child (under the age of eight) to be in an examination room alone. Watch the child who can open doors and wander off. Keep the lower shelves in the examination room locked or free of anything that might cause injury to a child, such as instruments, sharp objects, and things that can be ingested. Be alert for chairs that the child might climb on to reach a counter, shelf, or examination bed.

If the parent is with the doctor, someone should be available to watch the child either in the examination room or in the reception area. All too often, a parent will leave a child in the reception area, feeling that he is safe because he is occupied with a toy or a book. But children are mercurial, and when the toy loses their interest, they may take up something more dangerous. It only takes a moment for an injury to occur. Normally, you will not have time to assume the responsibility of watching a child.

All toys in the reception area or examination room should meet provincial or territorial safety standards and should be safe for children under three.

School-age children are more aware of danger but, depending on their age and upbringing, often lack the knowledge and awareness to meet all of their own safety needs. Their increased motor skills put more objects within their reach; however, they are increasingly receptive to explanations of danger. Keep in mind, however, that children with developmental delays may be at increased risk.

Visual and Hearing Impairment

Older adults are particularly prone to diminishing vision and hearing, but these difficulties can occur at any age. Do not assume that only senior clients suffer from these impairments. Often, people will underplay their disabilities, putting themselves at risk of injury.

Mobility Impairment

Mobility difficulties can range from the most obvious to the subtlest of impairments. The client may, for the most part, manage well and independently. Sometimes anxiety or a current health problem can turn a normally manageable impairment into a problem. Be especially alert for clients with impaired balance, weakness, or an unsteady gait.

Any client who has had a procedure requiring sedation should be assessed for the ability to navigate independently. Sedation may leave clients with slower reflexes such that they are unable to move quickly to avoid injury. Pre-existing mobility problems increase the risk. For procedures requiring sedation, always suggest the client bring along a family member or friend.

Altered Cognition

Some older, ill, or developmentally delayed clients may tend to be confused. What may normally be only mild confusion may be compounded by anxiety and stress in the health office. Whatever the cause, confused or very anxious people may not take in information properly or may misinterpret instructions. They may have poor judgment and fail to recognize danger. For example, a client may forget an assistive device and fall.

Fatigue

When people are overtired, accidents happen. People lose dexterity and agility and are more likely to drop things or stumble. Clients may misunderstand instructions or take the wrong medication.

It is not only clients who can become overtired. Try to show up at work rested. If you are tired, be doubly careful about handling sharp, heavy, or delicate objects, and double-check your work. If you sense that you are reaching the point where you can no longer work reliably, tell your employer. It is not heroic to keep working through your fatigue if you make a potentially dangerous mistake, such as handing someone the wrong medicine or dropping a sharp into the wrong container.

Overconfidence   Some people, particularly older adults with recent impairments, think they can do more than they really can. For example, a person with impaired balance might insist on walking out to the taxi or car without assistance. An understanding, tactful offer of help may be easily accepted.

Environmental Risk Factors

You will be largely responsible for maintaining a safe environment in the health office and reception area. Make sure the environment meets the needs of your specific clients; a pediatrician's office will have different safety needs than a gerontologist's. Be continually alert for areas you can improve upon. Listen to clients' complaints or suggestions.

Lighting   Dim lights in the reception area and halls may predispose clients to falls. Find a balance between dimness and bright, glaring lights.

Noise Level   Children and teens do not appear to mind a noisy environment, but loud noise may be irritating and distracting to adults and may hurt older people's ears or interfere with hearing aids. It may also reduce their ability to concentrate or to understand instructions. If you play music, keep it quiet enough so that people can be heard clearly without raising their voices.

Providing a Safe Environment

- Keep the floors clean and dry, especially during rainy or winter weather. It is fine to post a sign asking clients to remove their boots—but few will. No one wants to remove their boots to walk on a cold and perhaps wet or damp floor. Older people are at increased risk of falling because of mobility problems, poor balance, slower reflexes, and osteoporosis.

- If spills occur, clean them up without delay.

- Pay extra attention to clients with altered vision or mobility problems.

- Periodically check the reception area for scattered books, magazines, and toys.

- Avoid loose scatter rugs. Clients can easily slip and fall or trip over the edges. If you must have an area rug, have a smaller one that fits under a coffee table or some other heavy, fixed structure.

- Arrange furniture, such as coffee tables, out of the way of traffic.

- Do not rearrange the room too often. The unfamiliar layout can be a barrier to clients with poor vision.

Future Trends

Health Canada, through the Public Health Agency of Canada, sets guidelines for the private and public sectors to prepare for future disease outbreaks. The health-care sector and the workplace must have contingency plans in place that balance health safety with minimal adverse effects on the Canadian economy.

The mobile population of people who visit Canada or seek permanent residency affects the health of Canadians with diseases they may bring into the country. Health authorities are committed to monitoring the health of immigrants and visitors by identifying and screening for communicable diseases and providing prompt treatment.

>

Immunization remains the single most effect method of preventing disease. Essential immunizations, such as those for MMR, pertussis, varicella, diphtheria, tetanus, and hepatitis, are provided under the health plan in all provinces and territories. Although vaccinations are given to the majority of children, many adolescents and adults are under-vaccinated, particularly against hepatitis B, influenza, and pneumonococcal disease. Immunization protocols sometimes change (such as in Ontario in 2011)—be sure you are aware of the current immunization programs in your jurisdiction.

In 2007, a new vaccine research and development facility opened at the University of Saskatchewan. Its mandate is to develop vaccines for humans and animals. This level 3 laboratory is one of a few in the world to work with livestock. The lab will train medical doctors, veterinarians, and immunologists to deal with emerging diseases and find preventative and curative solutions.

Newer and improved vaccines are constantly being both researched and developed. For example, a newer versions of meningococcal vaccine is now widely in use across Canada—the previous vaccine was ineffective on both infants and small children. The newer version is effective and is recommended for all children under age five and for adolescents and young adults. Although there are several types of meningococcal disease, this new vaccine provides protection against Group C bacteria, which is most common in children and teens. In addition the Canadian Pediatric Society has recently advocated for public funding for a vaccine that would protect babies from rotavirus, the most common cause of diarrhea in babies and children. Recommendations for HPV are continuously evolving. Currently the NACL is recommending that Ceravix and Gardasil be administered simultaneously with other adolescent vaccines in an attempt to ensure that adolescents and young adults receive the vaccines as recommended. Funding for new and more effective vaccines varies across the country. In 2011 Ontario started funding an oral form of the rotavirus vaccine, as well as a second dose of varicella vaccine against chickenpox.

Probiotics is a new therapy to fight disease, including infectious diseases. It involves the colonization and administration of live bacteria to combat disease. One strain, *Lactobacillus,* has been shown to be effective in treating children who have infectious diarrhea. Some studies show that probiotics and prebiotics have some effect in preventing malignant tumours in the colon of animals.[1] Further research to apply this to humans continues.

Health and safety standards must continue to evolve to meet future challenges. Nosocomial infections are an ongoing concern. Risk-management programs in health-care facilities are continuously developing policies and procedures to reduce the risks of acquired in-hospital infections. Vigilance on the part of all hospital staff, screening of individuals who carry infectious organisms, and stringent isolation policies are instrumental in preventing and containing infections. As well, caring for individuals in the home whenever possible has been shown to reduce the chances of infection for the patient.

---

[1] *American Journal of Clinical Nutrition*, Vol. 85, No. 2, February 2007, 488–496.

SUMMARY

1. Quality assurance is a systematic process of checking to see whether a product or service meets requirements. Excellence in the health-care environment includes prompt treatment and reporting of laboratory tests, accurate prescriptions, reasonable waiting times, guidance in emergencies, and proper follow-up. Hospitals have formal quality assurance plans; health offices may use a more informal system.

2. Workers' compensation and occupational health and safety legislation together provide a safe environment for employees. Workers' compensation sets out rights and responsibilities for employers and employees, including the conditions under which

an employee may refuse work perceived as unsafe. Workplace Hazardous Materials Information System is federal legislation ensuring that employees are knowledgeable about hazardous materials in the work place.

3. Health-care settings pose risks of infection for both professionals and clients, some of whom are particularly vulnerable. Simple steps like wearing gloves, providing tissues and wastebaskets, and handling sharps properly can prevent exposure and break the chain of infection.

4. Disease-causing microorganisms include bacteria, viruses, fungi, and protozoa. Transmission of infection requires a pathogen, a host, a portal of exit, a mode of transmission, a portal of entry, and a susceptible recipient host.

5. Health professionals should keep routine immunizations up to date and should be vaccinated for common diseases, including the flu and hepatitis.

6. Proper hand washing is probably the single most effective way to protect yourself and your clients from infection. Wash your hands before and after preparing an examination room, assisting with a procedure, or assisting a client. Wash them after using gloves or handling specimens, waste, or potentially soiled instruments or other articles.

7. Levels of hygiene range from sanitization through intermediate-level disinfection to sterilization. The level needed depends on the material and the conditions of use. Proper procedure must be followed to insure disinfection or sterility.

8. Wear gloves when touching body fluids, secretions, excretions, and contaminated items. Change gloves between clients and between tasks. Remove gloves carefully to avoid contamination.

9. Consider the risks for injury to your clients, particularly young children, seniors, and those with physical or cognitive impairments. Ensure that all instruments, solutions, and medications are out of children's reach. Never leave a baby alone on a table or scale. Make sure children are supervised. Use proper lighting, and arrange furniture to reduce the risk of falls and other injuries.

Key Terms

active infection 113
acute infection 113
aerobic bacteria 114
anaerobic bacteria 114
antibody 119
antigen 117
antiseptic 126
asepsis 120
asymptomatic 113
autoclave 128
bactericidal 126
bacteriostatic 126
chronic infection 113
contagious or communicable disease 112
contamination 124

disinfectant 126
disinfection 124
exacerbation 113
immunity 112
immunoglobulin 119
infection 112
latent infection 113
local infection 113
microorganism 112
nonpathogenic 114
nosocomial infection 114
opportunistic infection 113
otitis media 113
pathogen 114

quality assurance 108
quarantine 122
recurrent infection 113
relapse 113
remission 113
sanitization 124
sanitizer 125
sharp 125
sterilant 127
sterile technique 124
sterile 124
sterilization 124
systemic infection 113
teratogenic 121
topical 113
virulence 114

Review Questions

1. What is meant by quality medical care?
2. Discuss the relevance of quality assurance in the health office.
3. What is the purpose of an incident report, and who would initiate it in any given situation?
4. Draw a diagram illustrating the chain of infection, and explain each step.
5. Describe how the health office professional should deal with used needles, soiled linen, and dirty surgical instruments.
6. What is a nosocomial infection?
7. Explain the different levels of disinfection.
8. In what circumstances should you wear gloves?
9. Why are small children at risk of injury? How can you reduce the risk in your office?

Application Exercises

1. In small groups, list and discuss all the services and policies you think are important for a high-quality general practice. Consider both clients' and professionals' perspectives in the office. On the basis of your discussions, draw up a quality assurance manual for the office.
2. Using the Public Health Agency of Canada website at the end of the chapter, prepare a reference chart that a health office professional could use for determining when children should be scheduled for immunizations. Research the benefits and risks of childhood immunizations.

   a. Joyce who has a three-month-old baby, decides not to have the child immunized. Discuss your own feelings about this decision. Do you think she is right or wrong in making that decision? Give reasons for your stand.

   b. Compare Ontario's schedule and that used in British Columbia. A 13-month-old and a 2-year-old have joined your Ontario practice from BC. What adjustments would you have to make to merge the two protocols? What adjustments would you have to make for the same children in your practice to accommodate just the Ontario changes, that is, to ensure that the child's immunizations were complete, in accordance with the current protocol?

3. Visit a health-care setting of your choice. (Alternatively, your professor may divide the class into groups and assign a variety of settings.) Prepare by researching the basic elements of WHMIS so that you know what to look for. Find out what materials in each setting are under WHMIS guidelines. How are staff informed about WHMIS? Where do they keep their Material Safety Data Sheets (MSDS)? (If a visit to an occupational setting is not possible, see what you can find by doing an internet search on the setting of your choice.)

4. Jacob, a co-worker on your busy medical unit, neglects to transcribe a doctor's order promptly. As a result, a client misses an important medication. Jacob claims he didn't see the order. You know he did. What would you do?

5. You are the administrative manager in a large family-practice clinic with four administrative assistants. Hanna, one of the administrative assistants, tells you that Jennifer, another administrative assistant, has confided that she may be HIV-positive. Hanna is upset; she does not feel safe working with Jennifer and feels she poses a threat to clients. She challenges you to "do something" or she will. Think of ways that you might effectively handle this situation. State your rationale for each action plan you propose.

6. In small groups, choose a health office setting (dentist, optometrist, urgent-care centre, family physician). Visit one or more offices (perhaps your own physician or dentist), noting the layout of the reception and office areas. Now design an ideal office, specifying layout and types of furniture. Take into account safety from injury, fire safety, employees' comfort, and safety from cumulative stress injury.

7. In small groups review the WCB website in your jurisdiction and in particular review the online forms. Contact your family doctor's office to see what forms they use most frequently. Create a fictitious case of a workplace injury where someone has to make a WSIB claim, including information from the persons family doctor. Download the forms you will need and fill them out using the information in the "case" you created.

Websites of Interest

International Organization for Standardization
www.iso.org/iso/en/ISOOnline.frontpage

WHMIS overview
www.hc-sc.gc.ca/ewh-semt/occup-travail/whmis-simdut/index-eng.php

An online course on WHMIS
www.whmis.net/

The Canadian Centre for Occupational Health and Safety
www.ccohs.ca/

Canada's National Occupational Health and Safety Website
www.canoshweb.org/en/

Association of Workers Compensation Boards of Canada
http://www.awcbc.org/en/*
Click on "Links to WCBs/Commissions" for access to the WCB in your jurisdiction.

Health Canada, TB Prevention and Control
www.hc-sc.gc.ca/pphb-dgspsp/tbpc-latb/index.htmlc

Public Health Agency of Canada: Immunizations and Vaccines
www.phac-aspc.gc.ca/im/is-cv/index-eng.php
This website has several informative links to vaccine protocols and related information. Click on NACI Recommendations for Infants & Children for the current list of recommended childhood immunizations.

Public Health Agency of Canada: Immunizations and Vaccines
http://www.phac-aspc.gc.ca/im/is-vc-eng.php
This website also provides information on provincial and territorial immunization programs.

Hospital For Sick Children: AboutKidsHealth
http://www.aboutkidshealth.ca/En/News/NewsAndFeatures/Pages/Flu-season-2011-2012.aspx
This webpage gives information about the influenza vaccination for children, with links to related articles and other features.

Public Health Agency of Canada: HPV Prevention and Vaccine
www.phac-aspc.gc.ca/std-mts/hpv-vph/hpv-vph-vaccine-eng.php

Dealing with AIDS
http://www.cdnaids.ca/files.nsf/pages/hiv-101/$file/HIV%20101.pdf

New HIV prevention technologies (PowerPoint presentation)
http://www.cdnaids.ca/welcome follow the links

Guidelines for Infection Control in the Physician's Office
http://cme.viha.ca/Hot_Topics/PDFs/Infection_Control_In_Physician_Office_Final.pdf

Chapter 6
Diagnostic Tests

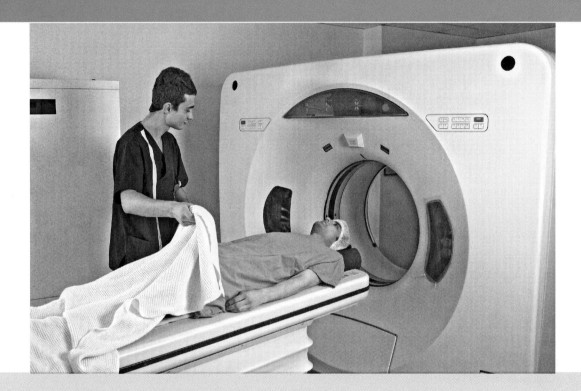

Learning Objectives

On completing this chapter, you will be able to:

1. Describe the role of diagnostic tests in client care.
2. Identify the departments of a laboratory, and list the tests associated with each.
3. Discuss the responsibilities of the administrative health professional with respect to diagnostic tests and procedures.
4. Educate clients about laboratory and diagnostic tests.
5. Demonstrate how to fill in requisitions with the required information.
6. Discuss how to receive and organize test results in the office and in hospital settings.
7. Explain how to deal with abnormal results.

This chapter gives an overview of diagnostic testing and highlights common tests. The purpose is to make you aware of the more commonly ordered tests and of your related responsibilities. Detailed information can be obtained from any laboratory and diagnostic manual. Specific tests are also discussed in context throughout this book.

❶ PURPOSE

MEDICAL PRACTICE IS BASED ON INFORMATION GATHERED FROM A VARIETY OF SOURCES, including client history and physical examinations. Diagnostic testing done by laboratory and diagnostic imaging departments provides another valuable source of information to establish a diagnosis and monitor a client's progress and response to treatment. Tests can visualize and analyze body structures, tissues, and fluids. Tests are an important part of health promotion and disease prevention in that they screen for disease, detect problems early, and facilitate prompt treatment. Diagnostic testing can also be used to establish baseline results for clients undergoing treatment or surgery. It may also be used for legal purposes. Results of lab tests are interpreted by a physician in the context of the client's clinical examination and history. The results may validate or invalidate an initial diagnosis; they may lead the doctor to adjust or change the client's treatment plan; they may provide the welcome information that the client is healthy.

A healthy body is said to be in a state of homeostasis, equilibrium, or balance. Each part of the body that is analyzed or examined has what is called a normal range, or a **reference range**. Results of tests are compared with this range. If they fall above or below this range, further investigation is often warranted. Various abnormal tests may, together with a physical examination and client history, lead to a diagnosis. Tests may be ordered individually or as groups, sometimes referred to as test profiles.

Different laboratories may use different reference ranges depending on the analysis type, reagents used, and client population. Thus, the normal ranges presented in this chapter may not be exactly the same as those used at any given laboratory. Always assess any lab result in the context of that laboratory's normal range.

All laboratories should provide normal ranges with test results and flag abnormal results.

reference range   the normal range; the values expected for a particular test.

❷ TESTING FACILITIES

DIAGNOSTIC TESTING IS DONE IN LICENSED CLINICAL LABORATORIES AND DIAGNOSTIC imaging facilities, both private and within hospitals. A limited number of tests are performed in physicians' offices.

Private laboratories are widespread in Canada. They may be centrally located, with satellite labs in medical buildings or large ambulatory/urgent care clinics. These facilities offer clinical laboratory services, including routine testing on blood and other body fluids and tissue analysis. Smaller satellite labs in some provinces and territories are referred to as specimen collection labs, and they simply collect specimens (e.g., blood, urine, stool, sputum) and send them to a central laboratory for analysis. Both private and hospital-based diagnostic imaging facilities offer such services as X-rays, **computed tomography (CT)** scanning, **magnetic resonance imaging (MRI)**, **ultrasonography**, and **mammography**. Diagnostic imaging provides a detailed view of structures beneath the skin. Continuing and rapid technological advances in this field have added to its versatility, diagnostic

computed tomography (CT) a type of X-ray that produces three-dimensional images of cross-sections of body parts.

magnetic resonance imaging (MRI)   a diagnostic tool that uses a magnetic field to produce images of body structures and organs.

ultrasonography   a procedure that uses high-frequency sound waves directed at an organ or object to produce a visual image.

mammography   a specialized X-ray of the breast.

capabilities, and complexity. Advances in diagnostic medicine have contributed significantly to the rising cost of health care in Canada, resulting in long waits for many of these tests.

Canada has national and provincial or territorial laboratories that provide specialized services. The Public Health Agency of Canada has two national laboratories—the National Microbiology Laboratory in Winnipeg and the National HIV and Retrovirology Laboratories in Ottawa, that provide specialized services. These centres provide services to all provinces and territories as requested. The labs can respond quickly to any health emergency, working collaboratively with other resources, and are linked to a government-wide emergency response system. The national laboratories conduct research as well as analyzing specimens sent from across the country. The Winnipeg National Microbiology Laboratory was the first in the world to decode the genetic makeup of the H1N1 flu virus. The Winnipeg lab is one of 15 centres worldwide equipped with facilities to deal with biosafety issues, including the most deadly infectious organisms. It is a facility where scientists and researchers can share and discuss information as they study established, emerging, and re-emerging diseases in both human and animal populations.

In most provinces and territories, hospitals have clinical laboratories and diagnostic imaging services. The larger the hospital, the more complex and varied are the testing services it offers. Hospital facilities serve inpatients, outpatients, and the general public. An average-sized hospital typically offers the following laboratory departments:

- Hematology
- Blood Bank or Blood Transfusions
- Chemistry
- Microbiology
- Histology/Pathology/Cytology

Larger hospitals also offer the most complete range of diagnostic imaging services. An average-sized hospital would likely offer the following radiographic studies:

- Routine/plain film X-rays
- Contrast techniques
- Fluoroscopy
- Computed tomography (CT)
- Magnetic resonance imaging (MRI)
- Ultrasonography

Cardiac and respiratory diagnostic services are also offered primarily by hospitals. Larger hospitals offer the most complete range of diagnostic imaging services.

Sometimes, the test may be performed at one facility but sent elsewhere to be processed and evaluated, often to another city or to a provincial or territorial lab. It may take several days to a week for the results to come back. Let your clients know when you expect the results back. This alleviates the anxiety of waiting and wondering why you have not called, particularly if the client expects undesirable results.

Clients often think that they must go to a hospital to have a test done if it is to be covered by their health plan. Provincial and territorial health plans cover most diagnostic services deemed medically necessary, regardless of where they are offered. Examples of exceptions in some provinces include PSA (prostate-specific antigen, a blood test used to diagnose prostate cancer); BAT (bioavailable testosterone, used to investigate erectile dysfunction); and the *Helicobacter pylori* test (used to isolate a specific bacterium involved in stomach ulcers). Physicians' offices and laboratories will have a current list of uninsured lab and diagnostic tests. It is important that clients are informed before they have tests if they will have to pay for them. This is the provider's responsibility, but the client may ask you for clarification.

❸ PROFESSIONALS INVOLVED

Allied Health Professionals

The primary duty of a *phlebotomist* is to draw blood specimens from patients. A phlebotomist may also collect specimens, prepare and maintain equipment, and do related data entry and clerical tasks. Phlebotomists are often trained on the job but may come from related health professions. They are employed in a public or private laboratory or a hospital. Medical laboratory technologists, medical technicians, or medical laboratory assistants frequently assume this duty as part of their general responsibilities.

A registered *medical laboratory technologist (MLT)* is knowledgeable in all areas of clinical laboratory work and can carry out specialized tests. Medical laboratory technologists have a three-year college diploma or a Bachelor's degree. An MLT makes independent decisions concerning the quality of laboratory results. Responsibilities often include education of peers, students, and subordinates; research and development of new techniques; and laboratory supervision.

A *medical technician* or *medical laboratory assistant* usually graduates from a college program with a certificate and performs more routine laboratory procedures, often under the supervision of a medical technologist.

Physician Specialists

Physicians who specialize in various areas of diagnostic testing work in almost every laboratory department.

A *hematologist* is a physician who specializes in the diagnosis, treatment, prevention, and/or investigation of disorders primarily of the blood and lymphatic systems. A hematologist may work in general practice or in a laboratory.

A *pathologist* is a medical doctor who examines tissue samples and interprets results. A pathologist also performs **autopsies**.

Radiology is the study of images of the human body, and a *radiologist* is a physician who specializes in interpreting these images. A radiologist may specialize in evaluating one particular area of the body. With diagnostic tests becoming more and more sophisticated, specialists are narrowing their fields to the interpretation of highly specialized tests.

autopsy   the examination of a body to determine the cause of death and/or to identify disease processes.

❷ COMMONLY ORDERED TESTS

YOU NEED A GENERAL UNDERSTANDING OF THE COMMONLY ORDERED TESTS, including where and how to order them and the type of information you need to book them. Your clients depend on you as a resource for information.

If you work in a hospital, you may be asked to obtain test results for the physician or to requisition a test that has been ordered. Knowing which laboratory department to call will save you both time and frustration. You should also be aware of **critical values** of common tests and how to read reports and note abnormal results. Rereading your notes or texts from any anatomy and physiology courses you have taken will help you understand these tests. Table 6.1 lists some of the more common test abbreviations you will come across.

Hematology

Literally translated, *hematology* means the study of blood. In the laboratory, hematology deals with the processing and evaluation of blood and blood components. The average human body contains five to six litres of blood. Blood is composed of serum, or plasma (the liquid portion of blood in which blood components are suspended), red and white blood cells, various proteins, hormones, antibodies, and other elements that perform specific functions. (Tests on blood plasma are usually done by the Chemistry Department.) Cells are examined and analyzed for their size, shape, functional ability, and numbers. The following are some of the more common hematological tests.

Complete Blood Count One of the most common and useful tests is the complete blood count (CBC). A CBC may be ordered to help the physician establish a diagnosis or as part of a routine medical examination for screening purposes. It can provide valuable information about the blood and blood-forming tissues (especially the bone marrow), as well as other body systems and the client's overall health. A CBC typically includes the following tests to analyze the various types of blood cells:

- Red blood cell count (RBC)
- Hematocrit
- Hemoglobin
- White blood cell count (WBC)
- Differential blood count (diff)
- Platelet count

There are, however, variations among laboratories; some, for example, do not include differential or platelet counts unless specifically ordered. Table 6.2 shows sample reference ranges for the main tests included in a CBC.

Red Blood Cell Count This test counts the number of red blood cells in a specific volume of blood. Most counts are performed using an automated system. Results of this test are closely linked to the client's hemoglobin and hematocrit. It is usually repeated at designated intervals in clients who are experiencing continued bleeding problems, and it plays an important role in diagnosing and evaluating clients with anemia. As with other tests, the normal range for RBCs varies with age and gender. Normal ranges may also vary slightly with the lab performing the test. Normal values might vary between 4.7 and 6.1 10^{12}/L for adult males and between 4.2 and 5.4 10^{12}/L for adult females.

Red blood cell indices are completed as part of most automated RBC analyses. They provide information about the size, weight, and hemoglobin concentration of RBCs. The *mean corpuscular volume* (MCV) reflects the average size of an RBC. The *mean corpuscular*

Table 6.1   Abbreviations for Commonly Ordered Laboratory and Diagnostic Tests

ABGs	arterial blood gases	LDH	lactic dehydrogenase
AFB	acid-fast bacilli	LDL	low-density lipoprotein
APTT	activated partial thromboplastin time (see PTT)	LP	lumbar puncture
BE	barium enema	LS	X-ray of the lumbosacral spine
BUN	blood urea nitrogen	MCH	mean corpuscular hemoglobin
C&S	culture and sensitivity	MCHC	mean corpuscular hemoglobin concentration
C&T	crossmatch and type (for compatible blood; see T&S)	MCV	mean corpuscular volume
CBC	complete blood count	Mg	magnesium
CK	creatine kinase	MRI	magnetic resonance imaging
CO2	carbon dioxide	Na	sodium
CRP	C-reactive protein	O&P	ova and parasites (often in stool specimens)
CSF	cerebrospinal fluid	OB	occult blood
CT	computed tomography	P	phosphorus
CXR	chest X-ray (PA: posterior-to-anterior; Lat.: lateral)	Pap	Pap smear
ECG	electrocardiogram	PCO2	partial pressure of carbon dioxide
ELISA	enzyme-linked immunosorbent assay	PFT	pulmonary function test
ERCP	endoscopic retrograde cholangiopancreatography	PSA	prostate-specific antigen
EMG	electromyography	PT	prothrombin time
ESR	erythrocyte sedimentation rate	PTT/aPTT/APTT	partial thromboplastin time (see APTT)
FBS	fasting blood sugar	RBC	red blood cell
GB/GBS	gallbladder series	S&A	sugar and acetone
GTT	glucose tolerance test	SGOT	serum glutamic-oxaloacetic transaminase
HbA1c	glycoylated hemoglobin	SGPT	serum glutamic-pyruvic transaminase
Hb	hemoglobin	T3	triiodothyroxine
HBV	hepatitis B virus	T4	thyroxine
Hct	hematocrit	T&S	type and screen (for compatible blood; see C&T)
HDL	high-density lipoprotein		
HIV	human immunodeficiency virus	TSH	thyroid stimulating hormone
INR	international normalized ratio	UGI	upper gastrointestinal series
IV-GTT	intravenous glucose tolerance test	US	ultrasound
IVP	intravenous pyelogram	VDRL	venereal disease research laboratory
K	potassium	VMA	vanilylmandelic acid (usually a 24-h urine test)
KUB	X-ray of the kidney, ureter, and bladder	WBC	white blood cell count

Table 6.2	Reference Ranges for the Common Elements of a Complete Blood Count (CBC)

RBC

male: 4.7–6.1 1012/L

female: 4.2–5.4 1012/L

WBC: 4.0–109/L

May be referred to as a leukocyte count (LC)

Hematocrit

male: 0.40–0.50/L

female: 0.36–0.44/L

Hemoglobin

platelet count: 100 000–450 000

male: 138–172 g/L

female: 121–151 g/L

Note: Reference ranges vary with testing methods. Use the ranges supplied by your laboratory. Some laboratories may also use different units of measurement; for example, hemoglobin is sometimes measured in mmol/L instead of g/L.

hemoglobin (MCH) is a variation on the MCV measurement and indicates the average amount of hemoglobin in a single red blood cell. The *mean corpuscular hemoglobin concentration (MCHC)* determines the average hemoglobin (Hb) concentration per 100 mL of packed red cells. The cell's weight is assessed by a test called random distribution of RBC weight (RDW), which measures the red blood cells for consistency in size. This index is available only on automated cell counting equipment. Cell counters categorize erythrocytes by volume as they are counted.

Hemoglobin (Hb)   Hemoglobin is a protein on the red blood cells that attaches to oxygen in the blood and carries it throughout the body. It also removes carbon dioxide. Hemoglobin gives blood its red colour and is the main content of the red blood cell. The amount of oxygen in the blood is determined by the concentration of Hb in the blood. Abnormal results indicate that something is wrong. Two common problems associated with a low Hb are anemia and hemorrhage. The normal range varies with gender and age and the altitude at which a person lives.

Hematocrit   The term *hematocrit* (Hct) comes from roots meaning "to separate blood." This test reflects the percentage of the total volume of blood occupied by cells. An Hct is almost always done together with an Hb as both are usually affected by the same underlying pathology. A low Hct may result from a diminished production of red blood cells, blood loss, or the abnormal destruction of the cells. In the case of hemorrhage, the results are most accurate several hours after the event. Often, the Hb and Hct are determining factors when doctors decide to give a person a transfusion with blood or blood products. Note that a low Hct in pregnant women is considered normal (within limits) because the pregnancy involves extra blood volume without a corresponding increase in red blood cells.

Red Blood Cell Morphology   Red blood cell morphology describes the appearance of the red blood cells on a blood film. This report may diagnose a condition, such as malaria, or suggest the need for further testing. A report of oval macrocytes, for example, suggests a vitamin B12 or folate deficiency.

White Blood Cell Count   The white blood cell (WBC) count determines the total number of white cells in the blood sample. White blood cells are the body's primary means of fighting infection. There are five main types of white cell, each of which plays a different role in responding to the presence of foreign organisms in the body. Elevations in the WBC count can result from stimuli, such as having a baby, stress, and infections. The normal WBC count varies with age. It is higher in babies and decreases as a person gets older. There are five main types of white cell, each of which plays a different role in responding to the presence of foreign organisms in the body. These cells are examined in the differential count.

Differential Count   A differential count estimates the different types of white blood cells as a proportion of the total white blood cell count. This count is valuable in determining what kind of disorder a client has (e.g., viral infection, bacterial infection, allergic response). It is usually split into neutrophils, lymphocytes, monocytes, eosinophils, and basophils.

Figure 6.1 shows a printed report of a complete blood count. Note that for each result, the normal values are listed as the "reference range." Abnormal readings are listed under the abnormal column. In this report, the RBC and Hct are flagged as L for low, and the WBC is flagged as H for high. Results posing considerable concern are also marked with an asterisk and addressed at the bottom of the report. The doctor has added notes for the administrative health professional (AHP). He wants to have the CBC repeated *stat* (immediately) and to see the client. The AHP should arrange the test and book the appointment, initial the request to indicate this has been done, and note what has been done on the client's chart.

Platelet Count   The platelet count is an actual count of the number of platelets or thrombocytes in a given volume of blood. Platelets, the smallest blood cells, play a vital role in the blood clotting system. A low platelet count may indicate a bleeding disorder.

Erythrocyte Sedimentation Rate   The erythrocyte sedimentation rate (ESR), or sedimentation rate (sed rate), is a measure of the settling of red blood cells in a saline or plasma solution over a specific period of time. Doctors often use this test to evaluate the condition of a client with nonspecific complaints or symptoms. An elevated rate is not usually diagnostic of any particular disease or condition or the involvement of any particular organ, but it does indicate that an underlying disease may be present, perhaps infection, cancer, kidney disease, or rheumatoid arthritis. This test is most frequently used along with others to monitor a client's condition or response to treatment.

Coagulation Studies   These tests measure the clotting time of the blood. They are used in particular for individuals on blood thinners or anticoagulants.

Partial Thromboplastin Time (PTT)/Activated Partial Thromboplastin Time (APTT/aPTT)   PTT/APTT/aPTT tests are used to evaluate a component of the clotting (coagulation) system. Coagulation depends on the action of substances in the blood called clotting factors. Measuring the partial thromboplastin time helps assess

RS LABORATORIES AND DIAGNOSTIC SERVICES
223 Lakewood Ave.
Vancouver, BC
V5R 6M1

Physician	Client: Perreault, Anne
Dr. D Singh	DOB: 11/4/56
43 Rundle Ave	Sex: F
Vancouver, BC	PH: 604-321-2232
	MCP # 4323432255
	Subscriber's Initial: A
	Date of Service: Sept 2/08
	Date Printed: Sept 3/08

Report Status: final

Test Name	Result	Abnormal	Reference Range	Units
Hematology				
WBC*	13.7×10^9/L	H	(4.5–11.0)	
RBC	3.81×10^{12}/L	L	(3.90–5.60)	
Hct	0.3480 L/L	L	(0.3500–0.4700)	
MCV	91 FL		(0.78–100)	
MCH	31.0 PG		(27.0–32.0)	
LYMPH	0.32		(0.20–0.45)	
NEUT	0.65		(0.25–0.80)	
MONO	0.02		(0.01–0.10)	
EOSIN	0.00		(0.00–0.06)	
BASOP	0.00		(0.00–0.03)	
PLATELETS	NORMAL			
ESR	31		(0–20)	

* note WBC
Call for repeat of CBC stat. See me Thurs.

Figure 6.1 Hematology report. Note that values vary slightly from one laboratory to another.

which specific clotting factors may be missing or defective. The APTT is a variation of the PTT, giving similar results that can be used interchangeably. Some consider these tests synonymous. Sometimes, a test ordered as a PTT will come back as APTT or aPTT, depending on the variation of the test the lab uses. These tests are also used to monitor therapy with **heparin**, an anticoagulant that prolongs the time it takes for the blood to clot. It is important to monitor the client's clotting time to keep the dosage within a therapeutic range. Too much heparin could cause bleeding problems; too little could lead to a blood clot. Critical values for either of these tests would be phoned in, and the doctor should be notified as soon as possible. Normal APTT/aPTT is usually between 28 and 38 seconds (varies with lab). The therapeutic range for heparin administration is 60 to 85 seconds.

heparin an anticoagulant (blood thinner) given to people who are at risk for developing blood clots.

International Normalized Ratio (INR) The international normalized ratio is a system established, in part, by the World Health Organization for reporting the results of blood coagulation tests. All results are standardized. For example, consider that Dr. Wong has a client taking warfarin (brand name Coumadin). The client travels to another province but is to have his INR levels done three times a week and to let Dr. Wong know the results (or have the lab call her with the results) so that she can adjust his warfarin dose. With the standardization of the INR, this client could have a blood test done anywhere, and Dr. Wong would know that the results are the same as those she would get in the lab she usually uses (unlike some of the values, for example, a CBC). The normal reference range is 0.9 to 1.1. The therapeutic range for someone on warfarin therapy is 2.0 to 3.0.

More recently low-molecular-weight heparin (a new class of anticoagulant) is being used both prophylactically and to actively treat individuals for actual and potential clotting issues and related conditions. As a prophylactic, low-molecular-weight heparin is as effective as standard heparin or warfarin but requires no monitoring (APTT or INR).

Blood Bank/Blood Transfusion

Blood and blood products are supplied to health-care facilities in Canada by the Canadian Blood Services (CBS), a not-for-profit, charitable organization that screens and collects blood used for all transfusions across Canada. The organization also manages the Canadian Bone Marrow Donor Registry. The CBS screens every donor and tests each unit of blood or blood product for a variety of transmissible diseases.

A hospital's Blood Bank or Blood Transfusion Department tests to ensure that blood or blood products given in transfusions are compatible with the client's. Transfusion of mismatched blood can result in a serious reaction, even death. The process of matching blood is called blood typing, crossmatching, or cross-typing.

There are four main blood types: A, B, AB, and O. These letters represent antigens on the red blood cell. If you have the A antigen, you are type A; if you have the B antigen, you are type B. If you have both the A and B antigen, you are type AB. If you do not have any antigen, you are type O. Each blood type carries antibodies to antigens present in the blood plasma of the other blood types. For example, if you are type A, you have anti-B antibodies and would react to any blood with the B antigen in it. If you are type B, you would have anti-A antibodies, therefore reacting to any blood with the A antigen in it. If you are type AB, you do not have any antibodies, making you the universal recipient. Each person's blood can also be categorized as either Rh positive or Rh negative. The rhesus, or Rh, factor is an antigen on the surface of the red blood cell. If you have it, you are positive; if you do not, you are negative. These factors must also be analyzed in the process of finding compatible blood or blood components for a client.

Clients are usually crossmatched if they present with a significantly low Hb/Hct resulting from a pathological process, before any major surgery, and in the event of hemorrhage. In emergency cases, the order would be stat. If there is no time for a crossmatch, the doctor would order type O negative blood, which is also known as the universal donor. Type O blood has no antigen (A or B) and no Rh factor and, therefore, will not react with other blood types.

A related test that may be done by the Blood Bank is the Coombs' test indirect, which measures a person's antibodies against red blood cells. This test is done for mothers who are Rh negative to determine whether they have developed antibodies against a possible Rh-positive baby. A Coombs' test direct is done on the baby after it is born and tells the doctor whether the baby has been sensitized by its mother's blood and, if so, how seriously. A baby with high levels of antibodies needs intensive observation for a condition causing pathological jaundice, which, if serious enough, requires exchange blood transfusions.

Chemistry

The Chemistry Department deals with tests on urine, blood plasma, and other body fluids. These include a variety of tests for blood sugar levels, electrolytes, blood urea nitrogen (BUN), creatinine, electrolytes, cholesterol and triglyceride levels, and various enzyme tests (microbiology). Timed and random urine tests are also completed in this department. Figure 6.2 shows a chemistry report. Note that the urea is considered abnormally high and appears under the abnormal column. This value may be given on a lab report as urea or as BUN (*blood urea nitrogen*). In either case, it measures in the blood the level of urea, a by-product of metabolism that builds up in the blood and is cleared by the kidney. Diseases that compromise the function of the kidney frequently lead to increased blood urea levels. Normal values range from 3.5 to 7.0.

RS LABORATORIES AND DIAGNOSTIC SERVICES
223 Lakewood Ave.
Vancouver, BC
V5R 6M1

Physician	**Client:** Perreault, Anne
Dr. D Singh	**DOB:** 11/4/56
43 Rundle Ave	**Sex:** F
Vancouver, BC	**PH:** 604-321-2232
	MCP # 4323432255
	Subscriber's Initial: A
	Date of Service: Sept 2/08
	Date Printed: Sept 3/08

Report Status: final

Test Name	SI Result	Flag	Reference Range
Chemistry			
GLUCOSE-RANDOM	12.2 mmol/L	H	3.6−7.8
PC BS	4.8 mmol/L		3.8−7.80
UREA	10 mmol/L	H	3.5−7.0
CREAT	60 mmol/L		50−110
SOD	137 mmol/L		135−145
POT	3.0 mmol/L	L	3.5−5.0
CL	104 mmol/L		99−108
Cholesterol*	5.03 mmol/L		< 6
Triglycerides	2.03 mmol/L		0.6−3.60
TOTAL THYROID (TOTAL T4) 0.30 mmol/L			60−155
T UPTAKE 0.30			0.22−0.34
FREE THYROXINE INDEX (FTI) 30			13−53
THYROTROPIN (SENSITIVE TSH) 2.34			0.50−5.00

*moderate risk category: cholesterol 5.20-6.20

Book for 5hr gtt. Note on chart diet counselling
DS

Figure 6.2 Chemistry report

Creatinine   *Creatinine* is a by-product of creatine phosphate, a compound found in skeletal muscle tissue that is produced continuously and excreted by the kidney. An increase in **serum** creatinine (the level of creatinine in the blood) indicates possible renal dysfunction. Levels can also become elevated as a result of some muscle diseases and congestive heart failure. Normal adult serum creatinine values range from 55 to 115 mmol/L for a female and 62 to 120 mmol/L for a male, depending on the lab. Creatinine and BUN are often ordered together to assess kidney function.

Electrolytes   Electrolytes are elements that are found in body tissues and blood in the form of charged particles. An order for electrolytes includes testing for levels of sodium, potassium, and chloride. Normal ranges for sodium are 135 to 145 mEq/L, for potassium, 3.5 to 5.0 mEq/L, and for chloride, 99 to 108 mEq/L. These will vary with laboratories. Electrolytes are discussed in more detail in Chapter 17.

Blood Glucose Levels   Blood glucose (sugar) levels are used to diagnose metabolic diseases, such as diabetes mellitus, and to monitor diabetics and adjust their medication. There are a number of tests for monitoring glucose levels. They differ depending on the time of day they are performed and what the client has had to eat or drink, as both factors affect glucose levels. One of these tests is a fasting blood sugar (FBS), meaning that the client must remain NPO (eat nothing) for at least eight hours before the test. (On occasion, a physician may allow a client to have sips of water or to take an important medication.) In hospital, this means delaying a client's breakfast until the test is completed. Blood is usually taken early in the morning so that breakfast does not have to be delayed long. The clinical secretary would also put an NPO or FBS notice at the client's bedside the night before the test. In the health office, make sure clients understand that not eating and drinking is important for accurate results. This test gives a value for blood sugar levels when they have not been immediately affected by food. Normal range for an FBS is 3.9 to 6.1 mmol/L for an adult, and 3.3 to 5.5 for a child. An FBS of less than 2.0 is considered to be critical.

Another common test for blood sugar, taken two hours after eating, is called a two-hour postprandial glucose level (2 h PC BS or 2 h PPG) and is used to diagnose early diabetes mellitus. Diabetics usually have elevated glucose levels two hours after eating, whereas the levels would return to normal within two hours in a person without the disease. Normal reference range for adults is 3.3 to 7.8 mmol/L.

A random blood sugar (RBS) may be taken any time. This is not as valuable a test as the FBS or the two-hour PC BS but will certainly reflect abnormal glucose activity.

Glycosylated hemoglobin is a test used to measure blood sugar control over an extended period in individuals with diabetes mellitus, and it is especially valuable in assessing a person's compliance with or response to treatment. It measures a component of hemoglobin known as A1c (which is on the RBC) that binds with glucose in the blood and indicates how much glucose has been in a person's blood during the previous two to four months (average being 120 days). The test is usually ordered as a HbA1c, GHb, or glycohemoglobin. No fasting is needed for this test. Normal levels range approximately between 4.5 percent and 6.5 percent.

You should be aware of critical blood sugar values, check reports diligently for abnormal results, and report levels that are a concern to the provider at the first opportunity. Critical levels would be telephoned to the office or hospital and should be given to the doctor as soon as possible. If the provider is unavailable, notify the doctor on call.

Glucose Tolerance Tests   The most common test in this category is the oral glucose tolerance test (OGTT). This test, a more detailed test to diagnose diabetes, assesses the body's ability to use glucose by measuring blood glucose levels at specified intervals after the person has ingested a glucose solution. The test is most often done on an outpatient basis, and must follow specific dietary recommendations. The client should be on a carbohydrate diet (at least 150–200 g per day) for at least three days before the test, and then remain NPO for 10 to 14 hours before the test. The outpatient client should be given a handout describing the dietary preparation. Fruits, breads, cereals, grains, and potatoes are some excellent sources of CHO to recommend. As well, some facilities ask the client to refrain from strenuous exercise and smoking 8–10 hours prior to the test. The procedure takes about four hours.

For the hospitalized client, you or the nurse would post an NPO notice by the client's bedside. Delay or cancel breakfast on the morning of the test. The client must not eat, drink coffee or tea, or smoke after drinking the glucose solution until the test is finished.

Cholesterol/Triglycerides   These tests measure types of fats (also called lipids) in the blood. Clients must usually fast for 12 hours, taking nothing but water and important medications. The two main lipids measured are cholesterol and triglyceride. Cholesterol is a waxy fat produced by the liver and is essential to the production of some hormones and to cellular growth. Cholesterol combines with proteins and is circulated throughout the body. In the circulating form, it is referred to as lipoprotein (and often appears on lab requisitions under this name). There are two types of cholesterol: high-density lipoproteins or HDL (called "good cholesterol" because it does not clog vessels and removes extra cholesterol from the body), and low-density lipoprotein or LDL ("bad cholesterol," which clogs arteries, increasing the risk of heart attack and stroke). The reference range for HDL is 1.0 to 1.80 for an adult male and 1.2 to 2.40 for an adult female; the reference range for LDL for an adult is 1.4 to 4.0.

Triglycerides are also lipids and are beneficial as long as they remain within normal ranges. Elevated levels are associated with heart disease, arteriosclerosis, and atherosclerosis. It is considered good control if a client's triglyceride level remains below 1.7 mmol/L. (Most lab values vary somewhat with gender and age.) Clients with high levels of either cholesterol or triglycerides may be advised to eat a low-fat, low-cholesterol diet. In Figure 6.2, the cholesterol result of 5.03, while within the normal range, is considered to present some risk for the client. The physician has noted on the bottom of the report that the client is to be booked for diet counselling.

Heart (Cardiac) Enzymes   When a person has a heart attack (also called a myocardial infarction, or MI), heart muscle is damaged. As a result of this damage, cardiac **enzymes** are released into the bloodstream. Measuring these enzymes can tell the doctor if a heart attack has actually occurred and, if so, how extensive the muscle damage is. Sometimes, measuring the enzymes is definitive in the diagnosis of a heart attack when ECG findings are absent or nonspecific. The enzymes most commonly measured are creatine phosphokinase (CPK, also known as creatine kinase [CK]) and troponin. The normal or reference range for total CK is 39 to 174 U/L for an adult male and 26 to 140 U/L for a female.

enzyme   a protein capable of initiating a chemical reaction that involves the formation or breakage of chemical bonds. When muscle damage or death occurs, enzymes within the muscle cell are released into the circulating blood.

Urinalysis

Urinalysis: Urine for Routine and Micro   A urinalysis is a valuable routine diagnostic and screening test that provides preliminary information about the kidneys and related processes. It may be ordered as "urine for routine and micro," or R&M.

```
RS LABORATORIES.
223 Lakeway Ave.
Vancouver, B.C.
V5R 6M1

Physician                          Client: Perreault, Anne
Dr. D Singh                        DOB: 11/4/56
43 Rundle Ave                      Sex: F
Vancouver, BC                      PH: 604 - 321-2232
                                   MCP # 4323432255
                                   Subscriber's Initial: A
                                   Date of Service: Sept 2/08
                                   Date Printed: Sept 3/08

                                        Report Status: final

Test Name          Result  Abnormal   Reference Range    Units
URINALYSIS: CHEMICAL

COLOUR             NORMAL
APPEARANCE         TURBID
GLUCOSE            NEGATIVE
KETONE             NEGATIVE
SPECIFIC GRAVITY   1.015
BLOOD              TRACE
PH                 5.0               (4.5 – 8.0)
PROTEIN            NEGATIVE
NITRITE            NEGATIVE
RBC                0                 (0 – 6.0)
WBC                0                 (0 – 6.0)
```

Figure 6.3 Routine urinalysis report from biochemistry

Routine testing includes examining the specimen for colour, clarity, specific gravity, pH, protein, glucose, and ketones. Microscopic analysis of the specimen involves numerous tests for the presence of red and white blood cells, casts, crystals, bacteria, yeast cells, and parasites—all not normally present. (See Figure 6.3.) Doctors order this test frequently, sometimes as a screening test, sometimes in response to either specific or vague symptoms as it provides information on a wide variety of potential problems. Some hospitals do this test on all admissions; others do it only if there are specific indications. Some facilities use the term *urinalysis* to mean only a routine test; others use it to mean a urine test for routine and micro. Note, as discussed below, that a routine and micro is a different test from a urine ordered for culture and sensitivity—although you frequently see these ordered together for example, "urine for R&M and C&S."

Timed Urine Collections Timed urine collections (also ordered as 24-hour urine collections) are quantitative tests done on urine collected over 24 hours. This test provides information about cumulative elements in the urine. Substances, such as hormones excreted by the kidney, are not excreted uniformly throughout the day, and so a 24-hour collection provides the physician with a more accurate picture of kidney function. Timed collections are analyzed for such things as creatinine clearance, protein, and hormone levels. The client is given a large bottle to put the urine in. The client should void in the toilet upon waking up. Thereafter, the client collects all urine up to and including the first void the next morning.

For example, if the test is to begin at 8:00 a.m., the patient empties his bladder then but does not collect that urine. All the urine produced in the next 24 hours is collected in a clean container. At 8:00 a.m. the next day, the patient collects the final sample. A 12-hour sample may also be ordered. For timed urine collections, stressing the procedure is vital. Even one discarded void will invalidate the test, as it is quantitative in nature. Every drop of urine counts.

Specifics regarding the urine collection will vary with the type of test. For example, the bottle may contain special solutions, be clear or opaque, or require refrigeration or protection from sunlight. To ensure accurate results, clients must follow instructions precisely. Urine specimens are best refrigerated or taken to the lab as soon as possible. The longer they sit around, the more likely the results will be inaccurate. Labelling them immediately reduces the chance of mixing up specimens.

You may need to call the lab to order the large sample bottles. In a hospital situation, ensure that the lab has sent the appropriate bottles (the client sometimes needs more than one) to the floor, and that they are clearly labelled. (See Chapter 19.)

Random Urine Collection A random urine specimen is one that is obtained any time, often in the doctor's office. A random test is usually done for preliminary screening purposes. Urine is collected in the same container as for routine and micro.

In the hospital setting you would make the necessary arrangements with the Dietary Department. The client may need assistance refrigerating the urine. If so, that is the nurse's responsibility. If you see the sample bottle sitting out, let the nurse know—or refrigerate it yourself if that is something you are allowed to do.

Early Morning Specimens Most often, a physician will ask the client to bring in a first morning void for a urine specimen. This specimen is preferred because it has a more uniform volume and concentration, and its lower pH helps preserve the formed elements. Abnormalities are easier to detect. These specimens are used, among other purposes, to diagnose and monitor pregnancies. Pregnant women are usually asked to bring in a specimen for testing with each prenatal visit. It is tested, usually in the office, for such elements as glucose, ketones, and protein.

Microbiology

Microbiology studies body fluids and tissues for infectious organisms, such as bacteria, viruses, parasites, and fungi. These organisms can be detected in a number of ways. A common type of test is culture and sensitivity (C&S). This is a two-step process in which any organism present in the specimen is grown in a controlled environment and then the susceptibility or resistance to various antibiotics is determined. Suppose the culture grew a pathogen, for example, *E. coli*, and the antibiotics used for the sensitivity portion of the test were amoxicillin, Bactrim, and Ciprofloxacin. Test results showed that the *E. coli* was

Tip

If you are asked to transport a urine test for culture and sensitivity to the lab, make sure you take it immediately or refrigerate it until you can transport it there. Left out, organisms can grow and invalidate the test. Likewise, if you see a sample sitting around, check with the nurse or refrigerate it.

resistant to the amoxicillin but sensitive to Bactrim and Cipro. This tells the doctor that treating the client with either Bactrim or Cipro would be effective but that treatment with amoxicillin would not be effective against that particular strain of E. coli.

When a client has a suspected infection potentially treatable with an antibiotic, it is usually best for the provider to have the results of the C&S before initiating antibiotic therapy. It is hard to make clients understand this, especially if they are in pain. Treating a sore throat with antibiotics when test results show the infection is viral is absolutely useless (and expensive). Prescribing an antibiotic that the organism is resistant to is also ineffective. Needless use of antibiotics contributes to the development of antibiotic-resistant organisms. Clients who understand the rationale behind waiting for test results may be less impatient to have the physician prescribe something. If an acute infection (such as a bladder or kidney infection) is suspected, it may be important to start treatment as soon as possible; in this case, the doctor will take a specimen but start the client on antibiotics without waiting for results. When the results are back, the doctor may change the prescription if indicated by the results.

Midstream Urine Tests   Urine specimens for culture and sensitivity are often ordered by the physician to diagnose urinary tract infections (see Figure 6.4). They are usually **midstream urine specimens (MSU)**, also called clean catch urine specimens, obtained by following specific instructions. Many offices use disposable specimen kits that include these instructions. To obtain a midstream urine specimen, the client must carefully wipe the area around the urethra with a cleansing solution. The solution used varies; often, washing with just soap and water is recommended. The client must start to void into the toilet, then stop and collect the middle part of the urine in a sterile container. Most people find it nearly impossible to void into a small bottle; so many kits supply a larger sterile container in which the person can catch the middle part of the urine stream. This is then emptied into the sterile bottle, taking care not to contaminate the urine or the container edges, and the lid is applied.

midstream urine specimen (MSU)   also called clean catch urine specimen; a urine specimen collected after cleansing oneself and discarding the first part of the urine stream in order to avoid contamination; used for culture and sensitivity tests.

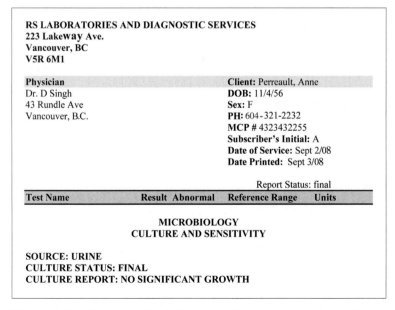

Figure 6.4   Normal urinalysis report for culture and sensitivity

Urine specimens for C&S *must be taken to the lab immediately or refrigerated*. If a specimen sits at room temperature, bacterial growth will interfere with the accuracy of test results. The lab will reject a specimen that has not been handled properly. Sometimes a client will be asked to obtain a midstream urine sample at home. It is very important for the person to understand the importance of refrigerating the specimen.

Sputum Tests

Culture and sensitivity (C&S) may be used to diagnose the cause of a chest infection, such as bronchitis or pneumonia. Sputum tests are also used to diagnose fungal infections, lung cancer, and tuberculosis. If a client is providing this specimen at home, be sure to tell her to produce an early morning specimen and to try to cough it up deep from the lung passages. Phlegm from the upper airways and throat are unacceptable specimens. Also advise the client not to use mouthwash prior to obtaining the specimen as antibacterial properties in the mouthwash will interfere with test results.

Chapter 20 discusses these tests as they relate to the hospitalized client; there is important information about these tests with respect to order entry procedures.

Blood Cultures   Cultures done on blood are ordered if a client is suspected of having septicemia, a blood infection. Infection can spread from various organs or result from surgery. Particularly dangerous is a condition called endocarditis, an inflammation and infection of the lining of the heart and/or heart valves. Although this infection is not common, people who have prosthetic heart valves or prosthetic joints are at increased risk. Blood cultures might be ordered on a client (in or out of hospital) with the onset of a high and otherwise unexplained fever. These are often ordered in groups of two or three to ensure the accuracy of the tests. They may be collected all at once or at designated intervals.

Stool Culture and Analysis   A stool culture and analysis is done to diagnose certain conditions affecting the digestive tract, including infection, poor absorption, or cancer. Lab analysis includes microscopic analysis and chemical and microbiological tests for such organisms as bacteria, fungi, parasites, and yeast. Other elements, such as mucus and blood, are also identified. A common test is stool analysis for occult blood (OB). Stool specimens are often ordered in groups of three, which would be separate samples, perhaps one each day. It is sometimes difficult to keep track of specimens obtained in the hospital; so the nurses usually note on the client's electronic or traditional Kardex (discussed in Chapter 19) when they have obtained a specimen. Most facilities provide disposable kits for clients to obtain stool specimens. Depending on the test, patients may be instructed to collect the sample in a container, scoop a small portion into a vial, or smear a small amount on special test paper.

Lung Function Tests

Spirometry   Spirometry is a test used for lung function screening and is one of many pulmonary or lung function tests. It is administered using a portable device called a spirometer. This easily administered, noninvasive test measures the air capacity of the lungs. The client breathes into a mouthpiece attached to a spirometer. The tests measures the volume of air exchanged, how fast it is exchanged, and the compliance of the respiratory muscles.

Spirometry is often ordered preoperatively to assess a person's surgical risk with regard to having an anesthetic, particularly for individuals who are older, who smoke, or who are morbidly obese. The test is also often done in conjunction with related physiotherapy procedures to determine client progress. Postoperatively, clients are sometimes given a portable spirometer to keep at the bedside and use to measure lung function after surgery as well as to encourage the client to practise deep-breathing exercises. A more detailed test called plethsmography is sometimes ordered if more accurate information is required.

Arterial Blood Gases   An arterial blood gas (ABG) assessment is done on a client to determine the amounts of oxygen and carbon dioxide dissolved in the blood. The test also calculates the blood's pH, or acid/base balance. The test is ordered on people who are hypoxic, often as a stat test. In many hospitals this test is done in the Respiratory Department—and usually for ER or inpatients. For that reason, details regarding this test are discussed in Chapter 20.

Lung Scan   A lung scan is performed in the Nuclear Medicine Department to diagnose pulmonary embolism (lung blockage) and to evaluate lung disease. This is a two-part test. First, the client inhales very small particles of radioactive material for three to five minutes through an aerosol. Then technicians take pictures of the lung fields with a special camera to record the distribution of the radioactive material. For the second part of the test, the client receives an IV injection of radioactive material. X-rays are then taken of the lungs, with the client assuming various positions.

Diagnostic Imaging

What was once the X-ray Department in most facilities is now called the Diagnostic Imaging Department because X-rays are only one of the imaging tools available. Other imaging techniques include computed tomography (CT), magnetic resonance imaging (MRI), and ultrasonography.

X-Ray   A X-ray is a visual test in which an image of a selected body part or region is created by using low doses of radiation reflected on film or fluorescent screens. X-rays can be used to diagnose a wide range of conditions, from pneumonia to a fractured bone. Common X-ray tests include chest X-rays, often ordered as "chest X-ray PA and lateral." This means the doctor wants a front and side view. (See Figure 6.5 for a normal chest X-ray report.) An X-ray can be done on almost any body part, for example, the abdomen, to evaluate trauma or a blockage of the bowel, or the bones, to assess for fractures. Most X-rays require little or no preparation, but you will likely have to book an appointment for a client to have one done. (See Chapter 9 for booking procedures.) In the hospital, if a client is acutely ill or cannot be moved, the doctor may order a "portable," or you may request a "portable" if the nurses deem it best for the client. The technologist will come to the client's room with a portable X-ray unit.

Chest X-ray   A chest X-ray is used to evaluate the status of the lungs and the heart and the surrounding anatomy. It can diagnose conditions including pneumonia, heart failure, pleurisy, and lung cancer, and can pick up heart abnormalities, especially in small children.

Endoscopic Retrograde Cholangiopancreatography (ERCP)   An ERCP is a test that uses an endoscope to visualize the liver and bile ducts. The client is required to remain NPO for eight hours before the test. Because a contrast dye is used, it is important

RS LABORATORIES AND DIAGNOSTIC SERVICES
223 Lakewood Ave.
Vancouver, BC
V5R 6M1
Diagnostic Imaging Dept.

Physician	Client: Perreault, Anne
Dr. D Singh	**DOB:** 11/4/56
43 Rundle Ave	**Sex:** F
Vancouver, B.C.	**PH:** 604-321-2232
	MCP # 4323432255
	Subscriber's Initial: A
	Date of Service: Sept 2/08
	Date Printed: Sept 3/08

Report Status: final

Examination Required

CHEST X-RAY – bilateral

The inspiration was suboptimal. The heart is not enlarged. The C/T Ratio is 15.5/26 cm, with a suboptimal inspiration. There is a 1 cm calcified granuloma in the left lower lobe. The lungs and the pleural spaces are otherwise clear.

U/S ABDOMEN

Examination was suboptimal as the client was not cooperative. Grossly, the gallbladder, liver, proximal abdominal aorta, interior vena cava, kidneys, spleen, and head and body of the pancreas are unremarkable. Distal abdominal aorta and tail of the pancreas are not imaged. The common hepatic duct is not dilated, the measuring 5.9 cm in calibre.

V.ss   Y.J. Henry MD, Radiologist.

Figure 6.5   Report of a chest X-ray and an abdominal ultrasound

to ask the client about related allergies. Many contrast dyes contain iodine, and so a history of allergies to iodine or past dye tests would be important. Clients find this test very uncomfortable. Despite a local anesthetic, and often an intravenous relaxant, gagging, nausea, and vomiting may occur when the endoscope is passed down the throat.

Cholecystography   For this test, the client must be given a contrast dye that helps visualize the gallbladder 12 to 14 hours prior to the test. Alternatively, the dye can be given intravenously just prior to the test. In preparation for either test, the client should remain NPO after the pills are taken or after 2200 h. As well, for either test, written consent is usually requested. Anyone with a previous reaction to a contrast dye or who is allergic to iodine or seafood should not be given the dye.

Tip

Sometimes an X-ray is ordered as a "portable." This is done when the condition of the patient is such that he is unable to be transferred to the Diagnostic Imaging Department. Keep the requisition on the floor and call the Diagnostic Imaging Department. This should be treated as an urgent or stat order.

Barium Enema   A barium enema visualizes the lower portion of the bowel. Barium is inserted through the rectum prior to the X-rays.

Protocols vary for preparing clients for this test. Some doctors order a fibre-restricted meal at noon the day before the test, followed by a clear fluid supper. Others require a full-fluid, low-fibre diet the whole day prior to the test. Still others have the client consume a special supplement up to two days prior to the test. Most clients are asked to take a laxative the night before. A common one is magnesium citrate, which is very salty. Many clients will tell you that the prep is worse than the test. Those who have experienced it suggest taking the laxative ice cold or sucking on a lemon afterward.

For the hospitalized client, you must put the client's existing diet orders on hold and initiate the preparatory diet orders. Make sure that the Dietary Department is aware of the changes. In some computerized environments, the Dietary Department is notified that a client is having a barium enema and automatically adjusts the diet. In some facilities, you must post a sign at the client's bedside about diet changes; for example, it might read "clear fluids" or "NPO."

Barium Swallow   A barium swallow is an X-ray of the throat and esophagus visualized using a contrast medium that is ingested as a drink with the consistency of a milkshake. The passage of the barium through the esophagus and stomach is monitored on the fluoroscope. Pictures are taken with the client in different positions to maximize the view of the GI tract. The test takes 30 minutes to one hour to complete. Similar tests may be ordered as a GI or upper GI series, which focus more attention to the stomach and duodenum.

The client must be instructed to remain NPO for eight hours prior to the test and may be placed on a restricted diet for two or three days prior. It is very important for the client to follow these instructions. Even swallowing a pill may interfere with the examination.

Clients must be advised to take a laxative following the test as the barium can be highly constipating. Let clients know that the first two or three bowel movements may be a greyish-white colour.

When booking both a barium enema and a barium swallow, whether for an inpatient or outpatient, you must book the barium enema first. Otherwise the barium from the swallow will interfere with accuracy of the barium enema.

Ultrasonography   Ultrasonography (US), frequently referred to simply as "ultrasound," is an imaging method that uses sound waves with frequencies above detection by the human ear to produce pictures of structures within the body. It is particularly effective in analyzing soft-organ tissue, such as the gallbladder, liver, kidneys, ovaries, and bladder. (See Figure 6.5 for an ultrasound report of the abdomen.) Ultrasonography is popular for pregnant women and is the most common investigative procedure in obstetrics and gynecology.

Usually, the AHP will book an appointment for a client's ultrasound. An ultrasound of abdominal organs, particularly for a pelvic examination, may require an empty stomach and a full bladder. The client is instructed to drink about six glasses of water one hour before the test. This fills the bladder, resulting in better visualization of some abdominal structures, especially the uterus. A full bladder is very uncomfortable (whether pregnant or not), and some clients find drinking that much water difficult. Advise the client not to go to the bathroom even if she feels she must. If the bladder is not sufficiently full, the test may be postponed or the client may be asked to drink more water and wait until the bladder is full enough.

Proton Emission Tomography (PET) This is a type of nuclear medicine imaging. The PET produces three-dimensional images of functioning body parts, such as a beating heart or blood flow. It is often done in conjunction with computed tomography (CT) or magnetic resonance imaging (MRI). The client is given a radioactive substance intravenously, by mouth, or by inhalation. There is no special preparation, but clients are asked to leave all jewellery at home. If they don't, it will be removed prior to entering the diagnostic area.

CT or CAT Scanning Computed tomography (CT), also called computerized axial tomography (CAT) or a CAT scan, is a technique using X-rays and a computer to produce cross-sectional images of any part of the body. It often provides more detailed information than conventional X-ray techniques. Common investigations include those of the head, spine, thorax, abdomen, pelvis, and joints. Not every facility has a CT scanner, and so you may need to arrange for a hospital client to have the test done elsewhere.

The part of the body being visualized is positioned inside a cylinder that tilts and rotates to facilitate various views. Claustrophobic people may not be good candidates for this test. The test is, however, less confining than an MRI. Examinations usually take between 20 and 40 minutes. The client may need to arrive an hour early.

Magnetic Resonance Imaging (MRI) The MRI machine produces a strong magnetic field. When a patient is placed inside this field and the body is exposed to short radio frequency pulses, some of the protons within the cells of the body realign with the external magnetic field. Cells from different parts of the body behave in different ways. Using modern high-speed computers, an analysis of this process can be used to produce images of different parts of the body. MRI is invaluable in diagnosing a wide range of conditions throughout the body and is particularly useful in diagnosing disorders of the brain, spine, and joints.

On the older MRI machines, which are closed in, the test involves moving the client into a tunnel approximately one metre in diameter. Most tests require the client to hold fairly still. Clients who are claustrophobic are poor candidates for the older model MRIs. Clients with metal devices in their bodies are also unable to have an MRI because of the strong magnetic field used for the scan. The doctor needs to know about pacemakers, metal pins or clips, and even tattoos (many contain lead) and IUCDs (intrauterine contraceptive devices). On occasion, a contrast dye may be used, which does not, however, contain iodine. Still, known allergies to any type of dye are important to note.

MRI is not readily available in many communities across Canada. In some regions, the wait for an MRI can be up to a year. If you have a client who is booked several months in advance for an MRI, make a note on your calendar or computer to give the client a reminder call a week or so before the test. Clients forget tests and appointments that are two weeks away, let alone several months. Many MRI machines are operated 24 hours a day to reduce waiting time. If a client does not show up, a resource that could have been used for someone else is wasted.

Mammography A mammogram is an X-ray of the breast that can be used as a screening mechanism to detect early-stage cancer. Most provincial and territorial plans will pay for periodic mammograms, usually for older women and those with family histories of breast cancer, who are considered at increased risk. This test must be booked, but waits are usually not long. The test takes about 10 minutes. Many women find the pressure used to compress the breasts painful. Clients may be advised to avoid caffeine for up to two weeks before the test to reduce breast sensitivity. It is also helpful to have the test a week after the client's period when the breasts are less tender. Women having the test for the first time are often quite apprehensive and may ask you if it will hurt. Remember that pain is very subjective and individual. Some women talk of feeling nothing but pressure; others describe the experience as excruciating. Avoid using the word "pain." Advise the woman that there is certainly pressure and that the level of discomfort varies from person to person.

Figure 6.6 is a report of a mammogram noting some irregularities. In light of the client's history of a breast lump, the radiologist recommends further investigation.

Bone Mineral Density Test   A bone mineral density (BMD) test uses very small doses of radiation to check the density of bone in the spine and hip. It is used to detect early osteoporosis and to monitor clients with osteoporosis. The exam takes about 20 minutes. Clients may be instructed to wear clothes without metal buttons, zippers, or buckles. Some facilities will delay a BMD if the client has had a barium swallow or enema or other radioactive studies within the preceding one or two weeks.

RS LABORATORIES AND DIAGNOSTIC SERVICES
223 Lakeway Ave.
Vancouver, BC
V4R 6M1

DIAGNOSTIC IMAGING DEPT

Physician	**Client:** Perreault, Anne
Dr. D Singh	**DOB:** 11/4/56
43 Rundle Ave	**Sex:** F
Vancouver, BC	**PH:** 604-321-2232
	MCP # 4323432255
	Subscriber's Initial: A
	Date of Service: Sept 2/08
	Date Printed: Sept 3/08

Report Status: final

Examination Required

MAMMOGRAM

The breasts are mildly dense bilaterally.
Benign-appearing calcification is demonstrated in the left breast. Both breasts are relatively symmetrical in appearance and appear unchanged when compared to previous mammogram of January 4 of last year. However, clinical history mentioned a lump in the left breast. It would be helpful to include a diagram of the left breast including the area of suspected lump so that it may be further analyzed with the ultrasound modality as it is possible for a clinically suspicious lump to be overlooked on plain mammography.

V.ss   Y.J. Henry M. Radiologist.

Book for appointment this week.
DS

Figure 6.6   Mammogram report

Other Tests

Colonoscopy   A colonoscopy is a visual examination of the entire large intestine, from the lowest part—the rectum—all the way up through the colon to the lower end of the small intestine. The procedure is used to look for early signs of cancer in the colon and rectum. It is also used to diagnose the causes of unexplained changes in bowel habits. Colonoscopy enables the physician to see inflamed tissue, abnormal growths, ulcers, and bleeding.

Preparation for this test involves dietary restrictions for one to three days before the test. Often, only fluids are allowed on the day prior to the test. The client must also be instructed to take a laxative the night before and perhaps the morning of the test and to be NPO (except for the laxative) for eight hours prior to the test. It is usually done in the hospital on an outpatient basis. The client will likely have an intravenous (IV) tube and receive sedation for cramping. The client can expect to be in the hospital for about four hours. A client who receives sedation should not drive for at least 12 hours and will need someone to provide transportation.

Gastroscopy   Also called an *endoscopy*, this is a very common procedure in which the lining of the esophagus, the stomach, and the first part of the small intestine are viewed using a flexible instrument called an endoscope, which is passed through the mouth and into the stomach. Most gastroscopies are carried out using a local anesthetic throat spray, sometimes supplemented by intravenous sedation. The client may feel like gagging when the scope is inserted. The test takes about 20 minutes. The client should have someone to drive him home in case sedation is required.

Tests for the Cardiovascular System

Electrocardiogram   An electrocardiogram (ECG or EKG) is a noninvasive test that records the electrical activity of the heart via electrodes placed on the chest, arms, and legs. This test helps the doctor evaluate a person's cardiac condition, including determining whether the person has had a heart attack and, if so, what part of the heart has been damaged. An ECG can also detect an irregular heartbeat and the presence of **ischemia**, a lower concentration of red blood cells because of a blockage.

ischemia   a local lack of red blood cells because of mechanical obstruction of the blood supply, usually caused by arterial narrowing.

Holter Monitoring Holter monitoring is a continuous tracing of heart activity. Electrodes are placed on the chest area with leads attached to a small transportable recorder. The client keeps a record of her daily activities and any relevant symptoms, such as chest pain or angina. This may be ordered for one or several days. After the test, a cardiologist examines the recording. This test is ordered by a physician and may be done in the hospital or on an outpatient basis. The equipment is usually hooked up in the Cardiopulmonary Services Department, and the client is given instructions. Book the appointment, and record it on the Kardex or PI screen.

Stress Test   Sometimes called an exercise ECG, this test measures the heart's response to the increased demands for oxygen caused by increased activity. The client is asked to walk on a treadmill (or ride an exercise bike) at various speeds. The test usually lasts about half an hour. Some clients experience such symptoms as angina or shortness of breath, so a physician and a technician should be present during this test, and the client should be carefully assessed afterward. This test is ordered by a physician and can be done on an inpatient or outpatient basis. Book the appointment with the lab, and record the information on the Kardex or PI screen.

Doppler Ultrasound The Doppler ultrasound is used, among other purposes, to assess peripheral pulses that are difficult to hear. The ultrasound unit has earpieces like those of a regular stethoscope. However, instead of a standard bell and diaphragm, the cord is attached to an audio unit with an audio transmission device called a transducer. This transducer picks up and amplifies the sounds of blood moving through vessels. The Doppler ultrasound is also used to detect a fetus's heartbeat. Similar devices are used to detect **bruits** (unusual sounds) that are not easily picked up by auscultation, such as the sound of blood passing over a rough spot in a blood vessel. Doppler tests are usually carried out by Cardiopulmonary Services. You need to book an appointment and arrange to have the client go to the department.

bruit a sound, especially an abnormal one, heard on auscultation or by ultrasound.

Echocardiogram An echocardiogram is a noninvasive procedure that uses ultrasound waves to evaluate cardiac function. An echocardiogram is essentially an ultrasound of the heart. Often referred to simply as an "echo," this test can display a cross-section of the beating heart, visualizing the chambers, valves, and major vessels.

There is no special prep for this test, and it can be done in a doctor's office or in the hospital. Gel is applied to the chest, and a wand-like apparatus called a transducer is moved over the chest area to produce images that are recorded and visible on a screen.

Cardiac Catheterization Also called a "heart cath" or an angiogram, this procedure is performed in a special lab. A thin wire called a cardiac catheter is inserted through an artery, usually in the thigh, and threaded into the heart. A dye is injected, and X-rays are taken of the arteries. The client usually requires some sedation. Smaller hospitals may not offer this test, and so the client may have to be transported to a larger hospital.

❹ HEALTH TEACHING

THE AHP'S ROLE IN DIAGNOSTIC TESTING WILL BE PRIMARILY ADMINISTRATIVE and includes completing and giving out requisitions, reporting and filing results (discussed later in the chapter), and educating clients. To fill this role, you need to recognize and understand the laboratory tests commonly ordered in hospitals and health offices. Clients need to know where to go for the test, how to prepare for it, and what to expect. They have many questions in mind: How long it will take? Exactly what will happen? Can someone come with me? Will I have sedation? How much discomfort will I feel? Will I be able to drive afterward? Do I have to do anything special afterward?

Client education is the single most important factor in successful tests. Tests can be accurate only if clients understand how to prepare for them. It may take you a few more minutes to explain clearly and carefully, but the time is well worth it. A client who does not understand the instructions may call the office several times to have them clarified. A well-informed client is likely to be less apprehensive, more compliant with preparation instructions, and more cooperative at the time of the test. For example, if a client does not realize that the test involves an IV, she may be frightened and require prolonged persuasion, throwing off the lab's schedule. She may even refuse the test. Others tests may have to be cancelled if the patient has eaten; for example, a fasting blood sugar will not give accurate results unless the patient has fasted for eight to 12 hours. Other procedures, such as a barium enema, an upper GI series, or a colonoscopy, also require that the client remain NPO, as food in the stomach could cause vomiting and gagging during the test. Most tests requiring sedation also require that the client be NPO because of the potential for aspiration (if the client vomits and inhales the vomitus into the lungs). Respiratory arrest and death can result. Likewise, some tests, such as a colonoscopy, require a laxative

THE ECHOCARDIOGRAM

Description of the Test

An echocardiogram uses ultrasound waves to assess the motion of the heart. A technician places a device, called a transducer, at different locations on the chest and directs sound waves toward the heart. These sound waves reflect back and create a picture on the monitor, which is recorded on video. This picture will be reviewed by a specialist. The picture shows the valves and the blood as it passes through the heart and shows how the heart muscle functions. This test takes about 1½ hours to complete.

Preparation

None. You may bring someone with you if you wish. You will not receive any sedation and will be able to drive if you so choose.

During the Test

This test is not painful. You will be required to lie down for the test. A gel is applied to your chest to facilitate the transmission of the ultrasound waves. The transducer will be moved over your chest to look at various portions of your heart. You will experience no pain, but often the transducer is pressed firmly against the chest wall and you may feel some pressure or tenderness.

After the Test

The technician will wipe off the gel. You may leave as soon as you are done.

Risks of the Echocardiogram Test

None; ultrasound is harmless.

Report

A detailed report of your echocardiogram will be sent to the physician who ordered the test.

Figure 6.7   A teaching handout

or enema the night before or the morning of the test. If the bowel is not properly evacuated, the colon cannot be adequately visualized, resulting in an invalid test that has been a waste of everyone's time (not to mention the cost of the test). Sometimes, medication must be discontinued for a specified time before a test. Other medications essential to the client's well-being may be permitted even for a client who is to be NPO.

Providing the client with written as well as oral instructions is helpful. Most laboratories keep handouts explaining the test preparation. If they do not, develop your own and give them to your clients as required. Although some diagnostic facilities do not mind the client calling them for instructions, it is better if you can give all the needed information. Figure 6.7 shows a teaching handout for echocardiography, a diagnostic tool used to visualize and assess the structure and function of the heart muscle, valves, and pericardium.

❺ REQUISITIONS

ALMOST ALL TESTS REQUIRE A REQUISITION, EXCEPT THOSE DONE RIGHT IN THE DOCTOR'S office, such as a hemoglobin or dipstick urine. These would be recorded on the client's chart. Tests ordered in the doctor's office, other than routine blood work and urinalysis, usually have to be booked. The protocol for booking tests is discussed in Chapter 9. It is essential to fill out the requisition accurately and completely. Always recheck the requisition to be sure that it is complete and correct.

Include the client's demographic information, health-card number, physician, test required, and any additional information requested on the requisition. In the hospital, the physician's name may be electronically added or may appear on the client's addressograph. If it is not—for example, if a consultant orders the test—add the name of any doctor who should receive test results. Usually, results are sent to the ordering physician's office, to the family doctor, and, for an inpatient, to the client's chart. If you work for a specialist, add the family doctor's name to the requisition, unless otherwise requested, to ensure that the lab sends the report to the family doctor as well as to the specialist. If the client is booked for surgery, indicate the date and time. A requisition for an electrocardiogram will ask you to list any heart medication or fluid pills the client is taking, sometimes including the dose and frequency. This information is relevant to the interpretation and, sometimes, the processing of the test. If the test is for a culture and sensitivity, you may be asked to identify any antibiotics the client is currently taking as these may affect the results. In a hospital, you would find this information on the client's medication administration record in the computerized environment, in the electronic Kardex, or in a separate field that lists the client's current medications. (See Figure 6.8, which illustrates an ECG requisition for a hospital inpatient.) Also include any specific reporting instructions, such as "Call doctor with results."

Other information required may include the date and time the specimen was collected (or time to be collected) and, sometimes, the name of the person who collected the specimen. In the computerized environment, if specific information is requested, a mandatory field will appear when you requisition the test. The physician usually orders the test, but several members of the health-care team may be in a position to collect it, or the client may collect the specimen herself (e.g., a urine specimen). If it is not readily identifiable,

CONESTOGA GENERAL HOSPITAL ELECTROCARDIOGRAM REAQUISITION	
Patient's Name: Health Card # Hospital #	Address: Version Code: Unit: Room: Bed#
Requisition Date	Appointment Date/Time
Elective O Priority O Stat O	Patient Ambulatory O Portable O Surgery Yes O No O Procedure: Date: Time:
Referring Physician (MRP)	
Phone and Fax No.	Other:
Copies To	Patients Ht. Patients Wt. (actual not stated)
Clinical History Patients Ht.	Patients Wt. (actual not stated)

Figure 6.8 Electrocardiogram requisition—paper format

URINALYSIS REQUISITION

HOSP. NO.	DR.		DATE COLLECTED		NURSE	
PATIENT SURNAME	GIVEN NAME / INITIALS		☐ ROUTINE ☐ URGENT ☐ PRE-OP		(O.R. DATE:) (O.R. TIME:)	

ROOM (ADDRESS)		24h COLLECTION		RANDOM COLLECTION
		START TIME	FINISH TIME	TIME

FAMILY / REFERRING PHYSICIAN(S)	DATE OF BIRTH			
	DAY	MONTH	YEAR	

DATE / TIME SPECIMEN RECEIVED	INITIAL	LAB NO.	CREATININE CLEARANCE ONLY:
			PATIENT - HEIGHT .... WEIGHT ....

☐ ROUTINE		REFERENCE RANGE	OHIP: ☐ YES ☐ NO	24h VOLUME .... mL	
COLOUR AND APPEARANCE				☑ TIMED COLLECTIONS	REFERENCE RANGE
GLUCOSE		Negative	LEUKOCYTES / hpf	CREATININE	7.1-15.8 mmol/d
KETONES		Negative	ERYTHROCYTES / hpf	CREATININE CLEARANCE	1.24-2.08 mL/s
SPECIFIC GRAVITY (SG)		1.010-1.030	EPITHELIAL CELLS / hpf	CALCIUM	<7.50 mmol/d
BLOOD		Negative	CAST / hpf	PROTEIN	0.01-0.1 g/d
pH		5 - 8		AMYLASE	<1100 u/d
PROTEIN		≤ Trace	MUCOUS THREADS/hpf		
NITRITE		Negative	AMORPHOUS CRYSTALS / hpf		
LEUKOCYTES		≤ Trace	CRYSTALS / hpf		
☐ BILIRUBIN		Negative	BACTERIA / hpf		
☐ UROBILINOGEN		≤ Trace	YEAST CELLS / hpf	PREGNANCY TEST	

FORM #2214 REVIEWED MAR '90   DATE OF REPORT   TECHNOLOGIST

HEALTH RECORDS

Figure 6.9   Urinalysis requisition—paper format
Huron Perth Healthcare Alliance

stat   (short for Latin *statim*) immediately.

the lab may want to know the exact source of the specimen and how it was obtained. For example, a swab could come from a wound, the throat, the ear, or elsewhere. A urine specimen may be a voided specimen or obtained from a urinary catheter; a sputum specimen may be coughed up by the client or obtained through a suction catheter. Figure 6.9 shows a requisition for a routine urinalysis, which could be used in an office or a hospital. Note that the requisition asks whether the test is urgent, routine, or preoperative. In-hospital requisitions often ask about the urgency of the test. Some are needed **stat**, meaning immediately; some may be *urgent,* meaning soon but not necessarily immediately; and others are *routine,* meaning that they can be done the next time the lab normally sends someone around to collect it. Computerized requisitions usually address this with a mandatory field.

In the office, the physician usually identifies the tests he wants done on the requisition, as well as relevant client information, leaving the AHP to fill out the rest. In the hospital setting, you will be filling out the entire requisition, either manually or electronically. Absolute accuracy is imperative.

Many paper requisitions have two or three copies. One can be kept for the client's chart as a record that the test has been requisitioned. This is especially useful in the hospital setting. If a specimen gets lost, it provides some measure of proof that it was indeed ordered. In the computerized environment, the computer will keep a record of all such transactions.

In the doctor's office, make a note on the client's chart that a test has been ordered and, if applicable, the time for which it was booked. The physician may note that the test has been ordered under "plan" or "treatment" on the chart, in which case you would only add the date and time. A client may call you because he forgot when the test was booked. This information is also useful if a specialist calls wanting a certain test done before she sees the client or wanting to know what tests were ordered. Sometimes, a diagnostic facility will call about a previously ordered test.

In computerized facilities, such as hospitals, lab tests are electronically ordered and therefore paperless. If a test is ordered stat, telephone the appropriate service to ensure that they are aware of the order. Electronic requisitions are sent into an "inbox" in the appropriate department and are only checked at specific intervals. If a stat test is electronically ordered at 1300 hrs (1:00 p.m.) and the next routine check of the inbox is at 1700 hrs (5 p.m.), the stat order would be missed. Because stat orders for tests often require a technician to come to the floor to collect the specimen, it is more efficient to print the requisition on the floor so that it is there when the technician arrives. (See Chapter 15 for more on electronic requisitions.)

Figure 6.10 illustrates a biochemistry/hematology requisition for a client in hospital. If you were transcribing a doctor's orders, you would tick off all the specific tests ordered by the doctor.

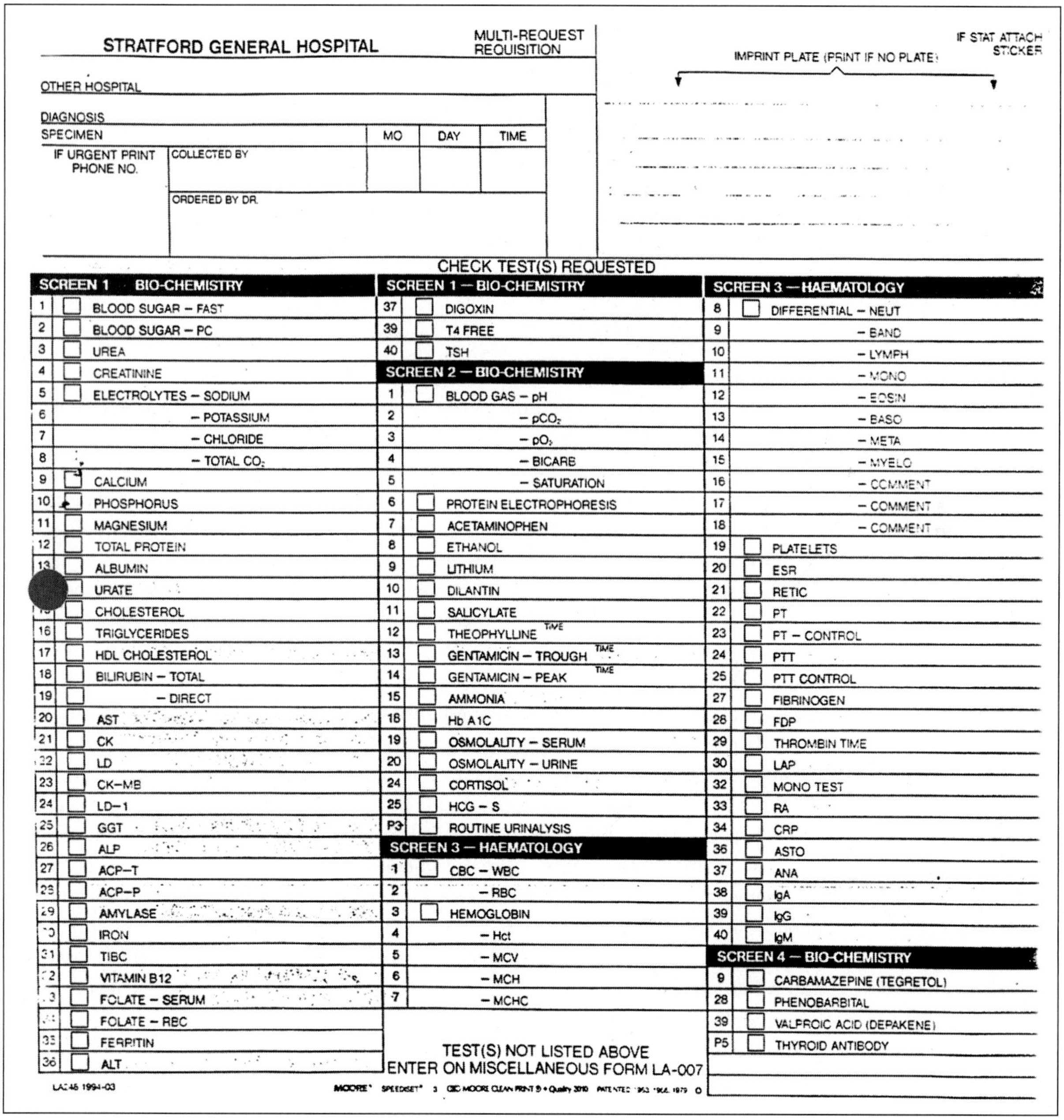

Figure 6.10 A multi-request paper requisition for a hospitalized client. Also used for outpatients.
Huron Perth Healthcare Alliance

PREPARING AND HANDLING SPECIMENS

IT IS UNLIKELY THAT YOU WILL BE ASKED TO HAVE MUCH TO DO WITH ACTUAL TESTING. In the doctor's office, you might, however, be asked to collect and label some specimens, such as urine specimens. The client will probably leave the specimen in the washroom or examination room. Some clients may bring the urine specimen to the office with them. It is essential to label the specimens promptly and correctly. If there are two bottles of urine in the bathroom and you are not absolutely certain which belongs to whom, you must discard them. The requisition itself should be filled out, at least in part, by the doctor. You may be asked to complete the client information. The requisition must be placed in a bag with the specimen or otherwise attached to it. The specimen container itself must also be individually labelled. Most labels have an adhesive backing so that they can be affixed to the container. Labelling the actual container before the test is sometimes a good idea. In the case of a urine specimen, sticking the label on after the specimen collection prevents the label from becoming soiled. Remember to refrigerate midstream urine specimens until the lab picks them up. Most laboratories will have a courier who picks up specimens and delivers them to the lab. *Remember to use Standard Precautions* (as described in Chapter 5) *when handling all specimens*.

❻❼ RECEIVING AND RECORDING TEST RESULTS

IN BOTH THE HOSPITAL AND THE HEALTH OFFICE, THE AHP MAY BE RESPONSIBLE for receiving and filing test reports. In the health office, reports of diagnostic tests will be faxed, emailed, sent by courier or mail, or telephoned to the office.

When you take a report on the phone, always repeat all reported information back to the caller, including the client's first and last names, hospital number, if appropriate, the type of test, and the values. Do not rush through this procedure. A misplaced decimal point or transposed numbers can have serious consequences. Even if you are certain that you recorded the numbers correctly, remember that the person giving you the report may have made a mistake reading them to you. Reading the values back can catch both kinds of error.

You may be required to sort test reports and place them on the doctor's desk for review. It is helpful to integrate this responsibility into your daily routine, perhaps first thing in the morning. Bring any abnormal results to the doctor's attention as soon as possible. Many doctors depend on their office staff to filter reports for them, prioritizing those that need immediate attention. The doctor may not review the test results until the end of the day. This is fine for normal or slightly abnormal results, but the client could be at risk if a critical value is not addressed immediately. For some tests, critical values are an emergency, and you must tell the doctor immediately, even if it means interrupting a client visit. Usually, a laboratory will call the office right away if a test comes back with a critical result. Printed reports will also make note of abnormal results. Review Figures 6.1 and 6.2 for an example of a white blood cell count and an elevated glucose level.

The doctor may ask you to check the test results again before filing them to ensure that she has dealt with them, particularly with abnormal results, and to deal with any physician's instructions. For example, the doctor may ask you to call clients to come in and discuss abnormal results. Be alert for such messages as you file the reports. If you notice an abnormal result that the doctor has not addressed, either verbally or in writing, bring it to her attention. Many offices also call clients with normal results to alleviate their concerns.

Report abnormal or critical values to the physician immediately. If the lab calls the doctor's office with a critical result, put the call through immediately.

Keeping a lab book may also helpful, both in the health office and in the hospital. This will depend on the degree of computerization used in your workplace. If lab results are faxed, recording abnormal results may be unnecessary; just be sure you bring them to the doctor's or the nurse's attention. If the policy is to document results in a book, use it only for recording telephoned test results. See Figure 6.11 for appropriate headings. Print, for clarity. Record each result on a separate line, and sign or initial each entry. If you are in a hospital, add the client's room number and hospital number. This also serves as a record if the physician or lab wishes to follow up on anything related to the recorded results.

In most offices, you will then file the printed reports in the client's chart or enter information received by phone on the chart. But first, *always* double-check that the person for whom you received results is the same as the person on the chart. Clients can have similar or identical names, and if you are busy it is very easy to enter information on the wrong chart. This kind of error can not only cause confusion but, in some cases, can put both clients in danger.

Offices have their own system of filing test results, but there are two basic methods. In *source-oriented filing*, separate results by category (e.g., blood, X-rays), with the most recent result in each category on top. In an *integrated format*, which most doctors prefer, sort all tests by date ordered, regardless of category, and place the latest test results in the front of the chart. Many physicians also want significant test results recorded, along with a list of the client's current medication profile, on a flow sheet kept in the front of the chart. Some lab reports are cumulative, showing previous tests results from the same department. Discard any duplicate results. Electronic charts use a similar order but often keep results on a page separated by a line or heading. Purge the charts periodically, removing duplicate reports.

Date	Client	Rm#	Test and Results	Recorded by	Time	Reported to & Time
Nov 8/xx	Mark Collier	304–1	INR 3.7	R Munroe	1120	Dr. Hanson @ 1145

Figure 6.11 A sample lab book for recording telephone reports from the lab and diagnostic imaging

Often, a lab will telephone test results to the office of a hospital client-care unit, particularly if the results are abnormal or if the results have been ordered stat. In the hospital setting, most reports are computer generated and added to the client's electronic chart. In noncomputerized environments, diagnostic reports usually arrive on the floor toward the end of the day. They must then be added to the client's chart. Most hospitals will have a specific order if traditional charts are used, with each department separated with a divider, for example, hematology, biochemistry, pathology, microbiology, radiology. Reports may be cumulative and show previous results on one page. Eliminate any duplicate records.

Recording Results for the Preoperative Client

When a client is booked for surgery, inevitably, there will be routine blood work that must be completed first, as well as other specific tests. Many hospitals have a comprehensive checklist to be completed before a client goes to the operating room. (See Chapter 15.) This list will include lab results, medication, mental status, and a note on where documentation is to be found for such things as consent, physical history, and consultations. The form may also note preop preparation, including not only whether the client is NPO and has voided or been catheterized, but also such details as removing contact lenses and dental work. You will be required (perhaps in collaboration with a nurse) to ensure that all the appropriate lab work is on the chart. If a test has not been ordered for the client, mark the line "NA" for "not applicable." Never leave it blank. The surgeon may assume it was not done but was necessary. Sometimes, especially with emergency surgery, test results may not be back yet. In this case, tick "call OR." Either you or the lab is responsible for ensuring that the results are telephoned to the operating room. Some tests results are very important for the surgeons to have prior to operating. Without certain test results, surgery may be cancelled.

Future Trends

Innovations in diagnostic technology are rapidly moving forward. We have become familiar with the CT scan, the PET scan, and the MRI, which have become commonplace diagnostic tools. Already another generation of scanners has been introduced that will produce higher quality scans at a faster speed. For example, the Achieva 3T MRI scanner can visualize the structure of individual blood vessels in the brain, nerves, and tissue. This scanner will aid in cancer and stroke research: it will provide insight into how cancer cells grow and spread, and how the vessels and tissue in the brain recover from a stroke.

Diagnostic tests are continually evolving. For example, there is a relatively new rapid test for tuberculosis (TB) that is expected to be rolled out worldwide over the next few years. The new test can be done while the client is in the waiting room. It is accomplished by using a small device that can determine the presence of bacterial DNA

in a person's sputum, and is cheaper, faster, and more accurate than the standard TB test. Two new tests (currently approved in Europe) for HIV have been developed by Abbott Pharmaceuticals. These tests give results sooner than the traditional ones.

Genetic testing is still an important part of diagnosing disease, using DNA or RNA as a biomarker for clinical testing. It can be used to diagnose problems ranging from infectious diseases and cancer to those that are genetically inherited. Genetic tests are also used to assess a person's risk level for acquiring certain diseases as well as to individualize treatment—this is called personalized medicine. More recently, genetic profiles are being offered directly to consumers online for those willing to pay for these tests. More information is available through the DNA Solutions website listed at the end of the chapter.

>

Although proven reliable, most of these tests and subsequent treatments are unavailable to Canadians because of both cost and access. Provincial and territorial plans are unlikely to provide coverage for the majority of these tests in the foreseeable future. The cost of diagnostic tests is factoring into decisions on what tests to order. Some newer and more sophisticated tests are not covered under provincial/territorial plans. Other tests are under scrutiny because of how frequently they are ordered versus how valuable the information actually is, as well as their cost. For example, recently some publications suggested that many Canadians were at risk for vitamin D deficiency. Requests for family doctors to order this test soared, to the point where the cost to Canadian taxpayers was astronomical. Many provinces including Ontario, Manitoba, and Nova Scotia have put limits on ordering vitamin D levels. Ordering PSA titres in men is also under scrutiny.

Computer-aided diagnosis is a major part of ongoing research in medical imaging. Physicians combine their diagnostic findings with computer output based on algorithms for what is called computer assisted diagnosis (CAD). This is an evolving technology.

SUMMARY

1. Diagnostic tests are ordered by a physician or other provider and give valuable information to diagnose and monitor clients' conditions. Tests are processed by medical laboratories, which may be part of a hospital or be independent. Laboratories have specialized departments, such as Hematology (blood work), Pathology (tissue samples), and Diagnostic Imaging (X-rays, ultrasound).

2. Among the more common tests are complete blood count, electrolytes, blood glucose levels, cholesterol and triglycerides, and culture and sensitivity (C&S) tests for the presence of pathogens in blood, urine, or swabs from wounds, ears, or throat. Diagnostic imaging includes conventional X-rays, barium swallow or enema, ultrasound, CT scanning, magnetic resonance imaging, mammograms, bone mineral density tests, and endoscopies.

3. Clear, concise, and complete client information saves time in the long run and is essential for effective, accurate testing.

4. Tests usually require requisitions and must often be booked. Make sure that requisitions include all necessary information, which often includes the client's medication and the urgency of the test.

5. You will likely receive test results both as printed and as phoned reports. Notify the doctor immediately of abnormal and critical values. File results with the most recent ones on top.

Key Terms

autopsy 145
bruit 165
computed tomography
    (CT) 143
critical value 146
enzyme 154

heparin 150
ischemia 164
magnetic resonance
    imaging (MRI) 143
mammography 143
midstream urine specimen
    (MSU) 157

reference range 143
serum 153
stat 168
ultrasonography 143

Review Questions

1. Identify three professionals who work with lab and diagnostic facilities, and explain what they do.
2. What role does diagnostic testing play in health promotion and illness prevention?
3. What tests are usually included in a CBC?
4. What are the most common tests ordered on a microbiology requisition?
5. What tests usually require a client to fast?
6. Discuss the basic information needed when booking a lab test.
7. What is the advantage of thorough client instruction about test preparation?
8. Why must the Dietary Department be notified when a hospital client is NPO for a test?
9. What is meant when a test is ordered *stat*?
10. What is the appropriate way to handle a midstream urine sample taken for culture and sensitivity?

Application Exercises

1. Contact a local laboratory facility or doctor's office and identify what lab and diagnostic tests are uninsured in your area. State the purpose of these tests and the cost to the client.
2. Choose four of the following diagnostic tests. Construct a client teaching handout for each. Include such information as how the test is done, what it is for, how long it takes, whether the client should have someone to take her home, any medications involved, and other specifics related to preparation for the test.
   - CT scan
   - Glucose tolerance test
   - Barium swallow
   - Barium enema
   - Colonoscopy
   - Other (your choice)

Websites of Interest

Mammogram instructions and explanation
www.imaginis.com/breasthealth/abnormalities.asp

Midstream urine
www.healthcentral.com/mhc/top/003751.cfm

Links to explanations of various diagnostic tests
www.nlm.nih.gov/medlineplus/diagnostictests.html
Click on the test/category of interest for further detail.

Information on lab and diagnostic tests
www.labtestsonline.org/map/index.html

This website provides links to look up screening tests and tests specific to a range of conditions. This site will also take you on a virtual tour of a lab—Click on Features, and then, under Inside the Lab, Follow That Sample: A Short Lab Tour.

DNA Solutions: DNA Testing—Canada
http://www.dnacanada.com/

Chapter 7
Pharmacology

Learning Objectives

On completing this chapter, you will be able to:

1. Discuss the role of the pharmacy team.
2. List and discuss four major sources of drugs.
3. Identify four categories of names given to drugs.
4. Describe Canadian legislation controlling drugs.
5. Outline the way prescription and over-the-counter medications are dispensed.
6. List and identify the major classifications of drugs by use and by action and function.
7. List and describe routes of administration.
8. Explain the elements of pharmacokinetics and the factors that affect drug metabolism.
9. Distinguish between side effects and allergies.
10. Summarize the health office professional's role in educating clients about herbal, over-the-counter, and prescription drugs.
11. Outline proper procedures for storing, handling, and disposing of drugs safely.

pharmacology a biological science and academic discipline that deals with the properties, uses, and actions of drugs and chemicals in living beings.

Pharmacology is the study and description of drugs, their composition, actions, and effects. Pharmacology involves research into the therapeutic and adverse effects of drugs on living beings, their curative potential, and their interactions with other medications. In short, pharmacology examines the effects drugs and chemicals have on living things. A basic knowledge of pharmacology is important for all health-care professionals. A *pharmacy* is a licensed business involved in dispensing drugs. *Dispensing* involves compounding, packaging, labelling, and selling and/or delivering a drug in response to a prescription written by a qualified health provider. Your responsibilities for medications will be varied. You may be asked to phone a prescription to a pharmacist, take phoned-in requests for repeats from a pharmacy or a client, and copy dictated medical reports. In the hospital, you will process physicians' medication orders.

One component of pharmacology is *pharmacokinetics*, which deals with the effects drugs have on people. It considers how the drug is taken and absorbed into the body, how the body metabolizes it, or breaks it down, and how it is distributed and excreted. *Pharmacodynamics* looks at the small scale: it is concerned with the study of molecular and physiological effects of drugs on cellular systems and how they act on these systems. *Toxicology* concerns the adverse effects of drugs and chemicals used for therapeutic purposes as well as in agriculture and industry. *Clinical pharmacology* is the study of various drugs and their effects on people. It includes the study of how they work, how they interact with other drugs, and their therapeutic effects on diseases and disease processes.

As a health office professional, you need a basic knowledge of pharmacology. You will often be the intermediary between the client and the physician, the client and the pharmacist, and the pharmacist and the physician, ordering new prescriptions, dealing with repeats and renewals, and passing on information. Clients will have questions about their prescriptions and about over-the-counter (OTC) drugs, vitamins, supplements, and herbal medications. You should be able to respond to basic questions knowledgeably; more importantly, you need to know when to direct the client elsewhere for answers.

You need to understand the components of a prescription, the information needed for renewals, which medications the physician may order over the telephone, which require a faxed or written script, and when the client should see the physician about medications. In both the hospital and the health office, you need to be familiar with the more common medications, their spelling, and classification. Table 7.1 lists some drugs commonly prescribed in Canada. It is also important to know what time of day drugs should be taken, which medications should be taken with food, and which should be taken on an empty stomach. In the hospital or long-term care facility you will be responsible for transcribing medication orders accurately to the appropriate medication administration record (MAR). You must understand the terminology that accompanies the medication order. You also need to understand the pharmacist's role in your setting and how to work effectively with the pharmacist.

❶ THE PHARMACIST

PHARMACISTS ARE THE EXPERTS IN DRUG INFORMATION. A PHARMACIST IS A HEALTH professional who is trained in the art of preparing and dispensing drugs. Licensing standards for pharmacists are set by the provinces and territories but are similar across the country. Pharmacists must graduate from a university program recognized by their governing body and must have practical experience. Provincial and territorial regulatory

Table 7.1 Some Drugs Commonly Prescribed in Canada

acetaminophen and oxycodone (Percocet)

alendronate (Fosamax)

amlodipine (Norvasc)

amoxicillin (Amoxil)

atorvastatin (Lipitor)

azithromycin (Zithromax)

budesonide (Symbicort)

celecoxib (Celebrex)

cephalexin (Keflex)

ciprofloxacin (Cipro)

citalopram (Celexa)

clopidogrel (Plavix)

codeine (comes in 15, 20 & 60 mg tabs)

diazepam (Valium)

digoxin (Lanoxin, Toloxin)

dimenhydrinate (Gravol)

donepezil (Aricept)

enalapril (Vasotec)

escitalopram (Cipralex)

esomeprazole (Nexium)

ethinyl estradiol and levonorgestrel (Min-Ovral, Alesse, Triphasil)

fexofenadine (Allegra)

fluoxetine (Prozac)

fluticasone and salmetrol (Advair, MDI)

fluticasone oral inhalation (Flovent)

fosinopril (Monopril)

furosemide (Lasix)

glyburide (Diabeta)

heparin

hydrochlorothiazide /HCT (Hydrodiuril)

hydromorphine

hydroxyzine (Atarax)

insulin preparations (Humulin, Novolin)

ipratropium bromide (Atrovent; also solution for nebulizer)

irbesartan (Avapro)

ketorolac (Toradol)

lansoprazole (Prevacid)

levofloxacin (Levaquin)

levothyroxine (Synthroid, Eltroxin)

loratadine (Claritin)

lorazepam (Ativan)

losartan (Cozaar)

losartan and hydrochlorothiazide (Hyzaar)

low macular weight heparin (LMWH)

meloxicam (Mobic)

meperidine (Demerol)

metformin (Glucophage)

metoprolol (Lopresor)

morphine (MS Contin)

naproxen (Anaprox, Naprosyn)

nifedipine (Adalat)

nitrofurantoin (Macrobid)

nitroglycerin transdermal (Nitro-Dur, Minitran, Trinipatch)

olanzapine (Zyprexa)

omeprazole (Losec)

oxycodone (OxyNEO; replaces OxyContin)

paroxetine (Paxil)

phenytoin (Dilantin)

pioglitazone (Actos)

pravastatin (Pravachol)

prednisone (Winpred, numerous generics for many of these drugs)

pregabalin (Lyrica)

propranolol hydrochloride (Inderal)

raloxifene (Evista)

ramipril (Altace)

ranitidine (Zantac)

Rh (D) immunoglobulin IV/IM (WinRho SDF)

risedronate (Actonel)

risperidone (Risperdal)

rosuvastatin (Crestor)

salbutamol inhalation (Ventolin)

sertraline (Zoloft)

sulphamethoxazole-trimethoprim (Septra; Bactrim)

tamsulosin (Flomax)

terbinafine (Lamisil)

Tylenol #3 (acetaminophen/codeine)

venlafaxine (Effexor)

warfarin (Coumadin, Taro-Warfarin)

zyloprim (Allopurinol)

authorities grant pharmacists licences, assess the competency of pharmacists, and ensure public safety. Pharmacists dispense drugs in response to prescriptions written by physicians, dentists, or other designated health providers. They are also an important resource for clients, physicians, and other health professionals. Although most medications are accompanied by explanatory literature, clients often do not understand the sheet or seek more information. Pharmacists will answer their questions, simplify written explanations, and provide more detail, as required. Clients may be confused about when to take a medication, whether it will interact with other medications they are taking, and its side effects. Pharmacists can reinforce physicians' information. They will also give advice about OTC drugs and herbal products. Medications are one of the fastest-changing components in health care: as fast as some are removed from the market, new ones are approved and introduced to the market. Even if a drug has been on the market for many years, there is still much new information about potential uses, adverse effects, and actions on the body that is learned each year.

A pharmacist will review the client's medication profile (based largely on the pharmacy's own records, the client, and information from the doctor) when filling a prescription and will notify the doctor of potential adverse interactions or of more effective medication. The pharmacist is often the first to pick up misuse or abuse of prescribed medications and, depending on the situation, will either speak to the client or notify the physician. Some provinces will pay the pharmacist to complete basic and advanced medication reviews for specific groups of clients following specific timelines (e.g., annually or biannually).

The pharmacist will advise the physician of new medications, more economical alternatives, changes in dosage recommendations, and alerts about medications. She collaborates with all levels of health professionals to effectively and safely manage clients' medications. She will act as an information resource for you, clarifying medication orders in the hospital and supplementing information in the health office.

Emerging Responsibilities for the Pharmacist

Currently, the scope of practice for pharmacists is expanding across Canada. To assume most of the extended responsibilities the pharmacist must have special training. Added responsibilities include giving flu shots and other immunizations (BC, Alberta, and Nova Scotia are leading this initiative), emergency prescribing (of previously prescribed medication), offering pharmaceutical opinions (e.g., advice on an existing or potential drug-related problem as well as suggesting possible interventions), ordering lab tests (to manage a patient's response to drug therapy), authorizing refills (during a physician's absence or for individuals in long-term care facilities and/or with chronic diseases), prescribing certain medications, and making adaptations to prescriptions (e.g., dose, duration). Pharmacists receive special training for giving immunizations. The other responsibilities require collaboration with the client's doctor(s), and depend on inclusive electronic medical records (EMR) access. As well, pharmacists can refuse to fill a legally completed prescription. This would occur if the prescribed treatment is deemed inappropriate by the pharmacist based on information available at the pharmacy (and would require consultation with the physician). Saskatchewan pharmacists were the first in Canada to receive provincial payment for assessing approved "minor ailment conditions" that result in a drug prescription. Currently approved treatable minor conditions include acne, insect bites, and cold sores.

Other members of the pharmaceutical team are *pharmacy technicians* and *pharmacy assistants*. Both work under the direction of a pharmacist. Assistants package medication and assist with other dispensary duties and clerical functions. Technicians have greater responsibilities and more extensive training, usually a one- or two-year postsecondary program. They procure supplies, maintain inventories, and help dispense and distribute medications. Regulated technicians can independently perform and sign off on the filling of a prescription. A pharmacist is required to sign off on its therapeutic appropriateness.

❷❸ DRUGS: AN EXPLANATION

A DRUG MAY BE DEFINED AS "A CHEMICAL SUBSTANCE THAT AFFECTS THE PROCESSES OF THE mind or body, and any chemical compound used in the diagnosis, treatment, or prevention of disease or other abnormal condition."[1] In common speech, *drugs* are sometimes thought of as illegal substances, and drugs taken for health reasons are more commonly referred to as *medicines* or *medications*.

Drug Sources

Drugs are derived from a variety of sources.

Plants   Much of the current knowledge about drugs came from herbalists, who used plants and herbs in years gone by. They knew through trial and error what herbs, plants, and plant derivatives were effective for various conditions. We use many of their concepts and discoveries in conventional medicine today. Drugs can be obtained from fungi and from the leaves, seeds, sap, stems, fruit, and roots of various plants. The willow tree, for example, contains a component originally used in the production of Aspirin. Digitalis is an extract from the leaf of the purple foxglove. Morphine is derived from a gummy substance extracted from the seed pod of the opium poppy. Other products of plants include **fixed oils**, such as castor oil, and **volatile oils**, such as peppermint and cloves.

Animal Sources   Animals are a natural source for some medications, such as hormones. Originally, insulin was obtained from the pancreases of slaughtered animals, primarily pigs and cattle. Some estrogen is obtained from the urine of pregnant mares. (Synthetic and plant-based forms of estrogen are also available.)

Minerals   Minerals also supply of wide variety of natural drugs, such as potassium and iron supplements, milk of magnesia (a commonly used antacid and laxative derived from magnesium), and lithium carbonate (a salt used to treat bipolar disorder).

Semi-synthetic   The term *synthesis* means that something is chemically reproduced. A semi-synthetic drug results when a drug from a natural source is combined with synthetically produced compounds to alter the effect of the medication. The net result of such combinations is a single new chemical formed from some reaction between those ingredients. For example, heroin is a semi-synthetic variant of morphine.

Synthetic   Synthetic drugs are completely formulated in the laboratory. Some are produced using chemicals and others by copying genetic activity in a living organism.

fixed oils   (also called base or carrier oils) oils, extracted primarily from plants, that do not evaporate.

volatile oils   oils, extracted primarily from plants, that evaporate

---

[1] *Miller-Keene Encyclopedia Dictionary of Medicine, Nursing and Allied Health*, 6th ed. Philadelphia: W.B. Saunders, 1997.

Examples of synthetic drugs include diazepam (Valium), ASA, ibuprofen, and fluoxetine (Prozac). Synthetic forms of insulin were introduced in 1981. Today, there is widespread use of insulin produced from genetically modified bacteria and yeast.

Drug Names

A single drug can have up to four names. Each refers to the same drug but from a slightly different perspective. These names are

- chemical,
- generic,
- trade, and
- botanical.

Chemical   The chemical name of a drug represents its exact formula. For example, the chemical name of bupropion (marketed as Wellbutrin or Zyban) is 1-(3Chlorophenyl)-2-[(1,1-dimethylethyl)amino]-1-propanone. The familiar acetaminophen (Tylenol) is N-(4-hydroxyphenyl) acetanamide. Not surprisingly, these names are seldom used, except by pharmacists and manufacturers in the context of chemical interactions and perhaps in research.

Generic   The generic name of the drug is the nonproprietary name given to a medication, or the official name assigned to it. Generic names for new compounds are given out by an international body to ensure that no two products have the same generic name. The name is much simpler than the chemical name and is not owned by anyone. It does not have protection by copyright. A pharmaceutical company can manufacture a drug (prescription or OTC) under its generic name and put its own trademark on it. Generic names are always spelled in lower-case. Some examples of generic names are

- acetaminophen (one trade name is Tylenol),
- digoxin (trade names are Lanoxin, Toloxin), and
- warfarin (one trade name is Coumadin).

Trade Name   When a pharmaceutical company develops a new drug, it applies to the government for a patent, which gives it the right to sell the drug without competition for a designated period, usually 20 years. (However, it takes roughly 10 years from the time a pharmaceutical company applies for a patent until the drug is approved for used, reducing the effective patent life of the drug to 10 years.) This system is designed to allow the company to recover its investment in researching and developing the drug and to encourage continued research and development. Most manufacturers select a proprietary (trade) or brand name for a drug once it has been approved for sale. This name receives a registered trademark and is, in most cases, legally protected forever. A brand name may be registered only in certain countries. Anyone can reproduce a drug once the patent has expired but cannot use the original company's trade name. The second company can manufacture the drug under its generic name or can apply for a trademark for a name of its own choosing. It takes a manufacturer two to three years to develop a generic, chemically identical copy of a patented drug at a cost of about $1 million.

Trade names are always capitalized. Often, the trade names are more familiar than the generic name: people are more likely to have heard of Valium than of diazepam or of

Tylenol than of acetaminophen. However, the use of generic names is encouraged over trade names to avoid confusion.

Generic drugs are generally less expensive than brand-name drugs, partly because the producer of the generic drug is covering only the costs of manufacturing, not of research, development, and extensive advertising. For example, generic acetaminophen is less expensive than Tylenol. Generic ibuprofen is less expensive than Advil, which is the trade name under which one manufacturer produces the same medication. Some companies claim that the trade-name drug is of better quality than a clone with a generic name. Some such claims may be valid. The exact ingredients may differ, resulting in an altered absorption and excretion rate and a slightly different therapeutic effect.

Even when a medication is prescribed by its trade name, the pharmacist may be legally obligated to fill the prescription with a less expensive generic form of the medication unless the doctor or patient specifies "no substitution." If a drug plan is contributing to cover some of the costs of the prescription, they may only pay for the cost of a generic product. The patient might have to pay for the difference if a particular brand product is requested.

Interchangeability in Ontario is regulated by provincial legislation. Interchangeability allows the pharmacist some autonomy in choosing which brand is dispensed. The ODB (Ontario Drug Benefit) Formulary/CDI (Comparative Drug Index) identifies which products are interchangeable. If a product is not listed as interchangeable, the generic version cannot be dispensed in place of the brand prescribed without first receiving the approval of the prescriber. This applies in all provinces and territories.

Botanical   This is the name used to refer to the natural substance or substances that a drug is made of. An example of this as previously noted, is *Digitalis purpurea*—herbs from which digitalis is derived.

❹ DRUGS AND THE LAW

THE REGULATION AND CONTROL OF DRUGS IN CANADA IS ACHIEVED JOINTLY BY THE federal and provincial and territorial governments.[2] The Health Protection Branch of Health Canada is responsible for drug quality, safety, and efficacy. It regulates the manufacture and importation of drugs for sale in Canada, as well as their distribution, including conditions of sale. The federal *Food and Drug Act (FDA)* and other regulations control the testing and introduction of new drugs to the Canadian market. Federal legislation covers all drugs and chemical substances, legal and illegal. Provinces and territories also have regulations governing the dispensing and control of medications.

In response to concerns about inconsistencies among provinces and territories, in 1995, the National Association of Pharmacy Regulatory Authorities (NAPRA) proposed a national drug scheduling prototype to standardize regulations across the country. Provinces and territories are in various stages of adopting these regulations. NAPRA's system sets out three schedules, explained in the next section.

The federal government issues standards and regulations, under the *Controlled Drugs and Substances Act (CDSA)*, that govern the use of controlled substances in Canada. Certain drugs are defined as **controlled drugs** under the *CDSA*. These are typically drugs with a high potential for addiction and abuse, often narcotic analgesics. Special rules,

controlled drugs drugs defined by federal law to which special rules apply because they are liable to be abused.

[2] Material for this section contributed by Steve Chapman, author of *Drug Control in Canada: A Chemical and Legislative Compendium*. Toronto: Isomer Design, 1993.

discussed later in this chapter, apply to prescribing, administering, handling, and storing these drugs.

❺ DISPENSING DRUGS

THERE ARE TWO METHODS OF DISPENSING DRUGS: BY PRESCRIPTION AND OVER-THE-counter (OTC).

Prescription Drugs

Federal laws make drugs that are dangerous, powerful, or habit forming illegal, except if prescribed by a licensed physician or other qualified health provider who is to monitor the client's condition. (These drugs correspond to NAPRA's Schedule I.) A prescription is an order written and signed by the practitioner for a particular drug to be dispensed to a particular patient.

The pharmacist can dispense most controlled drugs only with a written and physically signed prescription or a signed faxed prescription that can be verified as originating from the prescriber. The use of fax technology by prescribers to transmit new prescriptions to a pharmacy is now commonplace in practice. A pharmacist can receive any type of prescription from a prescriber by fax, including a straight narcotic or controlled drug.

A prescription is usually filled by the pharmacist and given or delivered to the client. In some cases, doctors ask the pharmacist to prepare ahead of time medication packs, which contain limited amounts of the medication and corresponding directions. They are then used when a pharmacist is not available to dispense drugs, for example, at night in an Emergency Department in a smaller hospital. A doctor may prescribe a pain medication and give the client a night pack to last until the next day when the pharmacy is open.

Over-the-Counter Medications

OTC medications are those considered safe for individuals to take without the specific advice of a physician. They are available in pharmacies and a variety of retail outlets. Remember that even OTC drugs can be harmful if used incorrectly. For this reason, most provinces and territories have categorized these drugs to provide some control over access. Note that because some private insurance plans cover only prescribed drugs, physicians will sometimes prescribe some medications, even though they are available over the counter.

Pharmacy Only: Restricted Access   Drugs in this category are available only from a pharmacist (though no prescription is required) and are kept behind the counter. Use of the drug may delay recognition or mask the symptoms of serious disease. The drug may cause important adverse reactions, including allergies, or interact with other drugs, foods, or disease states that cannot be adequately addressed through product labelling. Intervention by the pharmacist is necessary to assess patient risk to prevent such problems for an individual patient through interpretation and clarification of labelling. These drugs correspond with Schedule II of the NAPRA guide.

Pharmacy Only: Under Supervision   Other medications are available only in pharmacies and are sold in a self-serve section of the pharmacy. The initial need for these drugs is normally identified by the patient, physician, or pharmacist, but chronic, recurrent, or subsequent therapy can be monitored by the pharmacist. The availability of the pharmacist to provide advice can promote appropriate use of the drug, and the pharmacist can direct the patient to a practitioner for assessment if the treatment period has been inappropriate or the therapy has been ineffective. Medications in this category include those that could present risks to certain people if used without adequate knowledge. These drugs correspond to Schedule III of the NAPRA guide.

Sold Anywhere: No Restrictions   Other medications can be sold in any retail outlet—corner stores, department stores, gift shops—without any professional supervision. ASA (acetylsalicylic acid), acetaminophen, antacids, and other common drugs are in this category. These drugs are considered "unscheduled" in NAPRA's guide.

Client Education   Most OTC preparations have instructions and indications for use clearly outlined on the package label, but additional client education better ensures correct and safe usage. Any medication can be harmful if used incorrectly. Nonprescription medications can interact badly with prescription medications the client may be taking, with foods, or with disease states.

Client information becomes even more important as a number of former prescription drugs have been granted OTC status. Examples include vaginal creams, such as Monistat for yeast infections; Benadryl for allergic reactions; and the anti-inflammatory Motrin. Some drugs, such as ranitidine (Zantac), used for stomach problems, are available at lower doses than those prescribed by a doctor. There is always the danger that a person who needs to see the doctor will instead self-treat with OTC medications. A pharmacist can provide advice to promote appropriate use or can direct the patient to a practitioner for assessment. Clients must be encouraged to have any persistent problems checked out medically.

6⑦ CLASSIFICATION OF DRUGS

DRUGS CAN BE CLASSIFIED BY FUNCTION (HOW THEY ACT), BY EFFECTS, OR BY BODY SYSTEM. Because a medication may be used for more than one purpose and on more than one body system, categories often overlap.

Classification of Drugs by Use

Desired effects or uses of drugs include

- therapeutic,
- diagnostic,
- curative,
- replacement, and
- prophylactic.

Therapeutic Drugs   Therapeutic medications—whether prescribed or OTC—are taken to relieve symptoms. They are used to treat a wide range of conditions from life-threatening ones to minor ailments, such as a cold or a headache. Many of the drugs you deal with will fall into this category, especially in the office setting.

Diagnostic Drugs   Diagnostic drugs are used to perform diagnostic tests. Examples would include the barium in a barium swallow or the contrast media used in nuclear medicine.

Curative Drugs   Curative drugs are given to overcome a disease, infection, or other conditions. Antibiotics are a common example.

Replacement Drugs   Replacement drugs are taken to "replace" a hormone or other normally present substance that the human body can no longer produce. For example, people whose thyroid glands do not function well, or who have had the thyroid gland removed, take l-thyroxine (Synthroid, Eltroxin) to replace the thyroxine they lack. People with diabetes may take insulin to replace the insulin their pancreas cannot produce. Female hormones, such as estrogen and progesterone, are other examples.

Prophylactic Drugs   This category of medications is given either to prevent a condition or to decrease the severity of a condition. Examples of prophylactic drugs are immunizations, such as the measles–mumps–rubella vaccine.

Classification by Action or Function

- *Adrenergic*: Causes blood vessels to constrict and augments the strength and rate of the heart. Used for such conditions as bronchitis, asthma, and various allergies. Examples include epinephrine, adrenalin, salbutamol (Ventolin), and xylometazoline (Otrivin).

- *Analgesic*: Relieves pain. Analgesics include controlled or narcotic drugs, such as morphine sulphate (MS Contin), and non-narcotic drugs, such as acetaminophen (Tylenol, Anacin, Atasol, Tempra).

- *Anaesthetic*: Reduces or obliterates pain by reducing sensation. Can be given for local or systemic effect. When given locally, the client is conscious. General anaesthetics put the client to sleep, such as during major surgical procedures. Local anaesthetics include lidocaine (Xylocaine) and bupivacaine (Marcaine).

- *Antacid*: Reduces acidity in the stomach and gastrointestinal tract. May be used for dyspepsia or heartburn. Examples include aluminum hydroxide and magnesium carbonate (Maalox, Diovol).

- *Anxiolytic or Anti-anxiety*: Reduces stress levels and feelings of anxiety. Examples include diazepam (Valium), alprazolam (Xanax), and lorazepam (Ativan).

- *Anti-arrhythmic*: Controls abnormal heartbeats, known as arrhythmias, that affect the electrical conduction of the heart. Examples include amiodarone (Cordarone), verapamil (Isoptin), and propafenone (Rythmol).

- *Antibiotic*: Given to fight bacterial infections. Drugs that destroy bacteria in a person's body (Apo-Pen VK, ciprofloxacin [Cipro]) are known as bactericidal; those that inhibit the growth of bacteria, such as tetracyclines, are known as bacteriostatic. Erythromycin can be cidal or static depending upon concentration and the bacteria susceptibility.

- *Anticholinergic*: Reduces muscle spasm through central action. Examples include benztropine mesylate (Cogentin). Other drugs, such as antihistamines and antidepressants, also have anticholinergic properties.

- *Anticoagulant*: Commonly called blood thinners; given to prevent blood clots. These drugs are often given prophylactically following major surgery, particularly to clients with a high risk for developing clots. Warfarin (Coumadin) is an example of an oral anticoagulant, and heparin is an example of a parenteral drug. Another is fragmin. These drugs should not be taken with ASA and certain herbal medications, except under the specific direction of a physician.

- *Anticonvulsant*: Given to prevent, control, or relieve seizure activity, such as in an individual who is epileptic. Examples include carbamazepine (Tegretol) and phenytoin (Dilantin).

- *Anti-depressant*: Used in the treatment and control of clinical depression. Examples include bupropion (Wellbutrin), amitriptyline (Elavil), fluoxetine (Prozac), and venlafaxine (Effexor). These must *not* be taken with St. John's Wort, a herbal anti-depressant, because of the potential for serious interaction.

- *Antidiabetic/Antihyperglycemic*: Used to control diabetes mellitus. Insulin is a parenteral hypoglycemic, used for type I or insulin-dependent diabetes; oral antihyperglycemics, used for the initial stages of type II or non-insulin-dependent diabetes, include glyburide (Diabeta) and repaglinide (Gluconorm), which increase insulin secretion. Antidiabetic medications have different mechanisms. Some antihyperglycemics stimulate the pancreas to produce more insulin. Other medications, such as metformin (Glucophage), pioglitazone (Actos), and rosiglitazone (Avandia), work to improve the body's use of insulin and decrease the amount of glucose released by the liver.

- *Antidiarrheal*: Given to stop or control diarrhea. Perhaps the most common of these today is loperamide (Imodium).

- *Antiemetic*: Given to control or prevent nausea and vomiting. Dimenhydrinate (Gravol) is often given to prevent nausea after surgery. People also take it to prevent motion sickness.

- *Antifungal*: Used to treat fungal infections, either locally (e.g., athlete's foot) or systemically. Examples of topical antifungals include miconazole nitrate (Monistat) and clotrimazole (Canesten). Oral antifungals include terbinafine (Lamisil) and ketoconazole (Nizoral).

- *Antihistamine*: Used to relieve allergies. The drug blocks histamine, which is released when a person has an allergic reaction. A common side effect is drowsiness, although there are antihistamines on the market that avoid this side effect. Examples include diphenhydramine hydrochloride (Benadryl) and loratadine (Claritin).

- *Antihypertensive*: Taken to lower and control high blood pressure. There are a wide variety of antihypertensives on the market, with different modes of action. Some of these medications act to impede vasoconstriction or to cause vasodilation, increasing the ease of blood flow in the body. Others slow the heart rate and decrease the force of the heart's contraction. Others act on a hormone produced by the kidney called angiotensin that affects blood pressure. Examples of antihypertensives include propanolol (Inderal), lisinopril (Zestril), amlodipine (Norvasc), and ramipril (Altace).

- *Anti-inflammatory*: Controls various inflammatory processes in the body, such as joint inflammation and pain. NSAIDs, or non-steroidal anti-inflammatory agents, include ibuprofen (Advil) and naproxen (Anaprox). Prednisone, a steroid, also has anti-inflammatory properties, but because of the high potential for adverse effects, especially with long-term use, it is used only for serious conditions.

- *Antineoplastic*: Used in the treatment of some forms of cancer. Examples include cyclophosphamide (Procytox).

- *Antipyretic*: Reduces fever. Examples include ASA (Aspirin) and acetaminophen (Tylenol).

- *Antispasmodic*: Relieves muscle spasms, for example, in the lower back, that result from either injury or disease. An example is baclofen (Lioresal). Bentylol is for gut spasms.

- *Antitussive*: Controls or relieves coughing. Very few antitussives will totally eliminate a persistent cough, but they usually provide enough relief to allow the client to sleep or rest. Many of these medications are Schedule I or II medications. An example is a drug containing codeine or dextromethorphan, such as Benylin (Delsym) or Novahistamine DM Expectorant, which combines guaifenesin and pseudoephedrine. Some common pediatric antitussives containing these ingredients have been reformulated or withdrawn from the market altogether following an American Academy of Pediatrics study showing that many children were being accidently given too much medication by well-meaning care-givers (including parents), resulting in overdoses and serious side effects.

- *Bronchodilators*: Used primarily to treat chronic obstructive pulmonary disease (COPD) and asthma, these medications cause the bronchial passages to relax and ease breathing. An example is salbutamol (Ventolin).

- *Cardiogenics*: Strengthens the heart muscle and heartbeat. Effective in some clients in relieving the symptoms of congestive heart failure (CHF). Digoxin (Lanoxin) is an example.

- *Cathartic*: Another broad term for laxatives, such as Magnolax, which combines magnesium hydroxide and mineral oil emulsion, magnesium hydroxide (milk of magnesia), and bisacodyl (Dulcolax).

- *Contraceptive*: Used for birth control. Most common are oral contraceptives ("the pill"), such as Triphasil and Min-Ovral, which combine progesterone and estrogen. Various vaginal creams and suppositories also fall into this category.

- *Decongestant*: Used to alleviate sinus and nasal congestion. These medications act by reducing swelling of the nasal passages. Some of these drugs are also controlled, or kept behind the counter in pharmacies, because they contain pseudoephedrine, which is a precursor for the illegal manufacture of methamphetamine. Some examples of these medications include xylometazoline (Otrivin) and pseudoephedrine (Sudafed). Clients should be cautioned that nasal sprays and eye drops should be used for three to seven days only, depending on the medication. Longer use can cause a rebound reaction, which means that stuffiness and swelling can actually increase as the blood vessels enlarge even more than they did before taking the medication. Oral decongestants do not cause the rebound reaction.

- *Diuretic*: Aids in the excretion of excessive body fluid, which can relieve symptoms of hypertension and congestive heart failure. An example is furosemide (Lasix).

- *Emetic*: Used to induce vomiting, such as in the case of a drug overdose. Ipecac syrup is an example.

- *Hormone*: Used primarily to replace hormones that the body can no longer produce. Insulin (Humulin, Novolin) and levothyroxine (Eltroxin, Synthroid) are examples. Hormones are also used to treat symptoms of menopause and in individuals who are seeking sex changes.

- *Hypnotic*: Used as sleeping pills and/or for their sedative effects. Most of these drugs are controlled. Examples include zopiclone (Imovane) and temazepam (Restoril).

- *Immune system modulating agents*: Alters the body's immune system. These drugs are used in the control and treatment of certain autoimmune diseases, such as rheumatoid arthritis and systemic lupus erythematosus, in which the body attacks its own tissues and organs. They are also used to deal with transplant rejection. Examples are prednisone (Apo-prednisone) and methotrexate (Enbrel).

- *Miotic*: Used by ophthalmologists and optometrists to constrict the pupil of the eye. Pilocarpine is an example. It is also used to treat glaucoma.

- *Mydriatic*: Dilates the muscles of the eye, such as for an eye examination. Some are long lasting (up to 24 hours). The client is very photosensitive and should not drive. An example is atropine.

- *Narcotic*: Acts on the central nervous system, causing pain relief. In large doses, it can depress the respiratory system. These drugs have a high potential for addiction and abuse and are usually controlled. Examples include hydromorphone (Dilaudid), and OxyNEO, the drug replacing painkiller OxyContin in Canada.

- *Purgative*: More powerful than routine laxatives; often taken by clients preparing for diagnostic tests, such as a colonoscopy. Sodium phosphate (Fleet enema, Phosphosoda) is an example.

- *Vasodilator*: Causes the blood vessels to dilate, lowering blood pressure. An example is amlodipine (Norvasc).

- *Vasopressor*: Induces vasoconstriction and raises blood pressure. May be used for clients in hemorrhagic shock. Examples include epinephrine (adrenalin) and mitodrine, used to correct hypotension in people with Parkinson's disease.

Classification by Scope of Action

Drugs can be described as local, systemic, or cumulative on the basis of the scope of action.

Local   A local, or topical, effect occurs when the drug is stored and produces an effect only at the site of application. A local anaesthetic, for example, reduces sensation in the body area to be worked on. Creams used for a rash, such as a steroid cream, would be considered local.

Systemic   Systemically acting drugs circulate in the bloodstream to produce a general effect, such as a central nervous system stimulus or depressant. Most oral drugs have a **systemic** effect. Some drugs are ingested and carried by the circulatory system to the entire body but affect primarily one area or one body system. Some drugs are stored preferentially in certain areas to produce a desired effect. For example, antibiotics used for a genitourinary infection might affect the renal system more than other systems.

systemic   circulating through the bloodstream to produce a general effect on the body.

Cumulative   A cumulative effect happens when the drug accumulates in the body faster than it can be metabolized or excreted and exerts a greater effect than the initial dose. These heightened concentrations can cause drug toxicity, damaging the kidneys, liver, or other organs. Most drugs have a therapeutic window of blood levels in which they work most efficiently and safely. What varies is how wide that safe range is. Gentamicin, for example, has a narrow therapeutic window and has to be carefully dosed and monitored.

Higher levels cause damage to the balance and auditory organs and kidneys. In contrast, amoxicillin and ampicillin can be given in a wide range of doses, depending on the severity of the infection, without the client developing toxicity.

There are times when a cumulative effect is desirable. Sometimes a "loading dose" of an antibiotic is given at the onset of an infection to achieve therapeutic blood levels quickly. For example, azithromycin (Zithromax) might be prescribed at 500 mg day 1, then 250 mg daily days 2 to 5.

Classification by Route of Administration

Drugs may be administered via many different routes, listed below, and can be manufactured in different forms, for a number of reasons. Some drugs can be given in only one way. For example, insulin is ineffective given orally and must be injected or given intravenously. When more than one route is possible, the choice is determined by the action the doctor wants—for example, an intravenous medication may (not always) take effect faster than an oral medication—and by how the client is able to take it. For example, the oral route is unsuitable for a vomiting patient. Medications given intravenously or by injection start acting faster and are therefore best for medical emergencies, such as a heart attack, or for relief of intense pain. When transcribing medication orders in the hospital, make sure that the route of the medication is entered accurately.

Topical/Transdermal Route   Medication may be applied to the body surface, to be absorbed through the skin or the mucous membranes. The effects may be local or systemic. For example, a steroid cream may be applied to treat a local dermatitis or an antibiotic cream to treat a localized infection. A hormone patch or a cream absorbed through the skin can have a systemic effect in hormone replacement therapy. A fentanyl patch applied to the skin can give systemic pain control. Patches are commonly used for heart medication.

Transdermal Patch   A transdermal patch consists of bandage fabric that contains medication. An adhesive outer layer holds the patch onto a selected spot on the skin surface. The structure of the patch facilitates sustained and controlled delivery of the medication. Patches are commonly used for heart medication, pain control, motion sickness, and smoking cessation. It is important that clients understand the proper use of the patch. For example, to prevent overdose, any existing patches should be removed before applying a new patch or patches. Patches usually have specific storage instructions.

Ointments and Lotions   An ointment is usually an emulsion of semisolid consistency used externally. Most ointments use lard, petrolatum, white wax, or paraffin for a base. The other ingredients depend on the use of the ointment. Lotions are ingredients contained in a water base that are normally patted on. Calamine lotion used to treat itching is an example. A liniment is in a liquid base but contains more oil than a lotion. Compresses are applied on a pad of gauze or other material.

Inhalation Route   Drugs may be administered into the airway to be absorbed through the mucous membranes of the respiratory system. This route is used primarily to treat conditions of the respiratory tract, such as asthma and COPD. A variety of inhalation delivery devices, called puffers or metered dose inhalers (MDI), dispense a suspension by one of two different delivery systems. MDIs are propellant driven. The device will dispense a specific dose of the medication each time the client activates it. A dry powder device relies on the client to forcefully pull or inhale the drug from the device into the airway. Spiriva is an example of a medication in the powdered form. Medication can also be delivered by air or oxygen using a mask device with a reservoir for the medication that is diluted in a vehicle, such as normal saline (salt water). Sprays are often used for their local effects on the nose, throat, and lungs. An example is xylometazoline hydrochloride (Otrivin), used as a nasal decongestant.

Otic Route

Medications may be placed directly in the ear (the **otic** route) for local ear infections, such as otitis externa (infection of the outer ear canal, also referred to sometimes as swimmer's ear). They are usually in the form of drops, either in solutions or suspensions. Oil is sometimes carefully instilled into the ear canal to soften wax that is plugging the canal.

otic via the ear.

Ophthalmic Route

Eye drops or ointments are used to treat a number of conditions, including glaucoma. Antibiotics in the form of eye drops are applied via the **ophthalmic** route as a precaution after laser surgery.

ophthalmic relating to the eye.

Nasal Route

Medications may be sprayed or inhaled via the nostrils. Atrovent is a decongestant spray used for rhinitis and asthma. Systemic effects may also be achieved; pain medications, such as butorphanol tartrate (Stadol), may be given by nasal spray. Flonase is a topical anti-inflammatory steroid for treating seasonal allergic rhinitis.

Sublingual or Buccal Route

Sublingual means under the tongue, and *buccal* means between the cheek and the gum. This is a relatively quick-acting route and does not necessitate swallowing. Examples of medications designed to be absorbed under the tongue include the tranquilizer lorazepam (Ativan) and nitroglycerin, which is used to relieve angina.

Vaginal Route

Suppositories or creams are applied vaginally to treat local yeast or bacterial infections. Prostaglandin E is administered vaginally to induce labour in pregnant women who are well past their due date or who, for various reasons, need to deliver early. A variety of contraceptive creams and foams are also designed to be administered vaginally. Douches are no longer much used.

Rectal Route

Rectal suppositories dissolve and are absorbed by the lining of the intestine. The effects may be systemic or local. Suppositories are rocket- or oval-shaped to ease insertion. They melt at body temperature, and the medication is absorbed into the bloodstream. Suppositories are useful when a client cannot take drugs by other means. For example, a drug to combat nausea may be given as a suppository if a client is likely to vomit an oral medication. The effect of this would be systemic. A suppository such as hydrocortisone for hemorrhoids would have a local effect. Enemas for evacuating the bowel are also administered rectally. Another example is the use of 5-ASA products to treat inflammatory bowel disease at the distal end of the colon.

Oral Route

The most common means of administering medication is oral—by mouth. Oral medications are absorbed by the gastrointestinal system and can be ingested in a variety of forms. The effects of oral medication are influenced by a number of factors, such as the characteristics of the medication, motility of the bowel, and the presence or absence of food in the gastrointestinal (GI) tract. Medications given orally are manufactured to achieve desired effects.

Pills   *Pills*, to most people, mean any type of solid, oral medication, whether it is a tablet, caplet, or capsule. Historically, pills are pressed, usually round, solid medications. Many of them are *scored*, or marked, so that they can be easily divided to give half or quarter doses.

Pills are difficult to swallow for many people, who find they seem to stick in the throat. Doctors may recommend that pills be crushed and taken with something like jam or apple sauce. This is contraindicated for some pills, as they may lose effectiveness or harm the patient; the pharmacist would identify which pills should not be crushed. Many older people take calcium, and you may hear some refer to the large pills as "horse pills." Calcium comes in more easily ingested forms.

Enteric-coated medications are covered with a smooth coating that prevents the medication from dissolving until it is further down the GI tract, bypassing the stomach. This is useful for medications that irritate the GI tract, especially in individuals with a history of ulcers or gastrointestinal problems. Enteric coating is also designed to release the medication at a specific target, for example, Asacol for inflammatory bowel disease. ASA is commonly enteric coated. Enteric coating also protects some medications from destruction by stomach acid and allows release further along the GI tract where absorption can occur.

Sustained Release   Medications of various shapes and forms may also be encased in or mixed with substances that cause a delay in the active absorption of the medication to ensure slow but sustained action. This allows once-daily formulations, which enhances adherence to therapy in chronic conditions, such as hypertension. An example is metoprolol SR (Lopressor SR). It also allows for sustained pain control and prevention of the emergence of pain (Hydromorph Contin).

Caplets   A caplet is usually an oval-shaped solid medication, either with an outer coating or compressed. Some people find them easier to swallow than tablets.

Capsules   A capsule is essentially a medication in a powdered or liquid form encased in a hard or soft shell or outer coating, usually a form of gelatin. Capsules mask the taste and odour of medications. Some people also find capsules easier to swallow. Many time-release medications come in capsule form. Controlled-release capsules contain pellets of a drug in a protective coating that dissolves slowly in the intestinal tract. Release time of the medication can be spread over hours.

Liquid   Many drugs are available in liquid form. Any medication that is not solid or semisolid is considered to be a liquid preparation. The main advantage of liquid preparations is ease of ingestion, especially for children or anyone who has difficulty swallowing. They may be ordered or referred to as a *suspension*, meaning that small particles are suspended in the liquid base. Suspensions must be shaken before ingestion. An *emulsion*, which consists of droplets of oil and water mixed together, must also be shaken vigorously before use.

An *elixir* (ordered as such) contains alcohol, sugar, water, and sometimes an ingredient to flavour the medication. Syrups are a concentrated solution of sugar in water and do not contain alcohol.

parenteral   by injection or intravenous administration.

Parenteral Route   **Parenteral** refers to the administration of medications by various types of injection or intravenously. Medications delivered parenterally achieve the fastest and most accurate effect. The most common variations in giving medications by injection include the following.

Subcutaneous Injection (s/c)   This type of injection deposits a small amount of solution under the skin for absorption into the bloodstream. Some immunizations, such as the flu shot, are given subcutaneously, as are some drugs, such as morphine. Medications given subcutaneously are absorbed more slowly than those given into the vein or into the muscle. For this type of injection, a subcutaneous needle and syringe are used. The needle size is shorter (about 1.5 cm) and narrower (usually a 25 or 26 gauge) than those for other intramuscular injections. The barrel of the syringe usually holds about 2 to 3 cc of the medicine.

Insulin is usually given subcutaneously, using specially designed syringes calibrated in insulin units or a pen injector device, devised specially for insulin administration.

Intradermal Injections   The objective is to inject a small amount of solution between layers of the skin, usually at a 10- to 15-degree angle. Medications given intradermally include steroids for a skin rash and tuberculosis vaccination. Allergy testing is often done intradermally. Intradermal amounts range from 0.1 cc to 0.3 cc. Often, a tuberculin syringe is used for this injection; this is the smallest syringe available and holds only 1 cc. Needles are 27- or 28-gauge and are about 1 cm long.

Intramuscular Injections (IM)   This type of injection is given directly into a muscle. Medications given using this route are absorbed faster than those given subcutaneously and slower than those given intravenously. Larger amounts of medication can be given intramuscularly than by the s/c route. IM injections are given into larger muscles, such as the deltoid in the upper arm or the vastus lateralis, which is located on the upper lateral aspect of each leg. Injections in the hip, or gluteal muscle, have become less common because of the risk of damaging nearby nerves. The needle used is larger and longer, usually a 22-gauge needle 4 cm in length.

Z-Track   Occasionally, the physician will write an order for a Z-Track injection, a specific technique for intramuscular injections, used for medications that may irritate or stain the skin—usually iron. The skin and muscle are pulled to one side, the injection given, and the skin released. This techniques seals the medication in, preventing it from oozing back when the needle is withdrawn.

Intravenous   Medications administered intravenously—that is, straight into the vein—are more effective and faster than those by any other route. Therefore, this route is used in emergencies. Medication may be administered from a syringe or through intravenous tubing (referred to as an IV push). It can also be diluted in intravenous solutions and given slowly by way of a minibag or add-a-line, or closely through a special chamber called a buritrol (see Chapter 17) when doses need to be monitored.

❽ PHARMACOKINETICS

As noted earlier, pharmacokinetics deals with how the body processes and uses a drug, including the absorption, metabolism, distribution, and excretion of the drug.

Absorption

Absorption includes the processes by which a medication is taken into to the body and broken down. Factors include how the drug is taken into the body (route), the form in which the drug is taken (for example, ASA with an enteric coating is absorbed differently from plain ASA), and whether the medication is taken on a full or an empty stomach.

absorption   the process by which a medication is taken into to the body, broken down, and transformed into a form that the body can use.

Some foods or liquids interfere not only with the absorption of the drug but also with its therapeutic effect. The presence of food may also enhance the absorption and action of other drugs.

Metabolism

Many drugs are administered in their active form; some (e.g., enalapril) require transformation into active metabolites for effectiveness. Various organs in the body are responsible for **metabolism** or breaking down a medication further into these particles or metabolites. This is accomplished by various body enzymes. Age and health affect the process. The liver plays a major role in transforming drugs into a form that can be excreted from the body; for this reason, someone with liver disease may be unable to take certain medications. The kidneys, lungs, intestines, and other tissues also metabolize some drugs.

Distribution

The drug metabolites are then transported or "distributed" to various parts of the body. **Distribution** also determines how long it takes for a medication to begin acting, when the action of the drug is at its peak, and when the action/effects of the drug decline. A number of factors affect the distribution of a medication, including by which route it was administered, the physical characteristics of the drug itself, and the age and health state of the client.

Excretion

Excretion is the process by which the body disposes of a drug. This is accomplished primarily by the kidneys. Some medications are excreted by the GI tract. Medications can also be excreted in smaller amounts in saliva, tears, sweat, and breast milk. Although there are some legitimate concerns, nursing mothers are sometimes too afraid of medication and forgo necessary therapy because of fear of potential adverse effects on the baby. The efficiency of excretion is affected by the health and function of the kidneys and liver and by interactions with other medications. If a medication is not excreted efficiently, it can accumulate and produce adverse effects. This is sometimes called drug toxicity. Testing is commonly done for toxic and therapeutic levels of many drugs, examples include digoxin and gentamicin sulphate.

❾ EFFECTS OF DRUGS

Therapeutic Action

Every medication has a method of action. For example, an antibiotic may work by preventing bacteria from reproducing. A tranquilizer affects the part of the brain that deals with the transmission of nerve impulses. A therapeutic action is one considered desirable—the purpose for giving the drug.

Side Effects/Adverse Effects

Every drug has potential side effects. There are two main types: (1) those that are expected to occur as part of the pharmacologic action and (2) those that may be *unpredictable* in occurrence. Most people develop a tolerance for common side effects or use strategies that help to deal with them. Rarely will a person have to discontinue a medication for common, less serious side effects. Before making a decision, the client and doctor should consider how important the drug is for the client and how frequent, uncomfortable, or unmanageable the side effects are. Clients should not stop taking a prescribed medication without consulting the doctor.

Unpredictable events are much less common but could potentially be fatal. They may range from neurological responses to anaphylactic shock. It is important that clients report serious adverse effects quickly so that the physician can respond accordingly. Their attention should be drawn to the list of side effects that should be reported immediately.

Most drug resource manuals outline the side effects that may be experienced from taking each drug. Some list them by system and others by frequency of occurrence and severity. All pharmacies give out information about the drugs they dispense, including a list of potential side effects. Sometimes clients will read the side effects and decide they do not want to take the medication. It is important to explain to clients that many listed side effects are quite rare and to explain the strategies that help to prevent an anticipated side effect. For example, if it is important for the client to take a drug likely to cause nausea, she should be taught how to control the nausea. In some cases where the drug is for symptomatic relief or where other treatment options are available, it may be quite reasonable for the client to choose an alternative. In most cases, it should be pointed out that the benefits of taking the drug almost always outweigh the chances of developing minor side effects.

Allergies

It is important to differentiate allergies from side effects. A side effect might be an upset stomach or diarrhea. An allergy would be a serious reaction, such as chest pain, a skin rash, or ultimately, anaphylaxis, which is life threatening. It is important for the client to clearly describe and document reactions so that the doctor can decide whether the client can safely use the drug again. For example, codeine makes some people sleepy and gives others nausea, but these are not allergic reactions. Nausea and diarrhea are not contraindications for using an antibiotic again. In contrast, a client who experiences hives, shortness of breath, blood pressure alterations, or circulatory collapse should *never* use that drug again, unless careful testing under an allergist's supervision establishes that a reaction was not allergic or that the client has outgrown the allergy.

Food allergies are also important to note. An allergy to nuts, for example, is a contraindication for taking some medications. It is worth noting that Atrovent's reformulation does not contain soy lecithin, so there is no longer a cross-reaction with nuts.

Any allergies must be clearly indicated on the client's chart, either in the office or in the hospital. Allergies are also recorded at the pharmacy if the client is registered there. For this reason, as well as to maintain continuity of care, it is a good idea for clients to regularly use a single pharmacy. Clients should be fully aware of their allergies and should realize that the drug they are allergic to may have different names.

A client who has had severe allergic reactions should wear a MedicAlert bracelet or the equivalent. Most pharmacies have information about these devices, which can be purchased in the form of attractive jewellery. They may give information on conditions (such as diabetes), current medications, and severe allergies, including food allergies.

Because the devices can carry only a limited amount of information, clients have to select the information most important in an emergency. For example, knowing that a person has diabetes or is taking an anticoagulant could change a paramedic's response to an emergency, but knowing that the patient has arthritis would not. If clients ask you whether they should have a bracelet, where they can get them, and what should be on them, consult with the doctor before advising them.

Factors That Influence a Drug's Therapeutic Effect

Body Weight   The client's body mass is an important factor in calculating the appropriate dose. If a client weighing 40 kg took 10 mg of diazepam, the effects would be far greater than on a client weighing 100 kg.

Age   Older people and small children respond differently to medications from those in the middle, not only because of differences in body mass but also because their body systems process medications differently. Older people and very young children are less able to excrete drugs and so may reach toxic levels more quickly. Older children have livers that work even better than those of adults, so the calculated dose of a particular drug may be higher than for adults.

As well, developmental factors are sometimes a concern. For example, quinolones generally are not used in pediatric clients because of concerns that the drugs cause premature closure of growth plates. Tetracyclines are avoided in pregnant women (they can inhibit bone growth of the fetus) and children under 12 because of their effects on teeth.

Gender   Some drugs may affect men and women differently, not only because of differences in body mass but also because of different relative muscle masses and because of hormonal and metabolic differences. Pregnancy is important to consider; hormonal changes may alter drug effects, and drugs can present a risk to the fetus.

Time of Day   The time at which medications should be given is affected by the client's normal body rhythms, food intake, and level of activity. A fluid pill, for example, is best given earlier in the day so the client is not up to the bathroom all night. Some drugs are short acting and others long acting; thus, some are taken once a day and others several times a day. Some drugs, such as warfarin, should always be given at the same time each day. Antibiotics should be given at regular intervals to maintain therapeutic levels.

Some medications will be absorbed more slowly if taken on a full stomach than on an empty stomach. Drugs that should be taken on an empty stomach include some antibiotics, such as penicillin. The acid environment of the stomach degrades penicillin G, for example. The actual action of some drugs is affected by certain foods. For example, tetracycline should not be taken with milk products or antacids. Some cholesterol-lowering agents and many other drugs should not be taken with grapefruit juice or after eating a grapefruit, which increases blood levels of the medication. (It is important that clients avoid all forms of grapefruit at all times when taking these medications because the effects on the medication are long lasting.) A medication may also interact with other drugs taken at the same time. For example, calcium and iron may bind to many other medications to prevent their complete absorption.

Consider all these factors when transcribing medication orders. Most facilities will have a protocol to follow.

NATURAL HEALTH PRODUCTS

NATURAL HEATH PRODUCTS (NHPs) INCLUDE VITAMINS, MINERALS, HERBAL REMEDIES, and homeopathic medicines. Natural heath products are available and advertised freely, citing cures and relief of symptoms that are "natural" and "drug free." (Note that the term *natural* is used somewhat arbitrarily; many powerful prescription drugs are derived from plants and are, thus, natural.) Many of these drugs (and they are drugs) do have therapeutic effects. Some trials have shown that many of these drugs do work as indicated, but many herbal medications have never been tested in sound scientific studies, and many claims remain unsupported.

The *Natural Health Products Regulations* in Canada came into effect in 2004 with 53 recommendations to regulate natural health products. These include product licensing, manufacturing practices, product labelling (including recommended use and cautionary statements), reporting of significant side effects to Health Canada, and the implementation of clinical trials.

Licensing of NHPs requires the manufacturer to apply to Health Canada for a product licence. Once granted permission to market, the producer must label the product with the letters NPN followed by an eight-digit product licence number. Homeopathic medicines have the product number preceded by the letters HM. Encourage clients to look for the product number as it indicates the product has been approved for safety and effectiveness by Health Canada.

In 2008 the government introduced the controversial Bill C-51, which effectively overhauls the 50-year-old *Food and Drugs Act*. This bill included amendments to the *Natural Health Products Regulations*. The bill also renames a broad category of products including cosmetics and drugs as "therapeutic products."

There is stiff opposition to this bill on the part of providers and producers of herbal products. They feel the bill limits licensing and will lead to the progressive reduction of herbal products available to the consumer.

Many people are unaware that herbal remedies, like other drugs, can have side effects or *unpredictable* effects, interact with prescription medication, or cause adverse effects with some medical conditions. *Ginkgo biloba*, for example, can cause bleeding. Ephedra has been reported to cause insomnia, increased nervousness, high blood pressure, and an irregular heartbeat.

Interactions with Prescription Medications

Many herbal medications will interact in some way—sometimes adversely—with certain prescription drugs. It is important for doctors to ask clients about herbal medications and for clients to report accurately. Unfortunately, many doctors are not well informed about these substances.

St. John's Wort, for example, has been shown by some studies to be effective in treating mild to moderate cases of depression, but it should not be combined with other anti-depressants because one potentiates the action of the other. Toxicity and undesirable side effects may result.

With the number of medications many people (particularly seniors) are taking, and with the mix of acute and chronic conditions people live with, the use of herbal medications must be carefully monitored. This is not a case where "more is better." More might be fatal.

These are examples of herbal products that interact badly with certain prescription drugs:

Echinacea	Not to be used with prednisone or other corticosteroids, or in conditions where the immune system is involved (e.g., AIDS, rheumatoid arthritis, cancer).
Gingko biloba	Contraindicated in people who take aspirin. Many individuals do take aspirin prophylactically to prevent heart attack or stroke and when a mild anticoagulant action is deemed advantageous. Other anticoagulants, such as warfarin, should not be mixed with this herb either.
Garlic	Potentiates the action of insulin and of hypoglycemics, such as sulphonylurea. Also contraindicated in clients taking blood thinners.
Valerian	(Recommended for calming effects.) May potentiate the action of tranquilizers, such as diazepam (Valium), lorazepam (Ativan), other benzodiazepines, and barbiturates.

⑩ CLIENT EDUCATION

ASK CLIENTS TO BRING ALL MEDICATIONS TO SELECTED OFFICE VISITS. STRESS THAT OTC and herbal remedies are medications and must be included for the physician to complete an accurate drug profile. All drugs should be brought in their original bottles for verification. A dosette with the pills in it is not suitable, unless all the drugs are labelled on the dosette.

Pharmacies will dispense medications in weekly dosettes or sealed blister packs, with labels indicating when to take each. This is important for people, especially older people, who have memory problems or who have difficulty organizing and taking multiple medications.

Many people stop taking drugs when they feel better, take them inappropriately, or discontinue them if they have minor side effects. Again, client education is important. For example, antibiotics must be taken for the full period prescribed.

Some physicians advise clients to carry a list of their drugs with them at all times in case they are in an accident. You can help by periodically reviewing the list with the client to ensure that it is current and correct. (Keep the list of client's medications to up to date. The use of an electronic chart facilitates this.) You could also prepare the list for a client who has difficulty doing so.

People often feel embarrassed to ask questions about their medications, particularly if they feel the provider is busy or unapproachable. You can help by encouraging the clients to write down their questions before they come in for an appointment. Many doctors want their clients to bring their medications with them for each office visit. If the client appears confused about medications or asks you questions, take the time to direct the client appropriately. If you can answer the questions competently, do so; if it is a matter of clarifying written instructions, do so. The client may need to have the provider or the pharmacist review the medications again. Although most pharmacies do provide excellent instructions, some offices give out their own pamphlets on some medications (e.g., warfarin). These may cater to clients who speak another language, reinforce important points noted in the pharmacy handout, or include specific information related to the client's individualized plan of care.

DRUG RESOURCES

The *Compendium of Pharmaceuticals and Specialties*

The most common drug reference for professional offices and health-care facilities is the *Compendium of Pharmaceuticals and Specialties* (CPS), published annually by the Canadian Pharmaceutical Association and distributed to health-care practitioners. One will be available in hospital units and in pharmacies. It contains an updated list of most drugs used, with detailed information on actions, indications and contraindications, and side effects. However, the information is not exhaustive, and at times it may be advisable to consult other references, the primary literature, or a drug information centre. The CPS is intended for professionals and is not meant for laypeople. Information for the patient is available only in the online version.

Other

There are a variety of drug/pharmacology books on the market. Some are geared more to nurses and others to health professionals, such as you. If you deal frequently with prescriptions or transcribing medications, you may want your own reference book. You can become familiar with it and add your own notes and markers.

HANDLING PRESCRIPTIONS

PRESCRIPTION DRUGS ARE SO CALLED BECAUSE THEY CAN BE DISPENSED ONLY BY authorized prescribers, including not only physicians but also nurse practitioners, pharmacists, and some optometrists. If the client is in the office, the doctor is most likely to fax the prescription from his computer directly to the desired pharmacy, so the client does not handle the prescription at all. If this is not possible, the doctor will write the necessary prescription and give it to the client to take to the pharmacy. Either way, the doctor will ensure that the details of the prescription are recorded on the client's EMR.

Any prescriptions faxed must be sent in a secure manner. In some provinces, recent changes require that a prescription sent to a home must be received and signed for by someone at the home—not left in the mailbox, for example.

Physicians may fill in and download electronic prescriptions, but they must be signed and faxed to the pharmacy. Electronic signatures are unacceptable as yet. If the doctor is seeing another physician's client, an electronic copy of the prescription should be sent to the client's family doctor.

Prescription Forms

Although more prescriptions are written online, most doctors still have prescription forms or pads headed with their name, address, and other necessary information. Figure 7.1 shows the elements of a prescription. Figure 7.2 shows a prescription written in a formal format (e.g., with the words "sig" and "mitte" written in); Figure 7.3 shows a prescription written informally, with the names of the elements left out.

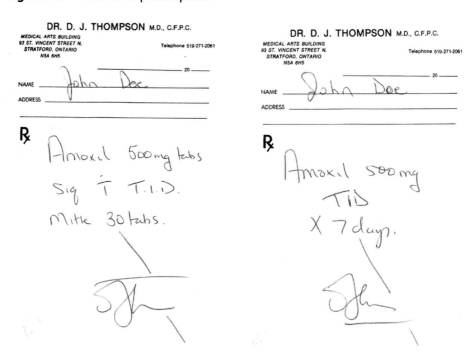

Dr. D. Smith M.D. C.F.P.C.
123 Anywhere St.
Calgary
Alberta

Date_____ 20____

Name ____ (Client) _____
Address_____

Rx: (Drug and dose) . . . .   **Diazepam 5 mg**

Sig (what dose to take, how often) . . . .   **1 tab b.i.d.**

Mitte: (how many tablets ordered) **30**

Rep X3

Signature . . . .   *D. Smith*

Figure 7.1   Parts of a prescription

DR. D. J. THOMPSON M.D., C.F.P.C.
MEDICAL ARTS BUILDING
93 ST. VINCENT STREET N.
STRATFORD, ONTARIO
N5A 6H5   Telephone 519-271-2061

NAME   *John Doe*   20

ADDRESS

℞ Amoxil 500mg tabs
   Sig ī T.I.D.
   Mitte 30 tabs.

Figure 7.2   A formal prescription
Courtesy of Dr. D.J. Thompson

DR. D. J. THOMPSON M.D., C.F.P.C.
MEDICAL ARTS BUILDING
93 ST. VINCENT STREET N.
STRATFORD, ONTARIO
N5A 6H5   Telephone 519-271-2061

NAME   *John Doe*   20

ADDRESS

℞ Amoxil 500 mg
   TID
   X 7 days.

Figure 7.3   An informal prescription
Courtesy of Dr. D.J. Thompson

Prescription forms must be kept safe because of the danger of theft and forgery, primarily by people who want narcotics, sleeping pills, and tranquilizers. Keep prescription pads out of sight and secure.

To convey most instructions on prescriptions, doctors use a set of standard abbreviations, listed in Table 7.2.

Table 7.2 Common Abbreviations Used in Medication Orders and Prescriptions

Ad lib	as needed by the client	q ___ h	every ___ hours (q4h: every 4 hours; q6h: every 6 hours, etc.)
bid	twice daily	qd or od	every day (every day; q2d every 2 days, etc. (also discouraged)
cap	capsule	qid	four times daily
–c	with	stat	immediately
gtt	drop	tab	tablet
hs	bedtime	tid	three times daily
hs prn	as required at bedtime	po	by mouth
od	daily (discouraged because of the potential to interpret as "right eye")	IM	intramuscular injection
prn	as necessary, or as required	s/c	subcutaneous injection
qhs	every bedtime	IV	intravenously
qs	quantity sufficient	SL	sublingual

Repeats and Renewals

Some prescriptions, such as antibiotics, are usually issued for a defined period of time. Once the specified period is over, the prescription is no longer needed. Medications for chronic conditions, such as diabetes, hypothyroidism, or hypertension, may be renewed many times. However, the doctor will want to review the client's condition and the dose from time to time. Prescriptions are often written with a certain number of repeats available (see Figure 7.1). If the client is starting a new medication, or a new dosage of a medication, and the doctor wants to check on the client's progress and response to the drug, he may write a prescription with no renewals, requiring the client to come in for an assessment and/or blood work.

Repeats and renewals differ slightly, although some people use the terms interchangeably. Repeats are continuations of long-term medications, while renewals are extensions of prescriptions that have run out, often of one-time or short-term medications. Medications for chronic conditions are usually prescribed with instructions that the prescription can be repeated or refilled a given number of times before a new prescription is necessary—for example, thyroxine, often prescribed for someone with hypothyroidism, a lifelong condition. Dr. Gifford prescribes Brenda 7.4 thyroxine with three repeats. This means Brenda can call the pharmacy three times and have her medication request filled without contacting the doctor. When the three repeats have been used up, the doctor must be contacted to authorize a renewal of that medication. The doctor may simply "renew" the prescription order or ask Brenda to come in for an assessment before he does that. As mentioned earlier in the chapter, in some provinces now the pharmacist may be allowed to renew the medication and/or order a related lab test (T3T4/TSH) before doing so. Note in Figure 7.4 that Marlene Blane wants more repeats on her levothyroxine, a hormone replacement she will be on for life. For an example of a renewal, Jorge deSantos

```
TUESDAY, JANUARY 20TH


Client                  Medication              Pharmacy/Comments

Celia Chan wants the following renewed:

232 Whitlow Cres        Valium 5 mg., t.i.d. po   Sinclair Pharmacy
Kitchener               Rx # 23443235            wants delivered after 5 pm
Ph. 519-231-0000                                 519-543-0999


Marlene Blane wants repeats on :

689 Lake St             levothyroxine 0.1 mg     Greens Pharmacy
Waterloo                po 1 tab q.a.m.          husband will pick up after work
Ph. 519-543-0000        Rx# 321422               519-232-0000


Clover Pharmacy called wanting renewals for the following scripts:
PH 321-0000
   1.  Jen Hartlow          digoxin 0 125 mg
   2.  Jorge deSantos       Voltaren 50 mg, q4h prn
   3.  Leonard Mihailovic   Wellbutrin SR 150 mg, h.s.
```

Figure 7.4 Computer-generated list of prescription requests

was prescribed Voltaren (diclofenac sodium) because his arthritis pain became severe. The doctor thought he might need only one prescription for the flare-up, but when he used up his prescription and went off the Voltaren, the pain became severe again.

Policies for prescription renewals vary with the physician. Many doctors will not renew a prescription over the telephone but insist that the client come in for an assessment. This is prudent because physicians are responsible for any reactions or adverse effects of the medications they prescribe.

When a doctor first writes a prescription, she will include an appropriate number of repeats at the time. When the repeats have been used up, it is time for the client to be seen and reassessed. For example, the doctor may feel it is time to do some blood work on Marlene Blane to see whether her thyroid medication is effective or whether the dose needs to be adjusted. Likewise, birth control pills are routinely prescribed for a year. At the end of that time, the doctor may want to give the client a Pap test and a gynecological examination.

Prescriptions for sleeping pills or tranquilizers will not normally be renewed without an office visit and assessment. You will likely be told to make appointments for clients in such situations.

Some clients resent the inconvenience of having to see the doctor for a prescription renewal. They may feel that it is a money grab on the part of the physician. Actually, the doctor can charge more for a telephone renewal than for a minor assessment. It may be necessary to educate the patient about the benefits they receive from regular assessment.

Most physicians will also refuse to order antibiotics without seeing the client. This is the responsible thing to do. Most often, a swab or other test is done to determine the cause of the infection and to identify the most appropriate antibiotic for the client. Some clients, however, will call stating that they have a sore throat and want an antibiotic to make them better. It is helpful to explain why the doctor wants to see the client before ordering or renewing an antibiotic. As explained in Chapter 5, antibiotics are not effective against viruses. Different antibiotics are also effective against different groups of bacteria. Putting a client on an antibiotic for an infection it cannot cure wastes money and leads to needless side effects. Worse, the bacteria in the patient's body can develop resistance to the antibiotic and can then be passed on to others. The overuse of antibiotics has become a major public health issue, as antibiotic resistance increases.

Sometimes, when requesting a renewal or a repeat, a pharmacy will simply fax the original prescription that the doctor had written, along with a copy of the information put on the bottle at the time the prescription was filled. Figure 7.5 shows a faxed request for a single prescription renewal.

A pharmacist may refuse to fill a prescription because she feels that it is outdated. There are no hard-and-fast rules, but many pharmacists consider prescriptions outdated a year after they are written. A reassessment by the prescribing health professional would be in the client's best interest. Some controlled substances do have a legally imposed time frame within which they can be filled.

CONFIDENTIAL

COLDWATER PHARMACY
1-222 Lansdowne Ave
Ottawa, ON K1V 1A4
Ph 613-332-3333

REFILL REQUEST

PATIENT: TANAKA   ALAN
BIRTH DATE: 1966/05/26
PRESCRIPTION NUMBER: 32102222   [Tx 1232222]
LAST REFILL DATE: 24-Aug-08
DRUG NAME: VIOXX 25 mg
GENERIC NAME: ROFECOXIB
QUANTITY DISPENSED: 100 TAB
DAYS SUPPLY: 100

DIRECTIONS FOR USE: TAKE 1 TABLET DAILY

PHYSICIAN: DR.   BROWN   DJ

PHONE: 613-222-2344
FAX 613-443-3333

Number of Refills Authorized	Days between Refills (if applicable)
100	100

PHYSICIAN'S SIGNATURE   DATE

PLEASE FAX BACK TO: 613-243-2333

Figure 7.5 Faxed request for single prescription renewal

Phoned and Faxed Prescription Requests

In the health office, you will receive many calls about prescriptions, from clients, pharmacies, and facilities such as nursing homes. Most will deal with renewals. Physicians will have different protocols on how to manage these calls.

Regardless of who is calling, you need to record all information clearly and accurately. Keep a system for recording information—either a book or binder by the telephone or a computerized notebook, as shown in Figure 7.4.

If the client is calling, you need to get the following information:

- Client's first and last name
- Address and phone number
- Medication (ask for the spelling if you are not sure. Even one wrong letter can identify a different medication)
- Prescription number
- Dose and frequency (e.g., 5 mg T.I.D.)
- Date issued
- Preferred pharmacy
- Pharmacy's location and phone number (or you may keep the numbers of local pharmacies handy)

You may also want to ask

- if the client wants the medication delivered or will pick it up;
- when the client will pick up the prescription or will be home for deliveries;
- how the client plans to pay (e.g., charge, cash on delivery); and
- whether the client has a drug plan.

Some health offices leave it up to the pharmacy to arrange payment and pick-up or delivery. Others pass on the information with the approval. You want to ensure that someone will be home when the medication arrives. Sometimes, clients will ask that the medication be left in a mailbox or between doors. In other jurisdictions, the pharmacy has a right to refuse to do this for certain medications (controlled substances, tranquilizers). Ontario, for example, requires that the pharmacy obtain a signature of acceptance for receipt of delivered prescription items—so delivered medication must be received by a person. If the client cannot find the delivered medication, the pharmacy assumes no responsibility for medications that are left according to the client's instructions.

When a pharmacist calls, you can assume that the pharmacy already has some of this information. You still need to get

- the client's first and last names,
- name of the medication (correctly spelled),
- the dose and frequency (e.g. 5 mg T.I.D.),
- the date issued, and
- the pharmacy's phone number (if you don't have it).

Write the pharmacy's phone number on the request to make it easy for the doctor to call if she has a question.

The doctor should personally review all prescription requests. Many doctors review renewal requests last thing in the morning, or just before starting office hours in the afternoon, and again late afternoon. Do not leave it too late, though: some pharmacies may be closed, or clients may be unable to pick up the medication. If you think a request is urgent, take it to the doctor as soon as possible.

Often, a client will call the pharmacy instead of the doctor's office for renewal of medications. (Some doctors ask their clients to do so.) The pharmacist then requests permission from the doctor, often for several clients at once, and often by fax. You should give the fax to the doctor, who will make notes beside each request granting or denying approval, and perhaps adding other comments, such as "Must see doctor before next renewal." Nursing homes and other health-care agencies also may fax requests for renewals.

Once the doctor has approved or rejected requests, telephone or fax the designated pharmacy with the information. There are special policies to follow for prescriptions for controlled substances.

Drug Measurements

There are three measurement systems used in pharmacology that physicians may use when writing medication orders. Canada generally uses the metric system; others sometimes use, at least in part, the apothecaries' measure or the household (imperial) system. You will not be asked to calculate doses, but you do need to recognize measurements so that you interpret and transcribe them accurately.

SI Units   The metric system, with which you are familiar, is also referred as the *Système Internationale* (SI). Drugs are commonly prescribed in milligrams (mg), millilitres (mL), or cubic centimetres (cc). A cubic centimetre is the same as a millilitre; the terms are used interchangeably. The abbreviation "eq" stands for equivalents, a unit of measure used in laboratories; "meq" stands for milli (1000 smaller). Drugs may also be prescribed in micrograms (μg; sometimes also mcg). Be careful not to misread micrograms as milligrams: there is a tenfold difference.

Be acutely aware of the presence of decimals. If in doubt, check. To avoid misreading, written orders involving decimals should use a 0 to precede a measurement: for example, instead of .5 mg, write 0.5 mg. It is all too easy to miss a decimal point and transcribe .5 mg as 5 mg. Prescribers should *not* use a 0 on the right-hand side of a decimal point. For example, write 5 mg, rather than 5.0 mg, because 5.0 mg can easily be read or transcribed as 50 mg.

Household Measurement   Household measurements refer to imperial measurements, such as teaspoon, tablespoon, cup, and drop (gtt), once the standard household and commercial measurements in Canada and still the standard for lay uses in the United States. These measurements often make more sense to clients, especially older clients. Table 7.3 shows common imperial measures and their metric equivalents.

Most of us think of body weight in pounds and ounces. You rarely hear a mother say, "My baby weighed in at 4500 grams." However, doctors usually use metric measurements in tracking body weights and calculating doses. Medications are often ordered as so much

Table 7.3 Household Measurements and Metric Equivalents

Household Measurements			Metric
Volume	1 teaspoon (tsp.)	= 60 drops (gtt)	= 5 cc = 5 mL
	1 tablespoon (tbsp.)	= 3 tsp.	= 15 cc = 15 mL
	2 tbsp.	= 1 fluid ounce (oz. or fl. oz.).	= 30 cc = 30 mL
	8 fl. oz.	= 1 cup	= 20 cc = 240 mL
Mass (weight)	1 ounce (oz.)		= 28.349 g
	1 pound (lb.)	= 16 oz	= 454 g = 2.2 kg

"per kg body weight," and so doctors like to have an up-to-date record of clients' weights, especially for children. You can tell a client his weight in pounds, but record the weight on the client's chart in kilograms, or in grams for babies.

Apothecaries' Measure   You may occasionally come across the apothecary system, which uses minims, fluid drams, and fluid ounces for volume, and grains, scruples, drams, pounds, and ounces for weight. Note that this system overlaps with the household system. Occasionally, a doctor will write a drug order using grains. For example, you may see a prescription for phenobarbitol written as "phenobarb gr. 1/2." Since one grain is equivalent to 60 mg, this means 30 mg of phenobarb. Or you may see "morphine 1/4 gr." (equivalent to morphine 15 mg) or "ASA gr. 5" (325 mg). You may see an order or prescription for 1 oz. of Magnolax. One ounce equals 30 cc or 30 mL. Do not do the conversion yourself; read or transcribe the order as written, and let the pharmacist interpret it. Table 7.4 summarizes the apothecaries' measure.

International Units   Some drugs, such as insulin, and nutrients, such as vitamin A and vitamin E, are measured in international units (IU). Each 1 mL of insulin contains 100 IU. In Canada, physicians write insulin orders using IU or the symbol U^-. (The Institute for Safe Medication Practices (ISMP) recommends writing the word "units" because many errors have occurred because of the use of these symbols. For example, if a U looked like a 0, 6U became 60 units.)

Table 7.4 The Apothecaries' Measure

Mass		Volume	
Symbol	**Measure**	**Symbol**	**Measure**
gr.	grain	min.	minim
sc.	scruple	fl. dr.	fluid dram
dr.	dram	fl. oz.	fluid ounce
oz.	ounce	pt.	pint
lb.	pound	qt.	quart
1 grain = 60 mg = 0.06 grams		480 min. = 1 fl. oz. = 30 mL = 30 cc	

⓫ HANDLING DRUGS SAFELY

BECAUSE DRUGS ARE POTENTIALLY DANGEROUS SUBSTANCES, THEY MUST BE HANDLED WITH special care, especially controlled substances.

Storing and Handling Drugs

- Keep all medications in their original containers until they are administered or dispensed. (This is not likely your responsibility, but if you see medications sitting out in unlabelled containers, consult with the nurse or physician, or discard them.)

- Check manufacturer's storage recommendations.

- Some drugs must be kept in dark containers or dark areas. Do not leave any drug for long in the sun or bright light.

- If noted on label, keep drugs refrigerated. Monitor the refrigerator temperature. If there is a power outage, transfer medications to a working refrigerator.

- Do not open bottles unnecessarily. Some drugs, like older forms of nitroglycerin, lose potency if opened frequently.

- Once a drug (such as a pill) is removed from its container, do not return it. This is a basic safety precaution employed by many facilities. There is the danger that it has been contaminated, or a chance that another medication could be returned to the container.

- Keep drugs and solutions for external use well separated from those used internally.

- Store disinfectants and cleaning agents well away from medication.

- Store drugs in an ordered arrangement: by classification or alphabetically by drug name.

- Store medications with the ones expiring first at the front of the cabinet or shelf. (All medication bottles should have expiry dates on the label.)

- Discard unused expired medication such as samples or those returned by clients. For safe disposal, return to a pharmacy. Do not place in the garbage or flush down the toilet. It can then be directed to disposal companies that incinerate surplus medications at high heat.

- Never leave medications out in an examination room. If the doctor leaves samples out, put them away before the next client comes in.

Controlled Drugs

Special rules apply to the use of controlled drugs, as defined by the CDSA. These involve drugs with a high potential for addiction and abuse, often narcotic analgesics. They are typically medications in pure form. For example, codeine is a controlled drug. However, combination drugs containing smaller amounts of codeine are not controlled. If controlled drugs are kept in a medical office, special precautions apply. The physician should

- keep a special record of controlled substances dispensed, administered, or prescribed, either in a daily log book or arranged by type of drug. For each entry, check that the physician has included the client's name and address, the name and quantity of the drug, diagnosis, and the purpose for which the drug was provided. Keep records for at least two years.

- store all controlled substances in a safe or an immovable, locked cabinet. Make sure it is locked after use.
- be alert to the risk of break-ins. Although most providers do not keep narcotics in their medical bags, on their person, or in their offices, they, their offices, and their vehicles are frequent targets for thieves looking for narcotics. And
- report the loss of any controlled substances immediately to the local law authorities.

Narcotic Control Records and Tracking Controlled Medications

In a few facilities, controlled medications may still be tracked manually. In such environments, when a nurse gives a controlled substance to a patient (for example, morphine), she must record the patient's full name, room number, the time, dose, and route by which it was given in a designated book such as a narcotic control book or binder. These stock medications are counted at the end of every shift by two nurses. The nurses must sign that all controlled medications are accounted for. When required, the Pharmacy Department replenishes these medications.

The majority of hospitals have dispensed with the manual system for dispensing all medications and now use barcode-enabled systems that receive medication orders, sort, and automatically distribute the medications. Doses may be individualized for each patient. Narcotics and other controlled drugs are also dispensed and tracked by the system—thus the need for a narcotic book has been eliminated. Controlled drugs are still counted at regular intervals, for example, weekly. A nurse must scan his index finger and/or enter a password in order to access narcotics and as well, in some facilities, the patient's routine medications.

Disposing of Medications

As mentioned above, expired or unneeded drugs in the office, as well as clients' medications, should be disposed of by an authorized agency (such as a pharmacy) and in an appropriate manner. Most pharmacies accept unused and outdated medications and dispose of them properly. Dumping drugs down the drain or the toilet is not acceptable because of the potential cumulative environmental effect.

Some clients save their medications and take them when they think they need them, for example, for a cold or sore throat. This often involves misuse of antibiotics. Others share their leftover medications with friends and family members. Explain to clients that these habits are dangerous. Their friends may be allergic to the drug or may be taking another drug that will interact badly with the new drug. If the doctor changes or discontinues a client's medication while a quantity of the original remains, encourage the client to bring the leftover medication to your office or to a pharmacy for disposal. Pharmacies often have certain days when they invite clients to bring in expired or unneeded drugs for disposal. Some clients see this as "wasting" money or medications and are reluctant to part with them.

It may be a good idea for family members to occasionally survey the medicine cabinet or medication box of older people and dispose of outdated medications as well as those the person is no longer taking. One woman found 30 or 40 bottles of unused medications in her grandmother's cabinet. She said that her grandmother would take some occasionally to self-treat. "Grandma thought that if a little is good, more would be even better, and different kinds might cure things that haven't even happened yet." This story is not unusual.

Preventing Drug Abuse

It may be your responsibility to keep records of all drugs prescribed and in what amounts. These records are especially important for drugs that may be abused by being overused or sold, including many controlled medications. Be alert for behaviours that may indicate a drug-seeking or drug-abusing client. Often, a person will ask for medications to be renewed early, perhaps saying the pills were lost, stolen, or spilled. Keep a record of such calls and the reasons given.

Physicians prescribing drugs with a high potential for abuse to unfamiliar clients usually prescribe a limited supply. Pharmacies will often dispense only small quantities at a time. Be suspicious of clients who plead for larger quantities of such medications stating that it is either too expensive or too difficult for them to get the prescription refilled.

Be wary also of anyone who walks into the office off the street, perhaps stating that they are visiting in town and forgot their medications at home or had them stolen. Other individuals will present with complaints of a severe, perhaps recurrent pain, and will name the exact drug they need to relieve it. They sometimes suspiciously have allergies to any drug of lesser potency. "Tylenol does nothing for me, doctor, but Percocet does." Or "I am allergic to codeine, but Demerol really helps."

Avoiding Drug Errors

Any error in drugs or dosages can be serious, even fatal. A number of factors can contribute to medication errors; you can help prevent some of these.

Errors are more likely when orders are taken orally (e.g., over the telephone) than when they are provided in writing or electronically. It is all too easy to mishear or to have a slip of the pen. In most health-care facilities, only an RN can receive oral orders (medication or other) from a physician, although this is changing. For example, in nursing homes, a practical nurse may be allowed to accept an oral order.

Errors can also occur in transcription because of poor handwriting (by physicians and other professionals), confusion between drugs with similar names, misuse of zeroes and decimal points, confusion of metric and other dosing units (see Drug Measurements above), and inappropriate abbreviations (see Tables 7.2, 7.3, and 7.4).

Thorough knowledge of the spellings, pronunciations, and typical ordering methods of medications, as well as measurements and symbols, will help you be accurate in reading orders aloud, writing down phoned-in information, and transcribing.

Be alert for drugs with similar names, when speaking about them, writing down phoned-in information, or transcribing. If you are responsible for arranging medications

Tip

Transcribing drug orders is a task you must take very seriously. Check and double-check to ensure that you have transcribed the order properly. Many drug names are similar. A mistake in the drug name, symbol, short form, or dose designation can result in a serious error. Do not expect the nurse to catch these errors. You must take responsibility for the work that you do. The ISMP website listed at the end of the chapter will provide you with excellent information that will keep you from making transcription/order entry errors. If order entry is one of your responsibilities, keep a hard copy of these resource sheets with you at work.

Future Trends

In 2012 Canada was held hostage by a shortage of a number of medications, impacting doctor's offices and hospitals—and ultimately clients. The shortage was due to problems at a company in Quebec that was the sole producer of a wide variety of medications, and which had scaled back production because it had to upgrade its facilities. Health Canada is currently taking steps to avoid a similar situation in the future. Among other strategies, it is fast-tracking new resources for some of these medications.

Advances in pharmacology over the past two decades have provided medical science with effective treatments and cures for myriad infirmities ranging from the most complex of cancers to asthma. New and more effective immunizations have all but eradicated formerly crippling and deadly diseases. Discoveries in pharmacology are enhanced by advances in other areas of science, such as molecular biology, molecular genetics, and diagnostic medicine. These discoveries give scientists a more detailed, focused view of the physiological and pathological functions of the body and cellular processes. Thus, scientists are better able to target specific cellular sites for pharmacologic action. New trends in treating health problems—including pain control with drugs—include tailoring drugs more specifically to the individual.

Newer versions of drugs are now replacing first- and second-generation pharmacologic treatments in the treatment of numerous conditions, including heart conditions, depression, diabetes, and infection.

An ongoing concern is the misuse of antibiotics, resulting in organism resistance to them. In Chapter 5 we discussed problems associated with resistance to various pathogens and the resulting insurgence of nosocomial infections. Pharmacists, physicians, and other health providers have a responsibility to educate the consumer about this continuing and increasing danger. All too often a person will "bully" the doctor into writing a prescription for an unnecessary antibiotic. Physicians need to stand their ground, and consumers need to understand that some conditions will clear up on their own. Recent studies have shown that the typical ear infection in a child will resolve itself without intervention. However, parents feel more comfortable giving the child an antibiotic, feeling that it will reduce the period of the infection.

As well, there are groups of people opposed to immunizations—which are probably the most significant single factor in disease prevention. Ongoing education to encourage childhood immunizations is essential.

in a doctor's office, write the generic name as well as the brand name on the container. Post a list of drugs that could be confused, such as Accutane and Accupril; Atarax and Ativan; Benadryl and Benylin; or Atrovent and Alupent.

Check your work. As mentioned earlier, when you take a prescription request on the phone, read it back to the caller. If you phone in information or orders, ask the person on the other end of the line to read it back to you.

SUMMARY

1. You will need a general knowledge of how to handle new prescription, repeats, and refills. You also need a general knowledge of prescription, over-the-counter, and herbal medications so that you can answer clients' questions or refer them appropriately. In a hospital or long-term care facility, you need to be familiar with spellings and resource manuals to transcribe medication orders effectively.

2. Pharmacists are important members of the health team, with up-to-date knowledge not available in print.

3. Drugs may be derived from animals, plants, or natural minerals, or may be partly or entirely synthesized in a laboratory.

4. Drugs may have four types of names: chemical, generic, trade or brand, and botanical. The generic and trade names are used most frequently. The generic name is nonproprietary; the trade name is assigned by the manufacturer and protected. Original manufacturers are protected by a patent, usually lasting 20 years; during this time, no one else may reproduce the drug. (Usually, medication is prescribed by generic name because it less expensive than the same medication dispensed under its trade name.)

5. The federal *Controlled Drugs and Substances Act* (CDSA) determines which drugs are illegal and places controls on narcotics and other drugs considered hazardous.

6. Regulations set out which drugs may be dispensed only by prescription and which may be purchased over the counter—that is, without the recommendation of a physician. Provincial and territorial regulations may vary slightly and may follow NAPRA guidelines. Some OTC drugs may be sold anywhere; some may be sold only in pharmacies; and some must be kept behind the counter in the pharmacy.

7. Drugs can be classified by use (therapeutic, diagnostic, curative, replacement, or prophylactic), by action or function (e.g., antihypertensive, antiemetic), by scope of action (local, systemic, or cumulative), and by route of administration.

8. The route refers to how a medication is to be given for a client. Some medications may be given by only one route. Where choice is possible, it is determined by the desired action and the patient's condition. Generally, the least invasive route of administration (usually po [by mouth]) is preferred.

9. Pharmacokinetics describes four stages in the body's use of a drug: absorption, metabolism, distribution, and excretion. Age, weight, gender, health, time of day, and presence or absence of food can alter the processing of a drug.

10. All drugs have the potential for side effects. In most cases, you should reassure clients who are concerned about potential side effects. Occasionally side effects require stopping a drug. Encourage clients to report unpredictable effects. It is important to distinguish between common and expected side effects, such as nausea with antibiotics, and allergic or serious reactions, such as hives, shortness of breath, and circulatory collapse.

11. Natural health products can be effective but, like all drugs, can have side effects and can interact, sometimes adversely, with other drugs. Many clients do not consider herbal medications to be real drugs and do not report them. Encourage clients to report all herbal and over-the-counter medications.

12. Keep drugs secure in the office. Keep prescription pads out of sight, number them, and use only one at a time. Be alert for potential client abuse of medications, especially controlled substances.

13. Store medications correctly, refrigerating those that require it. Keep medications in their original containers, and make sure labels are legible. Keep controlled substances locked up. Never use expired drugs. Dispose of medications properly.

Key Terms

absorption 191
controlled drugs 181
distribution 192
fixed oils 179

metabolism 192
ophthalmic 189
otic 189
parenteral 190

pharmacology 176
systemic 187
volatile oils 179

Review Questions

1. Differentiate between pharmacokinetics and pharmacodynamics.
2. What are the roles of the pharmacist and the pharmacy assistant?
3. List and explain four drug sources.
4. Explain the four categories of drug names. Give examples of three categories.
5. What are four routes by which medications may be given? Describe each.
6. What are three factors that may interfere with the therapeutic effects of a drug?
7. Differentiate between allergies and side effects. What should you do if you learn that a client has a medication allergy?
8. Why is it important to encourage clients to report any herbal medications they are taking?
9. Why is it important for a client to bring current medications when coming to the office for an examination?
10. Describe proper methods for keeping medications in the health office.
11. List the factors contributing to medication errors and the steps you can take to prevent them.

Application Exercises

1. Divide into groups of three or four. Divide the list in Table 7.1 into as many sections as there are groups. List each drug in a table similar to the one below. Use a drug reference manual (you may have purchased one for your course) or the websites listed in this chapter. For each drug in your group's section, list the trade and generic name, the action of the drug, the typical adult dose (if your instructor wishes), three to five major side effects, and helpful client teaching. Put the group lists together to compose a master list to distribute to the class.

Generic Name	Trade Name	Therapeutic Category	Typical Dose	Side Effects	Health Teaching

2. Ask a sales consultant in a local health store for a list of commonly sold natural health products. Individually or in small groups, select one product, or a group of related products from the list. Research this product at the library or on the internet. Make sure to assess the reliability of your sources, especially on the internet. Develop a teaching pamphlet for clients in a family physician's practice about the potential benefits and risks of this product, and, if applicable, the dangers of taking this medication with prescription drugs (e.g., St. John's Wort with anti-depressants).

3. a. In 2012 the manufacturer Purdue Pharma stopped production of OxyContin (known also as hillbilly heroin) in Canada. OxyContin is a powerful and highly addictive drug. OxyContin was replaced with OxyNEO, a drug Purdue claims was designed to reduce abuse of the medication. The company claims that OxyNEO is less addictive and of a composition that makes it less prone to abuse—a claim questioned by Health Canada. A number of provinces are removing this replacement drug from their public drug benefit plan. This will leave large numbers of people without access to this painkiller. There are fears that this move will promote the use of even more addictive drugs, particularly in First Nations communities. There are no concrete plans in place to deal with the problems of addiction withdrawal that will ensue. In small groups discuss how you would deal with this. Should provincial/territorial governments fund detox and

treatment programs? Should these governments research and fund drugs to assist individuals to withdraw from such addictive drugs? Should OxyNEO be included in provincial/territorial drug benefit plans? Was Purdue Pharma's decision to withdraw OxyContin from the market a good one? Come up with at least five recommendations.

b. What steps can do you think can be taken to tackle the issue of prescription drug addiction across Canada?

Websites of Interest

MediResource
www.mediresource.com
A Canadian site with consumer-oriented information on drugs, physicians, and resources.

MedicineNet
www.medicinenet.com/script/main/alphaidx.asp?p = a_pharm
Health and medical information; includes a searchable database of drugs by generic and trade names. This is an American site, and so some trade names will differ from Canadian ones.

Drug Index
www.rxlist.com/script/main/hp.asp
An American site with a list of 1300 prescription drugs, searchable by key word as well as by name. Includes discussion boards about several drugs. This site provides the following information about prescription drugs: drug class, brand names, pharmacology, clinical studies, indications, contraindications, warnings and precautions, adverse reactions, and dosage and administration.

WebMD
http://my.webmd.com/medical_information/drug_and_herb/default.htm
An American site that lists herbal as well as prescription drugs.

The Mayo Clinic
www.mayoclinic.com/
Along with general medical information, this site from a highly reputed source lists more than 8000 prescription and over-the-counter drugs. Although the site is American, information is given on Canadian trade names and availability as well.

Med Broadcast.com
http://canada.medbroadcast.com/drug_info_details.asp?brand_name_id = 1342
This informative Canadian website discusses a variety of diseases and related treatments and medications, with a video option.

NAPRA
http://napra.ca/pages/home/default.aspx
This site from the National Association of Pharmacy Regulatory Authorities spells out, among other things, the schedules for controlling prescription and over-the-counter drugs.

Controlled Drugs and Substances Act
http://laws.justice.gc.ca/en/C-38.8/index.html
This site gives the text of the federal legislation that regulates controlled substances and determines which drugs are illegal.

Institute of Safe Medication Practices Canada
www.ismp.ca
This website lists common symbols, has information about medication errors, and is devoted to safe medication use and the prevention of errors.
http://www.ismp.org/tools/errorproneabbreviations.pdf
This link leads to ISMP's list of error-prone abbreviations.

Part IV
Office Procedures

Part IV of the textbook gives more detail on the administrative aspects of work in the health office. If you work in a health office, you will likely be the first person that many clients see and interact with. Effective communication and client relation techniques are vital. In Chapter 8, you will learn appropriate verbal and nonverbal communication techniques to use in person and on the telephone

You will also gain strategies for dealing effectively with difficult or dissatisfied clients. The chapter also discusses effective handling of mail and other written communication and how to deal effectively with peers and other health professionals. Chapter 9 applies what you have learned in Chapter 8 to effective management of scheduling. It deals with how to schedule client appointments and the principles of triage. You will learn how to assess the urgency and nature of the client's health complaint and schedule the client appropriately. Various scheduling systems are discussed, along with the challenges clients present with when they want to see the doctor. Chapters 10, 11, and 12 prepare you for provincial/territorial billing. These chapters outline the principles behind provincial and territorial billing in Canada, discussing the common elements apparent in most provinces and territories. Chapter 10 explains how provincial and territorial health-care plans work. Chapters 11 and 12 detail the elements of a health-care claim and the process of billing, emphasizing electronic billing. The Ontario system is used to demonstrate the billing process; however, most exercises can be adapted to the structure of any provincial or territorial billing plan. Chapter 12 also discusses the principles and procedures for billing clients, insurance companies, and others for uninsured services. Chapter 13 provides an overview of health records management. Topics include the life cycle of the medical chart, basic chart content, security and confidentiality, and common filing systems.

Chapter 8
Communicating for Health

Learning Objectives

On completing this chapter, you will be able to:

1. Explain the effective use of fax, email, and postal mail.
2. Apply the principles of plain language to the health services setting.
3. Coordinate the use of telephone answering devices and services.
4. Screen, triage, and manage incoming calls.
5. Respond to the individual needs of callers and give appropriate telephone advice.
6. Maintain confidentiality in the health-care setting.
7. Organize and manage outgoing calls efficiently.
8. Respond effectively to difficult and angry clients.
9. Discuss strategies to effectively communicate with health professionals.

Communication in the health office takes many forms. Technologies, such as email, fax, cellphones, pagers, BlackBerrys, answering devices, and computers, have made communication easier, faster, and more efficient. A doctor can use an internet link to access a client's test results and X-rays from home or can download client information from a central hospital database before making rounds. Communication technology has also improved electronic medical records (EMR) systems dramatically. Many laboratory and diagnostic facilities send results directly to the physician in electronic format. If one of a physician's clients has been seen by another provider during an evening or weekend, the doctor can also receive notification of that—within hours of the visit. EMR systems also have electronic, internal messaging systems for providers and staff members. Yet any information exchange system is only as good as the people operating it. The medium of communication is less important than the tone and content of the message.

Excellent communication is critical to good health-care delivery in any setting. Although this chapter focuses on communication in a family doctor's office, the same skills and approaches apply whether you work in a specialist's office, a clinic, a hospital, or a dentist's office. In the health office, many of the responsibilities of the administrative health professional (AHP) revolve around use of the telephone and other communication devices to collect and relay information, communicate with clients, and coordinate activities. Communication affects client care, treatment plans, appointment scheduling, client education, and interchanges between professionals. Effective health communication is challenging both for clients and for health professionals. Your skill as a communicator is essential not only to make sure everyone gets the information they need, but also to make people comfortable.

It would be helpful to review Chapter 1, which details the importance of professionalism with respect to dress, general appearance, and manner (emphasizing the importance of professional communication with others).

❶ THE OFFICE AND THE FAX MACHINE

AFTER THE TELEPHONE SYSTEM, THE FAX MACHINE IS THE BUSIEST TECHNOLOGY IN THE office. Pharmacies, hospitals, and nursing homes in particular will fax reports, test results, and requests for medication repeats or refills. Doctors and dentists will fax requests for consultations and consultation reports. The number and types of reports faxed will of course vary depending on the use of both EMRs and EHRs (electronic health records) in a given community.

Note that if you are in the position of purchasing a fax machine for your office, consider purchasing the accompanying maintenance agreement. The vendor will maintain and repair the fax machine and help resolve problems with the related telephone line.

Receiving/Sending Faxes

When you receive a fax, check that you have the number of pages noted on the cover sheet. Call the sender if you are missing pages. When you send a fax, specify the number of pages on the cover sheet. Keep a log of all fax transmissions, noting the same information as on the cover sheet. This serves as a record in case a transmission is lost. Most machines will print out a report that the transmission went through, giving date, time, and destination. These reports should be filed as a confirmation of faxes sent and received.

Sending and receiving reports must be done so as to protect the confidentiality of all documents. Often, fax machines are used by a number of people; some are shared by several offices or hospital departments. It is easy for someone to scoop up a bunch of faxed documents and take someone else's material by mistake. To minimize this risk at your end, try to place your fax machine in a secure area. Watch for expected faxes. When you receive faxed reports, pick them up as soon as you can. Even better, some fax machines come with mailboxes accessible only by code. The sender punches in a code to designate where the fax is being sent. The receiver then punches in the code to activate the printer and receive the message.

Prescriptions and Pharmacies

Pharmacies typically fax requests for prescription refills/renewals for multiple clients at once—possibly on the same form. The doctor can respond to these prescription requests right on the faxed request sheet you received. You can fax the request form back to the pharmacy, once repeats have been authorized, altered, or declined. Remember (from Chapter 7) that whether a prescription request comes by phone or fax, you must pull the client's chart if your charts are paper based. With EMRs the doctor can patch directly into the client's chart if he needs medical information. In an EMR environment, the doctor can also send prescriptions directly to the pharmacy from his computer, eliminating the need for a paper prescription.

Even if the doctor has the capability to send prescriptions electronically, there are times when they have to be downloaded, signed, and faxed or given directly to the client. For example, a prescription for a narcotic must be signed and the original given to the pharmacist. Federal regulations in Canada require prescriptions to be written on paper or communicated orally by physicians. Until these regulations are changed, physicians will be limited in their options. Newer systems offer the internal faxing option to the administrative staff as well.

Specialty Appointments and Related Consultation Reports

Faxing and receiving consultation reports still requires significant use of the fax machine. If a client requires an appointment with someone—for example, a specialist, physiotherapist, or dietician—the physician must complete a request for consultation detailing relevant portions of the client's medical history pertinent to the reason for the consult request. You would fax this information to the appropriate destination—for example, the specialist. They would receive the consultation request, make an appointment, and fax back the appointment information. You would then call the client with that information. Once the consult is completed, the specialist's office will fax you a completed consultation report. This report must be scanned and uploaded into the client's EMR.

Tip
When scanning and filing a report to a client's EMR, you must be sure you have the correct chart. Validate this by looking up the client's EMR by both name and date of birth (DOB). You may have clients with the same name, so using the DOB as well is an additional safety check.

Faxed Reports and Scanning

In environments with EMR and EHR connectivity, reports can be sent right to the doctor's desktop and can then be directly filed into the client's EMR. Reports may come from a hospital, pharmacy, or public lab, for example. Otherwise all faxed reports must be scanned and uploaded to the client's chart. Most AHPs report that this process can take several hours a day, sometimes filing more than 200 daily reports for a single doctor. You must scan the reports into a batch or file. You would then select the client's electronic chart, and categorize the report. You must recheck the name on the report with the EMR you are dumping it into, and then file it appropriately. Categories you can choose for filing the report include imaging, operative, consultations, letters, hospital discharge, hospital diagnostic reports, history and physical, internal reports, and external reports.

❶ EMAIL

EMAIL IS USED IN MANY HEALTH OFFICES AND OTHER HEALTH-CARE SETTINGS FOR messaging purposes, not for sending confidential health information. Some practices make appointments and send clients' messages via email. Even if you make all appointments by phone, it is a good idea to have an email address as another way to contact the client.

If you are sending email messages that contain confidential information, you should have security features: encrypt the message, and label the message confidential. Never use a web-based email service. When receiving email, do not leave anything confidential showing on your screen or accessible to anyone for whom it is not intended.

If you send letters or reports by email, use the same standards as you would for any professional written communication. Use proper spelling, grammar, and capitalization. Too many people have become sloppy with email, treating it as casual conversation. That may be all right for a quick note to a friend, but not for professional messages. When formality is more appropriate, send a properly formatted letter by email attachment.

If you have only one computer in the office, email may not be as convenient. The computer may be needed most of the time for processing health cards, dental policy ID cards, billing, accessing clients' records, and making appointments.

There are rules to follow for proper email protocol:

- Ensure you have the proper email address. When you start entering the address, the auto function will insert the address the computer "thinks" you want. It is very easy to accept the wrong address, particularly if you are in a hurry. Try adding the email address before you write the message. Check it again before you send the email.

- Always use a subject line. Some computer security software will prevent entry of an email without one. As well, the subject line is handy to use for filing, retrieving, and tracking email. When you use the "reply" option, the subject field retains the original subject line—ensure it reflects the current content of the message.

- Keep the message short and to the point. In a busy office reading (and writing) longer messages takes time.

- Do not use email "lingo." Use proper grammar and punctuation. Improper abbreviations, jargon, and mistakes reflect poorly on you and your organization. Most email software has a spell-check option. Use it.

- Answer promptly. Prioritize email messages and respond accordingly. Always reply. Delayed responses make you appear inefficient and discourteous. If you do not have the information the sender requires immediately, let them know there will be a delay. For example, a message saying "I received your message and will follow up within two days when I have the information you require" is better than letting someone think you are slow or didn't receive the message. Respond to all of the questions in the email. Not answering questions requires unnecessary follow-up and wastes time.

- Keep the message thread intact. Keep the original message in your email reply. Do this by using the reply option, not the new message option. The original message serves as a reminder in case you forget the details of the original message. If you are sending the original email to others (using the "cc" option), however, ensure that there is nothing sensitive or confidential in the original message thread before you do so.

- Proofread your email. Always reread your email—just as you would any written document. You have a last chance to check wording, clarity, format, grammar, spelling, and punctuation.

- Be aware of security. Do not open email attachments if you do not recognize the source. Add a disclaimer to your email. A disclaimer should include a statement regarding virus transmission and breach of confidentiality. A confidentiality disclaimer can protect your office or organization against the improper use of confidential information. The recipient of the email could be held liable for misusing the information.

❶ WRITTEN COMMUNICATION

Printed communication in the health office has decreased with the use of the fax machine, email, and electronic medical records systems. However, even with electronic tools, you still need to fill out insurance forms, process return-to-work notes, and prepare dictated consultation reports, depending on the type of health office you work in. Many health offices use medical transcription or voice-recognition software for creating reports, and then fax them to their destinations.

If you are responsible for typing letters and reports, you need a thorough knowledge of medical terminology, anatomy, physiology, spelling, grammar, and formatting. Reports must be accurately reproduced, be professional in language and appearance, and follow the standard format used at your facility. For the most part, letters will be electronically dictated or, if short, handwritten by the doctor or dentist. You will likely be expected to edit them for grammar, punctuation, correct word choice, and clarity. Documents created using voice-recognition software must be checked for words that were not recognized properly. For example, one report, dictated and sent out unedited, said, "The baby died." It should have read, "The baby cried." It is a good idea to have a letter template on your computer. Most doctors have letterhead stationery.

Some offices send out quarterly newsletters that include information about the practice, updating clients on policies and new treatment options. Sometimes they also include significant events about the professional staff—those who leave, new staff members hired, and so on. This creates a friendly bond with clients and is, in part, a marketing tool. Marketing in offices (other than a doctor's office) is a vital component in building and maintaining a client base. You may also be responsible for creating client teaching information. Such material must be clear, relatively simple, and organized to make it easy to read. Remember that many laypeople have limited knowledge of medical concepts and terminology. Avoid jargon. If it is simpler to use specialized terms, explain them on first usage.

Signs

If there is something you want all your clients to know, it often makes sense to put a sign in the reception area or at the front desk. For example, you may want to ask clients to call at certain times to schedule appointments (see Figure 8.1). You may want to let them know about office policies, charges for uninsured services, or dates when the office will be closed. You may want to remind them to take off their boots, to show their health cards, or to wait in the office after an allergy injection. It is important to note that all primary care reform groups must clearly post signs related to office and clinic hours. Any other services that are part of the group benefit package must also be clearly conveyed to the clients—telephone help lines and services included in and excluded from the "basket of services" for which the provincial or territorial plan will pay. The sign needs to convey the message clearly while being appealing and leaving a friendly impression. A few suggestions follow.

- Make the sign large enough to be noticed.
- Make the lettering large enough for people with limited vision to read.
- Make the sign simple but attractive. A simple border can help, as can a little colour. Rounded, open fonts are usually more appealing than narrow, heavy ones. Do not use ornate fonts.
- Keep the words brief and to the point.
- Be clear. Ask several people what the sign means to make sure it cannot be misinterpreted.
- Keep a friendly tone. Such phrases as "Please," "Thank you," and "We appreciate," are more courteous than simple commands or words like "must" and "don't."
- Try a little humour. But make sure your wording is not confusing or offensive to anyone.

Incoming Mail

In most offices, mail is delivered daily and arrives either by courier, special delivery, or regular post, which includes priority post and registered mail. You will probably be responsible for sorting and dealing with the mail according to office guidelines. Like phone calls, most incoming mail falls into certain categories.

PLEASE CALL AFTER 10 A.M. TO MAKE OR
CANCEL APPOINTMENTS.

THANK YOU FOR YOUR COOPERATION.
Dr. D. Thompson

Figure 8.1 An office sign

Medical Reports Electronic reports may be received on consultations, operations, home care, lab results, and radiology reports, but many are still sent as hard copy. Sometimes lab reports arrive by courier. Any lab reports should have abnormal or marginal results flagged. The doctor may also be notified this by the lab directly to his desktop. Alternatively, the lab may also call the office if the results are alarming. You would either put the call through to the doctor or notify him (send a flag to his desktop or tell him yourself). Alternatively the nurse may be able to handle that call. Diagnostic reports (such as an X-ray or ultrasound) will be faxed or sent electronically to the doctor's desktop. If results are abnormal (for example, a pathology report from a Pap smear), flag them for review by the doctor (some offices use a highlighter). With respect to lab results, of immediate concern are abnormal blood sugar and blood coagulation results (e.g., INR, APTT, B.S.). Usually the doctor will ask you to contact the client regarding abnormal test results of any description. You may be asked to schedule an appointment for the client to discuss the problem, have the client go for a repeat blood test (e.g. an INR), or instruct the client—at the request of the doctor—to alter the dose of a medication (for example, withholding a dose of warfarin if the INR was too low).

Insurance Reports Insurance reports are the bane of most physicians' lives—and of yours. Completing insurance forms takes an inordinate amount of the doctor's time. They are sent by numerous sources including private insurance companies, workers' compensation boards, and government agencies. You should fill out as much of these forms as you can, usually limited to demographic information. For example, you can fill in the name, address, DOB, health number, and claim number (if there is one). Many of these forms require detailed medical information that only the doctor can provide. Often the client will come in with a wad of forms to be filled in, thinking that the doctor can do it while she waits. Clients often do not understand the time factor, and that the doctor cannot simply abandon his current schedule to sit down for half an hour to prepare the form.

Every insurance company has its own forms. The commonly used ones include those requiring a physical assessment of the client, functional assessment forms, return-to-work forms, and disability assessment forms.

Once the doctor completes and signs the forms, you will send them back. You may have to individualize a reply or attach such documents as medical reports. Where consent is required, do not forget to include the signed form. Dental, chiropractic, and optometry offices have a higher volume of insurance forms, because most of their services are covered by third-party carriers (rather than the provincial or territorial health plan). Most insurance forms are completed at the point of service and faxed to the carrier by the administrative assistant.

Tip

Organization is efficiency: When you receive an insurance form for the doctor to complete, fill out as much as you can, make an appointment for the client for the necessary assessment if required, tell the client when he can expect the report to be completed for pick-up (or if/when it will be mailed/faxed), and be clear about charges the client is expected to pay if applicable. Follow the doctor's protocol for filling out reports—he probably would like the forms to be neatly stacked on his desk so he can complete them throughout the day. Some forms require online completion, but most are done by hand.

WCB/WSIB Forms   You can view samples of the WCB/WSIB forms you will likely be dealing with most frequently on your provincial/territorial WCB/WSIB website. Look for a link such as Forms for Health Professionals (or a similar phrase). In Alberta the link is Health Care Practitioners, for example. Familiarize yourself with the forms most frequently used, such as Form 8 in Ontario (used for all clients claiming WCB/WSIB benefits for work-related illness or injury) and forms C050 (first report) and C151 (progress report) in Alberta. In British Columbia a commonly used form is Form 8/11, Physician's First Report (to see this report, follow the links at the WSIB/WCB Boards website listed at the end of the chapter to find the WorkSafeBC website).

In most jurisdictions, basic claims require a functional abilities form (FAF) be completed prior to the client returning to work. Looking at the forms commonly used in your jurisdiction will give you an idea as to how lengthy and time-consuming they will be for you and the physician to complete. WCB/WSIB claims may require you to photocopy parts of the client's chart—you may claim payment from the WCB/WSIB for this, as the cost is about 40 to 45 cents a page. You also bill for the amount of time it takes for the physician to complete the form, usually by the half-hour and in increments of 15-minute intervals. The payment changes if the report is accompanied with a medical opinion versus without. The WCB/WSIB and clients are always in a hurry for prompt return of these forms, as claims cannot be adjudicated without them. There is sometimes discord between the physician and client regarding the initiation and continuation of disability claims—both WCB/WSIB claims and others—which can be unpleasant for all involved. For example, the doctor may feel that from a medical perspective the client can return to work, perhaps with work restrictions, but the client feels he is not ready. Also, the employer may not want to accommodate work restrictions. Such situations may require the physician to fill out additional forms, make further assessments, or perhaps meet with WCB/WSIB officials and the client.

Forms Submission   You can submit claims by fax, mail, or electronically if your office has registered to do so. If you submit forms electronically you should keep a copy in the client's file and print a copy of the recommended pages for the client to keep (e.g., in Ontario for Form 8 this is only page 3). Keep a record in the client's file of when forms were completed and sent. In many jurisdictions the WCB/WSIB pays the physician more for electronic submissions (eProvider), probably to encourage this mode of submission.

Personal Mail   Place any letters or documents marked "confidential" and any letters you recognize as personal on the doctor's desk unopened.

Educational Materials   Educational materials can be for the doctor, for the staff, or for clients. If the client-oriented material seems generally useful, you can put it in a rack in the reception area. Some material may be suitable for specific clients only; it can be placed in the treatment and examination room or left with the doctor. It is best given out to selected clients as appropriate. Educational materials for the doctor include a never-ending supply of medical journals, notifications of seminars, updates on drug therapies, and medical newspapers. The doctor should sort through these. Always replace outdated materials.

Magazines for the Reception Area   Many medical offices receive subscription magazines for the reception area. Some of these are promotional and sent free of charge; others may be ordered by the doctor or office staff. You may be tempted to "borrow" the magazines that appeal to you. It is fine to read them, but make sure they find their way to the reception area while they are still current. If your doctor does not subscribe to any magazines, you might suggest it. The cost of subscriptions can be written off as a business expense. Reading material in the office should reflect general interests, keeping in mind your client population. For a medical office, cater to various interests with a selection of lifestyle magazines, such as *Canadian Living*, and magazines covering sports, health, travel, science, or culture. For younger clients, include storybooks at various levels. If you work for a gynecologist, you might have a similar selection but with more focus on women's interests. If you work for a pediatrician, you will want more picture books. Have a few board books or washable fabric books for babies. If you are working in a dental office specializing in aesthetic dentistry, you might consider some magazines highlighting smile makeovers.

Outdated magazines are a standing complaint among clients. Remove shabby or outdated magazines (generally more than three months old). Decline clients' offers to bring in old magazines unless they are relatively current. Some offices offer notepaper and pens so people who see a recipe or any other interesting item in a magazine can copy it rather than tearing out pages or taking away the magazine.

Junk Mail   As with any household or business, you will receive your share of fliers, notices, and other forms of junk mail. This clutters the office and, for the most part, is inappropriate for a health-care setting. Sort and discard such material as it comes in. If you shelve it to sort through later, it will pile up. Some doctors like to look over pharmaceutical advertising; if yours does not, it, too, is junk mail.

Cheques   Depending on the type of office you are working in, you will receive cheques and other forms of payment for deregulated services or other things the doctor charges for. You will also receive third-party payments from insurance companies and workers' compensation boards. (See Chapter 12.) Many AHPs will open envelopes containing cheques and place them on the doctor's desk for him to review.

In many dental, chiropractic, or optometry health offices, the client is asked to pay at the point of service and is reimbursed by the insurance company. The client may have a policy whereby the insurance company pays the doctor directly. This is called assignment of benefits, but not often used. It is an arrangement between the client and the insurance carrier whereby the client gives written permission for the carrier to send a cheque directly to the provider. When this occurs, there may be a portion of the fee that the insurance does not cover; thus the health office must also collect money from the client. A credit card or cheque is the preferred method of payment.

Usually, cheques are marked for deposit only and are added to the provider's account according to your office routine. Keep a careful log of all payments received—from whom, the date, and the amount. Accurate bookkeeping is a must.

Holiday Mail   Often, the office stays open even when the doctor or other provider is on vacation. Sometimes a locum looks after the practice, or other members of a group practice or clinic cover for the doctor. In most primary care reform groups, the office remains open, and clients are booked for appointments at the group's central clinic. Continue to sort the mail and review lab reports, radiology reports, and so on. Make sure you have clear instructions on contacting a doctor with any abnormal results or correspondence that requires immediate attention, such as time-sensitive insurance reports. If you cannot contact a doctor, call the correspondent, explain that the doctor is away, and make suitable arrangements to attend to the matter. Prioritize remaining correspondence so that the doctor can deal with the most important or immediate concerns promptly when she returns.

Outgoing Mail

Outgoing mail must be prepared and sent promptly. Much of the material that was once mailed—medical reports, lab reports, X-ray results, insurance reports—is now routinely faxed. Sometimes an original copy is needed; for example, insurance companies processing a claim usually require forms hand-signed by the doctor. Often, a report may be faxed and the original mailed. Keep and file a copy of all outgoing documents.

Clients who are moving to a new city or otherwise changing medical or dental offices will need a copy of their chart sent to their new health-care provider. Most offices keep the original chart and, after receiving a signed request from the client for transfer, either mail or fax the information. Sometimes, only a summary of the chart is sent. The client is usually charged for chart transfers. (See Chapter 10.)

Outgoing mail may include notices to clients, such as formal notification of missed appointments or recall notices—reminders that it is time for the next appointment. Few family doctors send such notices, but they are common in the offices of chiropractors, optometrists, dentists, and some specialists. Most recall notices are followed up with a telephone call. Figure 8.2 shows a sample letter reminding a client of a missed appointment. Offices that charge for missed appointments would also address this in the letter or invoice.

Ending a Doctor–Client Relationship   Occasionally, a doctor (or other provider) and a client part ways because of differing values and expectations regarding the client's health and care. Either the doctor or the client may initiate the separation. If a doctor feels that he cannot continue to provide quality care for a client, it is in the interests of both parties to terminate the relationship. This is not something a doctor will do lightly or just because a client is difficult. Usually, all efforts will be made to preserve the professional relationship. However, sometimes, doctors feel they can no longer work with clients who refuse to follow advice. Or the doctor may be uncomfortable with clients who demand ongoing care that the doctor does not feel is necessary, especially if they demand that the doctor, against his professional judgment, declare them unfit for work so they can receive insurance payments or workers' compensation. In other cases, the client may

---

Dear Mrs. Greenbaum,

Our records show that you are overdue for your periodic eye examination and that you missed your October 8th appointment.

Continued routine eye examinations are important to your visual health. If you have found another doctor, please let us know, and we would be happy to forward copies of your medical records at your request. If not, please call the office to book an appointment at your earliest convenience.

Sincerely,

Madge Oban
Office Manager

Figure 8.2   Notification of a missed appointment

> Dear Mr. Dykstra,
>
> I am writing to notify you that I am withdrawing as your family doctor. I feel that I am unable to continue to provide you with quality medical care as a result of our differing expectations and your refusal to follow my medical advice.
>
> I will be happy to provide you with any medical care you need until you find another doctor.
>
> You may also use the walk-in clinic if you require medical care.
>
> Please contact us to let us know where you want a copy of your medical records sent. You will be required to sign a release form before your medical records can be transferred.
>
> Sincerely,
>
> M. Adams, MD

Figure 8.3 Sample letter ending a client–doctor relationship

leave because she mistrusts the doctor's diagnosis and wants the kinds of treatment the doctor cannot provide. In a dental office, a client may be noncompliant with a treatment regime, such as wearing braces; in a chiropractic office, the client may refuse to wear a brace or do recommended exercises. Sometimes, personalities may clash. Usually, the decision is mutual: if the doctor has done all she can for the client and the client wants more or different care, the client will be just as eager to find a new doctor as the doctor is to be relieved of the responsibility of caring for the client.

Nevertheless, a parting of ways is tricky and must be handled with discretion, sensitivity, and an eye to legal liability in case the client sues, possibly alleging discrimination or negligence. A doctor withdrawing services must notify the client in writing and must continue to provide care until the client has found another doctor. With the shortage of doctors in most parts of the country, this can be a long time. Figure 8.3 shows a sample letter "firing" a patient.

Send such a letter by registered mail to ensure that the client receives it. Put a copy in the client's chart. If the client calls after getting the letter, document all contacts in the chart. If the client wishes to speak with the doctor about the situation again, have the doctor call him back.

❷ PLAIN LANGUAGE

A COMMUNICATIONS MOVEMENT CALLED PLAIN LANGUAGE IS MAKING ITS WAY INTO health care from the business and legal communities.[1] Plain language principles, although developed for writing, also lead to effective, clear oral communication.

Plain language is speaking and writing so that your clients understand you. It is organizing and presenting information that focuses on your clients' needs. It is keeping them in mind when you write letters, memos, phone messages, or instructions. Always ask yourself three essential questions when communicating with a client:

- What do they need to know?
- What do they already know?
- How will I present it to them so that they understand?

---

[1] This section contributed by Susan D. Milne, Plain Language Consultant.

Plain language means asking, "Is this clear?" as you explain something on the phone or in person. It is watching for nonverbal clues from your clients and paying attention to what they are telling you.

Why Plain Language?

Before you start, ask yourself what barriers might keep your clients from understanding you. These include the following:

- Literacy problems
- Language and culture
- Educational level
- Stress and self-esteem issues

Consider the following:

- A significant number of adult Canadians have trouble with literacy tasks, such as filling out a form, following instructions, or calculating a tip in a restaurant. Language barriers or medical terms further complicate this.
- Seniors are one of the fastest-growing population groups in Canada. Many have limited vision and require large print and simple graphics. Literacy problems are also somewhat higher among older Canadians because of previous limited educational opportunities.
- Some Canadians whose second language is English often have difficulty understanding written and spoken instructions, especially when the content is technical.

Using plain language is especially important in the health-care field because misunderstandings can be serious. Clients need to fully understand what you are telling them. For example, if you are referring them to a specialist, they need to understand why they are going, what they need to bring with them, and the date, time, and location. If they are getting a test done, they need to understand the purpose of the test and how to prepare for it. Clear instructions the first time will often eliminate the need for the client to call back.

When you help people understand what they are supposed to do—keep an appointment, follow medication orders, or fill in a form—you help them be responsible for their health care.

Using plain language also shows respect for clients. It tells them you will work with them to achieve their goals. No one likes to admit they cannot understand something, but lack of understanding can cause frustration and confusion. Using plain language and checking for understanding will avoid this.

Keep in mind, though, that there is a difference between plain language and talking down. As mentioned in Chapter 3, no one likes to be talked down to. Although clarity is always good, sometimes trying too hard to keep your language simple can alienate people. For example, one educated mother was given a prescription for her daughter by a specialist. When she expressed concern about possible side effects, the specialist told her, "It's good medicine. It's safe for children." She felt that the doctor was not taking her seriously and she was not reassured. Later, her family doctor told her, "This medication has been shown by large-scale studies to be highly effective, and it has an excellent side-effects profile." Although the family doctor said essentially the same thing as the specialist, the mother was reassured when she heard a reasoned explanation in the kind of language she was used to. If you are a good conversationalist, you will learn to listen to clients, gauge their vocabulary and verbal sophistication, and tailor your own style to suit.

Plain Language Tips

Here are some tips you can apply to your written and spoken communications with clients.

1. *Write as you speak, using a conversational tone.* Use "you" and "we" to make your communication friendly and direct. It is easier for clients to figure out what to do if you address them directly.

   Instead of Patients should complete the forms before seeing the dentist.
   Try   Please complete the forms before you see the dentist.

2. *Include one main idea per sentence.* Keep sentences short (around 10–15 words or fewer). The first example below contains three ideas and is 34 words long. The second example is easier to understand because each main idea gets its own sentence, and the sentences are shorter.

   Instead of This prescription gives you 30 days' worth of medication, and the doctor would like to see you before you finish the medication, so can we set an appointment for about three weeks from now?
   Try   This prescription gives you 30 days' worth of medication. The doctor would like to see you before you finish the medication. Can we set up an appointment for about three weeks from now?

3. *Use active verbs most often.* The subject of an *active verb* performs the action ("Joanne called the clinic"). The subject of a *passive verb* is acted upon ("The clinic was called by Joanne"). Often, the doer of the action does not appear at all in a sentence with a passive verb ("The clinic was called"). Sentences with active verbs are more direct and easier to understand because the people doing the action are named at the beginning of the sentence.

   Instead of The application form was processed by Human Resources. (passive)
                   All decisions pertaining to the payment of medical claims over $500 are the prerogative of your insurance company. (passive, unclear as to who decides)
                   This medicine is to be taken before every meal. (passive, unclear as to who takes the medicine)
   Try   Human Resources processed the application form. (active, direct)
                   Your insurance company will decide whether it will pay medical claims over $500. (active, clear as to who decides)
                   Take this medicine before every meal. (active, clear as to who takes the medicine)

4. *Group related information together.* Finish with one topic before you begin another. In writing, guide the reader through the material by using lists and descriptive headings. Think about how the design of your document can help make it easier to read. For example, notice the use of lists, headings, and tables in this book. Do they help you understand the information and to find sections easily?

5. *Tell people what to do, instead of what not to do.*

Instead of	We will not reimburse you for your dental expenses unless you provide us with all necessary receipts.
Try	Give us your dental receipts, and we will reimburse your expenses.

6. *Get rid of jargon and acronyms, wherever possible.* If you must use a technical term, explain it. And remember, some acronyms have more than one meaning, and so write them out in full (or explain what they mean) the first time. Professional communication is about being clear, not about impressing clients with how much you know.

accomplish	do
advise	tell
designate	name
due to the fact that	because, as
have a responsibility to	must
influenza immunization	flu shot
in the amount of	for
per annum	a year
pursuant to	following
remittance	payment
subsequent to	after
terminate	stop, end
to the extent that	if, when
with reference to, regarding	about

Plain language is a common-sense revolution in business and health communications. It is being driven by clients reacting to websites they cannot figure out how to use, statements and contracts they cannot interpret, forms they cannot complete, and health-care instructions they cannot follow.

❸ THE TELEPHONE

THE TELEPHONE IS ONE OF THE MOST IMPORTANT COMMUNICATION DEVICES YOU WILL USE in any health-care setting. The telephone provides a vital link among health professionals, clients and their families, and health resources. How you communicate with people on the phone is as important as face-to-face interactions. Often, people get their first impressions of you and the practice on the phone. If you learn to use the phone effectively, you will project a positive image of yourself, your employer, and the practice.

Tip

As well as using plain language, use terminology and abbreviations correctly and clearly. Be precise to avoid confusion whenever possible. For example, IUD, depending on the situation, can mean either "intrauterine contraceptive device" or "intrauterine death." IUCD is a better abbreviation for the contraceptive device.

Telephone Equipment

If you are choosing equipment for your office, you need to be aware of the choices on the market and choose those that suit your office's clientele and administrative style. You need to be familiar with the equipment in your office: how it works and its capabilities and limitations. This may involve some initial training. Although the principles are the same, each telephone system is different. Most systems include the ability to put a caller on hold and to transfer a call to an extension.

The typical health office has an ordinary touch-tone telephone with two or three extensions: one in the doctor's office and perhaps one in the lab or workroom, if you have one. Larger, multi-doctor practices will have more telephone lines, usually one or two for each provider. The telephone in the front office may receive several lines. In larger practices, often, one staff member is assigned the principal responsibility of answering the phone. This person usually uses a headset, leaving her hands free to access the computer, pull charts, and receive messages. There are also wireless telephone systems that offer even more freedom and flexibility.

Rarely will you find a telephone in an examining room. It would be disruptive to the doctor and the client and would pose confidentiality problems.

Because the main telephone line is so busy with incoming and outgoing calls, most offices also have a second "private" line with an unlisted number. This allows doctors to make and receive calls when they need to and is useful in an emergency. The private number is given to only a few individuals, such as the doctor's family and selected health professionals.

The second line is sometimes used for the fax machine as well, although many practices have a dedicated line for that purpose. Most telephone companies can provide you with a separate number for the fax machine on the same telephone line. If a fax is coming into the office, the fax machine answers that number after the first or second ring. If your system is programmed that way, do not answer that line until after the second ring. Other systems may use a separate line for the fax only or may signal a fax with a different ring.

Other optional services your office can purchase include call answer, universal messaging, call waiting, call display, call privacy, voice mail, and ident-a-call. These features may or may not suit your office.

Call Answer/Voice Mail   This service will take messages 24 hours a day, seven days a week even when the telephone is in use. You can retrieve the messages at your convenience. You need a touch-tone phone in order to use this service. You are signalled that there is a waiting message either by a flashing light or by an interrupted dial tone when you pick up the receiver. Most doctors opt not to have the option for leaving messages. Voice mail places the onus of contacting the client on you or the physician. This is time consuming and sometimes frustrating.

Universal Messaging   Some doctors prefer the consolidated services of universal messaging.

Universal messaging delivers phone messages, faxes, and emails to one place. This internet-based solution transforms media messages into digital files and sends them to an email box. The receiver can access them via email or through a private webpage. Messages can be sent on a delayed basis and provide a confirmation that a message has been received.

Call Waiting This service allows you to receive calls while you are talking on the telephone. You will hear a soft beep. You ask the other party to hold, and depress the flash button while you answer the incoming call. To return to your initial call, you press the flash button again. Some offices have visual call waiting, which shows the name and number of the caller, allowing you to decide which calls you wish to answer.

Call Display With a compatible telephone, you can see the name and number of the caller. This is not used extensively in health facilities but is useful in some.

Ident-a-Call This service allows you to have two additional telephone numbers on one line, each with its own distinctive ring. Some practices offering multiple services within the practice will use this feature.

Automated Attendant Callers outside the practice can dial directly to an internal extension without going to the receptionist first.

Automatic Call Distribution This gives you the ability to set up a call centre for incoming calls, which is practical for receptionists in a medium or large practice.

Conference Calling This connects three or more people for a group call. The usefulness of this feature is related to the practice style of the physician.

Electronic Medical Record (EMR) Integration A telephone system can be programmed to integrate with an EMR system so that information from the clients' EMR appears on the computer screen when they call in.

Call Forwarding This feature allows you to transfer incoming calls from one phone to another where you can be reached or where someone else can take a message. This is helpful in an office where extensions are limited. If you are in an area where there is another telephone, you can have calls from the main office line forwarded to the telephone within your reach.

Automated Routing There are a number of automated routing devices on the market. Some are designed for larger facilities, such as hospitals, while others are tailored to small and medium-sized offices. These devices will answer each call, offer the caller a selection of options, and direct the call accordingly. An office with four doctors could separate calls by doctor. For example:

> "Good morning, Hudson Medical Centre. Please choose from the following four options: for Dr. McArthur, press 1; for Dr. Santorelli, press 2; for Dr. Lisowski, press 3, for Dr. Feinberg, press 4."

The device allows a single number to link to four offices. It is efficient and remains relatively uncomplicated. Routing devices can be programmed to meet your office's needs. Most can direct callers who simply want routine information, such as office hours, to recorded messages. This saves you time since you do not need to take those calls. However, the more options you have available, the more complex the system becomes and the more frustrating for some of your clients. Many health-care consumers feel that the automated routing device in a health office is just one more step away from personalized care.

Telephone Answering Options

Every facility must have some method of answering the telephone when the office is closed or you are not available. A number of things must be considered when choosing which option works best for a practice. Whatever option you use, it is vital that the communication remains professional and friendly and meets the needs of your clients.

The Answering Service An answering service employs operators who answer calls for a broad range of clientele, ranging from doctors to churches and private companies. These operators usually have some training in dealing with medically related calls and have a protocol to follow. Use of an answering service has declined significantly in favour of automated answering options and electronic devices such as pagers.

Answering Devices There is a wide selection of answering machines on the market, in both analogue and digital format. Make sure the device is of good quality and is reliable. Some answering machines are used only to give a message to the caller. The message can be changed as required. Others allow callers to leave messages.

Another option is an automated service provided by communication companies such as Bell Canada or other telecommunications company (such as call answer, discussed above). This option eliminates the clutter of an answering machine.

Clients needing emergency or urgent care are directed to the nearest appropriate clinic or operating Emergency Department. The family doctor may not be involved at all. Thus, there is no need for any exchange of information, A recording in the doctor's office can give callers a simple message, directing them to the Emergency Department or after-hours clinic. Family doctors with EMR capabilities should receive an electronic summary of their client's visit to the clinic or the Emergency Department as soon as the information is entered by the attending physician. This does not always happen, contributing to fragmented client/patient care.

In all provinces and territories, those who want phone advice can call government-run services, such as HealthLine in Saskatchewan, HEALTHlink in Alberta and Newfoundland and Labrador, Telehealth Ontario, and British Columbia's NurseLine, and speak to a registered nurse or a nurse practitioner. In BC, the client is required to give his or her health number when accessing this service, but not in Ontario, Saskatchewan, or Newfoundland and Labrador.

Across Canada, telephone help lines have been established for most primary care reform groups, providing prompt, confidential advice and direction regarding health concerns. Rostered clients can call this number after hours for similar advice. In most instances, there is a doctor on call to handle situations referred to them by the nurse handling the call service. Sometimes the client must wait for a call back from the help line—this should

---

Tip

If you change from one answering system to another, or the options offered to your clients change, expect some confusion on the part of those in your practice. Be patient and reinforce the changes that have occurred. You may even want to provide a short explanation as a hand-out for clients.

occur within a designated time frame. This service may be offered during selected hours or on a 24-hour basis. Services of this type may also be referred to as teletriage.

Some offices do combine an answering machine with an answering service. For example, a practice's phone line may be answered with a message saying:

> "You've reached the office of Dr. McMichael and Dr. Bodnarchuk. The office is now closed. If this is an emergency, please call 911, or go to the nearest hospital Emergency Department. If you would like to speak to a doctor on call, please call the answering service at 905-555-5555. You may also call ONcall Healthline at 1-866-000-0000. If you wish to make an appointment, please call during office hours, which are 9 to 5 Monday to Thursday and 9 to 12 on Friday."

Using an Answering Device

Most offices activate the answering machine over the lunch hour and when the office closes for the day. The message that you leave on the answering machine should be friendly, clear, and concise.

Messages can be worded generally and left the same from day to day. Some offices prefer to create a new message for each day.

Closing Messages

1. "Dr. Thompson's office is closed until 9 tomorrow morning. If you have a medical emergency, please go to the Emergency Department at Stratford General Hospital."

2. "Dr. Thompson's office is closed until 9 tomorrow morning. If you have a medical emergency, please go to the Emergency Department at Stratford General Hospital. Dr. Thompson's office hours are Monday, Tuesday, and Thursday, 9 a.m. to 5 p.m., and Wednesday, 9 a.m. to 12 noon. The family health clinic, located in the Jenny Trout Centre, 123 Erie Street, Suite 4, is open for non-urgent medical matters weekday evenings from 5 p.m. to 8 p.m. and Saturdays from 9 a.m. until noon."

3. Dr. Jones's office is closed until tomorrow at 8 in the morning. If you have a dental emergency, please call the dental emergency number, 403-111-2222, or leave a message and someone will return your call as soon as possible.

Lunch-Hour Messages

Most medical offices close over the noon hour, allowing staff members and the doctor time to rejuvenate from the morning's activities. Messages for over the noon hour are fairly straightforward.

> "Dr. Thompson's office is closed for lunch and will reopen at 1:15. If you have a medical emergency, please go to the Emergency Department at Stratford General Hospital."

Using the Answering Device at Other Times

Every office will be busier at certain times than others. Do not be afraid to use your answering machine or service for brief periods when you are very busy with other responsibilities. The volume of incoming calls usually peaks first thing in the morning or before the doctor begins to see clients in the afternoon. You may be meeting with the doctor to review the day's schedule, dealing with mail or incoming lab test results (which come by courier or are faxed), and so on. Leave the answering machine on for an extra 15 to 30 minutes.

> "Good morning. This is Dr. Thompson's office. The office is open, but we are unable to answer the phone at this time. Please call back after 10 a.m."

You will be more organized in the long run and better able to deal with calls and other duties if you are not trying to juggle several things at the same time. Your clients will soon get to know what time you are ready to accept calls. If there is an emergency, they will call the appropriate facility as per your taped message. Callers with non-urgent agendas will call later.

In recording any message, speak clearly and at a moderate pace. Keep all messages as simple as you can. Directions should be simple, clear, and concise.

Pagers

Some doctors still carry pagers, also known as beepers. These small, portable message devices are a critical component of a communication network. They allow people who need direct access to the doctor to contact him directly, eliminating the need for an answering service. Often, the doctor gives the pager number to a short list of health professionals, hospital units, and facilities where he has clients.

A caller dials a designated telephone number and either leaves a voice message or keys in a message and/or telephone number. The pager notifies the carrier by beeping, flashing, or vibrating. The vibration option is especially useful in a theatre, operating room, or lecture hall, where noise would be disruptive. Pagers may be bought or rented. A pager and answering machine together still cost less than an answering service. Many physicians are using BlackBerrys or similar devices instead.

Breaches of confidentiality can occur with pagers, though perhaps not as easily as with other devices. People who carry pagers should keep them on their person and turn them off when not in use.

Pagers come with a variety of features. Numeric pagers, the cheapest and most basic, simply provide a number for the user to call. Alphanumeric pagers, which are slightly more expensive, provide a visual text message. This sometimes saves a call. The next step up offers voice messages as well. The most costly and most adaptable devices, e-pagers, offer email and internet access and link to a computer to allow the user to check schedules and information.

Cellphones

Cellphones, BlackBerrys, and iPhones (or other smartphones) have become as important to most doctors as their pagers—often replacing the pager. There is a wide selection of such devices on the market.

These devices offer a flexibility only dreamed about a few years ago. The doctor can respond to messages swiftly and conveniently. He can use text messaging and access email, the internet, and a number of other web-based tools.

The mobile number should be given out only by the doctor. Some doctors still prefer to be reached by pagers; many leave their mobile phones turned off. They prefer to use their mobile phone, if necessary, to return calls. Most hospitals do not allow the use of mobile phones inside the building. Current research, however, indicates that the use of mobile devices in hospitals is not as disruptive as many believe.

To ensure client privacy, many practices discourage the use of cellphones in the office because of the capabilities to take pictures and videos.

You may be required to contact clients or agencies in other jurisdictions. Be aware of differences in time zones across Canada, as shown in Table 8.1.

Table 8.1 Time Zones Across Canada

Time Zone	Location	Time
Pacific	Most of British Columbia, Yukon	1 p.m.
Mountain	Alberta, Northwest Territories, Northeastern British Columbia, and western part of Nunavut	2 p.m.
Central	Saskatchewan, Manitoba, part of Northwestern Ontario, and central part of Nunavut	3 p.m.
Eastern	Most of Ontario, most of Quebec, and eastern part of Nunavut	4 p.m.
Atlantic	New Brunswick, Nova Scotia, Prince Edward Island, most of Labrador, and easternmost part of Quebec (south of Labrador)	5 p.m.
Newfoundland	The island of Newfoundland and Southeastern Labrador	5:30 p.m.

Tip

if you are communicating with facilities or individuals in other provinces/territories, be sure you consider the time zone they are in. Faxing material may not be as important, but for telephone calls you will save yourself time if you call during their office hours. Consider time zones when calling long distance. A website listed at the end of the chapter will provide you with the current time in any town in Canada.

④⑤⑥⑦ TELEPHONE SKILLS AND TECHNIQUES

HANDLING TELEPHONE CALLS APPROPRIATELY AND EFFICIENTLY IS PRIMARILY THE AHP's responsibility. You need to control the volume of incoming calls, and triage and direct them while maintaining a positive, client-oriented atmosphere. Effective management of these calls is essential not only to the well-being of your clients but also to the management of your office. It is a challenging task that requires skill, knowledge, patience, and excellent communication skills. Dealing with the public in any situation can be both rewarding and challenging. When this is coupled with health-care issues, the challenge is even greater.

Improving Your Telephone Manner

Your attitude, mood, and stress level are clearly conveyed on the phone. People will react to the tone of your voice, your choice of words, and your response to them. If your manner is positive, chances are the telephone conversation will be positive. Even a grumpy, irritated client is apt to be easier to deal with when there is a pleasant, patient person on the other end of the line. This, in turn, will make your life easier and reduce job stress.

As with face-to-face interactions, effective telephone communication is a skill. Some of us are more natural communicators, readily perceived as warm, caring, and friendly. Think of someone you have spoken with who made you feel good. How did you feel? What made you feel that way? The tone of voice? Inflections? Choice of words? Was the person empathetic and supportive? How did that person show empathy?

When conversing with such people, you can feel their warmth and almost see them smile. You look forward to speaking with them. That is what you want to achieve in the health office. If you are one of those natural communicators, you bring a wonderful asset to your job. If not, you can develop your "telephone self" through practice.

- When the phone rings, stop what you are doing to answer the phone. This will help you focus on the call.

- Take a deep breath, and concentrate on the call.

- If someone comes into the office while you are on the telephone, make eye contact, nod, or wave, but remain focused on the caller. When you finish the call, you can attend to the newly arrived client.

- Do not push your mouth up to the mouthpiece of the telephone. This muffles your voice. Have you ever heard someone talk with her mouth on a microphone? A mouth on the mouthpiece produces a similar effect.

- Do not chew gum, eat, or drink when you are speaking on the telephone.

- Smile when you answer the phone, even if you do not feel like it. Some people claim that a smile will make you less tense and more patient and impart a lift to your voice.

- Practise speaking into a tape recorder with various telephone greetings. You might be surprised at how you sound.

- If you have a soft, quiet voice, practise putting more energy into your voice.

- Speak in a lower voice. A lower tone is more soothing and more easily heard and understood.

- Speak more slowly than you usually do. This gives the person at the other end time to take in what you are saying and adjust her thoughts.

- Pronounce each word clearly. Space your words carefully to avoid running them together and sounding garbled.

- Be expressive, avoiding a monotone. This gives interest and meaning to what you are saying and adds appropriate emphasis.

- Do not be embarrassed to use gestures when you are on the telephone; it may enhance the tone and organization of speech. Watch someone talking on the telephone to see how it works. For example, in giving driving directions, many people will sketch the turns in the air; this helps them sequence what they are trying to explain.

Your choice of words is also important (as it is in face-to-face interactions). Use proper grammar and sentence structure and choose your words appropriately. Though proper English usage has relaxed substantially over the last few years, slang and poor grammar have no place in professional conversation. "It don't," "youse guys," "her and I," and "I seen" are some of the errors that will make you sound uneducated and unprofessional. Older people, in particular, will notice this, and in almost every practice today, older people make up a large part of the clientele. If you are not sure about English grammar, take a remedial English course or work through an exercise book. People often fall into error when trying to speak properly. For example, people taught to avoid saying, "Me and Jane are going to the show" may compensate by avoiding "me" entirely, and may end up with sentences like "Please return it to Jane or myself"—which is just as bad.

Sound confident. Avoid muttering "I guess," "I'm not sure," "ummmm," or "I, uh, like, you know." Such vagueness makes the caller wonder whether you are a reliable

Tip

**Answering the Phone:
The Six P's**
Prompt
Polite
Precise
Professional
Positive
Patient

source of information. If you are asked something that you cannot answer, simply say, "I will have to check that with the doctor," or "I will recheck that policy, Mrs. Rubinoff, and call you right back." You want to convey the idea that if you do not have the information at hand, you know where to get it and will do so promptly.

Answering the Phone

Promptness   Try to answer the telephone before the third ring. This may not always be possible in a busy office, but making a conscious effort will pay off. You may tell yourself that the task you are completing will only take a moment, but it could be seven or eight rings later when you get to the telephone. The caller at this point may be disagreeable and upset, or, worse, it may be an emergency. Usually, it is better to answer the telephone and then get back to what you were doing. *Not* making answering the phone a priority may become a habit that will cause endless irritation in clients.

If you often cannot answer the telephone promptly, you can at least be upbeat about it. Make a bet with the client that you will answer by the fifth ring next time. Even if you do not, you can be sure he will be counting. In most cases, this or a similar technique will lighten the mood.

Greetings   Review the examples below. Which one appeals to you the most? The least?

- "Good morning, Dr. Tremblay's office. Lise speaking."
- "Dr. Tremblay's office, Lise speaking. How may I help you?"
- "Dr. Tremblay's office, Lise speaking."
- "Dr. Tremblay's office."
- "Doctor's office."

Most clients prefer the first, with the second and third ones close behind. The first greeting is complete and courteous. It identifies the doctor's office and the speaker, as do the second and third.

Giving your own name is not only friendly but helpful. The client may know you by name and feel more comfortable speaking with you. Furthermore, the client may be following up on an earlier phone call or visit and want to speak to the same person as before. Having to explain the reason for the call to someone else is frustrating and could waste your time as well as the client's.

"Doctor's office" is impersonal and lacks warmth. It also does not rule out a wrong number; it could be a different doctor's office. How can you name the doctor if you work for a number of doctors? Some group practices solve this problem with a different line for each doctor. If you have separate lines, answer each with the doctor's name. If you have a common line, answer with the name of the group or clinic:

"Rankin Medical Centre, Andrew speaking."

One office manager works for a group of three doctors and answers the telephone simply with "Doctor's office." She claims that this greeting saves time because it is short and direct. But does it? How often does the caller respond, "Is this Dr. Heine's office?" and then, "Is this Diane?" Usually, it saves time to establish identification immediately so that the client can get right to business.

Handling Incoming Calls

Dealing with Volume   You can reduce the number of calls you receive in the office by asking clients, other professionals, and agencies to fax information, if appropriate. Faxes are particularly useful for prescription renewal requests (see Chapter 7) and test results (see Chapter 6). A fax gives you a printed copy of the information or request and leaves the phones free for other calls if you have a separate fax line. Some offices are asking that people use email. This is efficient to a point but can become time consuming.

The Morning Rush   Be aware of peak times for incoming calls in your office, and make an effort to change some of these patterns. For example, many clients will call for an appointment first thing in the morning. This is likely a busy time for the office staff. You can ask your clients to call for appointments at certain times of the day or post a sign to that effect. (See the discussion of signs earlier in this chapter.)

Appointment Cancellations   You certainly want clients to call if they have to cancel an appointment. However, to reduce the volume of incoming calls, some health offices have a telecommunications system that asks clients who are calling to cancel or reschedule to leave a message. These messages must be checked at regular intervals.

Clients Calling for Clarification of Instructions   A common type of call will be from clients seeking information. You can help reduce this type of call by clearly and concisely explaining any instructions to the client about tests and appointments. (See Chapter 6.) Whenever possible, give out printed instructions. Highlight relevant areas. Avoid medical jargon that might confuse the client. It is worth taking a couple of extra minutes to explain something thoroughly if it saves having to explain it again over the phone.

Clients Calling for Test Results   Try reversing the process. Tell clients that you will call them if there is any concern about the test results. If clients want to know either way, tell them you will call with results within a certain time frame. This obviously depends on the type of test; results from simple blood work can be back within 24 hours, while biopsy results may take a week. You could also advise clients to call the office if they have not heard from you by a certain date. This still gives you the opportunity to call, but does not leave the client sweating for weeks if you forget or the test is delayed.

Handling Typical Calls

Most calls in a doctor's office fall into certain defined categories. Your first decision is regarding which calls to handle yourself and which to pass on to the doctor. If there is a nurse, she can take a number of the calls that you would otherwise route to the doctor. The nurse and the doctor should agree just what types of calls the nurse can handle—usually questions about immunizations and other health-related issues. If the nurse takes a call that she feels she cannot handle, she will direct the call to the doctor or have the doctor return the call when he is available. Most providers put aside a designated time for returning calls.

Table 8.2 assumes that there is no nurse in the office and divides typical calls into three categories: those that you or another AHP can usually handle, those that should be directed to the doctor (either immediately or as a message to call back), and those that fall into a grey area. The ones in the middle column of the table you may be able to handle after consultation with the doctor, or you may be able to handle in part before leaving a

Table 8.2 Routing Typical Calls

Calls You Can Handle	Calls That You Might Handle with Consultation	Calls to Direct to the Doctor
Drug reps	Clients asking for medical advice	Other doctors wanting to speak to your doctor (Always put through another doctor unless specifically advised otherwise.)
Clients calling to make appointments	Clients calling to request the results of lab tests	The hospital wanting orders on a client who has been admitted or asking to change or renew an order
Clients calling for information about family	Calls relating to prescription renewals/repeats	The hospital calling about a change in a client's status (Always put this through. It may be an emergency.)
Clients wanting to talk to staff members	Clients wanting to speak with the doctor	Community agencies calling to speak with the doctor about clients under their care
Individuals looking for a doctor	Laboratories calling with test results	Personal calls for the doctor
Laboratories or diagnostic facilities calling to confirm or change appointment times		

message for the doctor. The doctor should establish clear policies on how to handle different types of calls.

Drug and Supply Representatives   Drug reps are people employed by drug companies to promote their company's line of medications. They visit doctors' offices to discuss their products and sometimes leave samples. The reps may call for an appointment or simply arrive at the office. Most doctors set specific times—perhaps every Friday from 11:30 to 12:00—when they will meet with the rep. You need to know the policy, make sure the drug reps know it, and adhere to it. Encourage reps to call the day before to confirm the appointment. Remember to notify drug reps as well as clients if you have to cancel appointments.

Supply representatives also visit all types of medical offices. For example, dental supply representatives are employed by dental supply companies who provide equipment, sundries, and service support to the dental office. The representative will visit the office to collect orders, demonstrate new products, arrange for learning seminars for the dentist and staff and arrange for equipment servicing. It is more efficient if these reps have an appointment rather than arriving unannounced.

Clients Calling to Make Appointments   This type of call is generally straightforward, and the AHP would handle it. The only time you may want to check with the doctor would be if the client had spoken to the doctor with a special request for a visit outside of office hours. Unless the doctor had told you about this, you would confirm with her.

Remember that when clients call to make an appointment, it is for a reason, usually related to a health concern. One cannot overemphasize the importance of a pleasant telephone manner in this situation. Be positive and helpful. Try to accommodate the client's request, but remain in control by offering choices. Never use barrier words, such as "I can't," "you can't," "it's impossible." Instead, try the following:

Mr. Li, which would be better for you, morning or afternoon? I'm sorry, Mr. Li, I don't have anything for late morning. I can fit you in on Wednesday at 9. I realize that's somewhat early for you, but the advantage is that you won't have to wait. Later in the morning, on Wednesdays in particular, we get very busy and often run a bit late. Now, I could give you an appointment next Monday morning, but that's six days away. Would you prefer that?"

You are keeping control while offering Mr. Li choices.

Appropriate use of triage is essential. Anyone whose problem sounds urgent should be seen immediately or sent to the Emergency Department. Anything like chest pain, shortness of breath or other breathing difficulties, loss of consciousness, profuse bleeding, loss of function of body parts (for example, inability to effectively move one side of the body), or loss of sensation must be dealt with immediately as should earache, high fever, or UTI (urinary tract infection). The doctor should provide you with criteria for triage both in the office and over the telephone. Remember that it is not your responsibility to make medical decisions, but you should know how to direct clients with health concerns. You will gain experience at triage, but never second-guess a client in distress. When in doubt, err on the side of caution and assume it is an emergency: check with the doctor immediately, and/or send the client to the nearest ER. A needless emergency visit or a little disruption is better than a preventable death or permanent disability.

Clients Asking for Medical Advice The best advice here is "Don't." An exception is triaging obvious emergencies. Your employer may also define certain areas of knowledge and experience within which you may give advice. For example, if a mother calls asking when to bring her child in for the next well-baby check-up or for a set of immunizations, you should be able to answer by consulting a schedule of routine visits and the client's chart. However, if a child is ill and the mother wonders about going ahead with an immunization, check with the nurse or doctor if you have not been given clear guidelines.

If you have an office nurse, direct advice calls to her unless office policies dictate otherwise. If you do not have a nurse, make a note of the concern and tell the client that the doctor will call back, or make an appointment for the client to discuss the concern with the doctor.

Clients Asking for Cost for Dental Treatment Don't give quotes unless you have explicit guidelines and instructions. It is best to explain to the client that the cost will vary from person to person. Because each person's mouth is unique, it is difficult to quote for dental services. The dental office policy may be that you could present to the calling patient a range of fees; you might say, for example, "The cost of a dental cleaning varies depending on how many teeth are present and how much time is spent on your cleaning. The average range is between $75 and $150."

Tip

Think a smile, be upbeat and enthusiastic, negotiate, but remain in control while letting the clients think that they are making the decisions.

Clients Calling for Lab Test Results   The doctor should have a policy on which results you can give over the phone. Most policies allow you to give normal results on the phone. The doctor usually discusses an abnormal result with the client as it will probably require treatment or explanation. Some doctors may ask you to call the client, let them know of the abnormal result, and set up an appointment.

Clients Calling for Information about Family Members   The doctor more commonly delivers this type of information as it involves confidentiality issues, assessments, and perhaps a prognosis. Sometimes, the doctor may ask you to pass on straightforward information. Remember that information must not be given without the client's express permission. The exception is parents discussing a minor child—and this becomes a grey area as the child gets older. Generally, a doctor would not share information about a teenager without the teenager's permission, especially if it involved sexual activity or birth control.

Be polite but firm. You might suggest that the family member speak directly with the client. If he cannot, then probably the client wishes to keep the information confidential. For example, you could say, "I am sorry, Mr. Smith, but I am not authorized to give you that information. If you are able to supply us with written permission to release that information, you could come in and discuss the matter with Dr. Thompson. Perhaps if you speak to your son, he will be able to answer your questions."

Or, you may simply say, "I cannot provide you with that information as it is confidential. I can have the doctor call you."

Personal Calls for the Doctor   Assume that the doctor's spouse and other family members would not call unless it were important. Ask if they wish to speak with the doctor immediately or if he can call back.

Other personal calls may be to give the doctor information about something or to speak with the doctor. Unless it is urgent or the doctor has asked that the person be put through, take a message and telephone number. As with client calls, arrange an approximate time for the return call, and ask if there is a better number for that time.

Clients Wanting to Speak with the Doctor   Try to determine why the client wants to speak to the doctor. Most clients will give at least a general reason. You may be able to handle the call yourself, or it may be best for the client to make an appointment to see the doctor. If the client is seeking non-urgent medical advice and you have a nurse in the office, direct the call to her. If a client refuses to give a reason, do not press the matter. Respect the client's right to privacy, and have the doctor call back. Take the person's name and the phone number where she can be reached at the time you expect the doctor to return the call. Repeat the number back to the client to ensure accuracy. Pull the client's chart and leave it with the doctor.

Unless the case is urgent, most doctors will return calls after they have finished seeing clients for the day. If a client insists on speaking to the doctor at once, explain that the doctor is with a client. Be polite but firm. Remember that you are the filter between the doctor and the outside world.

New Clients   You need to know the doctor's policy on new clients. With the current shortage of doctors in Canada, most family doctors can hardly manage the practices they have now. If they take on more clients than they can handle, they will not have enough time to offer high-quality medical care to anyone.

Some doctors have an iron-clad policy of not accepting any new clients. Others will accept relatives of families already in their practice or will make the occasional exception. Sometimes, a doctor will be asked personally to take on a new client and/or family. She may agree and then forget to tell you. If someone calls for an appointment saying that the doctor has agreed to accept him as a client, check with the doctor.

If your practice is not accepting new clients, say so: "I am sorry, but Dr. Suzuki is not accepting any new clients at this time." Be firm but polite. It is also helpful to put a sign in the reception area to this effect. If there are doctors in your area accepting clients, you could add their names, addresses, and telephone numbers to the sign.

A newly established doctor will take new clients, usually until a certain client number is reached. If you work in such a practice, find out the doctor's policies. Some doctors interview clients before deciding to accept them; others may have specific criteria. When accepting new clients, you will have to initiate a client chart and speak to the client about transferring records from the former provider.

Unlike physicians, dentists are abundant in most communities. Most dentists welcome new clients and depend on a referral program. Dental offices have incorporated marketing strategies as a way of attracting new clients. Using a combination of both internal and external marketing has become the norm for today's practices. Individuals can call a general dentist and some dental specialists without a referral. Optometrists and chiropractors also take clients without referrals.

Laboratories Calling with Test Results   Most of the time, you can take these calls. Remember, accuracy is paramount when recording lab results. One mistake when writing down lab values—transposing two numbers, for example, or putting a decimal point in the wrong position—can change the value from critical to noncritical and vice versa. For example, suppose the lab phoned with a hemoglobin level of 12.4 (which is normal) but you wrote down 4.12 (which is critically low). The doctor would probably order needless follow-up tests and alarm the client. Writing down lab values for the wrong client can also have disastrous consequences. You might be telling the doctor that Mrs. Strugnel, 65, has tested positive for pregnancy.

- Have the caller spell the client's name if you are not sure.
- Always read the test results back to the caller. For example, "The Hb was 14.5, the WBC 13.000. The INR was 7.5 and the blood sugar 9. The client was Mr. Michael Cook." Asking for the date of birth is an added safety check. (This information is on most requisitions and therefore would be available to the caller.) There may be more than one client in the office with the same last name and first initial or even the same first name. The date of birth may be the only unique piece of identifying information.

Calls Relating to Prescriptions   A significant number of the incoming calls in a doctor's office concern prescriptions—although with most pharmacies faxing prescription requests, these calls are decreasing. These calls may be placed by the client, the pharmacy, or a health-care facility and may be requests for a renewal or a repeat of a prescription or, in some cases, for a new prescription. Attention to detail and accuracy is essential. Doctors will have different policies on how to handle these calls, but all prescription requests should be personally reviewed by the doctor. See the section on prescriptions in Chapter 7 for more detailed information.

Calls from Other Doctors   Under most circumstances, you would put a call from another doctor through to the doctor unless the caller is content just to leave a message.

Calls from the Hospital

Order Requests   An order is a directive provided by the doctor, usually to a nurse, concerning the care of a hospitalized client. Clients must have doctor's orders provided on admission and on discharge, as well as during their stay. These orders change, sometimes several times a day, depending on the client's needs and condition. If the nurse calling tells you the order is needed urgently, put the call through right away. For example, a client who is in pain may require an order for an analgesic, or a client with a critical test result may require insulin or an anticoagulant immediately. Even if not urgent, hospital order requests should be dealt with fairly quickly, but the doctor would probably prefer to deal with them between clients. If the nurse leaves a message to have the doctor call back, take the name of the hospital, the client-care unit, the client's first and last names, the diagnosis, the name of the nurse calling, and, if given the information, what the order is needed for.

Often, a hospital unit will call wanting discharge orders for a client. It is not uncommon for a doctor to tell a client she can go home and then forget to write the order. The client packs up and goes to the nursing station to announce she is leaving only to find that no discharge orders have been written. Sometimes, a doctor will write a discharge order for a new mother but forget to write one for the baby. The client is usually asked to wait until the nurse receives the discharge order. In these situations, if at all possible, put the call through to the doctor.

Report of Change in a Client's Condition   The hospital will call if a client's condition takes a turn for the worse or becomes unstable. Put such calls through immediately. Hospitals do not often call to let the doctor know that the client's condition has improved unless the doctor has requested such information for a very ill client.

Notification of a Surgery Date   You can handle such calls. Make note of the surgery date on the client's chart, and make a note for the doctor, who may be required to assist with the surgery. Make sure that a preoperative assessment has been completed on the client if required. (You may be responsible for booking this assessment.) Call the client with all necessary information. Make any other necessary arrangements, such as booking a pre-admission routine, which requires the client to complete forms and have required blood work done ahead of time.

Community Agencies Wanting to Discuss a Client with the Doctor   Usually, you should put this call through to the doctor unless the caller says the matter can wait. Often, it is related to a matter that the agency is dealing with at the time of the call. The office nurse, if you have one, may be able to handle this type of call.

The Telephone and Confidentiality

Conversations in any office are easily overheard. You will often be discussing confidential information with clients, perhaps peers, and other health professionals. Assess the potential for breach of confidentiality, and use your ingenuity to avoid problems. Try to speak in a low voice. If you are in an office with a window area that can be closed off, do so. Say as little as possible if it involves confidential information, and let the person on the other end of the telephone do most of the talking. Take or make highly confidential calls in a location that can be private. If your office has no such location, you may have to reserve some telephone calls for times when the reception area is empty (e.g., noon hour, just before closing), or use a phone in the doctor's office when she is out.

Remember that it is against the law to release any medical information about clients without their written permission or that of their designated authority. (This applies to any means of exchanging information. You cannot, for example, transfer medical records to a new doctor without the client's written permission.)

You can give information to specialists to whom the client has been referred or to anyone else directly and actively involved in the client's care. Give only the information needed. A physiotherapist probably needs to know about a client's hip problems but not her obstetrical history or the fact that she was on anti-depressants several years ago. You are not at liberty to discuss a client's condition with even another staff member, for example, just because the client is a mutual acquaintance or has an interesting case history. Even good news is confidential. It can be easy to slip into giving out confidential information, so think carefully. For example, Fatima was working in a hospital in a maternal/child unit. She went down for coffee. Renée (who worked in a medical unit) sat down beside her, and they began discussing mutual friends:

"I heard that Tia came in last night in active labour. Did she have her baby yet?"

Fatima thought for a minute and responded, "I can't give you that information, Renée. I am sure that Tom (Tia's husband) will get around to notifying everyone when the time is right."

"Give me a break, Fatima, we're not talking life and death here. I won't tell anyone."

"Sorry, I can't," Fatima replied. "I have to get back to the floor. See you later."

Fatima did the right thing. It can be tempting to share this kind of information with a friend or colleague, especially if you are pressured, but to do so is unprofessional, unethical, *and* against the law.

Never leave a message containing medical information about a client with another person (other than, of course, a child's parent on matters where confidentiality is not an issue) or on an answering machine unless special arrangements have been made. There are conflicting thoughts on how to leave messages. Even a simple message to call a doctor's office could be a problem if someone chose to impersonate the client in order to get the information. Besides, the client may not want others to know that she has been to see the doctor. Even if confidentiality is not an issue in the client's home, a client waiting for test results could become anxious, especially if she has to wait until the next day or after the weekend to call you back. One option is to simply leave a message to "call Laura" (using your first name).

Most health facilities will require that you sign a confidentiality form when you are hired. We will look at confidentiality in the hospital in Part V.

Taking Telephone Messages

Write down everything that requires action or a call back. *Do not trust anything to memory*. In a busy office, it is too easy to forget something. Never write a message on a scrap of paper. Murphy's law dictates that that piece of paper will get lost. Keep a notepad or notebook and a pen or pencil by each telephone in the office. You can buy commercially prepared notepads or design your own. (See Figure 8.4.) Some offices keep a dated notebook. Messages may be recorded in the order in which they are received, or the page may be

```
┌─────────────────────────────────────┐
│         Telephone Message           │
│  For ..............................  │
│  Time ................. Date .......  │
│  Caller ...........................  │
│  Ph # .............................  │
│  Call back ........................  │
│  Other ............................  │
│  Message:                           │
│                                     │
│                                     │
│                                     │
│  Taken by .........................  │
└─────────────────────────────────────┘
```

Figure 8.4   A message pad

divided into categories, such as personal, high-priority call-backs, and non-urgent call-backs. The notebook is less likely to be lost than a piece of paper and provides a record if the doctor wants to check a previous message. The primary disadvantage is that it may not be handy when you need it. If you are at another phone, you would have to write a message down and later transcribe it to the book. This takes time and can lead to errors. The popular "sticky notes" may work in some offices. They are transportable and can be stuck in prominent places. The downside is that they can get lost. One office used sticky notes but put them in a book.

Every message requires the following:

- Name of caller
- Name of client, if different from caller
- Telephone number
- Date and time

Name   Be sure that you write down the caller's name accurately. If you are in doubt, ask. If you are embarrassed to admit that you do not remember a client's name, ask for the spelling.

> "Regan, could you spell your last name for me?"
> "T-h-o-m-p-s-o-n"
> "Thanks. I wasn't sure if you spelled it with or without a p."

If someone is calling on behalf of a client, get the client's name as well. Ask whether the doctor should return the call to the caller or to the client.

Caller's Telephone Number   Read the telephone number back to the caller to ensure that it is correct. Make sure your writing is legible. If you are in a hurry, your "3" might look like an "8," for example, or you might transpose numbers. Try to approximate what time the doctor will return the call. This can be difficult with a doctor's uncertain schedule, but it is unreasonable to expect the caller to wait around indefinitely. Ask the caller for the number where he can be reached at the time you expect the doctor to return the call. Also, ask the caller to try to keep the line free at that time. I have often seen a doctor trying to return a call several times only to find the line busy. This is frustrating, and the doctor may not have the time to keep trying.

Date and Time   This is important because return calls are sometimes overlooked or delayed. Knowing the date and time the call was received will help the doctor return the call within a reasonable time frame.

Content of the Message   The types of messages you take will vary. The most common are requests for prescription renewals (discussed in Chapter 7) and the results of lab tests (discussed in Chapter 6). Repeat the message to ensure accuracy, especially if it involves numbers, such as a lab result. You can summarize a more general message, but make sure you include all important points.

Signature or Initials of the Message Taker   This is important in a large office. If the doctor has any questions about the message, she needs to know who took it. Including your signature also ensures that you take responsibility for what you have written.

Handling More Than One Call

If there are two lines into the office or clinic, it is inevitable that sometimes they will both be ringing at once or you will be on line 1 when line 2 rings. If you are the only person available to answer the phone, you need to deal with both calls and find out if either represents an emergency. Suppose you were talking to Mrs. Felipe on line 1 when line 2 rings.

"Excuse me, Mrs. Felipe, may I put you on hold for a minute?" (Answer line 2)

Dr. Patel's office, Theresa speaking. Are you able to hold?" (Wait long enough to hear the answer. Imagine a client complaining of acute chest pain or stroke symptoms only to be put on hold! If the caller hesitates, ask, "Is this an emergency?" If the caller identifies an emergency, then you must deal with it. If this necessitates a long delay, briefly return to line 1.)

"I'm sorry, Mrs. Felipe, I have an urgent situation to deal with and will call you back as soon as I can." (Don't say "something important to deal with," which suggests she is not important.) (If the caller on line 1 agrees to hold, go back to line 2 and complete the urgent call. Then return to line 1.)

"Hello, I'm sorry to have kept you waiting. How can I help you?"

Tip

Making Effective Calls

- Make the call at an appropriate time.
- Be sure that you are the best person to handle the call. For example, are there likely to be questions that only the doctor can answer? Are you in conflict with the person?
- Know whom you wish to speak to and if someone else can take the information. Place the call when the appropriate person is most likely to be available.
- If confidentiality is a concern, place the call from a phone with privacy.
- Have the information you need handy, such as a calendar, the doctor's appointment schedule, or the client's chart.
- Plan what you want to say.
- Write a list of information you need.
- If you are retrieving information, especially medications and lab values, write it down and read it back for accuracy.
- Be polite but brief and to the point. Avoid long social conversations.

The caller may not want to hold for reasons other than an emergency. She may be calling long distance or may be busy. These calls should be returned as soon as possible.

Ending a Call

Always bring some type of closure to the conversation. Thank the person for calling, or end with some other pleasant phrase, for example, "I look forward to seeing you on Thursday," or "I appreciate your calling with that information." Always say goodbye, and allow the caller to hang up first.

Handling Outgoing Calls

Most AHPs will tell you that there is no ideal time to make outgoing calls. Dealing with clients, answering the telephone, finding reports and charts, and responding to doctors' requests leave little uninterrupted time. But effective management of outgoing calls is an essential component of practice management.

You can eliminate the need for some calls by using other methods of communication. If fax or email will work well, use it. This usually saves time and provides a printed record.

Being organized and prepared will make your outgoing calls more effective and help you manage time. Have a plan for each call that you make. Outgoing calls, like incoming calls, tend to fall into certain categories:

- Making appointments for clients at other facilities
- Notifying clients of test results or appointment times
- Responding to insurance companies or lawyers
- Arranging file transfers
- Arranging meetings or speaking engagements for the doctor
- Responding to requests by the doctor (calling clients, other facilities, finding reports, and so on)

Keep Needed Numbers Handy Looking up numbers wastes time. If your telephone system has an autodial feature, program in frequently called numbers, such as hospitals, consultants you frequently refer to, pharmacies, laboratories and other diagnostic facilities, and community care agencies. Or you can create a file on your computer. Keep your telephone numbers up to date. Otherwise, you will forget and have to look the number up or call the operator. This applies to your clients' files as well. When you swipe a client's health card, check to see whether the address and telephone number are current.

When you are making appointments, write the client's daytime phone number and/or email address in the appointment book so that if you have to cancel, you will not need to look up numbers. Some offices skip this step because it takes time, but looking up 20 or 30 phone numbers (even on the computer) is considerably more time consuming.

Ensure that your numbers are current. Every few months, specifically ask the client if his phone number is still the same: "Mr. Kim, your number is still 647-444-4444 at work, and 647-333-3333 at home?"

Plan the Timing Make the call at the appropriate time. For example, unless the matter is urgent, do not call a hospital unit at 10 a.m., when RNs are likely giving out medications, or between 3:00 and 3:30 p.m., when some of the nurses are likely to be taking reports as shifts change. You will likely get a busy signal or an answering machine and just have to call again. Obviously, you cannot always time your calls, but you would be surprised how much time you save by doing so when you can. Prioritize calls, and make time-sensitive ones as soon as you can. Make the rest of your outgoing calls in a clump during a less busy time of day. Try to avoid interruptions. If there is a more secluded phone, use it, especially if there is a concern about confidentiality. If you are in the front office, close the window leading to the reception area (if you have one). If possible, have someone else (another AHP or an office nurse) receive clients while you make the calls.

Be Prepared   Have handy all the information you are likely to need. For example, if you are booking a consultation or a test, have the client's chart beside you so that you can answer questions. Also, find out beforehand when the client is available so you do not waste time rebooking. (You could ask the client to rebook, but some facilities prefer to deal with the office.)

Make Reminder Calls, If Needed   Many specialists, dentists, optometrists, and chiropractors, who often have appointments set up well in advance, have the office routinely call the client the day before an appointment with a reminder. Family doctors' offices are usually too busy. However, if you have a client who is repeatedly late or has difficulty remembering appointments (perhaps because of cognitive impairment), it might be worth your while to make that call.

Stay on Track   When you have the time, a brief social conversation is pleasant and helps build relationships with clients and other professionals. However, a few minutes here and there can really add up. If you are pressed for time, after a brief greeting, get right to the point of the call and end it politely but promptly.

Leaving Messages   If the person you are calling is not home, leaving a message—either with another person or on an answering machine—requires thought and adherence to confidentiality standards. Avoid leaving medical information unless explicitly asked to do so by the client. Simply ask the client (or designated person) to call the office back. Remember to speak slowly and clearly and repeat your number at the end of the message. Rarely is it a good idea to call the client at work unless you have the client's permission to do so. If confidentiality is a real concern, arrange for the client to call you if she is expecting a test result.

Controlling Telephone Time

Time on the telephone can easily get out of hand, especially if clients feel that you are free for a social conversation. A client may be lonely or may just like to talk. A brief social exchange is friendly and appropriate, but longer conversations will eat away at your workday. Be polite, but keep the caller on track. "You wanted the results of your lab test, Mrs. Pinder." Or, "Mrs. Pinder, when did you want that appointment for? I have an opening tomorrow afternoon." You can also politely indicate that you are ending the conversation. "Thank you for calling, Mrs. Pinder. I'll see you next week." Usually, the caller will get the message and facilitate ending the call.

FACE-TO-FACE COMMUNICATION WITH CLIENTS

COMMUNICATING FACE-TO-FACE DRAWS ON THE SAME SKILLS AND ATTITUDES AS telephone communication. However, face-to-face encounters bring the added dimension of vision. You are now communicating not only with your voice and words, but with your facial expression, body language, and even dress and presentation. Your responses to people are more perceptible. You may be able to modulate your voice to disguise distaste for a person or anger at a situation on the telephone. In person, you also have to control your facial expression, eye contact, and demeanour to create a positive impression. Some people find it easier to relate to people in person; others find the telephone easier. You need to learn to be comfortable with both. You will probably spontaneously establish an easy, pleasant relationship with most clients. You may feel no rapport with others and find still others irritating or difficult. There will always be a segment of the practice that takes up more of your energy and time because of personalities, needs, or maybe loneliness. There is an old saying among doctors: "Twenty percent of your practice will take eighty percent of your time." This applies to your time as well. These clients may call for appointments regularly or simply show up expecting to be seen. Some come to see the doctor for human contact, reassurance, and support. At times, it will be difficult to smile and be pleasant, but your job requires you to. You can improve client management by developing strategies to help you maintain a consistently professional and friendly manner.

Greeting the Client

What Not To Do   "The Doberman at Desk A" is a reputation you do not want! Whether you interact with individuals on the telephone or in person you are almost always the first point of contact for anyone entering or calling the office. While you have a duty to the physician to screen calls and visits, you are also responsible for being polite, reasonable, and approachable to clients and the public. This applies to any medical facility whether you work in a lab, in a family doctor's office, or for a specialist, and for any type of interaction: handling an appointment request, giving out information to a client, or directing a referral. Regardless of the situation, there are proper and polite ways to respond. Do not be responsible for a negative reputation either for yourself of the facility in which you work, where individuals are remiss to call or come in because of perceived Doberman-like characteristics: ferocious, snappy, protective, and impatient.

Appropriate Greetings

If possible, acknowledge each client as he enters the office. Always greet the client with a smile. If you are on the telephone when a client arrives, make eye contact, smile, nod, or use other appropriate nonverbal signals of recognition. When you are finished with the call, greet the client, and ask for his health card. Briefly answer any questions, and let him know approximately how long it will be before he sees the doctor. The exchange does not have to be a long one and may save you time in the long run. Give the client your undivided attention, even if for less than a minute. Have a brief conversation with the client about safe topics. Certainly, you do not want to discuss her latest round of radiation therapy or visit to the psychiatrist. For example, it would be inappropriate to comment to a newly arrived client, "Good morning, Keisha. You look like you've finally lost some weight!" Or, "Your sister-in-law was in this morning. I think her ulcer is clearing up." Thoughtless comments like these embarrass clients and breach confidentiality.

Develop strategies to personalize your client interactions. One way is to keep notes on a client's chart (sticky notes on a paper chart or incidental notes on an electronic chart) about the client's interests, hobbies, or family events. Imagine how valued the client will feel when you ask about his recent scuba diving trip or how her new granddaughter is doing. You will not always have the information or the time to do this, but when you can, it adds a personal touch and can make someone's day. For example,

> "Mrs. Janssen, may I have your health card please? Thank you . . . how is that new granddaughter of yours doing? She would be . . . what . . . six months old now? Here's your card, Mrs. Janssen, please have a seat. The doctor is running pretty much on time today."

The extra minute to inquire about her granddaughter establishes a warm, friendly feeling. You do have to keep the conversation short, though. If Mrs. Janssen starts telling you in detail about her daughter's struggles with child care, you can smile sympathetically and say, "Yes, it's a challenge. Here's your card, Mrs. Janssen."

Addressing the Client

Use the client's name whenever possible (but do not repeat it so often as to sound insincere). It personalizes the encounter and makes the client feel respected. There is a trend today, in stores, restaurants, and professional settings, to call everyone by their first name. Some clients are comfortable with first names; others are not. Older clients, in particular, and clients from certain cultures may find the familiarity disrespectful and impolite. For example, a clinical secretary came around the corner into the reception area of a hospital Radiology Department with a chart in hand. "Betty, Betty," she called, her voice getting louder, "is Betty here?" An elderly woman moved forward, dressed in a neat suit and a hat and using a walker. She looked at the secretary and said coldly, "Don't you have any manners? What gives you the right to be so familiar with me?" Other clients may feel the same resentment even though they do not express it. If you do not know the client, initially use Mr., Miss, or Mrs. (Glance at the next-of-kin section on the chart; a married woman will usually give her husband as next of kin; if the next of kin is a parent or sibling, you can try Miss or Ms.) For example, in the above situation, the clinical secretary might have said, "Mrs. Sheridan . . . Mrs. Sheridan . . . is Mrs. Sheridan here?" Mrs. Sheridan might reply, "Please call me Betty." Or, she might correct, "That's Miss Sheridan." If she does not, the secretary may ask her how she prefers to be addressed. When you meet a new client in an office, always ask about preference. Write the client's answer on the front page of the chart as a reminder to other staff members. Some people write their full names on their forms but prefer to be addressed by a nickname; others hate them. Some women prefer Ms. to Mrs. or Miss; others, especially older women, dislike the title.

It is also important to try to pronounce the client's name properly. If you are unsure of how to pronounce the name of a new client, ask the client to help you rather than mangling the name. Then, write down the name *the way it sounds, using phonetics*.

The Wait

If the doctor is running late or has been unexpectedly called away on an emergency, inform the waiting clients. Their time is just as valuable as the doctor's. Often, people take time off from work, get babysitters, and otherwise rearrange their schedule to come to see the doctor. A long delay may disrupt their arrangements. Letting clients know about delays shows respect and often avoids the frustration of an indeterminate wait. Offer alternatives, depending how long the delay is. If the delay is short, you can tell the client, "Ingrid, Dr. Levesque is running about 15 minutes behind." For a longer delay, you might suggest they go for a coffee, do some shopping, and come back at a certain time. Clients may have to alter some plans—perhaps phone the babysitter, the hairdresser, or the person picking them up. If the delay is more than half an hour, it is reasonable to give the client the choice of waiting or booking another appointment. You may also be able to avoid such waits by getting in touch with clients before they leave for the doctor's office to inform them of the delay and reschedule, if necessary. (See Chapter 9 for a discussion on scheduling.)

Escorting Clients to the Examination Room

Escorting clients to the examination room provides another opportunity for conversation. If your office has a nurse, this may be her responsibility, or it may be done by whoever is free. This applies to most health offices. In the dental office, for example, it could be the administrative assistant, dental assistant, hygienist, or the dentist. Watch the traffic flow. If you see a client leaving, you will know that the examination room is empty. If you are alone in the office, prepare the room for the next client *before* you usher her in. If there is a nurse but she is busy elsewhere, check the room first; the nurse may have already prepared it. Take the client's chart, call the client, and walk beside her, not in front of her, to the room. Walking side by side feels more equal and allows conversational exchange. Stop just outside the door, and allow the client to enter first. It may be your duty to obtain a brief history about why the client has come to see the doctor and record the information on the chart. You would then instruct her on how to prepare for the examination and give her a gown, if appropriate. Usually, only a complete physical requires that the client remove all clothing. For an examination of the upper body (such as the chest/lungs), clients are usually asked to remove everything from the waist up. The abdomen may be examined with clothing on, depending on the doctor's preference. If a woman is having a pelvic examination or a Pap smear, she would be required to remove everything from the waist down. Most clients appreciate privacy while undressing.

If you are simply escorting the client to the room, try to keep the conversation light and general. Answer any questions you can, and let the client know how long the doctor will be. Put the chart in the designated place, usually a chart holder outside the door of the examination room or on the doctor's desk.

When the Client Is Leaving

Unless clients have to book an appointment or a test, they often leave without saying goodbye. They may be feeling confused about the instructions they have been given or disturbed about some information the doctor has given them. Acknowledging their departure gives you the opportunity to pick up such cues and respond accordingly, answering questions or offering a comforting comment if appropriate. A smile, "Goodbye," "It was nice to see you," or even a wave is good client relations if you can manage it. In many dental offices, the client is asked to stop at the administrative desk after the appointment, either to pay for dental services or make another appointment—even for a check-up or cleaning six months away.

COMMUNICATION WITH CLIENTS WHO ARE MENTALLY ILL

FOR THE MOST PART, INDIVIDUALS WITH MENTAL ILLNESS ARE THE SAME AS ANYONE ELSE, and thus you communicate with them as you would with anyone else. Mental illness, however, as with any illness, can occur at varying levels. Individuals with a mental illness that is more clinically evident may indeed have altered communication patterns. These may include a short attention span, higher levels of frustration/impatience, and inability to internalize what is being said. This would require on your part patience, understanding, and perseverance. Understanding the typical behaviours and needs of the more common mental disorders, such as psychosis and schizophrenia, is helpful. Individuals coping with clinically evident psychosis, for example, can exhibit thinking disturbances. Thoughts may be unclear, following a conversation may be difficult, and the client may appear unresponsive or uncooperative; they may experience delusions or hallucinations. Schizophrenia affects perception, thinking, feeling, and behaviour. Some communication techniques include speaking calmly, clearly, and maintaining eye contact. Phrases such as "I would really appreciate it if you would . . ." are helpful.

It is important to remember that mental illness has nothing to do with a person's level of intelligence. Treat these individuals with the same level of respect and honesty that you would any other person. Trust, as with any client, is an essential ingredient to successful communication. Individuals with a mental illness may not like to be reminded of it, and certainly do not want to be branded as "sick" because of it. Being understood, respected, and valued is of great importance, especially if the person feels that having a mental disorder stigmatizes him.

Many are fearful of individuals with more pronounced mental illnesses. Having a mental illness does not increase the likelihood of offensive or violent behaviour (unless compounded by something by substance abuse). If you are working in an established medical practice, you will get to know the needs, attitudes, and communication styles of individual clients. There may be specific strategies for dealing with an individual, including "triggers" and topics to avoid. If the person's condition is complicated with substance abuse, interaction may become difficult. Seek the assistance of the health-care provider if you feel the conversation is getting out of hand.

❽ DEALING WITH DIFFICULT SITUATIONS

YOU MUST BE PREPARED TO INTERACT EFFECTIVELY, BOTH IN PERSON AND ON THE telephone, with clients in a variety of situations. Inevitably, some clients will be angry, rude, or just plain difficult. They may be upset, anxious, stressed, or confused. How a person reacts will reflect a combination of his personality and the situation he finds himself in.

If not handled sensitively, an angry and upset client may become increasingly louder and sometimes aggressive. Your challenge is to maintain your composure and try to contain the situation. Waiting to see the doctor is an ongoing source of irritation in many health offices. Some clients relax with a book, others mutter good-naturedly, and still others become openly resentful. Other issues upset clients as well: a lab test result that they were not notified about, a long wait before they can see a specialist, a mix-up in appointment dates, problems with prescriptions, or unmet expectations of health care. Sometimes, clients' distress about bad news may turn to anger.

Often, anger begets anger. Have you ever come home in a good mood only to find an argument in progress? You probably found your own mood deteriorated quickly. If a family member confronts you angrily, how do you respond? Most people will become defensive and show their own annoyance in word and gesture. But what can this entirely natural reaction lead to? An escalated argument.

Business people often say, "The customer is always right." In a sense, the same principle applies to health care. As discussed in Chapter 1, we no longer deal with *patients* who are expected to passively receive care, but with *clients* who are active consumers of health care. If your practice is client driven, your goal is client satisfaction and retention. Dealing effectively with difficult situations goes a long way toward achieving client satisfaction.

The key to dealing with angry or upset clients is to show genuine warmth, respect, and empathy. If you are taking or have taken a communications course, you will be familiar with these variables. Apply them to health-care situations.

Warmth is difficult to define but makes a world of difference. It can be displayed through words, voice, facial expression, and eye contact. Over the telephone, a soft tone of voice can convey warmth, as can words that express concern for the client. Emphasizing some words can also display warmth.

> "Mr. Martinez, I am so sorry that you were kept waiting so long."

Being treated with *respect* is a fundamental human right and is especially important in health care. A client who feels respected will be better able to calm down and deal with issues. One way to show respect is simply to pay full attention as you allow the client to express her thoughts and feelings. If the complaint is long, acknowledge that you are listening with the occasional "Uh huh" or "I see." You may also ask for clarification: "Miss Hakimi, I'm not sure I understood that last part. Would you repeat the part about the X-ray getting lost?" Using the client's name also signals respect for the individual.

Empathy is the ability to put yourself into the client's situation. Understanding where the client is coming from does not have to mean that you agree, but it does give you a deeper appreciation of how the client is feeling. If you can show that you understand where the client is coming from, without judging, the client will feel more accepted and valued. Try such phrases as the following:

> "I understand how you must be feeling, Mr. Amadou."
> "You seem very worried, Ms. Carr. Let's look at the options we can consider here and find out what would be best for you."

Met with warmth, respect, and empathy, most people have a hard time staying angry. Certainly, their problem does not disappear. However, the level of anger and anxiety may subside, paving the way for meaningful dialogue about solutions.

The Aggressive, Unpleasant Client

Remain calm. Remind yourself that the anger is not aimed at you personally. When people are angry, they often take it out on the nearest person. Separating yourself from the situation helps you keep your emotions in check. Speak as slowly as usual, and do not raise your voice, even if the client is shouting. The last thing you want is a shouting match. A technique that sometimes works is to actually lower your voice. The client will have to stop talking to hear what you are saying.

It is important to retain control of the conversation. Be firm, but do not argue with the client. Do not give the client something more to argue about; stick to the issue at hand. Sometimes, a response such as "I'm so sorry. That sounds like it was very upsetting for you," will take the wind out of the aggressive client's sails. Remember, often the client really does have a valid concern or complaint. If the complaint is justified and the office is at fault, acknowledge it and apologize. Try to find a way to rectify the problem immediately. In some situations, all you can do is apologize. If there is a reasonable explanation for the error, tell that to the client. It will not right the wrong, but it might help her understand why it happened. If there are steps you can take to prevent a similar error from occurring again, assure the client that you will take them.

As discussed in Chapter 2, sometimes the client's perspective may be altered because of illness or an emotional reaction to the illness of a loved one. That does not make the issue any less real for the client. Regardless of the situation, if you make clear to the client that you will work *with* him, you will usually get somewhere.

Ask the client what he sees as a possible solution. People will often calm down when they feel they have input and are listened to. If you have several options to deal with the issue, offer all of them, and ask the client which he thinks is most appropriate. If the issue is something that you cannot rectify, assure the client that you will look into the matter and get back to him with an answer or direct him to someone who can help. Give a time frame. "I understand, Mr. Premsyl. I will talk to Dr. Matthews when she gets in after lunch and call you back before four o'clock, if that's convenient for you."

Sometimes, writing down the concerns may help a client calm down and refocus. Assure the client that you will give what he has written to the appropriate person.

If the client is rambling and you cannot get a word in edgewise, try raising your hand into the stop position. The client's eyes will follow your hand, and usually, she will stop talking for a moment. Use this opportunity to interrupt: "Celina, I think I understand what you are saying. Let me rephrase the problem, just to be sure. I don't want to miss any of the facts here." This response requires the client to pay attention to what you are saying and lets the client know that her complaint has been heard and that you are taking steps to deal with it.

Remember, when you were little, how you felt when your mother said "No!" or "You can't" or "I won't allow you" or "Never"? You probably felt backed into a corner and more determined than ever to do whatever you were not allowed to do. To an angry person, these words are like a red flag to a bull. Instead, use conciliatory and nonjudgmental language.

The Threatening Client

If you are facing an angry or aggressive client across your desk, stand up. If you are sitting and the client is standing, that puts the client in a position of power, physically as well as emotionally, and makes you seem more vulnerable.

On a rare occasion, you will face a situation you cannot deal with. It is no shame to admit it. Remember that you matter, too. Patience has its limits; you should not tolerate being abused or threatened.

Some sources will advise you to put a disruptive client into a separate room, such as an empty examination room or the doctor's office. Although this might work in some situations, in your particular situation, use your good judgment. If possible, call the doctor out to support you and perhaps take control of the situation. Never enter a room alone with a client who makes you feel threatened. Do not let the client stand between you and the door of the room. If you ever feel that your safety is threatened, tell the client that you are going to call the police. Then, do it.

The Anxious Client

Skill and patience are also needed in dealing with anxious clients. Speak to them especially warmly and gently. People who are stressed, anxious, and preoccupied with thoughts of, for example, an illness or the prospect of an operation are less able to take in and retain information. This temporary loss of capacity will compound forgetfulness and confusion in anyone (elderly or not) with cognitive impairments. If you see that a client is anxious, carefully explain whatever she needs to know about medications, treatments, and subsequent appointments, and reinforce the information by writing it down.

The Client Wanting a Prescription Renewal

Clients will frequently call wanting a prescription renewal. You can look up the client's prescription history in her EMR. This will tell you when the prescription was last filled, how many repeats, and how many pills the doctor ordered. For the most part, this is an easily handled call. However, there are those who are seeking medications inappropriately—usually ones with addictive properties. The client is on a mission and will have every possible excuse: the medication was accidently flushed down the toilet, I forgot my medication in a cab, the dog knocked them over and ate them (poor dog), they were vacuumed up by accident, I am away and forgot them at home, I threw them out by mistake, I lost them, I had to take more because of increased pain—almost anything. The client is likely to become angry if you stall or suggest that he come in to see the doctor, saying that it is office protocol and the doctor will not renew without a visit (usually the case). Be polite but firm—you are in control. Ask the client to call later for an appointment if the conversation is going nowhere.

Know Your Limits

Throughout this section, we have emphasized the need to make the client feel important. But you are important, too. You are human, and you, too, have emotions. There will be times when your own concerns make it very difficult to maintain the calm, warm, unruffled manner you would like. If the problem is work related, try to resolve it promptly. The tension of an unresolved conflict in the office cannot help but affect how you relate to others. Approach the person(s) involved, and tactfully address the matter. If you do not feel the parties involved are able to deal with the issue fairly and responsibly, try to get a third party to help resolve the conflict, perhaps the office manager or the doctor.

Dealing with Difficult Clients

- Keep calm.
- Do not take it personally.
- Listen to the complaint without interrupting, and then restate it.
- Use the client's name from time to time.
- Keep your voice quiet, even if the client is shouting. Try lowering your voice.
- Try to put yourself in the client's shoes.
- Acknowledge the client's anger or frustration.
- Do not blame the client.
- Assure the client that you will do everything you can to help. Offer options.
- Never argue with the client or use provoking words or phrases, such as *never, can't, won't,* or *you're mistaken.*
- If the complaint is justified and the office is at fault, acknowledge it and apologize.
- If the client becomes verbally abusive, swears, or threatens, simply say, "Mr. Leung, I cannot help you if you continue speaking to me like that."
- If a caller continues to be abusive, say, "Mr. Leung, I will not listen to that kind of language. Please call back later. Goodbye." Then, hang up.
- If you cannot resolve an issue, consider passing it on to the doctor. Some clients feel that the doctor is the ultimate authority and that they have won the battle by being able to discuss the issue with the doctor.
- Document the complaints on the client's chart as soon as possible while the details are fresh in your mind. Do not record impressions or intangibles. Whenever possible, use direct quotes.
- Tell the doctor what occurred. The doctor may need to deal with the occurrence the next time the client comes into the office. It is important to work as a team. Even if you or the doctor is in the wrong, acknowledging the fact together reinforces your office's commitment to good client care.

Personal issues likewise cause strain and undermine your ability to deal with other people and their problems. If possible, deal with personal issues at home, and shelve them while at work. But recognize that this is not always realistic. You are not doing yourself or anyone else any favours if you ignore your personal problems when they adversely affect your performance. You have to balance your own physical and emotional health needs with the demands of your job, even if it means taking time off.

❾ PROFESSIONAL COMMUNICATION

YOU MAY WANT TO REVIEW THE PRINCIPLES OF PROFESSIONAL DRESS, APPEARANCE, AND manner discussed in Chapter 1. In this chapter, so far, I have emphasized the importance of communication with clients. It is equally important to communicate effectively with other health professionals. Even within the office, miscommunication can turn an otherwise pleasant workplace into a minefield.

What undermines good communication in the office? Stress, of course, is a factor. However, staff members who have a good working relationship will not take the occasional stress-induced flare-up to heart. Territorialism also leads to trouble when staff members guard their own job responsibilities so jealously that they resent anyone who tries to help. A health-care setting requires a certain amount of sharing. Teamwork is the backbone of any successful enterprise. If you see that a colleague is feeling pressured or overwhelmed, offer to help, if possible; it can make a huge difference.

Each staff member will have a certain level of expertise in a given area. Sometimes people, especially if they are insecure or lack self-confidence, will not ask for help because they do not want to acknowledge that someone else might know more than they do about a particular subject or procedure. Office professionals can end up working alone in the same office, isolated by defensive attitudes and not benefiting from cooperation. It is so much more effective to give each person credit for what she does well and to share knowledge and experience.

Always treat others with respect. Comment positively on what a co-worker does well. If you see someone doing something you think you could do better, assess the situation before you speak. Sometimes it is better to keep quiet. If you feel you must offer advice, do so constructively. Ask for help if you need it. Most of us are pleased to share knowledge with someone who appreciates it.

You may meet with a cold shoulder in a new job. Try not to take it personally. The other staff members may feel threatened by your arrival or resent the hiring of another staff member. They may miss the person you are replacing or may simply not adjust well to change. Sometimes, you just have to tough it out. However, if you are patient, polite, and persistent, usually a constructive relationship develops. Be positive. Be aware of your limitations as well as your strengths. Learn all you can from the staff members who have been there before you. They know the routine and are invaluable sources of information. Show respect for their knowledge and a desire to learn.

Never arrive in a new job setting, even if you are hired as the manager, and attempt to rearrange the office and its administrative structure on your first day. It may end up being your last day as well. Remember the saying, "You catch more flies with honey than with vinegar." Staff members need to get used to you, and you need to get to know them. Allow them to show you the ropes. If you must make changes, go slowly. Listen for clues about things they are satisfied with and those they are not. If someone complains about something, pick up on it. Ask the staff member to explain and to suggest improvements. Involve the staff members, make group decisions, and give credit for good suggestions. In the following example, Kamala has just been hired as office manager. Ellen, a long-time employee, does the appointment bookings.

Ellen: "That appointment book frustrates me sometimes."

Kamala: "Why, Ellen?"

Ellen: "It's so small. There just isn't enough space to write things in."

Kamala: (who had thought the appointment book was too small from her first day) "What kind of book do you think would be better?"

Ellen: "Well, I don't know. We've had this one forever. Natalie, the former manager, liked it, but her writing was almost microscopic."

Kamala: "It doesn't leave much space, I agree. Would you mind looking for something more suitable?"

Note that Kamala initially said nothing about her observation. When Ellen complained, instead of jumping in with a decision, which Ellen might have resented, Kamala drew out Ellen's opinion. Kamala showed Ellen respect by supporting her views and acknowledging her ability to choose something that would work for her. Kamala is secure enough not to need to show power; instead, she shares responsibility, which gives Ellen confidence and a sense of autonomy.

In the next example, Rita has just been hired by a busy pediatrician. She is partway through her first morning at work when Gail, the senior office professional, notices that Rita is having trouble filing a pile of claims. Consider these two responses:

"Rita, you've made a mess of those claims. Let me do that."

"Rita, I know that filing those claims can take forever. I used to hate doing it. You're faster than I was at first. I found a shortcut that really speeded up the process. Would you like me to show you?"

In the second response, Gail notes Rita's difficulty in a neutral tone. Rather than criticizing Rita, she puts herself in Rita's position and shares her own past difficulties. She keeps her tone conversational and does not claim superiority. Instead, she gives Rita a "warm, fuzzy feeling" that helps establish a connection and boosts Rita's confidence. Then, she offers a suggestion and gives Rita the choice of accepting or rejecting it.

INVENTORY

MAINTAINING AN ADEQUATE OFFICE SUPPLIES IS BOTH A DEMANDING AND A PRECISE TASK requiring excellent organization skills. It will be your responsibility to contact the appropriate resources to ensure that office supplies and other items are ordered as required. This will include everything from paper, labels, and pens to toilet tissue and cleaning supplies. In addition you will have to order such medical supplies as syringes, Pap smear kits, swabs, histology containers, fecal occult blood test (FOBT) kits, immunizing agents (vaccines), and patient information pamphlets. Keep information for reordering handy. Many offices fax reorder forms to the supplier.

Try to keep costs down by occasionally looking for better deals (for paper type products in particular, as for medical supplies there may be limited choices). Sometimes your local office supply store may be your best option. Remember though, that the best price may not mean the best product.

Tip

Take time every day to check inventory. Create a list of supplies on a spreadsheet. Analyze inventory for several months so you can adjust levels, reordering accordingly. If possible order online. If using a purchasing order, keep the orders filed so you can check your buying history. Always check delivered supplies against the purchasing order to ensure everything is there. It is best for one person in the office to be responsible for inventory.

Future Trends

The basic rules for effective communication will not change significantly over time, but methods will. The area in which we can expect to see the most change over the next 10 years relates to the use of electronic technologies in health-care communication. This will include ways in which all forms of health information are exchanged and the integration of networks that will accommodate the efficient and secure use of electronic health records.

Each year more health providers are moving from using cellphones and pagers to more sophisticated devices, such as a variety of smartphones, which are improved almost annually. According to a 2011 survey conducted by market

>

researcher Essential Research, 62 percent of Canadian physicians have smartphones. Of those, 86 percent use them for professional purposes. Health providers can now preview urgent laboratory and diagnostic images on these devices. A 2012 pilot project at Women's College Hospital in Toronto is using technology to follow selected postoperative clients. The clients are sent home with a customized smartphones and tablets on which to record their recovery. They have to submit answers to specific questions using touch-screen technology. Answers indicating potential recovery problems are flagged and the attending physician follows up with the client by phone or in person. As well, the clients took pictures of their incisions daily and sent them to the physician.

As an assistant, you can be more in touch when the doctor is away from the office by forwarding important emails, reports, and updates to his schedule; he then can access these items remotely.

Communication networks in doctors' offices are also becoming more sophisticated. Many reports, such as lab and consultation reports and X-rays, are being sent electronically. As the connectivity of networks improves, this practice will increase.

One of the latest health-care communication solutions is a technology that facilitates two-way internet communication between clients and their physicians. Supported by the Canadian Medical Association, this technology enhances clients' access to their own health information as well as to the doctor. The technology is referred to as an internet-based patient–provider communication system. Client access is through the use of patient portals. The doctor can upload lab test results, reports, and general comments about the client's condition. This reduces the number of enquiring phone calls to the office, allowing the administrative staff time for other duties. As well, secure online payment options will reduce accounts receivable tracking time and eliminate expenses associated with manual collection efforts.

Some facilities are beginning to use automated online scheduling systems to schedule office/facility appointments. These systems offer convenience to the client and reduce the number of calls into the office. Another option is using email to book, cancel, and change appointments. A little more time-intensive than automated scheduling systems, using email still offers clients some advantages over calling the office to make an appointment in terms of flexibility and convenience. This solution also eliminates frustration associated with multiple attempts to get through to the office on the phone. Look at the websites of the following offices that use the email option to get an idea as to how it is used: Thornhill Pediatrics (www.thornhillpediatrics.ca) and Lakeside Medical Clinic (www.lakeside.ca).

When the use of EMRs become more widespread and standardized, some of your office responsibilities will shift to being more online oriented. For example, there may not be any written prescriptions or faxed forms—they will all be delivered, filed, and stored electronically.

Electronic referrals (e-referrals) are direct digital referrals between (for the most part) family doctors and specialists that are being tested in pockets across Canada. Linked to EMRs, this method of communication is asynchronous and allows family doctors and specialists to exchange files digitally at their convenience. The technology facilitates dialogue between the family doctor and specialist. For example, the family doctor can ask the specialist a question about a client and attach a file (such a test result). The specialist can respond directly, ask for more information, and then decide if she needs to see the client or not.

Online access for clients to their own health information is a trend that is expected to grow. Certain portions of a client's health and treatment history will be available to them. Clients will be asked to monitor portions of their care at home and enter the relevant information into their charts to be reviewed by their provider. Devices such as digital glucometers for clients with diabetes, electronic scales and blood pressure monitoring devices for those with congestive heart failure (CHF), and digital spirometers for those with asthma help clients track progress and detect early changes in their condition. This type of monitoring will reduce the number of visits to the doctor for assessment and tracking. You may be required to log and organize digital feedback.

In some cities there is a new and growing trend: smartphone and tablet apps that provide clients with information about how long ER waits are at various hospitals. The app may also provide a map with directions to the person's selected Emergency Department.

Excellent communication skills—written and oral—will always be key to interacting in a positive way with clients and contribute to high quality, well coordinated, and comprehensive care. Never underestimate the value of person-to-person communication. Technology is only a device to improve the channels of data exchange and is only as good as the persons using and analyzing it.

SUMMARY

1. Communication, both written and verbal, is central to every health office and health-care facility.

2. Technology offers many options in the health office. Each office must choose that which suits its needs.

3. Because of speed and efficiency, faxes and email have taken over much of the correspondence, such as reports and lab results, that used to go by mail. However, confidentiality is a major concern.

4. Reports, letters, and other written material created in your office must be accurate, grammatically correct, and properly formatted.

5. Using plain language will help your clients understand your written and oral communications so they can take a greater role in their own care. Address people directly; use one main idea per sentence; choose active verbs; group related information; tell people what to do instead of what not to do; and limit jargon and acronyms.

6. Become familiar with the features of your office's phone system. More offices now use answering devices rather than human answering services. Make sure your answering message is clear, concise, friendly, and professional.

7. A friendly, professional telephone manner is essential to client relations. Tone of voice, volume, speed, expression, grammar, choice of words, respect for the caller, and confidence all play a role. Assess your own telephone personality, and work to improve it.

8. Identify yourself and the office when you answer the phone. Try to answer promptly. Stop what you are doing, and focus on the conversation.

9. Directing incoming calls requires knowledge, skill, and organization. You can probably handle certain types of calls, such as those from clients calling for appointments, drug reps, and laboratories calling with results. You should pass on to the doctor calls from other doctors and most calls from hospitals. You need to triage clients to ensure that emergencies and urgent concerns are dealt with promptly. Most doctors will provide guidelines.

10. Never trust anything to memory. Keep a notepad or notebook to take messages, and make sure you have complete information, including the phone number where the caller can be reached at the time you expect the doctor to call back. Always read back lab results and dosages.

11. To make outgoing calls efficient, make them in batches, and have all necessary information handy.

12. Find out how clients prefer to be addressed. When greeting clients, a brief personal conversation can build relationships. Tell clients when they will have to wait to see the doctor and offer options if the wait will be long.

13. In dealing with difficult clients, show warmth, respect, and empathy just as you do with all clients. Keep your voice level. Do not take it personally. Listen to clients, and show them that you understand their concerns and are willing to work with them to solve problems. Use conciliatory language. Recognize your own limits.

14. In a new office, listen to the staff and learn the ropes before you offer suggestions. Emphasize teamwork, mutual respect, and sharing of information.

Review Questions

1. Discuss the term *professionalism* as it applies to telephone communication.
2. Identify some strategies to enhance a positive impression over the telephone.
3. List four telephone services available today, and discuss how they would be useful in the health office setting.
4. Compare and contrast the advantages and disadvantages of an answering service and an answering machine in the health office.
5. Discuss confidentiality concerns relating to fax, email, cellphones, and pagers.
6. List the information that is essential when taking a telephone message.
7. List eight types of incoming calls to the health office. Discuss the appropriate methods of dealing with them and the rationale for each.
8. Describe the appropriate strategy for handling more than one telephone call at the same time.
9. Identify and discuss six methods to enhance efficiency when dealing with outgoing calls in the health office.
10. Discuss four ways to effectively deal with an angry client.

Application Exercises

1. Review the following directives. Think of a client-friendly way of putting these into a sign.
   a. Take off your boots at the door.
   b. There is a $10 charge for missed appointments.
   c. Notify reception when you arrive.
   d. You must show your health card at every visit.
   e. The doctor does not give prescriptions out over the phone.
2. In groups of three, create three scenarios of telephone conversations. They do not have to be related to health-care issues, but each should involve one person calling and one answering who must direct, explain, or deal with a complaint or request. Examples:

   A customer calls the bank wanting to know her balance. The teller refuses.

   A client calls the doctor's office complaining because he was sent a bill for a missed appointment.

   The responder should rate her own telephone personality, the caller should give her impressions, and the third group member should give a rating. Switch roles and repeat twice. How does your self-evaluation differ from others' evaluation of your style? What strengths do you have? What areas do you need to improve?
3. Jennifer accidentally opened a personal letter addressed to Dr. Ward (who is married with two young sons). It was from a client in the practice. Jennifer read the letter even though she knew she should not. The client, an 18-year-old female, was thanking the doctor for a wonderful evening out. She went on to say that she cared for him and was looking

forward to continuing the "relationship." Horrified, Jennifer put the letter back into the envelope and stuffed it into her pocket. She didn't know what to do. This is an ethical situation with potentially legal implications. What would you do? Using the problem-solving steps suggested in Chapter 1, outline a course of action for Jennifer.

4. Suppose you work in a busy family practice office. You receive the following calls. Respond to each call in what you think is the best manner. Think about how you should handle or direct the call and whether you need additional information. If the call is for the doctor, should you put it through? How should you respond to the caller's questions or demands? You may work alone or in small groups to complete this assignment. If you work alone, compare your responses with someone else's. Think about ways to improve your responses.

1 p.m.

▪ "My mother, Bertha Waters, was in to see Dr. Marino yesterday. She has been upset ever since. She won't talk to me about it. I want to know what's going on."

1:10

▪ Hi, this is Rosa from Labour and Delivery at the hospital. I have Mrs. Stein here, and I think she's in labour. Could I speak with the doctor?"

1:15

▪ "Hello, this is Sandra Moscati calling. I would like to make an appointment to see the doctor. I am having some chest pain, and I find it hard to catch my breath."

1:17

▪ "This is Gertrude Meyers. I have an appointment for Thursday afternoon to see the doctor, but I am not going to be able to make it. I thought you would like to know."

1:20

▪ "Hello, this is Ella. I would like to make an appointment to see the doctor. I had my X-ray yesterday, and oh, what an experience, I must tell you. First, I had a hard time getting down to the hospital. Then I got lost trying to find that X-ray department, but this nice lady. . . ."

1:25

▪ "This is Jim Cameron. I want to have my prescription for Valium renewed. You can phone it in to Lakeside Pharmacy. I will pick it up after 6 p.m."

1:30

▪ "I have been trying to get through to you for the last half hour. What's the matter with you people? Do you leave your telephone off the hook? Don't you realize that there are sick people wanting to get in touch with you? Can't you afford another telephone line? This is ridiculous, just ridiculous."

1:32

▪ "Hello, this is Rob Bruni. I am a drug rep with Abbot. I would like to drop around later with some samples and see the doctor."

1:34

▪ "Hello. This is Marg from MDS. I have some lab results on Martha Bowman:
  Hb 12.1
  WBC 15.00
  Blood Sugar 12.5. That's high, I thought you should know."

1:40

■ "This is Raj Anand. Could I speak to the doctor, please? It's important."

1:45

■ "Good afternoon, this is Dr. Mason. Dr. Marino, please."

1:50

■ "I would like to have some pills renewed. Would you ask the doctor to do that for me?"

2:00

■ "This is three north at the hospital calling. I need some orders on Mr. Walsh."

2:04

■ "This is Ayesha Mahmoud. I was wondering if you could give me the results of my Pap smear. It was done last week, and I am feeling a little anxious."

2:10

■ "This is Stephanie Pichette. I need my birth control pills renewed. I only have about three pills left."

2:15

■ "This is Denise Olson. My son Kyle has a sore throat, and I would like the doctor to phone in a prescription for an antibiotic."

2:20

■ "This is Jake Ellis. I have a bone to pick. You told me that Dr. Marino would call me back yesterday after hours, and he didn't. I waited for two hours for that call. I want an explanation!"

2:35

■ "My name is Samantha Kovacs. I am a relative of Josh Lemke. He's a patient of the doctor. I just moved to town, and I need a doctor. Josh said it wouldn't be a problem."

Websites of Interest

WSIB/WCB Boards across Canada
http://www.awcbc.org/en/linkstoworkerscompensationboardscommissions.asp

The Canadian Public Health Association
http://www.cpha.ca/en/default.aspx
This site includes a section about plain language health information, under "Plain Language Service."

The National Adult Literacy Database
www.nald.ca
This site has information about literacy and plain language resources.

Health Communication
http://www.healthypeople.gov/2020/default.aspx
This is a U.S. government website about health issues.

Dealing with Anger
www.ext.colostate.edu/pubs/consumer/10236.html
www.mala.ca/conflict/anger.asp

Time Zones Across Canada
http://www.timetemperature.com/directory/canada.html
Use this website to find the time zone of any location in Canada.

Managing Workplace Conflict

http://www.communicationdiva.com

This website has been created by Jennifer Swanson, who is an expert in health communication. Of particular interest are the following podcast episodes and webpages:

http://www.communicationdiva.com/19cd-podcast-episode-7-thing-not-to-say-when-someone-dies/
http://www.communicationdiva.com/18-cd-podcast-episodetone-of-voice-what-are-you-really-saying/
http://www.communicationdiva.com/17cd-podcast-episode-motivation-and-initiative/
http://www.communicationdiva.com/15-cd-podcast-episode-how-to-be-professional-in-the-workplace/
http://www.communicationdiva.com/12-cd-podcast-episode-on-customer-service/
http://www.communicationdiva.com/04-cd-podcast-episode-how-best-to-communicate-with-your-healthcare-provider/
http://www.communicationdiva.com/cd-podcast-episode-02-10-minutes-to-better-listening/
http://www.communicationdiva.com/what-is-a-nursing-unit-clerk-anyway/
http://www.communicationdiva.com/goal-setting-tips/
http://www.communicationdiva.com/9-ways-to-improve-workplace-professionalism/

Chapter 9
Scheduling Appointments

Learning Objectives

On completing this chapter, you will be able to:

1. Schedule client appointments.

2. Pre-edit an electronic appointment schedule.

3. Keep client health information secure.

4. Explain five protocols for scheduling appointments.

5. Determine the appropriate length of time for various appointments.

6. Triage clients in the health-care setting.

7. Explain how to cope with disruptions to schedules.

8. Schedule an appointment for a new client.

9. Schedule consultations, diagnostic tests, and surgery.

10. Discuss scheduling procedures specific to the dental office.

Efficient and organized scheduling is vital to the success of any medical practice. Proper scheduling and billing generate the main sources of income for the provider. Proper scheduling also improves service to your clients. Scheduling appointments is one of the main tasks of health office professionals and requires effective communication skills, people skills, good judgment, a general knowledge of medical diseases and conditions, and an understanding of the physician's own style of management. It is essential that you understand all components of the scheduling software you use to maximize its potential. In an office with several staff members, one person may be assigned the responsibility of scheduling, sometimes on a rotational basis; thus, everyone in the office should be able to perform this important duty.

❶ TOOLS FOR SCHEDULING APPOINTMENTS

THE TELEPHONE AND THE COMPUTER ARE YOUR PRIMARY TOOLS FOR SCHEDULING appointments. Most offices have two or more computers in the administrative area, one in the doctor's private office, and one in each examination or treatment room. How "electronic" your office is affects scheduling, charting, and billing procedures in the practice.

Computerized Scheduling

Most software systems offer a wide range of features that can be adapted to suit any physician. Paramount is ease of use, defined by an organized and logical approach to the various modules in the system. At the heart of any software system is the scheduling module. This module will connect with other modules in the system: e.g., pharmacy, client history, client encounter, billing, chronic disease management, referral and document management (where you would file all electronically received and scanned reports), flow sheets (e.g., diabetic flow sheet), desktop flagging (allowing you to send notes to the provider) and templates for forms/letters (which you can modify).

A software scheduling system should include features that enable you to

- block off the provider's time on a physician's schedule that interfaces with the electronic appointment schedule (some systems will prevent you from physically scheduling a client appointment if the doctor's time is blocked as unavailable);
- choose between single- and multi-provider formats;
- show all providers' availability at a glance in a multi-provider practice;
- view appointment screens for a day or a week at a glance (see Figures 9.1 and 9.2);
- copy and paste appointments, or otherwise duplicate appointments for future visits;
- print/view a day sheet from a selection of day sheet formats;
- electronically search for a client's appointment;
- compile a profile of a client's appointment history;
- prompt you for client recalls, reminder calls, or forms that need to be filled out (some systems have an automated telephone reminder system);
- schedule rooms and equipment and link them to providers' schedules and clients' bookings;
- track client flow considering arrival, check-in, visit, and departure time; can be time-stamped and recorded or simply colour-coded;

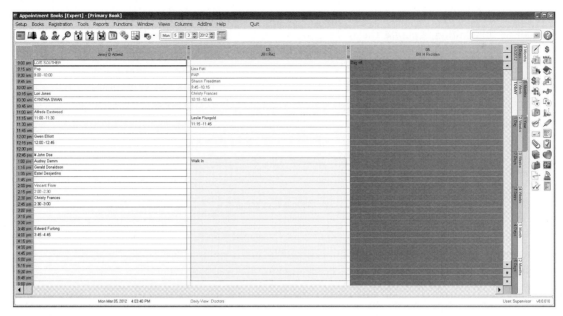

Figure 9.1 Calendar with daily appointments
Courtesy of P&P Data Systems

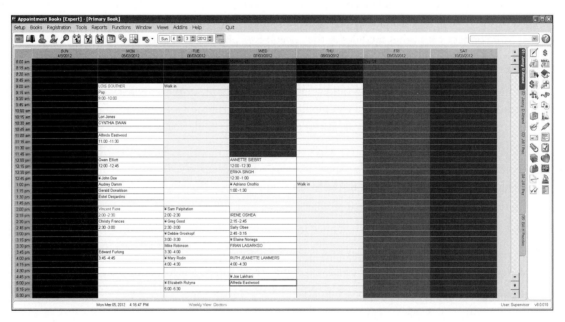

Figure 9.2 Days of appointments
Courtesy of P&P Data Systems

▓ create and apply scheduling templates using colour options;

▓ activate a billing option from the scheduler; and

▓ enter notes regarding missed appointments, requests for prescription renewals, phone calls and how they were handled, or other information relevant to the client's care.

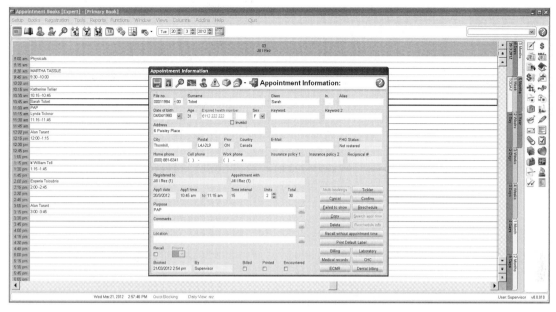

Figure 9.3 Short registration

Courtesy of P&P Data Systems

Figure 9.3 shows an electronic booking/scheduling module. The calendar on the left is used to schedule appointments and for claims submissions. In this example, the practice includes six providers (shown in the upper left). Clicking on the doctor's name brings up her schedule. Clicking on a particular appointment listing produces a pop-up with client information. You can click to note that the appointment is confirmed and that the client has arrived, is waiting, is being attended to, or has skipped the appointment (right upper corner of the pop-up). You can perform provincial/territorial and direct billing right from the client's appointment listing and automatically mark the appointment as billed.

Scheduling Templates

Most software systems will allow you to set up scheduling templates. These are pre-assigned appointment spaces used for specific types of appointment or procedures. It's like booking an appointment with no client attached to it. This allows you to search for specific types of blank appointment spaces. They can be used for myriad things, including physical examinations, diabetic assessments, prenatal assessments, well-baby assessments, or counselling sessions. For example, Anita calls the office wanting a physical. You can simply search for the next available spot for a physical examination and give Anita the time and date. Templates also allow you to control the number and type of appointment you are booking—thus not overloading the doctor's schedule. To effectively use templates, the doctor must be comfortable with a reasonably predictable pattern of scheduling. To set up templates it is necessary to create a plan with the doctor so that the schedule pattern fits with his needs and expectations. Figure 9.4 shows a morning with templates that predetermine times for more lengthy appointments such as physicals, Pap smears and counselling.

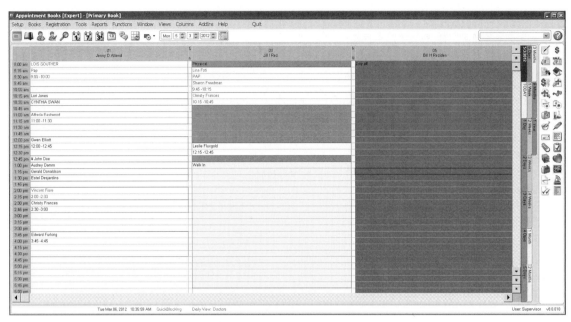

Figure 9.4 Physical appointment slots

Courtesy of P&P Data Systems

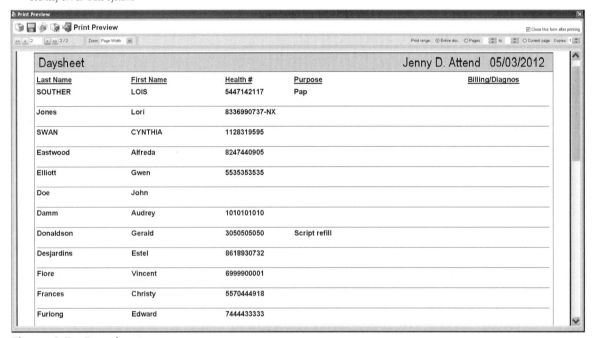

Figure 9.5 Day sheet

Courtesy of P&P Data Systems

Day Sheet

A day sheet is simply a computerized list of the provider's appointments for a day. See Figure 9.5. How the electronic day sheet is used depends on what view you choose from your view options. Many offices print a hard copy of the day sheet for referral purposes and for keeping notes. It is also handy if your computer system is down. This is not uncommon, particularly with more complex systems connected to a variety of other providers and organizations. It you can't use the computer, you do not have access to the scheduler. The day sheet can be a godsend in such situations. The doctor can keep her copy in her office and refer to it throughout the day. The day sheet helps the doctor keep to her schedule, gives her an idea of how many clients are left to be seen, and who is to be seen next. If you include the reason for the client's appointment, it also informs the doctor what she will be dealing with ahead of time. Keeping a copy yourself will enforce the habit of printing a day sheet for the doctor, and allow you to make note on your copy as well. Some physicians, as well as dentists, also use the day sheet to record notes, reminders, and claims information, such as the type of visit, diagnostic code, and so on, whether the office is computerized or not.

If a client cancels an appointment or you have to fit in an emergency, mark the change on the day sheet, adding it to the appointment schedule when you have access to the computer again. Remember that you should also note cancellations and no-shows on the client's EMR.

Alternatively, the doctor may keep track of scheduled clients and add notes using her own PC or PC tablet (also called a PDA—personal digital assistant). Any changes you make on the electronic schedule immediately show on the doctor's PC. (The doctor will have to click the "refresh" button to see changes.)

Appointment Cards

Appointment cards (see Figure 9.6) help reduce the number of clients who miss their appointments or show up on the wrong day or at the wrong time. They also save you time, because fewer clients will call and ask you when their appointments are. The doctor's phone number is on the card, which encourages clients to call if they are going to be late or miss their appointments.

Reminders

Some health-care providers—usually not family physicians, but specialists, optometrists, chiropractors, and dentists—will call, email, and/or mail postcards reminding the client of an upcoming appointment.

Dr. D. J. Thompson, M.D., C.F.P.C.
Medical Arts Building
93 St. Vincent Street North
Stratford, Ontario
N5A 5H5

Name:_____ has an appointment on
Date:_____ Time: _____a.m./p.m.

Please call if you are unable to keep this appointment.
There is a $20 charge for failure to notify this office
within 24 hours of an appointment cancellation.
Ph. 519-271-1111

Figure 9.6 An appointment card

❷❸ SCHEDULING PROCEDURES

Pre-editing the Provider's Scheduler

It is important to set aside a time to update the doctor's electronic scheduler. This applies to any other provider who is seeing clients (e.g., nurse practitioner, dentist, hygienist). Filling in the times you know the provider to be unavailable is called scheduling by exception. Most systems will allow you to do this "behind the scenes" on a separate calendar that interfaces with your client appointment scheduler. Some systems will provide an option wherein you will be physically unable to book a client appointment at a time when you have the doctor scheduled as unavailable. This saves time, and prevents you from accidentally bringing in a client only to find that Dr. Smith is away at a conference. This is easily done in a hectic office environment. Pre-editing the doctor's time can be done a month or so in advance and updated accordingly. You should review the doctor's schedule with her frequently to ensure accuracy. All too often the doctor will forget to tell you that she will be away at a meeting or is leaving early for an appointment. Items should include

- routine times when the doctor is not in the office (many physicians take Wednesday afternoons off);
- routine commitments, such as hospital rounds or medical seminars (often conducted weekly, usually around 0700 hours);
- on-call schedules, usually available several months in advance (It is vital that this schedule is accurately recorded. Doctors sometimes switch calls with another doctor and may forget to tell you. Discuss the doctor's call schedule at least every few days to ensure any changes are noted.);
- assigned days in the clinic or the ER (Most primary care reform groups have a clinic that operates five days a week, including evenings. Doctors from the group staff the clinic on a rotational basis. How often depends on the number of doctors in the group.);
- variable meetings and appointments; and
- statutory holidays (be sure to include new ones, such as those implemented in Ontario and Manitoba in early 2008). You can do this for an entire year, and it helps to avoid confusion.

If you are working for a multi-provider practice, ensure that you carefully edit each provider's schedule. In a dental or optometry office where allied health professionals are seeing clients, schedules depend on one another. For example, if a hygienist is off, the dentist's and dental assistants' schedules may also be affected.

Standard Terminology

To save both time and space (few appointment schedulers have enough space for long notes), use standard terms and abbreviations in scheduling as shown in Table 9.1. Though these abbreviations are fairly standard in physician's offices, not all dental practices use the same abbreviations.

Table 9.1 Common Medical Abbreviations Used in Scheduling

V/S	vital signs check	Can	cancellation	Ref	referral
CPx	physical examination	NS	no show	ECG	electrocardiogram
A/CPx	annual physical	FUp	follow-up	Lab/w	lab work-up
AHE	annual health	RS	reschedule	US	ultrasound
	examination	A/S	allergy shot	WB	well baby
PN	prenatal	Imm	immunization	Pap	Pap smear
PP	postpartum check	F/S	flu shot	Con	consult
NP	new patient	Inj	injection	BP	blood pressure
NC	new client				

Scheduling Considerations

In scheduling appointments, consider first the client's health concern. How soon should she be seen? How long an appointment will the doctor need to deal with the concern? If possible, try to accommodate the client's individual needs as well. For example:

- See school-aged children after school or on professional development days. High school students may have variable schedules.

- A mother of school-aged children may prefer to come in while the children are at school, as long as she can be home for their return.

- Clients with busy schedules and work-related commitments during the day may prefer appointments first thing in the morning before delays occur.

- Older clients or those who take a great deal of time with the doctor might best be seen at the end of the morning or afternoon.

- Never book an appointment for a pregnant woman back to back or even close in time with a client who may have rubella (German measles). Avoid even same-day bookings if you can. If a pregnant woman who is not immune to rubella contracts the disease, especially in the first trimester, the consequences to the unborn baby could be serious. If a child has symptoms suggesting rubella (rash, fever, crankiness) check your appointment scheduler to see if you have a prenatal appointment booked.

- Clients with disabilities might depend on others to get them to and from the office and therefore may need special consideration regarding their appointment times.

- Clients who need interpreters usually require a longer appointment. Schedule this at the end of the day or morning so that if the visit takes longer than expected other clients are not kept waiting.

If you are making an appointment for a new client or someone with whom you are not familiar, try to determine if they have special needs so that you can accommodate them as much as possible. I once made an appointment over the telephone for a client who had never been to the office. She arrived in her wheelchair only to find that the office was not wheelchair accessible. She had to return home without being seen. (The doctor made a house call later in the day.)

Pre-office Conference or Information Update   It is good to get into the habit of reviewing the day's appointments with the provider, using a day sheet or viewing the electronic schedule. An excellent time is at the beginning of the day and/or before the doctor starts seeing clients in the afternoon. Some physicians also like updates mid-morning and mid-afternoon. This quick meeting facilitates good communication and helps the day run smoothly. It lets the doctor know what is happening and how heavy the day is and gives both of you the opportunity to talk about other matters. You can ensure that the doctor knows about any activities he is scheduled for that day; he may have forgotten about a commitment made weeks ago. Also, ask if the doctor has anything to add to the schedule; he may have forgotten to tell you about something that came up at the last minute. Doctors have been known to encourage a client to "just drop in this afternoon," which plays havoc with your appointment schedule. You have to deal with these clients, try to fit them in, and often make scheduled clients wait. You need to communicate clearly with the doctor about the problem; you can request that he not do this, except in special circumstances. If he does, he should at least let you know so that you can pull the client's chart and be prepared. If clients are expecting to pick up forms, you can give them to the doctor or remind him to complete them. You can also present any abnormal lab tests to the doctor, receive instructions on dealing with them, and ask any questions you may have about other issues or reports.

Confidentiality and Scheduling

If you are using an actual appointment book, keep it out of view of clients, and at the end of the day, put it in a secure place. Otherwise, it can innocently be seen by the cleaning staff and anyone else with access to the office.

With an electronic scheduling appointment system, place the monitor at an angle that does not allow clients to read it. Turn the monitor off when you are not using it. Many offices store other client information and files on the computer as well, so limit computer access to appropriate individuals. Keep all passwords confidential and, if written down, stored securely. Most systems require that you change your password at regular intervals. A password that is alphanumeric (letters and numbers) is advised.

The appointment schedule is a legal electronic document and must be backed up and filed. If you make a mistake or change appointments, keep a record of the changes. In a manual situation, do not erase; instead, rule a neat line through the error, and write in above it. An alternative for computerized systems is to note no-shows and cancellations on the daily appointment schedule or day sheet. You should also note this information on the client's EMR or paper chart. Note that most physician-governing bodies across the country require you to keep a record of all appointments for 10 years.

❹ TYPES OF SCHEDULING

A NUMBER OF DIFFERENT SCHEDULING METHODS ARE CURRENTLY USED IN HEALTH CARE. Each has its own advantages and disadvantages and suits some types of practice better than others.

Fixed Office Hours, or Open Scheduling

With this method, the facility is open at certain hours, and clients may come whenever they like within those hours without an appointment. Few family practices use this method, but it is used in some group practices and is the norm in walk-in and urgent-care clinics based on the principle of providing care to clients when they need it. Clients first see the administrative health professional (AHP), have their health card validated, and explain the purpose of the visit. Clients in urgent need of care are seen first; otherwise, clients are seen in the order in which they arrive. The client must understand that barring an emergency, they will be seen on a first-come, first-served basis.

This method eliminates the work of maintaining schedules and the problems of missed or cancelled appointments and late arrivals. It suits some clients with busy and irregular schedules.

One obvious drawback to this method is the unpredictable variations in workload. There may be very slow periods, in which staff time is not used effectively, and times when both you and the doctor are so busy that it is difficult to cope. Another drawback is that you have no time to pull the client's chart ahead of time, no opportunity to validate the health card, and no idea what the presenting problem is. You have no time to prepare for procedures required for particular complaints, such as syringing an ear.

If you are working in a walk-in or urgent-care clinic, the client is unlikely to have a chart there. All information is recorded on a facility admission sheet and perhaps a progress, multidisciplinary, or fact sheet. You will take the necessary client information, process the health card, and record the reason for the visit. The physician will record the details of the visit on the appropriate record. Forward duplicates to the client's family physician.

Wave Scheduling

Wave scheduling is a compromise between open scheduling and scheduling by appointment. This method is so named because clients come in groups, like waves hitting a beach. A certain number of clients are booked to see the provider within a given time frame. (See Figure 9.7). Note that the schedule shows clients' names across the page; in this case, three clients are booked every half hour. Although this type of scheduling can occur in general practice, you are more likely to find wave scheduling in the office of an allergist or an endocrinologist. First, determine how many clients the provider can see in the time frame. (See the discussion later in this chapter.) For example, if Dr. Meiros usually sees one client every 10 minutes, he will see approximately six clients in one hour. You would then ask six clients to come in between 0900 and 1000 hrs, and another six between 1000 and 1100 hrs. They are not given specific times. The premise is that some clients will come earlier than others. It allows clients some flexibility, while still offering some structure and control. You can pull charts and validate health cards ahead of time. The drawback is that if all the clients in a wave arrive at the same time, some will have to wait longer.

wave scheduling scheduling several clients for the same block of time, typically an hour.

Modified Wave Scheduling

Modified wave scheduling uses a basic block of time, as does wave scheduling. However, clients are given narrower time slots to control traffic flow more closely. For example, you might ask two clients to arrive between 1 p.m. and 1:15 p.m., another two to arrive between 1:15 and 1:30, and so on.

Affinity Scheduling

Affinity scheduling, also called **cluster**, **categorization**, or **analogous scheduling**, involves scheduling clients in clusters on the basis of the type of service or reason for seeing the

affinity, cluster, categorization, or **analogous scheduling** scheduling similar appointments together, for example, scheduling physical examinations on a certain day.

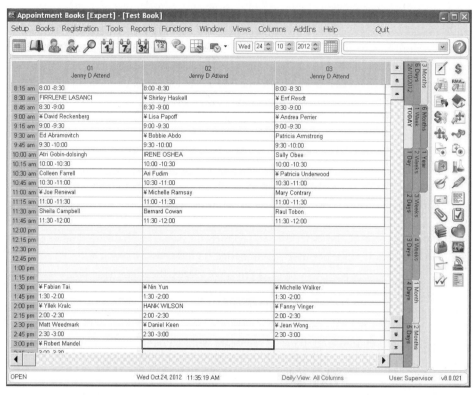

Figure 9.7 A scheduling screen showing wave scheduling with three clients booked every half hour

Courtesy of P&P Data Systems

doctor. Many dental offices, as well as some medical practices, use this method. For example, the dentist may see clients who need checkups on Monday and Wednesday mornings and those who require uncomplicated fillings on Tuesday and Thursday afternoons. Monday and Wednesday afternoons may be surgery days, and Fridays reserved for orthodontic procedures. A general surgeon might see all clients with breast lumps on a certain day, those with abdominal complaints another day, those who need follow-up assessments another day, and so on. Primary care physicians do not usually use this method of scheduling exclusively.

In some primary care reform groups using alternative payment plans, affinity scheduling is becoming more popular. Doctors in primary care groups (PCGs) are given bonus or incentive payments for meeting certain service milestones (e.g., completing a certain number of Pap smears and immunizations). Affinity scheduling allows the physician to efficiently schedule individuals that help him meet these criteria.

Affinity scheduling maximizes the use of special equipment that may be needed for certain procedures and makes it easy to determine how much time to allow for each appointment. It is helpful and saves time to use appointment templates for affinity scheduling. However, the repetition of affinity scheduling can become boring for the provider. Furthermore, in a given week, the range of clients' problems may not fit the affinity schedule. This form of scheduling also leaves fewer choices for clients.

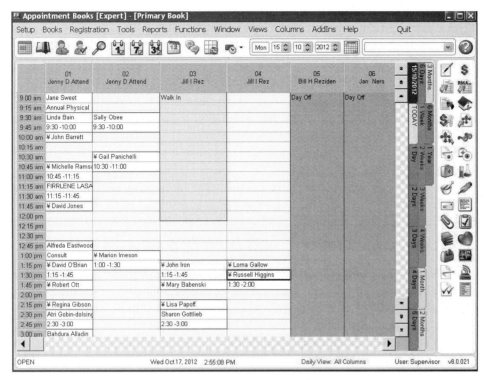

Figure 9.8 An appointment screen showing a blend of stream, or fixed, and combination, or blended, scheduling

Courtesy of P&P Data Systems

Combination or Blended Scheduling

Often, a medical practice will use a mix of randomly scheduled appointments with affinity scheduling to create what is called **combination** or **blended scheduling**. Many physicians will do annual physicals and preoperative examinations at certain times, perhaps Monday and Wednesday mornings. They may see prenatal clients and do well-baby examinations on Tuesday and Thursday mornings. Individuals who require allergy injections may be asked to come in on Tuesday and Friday afternoons. The doctor must be in the office when a client has an allergy shot in case there is an adverse reaction, but if there is a nurse to give the injection, the doctor does not usually have to see the client. The rest of the time is open for any type of complaint. Figure 9.8 shows a schedule with fixed or stream scheduling on Monday, and a combination of blended affinity scheduling the rest of the week. Of course, other clients can be fit in or double-booked any time, as the need arises.

Advantages to this type of scheduling include organization and making optimum use of specialized equipment. Annual medicals, for example, take anywhere from 20 to 30 minutes. Doing them on specific days allows the rest of the week to be used more efficiently for more routine encounters and avoids delays caused by lengthy appointments. Scheduling an annual examination in the middle of a busy afternoon when the reception area is full and you are already running 45 minutes late will only add to the stress for you and the waiting clients.

Assess the scheduling pattern in your practice. You may be able to introduce some changes that enhance efficiency.

combination scheduling
or **blended scheduling**   a combination of affinity and random scheduling.

Double, or Double-Column, Booking

Most scheduling modules allow you to book clients in the same time slot—the appearance of the screen will vary.

double scheduling or **double-column booking**   scheduling two client appointments at the same time, on the assumption that one of the appointments will involve little of the doctor's time.

Double scheduling or **double-column booking** is rarely used as the *primary* scheduling method in any facility. However, when a busy office or clinic already has a full schedule and has to accommodate emergencies, double-booking can lend a semblance of order to what could be a scheduling nightmare. The additional clients' names are entered into the same time slot, or a second column or row beside or beneath the names of the regularly scheduled clients. (See Figure 9.2.) On Monday at 1:15 p.m., Mr. Bakhshi's and Mrs. Dyck's names appear beside each other. On the computer screen sometimes it may look as though the doctor will see both clients at the same time. Of course, she will not, but the schedule will still work reasonably well as long as you double-book with a client who can be seen quickly. In this case, each client is estimated to take 5–7 minutes (a brief or minor assessment). An example might be a skin rash or a recheck of vital signs or an incision. Allergy shots and other injections are also appropriate for double-booking. If there is a nurse in the office who gives injections, the physician will often not see the client at all (although the doctor must be in the office in case the client has an adverse reaction).

Double scheduling is discussed further below with reference to times allowed for clients to see the provider. Explain the situation to regular clients who end up waiting, and thank them for their cooperation.

Stream Scheduling

stream or **fixed-interval scheduling**   allotting a specific, unique time slot for each client appointment; the most common method of scheduling.

Stream or **fixed-interval scheduling** is the most common method of scheduling appointments in offices. With this manner of scheduling, each client has a fixed, or specific, appointment time, and clients are supposed to come in a steady stream. In a well-organized office, client flow should be fairly smooth most of the time. Some disruptions and delays are unavoidable. However, if delays are chronic, a review is needed. There may be several causes:

- You may be allowing insufficient time for each client.
- The doctor may spend longer than she should with each client. You cannot change how the provider operates—although you can discuss it with her—but you can book more time with each client and fewer clients in the day. This will affect revenue and might motivate the provider to use her time more efficiently.
- Clients may be in the habit of mentioning one complaint when they book but present with additional ones when they arrive at the office. Remind clients that time scheduled with the provider is based on the original complaint. Offer to schedule another appointment for any other problems.
- Perhaps you are allowing too many walk-ins. Post a sign that clearly states that, except in emergencies, clients will be seen by appointment only—and stick to that policy.
- Clients may be bringing the whole family along to be seen "because I was coming anyway." If concerns are not urgent, book another appointment for the other family members. Remind them that if they want back-to-back appointments next time, they must request two appointments when they book.

The success of stream scheduling is contingent on accurate estimation of appointment times.

❺ STANDARD TIMES FOR APPOINTMENTS

HOW MUCH TIME A DOCTOR SPENDS WITH A CLIENT WILL DEPEND ON SEVERAL THINGS, INCLUDING

- the doctor's practice style;
- the type of practice (e.g., specialist, primary care physician);
- the type and number of individuals in the office helping the provider (dental assistant, hygienist, chiropractic assistant, nurse practitioner, optometry assistant, nurse); and
- the reason for the visit.

In a family doctor's office, most appointments are scheduled every 10 to 15 minutes. Some doctors take more time with clients than do others. Some very busy doctors may double-book two or more examining rooms every 15 minutes. The doctor may see the client briefly but have a nurse, nurse practitioner, or assistant do a lot of the preliminary work-up, health teaching, and part of the examination. If the assistant has done some testing, the provider would review the results with the client and complete any necessary parts of the examination.

Categories of Assessment

The reason the client has come to see the provider determines the length of time the doctor should spend. For example, it would take the doctor less time to assess a client with a sore throat than one who was complaining of abdominal pain. Each province or territory has different terms to categorize visits. Ontario terms are used here, as outlined in the chapter on health plan billing, but the principles are the same everywhere.

A *minor assessment* is something that the doctor can deal with relatively quickly and that may only require a quick look or a verbal investigation. An *intermediate assessment* takes more of the doctor's time. A *complete assessment* refers to an investigation of most (usually all) body systems, and/or a complete physical examination, and takes 20 to 40 minutes or more, depending on the provider.

The following list covers the most common types of visits to a family physician, with approximate recommended scheduling times.

- Minor assessments (usually limited and done quickly), 5–7 min.
- Intermediate assessments (requiring moderate amount of time), 10 min.
- Initial prenatal examinations, 20–30 min.
- Subsequent prenatal examinations, 10 min.
- Well-baby visits (progress check for a healthy baby), 10–15 min.
- Partial gynecological examination (e.g., Pap smear), 10 min.
- "Talks" or counselling, 30–60 min. (usually billed as units of time)
- Annual health examinations or complete assessments, 20–40 min. (sometimes longer if the client is a senior and/or has multiple-system health problems)
- Allergy shots/flu shots: often no appointment needed, especially if there is a nurse to give the injection
- Immunizations: usually given to children during routine checkups; no separate appointment is needed. (It may sometimes happen that immunization and checkup dates do not coincide; in this case, the nurse can give the immunization without the client seeing the doctor.)

How to Determine the Type of Visit

It is important to know the reason for the appointment so that you can book the appropriate amount of time. If a client seems reluctant to tell you, explain that you can better accommodate her if you know how much time she needs with the doctor. The client may then give you some indication: "I need to talk about a personal problem," "It won't take long, it's something simple," or "The doctor knows what to do, this only takes a few minutes." However, if the client still refuses to tell you, do not make an issue of it; just assume an intermediate assessment.

The majority of appointments in a family doctor's office are intermediate assessments, which require a moderate amount of time. An intermediate assessment involves a moderately detailed history and examination of one or more body systems. When you think about it, even an earache involves more than a transitory conversation and a quick look at the ear. The doctor must take a history related to the complaint, look in the ears, check the throat and neck for lymphadenopathy (elevated cervical nodes), and examine the chest to rule out related respiratory problems.

As discussed above, double-booking works well for certain types of visits. For example, if Amanda is coming in for an allergy shot but does not have to see the doctor, the nurse will give her the shot while the doctor is seeing Marysia for a well-baby visit. Likewise, the nurse can remove Simone's sutures and complete the charting. Unless there are complications, Dr. Devor will only need to spend a brief amount of time with Simone. (Remember that one examining room will be tied up while the nurse is removing Simone's sutures.) Thus, you can book her alongside Lillian, who is coming in for a follow-up to see if the antibiotic has cleared up her ear infection—usually a quick check. Dana, who has a rash, does need to be seen by the doctor, but the visit will probably be brief, and so she can also be double-booked.

Scheduling for Other Providers

If you are scheduling appointments for an optometrist, you need to be familiar with the various procedures and examinations done in the office so that you can book appropriate times. A complete eye exam usually includes dilating the client's eyes. This necessitates a 20- to 30-minute wait after the drops are instilled until the pupils are sufficiently dilated to conduct the examination. The optometrist would see other clients during that wait time. Often, staff members can complete some preliminary examinations, such as an automated refraction, and so client appointment times can overlap at certain points.

Scheduling for a dentist involves the same principles. The client can come in at a specific time to see the hygienist and then see the dentist. Likewise, the dentist may inject freezing before filling a client's tooth, then fill a tooth for another client while the freezing is taking effect. Dentists book using units of time, usually 15 minutes. Certain procedures would take two units of time, others perhaps three or four.

A chiropractor may complete an adjustment and then have the client move to another room for some physiotherapy but see the client again before she leaves the office. If the chiropractor uses acupuncture, the client may have to remain in the office for half an hour or more. In the mean time, the chiropractor would see other clients.

INFORMATION NEEDED TO BOOK AN APPOINTMENT

Some offices that use a manual scheduling system take more information than others do. The more complete the information (within reason), the easier it is to get in

Some clients may be evasive if you ask them the reason for the visit. The reason may be something very personal. Explain you want to ensure that you schedule the appropriate amount of time with the doctor, and have ready any equipment or material the doctor may need. If this doesn't work, try to get a general sense as to what the reason is. "Do you think the visit will require a physical examination of any description?" or "Do you think that you will require a fair bit of time talking with the doctor?"

touch with the client if you need to cancel or change the appointment, or for any other reason. Record first and last names of the client and pertinent phone numbers (e.g., work, home, cell). You need to have the client's permission to call them at work. Some clients may prefer to be contacted using their email address.

An electronic scheduler allows you to easily access contact information, usually by clicking on the client's name and then accessing the client registry database.

Some offices do not ask the reason for the appointment. This information, however, helps the AHP not only book the appropriate length of appointment but make any special preparations for the visit. For example, if a client has a sore throat, the doctor will probably want to take a throat swab. You or the nurse could put out the needed equipment, making the visit more efficient. Likewise, if a client is coming in to get her prescription for birth control pills renewed, the doctor will probably do a Pap smear if it has been a year since her last visit. You would need to know this so that you or the nurse can prepare a speculum and put the client into the appropriate examination room. A well-baby check needs to take place in the examining room where the baby scales are located. If you have to reschedule an appointment for a physical examination, you would want to choose another day when the doctor is doing physical examinations. Knowing the reason for the visit is necessary for affinity scheduling or if you are using scheduling templates.

❻ TRIAGE

Occasionally, a client will just show up at the office wanting to see the doctor.

If a client is in distress or clearly has an urgent need to see the doctor, let him in as soon as possible, even if it means making others with scheduled appointments wait. Otherwise, treat him the same way as a client who phones in, and book the earliest available appointment. If he is not satisfied, advise him that he may wait but you cannot guarantee that the doctor will be able to see him and that next time he should call for an appointment. If you handle the incident in this manner, most clients will only do it once. If you squeeze the client in, there is no incentive for him to change his behaviour. Why should he? It gets him what he wants.

If a client telephones the office wanting to see the doctor right away, the urgency of his need to be seen must be assessed. A nurse or the physician would most likely do this. In some health offices, however, the AHP would be given triage guidelines. Direct acute emergencies, such as chest pain, difficulty breathing, profuse bleeding, or stroke symptoms, to the nearest Emergency Department. If in doubt, involve the doctor in making this decision. Never make decisions without clear guidelines, and never make decisions you are unsure about without appropriate consultation. Health advice is the domain of the doctor and/or the nurse.

What about the client who wants a same-day appointment when your schedule is already full? Determine the reason and assess the need using the triage guidelines, or ask the client to speak to the nurse. If the problem is not serious enough to justify a trip to the hospital Emergency Department but still sounds quite urgent, double-book the client. High temperature, earache, and UTI are usually considered urgent. For example, if a mother calls about a baby with a fever who is pulling at his ears, tell her to bring him in. This child must be seen. Generally, ailments involving small children should be assessed as soon as possible. On the other hand, an adult who has had a cough and a sore throat for a couple of days, in the absence of other serious clinical signs is probably not an emergency. You need to be firm. It is not reasonable to make other clients wait to accommodate this client. If you allowed every client who asked for an immediate appointment to get one, chaos would result. Give the client the earliest available appointment. If he remains insistent, suggest a walk-in clinic. Make sure that you do not, in any way, imply that the complaint is trivial. The client may be worried and upset; to him, the complaint is troublesome. Show that you are concerned and are doing your best to help. One strategy that appeases clients is to offer an appointment several days away initially and then one a little sooner. For example:

> "Mr. McIvor, I am sorry, the earliest opening I see here is Friday afternoon at 2 p.m., but let me see if there is anything I can do (pause). Actually, I think I can squeeze you in on Thursday morning at 10:30. Would that be better for you?"

Or

> "Mr. McIvor, I am sorry, but the earliest available appointment I have is Friday afternoon at 2 p.m. What I can do is make a note that you want to get in as soon as possible and call you if I get a cancellation. Now, which is the best place to reach you?"

You are offering alternatives and asking the client for input. At the same time, you are sticking to your guidelines.

If squeezing someone in makes other clients wait, explain that an urgent problem has come up without going into details. If the doctor is going to be delayed by more than half an hour, ask the waiting clients if they wish to schedule another appointment.

❼ DISRUPTIONS

As THE GREAT SCOTTISH POET ROBERT BURNS SAID, "THE BEST LAID SCHEMES O' MICE AND MEN GANG AFT AGLEY." I wonder if Burns ever worked in a health office. The most organized office manager cannot predict what the next hour, or the next phone call, will bring. Contingency plans are necessary to keep the office running efficiently and, in some cases, to ensure the well-being of your clients.

Catch-Up Time

It is a good idea when pre-editing the appointment book for the week to set aside some catch-up-time slots, or buffer zones. These vacant time slots give you some flexibility. They may be used to

- let the doctor catch up if she is running late;
- provide a much-needed coffee break (although that rarely happens, except for quick gulps between clients and phone calls);

- give the doctor the opportunity to return important phone calls or to review messages and prescription requests; and
- squeeze in clients who need immediate attention.

Cancellations

A cancellation represents lost revenue if the slot is not filled—a concern, especially if it is a long period, as it may be in a specialist's or a dentist's office. In a specialist's office, you would likely fill the slot from a wait list. In a dental office, you may also have a wait list of clients with a toothache or a filling that has fallen out. If not, you may call clients to see if they would like to move up their appointment. In a family physician's office, the spot can usually be filled almost immediately with clients calling for appointments or walking in. Indeed, in the family physician's office, a cancellation is usually a welcome opportunity to catch up. Draw a neat line through the client's name and write "can." beside it.

No-Shows

Sometimes, a client does not show up for an appointment and does not call to let you know. As with cancellations, in a manual environment draw a neat line through the client's name in the appointment schedule and write N/S beside it. On a computerized system, check "no show," so that it is recorded on the appointment screen and/or day sheet. Add the information to the client's EMR or paper chart.

It is frustrating when clients do not show up. You rarely have time to offer the slot to clients who may be on a long waiting list. So, the client loses the opportunity, and the provider loses revenue. No-shows can also be worrying. You will get to know your clients. Some people are chronically forgetful or late. If the client is usually punctual, missing an appointment may signal trouble. I recall one case when an older diabetic gentleman, usually reliable, did not show up for an appointment. The office manager called his home. Not getting an answer, she called a relative. The man was found unconscious, in the bathroom, having experienced an insulin reaction. Without prompt treatment, the outcome could have been very serious. Though few causes will be this serious, it is always a good idea to at least call the client. You can use this opportunity to rebook the appointment, which will help the client get the health problem looked after and will help the provider maintain revenue (especially for those not funded provincially/territorially).

Chronic offenders are difficult to deal with. Posting a sign indicating that there will be a charge for missed appointments may motivate some individuals to call ahead or to simply show up. Most offices that charge for missed appointments require 24 hours' notice unless the reason for missing is beyond the client's control. Family doctors are less likely than specialists and other providers to charge for missed appointments. However, if this is your office policy, you must follow through and charge the client. Some offices do let the client off with one warning, but only one. If you have time, a reminder call the day before may help. Many optometrists, dentists, specialists, and chiropractors do give reminder calls, but the majority of family physicians do not.

The Family Visit

Often, a client will make a single appointment and then come in with another family member (or two) in tow expecting the doctor to see them both. For example, a mother may make an appointment for one child and then bring one or two more. "Kyle has an earache, and Jessica has this rash on her arm. It will just take the doctor a minute to have a peek." You must discourage this behaviour. Unless the other complaints are urgent, you could respond with, "I am sorry, Mrs. Miklos, Dr. O'Brien is already running late and simply does not have time to see both Kyle and Jessica today. I do have an opening tomorrow afternoon, though." If you see that a client prefers to bring the whole family together, you can ask when she calls next, "Did you want to combine your appointment with the follow-up visit for Kyle? I have two appointments available back to back next Tuesday, if you prefer."

The Client with Multiple Complaints

Clients sometimes make an appointment to see the doctor about a specific problem. When they arrive, that problem has blossomed into several. When you are recording the client's presenting problem, tell the client that the doctor has only enough time to deal with the original problem. If the other complaints are not urgent, tell the client that you would be happy to book another appointment. The doctor should also be firm about this. If he relents and deals with each issue every time, all of your efforts will be to no avail. Clients will get away with what they can because "The doctor doesn't mind. He always has time for me." Perhaps, but at the expense of other waiting clients. A united front, with physician follow-through, is essential. If the client tells you that she has two problems to see the doctor about, an alternative is to book a double slot if one is available.

Physician's Absence

Occasionally, the physician may be called away or unable to come into the office at all. You are then faced with a scheduling nightmare: cancelling appointments on short notice and rescheduling.

If the physician is called away suddenly, perhaps to the emergency or delivery room, first, try to contact clients who may not have left for the office yet. If the reason for the visit is fairly urgent, refer the client to another physician—the group's clinic, if there is one, or a walk-in clinic. Reschedule the rest as soon as conveniently possible. When you call clients, explain the physician's absence (in general terms) so that they realize that the situation is beyond anyone's control. Most clients are good-natured about the inconvenience. Offer the same explanation to clients already in the office, apologize, and reschedule their appointments. Inevitably you will not reach all the clients. All you can do is apologize when they arrive and reschedule. Do not leave a message at a client's workplace unless you have permission to do so.

❽ SCHEDULING VARIATIONS

New Clients

Ask new clients to come 15 to 20 minutes before they see the provider to fill out a questionnaire or health history sheet, which gives the physician important information. (See Figure 9.9.) The physician or other health professional should carefully review the history sheet with the client to ensure that the information is complete and accurate. Some offices have the AHP fill the form out online, while interviewing the client. Others scan the completed form and add it to the client's EMR. Clients may leave a question unanswered if they do not understand it, or they may give an incomplete answer. For example, a client may answer the question, "Have you had any previous surgery?" with a simple "Yes." A review can elicit more useful information. Obtain demographic information, add the client to your computer records, and start a chart. If you do not have the client's medical records, ask him to sign a release so you can get them from his former doctor. It is important for the doctor to have this information to ensure continuity of care.

For some providers, the first appointment is long because the provider needs to take a complete history and discuss diagnosis and treatment plans. Some providers, such as an orthodontist or a chiropractor, may also need a long second appointment because they review X-rays and other data gathered from the initial examination to construct a treatment plan and explain it to the client on the second visit.

Some practices have a sheet or booklet containing information about the practice, such as the doctor's office hours, policies, charges for uninsured services, the doctor's on-call schedule, and where to go or call in an emergency. If your office does not have such a booklet, consider creating one. It prevents confusion, saves everyone time in the long run, and helps the client feel comfortable. Some practices call clients the day before the appointment and remind them to bring any medications they are taking. If clients have difficulty communicating, perhaps because of language difficulties or cognitive problems, ask that someone who can provide information accompany them.

Appointments for Clients' Forms

In any practice, there will be forms for the doctor to fill out: private insurance forms, sick notes, back to work/school notes, workers' compensation (WSIB) forms, forms for placement in long-term care facilities, home care forms, and physical examination forms for work, school, summer camp, and so on. Most forms require the doctor to examine the client, either partially or completely. Filling out these forms can be time consuming and frustrating for the doctor. Rarely will the doctor have time to fill them out on the spot—many clients can't understand this. Explain that the doctor will complete the form as soon as possible, and give a time frame. "May I tell Dr. Amiri that you will be in Thursday afternoon to pick up the completed form?"

Most practices charge to prepare such forms and notes. Post a sign in the reception area listing the cost of all such services. See Chapter 12 for a discussion on collecting payments.

Dr. D. Thompson

Family Medicine
Medical History

Client's Name:

Height   Weight: Date of Birth: Today's Date:

Medication Allergies:

Please List:

Present Medications	**Medical Problems** (e.g., diabetes, hypertension, etc.)	**Previous Surgeries**
1.	1.	1.
2.	2.	2.
3.	3.	3.
4.	4.	4.

Do you use tobacco products?   YES   NO   Amt:

Do you drink alcohol?   YES   NO   Amt:

Are you pregnant?   YES   NO

Marital Status: Single   Married   Divorced   Separated   Widowed

Number of children?   Occupation:

Family History

High Blood Pressure	YES	NO	Cancer	YES	NO
Heart Disease	YES	NO	Skin Rash	YES	NO
Vision/Eye Problems	YES	NO	Hearing Loss	YES	NO
Migraine Headaches	YES	NO	Irregular Heart Beat	YES	NO
Epilepsy	YES	NO	Shortness of Breath	YES	NO
Dizziness	YES	NO	Wheezing	YES	NO
Blood Clots in Legs	YES	NO	Pneumonia	YES	NO
Tuberculosis	YES	NO	Stroke	YES	NO
Heart Attack	YES	NO	Swelling of		
Diabetes	YES	NO	Feet or Ankles	YES	NO
Weight Loss	YES	NO	Gout	YES	NO
Blood in Stool	YES	NO	Thyroid Disease	YES	NO
Vomiting of Blood	YES	NO	Blood in Urine	YES	NO
Kidney Stones	YES	NO	Depression	YES	NO
Numbness	YES	NO	AIDS	YES	NO
Anxiety	YES	NO	Arthritis	YES	NO
Bleeding Disorder	YES	NO			

Figure 9.9 A health questionnaire

Courtesy of Dr. D.J. Thompson

Appointments for Drug Representatives

Drug reps are discussed in Chapter 8. If the doctor sets aside time to meet with drug reps, remember to slot it in when pre-editing. If you do not know a drug rep, take her business card so that you can call to cancel if you have to.

House Calls

Many, but certainly not all family doctors will make house calls when they consider it necessary, perhaps when a client with limited mobility or a client recovering from an accident or illness cannot leave home. However, most other clients who want the doctor to come to their home are asked to go to the Emergency Department, by ambulance if necessary. It is a reasonable assumption that ambulatory clients will come to the office unless their complaints are fairly serious. The doctor can assess the client more efficiently and effectively with access to a hospital's equipment and diagnostic services.

If a client requests a house call, gather all relevant information about the client's presenting problem, and check with the doctor before scheduling a house call. If the doctor agrees to see the client at home, clearly write down the client's name, address, phone number, and, if possible, directions to the house. Give the client an approximate time when the doctor will come. If the client is immobile, request that someone be at the house to let the doctor in. It is often best for the doctor to have another person in the house for legal reasons. One doctor made house calls to an older client who began giving him gifts and behaving in a suggestive manner. When this pattern became clear to him, he asked that someone be present for all visits. The doctor may want a printout of the client's health profile and a record of the client's latest medications and lab reports. In the manual setting, pull the client's chart. The doctor may want to review the client's medical history or take the chart along. Remember to note all house calls on the physician's electronic scheduler.

❾ APPOINTMENTS WITH OTHER PROVIDERS

Appointments with Specialists

A family doctor usually refers a client to a consultant for a more thorough investigation into a health problem that requires specialized, detailed attention. Appointments with specialists are likely to last from half an hour to an hour. Specialists therefore see fewer clients in a day than do family physicians. You will often make the appointment with the specialist. As noted in Chapter 8, most consult requests are faxed to the specialist; they will schedule the appointment and fax the information back to you. You will then have to contact the client. This may take up to a day. If the appointment date/time is unsuitable for the client, they can call the specialist's office and rebook. Alternatively, you could ask the client if there is a specific day they are unavailable and note that on the consult request prior to faxing. Given the long waits for appointments with specialists, most clients have enough time to shift their schedule. Across Canada, waits to see consultants average four to six months. Specialists triage, and so if the client's needs are urgent, clearly tell the specialist's office. If an early appointment is not available, you can ask that the client be added to a wait list in case of cancellations.

Over the telephone, give basic information (or fax the information). If you have a secure internet connection, you can send the information electronically:

- The client's name
- Telephone number
- Address
- Diagnosis

As well, you may fax or mail other medical information:

- Consultation request form letter
- Relevant previous test results
- Tests the family doctor has ordered in preparation for the consultation
- Relevant history

Make sure that the information reaches the specialist's office before the appointment. Add the specialist's name to any test requisitions so that the laboratory will send the specialist a copy of the test results. Call the specialist's office to ensure that the results have been received. Advise the client of anything else she should bring with her, such as medications or X-rays. Ensure that the client has the specialist's phone number and directions to the office.

Because specialist appointments may be made weeks or months in advance, it is easy for clients to forget. Given the long waiting periods, this is a wasted opportunity, as well as a loss of revenue for the provider. Some specialists' offices call the client the day before the appointment. Some family doctors' offices will do this instead. With computerized appointment scheduling, you can enter a reminder to yourself to call the client. The note will automatically appear on your screen on the appropriate day. If for any reason the client cannot keep the appointment, make sure she calls the specialist in advance. When you schedule the appointment, ask about charges for missed appointments. If the specialist has such a policy, you must notify the client in advance.

If you work for a specialist, notify the family doctor if a client cancels an appointment or fails to show up. The family doctor's AHP should note this on the client's chart and let the doctor know. The family doctor can then investigate the reason and will not be awaiting a letter from the consultant.

Scheduling Appointments for Tests

Physicians routinely order procedures or laboratory tests for clients. All tests require a requisition, as discussed in Chapter 6.

Blood Work   Routine blood work does not usually require an appointment with the lab. However, the client may need directions to the laboratory and the hours of operation. The client may have a choice of laboratories, which may be in-hospital or private facilities. If your office is in a medical building, you may have a laboratory on site (sometimes called a satellite lab). Provincial and territorial insurance covers the cost of most tests at any lab. The client can choose whichever is more convenient. You can give the requisition to the client, fax it, or send it electronically to the lab. Sending the requisition reduces the chance of the client misplacing it.

Diagnostic Tests Diagnostic tests are more likely to require appointment times, and some require special preparation. (See Chapter 6.) Before scheduling the appointment, ask the client for a range of convenient days and times. The exception is for such tests as MRIs, which, in some parts of the country, currently have waiting periods of up six months for non-urgent cases. In this case, take whatever appointment you are offered. Once the appointment is made, give the client written verification of the date and time. Send or fax the requisition to the appropriate facility.

Scheduling Clients for Surgery

A client who is scheduled for surgery has already been to see a specialist to determine the nature of the surgery required. The surgeon's AHP will book the procedure with the appropriate facility. The surgeon's office may notify the client of the date or may notify the family doctor's office, in which case you would relay the information to the client. Often this done by fax. You will also provide them with details about their admission. Depending on the procedure, the client may be booked for day surgery (in and out the same day) or as an inpatient. Most often inpatients are asked to come to the hospital the morning of the surgery and are admitted at that time. Preoperative preparations are completed in a pre-admit clinic, then the client goes to surgery, and then postoperatively to a patient care unit.

Some basic information is needed in scheduling surgery:

- The client's name
- Address
- Phone number
- Date of birth
- Provincial/territorial health plan number
- Private insurance coverage, if any
- Type of accommodation requested if an overnight stay is required (standard/ward, semi-private, private room)
- Referring physician's name
- Surgeon's name
- Provisional diagnosis
- Name of the procedure (e.g., hysterectomy, left total hip replacement, laparoscopy)

A client may have a **provisional diagnosis** of an ovarian cyst and be booked for a laparoscopy. The procedure may reveal that she has an ectopic pregnancy. The postoperative diagnosis then would be an ectopic pregnancy.

provisional diagnosis a tentative diagnosis made before a procedure is done, which may be confirmed or changed by findings.

You may need to book an appointment for a client to come in to the family physician's office for a preoperative assessment. In some provinces and territories, if the client has had an annual physical within a certain number of days prior to the surgery, he will not have to have a preop assessment repeated. Clients having a major operation must have a complete assessment to provide current information about their medical conditions and to determine if they are a good surgical candidate. Most hospitals have a preop teaching program, usually outpatient, for surgical clients. The client will have to make an appointment at the hospital to have orientation, fill out some preliminary forms, and be told what to expect before and after the operation.

⑩ SCHEDULING IN THE DENTAL OFFICE

Much of what is discussed in this chapter applies to a number of providers, including dentists—from greeting the client in a positive, pleasant, and proper manner, to the use of a computerized scheduling system. There are some differences that are worth noting.

In the dental environment, units of time are used to refer to basic time segments. A unit of time can be 10 or 15 minutes, according to the dentist's protocol. Using 10 minutes as a unit of time offers more flexibility in scheduling and affords tighter control of scheduling. Clients are scheduled according to the length of the procedure. These times are average allotments, general in nature, and based on the dentist's or the hygienist's experience. A dental office—even with one dentist—can be a scheduling challenge! One dentist may have as many as three or four hygienists and two or three dental assistants (some of whom have extended responsibilities). Thus, scheduling involves the use of several columns in the electronic scheduler.

Some practices have production goals; this maximizes both chair time and use of the professional staff. Goals are best accomplished in a cooperative environment wherein each staff member has clear responsibilities. At the heart of success are organized and efficient scheduling techniques. The use of templates is most helpful, particularly with more complex procedures, such as crowns, bridge preparation, impacted molars, and some appointments involving root canals. (Root canals are often done in steps, some more lengthy than others.)

Usually, the dentist has two or three clients in chairs at the same time. He may be seeing John to complete a filling. He freezes John's tooth and then has to wait three to four minutes for the freezing to take effect. During that time, the dentist can see another client. For example, Assyria in the next operatory has had her teeth cleaned by a hygienist. The dentist will check her teeth then move back to John and proceed with filling the tooth.

In dentistry, clients usually require a series of appointments. Consider Daniel who has come in for an annual examination. The dentist has determined that Daniel has five cavities and needs one root canal and a crown. It is best to try scheduling all of Daniel's appointments at one time. You will need to know how many appointments are needed and the time units for each appointment. You will also need to be aware of any time required between appointments. This includes time for lab work, if indicated, or scheduling particulars for a root canal (e.g., if the tooth is infected, the dentist may put a medication into the root cavity to kill the bacteria and then wait until it has cleared to proceed). This approach also ensures that the client is available to have the work completed within a reasonable time frame.

Scheduling the hygienist's time should be discussed with her, to determine average times needed for her to carry out her responsibilities: everything from a general examination and taking X-rays to cleaning teeth and doing fluoride treatments.

As with a medical practice, new clients are asked to come in early to complete a history form. This history is reviewed annually. A good time is when clients are recalled for routine cleaning and checkups. Recall lists are computer generated, and calling clients is part of the daily routine. As well, dental offices frequently call clients a day ahead to remind them of their appointments. A client who forgets his appointment is lost revenue for the practice. With effective scheduling so dependent on teamwork, a missed appointment can also cause a ripple effect for other dental professionals.

The general principles of scheduling apply to the dental office. Children appear to be best treated in the morning, especially young children. As the day progresses, small children become tired, and are more out of sorts when they arrive at the office. At the best of times, the dental office is not a child's favourite place to be. Catch-up slots are also used in the dental office, but specifically for emergencies—clients in acute pain, or someone who falls and fractures a tooth, for example.

Most dental offices have policies and guidelines in place, and run relatively smoothly. Fitting in and becoming familiar with the scheduling system may take time. Supportive staff and an optimistic attitude will contribute to a successful transition.

Future Trends

In an attempt to reduce the stress on emergency rooms, an initiative called advanced access booking, same-day booking, or open access booking has been introduced in some provinces. The project was initially introduced in Cape Breton Island. The goal is to shift physicians to this booking concept. First the office must clear the backlog of pre-booked appointments. Much of the responsibility for the success of the method rests with the administrative health professional, and she must be committed to making the concept work. Results in the Cape Breton study showed a higher level of patient/client satisfaction, fewer visits to the ER, a higher level of satisfaction for the doctor and administrative staff, and improved continuity of care.

Nurse practitioner–led clinics are appearing in several jurisdictions. These alleviate the pressure on physicians and provide more people with access to primary care. These clinics are run collaboratively with nurse practitioners, registered and practical nurses, family doctors, and other members of the health-care team. A variety of scheduling models may be used, from walk-in to scheduled appointments.

Medical software is constantly changing, with more options available that are efficient and user friendly. Keep current with the latest technology. Almost all vendors conduct inservice seminars on updates and changes to their software system. Try to embrace these changes, as frustrating as they may be. The continual advances are a prime example of "if you don't use it, you lose it." The more informed you are with your software, the easier all aspects of running your office will be. Most groups have what they call "super-users" who act as resources when you need help/have questions. A couple of systems do automated forms processing, which dramatically cuts down on the time it takes an AHP to scan and file reports. It automatically identifies the client to whom a scanned or faxed document belongs, files the document in the client's record, and generates the appropriate follow-up tasks required.

Some jurisdictions are considering implementing a plan to track how long it takes clients to see their family doctors. Similar to posting the wait times that have been established for hospitals, this is seen as a movement to bring family doctors under a single quality movement process and a method of improving primary care access. It will involve teamwork on the part of the AHP and the physician—clearing the backlog of clients and keeping more daily time slots free for SDA (same-day appointments). The AHP will have to take accurate information from the client to determine how much time they need with the doctor.

>

The doctor must be on time and keep to the schedule. This initiative, it is thought, will keep more individuals out of hospital.

Another emerging technology is scheduling software connected to a kiosk located in the reception area. P&P Data Systems is one of the first companies to implement this technology. Similar to pre-boarding kiosks in large airports, clients can sign themselves in with a swipe of their health card. The information is transmitted to your computer, updating the visit status of the client, including verification of arrival, check-in, and check-out. The software also offers options of sending visit reminders and a place for clients' comments. Options at some kiosks include instructions in up to six languages.

SUMMARY

1. Scheduling appointments is one of the AHP's main responsibilities and takes knowledge, judgment, and people skills.

2. Computerized scheduling is the norm. It allows direct links with billing and is more flexible. Although the doctor can view the day's schedule on his desktop or portable device, some practices still use a printed day sheet. This is an asset if the computer system isn't working—something that happens more frequently than most health professionals would like.

3. Pre-edit the physician's electronic scheduler to block off prior commitments and time off.

4. Keep all appointment schedulers away from public view and keep the information they contain confidential. The information on an appointment schedule should be kept for at least 10 years. Electronic scheduling files must be appropriately stored.

5. Ambulatory care and urgent-care clinics usually have open scheduling within fixed hours. Specialists may prefer affinity booking—grouping appointments for similar purposes—and family doctors may blend affinity with random scheduling. Double scheduling is used to cope with a busy day; it assumes that some clients will take less of the doctor's time. Stream scheduling, in which each client is assigned a specific, unique time slot, is the most common. Each method has advantages and disadvantages. You may be able to modify your office's scheduling method to enhance efficiency.

6. The time required for an appointment depends on the type of practice, the provider's style, and the reason for the visit. Typically, a minor assessment may take 5 to 7 minutes, an intermediate assessment, 10 to 15 minutes, and a complete assessment or annual health exam, 20 to 40 minutes or longer. You need to ask the reason for the visit to book appropriately.

7. Triage is an important skill. It lets someone with an urgent problem see the doctor out of turn. On the phone, direct acute emergencies to the Emergency Department. If in any doubt, consult the doctor or nurse.

8. If a client's concern is not urgent, stick to your scheduling policy. Be firm but tactful, and offer alternatives. Unless concerns are urgent, do not allow clients to bring extra family members to be seen or to discuss additional problems.

9. Scheduling catch-up time helps you deal with unpredictable events. If the physician is called away, try to contact clients to cancel appointments. Apologize and reschedule.

10. Ask new clients to come in early to fill out a health questionnaire. Consider creating a sheet or booklet outlining office hours and policies.

11. In scheduling specialist appointments and diagnostic tests, first find out when the client is available. Make sure the specialist gets all necessary information and that the client knows the date, location, and what to bring. In scheduling surgery, you may need to schedule a preop assessment.

12. Scheduling clients in the dental office uses time measurements called units of time. Clients often require several visits, which are best booked together to ensure timely completion of the proposed treatment regime. Sometimes setting up appointments requires you to coordinate the client's treatments with other members of the dental team.

Key Terms

affinity (cluster, categorization, or analogous) scheduling 271
combination scheduling or blended scheduling 272

double scheduling or double-column booking 273
provisional diagnosis 285

stream or fixed-interval scheduling 274
wave scheduling 271

Review Questions

1. What steps can you take to ensure that the appointment book remains confidential?
2. What is affinity scheduling, and how does it relate to stream scheduling?
3. What is meant by double scheduling?
4. List the advantages of using catch-up or buffer zones in the daily schedule.
5. How should you handle a client who walks into the office wanting to see the physician immediately?
6. What information should you take when scheduling an appointment?
7. What information should you take when scheduling a house call?
8. What administrative steps do you take when a new client first arrives in the office?
9. Discuss the importance of reviewing a health history with a new client.
10. What information is necessary when scheduling a diagnostic test, such as a mammogram?

Application Exercises

1. Fill out the health history questionnaire in Figure 9.9. Review it with a peer. Were there any areas of the questionnaire that you did not complete in enough detail? Did you note allergies? If you are uncomfortable with revealing your own medical history, answer in the role of a fictitious client.

2. **a.** Design an appointment book page on your computer, or choose a design from a local stationery store, suitable for the office of a primary care physician.

   b. Pre-edit the next week, using the following information:

   i. Dr. Schumacher does hospital rounds from 8:30 a.m. to 9:30 a.m. every day.

   ii. He likes to do physical examinations in the morning on Tuesdays and Thursdays, but no more than two per day.

iii. On Thursday, he has a client-care conference 11:00–11:45 a.m. in his office.

iv. He must be out of the office by 5:00 p.m. on Thursday for another meeting.

v. He is seeing a drug rep from 10:00–10:15 a.m. on Friday.

c. Book the following appointments. Assume that Dr. Schumacher's style is to take an average length of time with clients or just a little longer. For each client, consider

■ what level of assessment is needed (minor, intermediate, major),

■ how long an appointment to book, and

■ the best time to book it.

i. Mr. Reynolds wants to have his annual physical examination. H: 416-432-4444; email: reynolds@sunshine.on.ca. Retired. At home most of the time.

ii. Donna Kim needs an appointment for her first prenatal visit. W: 416-332-3432, H: 416-343-3333. She works full days and has three other children.

iii. Elaine Yang is due for her allergy shot. She does not have to see Dr. Schumacher. She is at school full time. H: 416-332-3332.

iv. Maya Appleton has had a cold and sore throat for three days. She has experienced a pain in her left ear for the last 24 hours. She is 13 years old. H: 416-222-2222.

v. Jessica Zehr has a rash on her left forearm. Homemaker. H: 416-333-2222.

vi. Mihail Reznikoff complains of diarrhea and abdominal cramps that he has had for 24 hours. H: 416-333-3333, W: 416-333-2222.

vii. Elisabeth Walker, who is a diabetic, has been having trouble with regulation of her blood sugar level. She states she has been hypoglycemic twice in the past three days. She also has a sore on her left foot.

viii. Rachel Desmond is planning to become pregnant. She is coming in for advice and genetic counselling. She prefers Thursday.

ix. Marnie McLaughlin needs an appointment for a well-baby exam for Karen, who is 3 months old. H: 416-222-5555. Marnie is on maternity leave. Wednesdays work best, she says.

x. Emily Lawton is coming in for a physical examination. She is 88 years old. H: 416-111-2222.

xi. Mr. Anatoly wants an appointment. His left knee is swollen, and he is having difficulty walking. H: 416-234-3333, W: 416-943-9969. Thursdays are good.

xii. Mrs. Hazel calls and wants an immediate renewal for her Valium. H: 416-323-4444 W: 416-321-0222.

xiii. Cathy Evans needs an appointment to discuss placing her aged mother in a nursing home. Any day is good.

xiv. Jeremy Karsch wants an appointment for what he thinks is a recurrence of his bronchitis. email: jhewitt.@sympatico.ca.

xv. Mario Liotta wants to see the doctor. He is complaining of redness and swelling in his left leg. H: 416-432-3233.

xvi. Phil Ioannou needs an allergy shot. H: 416-111-2441.

xvii. Georgina Gould wants an appointment for a gynecological examination, Pap smear, and insertion of an intrauterine contraceptive device (IUCD). Any day but Mon./Tues. works for her. H: 416-426-9214.

xviii. Gary Janacek was asked to come in today for a blood pressure check. H: 416-421-6666.

xix. Betty Nguyen calls with vague symptoms of fatigue. H: 416-944-2111. Wants Tues. appt.

xx. Shaundra Ladouceur comes in complaining of a plantar wart (a wart on the sole of the foot). H: 416-111-9472. Any day is OK.

d. In groups of three to four, compare your appointment books. Do your partners see any problems with your scheduling? In particular, note any differences in how long an appointment each of you assigned to a given client. Was this because you came to different conclusions about what level of assessment was needed? Decide as a group which level is accurate. Adjust your schedule to solve any problems pointed out by your partners.

3. In small groups research the educational requirements, role function, and responsibilities of a dental hygienist, a treatment coordinator, and a dental assistant. Consider contacting a dental office and interviewing these health professionals, with each group member contacting a different office. Prepare three or four questions for each professional. For example, ask what their specific responsibilities are. For professionals treating clients independent of the dentist, ask how long they like the client to be scheduled for each procedure. Ask the administrative assistant to briefly describe her role. Discuss scheduling guidelines. Prepare a summary of your findings for comparison.

4. Dr. Hanoi has just opened a medical practice. He is part of a primary care reform group who rosters clients. He instructs you to begin scheduling appointments so he can begin his "interview and screening" procedures. Dr. Hanoi tells you to find out a little about the person before you schedule an appointment. He gives you criteria of people he is not prepared to interview: those over 40, individuals with chronic health problems, people on WSIB (WCB) claims, or those on social assistance. You feel very uncomfortable about this process, and you are unsure you want to be a part of this. In small groups discuss the ethical and moral implications of this policy. Is the doctor upholding his code of ethics? Are his actions violating the rights of health consumers? Are his actions morally or legally right or wrong? Try to find out whether the College of Physicians and Surgeons in your jurisdiction has guidelines about this type of action. Are you obliged to comply with his wishes? What courses of action do you have?

Websites of Interest

Principles of Confidentiality
http://www.gp-training.net/training/communication_skills/consultation/confidentiality.htm
This website outlines principles and techniques of patient confidentiality.

C.A.S.A. Vision Inc.
www.casa-vision.com/article.asp?articleid=55
This site offers scheduling tips for physicians and medical office staff.

Physician's News Digest: Develop a triage system in your office
www.physiciansnews.com/business/898anwar.html

KevinMD.com
http://www.kevinmd.com/blog/2010/04/patient-appointment-scheduling-flexibility.html
Discussion on the need for flexibility in appointment scheduling

Chapter 10
Health-Care Plans

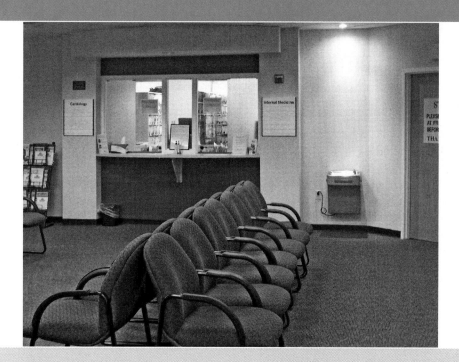

Learning Objectives

On completing this chapter, you will be able to:

1. Explain what is meant by "medically necessary."
2. List common insured and uninsured health services.
3. Discuss some of the additional health benefits covered by some provincial/territorial health-care plans.
4. Explain the criteria used to determine the value of an insured service.
5. Outline the eligibility criteria for provincial/territorial health-care coverage.
6. Discuss the format, purpose, and use of health cards in Canada.
7. Detail the process of applying for health insurance.
8. Discuss the three-month wait for health-care coverage and give exceptions.
9. Explain how health coverage works for individuals travelling within Canada and outside Canada.
10. Explore the billing implications of the reciprocal agreement.
11. Identify health-care services covered by private insurance companies in Canada.

This chapter expands on the information in Chapter 4, giving more detail about the structure of territorial and provincial health-care plans and the system of remunerating physicians. It will give you the background knowledge you need for Chapter 11, Preparing for the Billing Process, and Chapter 12, Billing.

FEE-FOR-SERVICE REMUNERATION

As discussed in Chapter 4, physicians in Canada are remunerated in a number of ways but primarily by provincial and territorial health-care plans through a payment system (**provincial or territorial billing**) referred to as fee-for-service; that is, the physician is paid a set fee for each insured service provided to an insured client. For example, Dr. Tse sees 25 clients on Monday. His health office professional submits claims to the provincial health plan for each insured encounter. How much he is paid for each service will depend on the service and the criteria set out in his province's fee schedule.

> **provincial or territorial billing** the process whereby a health-care provider submits a claim to a province or territory for insured health services rendered.

Chapter 4 lists the types of eligible providers (EPs) who can bill provincial or territorial health-care plans on a fee-for-service basis. To be eligible to submit claims, providers must be licensed by, and in good standing with, their professional colleges and be registered with their province or territory. Provinces and territories issue billing numbers to providers, either individual providers or groups, which must be cited on all submitted claims. In some provinces, a provider cannot bill under another provider's number. Other provinces allow a locum to bill under the regular doctor's number. The provider whose number appears on the claim assumes responsibility for that claim.

❶❷ INSURED AND UNINSURED SERVICES

The Ministry of Health in your province or territory (or a division of the Ministry) is essentially the insurance company that is responsible for claims assessment and payment. Health-care plans pay only **insured health-care services**—normally those they also define as *medically necessary*. Both the list of services considered medically necessary and the fees for these services are negotiated by the Ministry and representatives from provincial or territorial medical associations. Services covered under workers' compensation or certain other federal legislation are excluded, although some provinces act as payment agencies for workers' compensation claims (discussed later in this chapter). For the specific services insured in your province or territory, see the relevant website listed at the end of this chapter. Lists of services are updated annually.

> **insured health-care services** medically necessary hospital, physician, and surgical-dental services provided to insured persons.

The *Canada Health Act* defines *physician services* as "medically required services rendered by medical practitioners." A service includes the physician's time and expertise. The physician must maintain appropriate and detailed records of every service rendered, unless otherwise noted.

Services considered *assessments* generally include direct physician–client contact. For example, Darlene came into Dr. Atkins' office for a blood pressure checkup. The nurse took Darlene's blood pressure and recorded the results. If Darlene then left without seeing the doctor, Dr. Atkins could not legally claim that visit as an assessment because he did not see Darlene. In some provinces, the blood pressure checkup could be billed, but not as a physician encounter. The physician must be present, either directly supervising or available, and the procedure must be appropriately documented with a record of who performed it. If Dr. Atkins came into the examination room and discussed

Darlene's blood pressure with her, even briefly, he could submit a claim for the related assessment.

Naturally, the extent of the assessment will vary with each encounter. Normally, an assessment requires that the doctor examine the client and/or take a history, make a diagnosis, implement appropriate treatment (including giving advice and support and/ or counselling), and make an appropriate record. (See Chapter 13.) It may or may not include a procedure, such as an injection.

The term **medically necessary**[1] has not been formally defined by the *Canada Health Act*. Though the parameters of "medical necessity" are constantly debated, the Canadian Medical Association defines a medically necessary service as "one that a qualified physician determines is required to assess, prevent, treat, rehabilitate, or palliate a given health concern or problem." Services considered medically necessary in a given province or territory at a given time may not be considered so in another province or territory or at another time.

For example, if Jacob went to the doctor with a sore throat, he would be examined and perhaps have a swab taken. The doctor might choose to put Jacob on an antibiotic and/or give him advice on how to relieve the pain. This whole process would be considered a *service* and the visit by the client an *encounter*. (See Chapter 4.) The assessment, diagnosis, and treatment, including any tests and/or follow-up, would be covered because they are considered medically necessary.

If Jacob went to see the doctor to get a note to return to school after being absent, the visit or encounter would *not* be considered medically necessary and would therefore not be insured. Clients can expect insurance coverage only for services deemed medically necessary as outlined in the provincial or territorial fee schedule.

Another common insured physician service is called a *consultation*. This service in most provinces and territories is provided by a specialist (also called a consultant) only upon written request from a referring physician, usually the family doctor. This occurs when the referring doctor feels that he does not have the expertise to deal with a particular health problem. Levels of consultations will be discussed in Chapter 11.

Though each province and territory has some latitude in deciding what services to insure, the *Canada Health Act* sets out categories of services that must be covered, specifically *medically necessary* physician, hospital, and surgical-dental services (the latter includes only those that must be performed in a hospital). Insured health services include physician services, including home and hospital visits, and inpatient services provided in an *approved* hospital facility.

Insured services are also referred to as regulated services. Ministries review services regularly to consider whether they should continue to be insured and whether the fee should be adjusted. A service that is no longer insured is removed from the fee schedule, or **deregulated**. For example, a few years ago routine infant circumcision was removed from the Ontario fee schedule because it is not considered medically necessary.

Hospitals and doctors also provide services that are not defined as medically necessary and are not covered by provincial or territorial insurance. These services, whether performed in a hospital, clinic, or physician's office, must be paid for by the client or by private insurance.

---

[1] Library of Parliament, Parliamentary Information and Research Branch, The Canada Health Act: Overview and Options (94-4E). www.parl.gc.ca/information/library/prbpubs/944-e.htm.

Long-Term Care Facilities/Residential Care Facilities

All jurisdictions offer long-term care (LTC) facilities to their residents. A LTC facility provides 24/7 nursing care and supervision as required to individuals unable to remain in their homes because of illness or disability. All provinces and territories have residency criteria that must be met—Alberta with the most detailed. All jurisdictions subsidize the cost of the facility based on an income/assets analysis. There are differences, for example, Ontario and BC consider only annual income (not assets) when a person applies for a subsidy. New Brunswick considers both assets and annual income. LTC is fully subsidized in Nunavut. In most jurisdictions, if an individual is eligible for a subsidy it is for basic accommodation only—if their entire income goes towards their basic accommodation, the person must be left with a nominal amount of money to cover the cost of personal and other items (e.g., television, telephone, and sundries).

Hospital Services

Insured hospital services include medically necessary services to inpatients and outpatients.

Insured inpatient services include

- standard ward accommodation and preferred accommodation, if medically required;
- meals;
- nursing services (including private nursing care, if deemed medically required and ordered by the physician, or as determined by the nursing staff for the client's benefit);
- drugs and related preparations when administered in the hospital;
- use of an operating room, delivery room, or case room and anaesthetic facilities;
- laboratory, radiological, and other diagnostic services, along with the necessary interpretations;
- use of other therapies, such as physiotherapy, occupational therapy, speech therapy, and audiology;
- medical and surgical equipment and supplies; and
- services provided by persons who receive remuneration from the hospital.

Insured outpatient services vary across provinces and territories but typically include

- laboratory, radiological, and diagnostic procedures;
- physiotherapy, speech therapy, occupational therapy, diet counselling services (if considered medically necessary);
- renal dialysis (in hospital and at home, including equipment);
- medications for clients with specific conditions, such as cystic fibrosis; and
- administration of rabies vaccine.

Hospitals also offer services that are not insured. These also vary by jurisdiction but typically include

- private or semiprivate accommodation (many Canadians have private insurance to cover the additional cost);
- private duty nurses, unless ordered by the physician;
- grooming services, such as a pedicure or a haircut;
- telephone and television;
- accommodation for cosmetic surgery (not deemed medically necessary); and
- medications to take home (may be some exceptions).

To contain costs, some facilities are asking clients to bring personal items they might expect to be provided, such as tissues and soap. On some obstetrical units, new mothers are asked to bring diapers, breast pads, and sanitary supplies.

Physician Services

The following services are insured across the country:

- Physical examinations, when done to investigate symptoms or for disease prevention/screening (with some conditions—not all provinces cover annual preventative general assessments)
- Home visits and physician visits to other health facilities (with some conditions)
- Major and minor surgeries
- Obstetrical services
- Complaint-driven office visits

Provinces and territories may cover other services, but Table 10.1 lists some common services that are not usually covered. One major variation is the handling of physical assessments of well adults. Ontario, for example, insures one annual physical examination as a screening and preventive measure. Some provinces do not cover such examinations.

You need to be aware of which services are not covered in your area. These services may be covered by private insurance or may be paid for by the client. (As discussed later, clients must be notified in advance of charges.) Physicians may charge clients directly for services not covered under their provincial/territorial health insurance plans. (This is not to be confused with illegal user fees for insured services.) How much the physician is allowed to charge varies with the province or territory and the situation, but it is usually based on the nature and complexity of the service (and amount of the physician's time) and the qualifications of the provider. For example, a specialist may charge more than a family doctor would. The physician may also charge associated costs (plus taxes where applicable) and a reasonable mark-up to cover administrative costs incurred as a result of the service. Some provincial and territorial medical associations have recommended fees for uninsured services, which may often be found on the association's website.

Procedures for collecting fees from third parties and directly from clients are discussed in Chapter 12. Clients may also pay for other types of services and facilities, such as home care, which may be partially covered by a provincial/territorial plan. Clients may also pay for enhanced services. An example is cataract surgery at a private facility. The surgery itself is covered by the provincial/territorial health plan, but the client may purchase a superior lens and pay for additional levels of postoperative care. Some provinces allow payment for an MRI. The rationale is that although an MRI is deemed medically necessary within a

Table 10.1 Services That Are Usually Uninsured

- Back-to-school/work notes/certificates

- Physical examinations requested by a third party (e.g., for school, camp, driver's licence) or in preparation for travel
- Completion of insurance/disability forms
- Transfer of files when a client changes physicians (includes the doctor's time as well as photocopying, faxing, or mailing costs)
- Legal proceedings

- Telephone advice/consultations (with certain exceptions, such as the supervision of ongoing medication)
- Charges for long-distance calls related to the client's treatment
- Assessment relating to fitness to continue employment

- Missed appointments/procedures
- Renewal of prescriptions when the client does not see the physician
- Any duplication of service that is contrary to the guidelines outlined in the fee schedule

- Devices, such as an intrauterine contraceptive device (IUCD)
- The newer types of removable fibreglass cast (Standard plaster casts are covered; the more expensive, light-weight, waterproof fibreglass casts are considered a convenience, not a medical necessity.)

- Preparation or provision of a drug, an antigen, or an antiserum used for treatment that is not used to facilitate a procedure (hepatitis B vaccines, WinRho for RH-negative mothers)
- Allergy treatments (Generally, the doctor's or nurse's service is covered, but the serum is not.)

- Drugs used in infertility treatments
- In most cases, psychoanalysis

- Circumcision of male newborns (unless deemed medically necessary)
- Reversal of vasectomies

- Reversal of tubal ligations

- Gastric stapling or gastric bypass (covered in some provinces and territories depending on the client's condition)
- Removal of superficial veins for cosmetic purposes
- Removal of warts other than plantar and venereal warts

- Immunizations not considered medically necessary (Criteria vary with jurisdiction and from time to time. Often, provinces cover immunizations to groups deemed at high risk. Where immunizations are not fully covered, usually the client must pay only for the serum.)
- In some provinces, interviews not considered medically necessary
- Alternative therapies, such as acupuncture, even if provided by a physician

"reasonable" time frame, an earlier MRI appointment can be considered an "enhanced" service, and therefore a facility can legally charge anyone who is willing to pay for one. A client would also have to pay for an MRI if the physician did not feel it was medically necessary.

❸ OTHER HEALTH BENEFITS

MOST PROVINCES AND TERRITORIES COVER A RANGE OF RELATED HEALTH SERVICES. Programs vary.

Travel Assistance

Canadians who must travel great distances for medical treatment are often compensated. For example, clients who live in designated areas of Northern Ontario are eligible for compensation from the Northern Health Travel Grant to offset some of the cost if they must travel more than a given distance to access a medical service. The grant pays a specified amount of money per kilometre travelled, after a deductible distance (e.g., 100 kilometres), but does not cover the costs of meals or accommodation. The client must go to the nearest provider who can render the required service and must have a letter from a doctor, dentist, optometrist, chiropractor, midwife, or nurse practitioner giving the reason for the referral. Newfoundland and Labrador has the Medical Transportation Assistance Program, which provides financial assistance for residents who incur substantial costs when travelling for insured medical services, such as cancer treatment or surgery. British Columbia has two such programs, the Medical Travel Assistance Programs for B.C. Residents and the Ministry of Health Travel Assistance Program.

If your area has such a grant program, make sure your clients know about it. A surprising number of people who could use the help do not know about it. Keep up to date on program criteria and eligibility, which often change.

Drug Benefit Plans

catastrophic drug   a catastrophic drug plan is a plan that would cover overriding drug costs causing impending financial hardship on individuals.

Currently there is no national plan to cover what is termed **catastrophic drug** costs (initially proposed by the Romanow Report). However, each province and territory has a drug benefit plan for seniors and other designated groups. Eligibility for such plans will vary, and criteria often change.

PharmaCare in British Columbia provides income-based financial support to eligible BC residents (which includes all residents registered with the Medical Services Plan) for a range of specified prescription medications and medical supplies. Fair PharmaCare is a specialty plan offering income-based benefits to families who need it the most. The coverage is more comprehensive than the PharmaCare program. Many families do not have a deductible under the Fair PharmaCare plan. Families who do have deductibles have the option of paying for those costs under a monthly deductible payment plan.

Manitoba also calls its drug benefit program Pharmacare (as does Nova Scotia); benefits are based on a family's income and the amount paid for eligible prescription drugs. Under Newfoundland and Labrador's Prescription Drug Program, a new program called the Access Plan also provides more comprehensive coverage to eligible low-income residents.

deductible   the portion of a benefit that a beneficiary must pay before receiving coverage.

The Ontario Drug Benefit (ODB) Plan covers, among other groups, seniors and residents of long-term care facilities. Ontario's Trillium Drug Program covers part of the cost of drugs for individuals not eligible for the ODB but who have high prescription drug costs in relation to their income. Some provinces and territories use annual **deductibles**. For example, if the cost of a family's drugs was $2000 and the deductible was $500, the family would pay the $500, and the province or territory would then pay the remaining $1500. Another method used by some provinces and territories is called a co-payment. This requires that the client pay a portion of the cost of each drug prescribed.

The Drug Benefit Formulary

Most provinces and territories have a formulary that lists selected prescription and non-prescription drugs covered by drug benefit plans. The formulary may sometimes include a variety of medical supplies and devices. Each province and territory has a committee that reviews new drugs on the formulary and recommends additions to and deletions from the formulary. Purdue Pharma is the drug company that made Oxycontin, a highly addictive but widely used painkiller (also called hillbilly heroin). In April 2012 the company stopped making Oxycontin and introduced OxyNEO, a supposedly less addictive replacement. Ontario, with other jurisdictions following, has delisted OxyNEO from its drug benefit plan.

If the physician feels the client should have a drug not on the formulary, she can seek approval for funding the drug for that client. This is called a restricted listing drug. The doctor must fill out a form requesting the drug for the client—sometimes called a limited use, or LU, form. There are other drugs not on the restricted-use list. For these the doctor must write a letter requesting the drug and/or submit another form. There are still more drugs that are entirely off limits to those on provincial/territorial drug plans; the only option for use of these would be the client paying for them. These are the newer, more expensive drugs. A doctor would seek use of a drug not on the formulary for a couple of reasons. The first is if the client is allergic to or otherwise cannot tolerate the available drug. The second is a situation wherein the client doesn't respond favourable to the available drug. For example, Sandra is on a hypoglycemic agent (from the formulary list), but it isn't controlling her blood sugar properly. The doctor feels that a newer drug on the LU list would be more therapeutic, so he requests permission to use that. If that drug fails to control Sandra's blood sugar levels properly, the doctor would then seek permission to use a drug that isn't on the LU list.

Clients sometimes wonder why the doctor does not prescribe specifically requested medications. Encourage them to ask the physician for clarification. You should be aware of clients who are on provincial/territorial drug benefit plans and of any special forms (such as for restricted listing drugs) the physician must fill out.

Physiotherapy

Coverage of physiotherapy varies across the country. Generally, physiotherapy services provided in a hospital are covered by provincial/territorial health insurance plans, whereas community-based services may or may not be. Most jurisdictions cover this service for outpatients in an approved clinic. In provinces and territories that cover physiotherapy, the client must be referred by a physician, and the service must be considered medically necessary.

Ambulance Services

Most provinces and territories completely or partially cover emergency ambulance services, whether ground or air, and ambulance transfers from one facility to another to obtain medical services. Services include medical and paramedical personnel deemed necessary on a particular trip. The client may have to pay part of the cost. This is called a co-payment. Some provinces and territories completely cover ambulance services for designated groups. In some jurisdictions, municipalities pay most of the cost of ambulances; some have banded together to jointly cover the cost.

Optometry

Many provinces and territories have reduced the optometry services they will insure. Across Canada, the majority of individuals from age 20 to 64 have no provincial or territorial coverage for eye examinations. In Ontario and British Columbia, individuals in the 20 to 64 age category are partially covered for eye exams if they have any selected medical conditions, such as diabetes, glaucoma, macular degeneration, or cataracts. In Alberta and Quebec, there is no coverage for this age group even if these conditions exist. People who want more frequent assessments must pay for them. New in some provinces and territories is the requirement that a person must pay for some minor eye assessments. For example, Katryna, who lives in Ontario, wakes up in the morning with conjunctivitis and makes an unexpected visit to an optometrist. The optometrist can charge up to $50 for that assessment. Some provinces, such as Alberta and Quebec, have had that policy in place for several years. BC covers medical services for minor eye irritations up to approximately $22. The provincial plan will not cover eye damage related to wearing contact lenses.

If you work for an optometrist or oculist and your region's health-care plan restricts eye examinations, you need to keep accurate records and notify clients when they are due for a routine assessment. If clients request assessments earlier than allowed, you have to let them know that they are responsible for payment. For example, suppose Ashley, who is 19 years old, had a complete oculo-visual assessment on July 15, 2008. Because she is going away for the summer, she wants to have her next checkup done in June 2009. It is your responsibility to explain that because it is less than 12 months later, she will not be covered. Her choices are to have the assessment in June and pay for it herself (considered an assessment requested for personal reasons) or to wait until she gets back. "Aw, come on," she may say, "why don't you just do the checkup in June and send the bill in July?" Altering data like that is illegal; if it were discovered, the plan would not pay the fee, and you could be charged with an offence. The same principle applies to any service with a time restriction, such as annual physical examinations.

❹ DETERMINING THE VALUE OF AN INSURED SERVICE

EACH INSURED SERVICE IS ASSIGNED A MONETARY VALUE, REFLECTED IN A SERVICE CODE, item code, or fee code (they all mean the same thing) that determines how much the provider can charge for the encounter. How this value is determined varies across the country. Most systems take into account the nature or complexity of the client's problem and the depth of the assessment and/or the age range of the client. Other elements (sometimes combined) considered may include

- the time the physician spends with the client,
- the client's age,
- any additional interventions rendered at the time of the service, and
- special circumstances, such as where and when the service is rendered.

Complexity of the Assessment

Generally, the time spent with a client depends on the complexity of the assessment. Many provinces and territories have two or three categories based on the complexity of the assessment and time spent with the physician. A visit of a type that usually requires minimal time with the doctor would be considered a minor assessment. In Ontario, a minor assessment usually includes a brief history and examination of the affected body part or region, a brief examination and history of a mental or emotional disorder, and brief advice or information regarding health maintenance, diagnosis, treatment, and/or prognosis. An intermediate assessment is more complex and requires a history of the presenting physical, mental, or emotional complaint and an inquiry about and examination of the affected body part or system to establish a diagnosis. The physician would receive a higher payment for a complete physical examination, either symptom driven or done for preventive assessment. In British Columbia, the categories are somewhat different: the category of partial or regional examination includes what would be called minor and intermediate assessments in Ontario. British Columbia has special categories for emergency care, which is divided into level I, II, and III assessments.

Time-Based Services

Fees for some services, such as counselling, surgery, and providing anaesthesia, are based, at least in part, on the physician's time. The physician is paid so much per unit of time (e.g., 15 or 30 minutes) spent rendering the service. Different jurisdictions calculate units slightly differently. Time-based payment may apply after an initial base fee. For example, suppose a surgeon is paid a set amount to remove an appendix. However, if the surgeon runs into complications and takes longer to complete the procedure, she could bill the province or territory for the extra time spent in the operating room. Some jurisdictions also allow physicians to charge extra if they are required to spend extra time assessing, treating, or monitoring a client. These claims are usually reviewed individually. For example, in Ontario, if a doctor is required to spend more than 30 minutes on what should have been a minor or intermediate assessment, he can submit this claim for special consideration for time-based remuneration. Most jurisdictions require doctors to note start and end times.

The Client's Age

Most provinces and territories assign different service codes bearing higher fees for the same service depending on the age of the client. For example, there may be a premium code attached to the fee code for services to older adult clients. In British Columbia, assessments have different fees for clients in five different age groups.

Additional Interventions

Providers in all provinces and territories can bill for diagnostic and therapeutic procedures, ranging from complex to minor, such as taking a urine sample or giving an injection. (Procedures considered a routine part of an assessment, such as a Pap smear as part of a woman's complete physical, may not be billed separately.) These services are billed using what many jurisdictions call a procedural code. Procedures done in conjunction with a physician visit are billed at a lesser amount than those done separately. For example, if a client visits the doctor for an assessment and also gets a flu shot, the doctor charges for the visit (service code) and for the flu shot (procedure). If the client comes into the office only to get a flu shot (whether from the doctor, a nurse, or a medical assistant), the physician does not submit a service code but can charge a slightly higher amount for the procedure.

Time, Location, and Special Circumstances

Most fee structures make allowances for services that must be provided at inconvenient times and locations. For example, a premium may be charged in addition to the regular fee if the doctor has to travel to another facility or the client's home or if a service must be done outside of office hours. Services provided after midnight often have higher premiums. A premium may also be chargeable if the doctor has to cancel office appointments to provide emergency service out of the office.

Independent Consideration

In most provinces and territories some services do not have a fee attached to them. Remuneration for these services vary with the situation, thus the provincial or territorial payment agency reviews each submission independently. These services are marked with a region-specific identifier.

Many jurisdictions refer to this as requiring independent consideration (IC). This is different from requesting a manual review—also requiring individual consideration for some services.

Policies, regulations, and statistics are subject to frequent change. It is impossible to keep any printed document absolutely current. Consult your province's or territory's fee schedule and website for up-to-date information.

The Fee Schedule

Every province and territory has a manual that outlines its rules and regulations regarding billing for insurable services. This resource manual is often referred to as a fee schedule. The proper name of this resource varies. In Newfoundland and Labrador, it is referred to as the *Medical Payment Schedule*, in Saskatchewan, the *Physician Payment Schedule*, and in Ontario, the *Schedule of Benefits*.

Your province's or territory's fee schedule is a valuable resource. It is provided to physicians and facilities at designated intervals or can be purchased at most government bookstores. *Schedules are now available on the internet*, and as a student, you may legally download for study purposes your province's or territory's fee schedule or only the components used in your program.

❺ ELIGIBILITY FOR HEALTH-CARE PLANS

Although there are some variations from one jurisdiction to another, generally, people who are Canadian citizens or landed immigrants and are permanent residents of a province or territory are eligible for health insurance in that jurisdiction. Some jurisdictions also extend eligibility to temporary residents in certain categories, such as temporary workers, holders of a Minister's permit, foreign students, and refugees whose status has been confirmed by the Immigration Refugee Board. Provincial and territorial health plans do not cover certain designated groups for which the federal government is responsible:

■ Aboriginal Canadians living on reserves

■ Members of the Armed Forces

■ Members of the Royal Canadian Mounted Police (but not their families)

■ Inmates of federal correctional institutions

Payment of Premiums

In Canada, there are two models for the payment of provincial and territorial premiums: (1) residents paying insurance premiums, and (2) government covering health-care costs through blended taxation.

As mentioned in Chapter 4, only British Columbia and Ontario residents pay insurance premiums. In all other provinces and territories, health care is paid for by tax money—including sales taxes, employer levies, and property taxes—from the federal, provincial /territorial, and municipal governments. Coverage is universal for legal residents, regardless of employment status.

❻ HEALTH CARDS

ALL PROVINCES AND TERRITORIES GIVE ELIGIBLE INDIVIDUALS A HEALTH CARD (IN SOME provinces referred to as a care card). This card must be presented each time the person seeks any insured health service. It is required across Canada that the user have a valid health card at the point of service. Some facilities enforce this policy more stringently than others. Follow your employer's policy. Even if your employer is willing to provide treatment to clients without cards, encourage the clients to remember to bring the card next time. A posted notice in a prominent place also helps remind clients. Some clients do not believe they need the card; they feel that you know them and can simply look up their information. That may be so in your office, but you are doing clients a disservice if you let them develop the habit of leaving the card at home. Sooner or later, they will probably be refused a non-urgent service at some other facility.

You may be able to convince clients that the health card is necessary by comparing it to a credit card. Suppose a customer went to buy a pair of shoes in a department store, but at the cash register she said, "Sorry, I left my credit card at home. I'll take the shoes now and pay you next time." Or suppose she presented an expired credit card. It is unlikely the cashier would let her walk out with the shoes unless she paid cash. A health card is no different.

Card formats vary, but generally a health card includes name (card must be changed if the person's name changes), health number (in many jurisdictions, assigned for life), and expiry date. (See Figure 10.1.)

Health Numbers

Each health card has a personal identification number on it. Depending on the province or territory, this number ranges from 7 to 12 digits. (See Table 10.2.) This number may be referred to as a health card number, a care card number, or a personal identification number (PIN). Some jurisdictions issue a separate health number for each eligible individual; others issue family numbers. In Manitoba only adults are issued a health card, which contains the name of each family member and their own personal health number. It is particularly important with a family number to report changes in family status, such as marriage and divorce.

All jurisdictions issue a health number; some also issue a separate account number. In Saskatchewan, individuals are assigned for life a unique health number, which is shown on the health card. They are also assigned a family identifier, which consists of a six-digit family number followed by a two-digit **beneficiary** number. It is used internally to configure family units on the provincial health registry and to determine eligibility for

beneficiary a person eligible to receive insurance benefits under specified conditions.

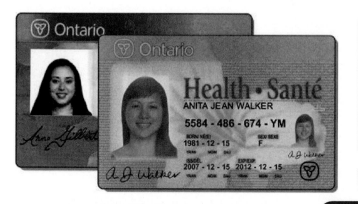

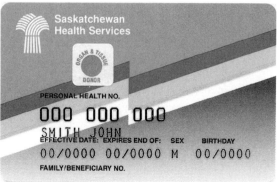

MCP Identification Card

This card identifies the person whose name appears on the reverse
side as being registered under MCP.

THIS CARD MUST BE PRESENTED EACH TIME YOU RECEIVE MEDICAL SERVICES

Please notify the Newfoundland and Labrad or Medical Care Plan
of any change of address. Forms are available from
MCP, physician's offices, or http://www.gov.nl.ca/mcp/
Toll free # 1-800-563-1557

Figure 10.1 Sample health cards from Ontario, Saskatchewan, Prince Edward Island, and Newfoundland and Labrador

family-based programs, such as Prescription Drug Plan deductibles. It is considered that at 18 years of age individuals move to a new family unit and therefore receive a new family identifier. When a couple marries, the health number of the older person is retained for family use. If the couple legally separates or divorces, the spouse who dropped his or her personal account number is reassigned that original number.

Alberta, too, uses both unique personal health numbers and family account numbers for billing purposes. On turning 21, a person must apply for a different billing account number but retains the personal health number. In Ontario, each person has an OHIP card number for life; there is no account number.

Table 10.2 Abbreviations and Formats for Health Numbers in Canadian Jurisdictions

Jurisdiction	Abbreviation	No. of Digits	Registration Unit
British Columbia	BC	10 or 11	Individual
Alberta	AB	9	Individual
Saskatchewan	SK	9	Individual
Manitoba	MB	9	Subscriber/family group
Ontario	ON	10	Individual
Quebec	QC	10	Individual
New Brunswick	NB	9	Individual
Nova Scotia	NS	10	Individual
Prince Edward Island	PE	9	Individual
Newfoundland and Labrador	NL	12	Individual
Yukon	YT	9	Individual
Nunavut	NU	9	Individual
Northwest Territories	NT	7 + 1 letter	Individual

Expiry Date/Renewal Date

Most health cards have an expiry date noted right on the card. After the expiry date, the health card is invalid and must be renewed. In some jurisdictions, cardholders are notified by mail when the expiry date is approaching. Record the expiry date on the client's chart, and if the client comes in close to that date, remind her that the card will soon expire. Although renewal is the client's responsibility, you will not only be doing the client a service but also saving yourself the time and trouble of having claims rejected because of an invalid card. Many office software programs will alert you when a client's card is nearing its expiry date when you swipe it.

Version Code

On the newer Ontario card, the version code is represented by two alpha characters that follow the health number. The purpose of this code is to reduce health card fraud. If a card is lost, the replacement card will bear the same health number but a different version code. If someone tried to use the lost or stolen code, it would be immediately picked up when the card was checked.

Privacy and the Health Card

A health card is an important personal document that must be treated as private and confidential. It is to be used for health-care purposes only. It is illegal to ask someone to show a health card for identification purposes (e.g., cashing a cheque, applying for a charge card, proof of age). An exception is that seniors in Ontario may use their Health 65 card as proof of age for seniors' discounts. Showing the card, however, is voluntary. This does not hold true in all provinces and territories.

❼❽❾ REGISTERING FOR PROVINCIAL OR TERRITORIAL HEALTH INSURANCE COVERAGE

YOU WILL LIKELY BE ASKED ABOUT REGISTERING FOR HEALTH COVERAGE. ALTHOUGH THE information is publicly available, it is helpful to understand the process so that you can explain it to clients.

Each province or territory has its own application form, usually available at doctors' offices, hospitals, and Ministry offices in cities and larger towns (see your local phone book). Many jurisdictions have the application form online as well. Figure 10.2 shows an application form for Prince Edward Island. In some jurisdictions, the form may be mailed, faxed, or brought in to the approved location along with the appropriate identification and citizenship or immigration documents.

Each applicant must supply the Ministry with specific information and validate this information. This information is stored in a central electronic database and is confidential. The insured person must supply accurate, current information.

Stress the importance of bringing all the required documentation. Without it, applications will not be processed, which will lead to delays and frustration. Clients are often surprised at what is accepted as documentation. Applicants need documentation from three categories, a fact that confuses many people.

Applicants must bring one document from each of the three following categories. (Detailed lists of specific examples of documents are on your provincial/territorial Ministry of Health website.)

1. Proof of Canadian citizenship or immigration status

2. Proof of residency in the province/territory (varies somewhat; check the local form)

3. Proof of personal identity (i.e., that you are who you say you are)

Temporary Health Cards

In most jurisdictions, a paper health card similar to the plastic card is issued for clients who need a card immediately (for example, those whose cards are lost or stolen) or who are eligible for coverage for only a short period of time. In some provinces, a validated copy of the application form accepted by the Ministry serves as a temporary card.

Registering Newborns

When a baby is born, the birth must be registered. Newborn registration must be completed before a birth certificate can be issued. Newborns are covered immediately by the provincial or territorial health insurance plan of the jurisdiction in which at least one parent is eligible to receive health care. In some jurisdiction, including Ontario, hospitals and midwives have forms with pre-assigned health numbers, which they complete when a baby is born. There is a tear-off portion that serves as the baby's health card until an actual health card is issued. In Ontario, OHIP will enter the baby's name and information into the system and should send a health card for the infant within three months after receiving the completed top portion of the form. When the baby's card expires, the parents will be asked to show a birth certificate when they make an application for a new health card. In jurisdictions that do not use pre-assigned health numbers, parents should apply for coverage for the child as soon as possible. (See Figure 10.3.) In Alberta, coverage

Health PEI

PO Box 3000
126 Douses Road, Montague
Prince Edward Island, C0A 1R0 Canada
Telephone: (902) 838-0900 / 1-800-321-5492

Personal Health Card Application
•
Carte santé personnelle Formulaire de demande

Santé Î.-P.-É.

C.P. 3000
126, chemin Douses, Montague
Île-du-Prince-Édouard, C0A 1R0 Canada
Téléphone : (902) 838-0900 / 1-800-321-5492

Please print all information clearly.
Complete in full and return to above address.

Prière d'écrire clairement en lettres moulées.
Veuillez remplir en entier et renvoyer à l'adresse ci-dessus.

For Office Use Only • À usage interne seulement

Document No. • *Document n°*	Household No. • *Ménage n°*
Date eligible • *Date d'admissibilité*	Status • *Statut*
Day • *Jour* Month • *Mois* Yr. • *Année*	
Date entered • *Date de saisie*	Entered by • *Saisi par*
Day • *Jour* Month • *Mois* Yr. • *Année*	
Date approved • *Date d'approbation*	Approved by • *Approuvé par*
Day • *Jour* Month • *Mois* Yr. • *Année*	

Name (surname, first name, initials) • *Nom (nom, prénom, initiales)*

Birth Date • *Date de naissance*	Sex (M/F) • *Sexe (M/F)*	Country and Province of Birth *Pays et province de naissance*	Personal Health Number *Numéro de la carte santé*
Day • *Jour* Month • *Mois* Yr. • *Année*			

Mailing Address • *Adresse postale*	City/Town • *Ville*

Postal Code • *Code postal*	Telephone No. • *Téléphone* Home • *Maison* ( ) Work • *Travail* ( )	

Spouse (surname, first name, initials) • *Conjoint(e) (nom, prénom, initiales)*

Birth Date • *Date de naissance*	Sex (M/F) • *Sexe (M/F)*	Country and Province of Birth *Pays et province de naissance*	Personal Health Number *Numéro de la carte santé*
Day • *Jour* Month • *Mois* Yr. • *Année*			

1. Dependant (surname, first name, initials) • *Personne à charge (nom, prénom, initiales)*

Birth Date • *Date de naissance*	Sex (M/F) • *Sexe (M/F)*	Country and Province of Birth *Pays et province de naissance*	Personal Health Number *Numéro de la carte santé*
Day • *Jour* Month • *Mois* Yr. • *Année*			

2. Dependant (surname, first name, initials) • *Personne à charge (nom, prénom, initiales)*

Birth Date • *Date de naissance*	Sex (M/F) • *Sexe (M/F)*	Country and Province of Birth *Pays et province de naissance*	Personal Health Number *Numéro de la carte santé*
Day • *Jour* Month • *Mois* Yr. • *Année*			

3. Dependant (surname, first name, initials) • *Personne à charge (nom, prénom, initiales)*

Birth Date • *Date de naissance*	Sex (M/F) • *Sexe (M/F)*	Country and Province of Birth *Pays et province de naissance*	Personal Health Number *Numéro de la carte santé*
Day • *Jour* Month • *Mois* Yr. • *Année*			

4. Dependant (surname, first name, initials) • *Personne à charge (nom, prénom, initiales)*

Birth Date • *Date de naissance*	Sex (M/F) • *Sexe (M/F)*	Country and Province of Birth *Pays et province de naissance*	Personal Health Number *Numéro de la carte santé*
Day • *Jour* Month • *Mois* Yr. • *Année*			

See other side • *Voir au verso*

Figure 10.2   Application for health coverage in Prince Edward Island *(Continued)*

Used by permission of Health PEI.

Residential Status • *Résidence*

☐ New Resident
Nouveau résident

☐ Returning Resident
Résident de retour

☐ R.C.M.P., Armed Forces, Penitentiary
G.R.C., Forces armées, établissement pénitentiaire

Day • *Jour*   Month • *Mois*   Yr. •

(Please indicate release date if any of the above apply • *Veuillez indiquer la date de libération, le cas échéant*)

Province/Country of last residence • *Dernier lieu de résidence (province ou pays)*

Mailing Address • *Adresse postale*	City/Town • *Ville*	Country • *Pays*	Postal Code *Code postal*

Former Provincial Health Care No. (if applicable) • *Ancien numéro de la carte santé provinciale (le cas échéant)*

Reason for coming to Prince Edward Island • *Raison de la venue à l'Île-du-Prince-Édouard*

☐ Internship
Stage

☐ Student
Études

☐ Employment
Emploi

☐ Other
Autre

(Please specify • *Veuillez préciser*)

Length of stay on Prince Edward Island • *Installation à l'Île-du-Prince-Édouard*

Permanent • *Permanente*
☐

Temporary • *Temporaire*
☐

Date of arrival on Prince Edward Island • *Date d'arrivée à l'Île-du-Prince-Édouard*

Day • *Jour*   Month • *Mois*   Yr. • *Année*

Citizenship Status (must attach copy of immigration record or proof of Canadian citizenship before applications may be processed)
Citoyenneté (*La demande ne sera traitée que sur la foi des dossiers de l'Immigration ou d'une preuve de citoyenneté canadienne.*)

☐ Canadian Citizen
Citoyen canadien

☐ Working Visa
Visa d'emploi

☐ Canadian citizen returning from another country
Citoyen canadien de retour de l'étranger

☐ Landed Immigrant
Résident permanent

☐ Other
Autre

(Please specify • *Veuillez préciser*)

I hereby authorize the details of this application may be discussed with the Federal Department of Employment and Immigration Canada.
J'autorise par la présente la discussion des détails de la présente demande avec le ministère fédéral de la Citoyenneté et de l'Immigration.

Signature _____

Declaration • *Déclaration*

I hereby state that I am legally entitled to remain in Canada, I am permanently residing and making my home in Prince Edward Island and I understand that it is an offence to give false information in this application.

Je déclare par la présente que je suis légalement autorisé à demeurer au Canada, que je réside en permanence à l'Île-du-Prince-Édouard et que je comprends que de fournir des renseignements faux dans la présente demande équivaut à commettre une infraction.

Signature _____

Day • *Jour*   Month • *Mois*   Yr. • *Année*

Personal information on this form is collected under Section 8 (Registration of Entitled Persons) of Prince Edward Island's Health Services Payment Act (Regulations) and will be used to ensure a resident's entitlement in respect to basic health services. If you require additional information, please contact Medicare Services, 126 Douses Road, Montague, PE C0A 1R0, 1-800-321-5492. • *Les renseignements personnels apparaissant sur le présent formulaire sont recueillis en vertu de l'article 8 (Inscription des personnes autorisées) de la Health Services Payment Act de l'Île-du-Prince-Édouard et de ses règlements, et ils seront utilisés pour assurer le droit d'un résident aux services de santé de base. Si vous avez besoin de renseignements supplémentaires, veuillez communiquer avec Medicare Services, 126, chemin Douses, Montague (Î.-P.-É.) C0A 1R0, 1-800-321-5492.*

Figure 10.2   *(Continued)*

GOVERNMENT OF NEWFOUNDLAND AND LABRADOR
Department of Health and Community Services

mcp

NEWBORN / ADOPTED CHILD REGISTRATION FORM
Please Print

MAILING ADDRESS

Street/P.O. Box		City/Town	
Province	Postal Code	Telephone Number (Home)	Telephone Number (Work)

PARENT OR GUARDIAN

MCP Registration Number	Surname	Given Name and Initials	Birth Date (YY/MM/DD)

CHILD/CHILDREN TO BE REGISTERED

Surname	Given Name and Initials	Sex (M/F)	Birth Date (YY/MM/DD)

DECLARATION (It is an offense to give false information for the purpose of obtaining coverage under the Newfoundland and Labrador Medical Care Plan)

I hereby declare that the information given is correct and the person(s) listed on this form are residents of Newfoundland and Labrador.

Signature   Date

REQUIRED DOCUMENTATION

If registering a child/children through adoption, a copy of the official adoption papers, or the birth certificate, is required for each child.

If the surname of the child/children is different than the registering parent or guardian, a copy of the birth certificate is required for each child.

Medical Care Plan
22 High Street, P. O. Box 5000
Grand Falls-Windsor NL Canada A2A 2Y4
Tel: 1-800-563-1557 Fax: 709-292-4052

http://www.gov.nf.ca/mcp

Medical Care Plan
57 Margaret's Place, P. O. Box 8700
St. John's NL Canada A1B 4J6
Tel: 1-800-563-1557 Fax: 709-758-1694

Figure 10.3 Application to register a newborn or adopted child in Newfoundland and Labrador
Government of Newfoundland and Labrador

is provided from the date of birth if notification is received within one year. Otherwise, coverage begins on the first day of the month in which notification is received. In BC either parent must complete a registration of birth form (given to the mother at birth) and return it to the Vital Statistics Agency within 30 days of the baby's birth. In BC and other provinces and territories, parents can apply for a SIN (social insurance number) for the baby at the same time.

Registering Adopted Children

Adopted children are normally registered for coverage in the same way as babies. The adoption process requires the collection of sensitive information, including the birth mother's identification. Even if an adopted child already has a health card, his adoptive parents would apply for him as a new registrant. This approach prevents accidental disclosure, as identifiable information will not be on the application form.

Updating and Correcting Cards

It is important to ensure that health cards are kept current, which, in some jurisdictions, means renewing them from time to time, and that the information is kept up to date.

Name Change   In most jurisdictions, insured persons who change their names must fill out the appropriate form to ensure that health coverage eligibility is maintained. You can find the relevant form on the Ministry of Health website for each province or territory. For name changes because of marriage, applicants must provide one of the following:

- Marriage certificate
- Certified statement of marriage
- A record of marriage form (This must be the original, signed by the person who conducted the marriage [e.g., clergy], and must include the name of the spouse, date of the marriage, and marriage licence number.)

For other name changes, the applicant would supply a change-of-name certificate.

Marriage is, of course, the most common reason for name changes—at least for women. After getting married, a surprising number of women begin to use their husbands' names without thinking about their health registration. You can help by asking any woman you know who is getting married if she is changing her name, and, if so, tell her that she needs to have her health card changed. If a male or female client asks you to use a new surname, or if you hear that a client has taken Canadian citizenship, you can also explain that a new card is needed.

In Ontario, if the client still has the old-style, red-and-white card, she will need to register for a photo ID health card at the same time, bringing documents of the same type needed to apply for a new card.

Some newly married women, although they are using the married name, continue to use their old card for a while. Keep both names on your computer system and records to avoid confusion when looking up the client's information. Keep in mind, however, that not all women change their names when they marry. When spouses have different surnames, it is usual to cross-reference family units by making a note on the clients' charts and linking them in the computerized database.

There is a similar process to follow if the marriage dissolves and the client wishes to return to her original name. Details can be obtained from your Ministry. Usually, a copy of the final divorce certificate is required.

Address Change Residents changing only their address need not go to an OHIP office. In Ontario, they have three choices:

- Fill out and mail a change-of-information form.
- Send a letter to the nearest OHIP office, including name, health card number, phone number, and full address (old and new).
- Update the card at a Service Ontario kiosk. The client will need the new postal code and the health cards of all family members.

When you find out that clients have moved or plan to move, remind them to update their cards. Increasingly, health-care facilities are refusing to accept health cards that lack current information. Manitoba, for example, specifically states that any change in location or family status, such as marriage, birth, adoption, death, divorce, or separation, must be reported to the Insured Benefits Branch. A client with an incorrect card will not be refused the service but may be required to pay and seek reimbursement from the province. New Brunswick specifically requires that individuals report any incorrect spelling of names, wrong date of birth, and out-of-province or out-of-country moves by one or more members of a family.

If you are dealing with another province or territory, be sure to check the specifics. For example, if you work in British Columbia and one of your clients is moving to Nova Scotia, check with the Ministry in Nova Scotia before advising your client about how to apply for health-care registration in that province.

Lost or Stolen Health Cards

Health cards should be kept as secure as credit cards. Across Canada, health card fraud is a concern. If one of your clients loses a health card or has it stolen, advise the person to report it immediately to the appropriate government office. Usually, there is a toll-free number. In Ontario, clients who had a photo health card will be issued a new photo card. Clients who had a red-and-white card will have to go to a Ministry office to register for a photo card.

New Brunswick has a specific form for replacing lost or stolen cards. Some other jurisdictions use the same form as for original application. Prince Edward Island charges a replacement fee, with a maximum amount per family.

The Three-Month Waiting Period

Moving from outside the Country Individuals moving to Canada, or Canadians returning after living out of the country, have a three-month wait before being eligible for provincial health insurance if they move to Ontario, British Columbia, Quebec, or New Brunswick. These individuals should be encouraged to apply for private health insurance for that period. Many private health insurance companies will not provide coverage unless the applicant purchases the insurance within five days of moving to Canada.

Refugees, refugee claimants, and immigrants from "humanitarian designated classes" who live in those provinces can receive emergency and essential health services through the Interim Federal Health program. People moving from out of the country to the other provinces and territories are eligible for health coverage immediately.

Moving within Canada People who move from one province or territory to another will face the three-month waiting period before their new health coverage comes into effect. They will still be covered by their province of origin. Unless they are moving from or to Quebec, providers in the new province can be paid through the reciprocal agreement (discussed below).

The three-month waiting period does not generally apply to individuals discharged from the Canadian Armed Forces or the RCMP or to people moving to become residents of homes for the aged, nursing homes, homes for people with disabilities, or other homes designated as charitable.

Absences from Province or Territory of Origin

Provincial or territorial health insurance plans provide coverage for residents during absences both within and outside Canada. Criteria may differ with each region. Residents are generally covered for vacations and for absences for education or work for a specified length of time. In some provinces, "snowbirds" who spend the winter in warmer climes must reside in the province for at least six months plus a day each year to be eligible for continuous coverage. Long absences—for extended vacations, employment, academic studies, and missionary work with approved charities—should be reported to the health-care plan, with supporting documentation. In Ontario, this is done on the change-of-information form. With approval, coverage may be extended as long as five years for employment.

Out-of-country medical services are usually paid at the rate that would be paid for the service in the resident province or territory. If the provider charges a higher fee, the client may be responsible for the difference. Usually, the client must pay when receiving the service and then submit receipts to the provincial or territorial health plan for reimbursement.

What is considered an insurable service in one jurisdiction may not be in another, perhaps providing incentive for residents in one jurisdiction to seek an otherwise uninsured service in another jurisdiction. This is not normally permitted. For example, a client whose home province does not cover routine infant circumcision cannot get it covered by travelling to a province that does cover the procedure.

Clients sometimes have elective surgery done in the United States to avoid long waits in Canada. Many have applied for authorization for such out-of-country surgery and been refused. On occasion, however, provinces or territories will authorize payment for a medically necessary procedure to be done outside the province or territory or country when the treatment is not available in the province or territory or country of origin or within the time frame considered medically necessary.

❾ BILLING FOR OUT-OF-PROVINCE/TERRITORY CLIENTS

A RECIPROCAL AGREEMENT AMONG ALL THE PROVINCES AND TERRITORIES, EXCEPT QUEBEC, allows providers to bill their own ministries for services rendered to insured residents from other parts of Canada. This covers medical and related diagnostic services. (Hospitals are covered by a similar separate agreement.) Prior approval is not normally needed. Physicians will normally be paid at the fee rate in their own province or territory.

Out-of-province/territory reciprocal claim forms are available, but if your billing is normally done by electronic data transfer (EDT), out-of-province/territory claims can be handled this way too. Clients must present a valid health card. Insist on seeing the physical card, not just a number. Check that the card has not expired. (Some jurisdictions issue lifetime cards; other have expiry dates.) Swipe the card or record the client information, enter the complete billing information, such as the diagnostic and service codes and the provincial or territorial initials, and bill your own jurisdiction directly.

If the client does not have a health card, collect payment. Give the client a receipt, which he can use to claim reimbursement from his own province or territory.

Participation in the agreement is voluntary. Physicians who do not want to participate in this program may bill the client directly.

Quebec has not signed a reciprocal agreement with any other province or territory for insured physician services. If you work for a provider in Quebec, charge out-of-province/territory clients directly, and advise them to keep the receipts and seek reimbursement from their own health plan. If clients mention that they will be travelling in Quebec, let them know that they should be prepared to pay for any medical services, and remind them to keep the receipts. Physicians outside Quebec who render services to Quebec residents should take all the client and diagnostic information, charge the client, and provide a receipt and record of the service provided. The client can claim reimbursement from the Quebec Ministry.

⑪ PRIVATE INSURANCE

ALTHOUGH MEDICALLY NECESSARY HOSPITAL AND PHYSICIAN SERVICES IN CANADA ARE covered primarily by public health insurance, private health insurance plays a significant role in covering services not eligible under provincial or territorial plans. Private insurance becomes increasingly popular as government health plans drop services once covered, such as routine eye examinations and chiropractic services in most jurisdictions. Many general insurance companies offer health insurance. However, a few companies specialize in it.

Blue Cross and Liberty Health Insurance are two of the larger companies in Canada that provide supplementary health-care insurance. They cover services ranging from home nursing care and health-care aids to semiprivate and private hospital accommodation and a television and telephone while in hospital. They may also cover co-payments and deductibles for services only partly covered by the government, such as prescription drugs, alternative therapies, and accommodation in long-term care facilities, such as nursing homes. The extent of the coverage is reflected by premiums paid. Many companies provide health insurance through group policies, often included in employee benefits packages. These policies may cover alternative health-care services, such as chiropractic, massage therapy, and acupuncture, as well as comprehensive dental and eye care and medications.

Blue Cross was organized in 1939 as a non-profit prepaid health insurance plan. Policies can be obtained through independent member benefit plans in each province or territory. Like other companies, they provide supplementary benefits, dental benefits, prescription drugs, medical care outside Canada, and critical illness coverage.

Liberty Health is another major player in the health-care industry. The company's main business is group insurance through employers, but they also offer health insurance for individuals and families, as well as life and disability insurance. Liberty Health offers drug and dental insurance in various packages, with higher-premium plans paying a higher percentage of potential expenses, as well as coverage for paramedical services, ambulance services, physiotherapy, vision services, and additional hospital coverage.

Most insurance companies will require medical information from the claimant's physician. This may be directly related to the reason for the claim, or involve additional information. Release of this information requires a release of personal information form, completed by the doctor and signed by the client. Figure 10.4 is a generic example of such a form.

Motor Vehicle Insurance

Insurance for injuries sustained in motor vehicle accidents is carried by most large insurance companies. Such claims can represent a significant portion of those you deal with in the office. In British Columbia, for example, the Insurance Corporation of British Columbia is a provincial Crown corporation providing, among other services, auto insurance to many BC motorists. Forms you will be required to deal with include those

---

CONSENT FOR DISCLOSURE OF PERSONAL HEALTH INFORMATION

I _____ give Dr. _____ (name of patient/client) full name of physician

    Permission to disclose the following health information

_____
_____
_____
_____
_____
_____
_____.

To (name of recipient of the information)

_____
_____
_____

    I understand the purpose of disclosing this health information, and that I am signing this document on my own free will in that I can refuse to sign this form. The reason for disclosure of this health information, how it will be used, and the benefits and consequences of disclosing this has been explained to me in terms that I understand and accept.

My Name: _____
Address: _____
Home Tel.: _____ Work Tel.: _____

Signature: _____ Date: _____
Witness Name: _____ Address: _____
Home Tel.: _____ Work Tel.: _____
Signature: _____ Date: _____

Figure 10.4 Sample of a release of personal health information form

requiring a physical assessment for special driver's licenses as well as those related to injury-generated claims. Forms for each company will have common elements, for example, the demographic information you can fill out for the physician. Ensure that the client has completed any release of medical information forms, and keep a note of when forms have been completed and sent and to whom. If medical information is to be faxed or mailed directly to the company, explain this to the client. She may be under the assumption that she can take the information and send it herself. There are situations wherein this is contraindicated.

Workers' Compensation

Workers' compensation is another type of insurance in Canada. (See Chapter 5.) Every jurisdiction has a workers' compensation board (WCB), although names vary somewhat: in Ontario, the body is called the Workplace Safety and Insurance Board (WSIB); in Yukon, it is the Yukon Workers' Compensation Health and Safety Board, and in British Columbia, WorkSafeBC. Through premiums paid by employers, WCBs/WSIBs insure workers against work-related injuries, paying partial replacement of wages as well as covering medical and other health-care expenses resulting from injuries. Services covered under the *Workers' Compensation Act* are usually billed directly to the Ministry of Health, which is then reimbursed by the WCB. There are exceptions that vary somewhat by jurisdiction. (See Chapter 12 for more detail.) An injured worker must sign a form allowing the treating physician to release to the WCB medical information relating to the claim. See Chapter 8 for details regarding common forms and links to these forms.

Future Trends

Coverage for services not mandated under the *Canada Health Act* remains a concern for Canadians and governments alike. At the top of the list are prescription drugs and home-care services.

All jurisdictions are attempting to improve their health-care services. For example, the Alberta government is providing funding for a new five-year health action plan that defines both short- and long-term goals for Alberta Health Services. These goals include a plan to reduce wait times for hip surgery and cancer treatment, shortening the wait for clients requiring hospital admission after being seen in the ER, providing clients with faster access to long-term care beds, and faster access to mental health services for children.

Alternative payment plans for physicians have gained popularity over the past ten years, and continue to do so. Fee-for-service payment has been around since 1966. Other payment models such as blended funding, capitation, and salaries are increasing in popularity, especially among female doctors. According to the Canadian Health Services Research, overall the "modern" doctor does prefer alternatives to the fee-for-service model. Capitation funding and working in groups (e.g., in family health teams/organizations) provide the physician with more job satisfaction, less stress, and a more reasonable lifestyle. Still, all jurisdictions continue to experiment with payment models, and it is fairly certain that a mix of models will remain—no one model will meet everyone's needs.

All jurisdictions are doing what they can to reduce health-care costs: moving more care into the community and providing more funding for these initiatives, having routine procedures done in non-profit clinics instead of the hospital, providing more money for home care, using non-physician practitioners to provide care, such as in nurse practitioner–led clinics, and allowing more private health care. The new health accord has been received with mixed reviews, along with great concern that aligning funding with the GDP will undermine the quality of health care and prove to be insufficient funding. First ministers have pledged to hold regular meetings to share ideas and innovations for cost-effective health-care delivery.

SUMMARY

1. Licensed physicians and other providers in good standing are eligible to receive fee-for-service payment from provincial or territorial health plans. All jurisdictions' health plans cover hospital services and physician services deemed medically necessary.

2. Uninsured services vary but usually include back-to-school/work notes, completion of forms, transfer of files, telephone advice, and infant circumcision (unless medically necessary). Some jurisdictions cover preventive physical examinations; others do not. It is helpful to post a sign listing the more common of these services, along with the charge for each.

3. Extended benefits vary. Most jurisdictions have a drug plan, long-term care coverage, ambulance coverage, travel assistance when necessary medical services are at some distance, and some optometry coverage. You should be able to inform clients about such benefits.

4. Many provinces and territories base physician payment on the complexity of the service performed, while some pay higher fees for older clients. Fees may be higher for services performed under special circumstances.

5. Canadian citizens and landed immigrants, as well as foreigners meeting certain criteria, are covered by provincial or territorial health plans. Members of the RCMP and the armed forces, Aboriginal people living on reserves, and inmates in federal prisons are covered by the federal government.

6. All health cards contain similar basic information. Several provinces have introduced photo ID health cards for greater security. Generally, an individual is issued a unique lifetime health number, but cards must be renewed every three to five years. Cards should be kept secure and should be presented every time a client seeks health services.

7. An applicant for health insurance must show documents proving Canadian citizenship, residency in the province or territory, and personal identification. People should report lost or stolen cards immediately and should report changes in name, address, or citizenship status.

8. People moving from one province or territory to another retain the original coverage for three months, after which they are eligible in their new place of residence. Ontario, New Brunswick, and British Columbia are the only provinces that enforce a three-month wait for individuals moving to Canada. Babies have coverage immediately.

9. Reciprocal billing, an agreement among all provinces and territories except Quebec, allows physicians to bill their own Ministry for providing services to clients from other jurisdictions. Clients must have valid health cards. Insured persons are covered outside the country during brief absences or authorized longer absences.

10. Many Canadians have private insurance to cover services that provincial or territorial plans do not cover, such as preferred accommodation in the hospital, additional nursing care, drug and dental benefits, optometry, and chiropractic.

Review Questions

1. List and explain six hospital and medical services that are not covered under most provincial or territorial plans.

2. What is the purpose of a drug benefit plan, and what segment of the population are such plans generally created to support?

3. What does a health office professional have to consider in scheduling vision checks?

4. List the three categories of documentation a person must present when applying for health-care coverage, and give three examples from each category.

5. Describe the process of registering a newborn.

6. What province does not participate in the reciprocal agreement? How does that affect clients from that province and clients travelling in that province?

7. List four groups of people who are exempt from the three-month wait.

8. Describe the process to follow if your health card is lost or stolen.

9. What can you do in the health office to reduce fraudulent use of health cards?

10. What are three organizations that provide private insurance for Canadians, and what types of services do they cover?

Application Exercises

1. Using the internet or other resources, develop a list of the extended health services covered in your province or territory. Explain who is eligible for coverage of each and the range of services offered.

2. Research how ambulance services are managed in your own province or territory and three others. Make a list comparing what is covered in each jurisdiction and the cost to the Ministry and to the client.

3. Amrini, who arrived in your province/territory two months ago, has two part-time jobs and is supporting a wife and three children. He has not applied for health insurance, not knowing how to do so or where to go. His combined salaries would give him about $24 000 a year. One child, aged 6, is diabetic, the other, aged 12, is asthmatic, and his wife is six months pregnant. He can't afford to pay for the medications. He doesn't know where to turn for help. He has paid cash for services at your office (family medicine). You suspect his wife has used his sister's health card for prenatal checkups at a walk-in clinic. Describe the steps you would take in this situation. Include corrective measures, such as helping Amrini access your provincial/territorial health plan. Review the drug benefits in your jurisdiction and identify which plan would best suit his needs. List the necessary steps Amrini would have to follow to register. You can start at www.hc-sc.gc.ca/hcs-sss/delivery-prestation/ptrole/index-eng.php#card.

4. Hinder has injured her back at work. She is diagnosed with a slipped disc and must be off work for at least three weeks. Outline the steps she would take to

   ■ report her accident initially,

- obtain the forms she would require the doctor to fill out, and
- apply for compensation (include the location of the nearest workers' compensation office).

Summarize your responsibilities as the AHP working in the doctor's office.

Websites of Interest

Canada Health Act Annual Reports
http://www.hc-sc.gc.ca/hcs-sss/pubs/cha-lcs/index-eng.php

Provincial and Territorial Health Care in Canada Links
www.hc-sc.gc.ca/hcs-sss/delivery-prestation/ptrole/index-eng.php#card

Alberta Schedule of Medical Benefits
http://www.health.alberta.ca/professionals/SOMB.html

Health Forms for Ontario
www.health.gov.on.ca//en/
For health forms, click on Forms in the menu on the left side of the screen.

Health Forms for British Columbia
https://www.health.gov.bc.ca/exforms/

Medical Services Payment Schedule BC
www.health.gov.bc.ca/msp/infoprac/physbilling/index.html

Directory of information about health cards and eligibility for provincial or territorial coverage in Canada
http://www.hc-sc.gc.ca/hcs-sss/delivery-prestation/ptrole/index-eng.php#card

Links to the Canada Health Act
http://laws.justice.gc.ca/en/C-6/

Canadian Health-Care System
www.hc-sc.gc.ca/hcs-sss/medi-assur/index-eng.php

Provincial/Territorial Ministries of Health
www.hc-sc.gc.ca/hcs-sss/delivery-prestation/ptrole/index-eng.php
This site lists provincial and territorial ministries of health. It includes a tab linking to information regarding eligibility and acquisition of health cards in each province and territory.

Alberta's 5-Year Health Action Plan
http://www.health.alberta.ca/documents/Becoming-the-Best-2010-Highlights.pdf

Globe & Mail Catastrophic Drug Coverage Series (Week of April 4, 2011)
http://www.bestmedicines.ca/node/152

Catastrophic Drug Coverage in Canada
http://www.parl.gc.ca/Content/LOP/ResearchPublications/prb0906-e.htm

LTC facilities, Retirement Homes, and Home Care Information for all Provinces and Territories
http://www.manulife.ca/canada/ilc2.nsf/Public/lc_cost

Chapter 11

Preparing for the Billing Process

Learning Objectives

On completing this chapter, you will be able to:

1. Explain how ministries monitor the validity of submitted claims.
2. Discuss three methods of health card validation.
3. State the benefits of health card validation.
4. Respond appropriately to clients who do not have valid health cards.
5. Explain the function of physician registration numbers.
6. Explain the purpose of service codes.
7. Distinguish among general, intermediate, and minor assessments.
8. Recognize the purpose and usefulness of the ICD system.
9. Explain when to use premium codes.

Chapter 10 gave an overview of health coverage, especially provincial or territorial coverage. This chapter explains the principles of billing. General rules and policies are similar across Canada, as are definitions for such things as an encounter, consultation, and a comprehensive visit. All provinces and territories use physician numbers, service codes, and diagnostic codes, discussed in this chapter. Chapter 12 will describe specific billing procedures using current software. Table 11.2 illustrates commonly used International Classification of Diseases (ICD-9) diagnostic codes.

❶ THE CLAIMS REVIEW PROCESS

A HEALTH CLAIM IS SUBMITTED TO A PROVINCIAL OR TERRITORIAL PLAN IN MUCH the same way as you would submit a claim to any insurance company. The body or bodies responsible for health insurance are the payment agencies (either the Ministry of Health or an organization designated by the Ministry). They accept, approve, monitor, and sometimes investigate claims and participate in deciding what services are insured.

The cycle of provincial or territorial billing *begins* with the submission of a claim for services rendered. The payment agency then reviews the claim. The cycle ends with payment to the provider for all valid claims. The payment agency examines each claim submitted to ensure that the

- provider has a valid billing number,
- service claimed is authorized by provincial or territorial guidelines,
- fee claimed is the one determined by the fee schedule,
- client has a valid health card, and
- claim is submitted in a technically correct manner.

All claims must be submitted in a certain format (usually electronically) and within a designated time frame.

❶ CLAIMS MONITORING AND CONTROL

ALL PROVINCES AND TERRITORIES USE SIMILAR METHODS TO MONITOR FEE-FOR-service claims submitted. The monitoring body (usually the Ministry of Health) must ensure that claims are made properly and honestly and that payments are for health services authorized by provincial or territorial guidelines. The monitoring process helps identify irregularities and fraud.

Inappropriate billing by organizations and physicians and the fraudulent use of health cards are ongoing problems that cost the provincial and territorial plans dearly. All claims submitted are routinely subjected to computer checks, and if they do not meet health plan requirements, they may be rejected or only partially paid. Selected claims may be forwarded to a medical review committee to determine whether the claim is valid and should be paid. Periodically, physicians will be asked for copies of their records or be audited. As well, British Columbia produces an annual profile report for each practitioner who receives fee-for-service payment. Physicians are divided into peer groups, and a profile of each group is created and compared for billing practices.

Ministries investigate reports of inappropriate billing promptly and thoroughly. Both the medical associations and the ministries may take disciplinary action.

Ministries also try to reduce invalid claims by educating and supporting physicians and their administrative staff. Most jurisdictions have a regional information service to answer questions about claims and provide clarification. Contact this service if you are not sure whether a service is insured or how to submit a particular claim.

Prior Approval   Each province and territory also has a list of health services that must be individually reviewed and approved in advance. Breast reduction is one example. If the proposal is rejected and the client still wants the service, she must pay for it or appeal the decision. A physician who fails to seek approval for an otherwise unapproved service risks not being paid for it.

Clients also need prior approval to seek some treatments outside their own province or territory—usually major services, such as surgery. Claims for minor ailments (sore throat, earache, etc.) are submitted at point of service and paid for by the client's province or territory of origin under the reciprocal agreement (except in Quebec).

Verification Letters/Service Verification Audits

Some jurisdictions send computer-generated letters to randomly selected clients, who are asked to verify that the physician actually provided the service he billed for. (Letters will not be sent about services that clients may regard as especially private, such as abortion; treatment of sexually transmitted diseases, AIDS, or dementia; assessment of genitalia; or organ retrieval after death.) Moreover, individually prepared letters may also be sent to the clients of physicians who are under review or are suspected of inappropriate or fraudulent billing.

❷❸❹ HEALTH CARD VALIDATION

Some provinces and territories try to control health card fraud by using health cards that have expiry dates and that incorporate photographs and version codes. Only Alberta, BC, and Manitoba do not require health card renewal. As emphasized in Chapter 10, clients should *always* be asked to present their health card before receiving a medical service.

Health card validation (HCV) means checking the card to make sure that it is authentic, current, and matches your information for the client. This confirms that the client is eligible to receive the service. All jurisdictions have methods for validating health cards.

You may feel that validating every card is a waste of your time and the client's time. However, the process offers real benefits for both the provider and the health system. The health-care system benefits because validation reduces the fraudulent use of cards. You benefit because you significantly reduce rejected claims. (Invalid cards are one of the most common reasons for claims rejection.) This improves your provider's cash flow and saves the time and expense of sorting out and resubmitting rejected claims. You are also prompted to verify the client's current address, which keeps your records up to date. Although you should validate all cards, the process is especially important for out-of-town clients, new clients, and referred clients you do not know personally.

Note: Any health card validation system needs to be secure because it grants query access to a secure database, which contains confidential information, such as health card numbers. Ministries require that users have a password, which must be changed periodically. *Keep track of when your password expires, and change it before it does.* Keep it confidential; if you write it down, ensure that only you have access to it.

Methods of Validation

In most jurisdictions there are several ways that you can validate a client's health card. Which method will suit you best depends on the size of your practice or clinic, the speed of response required, and whether your clients are mostly long-term, transient, booked in advance, or walk-in. Efficient validation methods are part of most primary care reform initiatives. The following is a summary of the more commonly used validation systems.

Electronic Validation through a Web-Based Telecommunications System   This method is available in some jurisdictions as part of the electronic claims submission process. You submit an electronic file to the Ministry containing each client's name and health card information. Some validation checks are done overnight, and the checked file is deposited in your "pick-up box" for review the next morning. This process takes little of your time, making it particularly attractive if you have a high client volume. Although effective, it validates only clients who have made appointments for a service ahead of time. Therefore, it would not work well in a walk-in clinic or an office that takes a lot of same-day bookings. When the Ministry is busy with end-of-month processing, the validation may take longer than overnight.

Interactive Voice Response   Interactive voice response (IVR) is a popular choice for smaller practices. This is an automated method of health card validation that is available 24 hours a day, seven days a week, using a touch-tone phone to call a toll-free number.

- Key in your personal identification number (PIN). This ensures that the information exchanged remains confidential.
- You will then be asked to key in the health card number and the version code of the card you are validating.
- A pre-recorded, coded response will notify you whether the card is valid.
- You can also access bulletins posted by the Ministry.

This system is inexpensive and does not have to be integrated into the office's software system. Another advantage is that it allows you to enter a fee schedule code to determine whether a client is eligible for a service that is covered only once in a given period, such as a routine checkup or a vision examination. For example, suppose your province allows checkups every two years. Sally has booked a routine checkup on September 12, but her two years will not be up until January 18. You will be given this date and can offer Sally the option of rescheduling or, under certain circumstances, paying for the service herself if she does not want to wait. However, IVR does tie up the telephone line and takes up your time because the process is manual.

Tip

For IVR validation you can never use a cellphone, because the line is not secure and confidential information may be intercepted by others.

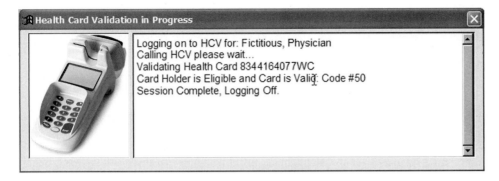

Figure 11.1 Magnetic card reader and response

Health Card Reader (HCR)/Point-of-Service Device A range of devices, called magnetic card readers or point-of-service (POS) devices, are available for health card validation. Some stand alone; others are integrated into the office's software.

Stand-Alone Devices The stand-alone POS device uses a dedicated phone line and is much like the one stores and restaurants use for processing credit card purchases. You swipe the health card and the device reads the information on the card's magnetic strip and transmits it to the Ministry's computer. The validity of the health card is assessed and a response sent back.

PC POS Device The PC point-of-service device uses a standard PC with a modem and special software. A card is swiped in a wedge device (Figure 11.1) that attaches to the computer keyboard. If the health card is not available, the number can be entered using the keyboard. This process can be integrated within a client registration system or run in a Windows environment in conjunction with other applications. The software enables the PC to submit the card data and receive a response from the Ministry's health card validation service. A patient's health card status is also updated as billings are accepted using the stored health card information. This ensures that a patient's health card status is always as up-to-date as possible. Figure 11.2 shows a return message noting a valid card and client information.

Checking Client Information

Validating and updating card information at every visit also helps keep your client records current and valid. When the client comes into the office and you swipe her card, you have an opportunity to review the information. "Your address here is 123 Anywhere Street. Has this changed? Same telephone number, 905-123-3486?" If you are dealing with a client you do not know, look to see if the face matches the photo on the card, if your jurisdiction uses photo ID cards. Asking for the information can also help prove that the card is really the client's. "Mrs. Oakley [using the name on the card], can you give me your address, please? Your telephone number?" Someone who had stolen a card may not know this information.

At the same time, look at the expiry date, if applicable. If it is coming up, remind the client to get the card renewed. (Many people never look at the expiry date on their

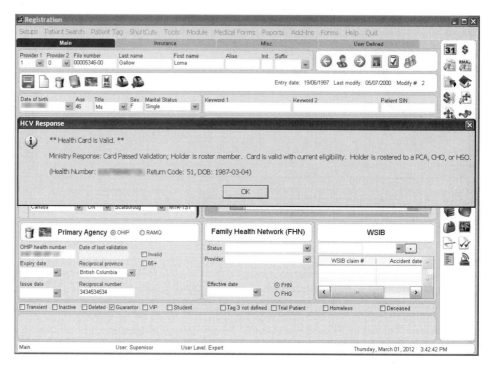

Figure 11.2 A message showing that a client's health card has been validated via a PC POS device

Figure courtesy of P & P Data Systems Inc.

cards.) It is helpful to offer clients a handout containing a list of locations where cards can be renewed or updated and the identification documents they will need to bring. Many software systems will alert you when you swipe a card that is about to expire.

Invalid Cards

A common reason for health card rejection is an invalid health card. Reasons for this include an invalid health number and/or (in Ontario) version code, or an expired card. Anywhere in Canada, each time a card is reported lost or stolen, the Ministry immediately invalidates the card to prevent fraudulent use. Within four to six weeks the client receives a new health card with a different number or other changed identifier. If a client finds her old card and tries to use it while waiting for the new one to arrive, it will be rejected when you do a health card validation or submit a claim. Likewise, when a client's card expires, it is automatically invalidated. Just as you cannot make a purchase with an expired credit card, you cannot obtain health care with an expired health card. Yet many people never look at the expiry date on their cards. Moving or changing your name can also be the cause of an invalid health card. Some jurisdictions crosscheck driver's licence addresses with those registered to a client's health card. A mismatch may result in the Ministry invalidating a person's health card.

Clients may be issued a temporary card or a new number to use until their new health card arrives. In some provinces, the issuing office may puncture the expired card, indicating that its expiry date has been extended until a new card arrives.

In some provinces you can use a health number release form to obtain the client's health card number. If a client with an invalid card or no card is in the office, you can have him sign the health number release form; fax it to the appropriate Ministry office, and they will provide you with the required information.

If this process does not produce a valid health number or, if a client repeatedly fails to correct a problem with his card, charge him for the visit. (You must inform clients *before* they go in for the visit that they will be charged.) The client can pay by cash, cheque, or credit card. (If the client pays cash, provide a receipt.) Many offices hold cheques or credit cards slips for 7 to 10 days to give the client time to present a valid card. If the client presents a valid health card number within that time, do not process the charge and return the cash or cheque. If the client does not present a valid number within that period, process the charge. If the client later produces a valid health card, he can seek reimbursement from the Ministry himself.

Alberta has a "good faith" claim policy. If a resident whom the doctor believes is covered by the Alberta Health Care Insurance Plan (AHCIP) cannot produce her Personal Health Number (PHN), the claim can be submitted using a "Y" indicator. The administrative health professional (AHP) should ask the client for proof of Alberta residency and personal ID. Individuals covered by other resources (for example someone who has moved recently from another province/territory) are not eligible for this consideration. In this case the province of origin is responsible for health payments until the three-month waiting period has expired.

Fraudulent Cards

You may be presented with two types of fraudulent cards. The first is a real health card that appears to be stolen. You may suspect this either because the version code does not match the one on record or because the person presenting the card does not know the address and telephone number. The second type is a counterfeit card. These cards are usually of poor quality and will differ from real cards in weight and colour or may lack the magnetic strip. There is no legitimate reason for anyone to have such a card, as real health cards are supplied free of charge in most parts of the country and replaced for free if lost. You and your employer are permitted to take possession of a health card that is fraudulent or fraudulently used if it is voluntarily surrendered. You are also required by the *Health Disciplines Act* to report fraudulent use of a health card. If you are presented with a fraudulent card,

- collect the card, if the client will give it to you,
- try to determine where and when the card was obtained, and
- report the incident to your Ministry's fraud hotline, if it has one, or to your district office.

A NOTE ON CONFIDENTIALITY

In submitting a claim, you need to provide relevant information to the Ministry about the client and the treatment. In receiving insured services, clients are understood to be authorizing the release of this information. You do not need specific permission to release this information and have no legal liability for doing so.

❺ PHYSICIAN REGISTRATION/BILLING NUMBER

THE BILLING PROCESS CAN BE INITIATED ONLY IF THE PHYSICIAN HAS A VALID **physician registration number**, also called a **billing number**. He must first register with the College of Physicians and Surgeons in the province or territory where he is practising and then apply for a billing number. In many jurisdictions the physician must also have a practice address. The physician is then issued a unique billing number that must appear on every claim he submits. Usually this number is added automatically as a function of the electronic billing process. The process is the same for dentists and other providers eligible to bill a provincial or territorial plan. In Alberta, an osteopath is also included in the definition of *physician*. As noted in Chapter 10, some jurisdictions will allow one physician to bill under another physician's registration/billing number (e.g., as a locum), and others will not. The provider whose number appears on the claim assumes full responsibility for the service provided to the client. A physician who moves to another province or territory must apply for registration in the new jurisdiction. Numbers differ in structure from one jurisdiction to another but usually cover similar information.

In BC and Alberta, for example, the physician billing number consists of two parts. One is the unique practitioner number that identifies the provider rendering the service; the second is a payment number, identifying the person to whom payment is to be made. Most of the time, however, these numbers are the same. They differ if the provider rendering the service assigns another physician (e.g., a locum), clinic, hospital, or diagnostic facility to receive payment for fee-for-service services she has claimed. This is called assignment of payment.

In Ontario, the number consists of three segments:

1. The first four numbers represent the provider's group registration number (if applicable).
2. The next six numbers represent the provider's unique registration number.
3. The last two numbers reflect a specialty code, identifying the physician's field of specialty.

Review the following example for Dr. Thompson, who is a family physician in private practice. He might have the following number:

0000-543993-00

Analysis:

0000 = the group identification number (he is billing independently)
543993 = the unique physician registration number (or billing number)
00 = the specialty identification number (family medicine)

Specialty Codes

Each physician is a **specialist** in a particular area, such as family practice, general surgery, or obstetrics. This specialty is represented by the specialty identification number, or specialty code. 00 represents family practice. In the example above, Dr. Thompson's specialty number, therefore, is 00 (family practice). Table 11.1 shows common specialty codes. These codes are approved by the Royal College of Physicians and Surgeons of Canada.

Table 11.1 Specialty Codes from The Royal College of Physicians and Surgeons of Canada

00	**Family Practice, General Practice**	The practice of a family physician, also called a primary care physician, general practitioner, or family doctor. These physicians complete postgraduate studies in family medicine and are generalists—usually the first contact when someone seeks medical care.
01	**Anaesthesia**	Pain management and the use of anaesthetics and client monitoring for surgical/diagnostic procedures. An anaesthesiologist (or anaesthetist) may give regional or general medications to achieve complete or partial loss of sensation during procedures. An example of a regional anaesthetic is an epidural, which is often given to women for pain control during labour and delivery. A general anaesthetic is one that renders the client unconscious and is used during major surgeries. The anaesthetist is primarily hospital based and does not usually have a private practice.
02	**Dermatology**	Practised by a physician who has completed postgraduate studies in diseases/conditions of the integumentary system, or the skin. These conditions include rashes, injuries, allergic reactions, and diseases of the skin, nails, and hair. A dermatologist also removes moles, cysts, warts, and malignant growths, addresses cosmetic problems, and is involved in skin grafting for such conditions as burns.
03	**General Surgery**	Performed by a specialist in general surgical procedures. These procedures can relate to curative, preventive, or palliative treatment of diseases/conditions. Does not usually include more specialized surgical procedures, such as neurosurgery or vascular surgery.
04	**Neurosurgery**	Concerned with operative intervention of conditions of the central nervous system and the brain.
05	**Community Medicine**	A specialist in community medicine does not usually deal directly with individuals, but with groups or populations. He assesses and evaluates the health needs of sectors of a population or specific groups of people, considering among other things, social, environmental, biological, and behavioural factors. He then develops, implements and evaluates programs and treatments to address these needs based on the occupational, social, and economic needs and the political climate affecting the designated population or group.
06	**Orthopedic Surgery**	This specialty deals with surgical procedures of the musculoskeletal system. Treatment and procedures may be restorative, preventive, or supportive. An orthopedic surgeon (sometimes called an orthoped) will, among other things, do hip and joint replacements, conduct back surgery, and repair complex fractures.
07	**Geriatrics**	The study and treatment of older people and related conditions. The physician is called a gerontologist. This is a relatively new field in medicine, and there are not many gerontologists in Canada. The gerontologist can generally see only a few clients in a day because meeting the needs of the older client is very time consuming.
08	**Plastic Surgery**	Deals with cosmetic and reconstructive surgery involving skin, muscles, and, at times, the reshaping of bones. Cosmetic surgery is not covered by provincial or territorial health plans, but reconstructive surgery, in many cases, is. For example, if a woman wanted a breast reduction to enhance her appearance, the provincial or territorial plan would not cover it. However, if the reduction was deemed medically necessary because of excessive back pain from the weight of heavy breasts, the health plan may cover it. Anything that is deemed to be medically necessary is covered, even if it is somewhat cosmetic in nature. Plastic surgeons operate on burn and trauma victims.
09	**Cardiovascular and Thoracic Surgery**	Deals with surgical procedures specific to the heart, vascular system, and the chest (thoracic cavity). Some of these procedures would include bypass surgery and procedures related to lung cancer.

(continued)

Table 11.1 *(continued)*

12	Emergency Medicine	A hospital-based specialty increasing in popularity. Hospitals in some provinces and territories are hiring doctors to work full-time in Emergency Departments. The physician who practises emergency medicine is called an emergentologist or trauma physician.
13	Internal Medicine	Deals with diseases or conditions, usually nonsurgical in nature, relating to the internal structures of the body, including gastrointestinal and metabolic disorders, such as ulcers and diabetes.
18	Neurology	Deals with diseases/conditions relating to the central nervous system, usually of a non-surgical nature.
19	Psychiatry	Deals with behavioural, emotional, and mental conditions, such as bipolar disease, depression, and psychosis. A psychiatrist, unlike a psychologist, is a medical doctor who has completed a specialty in psychiatry and can prescribe medication.
20	Obstetrics and Gynecology	Obstetrics deals with childbirth and related conditions. Gynecology deals with conditions of the female reproductive system. A physician may specialize in one field or the other or in both (called an ob/gyn). An obstetrician might care only for high-risk pregnant women or for any pregnant women referred to him. Usually, a family doctor will refer a pregnant woman to the obstetrician at about 20 weeks into the pregnancy. The obstetrician will care for the mother until after the baby is born but does not care for the baby. Many family doctors have, for a variety of reasons, given up doing deliveries, increasing the number of low-risk or normal deliveries for the obstetrician. In some provinces and territories, midwives care for mothers considered low risk.
22	Genetics	Deals with conditions and diseases that are inherited.
23	Ophthalmology	Deals with diseases and conditions of the eye. An ophthalmologist is a physician with a postgraduate specialty in ophthalmology and can do ocular surgery, for example, cataract removal. (Not to be confused with an optometrist or an optician, neither of whom is a physician. Optometrists care for low-risk cases and deal with routine eye examinations and corrective measures, such as prescriptions for glasses and contact lenses. An optician can only fill prescriptions for corrective lenses and does not do eye refractions.)
24	Otolaryngology	Deals with conditions/diseases of the ears, nose, and throat. (A pediatrician may specialize in otolaryngology and treat these conditions only in children.)
26	Pediatrics	Deals with diseases and conditions involving children (usually up to the age of 19 years). A pediatrician treats nonsurgical conditions. There are also a variety of pediatric specialists who treat only one body system in children.
28	Laboratory Medicine	Deals with the study of structural and functional changes in body tissue, especially those caused by disease. A pathologist usually works in the Pathology Department of a laboratory and studies tissue samples to determine what disease process(es) are present. For example, if a client had a lump removed, the surgeon would send it to a pathologist to determine whether the lump was malignant or benign.
29	Microbiology	The study of microorganisms. A microbiologist usually works in the Microbiology Department of a laboratory.
30	Clinical Biochemistry	Deals with chemical pathology. A clinical biochemist works mostly in a laboratory.
31	Physical Medicine	The treatment and diagnosis of diseases by physical, rather than surgical or chemical, methods. Specialists in this field may work in sports medicine.
33	Diagnostic Radiology	The interpretation of X-ray, MRI, ultrasound, and diagnostic procedures, such as a barium swallow and upper GI series. When you receive the results of such tests in the office, they have been prepared by a radiologist. A radiologist usually works in the Diagnostic Imaging Department or a related department of a hospital or private diagnostic facility.
34	Therapeutic Radiology	The planning and implementation of radiation treatment for cancer patients.

Table 11.1 *(continued)*

35	**Urology**	The study of the genitourinary system. A urologist specializes in the surgical and non-surgical treatment of diseases and conditions of the renal system (kidneys, ureters, and bladder) in both males and females. A urologist would diagnose and treat problems relating to the prostate gland in men, for example.
41	**Gastroenterology**	The study of the gastrointestinal system. A gastroenterologist has completed post-graduate studies dealing with the digestive system. Sometimes, the conditions seen by an internist will overlap with those treated by a gastroenterologist. Internists may refer clients to gastroenterologists for their more specialized knowledge.
47	**Respiratology**	Deals with diseases of the respiratory system, such as chronic obstructive pulmonary disease (COPD) and asthma. The physician is called a respirologist.
48	**Rheumatology**	Deals with rheumatic diseases, primarily arthritis.
60	**Cardiology**	Deals with diseases of the cardiovascular system, such as cardiac ischemia or myocardial infarction (heart attack). A cardiologist usually does not do surgery but is often asked to assess a client's cardiovascular status before surgery, particularly if the person has a history of cardiovascular disease.
61	**Hematology**	Deals with conditions and diseases of the hematopoietic system (blood and related structures), such as leukemia and anemia. A hematologist outlines the course of treatment (usually chemotherapy) for someone with leukemia. Hematologists work in research and laboratory settings as well as in private practice.
62	**Clinical Immunology**	Deals with diseases and conditions of the immune system. Increasing numbers of diseases are now thought to be related to the immune system. Much of this involves research.
63	**Nuclear Medicine**	Deals with diseases relating to unsealed sources of radionuclides. Physicians with this specialty usually work in a hospital (overseeing the Department of Nuclear Medicine), a laboratory, or research company.
64	**General Thoracic Surgery**	Dealing with surgery for conditions of the thoracic organs, primarily the lungs and related structures.

Diagnostic Codes   Every jurisdiction uses a diagnostic code when submitting provincial or territorial claims; they are similar in most regions. Diagnostic codes are based on the ICD-9 coding system and usually consist of three digits. Most medical software billing systems have a look-up option for diagnostic and service codes.

The diagnostic code represents the physician's diagnosis of the client's condition on which treatment decisions are based—for example, angina, congestive heart failure, diabetes mellitus symptoms. Sometimes client symptoms are vague, however; thus each system has a diagnostic code for ill-defined symptoms.

Certain diagnostic codes lend themselves to specific service codes. For example, in Ontario, the diagnostic code 388 (wax in the ears) goes with the procedural code for syringing the ear. Diagnostic code 477 (hay fever, rhinitis) often accompanies the corresponding code for allergy injections. Diagnostic code 487 (the flu) in many provinces and territories accompanies flu vaccine. In BC, the code 11A is used if nothing abnormal is discovered, whereas in Ontario, for vague complaints the physician would use the code 799.

When a physician submits a claim for a pronouncement of death, the cause of death would determine the diagnostic code used. Some jurisdictions require the underlying, rather than the immediate, cause of death. For example, if a client suffering from chronic obstructive pulmonary disease (COPD) died of heart failure caused by the lung disease, the diagnostic code would be 496 for COPD, the underlying cause.

❻❼❽❾ BILLING CODES

As well as a client's valid health card number and a physician's billing number, every claim to a provincial or territorial health plan must have a billing code (also referred to as **service code, fee code,** or **item code**). The structure of the billing code can be made up of alphanumeric or numeric components. The format of these codes varies significantly from one jurisdiction to another.

The billing code, depending on its format, can identify a number of things, including the type of service performed, the location of the service, and/or the age group of the person receiving the service. In Newfoundland and Labrador, billing codes consist of six digits, with the first three representing the service and the next two the physician specialty. The last digit is usually 0. When the last digit is 1, it indicates time units. In BC, most service codes consist of five numeric characters. The last two digits usually reflect the type of examination, the middle digit the location of the service (1 in the office, 2 out of the office); the first two the various age groups, with some exceptions. Figure 11.3 shows an electronic billing screen; the billing code entered A003A.

In Ontario, most service or fee codes consist of five alphanumeric characters:

Configuration:	1 alpha prefix
	3 numeric service identifiers
	1 alpha suffix
For example:	**A003A**

Prefix

The service code prefix can represent one of several things, such as

- the type of assessment,
- where the assessment occurred or under what circumstances, and
- the profession or specialty of the provider.

Numeric Component

The three numbers in the service code identify the type and/or complexity of the service rendered. For example:

- 003 refers to a general assessment (a complete or comprehensive physical examination and history),

Tip

Be aware that there are many more codes that are specific to the setting in which you are working, as well as to other jurisdictions. Do not let the huge numbers and types of codes overwhelm you. You will become familiar with the billing codes used in your own occupational setting. Use your province's/territory's schedule of benefits to locate codes you are unsure of; alternatively, your computer software system may have a look-up option to locate these codes. If you are still in doubt, ask another health professional—perhaps someone in the same office, or in another practice. Most people are glad to help.

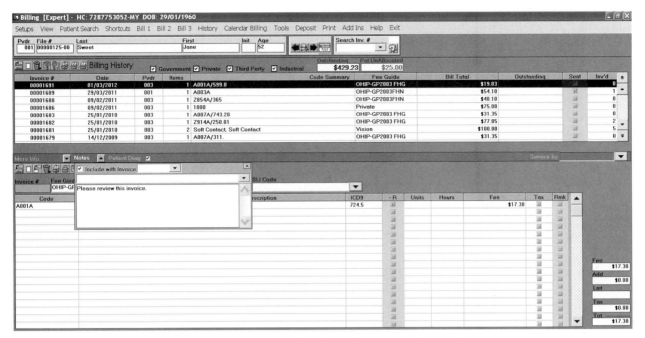

Figure 11.3 A screen from a billing program showing the entry of a service rendered and a request for a manual review

Figure courtesy of P & P Data Systems Inc.

- 001 is a minor assessment, and
- 007 is an intermediate assessment.

Suffix

Most jurisdictions use a suffix as a special identifier. A good example comes from Ontario.

The last component of the service code, an alpha character, records who rendered the service or examination.

A   Physician/provider rendered the service.

B   Assistant rendered the service.

C   Anaesthetist rendered the service.

The most commonly used suffix, particularly in a health office, is A, meaning that the doctor rendered the service or completed the assessment. Consider the following example. Dr. Surry called Dr. Traub in to assist with a caesarean section. Dr. Mohan was the anaesthetist. When they submit claims for the operation, all three use the prefix P, which represents obstetric care, and the numeric code 018, which represents a caesarean section. Dr. Surry uses the suffix A because he did the surgery. His service code is P018A. Dr. Traub uses the suffix B because she assisted with the surgery; her service code is P018B. Dr. Mohan uses the suffix C because he is the anaesthetist; his service code is P018C. (*Note*: Some software systems do not show the suffix. Unless otherwise stated, it is assumed that the physician billing is the one doing the assessment/procedure, thus it defaults to "A.")

B can also indicate that the doctor is billing for the technical portion of a diagnostic and therapeutic procedures code, such as performing a pulmonary function test or an ultrasound (discussed later). C can also indicate that the physician performed the professional component of a diagnostic and procedures code.

Diagnostic and Therapeutic Procedures   The suffix can also have a specific meaning in codes for diagnostic tests.

- A   Technical and Professional Components
- B   Technical
- C   Professional

Technical and Professional Components

In all provinces and territories, diagnostic tests can be billed as one or two components. In some circumstances, a diagnostic test has two insurable components, claimed separately. (In the Ontario fee schedule, codes marked with # can be delivered and billed in two components.) This is common in such specialties as nuclear medicine and diagnostic radiology. For example, if a doctor ordered an X-ray for a client, the doctor would bill for his services, and the diagnostic facility would bill for its services. In many jurisdictions, these two components are referred to as technical and professional. The technical element can include preparing the client for the test, performing the test, making arrangements for follow-up care, completing records resulting from the test, providing health teaching or advice, or preparing and transmitting a written report to a referring physician. The professional component can involve supervising and monitoring a test, performing any associated clinical procedure that is not separately billable (this may include monitoring the client after the procedure is complete), or interpreting the results of a diagnostic procedure. (To claim the professional component, the physician herself must interpret test results.) Another example is an electrocardiogram. Juanita had an ECG in Dr. Moore's office. Dr. Moore was also able to read or interpret the tracing. In this case Dr. Moore would claim both components. In Saskatchewan the claim would be 03.52A for the technical portion of the test (doing the test) and 03.52B for the interpretation of the test (the professional component).

When the doctor orders a test from a separate facility, the doctor's billing would use a C suffix for the professional component, and the diagnostic facility, a B suffix for the technical component. Diagnostic and therapeutic procedures in a family doctor's office are generally submitted as one claim using the A suffix. For example, if a doctor in Ontario completed a urinalysis in the office, the claim would be submitted as G010A.

Commonly Used Services

Each of the many services that doctors provide for clients has a distinct definition, guidelines, and parameters. The definitions of many of these services are the same across Canada. Detailed descriptions of most of these services can be found in the general preamble of the fee schedule in your jurisdiction—see the appropriate website at the end of this chapter. Brief descriptions of the more commonly used services are given below.

Consultation   A consultation is a service provided in response to a written request (called a referral) from a physician—often, but not always, a general practitioner. (It could be a chiropractor, midwife, or nurse practitioner, for example.) The referring practitioner must decide that the client needs the services of a specialist, someone with specialized knowledge in a particular field. For example, a pregnant woman who develops diabetes might be referred to an internist, an obstetrician, or both. A person complaining of chest pain might be sent to a cardiologist. A child diagnosed with leukemia by the family doctor would be referred to an oncologist and/or a pediatrician.

Family doctors themselves sometimes provide consultations, especially if they have advanced training or experience in a field, such as sports medicine or tropical medicine. Generally, however, a family doctor seeks a consultation with a specialist. A specialist may request a consult from another specialist as well. For example, suppose Joanne went to see her family doctor because of stomach problems. He requested a consultation from Dr. Abdul, an internist. Dr. Abdul conducted an assessment, decided the problem required investigation from a surgeon, and sent Joanne to see Dr. van Dyck, a general surgeon.

A specialist must perform a general or specific assessment, depending on the nature of the referral, and submit findings and recommendations in writing to the referring doctor. In some jurisdictions (e.g., BC) a written report must be generated by the specialist within two weeks of the consultation, although some exceptions are made. A specialist may continue to care for the client if this care is deemed necessary by both the referring practitioner and the specialist. Periodic written reports must be submitted to the referring provider. Client care would be transferred back to the provider as soon as appropriate.

A specialist may generally bill for only one consultation for a client in a 12-month period. In some regions, this time frame is six months. However, a second consultation is allowed for an entirely different complaint. For example, Su-Mei was referred to Dr. Hugh, a gastroenterologist, for chronic indigestion. Later in the year, she was again referred to him for unrelenting diarrhea, considered to be unrelated. Table 11.3 contains useful definitions used in physician–client care, transfer of care, and related timelines.

A consultation is not payable by most provincial or territorial plans if

■ the client arrives at the consultant's office without a referral from the primary doctor;

■ the client does not ask the primary doctor for professional advice but simply wants to see a specialist for personal reasons;

■ the client arrives for a consultation more than six to nine months after the referral (usually the referring physician would make a new referral); or

■ the referral is made at the request of a third party.

In these cases, the client or the third party would have to pay.

Repeat Consultation   A repeat consultation includes the same elements as a full consultation and involves periodic assessments of the client and a *repeat referral by the primary care doctor*. In most jurisdictions a specialist cannot charge for a full consultation until at least six months after the initial visit for the same problem. For example, suppose Su-Mei's family doctor sent her to Dr. Hugh for a consultation about her indigestion.

She then continued to see the family doctor, who monitored the problem. Su-Mei did not improve; in fact, the doctor thought the problem got a bit worse. He referred her to Dr. Hugh again for the same complaint. This would be noted as a repeat consultation. In Saskatchewan, a repeat consultation is a formal consultation for the same or a related condition repeated within 90 days by the same physician.

It is not a repeat consultation if the specialist asks the client to return for a repeat visit. The specialist would be paid the accepted provincial or territorial rate for an intermediate assessment.

Limited Consultation   A limited consultation involves all the elements of a full consultation but takes much less of the doctor's time. In some jurisdictions (e.g., Ontario), it applies to a noncertified specialist asked to investigate a specific problem. For example, Don's family doctor sends him to Dr. Lemaich, a family doctor with expertise in sports medicine, because of a knee problem. Dr. Lemaich need only examine Don's knee. In most jurisdictions, the fees charged would be the same as those for a regular visit to another family doctor.

In most provinces and territories, a limited consultation would be claimed for a re-examination of a client for the same condition within six months of the original visit.

General Assessment/Complete Examination   In many provinces and territories, a general assessment can be in response to the investigation of a health concern or for an annual health examination (AHE). Not all jurisdictions allow annual health exams—in some they must be complaint driven (e.g., BC). A complete examination usually takes place in a doctor's office. It requires a full history (medical, family, and social) and examination of all body parts and systems. It may include a more detailed examination of one or more parts or systems if the client has a specific complaint.

In provinces and territories that allow an annual health examination, a person is allowed only one general assessment in a specified time frame. This is a12-month period in Ontario and once every 180 days in Alberta. Most jurisdictions will pay for a second general assessment within the same period if a client presents with clinical signs and complaints that result in a diagnosis unrelated to the diagnosis made during the first general assessment. For example, Ryan, who is 33 years old, had his annual physical examination done in March. He returned nine months later with complaints of fatigue, insomnia, and weight loss. Because these complaints were new and were nonspecific enough to warrant a full investigation, a second checkup would be insured. A second checkup would also be insured if it is done in hospital as an admission assessment, assuming at least 90 days have passed since the client's general assessment.

General Reassessment   A general reassessment is the same as a general assessment except that only a limited history is needed. This category of assessment does not apply in all jurisdictions. It may be called a partial or regional examination. Usually, this is a follow-up. For example, Todd had a general assessment done because of vague symptoms of abdominal cramping, fatigue, and anorexia. If he returned four months later saying his symptoms were a little worse, the doctor would again do a thorough physical examination because the physical findings may have changed; however, instead of taking a detailed history, he would merely focus on any changes.

Preoperative/Pre-dental General Assessment   This category applies in most jurisdictions in Canada. Any client who undergoes general anaesthesia for surgery must have a general assessment to determine whether the anaesthesia and surgery present risks. In most provinces and territories, a preop assessment for **elective surgery** is done by the family doctor unless the client has had a comprehensive assessment within a given time frame (usually a month) prior to the surgery. In this case, the doctor may claim only a partial assessment. In cases of emergency surgery, the assessment would be done in the hospital. If the preoperative assessment is for a dental procedure, a diagnosis is not required when submitting this claim. In most jurisdictions there is a limit on how many preop assessments can be done in a year. In Ontario the number is two.

elective surgery surgery that is necessary but not an emergency and that can therefore be booked in advance. Examples of elective surgery include removal of a tumour, a hip replacement, or a hysterectomy. Appendicitis usually necessitates emergency surgery.

Telehealth Services   Telehealth offers a variety of services to people living in remote places. Most recently, it has broadened client access to specialists and other health-care providers who would be otherwise inaccessible unless the client was transported to a health centre outside of his or her community. Newer technology transmits live images and sound using the internet, other devices, and advanced technology.

The service(s) rendered must be on an approved list. If a specialist at the receiving site requires a family doctor to be with the client to assist with the distance examination, he can fill in the referral field that a request was made for another physician to assist. Specific rules may apply in various jurisdictions.

Special Premium Visits   When a doctor must travel from one place to another to see a client, he is compensates for this by charging for a special premium visit by virtue of a premium code. This includes emergency and non-emergency situations. What premium code is charged depends on the circumstances related to the visit, and the day and time of day on which the visit is made. The special premium visit codes are applied in addition to those claimed for services rendered. In some jurisdictions, a separate premium code is applied to visits for palliative care clients seen in their home. In Ontario this code is B998, for example.

House Call Assessment   In most regions this is considered a primary care service and usually done by family doctors or nurse practitioners. This can be an elective or an urgent home visit, initiated by the physician or generated by client request. If elective, the visit is planned at a time convenient to both the doctor and the client. If the visit is more urgent in nature, the doctor will go as soon as possible, sometimes having to cancel office appointments. Because the physician must travel and, depending on the time of the visit, she may also charge a premium (discussed below). A home visit is almost always billed as an intermediate (limited or regional) assessment. In most jurisdictions, if someone else in the household is seen during that visit, it is billable at a lower rate. For example, Dr. Morley visits Molly, who is 84 and having some shortness of breath. While the doctor is there, Molly's husband John complains of a sore back. Dr. Morley can bill for Molly at the full rate for a house call and for John at a lower rate. In Manitoba this visit is referred to as a Special Call.

House Call Assessment—Pronouncement of Death   The doctor goes into a home to pronounce a client dead. In some jurisdictions this is billed as a home visit, with no extra remuneration for filling out a death certificate. In Ontario however, a special code (A902) can be used. This visit includes counselling those involved with the client. See discussion of diagnostic codes below. A premium (discussed below) may apply depending on the time of day.

Pronouncement of Death—Intermediate Assessment   This is a new code in Ontario (A777) used when the pronouncement of death takes place elsewhere than the client's home. It has a lower value than A902.

Intermediate or Regional Assessment/Limited Visit   An intermediate assessment is considered a primary care assessment and is probably the most frequently used code in a general practitioner's office. It is less extensive than a general assessment but more extensive than a minor assessment (discussed below) and entails

- a history of the presenting complaint;
- current information related to the complaint and body parts/systems examined; and
- an examination of one or more body parts (the affected body part[s], system[s], or mental or emotional disorder, as needed to establish a diagnosis) or direct further tests to establish a diagnosis.

In BC, a similar service is called a partial/regional examination.

Consider two other examples of intermediate/regional assessments:

> Arlene comes into Dr. Tran's office complaining of vague gastrointestinal symptoms, including diarrhea and epigastric burning (a burning sensation below the sternum, or breastbone). Dr. Tran does a related history about her eating and bowel habits. He asks some questions related to the cardiovascular system. He does an abdominal examination, perhaps a rectal examination as well, and listens to the heart and chest. This would constitute an intermediate assessment because the doctor took a detailed history of the complaint, made inquiries regarding the cardiovascular system and the respiratory system, and examined the gastrointestinal, cardiovascular, and respiratory systems.
>
> Paul arrives complaining of an earache and a sore throat. Dr. Lyons examines his ears, throat, and lymph nodes, and probably listens to his chest and takes vital signs. She takes a related history. This would also be an intermediate assessment because the doctor examined more than one system (ears, throat, lymph glands, and the respiratory system) and asked questions related to each system.

Well-Baby Visits   In most provinces and territories, a *well-baby visit* is similar in time and complexity to an intermediate or a limited assessment. This involves routine periodic assessment during the first one to two years of life. It includes a complete examination, with weight and measurements, and instructions to the parent(s) or caregiver regarding related health care and health teaching and appropriate immunizations covered routinely by the provincial or territorial plan.

In BC the code 12101 is used up to the first year of life for a complete assessment; after that, 00101 is used for a complete examination. 12100 is used for a partial exam in the first year. In Alberta, when a newborn visits a doctor's office for whatever reason within the first 14 days of life, the visit is billed as a limited visit if the doctor billed for newborn care in the hospital. Subsequent visits are billed under the appropriate service code. In Saskatchewan the visit code 4B is used for periodic visits during the first year of life.

Annual Health/Physical Examination (Child)   This category does not apply in all jurisdictions. In Ontario for example, an AHE for a child is a general assessment of a child 2 to 15 years of age who does not present with health problems. The code is K017 with no diagnostic code used. It includes all relevant instructions and health teaching.

This assessment code includes primary and secondary school examinations. In BC, these examinations are complaint generated. The service code 00101 is used for a complete assessment after the child is a year old, and 13201 for a partial assessment.

Minor/Brief Assessment

A minor or a brief assessment is also considered a primary care assessment and is used in many jurisdictions for an office visit. This code is used when the encounter involves a brief history, examination of the affected part or region or mental or emotional disorder, and/or brief advice or information regarding health maintenance, diagnosis, treatment, or prognosis.

Examples of a minor assessment:

Trudy had been diagnosed with pneumonia and was treated with an antibiotic for 10 days. She comes back in so that Dr. Dumont can quickly assess her recovery. He asks her how she is feeling, if she has any shortness of breath, fever, and so on. He listens to her chest and, finding nothing, concludes the assessment.

Victor is going abroad and comes in to see Dr. Dumont to ask what immunizations he will need.

Mei-Lin has been having trouble with a skin rash, and Dr. Dumont prescribed some new medication for it. She comes in so that he can assess her progress. He checks her rash, asks a couple of questions, and concludes the assessment.

Mini Assessment

In some jurisdictions, a mini assessment is applied if the doctor has to examine the client for a completely unrelated problem during the same office visit for an examination of a Workplace Safety Insurance Board (WSIB) assessment. It can be claimed only in conjunction with a WSIB claim, for which the WSIB will pay only for a minor assessment during the same visit. It cannot be claimed if the WSIB claim is complex or requires a comprehensive examination.

Prenatal Visit—Initial Assessment

This is the initial assessment once a diagnosis of pregnancy has been established. This visit is more detailed than subsequent visits and should entail a comprehensive history and physical assessment of the mother-to-be and related health teaching. In most jurisdictions this visit may only be claimed once per client per pregnancy.

Routine Prenatal Office Visits

These visits for a routine pregnancy are specific and do not involve an in-depth assessment. They equate to a regional or limited assessment in depth and complexity. The assessment primarily includes testing a urine sample for protein, glucose, and acetone, taking the woman's weight and vital signs, taking fetal heart rate (once audible), measuring the height of the **fundus**, asking a range of related questions, and answering any concerns the woman might have.

fundus the top of the uterus. Measuring how high the fundus is in the abdomen provides valuable information about the size of the uterus and the progression of fetal growth.

Antenatal Preventative Health Assessment

This visit option, offered in some jurisdictions, is for a client who is considering becoming pregnant (**antenatal** means "before birth"). The physician conducts an examination, reviews the client's history, and assesses genetic, psychosocial, and medical risks. There may be some restrictions on this visit.

antenatal before birth.

Counselling

This is defined as a visit to discuss the client's problems and help the client develop an awareness of them and consider solutions. Counselling can be individual or group (two or more persons). For billing purposes, counselling is usually based on time units, with a minimum of 20–30 minutes. If it is less than

20 minutes, the practitioner should only charge for an intermediate or limited visit. In Saskatchewan, for example, the first unit of time is 15 minutes (40-B), the second 15 minutes, or major portion thereof (41-B). Most jurisdictions will pay for a specific number of counselling sessions in a calendar year. There are sometimes different codes for counselling based on specific medical problems and general counselling for healthy lifestyles.

Services to Hospital Inpatients

In all provinces and territories, physicians attend to clients within the hospital setting. Most often the MRP (most responsible physician) is a specialist, but the family doctor may still visit the client in hospital, providing some element of care. You would bill your provincial or territorial plan for this care (a concurrent visit). The doctor would provide you with the information on how many visits he has made and when. Each province and territory will have unique codes for services provided to clients in hospital, both inpatients and outpatients. If you are working for a general practitioner, it is your responsibility to ensure that all claims for hospital visits and procedures are submitted. The types of visits you can bill for may include

- admission assessment. (If necessary the family doctor can complete and claim for a complete physical assessment.)
- subsequent hospital care (usually limited to one visit/client/day).
- concurrent or supportive care. (Family doctor provides services in collaboration with the specialist.)
- long stay in hospital. (The number of visits allowed is reduced unless acute episodes related to the admission or another illness arise.)
- attendance in labour and delivery. (Many family doctors assist with a delivery, particularly a caesarean section. Codes used may be time based and/or have a premium code depending on the time of day of the delivery.)
- newborn hospital care. Usually a specialist delivers a baby in hospital but does not care for the baby. (The family doctor often assumes immediate newborn care. He can claim for the newborn assessment and daily visits as required up to a maximum number of days—usually 10.) Note: if a midwife delivers the baby, she will provide newborn care as well as looking after the mother.
- operative assist. Some family doctors assist in surgery for their own clients. These claims may be calculated on units of time and would likely have a premium code depending on the time of day of the surgery.
- palliative care in hospital or another place. Palliative care visits are to a client suffering from a terminal disease (e.g., cancer, AIDS) who is not being actively treated. Visits can be made daily. Usually these visits are billed after the client has died.

Services in Long-Term Care Facilities

Doctors can claim a facility visit for seeing clients in long-term care facilities, such as nursing homes. The permitted frequency of these visits may vary but ranges from a visit every two weeks to once a month. If required, more frequent visits can be claimed with supporting documentation.

Special Service Code Notifiers

Some jurisdictions use a special service code notifier to point out parts of a service that are included in the visit and thus must not be billed separately. (An example would be doing a Pap smear as part of an annual health exam).

UVC stands for Use Visit Code. Beside some items in the Schedule of Benefits in Ontario, for example, this code appears instead of a specific procedural code. Do not claim for these items separately; they are considered to be part of a visit. For example, removing a Shirodkar suture (a stitch put into a woman's cervix to prevent spontaneous abortion) is marked UVC in the schedule. You would not submit a claim for this procedure but would simply bill the appropriate code for the office visit during which the stitch was removed.

Independent Consideration Claims Most jurisdictions have services that require special evaluation before a fee can be determined.

IC stands for independent consideration. Independent consideration may be given when a set fee is not listed in the provincial or territorial schedule, or the service isn't listed at all. Each IC claim is reviewed by a consultant at a district or regional office. These claims must be sent with a letter and either an operative report or a consultation report detailing relevant data. This can be done electronically, but the Ministry may still require a faxed explanation for the request.

Manual Review

Sometimes a physician will submit a claim for a service that contravenes the policies and regulations of the provincial or territorial billing guidelines. The doctor must mark the claim MR (usually a field option on the computer)—which stands for manual review. This signals that there is an irregularity with the submitted claim. The doctor must fax an explanation for the claim. In some jurisdictions the explanation can be submitted electronically. For example, Jeremy came to see Dr. Ward for a limited assessment for headaches Wednesday morning. Wednesday afternoon he returned because he developed severe abdominal pain. Most provinces and territories pay for only one visit per person per day. In this case, Dr. Ward marked the second claim as MR. He faxed an explanation for the circumstances under which Jeremy came back for another visit. The examiner reviewed this and the claim was accepted.

Diagnostic and Therapeutic Procedural Codes

There is a special category of codes in all jurisdictions for a group of actions/services that come under the umbrella of diagnostic and therapeutic procedures. They are often referred to as procedural codes. Services related to diagnostic procedures range from simple tests done in a doctor's office to ultrasounds and more complex services. Thera
procedures include any services or actions that contribute to the cure and
of a disease or condition; these include syringing a client's ear to clear t
a laceration, giving an immunization or injection, putting on a dressin
infected wound.

The listings under the Diagnostic and Therapeutic Procedures are cl
to an office visit, when performed during that visit. Thus, the doctor ma

appropriate fee code *as well as* the related procedure code. If the procedure is the only reason for the visit, then only the procedural code can be claimed. The listed value for the procedure will apply. For example, if a client comes in for an allergy shot and nothing else, then only the procedural code can be claimed. If a client comes in complaining of an earache and also has an allergy shot at the same visit, then the doctor can claim for the fee code for office visit and assessment related to the earache and for the procedural code for the allergy shot. In most jurisdictions the amount paid for the procedure without a physician visit is more than would be paid if the person saw the doctor as well. For example, if Mary came in for an allergy shot and did not see the doctor, the amount claimed would be $5. If Greg came for an allergy shot but saw the doctor because he needed his inhalers reviewed, the amount that could claimed for the allergy shot is only $3, but the doctor could also submit a claim for an assessment.

Sometimes, a diagnostic code is necessary, and sometimes it is not. Some procedures, such as a flu vaccine and other immunizations, may require specific diagnostic codes designated by the Ministry. Otherwise, use the diagnostic code that best relates to the condition or suspected condition for which the test or procedure is being done. For example, if a urinalysis is done in the office as part of a prenatal examination, then the diagnostic 650 (normal pregnancy) could be used for the urinalysis. Each procedure (diagnostic or therapeutic) will have a unique billing code, either numeric or alphanumeric. For example, in BC the first three digits of the codes for lab procedures done in a doctor's office are usually 151, minor procedures 136. If preceded by a B in the schedule, that indicates the procedure is part of the visit. In Ontario, the prefix G or Z is often used in conjunction with a numeric component. See Table 11A.1 in Appendix 11A for Ontario procedural codes.

Codes and Primary Care Reform Groups

As mentioned in Chapter 4, the billing for primary care reform groups is complex. As well, the billing format and the codes used are constantly changing. What is current in 2010 may well be outdated in 2012.

Services claimed in these groups have unique codes, some common and others specific to each primary care reform model. These codes apply to the following:

- After hours, holidays, and weekend services (including working in the clinic)
- Client enrolment (includes several categories)
- Diabetic management
- Smoking cessation (simple discussion and counselling are separate codes)
- Primary mental health services

Ontario has made more headway than many other jurisdictions in implementing patient enrolment models and in developing a related billing format. Most PEMs (primary care enrolment models) are paid for each client they enrol. In Ontario the code for this is Q200A, and OHIP pays about $5 per client for the first year only. New doctors get more for enrolling clients, and use the code Q033A. This is called the New Physician–New Patient Agreement. In addition, all doctors can claim for taking on a new client who has ⌐ doctor and who has been discharged from a hospital; that person must enrol with the ⌐ctor within three months of his hospital discharge. Q023A, the unattached patient ⌐uisition code, would be used. Diabetic management is Q040A. Discussing smoking cessation is Q141A, and counselling about smoking cessation is Q142A. Q016 can be added to existing visit codes for clients seen on weekends, and after hours (e.g., intermediate assessment).

As mentioned in Chapter 4, most jurisdictions use numerous tracking codes. Use of the codes is voluntary and intended to make it easier for the administrative staff to monitor and calculate cumulative bonus payments for preventative-services goals achieved. These codes include exception codes as well. For example, the tracking code for a Pap smear is Q11A (for women between 35 and 70 years of age). The exception code is Q140A (women who have had a hysterectomy). Any woman who has had a hysterectomy obviously would be excluded from the list of eligible women for whom the Ministry expects the doctor to complete Pap smears, unless the cervix has been retained.

Time Units

Time units are used for some services rendered by a family doctor (e.g., counselling). They are, however, most often used for specialists, such as surgeons and anaesthetists. For example, 15 minutes might be one time unit. An hour would be four time units. Sometimes, a hardship benefit may apply after a certain point. For example, suppose the time unit is 15 minutes and the cut-off point is 2 hours; the hardship point allows doubling the units. For example, a doctor assisting with a surgical procedure is allowed 3 hours. The total number of units should actually be 12 (3 hours × 4 time units). However, you would count the first 2 hours as 8 units, and then double the units in the last hour to count as another 8 units, producing a total of 16. In most jurisdictions, there is also a preset number of base units. If 4 base units are allowed for this procedure, you would bill for 20 units (16 time units + 4 base units).

Premium Codes

A premium code is a code that, under special circumstances, may be claimed *in addition to* service codes listed under "consultations and visits" and "diagnostic and therapeutic procedures." It is payment to a provider for services over and above the routine—for example, services provided after hours, away from the office, or at the expense of office hours—for emergency work and for added responsibility. Certain premium codes are based on time units.

Premium Codes for Care of Older Adults Premium codes also apply to some assessments done for older patients, on the reasoning that they often have more complex medical problems and take more time to assess. In many jurisdictions, premium codes for care of complex, time-consuming clients have been eliminated, and remuneration for service for designated age groups has been increased.

Premium Codes Plus Diagnostic and Therapeutic Procedures Most provinces and territories allow a premium code as an "add on" for certain procedures. This involves more complex procedures for which the basic procedural fee is deemed inadequate. A premium code may also apply to a "tray fee," and is compensation for the use of equipment that is disposable or that must be autoclaved. A tray fee could apply to a service claimed for doing a complex dressing or removing sutures, for example. The procedures that the extra premium code applies to will be clearly marked in your province's or territory's fee schedule. For example, taking blood from a baby is considered more

Table 11.2 Common Diagnostic Codes

(From ICD-9)

Abdominal pain	787	Cataracts	366	Exhaustion	796
Abrasions, contusions	919	Cellulitus	682	Family planning	895
Abscess (skin)	685	Cervicitis	616	Fatigue	796
Acne	706	Chest pain	785	Fever	796
Adenitis	289	Chicken pox	052	Flu	487
Adverse drug reaction	977	Cholelithiasis	574	Gall stone	574
AIDS	042	Cirrhosis	571	Ganglion	727
Alcoholism	303	Colon cancer	153	Gastric Ulcer	531
Amenorrhea	626	Concussion	850	Gastritis	535
Anemia (iron deficiency)	280	Congestive heart failure	428	Gastroenteritis	009
Angina pectoris	413	Conjunctivitis	372	Gastrointestinal symptoms—vague	
Ankle strain	845	Constipation	564	(includes jaundice, N&V)	787
Anorexia	787	Contraception	895	Gout	274
Anxiety	300	Contusion	919	Grief reaction	611
Appendicitis	540	COPD	496	Gynecomastia	611
Arrhythmia	427	Coronary artery disease (CAD)	412	Head injury	854
Arteriosclerosis	440	Cough	786	Headache (migraine)	346
Arthritis (osteo)	715	Crohn's disease	555	Headache (tension)	307
Arthritis (rheumatoid) (RA)	714	Croup	464	Headache NYD	780
ASHD	412	CVA	436	Heart failure	428
Asthma	493	Cystitis	595	Heart murmur	429
Athletes foot	110	Deep vein thrombosis or DVT	451	Heartburn	787
Back pain	847	Dementia	290	Hematoma	959
Baker's cyst	727	Dental caries	521	Hemiplegia	599
Behaviour disorder	313	Depression	311	Hemorrhoids	455
Benign prostatic		Dermatitis (contact)	692	Hepatitis	070
hypertrophy (BPH)	600	Diabetes	250	Hernia (inguinal)	550
Birth control	895	Diaper rash	691	Hernia (other)	553
Bites (insect)	989	Diarrhea	009	Herpes genitalis	099
Bleeding (postmenopausal)	627	Disc disease	722	Herpes simplex	054
Breast cancer	174	Diverticulitis	562	Herpes zoster	053
Breast lump (benign)	217	Divorce	901	HIV	279
Bronchitis (acute)	466	Dysmenorrhea	625	Hives	708
Bronchitis (chronic)	491	Dyspepsia (indigestion)	536	Hyperactivity	314
Bunions	727	Dyspnea	786	Hypercholesterolemia	272
Bursitis	727	Eczema	691	Hyperemesis	643

Table 11.2 *(continued)*

Cancer of the cervix	180	Edema	785	Hypertension	401
Cancer of the prostate	185	Emphysema	492	Hypertensive heart	402
Candidiasis	112	Epistaxis	786	Hyperventilation	486
Carpal tunnel syndrome	739	Esophagitis	530	Immunization	896
Impetigo	684	Peripheral vascular disorder	443	Sprain (neck)	847
Incontinence	788	Personality disorder	301	Sprain (shoulder)	840
Influenza	487	Pharyngitis	460	Sprain (wrist)	842
Ingrown toe nail	703	Phlebitis	451	Sprain, Strain (other)	848
Intervertebral disc disorders	722	Pilonidal abscess	685	Strep throat	034
Joint pain	781	Pneumonia	486	Stress incontinence	625
Knee Pain	844	Pregnancy (normal)	650	Stroke	436
Laryngitis	464	Prostatis	601	Syncope	785
Leg cramps	781	Pyrexia	796	Tachycardia	427
Legal Problems	906	Rash	691	TB test, conversion	010
Low back pain	724	Renal colic	788	Tendonitis	727
Malaise	799	Renal failure (acute)	584	Tennis elbow	739
Marital problems	898	Rheumatoid arthritis	714	Tension headache	307
Measles	055	Rhinitis	477	Tonsillitis	463
Menopause	627	Rosacea	695	Toothache	525
Menorrhagia	626	Rubella	056	Threatened abortion	635
Menstrual disorder	626	Scabies	133	Thrush	112
Migraine	346	Sciatica	724	Transient ischemic attack	435
Mononucleosis	075	Sebaceous cyst	706	Upper respiratory infection	460
Mumps	072	Seborrhea	690	Urinary infection	599
Muscle spasm	728	Seizure disorder	345	Unemployment	905
Nosebleed	786	Senility	797	Vaginal bleeding	626
Obesity	278	Sexual dysfunction	306	Vaginitis	616
Occupational problem	905	Shingles	053	Varicose vein	454
Oral ulcers	528	Shortness of breath	786	Venereal disease	099
Osteoarthritis	715	Sinusitis (acute)	461	Vertigo	780
Osteoporosis	730	Social maladjustment	904	Viral illness	079
Otitis externa	380	Sprain (foot, ankle)	845	Warts	078
Otitis media	381	Sprain (leg, Knee)	844	Wax in ear	388
Pain (chest)	785	Sprain (lumbar)	724	Weight loss	796

complex in most jurisdictions. If this is the case the procedural code for this service would be identified with a marker indicating that you can also claim a premium code (sometimes called a basic fee-for-visit premium).

Table 11.3 Useful Terms and Definitions

Useful Terms and Definitions

Year:	a calendar year beginning January 1
Month:	a calendar month
Sole reason for visit:	applies when the client sees the physician with a specific complaint and the physician assesses and treats that complaint only
Most responsible physician (MRP):	the attending doctor who is primarily responsible for the day-to-day care of a client in hospital; this may change depending on the client's condition and progress
Concurrent care:	a physician other than the MRP directs care for a hospitalized client. In some jurisdictions (e.g., Saskatchewan), the doctors must prove that the client needs care by more than one doctor before the provincial or territorial plan will pay for services rendered by the second doctor.
Transfer of care:	exchange of information when the responsibility for a client's care is transferred from one provider to another, for example, if the original provider goes on vacation; note that any consultations involved cannot be billed

In Ontario G700 is the basic fee-for-visit premium related to certain procedures marked (+) in the Schedule of Benefits. The procedural code for performing venipuncture on an infant is G480. In the schedule it appears as +G480. That means that you can also submit a claim using the code G700 in addition to the G480 for the procedure. These codes apply only to visits where an applicable therapeutic or diagnostic procedure was completed.

Surgical Assist Premium Codes A premium code also applies if a doctor assists a surgeon with an operative procedure after hours or at the cost of office hours. For emergency surgery, in particular, a surgeon will often call in one or more other physicians to assist. In smaller communities, this is often a family doctor. As with special visit premiums, there is recognition given for the time of day or night the physician must work and how long the physician must work. The assistant's fee is calculated by a formula including a basic rate and time units. Premium payments are usually determined as a percentage of a calculated or predetermined fee.

Premiums and Detention "Detention" occurs when a physician must spend longer than the usual amount of time with a client. The physician may claim a premium for the extra time, usually calculated by time unit.

Special Visit Premium Code/Call-Out Premiums

A special visit premium code may be claimed in addition to specified services when, for medically necessary reasons, a physician must travel to render a service. This includes visits to a client at home, in a hotel, in a vehicle at the side of the road, or in a health-care facility. This premium can be claimed only when the client cannot realistically visit the doctor's office. Usually, there is one code for the first client seen during a special visit and another one (with a lesser premium) for any other clients seen at the same facility on the same visit. Moreover, the doctor may claim only one premium code for a single visit to a client. For example, if Dr. Paquette saw Genevieve to suture her laceration and she complained of a sore throat that had to be examined, he could charge only one premium code related to that visit.

Special visit premium codes also reflect the time of the service: during the day (0700–1800), evening (1800–2400), and night (0000–0700). The evening code is often the same one used for weekends and holidays. Hours may vary. In BC, 0800–1800 and 1800–2300 hours define the day and evening premiums, 2300–0800 the night premium; another premium rate applies for services rendered on weekends and statutory holidays between 0800 and 1800 hours.

In BC, premiums paid for home visits are called call-out charges. The codes used are 01200, 01201, and 01202 in addition to the service code for out-of-office visits. Table 11A.3 shows common premium codes.

Age-Related Premiums

Age supplements are given to physicians in some provinces and territories caring for older people with more complex needs. They are based on the value of the visit (a brief or limited visit compared with a comprehensive visit), excluding other premiums and charges. The rationale is that older people take more time because they require more intensive medical assessment and care. In Alberta, for example, the special code 03.03Z is used for a limited visit with a client over the age of 75.

BILLING EXAMPLES

THIS SECTION INCLUDES EXAMPLES TO WHICH YOU CAN APPLY THE VARIOUS CODES relevant in your province or territory. Work in class with your professor to complete the sample blank billing screens. Use the links listed at the end of the chapter to look up the fee and diagnostic codes.

Submit the appropriate claim information as requested by each of the following examples, using your medical software program or a hard copy of a claims form designed by your professor.

Intermediate Assessment in the Office

Example #1: Scratchy Throat   Helen, 52, comes in to Dr. Cardinal's office complaining of a scratchy throat and chest tightness. The doctor takes a history related to her cardiovascular and respiratory systems. He listens to her heart, checks for swelling in her feet and ankles, and listens for bruits (sounds) in the neck region. He listens to her chest. He looks at her throat and palpates for swollen glands.

Note that, to reach a diagnosis, the doctor

■   took a history of the presenting complaint and related systems, and

■   examined one or more body systems.

This is an intermediate or a regional/limited assessment. The diagnosis is acute bronchitis—use that diagnostic code.

Example #2: A Sore Knee   Jack, 25, comes in to see Dr. Connelly about a sore knee. It is swollen, and he has been having difficulty bearing weight. The doctor does a thorough investigation into the history, asking about recent injury, onset of clinical signs, and so on. He does a thorough examination of the knee, compares it with the other knee, and checks Jack's ability to walk and bear weight. Dr. Connelly makes a diagnosis of bursitis (inflammation of the bursa). Use the diagnostic code for bursitis.

This is an intermediate or partial/limited assessment because the doctor

- took a detailed history relating to the complaint, and
- did a thorough examination of the knee, joint, and leg.

Minor or Brief Assessment in the Office

Example: Itchy Skin   Asha is 80 years old. She saw Dr. Connelly on April 28. Her complaint was itchy skin on her right forearm.

Dr. Connelly looked at the area but did not see anything significant. He prescribed a cream. The visit was quick. No in-depth examination was done. He questioned her briefly about possible causes. This fits the criterion for a minor or a brief assessment. The diagnosis is pruritis—use that diagnostic code.

Office Visit for a Procedure

Example #1: Procedure with Assessment   Leslie is 32 years old. She comes in to see Dr. Simanek for an allergy shot. She also sees the doctor about a brief assessment of her allergies. You have a brief visit to discuss allergies, and a procedure (allergy shot) Use the diagnostic code for rhinitis.

Example #2: Procedure without Assessment   The following week, Leslie comes in for her second allergy shot. The nurse gives her the injection, and she does *not* need to see the doctor. Will the value of this procedure be more than for the same injection when the doctor could also charge for a minor assessment? This is a visit only for a procedure. Use the diagnostic code for rhinitis unless otherwise directed.

Example #3: Procedure with Unrelated Intermediate Assessment   Ethel is 7 years old. She arrives at the office with her mom for an immunization and a visit to have her asthma medication adjusted. Use the diagnostic code for asthma. You would bill for the intermediate assessment.

You also submit a procedural code for the immunization.

Example #4: Intermediate Assessment with Related Urinalysis   Marco is 32 years old. He comes in complaining of low back pain and burning sensation on urination. The doctor completes an intermediate assessment and does a urinalysis in the office. Use the diagnostic code for urinary tract infection (UTI). You would also claim a procedural code for a dipstick urine test. Is a diagnostic code required?

Premium Codes

Example #1: House Call after Office Hours   Margaret calls Dr. Baird and requests he come to see her at home outside of normal office hours for complaints of generalized weakness. Dr. Baird goes to see Margaret at 1730, just after the office closed.

What is the service code for a home visit? Select the premium code for a visit between 0700 and 1800 hrs.

Example #2: House Call during Office Hours   Margaret asks Dr. Baird to come during office hours. She has fallen down and cannot get up. Use the same service code for a house call. Select the premium code for a house call at the sacrifice of office hours.

Example #3: House Call on a Weekend Evening   Dr. Baird makes a house call to see Margaret at 2000 on Saturday because she complains of abdominal pain. Use the same service code for a house call. Select the premium code for visiting a client during the evening on a weekend or holiday.

Example #4: Visit to an LTC after Office Hours   Dr. Baird goes to see Tomas at a nursing home at 1700, after office hours, for complaints of generalized weakness. Find the service code for a visit to a long-term care facility. Select the premium code for a daytime visit that is not at the expense of office hours.

Example #5: Visit to an LTC during Office Hours   Dr. Baird goes to see Tomas at the nursing home because he has fallen down. It is an emergency, and the doctor goes during office hours. Use the same service code for a visit to an LTC. Select the premium code for a visit at the expense of office hours.

Example #6: Visit to an LTC Late at Night   Dr. Baird is asked to come and see Tomas at the nursing home at 3 a.m. Use the same visit code for the nursing home. Select the appropriate premium code for a 3 a.m. visit. Format a claim for this visit.

Example #7: Late-Night Normal Delivery   Sarah delivered a healthy baby boy at 3:30 Wednesday morning. Select your provincial or territorial visit code for a vaginal delivery with no complications. Because the delivery occurred between 0000 and 0700 on a weekday, the physician can also claim a premium code—select the appropriate code.

Example #8: Pronouncement of Death with Premium for Sacrifice of Office Hours   Dr. Hoffman is called to Elena's home during office hours. She pronounces Elena dead, the underlying cause of death being COPD. Use the diagnostic code for COPD. Format a claim for the appropriate service code for pronouncement of death at home and a premium code for sacrifice of office hours. The same diagnostic code is applied to both items.

COMMON FORMS USED IN CLAIMS SUBMISSION

Reciprocal Claim Form

Although reciprocal claims are usually submitted electronically, a reciprocal claim form is used occasionally by a provider who renders care to an individual from another province or territory. (Remember that Quebec does not take part in the Reciprocal Medical Billing System.)

Out-of-Province/Territory Claim Form

An out-of-province/territory claim form is used by a provider who provides services to someone from out of the province or territory if the client's home province or territory does not participate in the Reciprocal Medical Billing System or if the services are excluded from the billing system (see Figure 11.4). The claim may be sent directly to the client's home province or territory. The provider may also bill the client directly; the client can then apply to her Health Ministry for reimbursement.

Request for Approval of Payment for a Proposed Dental Procedure

This form is used by a dental provider seeking coverage for a service not routinely covered by the provincial or territorial health plan. The provider must present a good argument as to why the Ministry should cover the costs of the proposed procedure. The request will be reviewed and the provider notified. Normally, the dentist would wait for approval before proceeding. If the request is turned down, the client would have to pay if she still wants the service.

Request for Approval for Proposed Surgery

Similarly, a doctor may request coverage for a surgical procedure not normally covered. An example might be a breast reduction surgery or reversal of a sterilization procedure. Again, the doctor must argue why the procedure should be covered in this case and should wait for approval before proceeding. If the proposed claim is rejected, the client can decide whether to pay for the surgery himself.

Request for Prior Approval for Out-of-Country Health Services

This form is completed by a physician on behalf of a client for a procedure to be rendered out of the country, usually for a medically necessary service that is not available in Canada.

Health Card Number Release Form

These forms are used in every province and territory (see Figure 11.5). They allow you legal access to the client's health card number and version code. This would allow you to process a claim if the client forgot to bring his health card or if it was lost or stolen. The client will likely not know his health card number and version code; even if he does, you will likely want to check that the information is correct. If you do not know the client, perhaps because he is a walk-in or from out of town, it is important to check whether he is eligible for coverage.

Consent is necessary because, under the *Freedom of Information and Privacy Act*, the health card number and version code are confidential information that belongs to the client. When the client presents you with his health card, the act of presenting it indicates consent. However, if he does not have the card to give you, written consent is needed.

Copies of these forms are supplied by the Ministry or a designated office. Most jurisdictions also have them available on the internet. The form must be completed and signed by the client at the point of service. You may *not* charge for completing this form. Often specialists' offices seeking health card information will request it from the client's family doctor, which may also necessitate accessing the information from the provincial or territorial Ministry.

Ministry of Health and Long-Term Care

Out-of-Province/Country Claim Submission

- Do not submit receipts for prescription drugs as they are not an insured Ontario Health Insurance Plan (OHIP) benefit.
- Complete, sign and return this form with your *original* detailed statement that gives a complete breakdown of all charges to a Ministry of Health and Long-Term Care office. Keep copies for your records.
- If the *original* statement is not in English or French, for accounts:
  - Under $1000 Canadian, a non-certified translation with a signed statement is acceptable.
  - $1000 and over, a certified translation is required.
- If the other criteria for payment set out in the *Health Insurance Act* and Regulations are met, the ministry will pay the amount payable under the Act to an eligible hospital or health facility *directly* upon receipt of an itemized invoice and the signed authorization and direction (see below). The ministry will not make payment directly to an out-of-country physician.
- If the other criteria for payment set out in the *Health Insurance Act* and Regulations are met, the ministry will pay the amount payable under the Act to the client *directly* for *hospital* or *physician* charges upon receipt of an itemized invoice and *original proof of payment*.
- Accounts must be submitted within 12 months from date of service. Please allow 6–8 weeks for payment. All payments will be in Canadian funds.

Patient Information

Health Number		Version	Patient's Last Name	First Name

Date of Birth — year / month / day

Sex: ☐ Male ☐ Female

Telephone No. (home) ( )

Telephone No. (business) ( )

Mailing Address — Street Name | City | Province | Postal Code

Residence Address Street Name | City | Province | Postal Code

Date of Departure from Ontario — year / month / day | Date of Return to Ontario — year / month / day | Country/Province Where Treatment Provided | Type of currency paid

In the previous 12 month period, have you been absent from Ontario for a period of more than 212 days?   ☐ No   ☐ Yes ▷   If yes, provide details.

Are you covered by any travel/supplementary insurance?   ☐ No   ☐ Yes ▷   If yes, name of insurance company | Policy Number

Treatment Information *(Complete this section in full)*

Was this treatment required due to a condition which arose outside Ontario, was acute and unexpected, and required immediate treatment?   ☐ Yes   ☐ No

Reason for Visit/Diagnosis *(nature of illness)* | Type of Treatment Received

Place of Treatment: ☐ Office ☐ Home ☐ Hospital ☐ Other *(specify)* _____ | Treatment Date — year / month / day | Time of Treatment _____ : _____ ☐ A.M. ☐ P.M.

Hospital Information

Hospital Name | Admission Date — year / month / day | Discharge Date — year / month / day

Hospital Address | Please Check (✔) One ☐ inpatient ☐ outpatient

Knowingly providing false information is an offence punishable by fine and/or imprisonment. The information given on this form is true and accurate.

Signature of Patient/Guardian   X _____ | Date _____

Authorization and Direction *(The ministry will pay the amount payable by OHIP directly to an eligible hospital or health facility upon receipt of an itemized invoice and the signed authorization.)*

I, _____ authorize and direct the Ministry of Health and Long-Term Care to pay the
      Name of Patient *(print)*

amount of my hospital / health facility bills that are payable by OHIP directly to _____ .
                                                                          Name of Hospital/Health facility *(print)*

Signature of Patient/Guardian   X _____ | Date _____

For more information, contact a claims processing office (collect calls accepted) or visit our web site at: www.health.gov.on.ca

London	**Oshawa**	**Ottawa**	**Thunder Bay**
217 York St. 5th floor, N6A 5P9	419 King St. W., L1H 8L4	75 Albert St., 7th Floor, K1P 5Y9	435 James St. S., Suite 113, P7E 6T1
519 675–6800	905 576–2870	613 237–9100	807 475–1353

0951–84 (2010/09)   ©Queen's Printer for Ontario, 2010   ©Imprimeur de la Reine pour l'Ontario, 2010   7530–4568

Figure 11.4   Out-of-province claim form

© Queen's Printer for Ontario, 2010. Reproduced with permission.

Ontario

Ministère de la Santé et des Soins de longue durée

Demande de remboursement en cas de traitement hors de la province ou du pays

- N'envoyez pas de reçu pour les médicaments sur ordonnance, car ils ne sont pas couverts par l'Assurance-santé de l'Ontario.
- Vous devez remplir, signer et envoyer le présent formulaire avec votre déclaration *originale* détaillée donnant une ventilation complète des honoraires à un bureau du ministère de la Santé et des Soins de longue durée. Conservez-en une copie pour vos dossiers.
- Si la déclaration *originale* n'est ni en français ni en anglais, il faut y joindre une traduction.
  - Pour les demandes de moins de 1 000 $CAN, une traduction non certifiée est acceptable si elle est accompagnée d'une déclaration signée.
  - Pour les demandes de 1 000 $CAN et plus, une traduction certifiée est nécessaire.
- Si les autres critères de paiement énoncés dans la *Loi sur l'assurance-santé* et les règlements ont été satisfaits, le ministère versera le montant payable en vertu de la Loi directement à l'hôpital ou à l'établissement de santé admissible sur réception d'une facture détaillée et de l'autorisation et de la demande ci-dessous dûment signées. Le ministère ne paiera directement aucune somme à un médecin pratiquant à l'étranger.
- Si les autres critères de paiement énoncés dans la *Loi sur l'assurance-santé* et les règlements ont été satisfaits, le ministère versera le montant payable en vertu de la Loi directement au client ou à la cliente pour les frais d'hospitalisation ou les honoraires de médecin sur réception d'une facture détaillée et d'un *reçu original comme preuve de paiement.*
- Les demandes de remboursement doivent être transmises dans les 12 mois suivant la date de traitement. Veuillez prévoir de six à huit semaines avant de recevoir les paiements. Tous les paiements sont effectués en dollars canadiens.

Renseignements sur le patient ou la patiente

N° de carte Santé	Version	Nom de famille	Prénom

Date de naissance (année mois jour)	Sexe ☐ homme ☐ femme	Téléphone (domicile) ( )	Téléphone (travail) ( )

Adresse postale — Rue	Ville	Province	Code postal

Adresse personnelle — Rue	Ville	Province	Code postal

Date de départ de l'Ontario (année mois jour)	Date de retour en Ontario (année mois jour)	Pays/Province où le traitement a été reçu	Devise utilisée pour le paiement

Au cours des 12 derniers mois, avez-vous été à l'extérieur de l'Ontario pendant une période de plus de 212 jours? ☐ Non ☐ Oui ▷   Dans l'affirmative, veuillez fournir des détails.

Avez-vous une assurance de voyage/supplémentaire? ☐ Non ☐ Oui ▷   Dans l'affirmative, veuillez indiquer le nom de la compagnie d'assurance.   Numéro de la police

Renseignements sur le traitement *(Remplir cette section en entier)*

Le traitement a-t-il été nécessaire en raison d'un état grave et imprévu qui s'est déclaré à l'extérieur de l'Ontario et qui a exigé un traitement immédiat? ☐ Oui ☐ Non

Raison de la consultation/du diagnostic *(nature de la maladie)*   Genre de traitement reçu

Lieu du traitement ☐ bureau ☐ domicile ☐ hôpital ☐ autre *(précisez)* _____ | Date du traitement (année mois jour) | Heure du traitement : ☐ A.M. ☐ P.M.

Renseignements sur l'hôpital

Nom de l'hôpital	Date d'admission (année mois jour)	Date de sortie (année mois jour)

Adresse de l'hôpital   Veuillez cocher (✓) une case ☐ hospitalisation ☐ clinique externe

Le fait de fournir sciemment de faux renseignements constitue une infraction passible d'une amende ou d'une peine d'emprisonnement, ou les deux. Les renseignements donnés dans ce formulaire sont justes et précis.	Signature du (de la) patient(e)/tuteur(trice) X	Date

Autorisation et demande *(Le ministère versera le montant payable par l'Assurance-santé de l'Ontario directement à un hôpital ou un établissement de santé admissible sur réception d'une facture détaillée et de l'autorisation signée.)*

Je, _____ autorise le ministère de la Santé et des Soins de longue durée à verser le montant de mes frais
    Nom du (de la) patient(e) *(en lettres moulées)*

d'hospitalisation ou de séjour dans un établissement de santé payable par l'Assurance-santé de l'Ontario directement à

_____ et lui demande d'effectuer le paiement.
Nom de l'hôpital ou de l'établissement de santé *(en lettres moulées)*

Signature du (de la) patient(e)/tuteur(trice) X	Date

Pour obtenir plus de renseignements, communiquez avec l'un des bureaux chargés du traitement des demandes de remboursement (Nous acceptons les appels à frais virés) ou consultez notre site Web à l'adresse : www.health.gov.on.ca

London	Oshawa	Ottawa	Thunder Bay
217, rue York, 5ᵉ étage	419, rue King Ouest	75, rue Albert, 7ᵉ étage	435, rue James Sud Bureau 113
N6A 5P9	L1H 8L4	K1P 5Y9	P7E 6T1
519 675–6800	905 576–2870	613 237–9100	807 475–1353

0951–84 (2010/09)   ©Queen's Printer for Ontario, 2010   ©Imprimeur de la Reine pour l'Ontario, 2010   7530–4568

Figure 11.4 *(Continued)*

| Ministry of Health and Long-Term Care | Ministère de la Santé et des Soins de longue durée |

Health Number Release
Divulgation du numéro de carte Santé

| Health Number/Numéro de carte Santé | Version |

Ministry Use Only/Réservé au ministère

This form may be submitted to the Ministry of Health and Long-Term Care when the Health Number of a patient is not available.
La présente formule peut être envoyée au ministère de la Santé et des Soins de longue durée lorsque le numéro de carte Santé d'un patient ou d'une patiente n'est pas disponible.

Confidential when completed/Renseignements confidentiels

1. Patient/Patiente

A. General Information/Renseignements généraux

Last name/Nom de famille

First name/Prénom

Middle name/Deuxième prénom

Sex/Sexe
☐ M   ☐ F

Birth date/Date de naissance
year/année   month/mois   day/jour

If an alternate last name is known, please provide/Si vous avez un deuxième nom de famille, inscrivez ici

B. Health Number Disclosure/Divulgation du numéro de carte Santé

The Ministry of Health and Long-Term Care will give your Health Number to the health care provider/facility.

I agree to allow the Ministry of Health and Long-Term Care to release my Health Number to the health care provider/facility listed below.

Le ministère de la Santé et des Soins de longue durée donnera votre numéro de carte Santé au fournisseur/à la fournisseuse ou à l'établissement de soins de santé.

J'autorise le ministère de la Santé et des Soins de longue durée à divulguer mon numéro de carte Santé au fournisseur ou à l'établissement de soins de santé dont le nom figure ci-dessous.

Collection of the information on this form is for the assessment and verification of eligibility for Health Insurance and Drug Benefit and administration of the Health Insurance and Ontario Drug Benefit Acts, and for health planning and coordination. It is collected/used for these purposes under the authority of the Ministry of Health Act, section 6(1,2), Health Insurance Act, section 4(2) (b,f), 10, 11(1), and Regulation 201/96 under the Ontario Drug Benefit Act, section 2. For information about collection practices, call 1 800 268–1154, in Toronto (416) 314–5518, or write to the Director, Registration and Claims Branch, P.O. Box 48, 49 Place d'Armes, Kingston ON K7L 5J3.

Les renseignements demandés dans cette formule sont réunis aux fins d'évaluation et de vérification de l'admissibilité à l'assurance-santé et aux prestations de médicaments gratuits, aux fins d'administration de la Loi sur l'assurance-santé et de la Loi de 1986 sur le régime de médicaments gratuits de l'Ontario, et aux fins de planification et de coordination des services de santé. Ces renseignements sont réunis ou utilisés à ces fins en vertu de la Loi sur le ministère de la Santé, paragraphes 6(1),(2), de la Loi sur l'assurance-santé, alinéas 4(2)b),f), article 10, paragraphe 11(1), et du Règlement 201/96 pris en application de la Loi de 1986 sur le régime de médicaments gratuits de l'Ontario, paragraphe 2. Pour plus de précisions sur la collecte de ces renseignements, faites le 1 800 268–1154 ou, à Toronto, le (416) 314–5518, ou écrivez au directeur ou à la directrice de l'inscription et des demandes de règlement, C.P. 48, 49, Place d'Armes, Kingston ON K7L 5J3.

Signature of
☐ applicant   ☐ legal guardian
☐ parent   ☐ power of attorney   **X**

Date

Home phone number / Téléphone (domicile)
(   )

Business phone number / Téléphone (bureau)
(   )

A parent or guardian may sign for a child under 16 years of age. An attorney under continuing power of attorney, an attorney under power of personal care, or a legal guardian may also sign on behalf of an individual of any age.
Le père, la mère ou le tuteur, la tutrice peuvent signer pour un enfant de moins de 16 ans.

2. Provider/Facility / Fournisseur/Fournisseuse/Établissement

Provider no./N° du fournisseur

Provider's phone number
N° de téléphone du fournisseur
(   )

Facility no./N° de l'établissement

Facility phone number
N° de téléphone de l'établissement
(   ) –

The Health Number of the patient will be returned to the provider/facility listed here.
Le numéro de carte Santé du patient/de la patiente sera transmis au fournisseur/à la fournisseuse/à l'établissement de soins de santé dont le nom figure ci-dessous.

Date of service/Date de prestation du service
year/année   month/mois   day/jour

Provider/Facility name and address/Nom et adresse du fournisseur

| Ministry Use Only/Réservé au ministère |
| Date received |
| Date processed | Processed by |

1265–84 (05/03)

©Queen's Printer for Ontario, 2005

©Imprimeur de la Reine pour l'Ontario, 2005

7530–4626

Figure 11.5 Health number release form, Ontario

© Queen's Printer for Ontario, 2005. Reproduced with permission.

Future Trends

Primary care models (PCMs) will continue to evolve over the next several years. It is a well-accepted fact among health professionals that there will never be a one-plan-fits all" model. Doctors are fiercely protective of their autonomy and want to work in an environment that balances that autonomy with excellent, cost-effective care. Nonetheless, patient enrolment models that use the multi-disciplinary team approach to care are becoming the norm across Canada. However, even subtle differences in how a PCM is funded distinguish one PCM from another.

Tracking codes, incentive codes, codes for selected services, enrolment codes, and others are part of the claims submission process in PCMs, making it a billing nightmare for both doctors and administrative staff. These codes change constantly. The only time you will even begin to truly understand these codes is when you work in a primary care model setting—and even then it's a challenge.

Just when you think you have a handle on some of these codes, they are eliminated or a different criterion emerges. The unfortunate consequence of not knowing how to use these codes properly, however, could be your employer losing thousands of dollars.

Provincial and territorial governments are providing funding to PCMs to improve care and broaden services. Many governments are paying, at least in part, for doctors to hire nurses, nurse practitioners, pharmacists, podiatrists, nutritionists, and so on, as part of the team. Over the next few years these professionals will more clearly define their scope of practice and level of responsibility within the primary care environment. How these professionals are remunerated may also change. Government funding will only last for so long—after it is reduced or eliminated, other funding mechanisms must be implemented.

SUMMARY

1. Provincial and territorial Ministries of Health can be regarded in the same way as an insurance company. When a person receives a medical service, the physician makes a claim that is paid by the Ministry.

2. Ministries monitor claims to ensure that they are valid. Methods include screening claims, periodically reviewing physicians' records, and periodically sending clients letters to verify that claimed encounters took place.

3. Health card validation is an important part of the claims submission process. Invalid cards lead to rejected claims and lost time and revenue. Several methods of validation are available.

4. A client who does not have a health card or who presents with an invalid health card should be billed for the service. The credit card imprint, cheque, or cash payment can be held for a set time to give the client a chance to present a valid card.

5. Each physician eligible to bill a health plan has a physician registration number. In Ontario, the number includes a specialty designation and, if the physician is part of a group, the group number.

6. Each claim must have a service code to identify the type of encounter. Likely the most common encounter in a doctor's office is the intermediate assessment (in Ontario, code A007). This involves an investigation into one or more systems and a detailed history of the client's complaint. If the physician does not enter the appropriate service code for you, select a code based on accurate information about the assessment.

7. Therapeutic and diagnostic codes may be claimed in addition to service codes or by themselves depending on the circumstances. A different code with a different fee applies, depending on whether the procedure is done on the same visit as an assessment.

8. Premium codes apply when doctors see clients at home, at a hospital, or in a nursing home. Different premium codes apply at various times of the day. A physician delivering a baby in the middle of the night may also use a premium code.

Key Terms

antenatal   337
billing (service, fee item)
   code   330

elective surgery   335
fundus   337
physician registration
   number/billing
   number   326

specialist   326

Review Questions

1. How do Health Ministries monitor claims in your jurisdiction to ensure that they are valid?

2. Compare and contrast the advantages and disadvantages of the three methods of health card validation noted in this chapter.

3. What are the most common causes of an invalid health card?

4. What options do you have if a client has forgotten his health card?

5. Explain the structure of the physician billing number in your province or territory.

6. Discuss the format of billing codes for limited visit, intermediate visit, and a complete assessment in your province or territory.

7. What are the criteria for a house call assessment in your jurisdiction?

8. List the various premium codes used for out-of-office visits to a home and to a LTC facility in your jurisdiction.

9. What is meant by concurrent hospital care?

10. What are diagnostic and therapeutic procedural codes used for?

Application Exercises

1. Independently, or with a peer, think of effective ways to encourage clients to present their health cards. Consider a creative sign for the reception area. Plan two responses to clients who repeatedly do not update their health card information or who leave their cards at home.

2. Marty is 70 years old and lives in Spruce Lodge, a nursing home. The nurses call Dr. Thompson at 0200 to say that Marty is short of breath and complaining of feeling weak. Dr. Thompson arrives at 0230.

   a. What service code would you use?

   b. What premium code would you use?

3. For each of the following scenarios, using your medical billing software program, fill in the service code, procedural code (if applicable), diagnostic code (if applicable), and premium code (if applicable). Use the sites listed under Websites of Interest and/or the tables in this chapter.

a. Leigh came to see the doctor complaining of an earache in the left ear. She was also having difficulty swallowing. The doctor examined her ears, looked at her throat, and listened to her chest. He took a detailed history relating to her complaint and asked questions about her respiratory system. He diagnosed otitis media and tonsillitis and sent her home with a seven-day prescription of antibiotics.

b. Ivan came in because he was experiencing lower back pain. The doctor obtained a detailed history related to the complaint and noted on the chart that Sam also had dysuria and was febrile. A urine sample was tested in the office. The doctor diagnosed cystitis and prescribed antibiotics.

c. Bill came to the doctor and complained of a skin rash on his forearm. The doctor looked at it and asked some questions related to the complaint. She quickly diagnosed contact dermatitis.

d. Kersti came in complaining of a sore stomach and diarrhea. The doctor completed a history about the complaint and related system. He examined her abdomen. He concluded that she had the flu.

e. Ardelle came in with her one-year-old son Zachary for a well-baby checkup.

f. Ravi came for an annual medical examination.

g. Latoya came in for an allergy shot. The nurse gave it to her. Latoya did not see the doctor.

h. Mrs. Purves came in for her annual physical examination. Mrs. Purves is 90 years old.

i. Gregory came in complaining of dysuria (pain on voiding), low back pain, and some hematuria (blood in the urine). The doctor diagnosed pyelonephritis and started Gregory on an antibiotic. He also had the nurse complete a dipstick urinalysis in the office.

j. Agnes Morrow called the office and asked if the doctor could come visit her after office hours. She was bedridden and had noted some increased shortness of breath. The doctor made the house call at 2000.

Websites of Interest

Provincial Health Care in Canada
http://canadanews.about.com/cs/provhealthcare/index/htm
This is a "one stop" link to all the Ministries of Health.

About the Websites Below
Each province and territory has a comprehensive manual outlining billing procedures, rules, regulations, and fee codes. Although they are complex, it is essential that you understand the manual in your jurisdiction. This manual will become your major resource for billing purposes if you are working for a doctor. Each begins with an introduction, general preamble, or something similar. It is important to read this section thoroughly—and the sections on definitions if separate. These sections explain, among other things, the various types of visits (e.g., a consultation, limited visit, comprehensive visit), what they entail, and billing exceptions. The manual will have an index, either on the side of the screen, or at the beginning of the site. The sections on therapeutic and procedural codes and explanatory codes are ones you will probably use. If your course focus is on general billing procedures (versus for a specialist), you will use the section on general practice. There you will find the visit types, codes, and rules applying to those visits and codes.

Some jurisdictions have a site for diagnostic codes, others do not. The diagnostic codes are the same across Canada. For an excellent resource (if you do not have one in your own province or territory or access to them on your computer software), use the *Ontario Physicians Resource Manual*. These codes are the same in your jurisdiction.

Ontario Physicians Resource Manual
www.health.gov.on.ca/english/providers/pub/ohip/physmanual/physmanual_mn.html
Go to section 4, page 40. The codes are clear and in alphabetical order.

ICD-9 Diagnosis Codes
http://icd9cm.chrisendres.com/
Alternatively, try this website. These diagnostic codes are the same but are broken down into detail. To test accuracy in your region, try a few to see if they match diagnostic codes used for various conditions in your jurisdiction. For example, compare acne rosacea and vulgaris, amenorrhea, dysuria, and vomiting. Consider vomiting: it can have several codes; 787 is under symptoms of the digestive system and can be used, but so can 586 for persistent or habitual vomiting.

British Columbia

British Columbia Medical Services Plan—Information for Physicians
www.health.gov.bc.ca/msp/infoprac/physbilling/index.html
Access page to fee schedules, billing information. Click on "MSC payment schedule." You can choose areas applicable to your learning. The preamble (important to read) describes various services as well as outlining policies and guidelines. General practice includes the office fee codes that you will use for provincial or territorial billing.

Explanatory Codes for BC
www.health.gov.bc.ca/msp/infoprac/physbilling/payschedule/explancodes.pdf

Diagnostic Codes Used for Billing in BC
www.health.gov.bc.ca/msp/infoprac/diagcodes/index.html

Alberta

Alberta Health
www.health.gov.ab.ca/

Schedule of Medical Benefits—Alberta
www.health.alberta.ca/professionals/somb.html
"Medical Governing Rules" gives you an overview of how to use the rest of the schedule; click on "Medical Benefits Procedure List" for service codes. You will need to familiarize yourself with services performed by a family doctor, for example, immunizations (13.42); comprehensive office visit (03.04A). You can do a search in the box at the top to quickly find what you are looking for—by code, word, or phrase.

Alberta NetCare
http://www.albertanetcare.ca/default.htm
This website will provide you with current information on the technical and practical applications of HER in Alberta.

Alberta Medical Association
www.albertadoctors.org
The *Alberta Doctor's Digest* (under Publications) is a terrific resource for general information regarding what is happening in primary care and other medical topics.

Alberta Diagnostic Codes
http://www.health.alberta.ca/documents/Diagnostic-Code-ICD-9.pdf
Useful for finding diagnostic codes for billing purposes.

Alberta Health and Wellness: Physicians' Resource Guide
http://www.health.alberta.ca/documents/Physician-Resource-Guide-2011.pdf
Resource manual for physicians (and health professionals) on how to handle Alberta fee-for-service-claims.

Saskatchewan Health
www.health.gov.sk.ca/physician-information
Under Physician's Document Archive, click on Physician Payment Schedule. On the left-hand side is an index. Read through the introduction and definitions, which give you insight into the rest of the manual. Under the

list of insured services, you will see general practice in section B. Under Explanatory Codes at the bottom or the index click on Section B and it will direct take you to the general practice section of the manual.

Manitoba Health—Physicians Manual

www.gov.mb.ca/health/manual/index.html

Contains descriptions of visits, fees, codes, and more. The preamble (general information), starts on page 96. General Practice information is in section 11. (You can click on that link in the index, and it will take you to that section.)

For easier searching, click on bookmarks at the side of the screen. You can select and click on the desired selection.

Ontario

Online Resource Manual for Physicians

http://health.gov.on.ca/english/providers/pub/ohip/physmanual/physmanual_mn.html

This is an excellent resource for essential information for the family doctor's office. It has been extracted from the schedule of benefits. It includes explanation of various visits, billing procedures, fee codes, diagnostic codes, and more. (Section 4 has diagnostic codes.)

Ontario Schedule of Benefits

www.health.gov.on.ca/english/providers/program/ohip/sob/physserv/physserv_mn.html

Under the table of contents, click on "General Preamble." *Read this section carefully.* Page 15 of the preamble begins explanations about the various types of visits. Of note: page 22 has a table of diagnostic codes that OHIP requires you submit with the related fee code; page 25 discusses E080 code for hospital discharge; page 40, data on time units; page 40, delegated procedures; page 47, special visit premiums. Section A is family medicine.

New Brunswick Physician's Manual

www.gnb.ca/0394/pdf-en/PhysiciansManual-e.pdf

The General Preamble begins in section 03 on page 45. On page 51 (General Practice Guidelines) the manual states that the fees cannot be interpreted without knowledge of the preamble—read that section carefully. Section 03.3 outlines the definitions for various types of visits. Note also, sections 04 (information common to all physicians) and 05 (family medicine). Page 88 covers visits to vessels in harbour and at wharf.

Newfoundland and Labrador

Medical Care Plan

http://www.health.gov.nl.ca/health/index.html

This is the main site for all information related to the medical care plan in Newfoundland and Labrador. General information that clients may ask for, as well as links to information for health professionals, is contained here.

Physician's Information Section

http://www.health.gov.nl.ca/health/mcp/providers/index.html

This site provides you with links to the *Physician's Information Manual*, the physician On-Call Payment program, the Medical Care Plan Medical Payment Schedule, physician Registration, Claim Submission, and Claim Payment, and Provider Audits.

Medical Payment Schedule

http://www.health.gov.nl.ca/health/mcp/providers/mcpmedpymt.html

This is the direct link to the payment schedule. The site contains almost all the relevant information required for billing for medical services. The preamble is particularly important.

Physician's Information Manual

http://www.health.gov.nl.ca/health/mcp/providers/physicianinfoman.html

This site provides information for health-care providers in Newfoundland and Labrador. It offers links to everything from forms to claims submission and payments. There is also a link to the provincial physician information manual. This manual contains information valuable to anyone working on a physician's office.

APPENDIX 11A Service and Premium Codes

Table 11A.1 Service Code Prefixes Commonly Used in Family Practice (Ontario)

Prefix	Code Definition
A	General listing (consultations and assessments)
	Special office visits
	Oculovisual assessments
B	Special visits to a home
C	Visit to a client in hospital
E	Extra procedures/premiums paid in addition to other procedures
	Premium for Emergency Department or equivalent
F	Fractures (family doctors frequently set simple or moderately complex fractures)
G	Diagnostic and therapeutic procedures (injections/immunizations, urine testing, etc; also referred to as procedural code)
H	Emergency Department assessments
	Care of newborns and premature babies (family doctors often care for babies even when an obstetrician handles the birth)
	Rehabilitation management (e.g., for stroke recovery victims, clients recovering from a hip replacement)
	Outpatient Department
J	Clinical procedures associated with diagnostic radiological examinations
	Pulmonary function studies
	Diagnostic ultrasound
	Special visits to the ER (if the doctor is called to see a client in emergency)
	Counselling/interviews/primary mental health assessment
	Psychotherapy (may be used by family doctors, but more often by specialists)
K	Forms for the Ministry of Community and Social Services
	Sexual assault assessment
	Some health examinations
W	Special visits to chronic and convalescent hospital/long-term care, nursing homes, and homes for the aged

Table 11A.2 Commonly Used Service and Therapeutic/Procedural Codes

Fee Codes	Description of Service
Visit/Service Codes (ON)	
A001	Minor assessment
A007	Intermediate assessment
A003	General assessment (917 if AHE)
A004	General reassessment
K017	Annual health exam—child over 2 years old
A002	++* 18-month developmental assessment
A008	Mini assessment—billed with WSIB minor assessment
E080	++* First post-hospital premium—billed within 2 weeks
A888	++* ER visit equivalent
A903	Preop assessment
K005	Primary mental health care
K007	Psychotherapy
K013	Counselling—up to 3 units/year
K033	++* Counselling—when billing over 3 units units/year
K022	++* HIV primary care
K037	++* Chronic fatigue/fibromyalgia
K030	++* Diabetic management—4 per year
E079	++* Smoking cessation premium
K039	++* Smoking cessation follow-up
Q150	++* FOBT kit distribution and counselling
Q152	++* FOBT completion
K051	++* Health status report
K055	++* Special diet application form
K070	++* Home care application form
K002	* Interview with authorized person
A901	* House call assessment + premiums
A902	* Pronouncement of death in home + premiums
K035	++* Ministry of Transportation mandatory reporting of medical condition
K036	++* Northern Travel Grant application
K038	++* Long-term care report/application
Hospital Care	
C003	++* On-call admission assessment
C122	++* MRP Day 1
C123	++* MRP Day 2
C124	++* MRP Discharge Day
E082	++* Add to admission assessment by MRP
E083	++* Add to subsequent visit by MRP

Table 11A.2 (continued)

C002	++* Subsequent hospital visit—first 5 weeks
C010	++* Supportive care
C008	++* Concurrent care
H001	++* Newborn care—hospital or home

Long-term Care

× W010	++* Monthly management fee
W003	++* First 2 visits/month
W008	++* Additional 2 visits/month
W892	++* Palliative care visits—no limit

Obstetrics

P006	++* Vaginal delivery
P009	++* Attend L&D and/or section
P023	++* Oxytocin stimulation
P030	++* Cervical ripening—once per pregnancy
C989	++* sacrifice of office hours
P007	++* Postpartum care in hospital
P008	++* Postpartum check in office
P003	++* Major antenatal assessment

Office Procedures

+ G700	++* Basic fee
> E542	* Office premium (tray fee)
> Z101	Abscess, haematoma I&D
G271	Anticoagulant supervision
G202	Allergy injection with visit—1 or more
G212	Allergy injection—no visit
Z113	* Biopsy without sutures
> Z116	* Biopsy with sutures
Z139	++* Breast cyst aspiration
+ G370	Injection of bursa
Z153	* major dressing
+ G420	Ear syringe, curette (use with 388)
Z315	* Epistaxis—unilateral anterior packing
> Z114	Foreign body removal
+ G310	* ECG technical
G313	* ECG professional
G538	Immunizations not otherwise listed—each injection (if sole reason for visit add G700—see Ontario immunization codes in Table 11A.4)
G590	++ Flu shot with visit (if sole reason for visit add G700)
G372	Injection with a visit

Table 11A.2 *(continued)*

G373	Injection, no visit
> G378	* I.U.C.D. insertion
+ G365	Pap smear (annual)
+ G394	++* Pap repeat, previous abnormal result
E430	++* Tray fee for Pap
> Z176	Suture
Z117	* Chemical RxWart (plantar, genital)—for others, charge client

Lab Procedures in Office

G010	Urinalysis
G002	Glucose
G481	Hemoglobin
G004	Stool for O.B.
G005	Pregnancy test
G014	Rapid strep

Note
* Fees charged outside of the FHN basket (for a FHN these fees can be billed)
++ Fees charged outside of the FHO basket (for a FHO these fees can be billed)
∞ applies to C002, C122, C123, C124
× Cannot bill if you are billing W003 or W008
> E542 may be charged with these fees
+ add G700 to these fees if sole reason for visit

Table 11A.3   Common Premium Codes

British Columbia Call-Out Charges

01200	Days 0800–1800 and evenings 1800–2300
01201	Nights 2300–0800
01202	Weekends and statutory holidays 0800–1800

Premium Codes

Home Visits (Ontario, Prefix B)

B990	Special visit to a client's home or a multiple dwelling, such as an apartment block or seniors' residence, during the day, 0700–1800. Payable for first client seen in that location (e.g., if a doctor visits two clients in the same apartment building, he can charge a house visit for each but a premium code only for the first seen).
B990	* Days Mon–Fri 0700–1700
B992	* Sacrifice office hours
B994	* Evenings Mon–Fri, 24 hours Sat, Sun
B996	* 0000 to 0700 every day
B998	++* Special visit to palliative care patient

Office Visit Premiums (Physician makes unscheduled visit to own office or other facility)

A990	Days 0700–1800
A994	Evenings 1800–2400 (Sat/Sun/holidays)
A996	Nights 0000–0700

Table 11A.3 (continued)

Hospital Visit Premiums (Special visits to the hospital, prefix C)

C990	Special visits to a hospital 0700–1800
C992	Emergency call, sacrifice of office hours
C994	Evenings (Mon–Fri), daytime/evenings on Sat/Sun/holidays
C996	Nights 0000–0800

Long-Term Care Facility (LTC) such as a nursing home (prefix W)

W990	Special visit to see someone in an LTC, 0800–1800
W994	LTC visit evenings, 1800–2400 (Sat/Sun/holidays)
W996	LTC visit, 2400–0700
W992	Emergency visit to LTC at the sacrifice of office hours

Premium Codes for Delivery of a Baby and Surgery (prefix C indicates service in hospital)

C989	Normal delivery of a baby at the sacrifice of office hours (C prefix indicates service in hospital)
E410	Delivery of a baby, 0000–0700
	Nonelective surgical procedures (e.g., fractures, dislocations) or ambulance transfer, 0000–0700
E400B	Assisting with surgery, 1800–2400 (B suffix indicates assisting, rather than doing procedure)
E401B	Assisting with surgery, 0000–0700

Table 11A.4 Ontario Immunization Codes

ONTARIO NEW IMMUNIZATION CODES

G840	Quadracel
G841	Pediacel
G842 B	Hepatitis
G843	Gardasil
G844	Menjugate (Men-C)
G845	MMR, Priorix
G846	Prevnar 13
G847	Adacel, Boostrix
G848	Varicella
G538	Other immunizing agents
G590	Influenza + G700 if immunization is sole reason for visit

Table 11A.5 Q Codes for Ontario's Enrolled Primary Care Models

These "Q" codes and explanations apply to enrolled models of care in Ontario: family health organizations (FHOs), family health groups (FHGs), family health networks (FHNs), and comprehensive care models (CCMs) (see Chapter 4)

Q200A	1st year enrolment fee
Q013A	New client premium—over 60 years of age
Q023A	Unattached client fee from hospital—no limit on number of patients
Q033A	New grad new patient fee—maximum of 300 clients first year only
Q043A	New client seen for fecal occult blood test and who is at risk for colorectal disease (payment varies with age of client—more for those over 75, less for those 64–75, and even less for those under 64)
Q053A	new client with complicated conditions requiring comprehensive care (same payment applies regardless of client's age)
Q150A	Distributing kits for FOBT and counselling fees
Q050A	Incentive code for detailed managing/counselling clients with heart failure
Q040A	Incentive code for comprehensive management of diabetic clients—includes keeping a current diabetic flow sheet in the clients EMR
Q402A	Incentive for counselling and management for smoking cessation
Q014A	FHNS only: periodic care for babies under one year of age—maximum 8 babies per year
Q015A	FHOs only: periodic care for babies under one year of age—maximum 8 babies per year

These incentive codes are for tracking purposes for enrolled clients who are rendered certain services.

Q130A	Influenza vaccine over 65
Q011A	Pap smear 35–69
Q131A	Mammogram 50–69
Q132A	Immunization 18–24 months
Q113A	Colorectal screening 50–74

Incentive Payments

Physicians are monetarily remunerated if they maximize their services related to preventive medicine. This involves encouraging their clients/patients to have screening tests, for example, Pap smears, mammograms, and fecal testing for occult blood (to diagnose early colon cancer). Incentive payments are also designed to motive physicians to better manage treatment of chronic diseases such as hypertension and diabetes. Smoking cessation initiatives are included as well.

Method

Physician's offices must keep track of the number of all visits that relate to these incentive programs, for example, the number of patients who had Pap smears or mammograms, or who were seen for chronic disease management. You track these visits using the appropriate "Q" code designed for specific conditions. The number of visits for each incentive is totalled yearly. You submit a code based on the number of enrolled clients serviced for each category; this is calculated as a percentage of the total number of eligible clients for each category. (e.g. if you saw 60 percent of all clients eligible for the flu vaccine you would bill Q100A. If you saw 80 percent of eligible clients you would bill Q104A (see below for more of these preventive care service enhancement codes).

The Responsibilities of the AHP

In most practices, only a certain number of clients will call for appointments related to these services. You can prepare and send computer-generated letters to clients reminding them if and when they are due for such an appointment, such as a Pap smear or FOBT.

Table 11A.5 *(continued)*

You must be sure to carefully review the letters prior to sending them to ensure that they go to the proper individuals. Mr. Smith would not need a Pap smear, nor would Mrs. Brown, who had a complete hysterectomy. Exclusion codes can facilitate this process.

Exclusion Codes

Exclusion codes are applied to clients who should be excluded from a target population for certain services. Use of the codes assists you in accurately summating the number of clients seen for target services when submitting your numbers to the Ministry. As well, they serve to exempt clients from inappropriately receiving reminder letters.

Q140A	Pap smear 35–69
Q141A	Mammogram 50–69
Q003A	Influenza vaccine over 65
Q142A	Colorectal screening 50–74

Table 11B Common British Columbia Office Codes

British Columbia

Complete In-Office Examination Service Codes

IN BC

12101	(age 0–1)
00101	(age 2–49)
15301	(age 50–59)
16101	(age 60–69)
17101	(age 70–79)
18101	(age 80+)

Regional Examination and History In-Office

12100	(age 0–1)
00100	(age 2–49)
15300	(age 50–59)
16100	(age 60–69)
17100	(age 70–79)
18100	(age 80+)

Call-Out Charges

01200	days 0800–1800 and evenings 1800–2300
01201	nights 2300–0800
01202	weekends and statutory holidays 0800–1800
Revised	Immunization Codes
P10027	Diphtheria, Tetanus, Pertussis, Hepatitis B, Polio, Hib (Hexavalent)
P10010	Diphtheria, Tetanus, Pertussis, Polio (Quadrivalent)
P10011	Diphtheria, Tetanus, Pertussis, Polio, Hib (Pentavalent)

Table 11B	*(continued)*
P10016	Hepatitis A (HA)
P10017	Hepatitis B (HB)
P10018	Hib (Haemophilus influenzae type b)
P10015	Influenza (Flu)
P10020	Meningococcal – Conjugate – C (MEN-C-C)
P10021	Meningococcal – Conjugate – ACYW135 (MEN-C-ACYW135)
P10022	Mumps, Measles, Rubella (MMR)
P10023	Pneumococcal Conjugate (PNEU-C-7)
P10024	Pneumococcal – Polysaccharide – 23 (PNEU-P-23)
P10019	Polio Vaccine (IPV)
P10025	Rabies (RAB)
P10012	Tetanus, Diphtheria (Td)
P10014	Tetanus, Diphtheria, Pertussis (Tdap)
P10013	Tetanus, Diphtheria, Polio (TdP)
P10026	Varicella (VAR)

Chapter 12

Billing

Learning Objectives

On completing this chapter, you will be able to:

1. List four methods of claims submission.
2. Discuss the process of claims submission by electronic data transfer.
3. Understand the stages of the billing cycle.
4. Discuss the process of client registration in the health office.
5. Describe software options used in client registration and billing.
6. List the information components of a health claim.
7. Describe how to handle reciprocal claims and workers' compensation claims.
8. Discuss claims reports received from the Ministry of Health.
9. Explain the process of billing a third party.
10. Explain how to collect unpaid accounts.

Chapter 10 outlined the provincial and territorial health-care plans; Chapter 11 introduced the elements of billing. This chapter discusses the actual process of claims submission and the technologies available to facilitate it, as well as outlining approaches to billing payers other than through provincial or territorial health plans.

The billing process is the same in all provinces and territories. The basic billing cycle is relatively simple: you collect information needed for a claim, store the claims forms on your information system, put the files together, and send them to the Ministry responsible. The Ministry reviews your claims according to a schedule and reports which ones are approved and which are rejected. The Ministry will send out a list of the rejected claims, allowing you to correct and resubmit them within the billing cycle. The Ministry processes the corrected statement and then sends out a final statement and payment to the provider. You have an opportunity to review and correct again, and resubmit rejected claims. Payment for these resubmissions will occur in the next billing cycle.

In this chapter, the processes and elements of billing are described in generic terms. The preamble to your jurisdiction's fee schedule will give more details. It is important to know your schedule and use it when in doubt. You may find it easiest to use online.

CLAIMS SUBMISSION: THE PROCESS

THE MECHANICS OF SUBMISSION IS PRIMARILY THE RESPONSIBILITY OF THE ADMINISTRATIVE health professional (AHP). You need to be familiar with the method of claims submission used by your provider. Even if you are familiar with the general process of claims submission, when you start a new job, you will need some orientation to the particular system. Be sure that you are comfortable using the computer, the specific software, and the billing procedures before you try the process alone.

In the claims process, there are a number of codes that have not been discussed elsewhere in detail but that you will need to know. These will be specific to your jurisdiction. Rejection codes appear on reports explaining why a claim was not accepted for payment or why it was partially paid. They indicate a range of reasons and may be categorized into groups of rejection criteria. For example:

Explanatory codes: eligibility rejections (the service date was not within an eligible period, the claim was stale-dated, or client coverage has lapsed); general reasons (service is not an insured benefit, it was claimed by another physician within group, claim under review); diagnostic and therapeutic (allowed as a repeat procedure, payment reduced, limit of payment for this procedure reached, not allowed in addition to visit fee). The structure of explanatory codes differs but the principles for claim rejection remain the same. Remember the good-faith policy Alberta has for clients who cannot present their valid health card number, discussed in Chapter 11? The explanatory code 01C indicates a claim rejection if a good-faith claim was previously paid for that client, or the client was covered by another plan (e.g., an RCMP officer who is covered by the federal government).

Error codes: assessment rejects (wrong sex for service, no such service code, duplicate claim); reciprocal medical billing (RMB) rejects (missing province or territory code, service excluded from RMB); validity rejects (error in claim number, expired card, missing payee address, invalid surname).

You must also have a solid understanding of the service and diagnostic codes used in your province or territory and how and when to use them. If you are working in a primary care reform group, you will need to thoroughly understand the various codes used for both billing and tracking. Your provider may not understand them completely and will rely on you to use them efficiently. When you start a new job, an orientation period with the staff member you are replacing or another staff member in the office is necessary. (Refer to Chapter 11 for details on the codes.) Most software supplies the coding information; you will find this feature a tremendous time saver. If your software does not have this feature, check your fee schedule when you are not sure of the code. Many vendors will supply a summarized list of the commonly used codes in your province or territory. Accuracy and attention to detail are vital in the claims submission process. Omissions or coding mistakes can result in extra work for you and a significant loss of revenue for the physician. With time, you will become familiar with the codes and know when to use them, as well as the exceptions. When you are starting out, go slowly, and focus on accuracy.

You will find claims submission most effective if you do it promptly and follow a regular routine. Some AHPs enter claims into the computer at the end of the morning and again at the end of the day. Regardless of when you submit batches to the Ministry, it is best to enter the data into your files on the day of the encounter.

Applying the appropriate code for claims can happen in four ways—you do it, the physician does it, you both do it, or your office hires someone apart from the administrative staff to carry out billing responsibilities.

As discussed in Chapter 11, you need certain basic information to submit a claim. You and the provider should work as a team. If the doctor relies on you to add codes to the claims, she should get you the information you need as soon as possible (diagnosis and details of the encounter), and you should process it according to a regular schedule. The software adds the physician's billing number to each claim as the claim is initiated. The client information (date of birth, health card and version number, and so on) is added to the claim screen when you swipe the health card. The remaining information—service or billing code and diagnostic code—is collected after the encounter. It helps if the physician charts quickly and regularly. You cannot submit a claim until you have the diagnostic and service codes from the client's chart or the doctor's day sheet.

In a computerized office, the provider can enter that information into a computer in the examination room or in her office as soon as the encounter is complete. This information is entered into the computer and stored with other claims until you are ready to batch and send them to the Ministry for review and payment.

❶❷❸ METHODS OF CLAIMS SUBMISSION

Web-Based Submission

Recently, many physicians, particularly those starting out, work for multiple clinics and various fractional practices. The result is a demand for a "virtual office." Web-based access to provincial billing is available; organizations such as BillitNow offer such a service. It allows physicians to bill and track invoices for provincially/territorially insured health services. The service requires only a computer and an internet connection. Physicians can submit invoices from anywhere through a single portal. The organization offers similar services to those offered by computer software systems used for other modes of bills submission, including customer service and support to answer billing-related questions. The cost of this service is 0.25 percent of billing to a maximum of $580 per year. QuickClaim is another web-based service. It requires a program to be installed on the physician's computer, and requires users to use only the computer with the software.

Machine-Readable Input/Output

To make the billing and payment process more efficient, all ministries use computers to process claims. These systems require you to send your billing information as **machine-readable input (MRI)**. In return, you get back from the Ministry machine-readable output (MRO), also referred to as output response files.

Machine-readable input may be submitted in most provinces and territories on tape cassette, magnetic tape cartridge, or disk, or by **electronic transfer** or **ET** (the information is sent by modem to the Ministry's mainframe computer). Usually, you will get information back from the Ministry in the same form in which you send it. For example, if you send disks, you will get reports back on disk.

machine-readable input (MRI) any information that can be read by a computer.

electronic transfer (ET) vehicle for the electronic transmission of medical claims from the source computer to the Ministry's mainframe computer.

Tape Cartridge and Disk

In most provinces and territories, tapes and disks may be obtained from the Ministry. They are erased for reuse after the files are downloaded for processing. Tapes come in two forms: (1) regular tape cassettes and (2) magnetic tapes, which are tapes coated with iron oxide. Magnetic tapes are used primarily by larger facilities, such as hospitals. Disks are more commonly used than tapes and are the regular 3.5-inch type.

Use your software to compile the billing information and store the files on tapes or disks, and then send them, usually by courier, to the Ministry within a designated time frame for processing. Bundle up the package securely, but do not use so much tape that it is hard for Ministry staff to open it.

Label each tape or disk with the following information (see Figure 12.1):

- Health-care provider or group name
- Provider's registration number
- Phone number
- Number of claims submitted
- Number of records submitted
- Date of submission
- Sequence number (e.g., if you are sending two disks, label them "1 of 2" and "2 of 2")

Electronic Transfer

Electronic transfer (ET) is fast overtaking disks as the billing method of choice across the country. In British Columbia, for example, 98 percent of claims submissions are elec-

```
M.O.H. Ottawa
Provider Name: Dr. D. Thompson
PROV/GRP ID: HA345432.002      PH 613-343-3333
#Claims/Records: 190 / 32
Disk 1 of 2

Date: 01/16/XX
```

Figure 12.1 Sample label for disk or tape claims submission

tronic. In Prince Edward Island, only electronic submissions are accepted. You connect to the electronic claims submission system from your computer, using communication software and a modem. It is as simple to use as email. There is nothing to mail or courier.

To log on and send files, you will require a password. Information being returned to you from the Ministry will be sent to a secure mailbox. You log in to this mailbox by using your password and download the files or reports so that your software system can interpret or read them.

Different jurisdictions use different names for their electronic systems. In Ontario, it is referred to as EDT or electronic data transfer; in British Columbia, the system is called Teleplan. In some provinces, this system parallels and/or links with others that provide more comprehensive client care. For example, in BC, Teleplan links with a secure computer network system linking pharmacies throughout the province to Emergency Departments and the College of Pharmacists. This system is being expanded to include physicians' offices and will allow pharmacists access to a client's complete medication record, as well as allowing online adjudication for claims for prescription drugs. To use electronic transfer, you can connect through a private internet service provider (ISP) via dial-up or high-speed access.

Electronic billing has many advantages for the provider and for you:

- It simplifies the billing process.
- In most provinces and territories, claims can be submitted any time except on Sundays.
- Security is enhanced for both sending and receiving information because only authorized individuals have access.
- There is nothing physical to send: you save courier costs and packaging time.
- Claims are transmitted and received much more quickly.
- You receive timely confirmation that your file has been received.
- If one of your files is rejected, you get a File Reject message within hours, allowing you to correct the problem and resubmit the file promptly.
- A Batch Edit report is returned to you, usually within 24 hours, notifying you of acceptance and rejection of claims batches.
- Remittance Advice reports are available earlier, allowing reconciliation of accounts.
- Error reports are sent in a machine-readable format so that your software can be programmed to reconcile automatically.
- You can use electronic validation through a web-based telecommunications system (described in Chapter 11), thus reducing claims rejections.

Claims Deadlines

Claims must be submitted by a specific date determined by the payment agency to guarantee reimbursement within the next billing cycle—monthly in most jurisdictions. This date is usually the 18th to 20th of the month. (Some jurisdictions including Newfoundland and Labrador and British Columbia, however, have a two-week cycle.) The Ministry makes every effort to ensure that the monthly payment includes all correctly submitted claims received by the designated deadline. In British Columbia, a payment for claims submitted electronically using Teleplan includes all correct claims received at least seven days prior to the next payment date.

Those using tapes or disks usually submit claims weekly, perhaps bimonthly. Rejected claims cannot usually be identified, mailed back to the provider, corrected, and sent back to the Ministry by the cut-off date. The provider would therefore not be paid for those claims until the end of that next billing cycle.

In contrast, electronic transfer users are encouraged to submit claims *daily* or *several times a week*. More frequent submission has two benefits. First, the earlier in the cycle the Ministry receives your claims file, the sooner you will get your error report and other files back. Thus, you will often have time to correct and resubmit rejected claims by the guaranteed payment date. Second, you are more likely to receive payment within the billing cycle for claims sent late in the month. Although the Ministry *guarantees* payment only for claims received by the stated date, if time and volume permit, it will continue processing claims, sometimes up till the month-end computer cut-off date. Thus, some months, you may receive payment for claims sent as late as the 28th of the previous month.

Changing Methods

If your provider is switching from disk or tape to electronic transfer, she must fill out an application form and send it to your local Ministry office. Most ministries will provide sign-up kits that help you make the transition to electronic transfer. Once your provider's application is processed, you will be given a user manual and assigned a password. Your local Ministry office can answer questions about the process or about claims submissions or payments. Your software vendor should also provide technical support.

④⑤ CLIENT REGISTRATION

THE FIRST STAGE OF PREPARING A CLAIM BEGINS WHEN YOU REGISTER A CLIENT. REGISTERING the client can be combined with acceptance, review, and validation of the health card. Much of the information contained on the magnetic strip of the health card is the information you need for registration and billing.

If your card validation system (discussed in Chapter 11) is integrated with your computer system, then when you swipe the client's health card, your computer screen should show the information contained by the health card (health card number, version number, name, date of birth, and gender) on the same screen as the remaining information required for client registration.

Figure 12.2 shows a basic registration screen. Once the data are entered, the system will store the required data until you choose to remove any. It can be updated and/or changed as necessary. Some software programs have the capability of storing a photo of the client as well, which is helpful in preventing health card fraud. It is also convenient if your software allows you to paste selected information, such as name and address, to documents in other applications, such as letters and insurance forms.

Basic registration information includes the following:

- First and last name, initial or middle name
- Title (Mr., Mrs., Ms., Dr.)
- Date of birth
- Gender
- Address

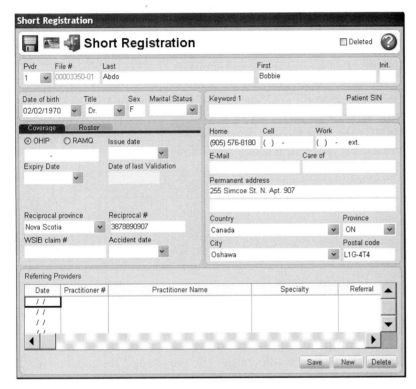

Figure 12.2 Short client registration screen

Figure courtesy of P & P Data Systems Inc.

- Phone number (home, work, cell)
- Greeting (This field is not standard on all medical software programs. It is meant to indicate how the client prefers to be addressed, e.g., Mrs. Smith or Suzanne; Catherine or Katie.)

You can search for a client's record on the system by entering any part of the registration information:

- First or last name, in part or in full
- Date of birth
- Telephone number
- Chart number
- Address

When a client comes in, scan or swipe her health card. To scan the card, run it through your card scanner at a steady speed, being careful to keep the card level. The health card information appears automatically on the screen; check to make sure it is current and correct. Figure 12.2 shows the information that will be displayed when a card is swiped. If the client is already in the registry, other information will also appear, such as the default provider (the client's usual doctor) and the client's address, phone numbers, and billing defaults. If the client has not been registered before in your office or if information is missing, you will see empty fields. Once you have filled them in, you can save the updated client information to your registry.

If the Card Will Not Swipe

Occasionally, the health card will not register on your screen when you swipe it. This often happens with a bent or worn card. In Ontario, it often happens with the older red-and-white cards. Try to swipe the card two or three times. Sometimes, putting a thin paper over the magnetic strip will help it be swiped properly. If this does not work, you can enter the information manually. Suggest that the client get the card replaced.

❺ SOFTWARE BILLING OPTIONS

A VARIETY OF SOFTWARE IS AVAILABLE TO HELP WITH CLAIMS SUBMISSION. GET TO KNOW the capabilities of your system. It will probably do more than you think if you become comfortable with the computer and take the time to learn its features. Most software systems offer the features described below. Figure 12.3 shows a client-specific billing screen that also captures the client's billing history.

Billing Day Sheet/Calendar Billing

When you schedule a client's appointment, you are collecting much of the information you will need to submit a claim. The booking/scheduling module automatically creates a list of clients whom you need to bill. Day-sheet-based or calendar billing (see Figure 12.4) uses the information the system already contains. When you select a billing provider and a date, the day's list of appointments is presented on a spreadsheet. You can then go through the list and enter service and diagnostic codes for each appointment. Identify no-shows and delete them from the billing record. Once you are satisfied with the billing record, you can file all of the claims simultaneously, submitting them to the Ministry with your next cumulative submission.

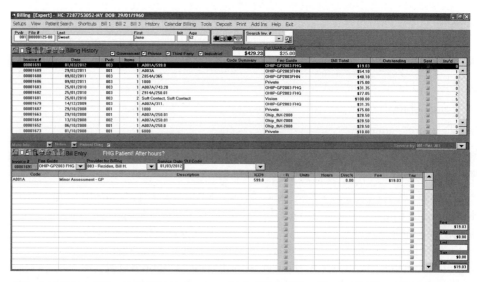

Figure 12.3 Client's billing screen, including the client's billing history

Figure courtesy of P & P Data Systems Inc.

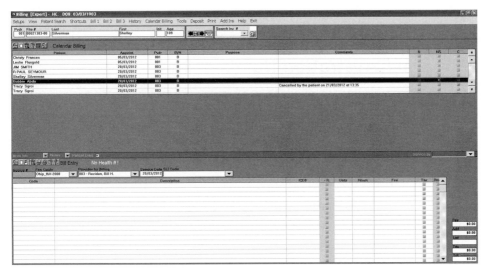

Figure 12.4 Calendar billing screen

Figure courtesy of P & P Data Systems Inc.

Day-sheet-based billing works well if you have high volume and mostly straightforward billing.

Billing

This is undoubtedly one of the most valuable and essential features to have on any software system. It follows the old system of paper-based claim submission but is much more efficient. This programming capability is designed to sequentially complete the billing process as directed by the user. The software is written to be specific to your province or territory and reflects your own jurisdiction's coding and billing format, including service codes and their value and procedural and diagnostic codes. This saves a great deal of time. Some systems will review entries to ensure that they do not conflict with other billings. For example, ministries will not generally accept two billings for the same client on the same day. If you enter two such billings, the computer will point out the conflict and ask if you are sure you want to proceed with that claim submission.

Electronic Records

Most software programs offer the capability of storing a client's entire file, including laboratory and radiology reports, making some offices virtually paperless. These are discussed further in Chapter 13. One advantage of electronic records is that information used in billing is integrated with client records.

❻ INFORMATION COMPONENTS OF A CLAIM

SOFTWARE PROGRAMS DIFFER SOMEWHAT IN WHAT INFORMATION SHOWS ON THE SCREEN and what the fields are named.

Note: Provincial and territorial billing computers need numbers, dates, and so on, in a specific format. However, your computer screen may not show information in this format.

Some programs display data in a form easier for readers to deal with; on submission, it automatically converts the data to the required format.

Physician Registration Number

This number is shown on some billing screens; others show the provider's name or may show neither. This number must be on every submission to the Ministry, whether the physician bills individually or as part of a group. Software programs that do not show it on the billing screen will add it when claims are batched.

Date of Birth

For cards and older systems, OHIP requires date of birth to be entered with two digits each for year, month, and day, with no punctuation or spaces. For example, November 9, 1950 would be 501109. Your software program may have a specific format for dates.

Accounting/Claims Number

Automated systems will have a computer-generated number (generally up to eight alpha-numeric characters) used for accounting and claims reconciliation.

Chart Number

This item is not needed for claims submission but is used internally if your office assigns a number to each client's chart for filing purposes. Some filing systems file by name and/or colour-coded charts instead.

The Payment Program

The software will offer three choices:

- HCP—health-care plan
- RMB—reciprocal medical billing
- WCB—Workers' Compensation Board or your jurisdiction's equivalent

Most often, the payment plan is HCP, and most software programs select this choice by default. If the encounter is related to a workplace incident covered by workers' compensation, select WCB/WSIB. If the service was provided to an out-of-province/territory client (assuming neither you nor the client is from Quebec), select RMB. Some programs will automatically change the setting to RMB if you swipe an out-of-province/territory health card. Computerized billing can handle reciprocal billing electronically in the same way as claims to your own jurisdiction. If you have a client with a WCB/WSIB claim and an unrelated medical claim on the same visit, the claims must be submitted separately by using the appropriate codes for your province or territory.

RCMP Billing

Uniformed RCMP officers (not their family members) are covered for health care under the federal government through Blue Cross. They will present a health card distributed by the RCMP. Their health record and health information can be kept as an EMR, as for any other patient. Billing for services rendered for an RCMP officer, however, must be submitted by mail to the head office for Blue Cross in Moncton, New Brunswick. A Medical Services Program 06 form allows you to document several visits. You would submit the form at designated intervals. Information requested includes the date, benefit/fee code, and the number of units for the service (if applicable, e.g., counselling) and the amount you are billing to the RCMP Health Benefits Program. The provider's information, including the provider's number, must be recorded, along with detailed information about the client (name, unit/detachment/collator code, DOB, and their RCMP health card number. For major surgery and other designated procedures, you must send in a Request for Treatment form to the RCMP.

The Payee

The payee is the party paid for the encounter or service. It rarely changes from "P," meaning the submitting provider. ("S" means pay the client.) In fact, the payee is not shown on newer billing modules. If you are using an older computer program or billing cards, enter "P." Even with workers' compensation claims in provinces or territories where the Ministry of Health acts as the payment agency, the payee is still "P" because the provincial or territorial plan pays the provider.

Referring Physician

If the client has been sent to a specialist for a consultation, the Ministry will want to know who made the referral—usually the family doctor. Insert the referring doctor's physician registration number.

Facility Number

This is a number assigned to a facility, such as a nursing home or a hospital. It is added when claiming for services rendered at the facility for inpatients or outpatients.

Inpatient Admission Date

This field, which may appear as "Admin Date" on the computer screen, represents the date a person is admitted to a hospital or other facility. Include two digits each for year, month, and day. As with birth dates, the claim uses no punctuation; however, your screen may show a specific format.

Tip

When submitting a claim for an RCMP officer, double-check to ensure that the date and provider's signature are on the claim. Keep a copy for your files for audit purposes. See the website listed at the end of the chapter for information about RCMP claims and forms (applicable to all jurisdictions in Canada).

Manual Review Field

The manual review field is used to flag or identify claims that deviate in some way from programmed billing criteria and require an explanation of the circumstances. With this box checked, someone at the Ministry will review the claim individually. Any claim marked for manual review must have supporting documentation, which should be sent (usually faxed) the same day the claim is submitted. (Instead of faxed documentation, the physician can fill out a form intended specifically for that purpose. Some programs have a manual review feature that will support the entry of review comments for printing at the time of submission. In Ontario, it is called a Claims Flagged for Manual Review Form.) For example, in some jurisdictions, circumcision is no longer covered unless deemed medically necessary. If a doctor performs a circumcision for medical reasons, you would check the box and submit an explanation as to why the doctor considered the procedure medically necessary. Similarly, if you billed for two services for the same client on the same day or submitted a premium claim for a surgical procedure that took longer than usual, you would need to explain the circumstances. Figure 12.5 shows a screen with a space for such an explanation. Some programs have a manual review feature that will support the entry of review comments for printing at the time of submission.

Independent Consideration

Independent consideration claims were addressed briefly in Chapter 11. Some services are marked as IC on the Schedule of Benefits. (Some jurisdictions may use a different symbol.) This means "independent consideration," and such claims are also reviewed manually. This is sometimes referred to as being marked with a "Y" indicator. If you submit claims electronically, remember that you must fax the supporting documentation when you submit that claim. If your claims are submitted on disk or tape, send the supporting documentation the same time as you send the tape or disk.

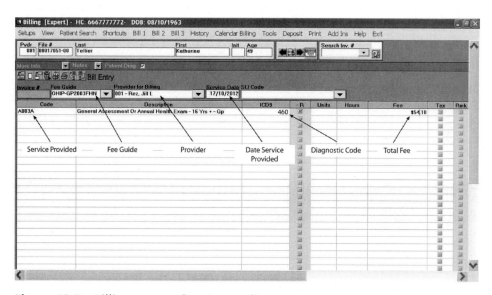

Figure 12.5 Billing screen showing coding

Figure courtesy of P & P Data Systems Inc.

Shadow Billing

Shadow billing or a similar billing format is used in practices that have entered into primary care reform agreements. It helps direct comparison of the capitation fee or other alternative payment plan the Ministry is paying the provider with the costs that would be incurred if the provider were billing fee-for-service. Precisely how this billing is formatted may vary. There may be a special code used for rostered clients and a shadow billing option on the computer software system. For rostered clients, you will enter other information as usual but click the "shadow" tab. A zero balance is submitted. Not all software programs have this option. In some jurisdictions, billings are done for rostered clients as if they were fee-for-service, and the Ministry's computer identifies them and separates them from fee-for-service clients.

Example Dr. Chen is working in a primary care reform group. In one calendar year, she was paid $300 000 under the capitation formula to take care of 2000 clients while providing extended hours and other health-care services to her clients. The shadow billing for her practice year showed that under the fee-for-service system, she would have billed the Ministry of Health $350 000. In this case, capitation saved the Ministry $50 000.

Service Date

This is the date the service was provided. Make sure it is accurate. An incorrect date could result in the claim being rejected. Generally, it is best to process claims every day so that the service date will be the current date—which your software program will show automatically. However, there may be days when you just do not have time to complete the claims. If you are doing claims for the previous business day or if, for any other reason, you are claiming for a service provided earlier, be sure to change the service date manually. You can usually select a calendar and just click on the date you want.

Service Code

As described in Chapter 11, this code identifies the type of service or encounter that is claimed and generates the amount charged for the claim. (See Figure 12.5.)

Diagnostic Code

As discussed in Chapter 11, this is usually a three- or four-character code that indicates the diagnosis made at the time the service was rendered. If there is more than one diagnosis, use the primary one. In Figure 12.5, the diagnostic code is 460, which refers to a cold or acute nasopharyngitis. Diagnostic codes are discussed in more detail later in the chapter.

Number of Services

The number of services refers to the number of encounters the client has had with the physician. Usually, the number of services is 1. For example, Chad visits the doctor in the office because of an earache. The doctor assesses and treats Chad. That is one service or encounter. (If Chad also mentions that his knee is troubling him, the provider cannot bill for two assessments. If the doctor performs both an intermediate and a minor assessment, bill for the intermediate assessment.) However, as noted in Chapter 11, you may claim for a number of services if they are on consecutive days for inpatients in health-care facilities. For example, if Helga was in hospital for five days, the most responsible physician (MRP) might visit her daily. You would submit a single claim for five services. However, you would submit separate claims for visits that are not on consecutive days (e.g., you would submit separate claims for a visit on November 9 and one on November 11). Some software systems require that the number of services consist of two digits. If there are fewer than 10, use a zero followed by the number (thus, the most common entry is 01). For other software systems this is irrelevant. You may enter the number of services as they appear (e.g., 1). Provincial or territorial billing software will customize the format as required.

PPU, or Price per Unit

For most services, a "unit" is the service, and the price per unit is the amount allowed in the fee schedule for that service. For time-based services, a unit is the amount of time designated in the fee schedule; for example, a unit of time might be designated as 15 minutes. Each 15-minute period spent with a client would be worth a certain value. Extra units sometimes have a different code from that for the base unit.

In Figure 12.5, the service is A003A, an intermediate assessment. The fee for this assessment is $54.10; this is the PPU.

Fee Submitted

This is the amount paid for the service provided, and it relates directly to the service code submitted for a particular encounter. The amounts are listed in the Schedule of Benefits/ Tariffs. In Ontario, there may be a maximum of nine digits. Your software program may automatically insert the fee when you enter the service code.

For most services, the fee submitted will be the same as the price per unit, as shown in Figure 12.5. However, if more than one service is claimed, as in consecutive hospital visits, or if the service is a time-based one and the provider spent more than one unit of time, the fee will be the price per unit times the number of services.

The input required for the health plan's computer uses neither dollar signs nor decimals. Thus, $27.05 would be simply 2705. However, as with birth date formats, your program may show prices in a more reader-friendly format but will convert them to the required format before submitting.

❼ TYPES OF CLAIMS

Physicians submit three types of claims to the provincial or territorial plan, which correspond to the payment programs discussed above. The majority of claims apply to the health-care plan itself; the others are reciprocal billing (RMB) and workers' compensation claims.

Reciprocal Claims

The reciprocal billing format is the same across Canada. If your office is computerized, you will claim for out-of-province/territory clients just as if you were billing your own health-care plan, except that you need to make sure that RMB is selected as the payment program. Also check that the client's province or territory of origin appears in the appropriate field. Usually, the software will automatically insert the province or territory code when you swipe the card; if it does not, insert it manually. (See Table 10.2 for a list of two-letter province and territory codes.)

If you bill manually, use a reciprocal claims form. Double-check your form to be sure that you have included the following:

- The code of the province or territory
- The client's health card number or the equivalent
- The client's name, gender, and date of birth
- The client's home address
- Payment program (RMB)
- Payee (P)

Always validate the client's health card, as discussed in Chapter 11. If the card is not valid, charge the client, and let her know she can seek reimbursement from her home province or territory when her eligibility is re-established. Most plans will not accept reciprocal claims submitted after 90 days.

Services Excluded from RMB   Check to see that the service in question is covered under RMB. Some services, even though they may be covered by your jurisdiction, are excluded from RMB. If the client is not willing to wait to have the service done in his home province or territory, bill the client directly. Some of the more common excluded services are as follows:

- Cosmetic surgery
- Sex reassignment surgery
- Therapeutic abortion
- Annual health exams or physicals and periodic ocular assessments
- In-vitro fertilization and artificial insemination
- Lithotripsy for gallstones
- Acupuncture, acupressure, hypnotherapy services to individuals covered by other agencies such as WSIB or Veterans' Affairs
- Genetic screening

WCB/WSIB Claims

Workers' compensation claims, as discussed in Chapter 10, relate to on-the-job injuries. In most jurisdictions, the Ministry of Health act as a payment agency for the WCB or WSIB. Doctors submit workers' compensation claims directly to the local Ministry of Health, as long as the client has valid provincial/territorial health coverage. In some jurisdictions, the billing is the same as for provincial/territorial claims except that you must make sure the payment program selected is WCB/WSIB. In jurisdictions, you would submit the claim to the WSIB/WCB using preferred codes. In BC, for example, a telephone consultation initiated by a medical advisor has a fee code of 19508; an office consultation would be coded as 19919 (this is time based for up to 15 minutes); a return-to-work (RTW) consultation is 19950; if a physician reviews an RTW plan, you would use the code 19976. (note that visit, conversation, or consult has more detailed parameters attached to the billing criteria; see the WorkSafeBC *Physicians Reference Guide*, available at the website listed at the end of the chapter.

If a client cannot produce a valid health card, the provider would bill the workers' compensation board directly. Physicians must bill the workers' compensation board directly for services not covered by the health-care plan, such as medical–legal reports or office interviews with WSIB/WCB representatives, and for selected services noted in the Schedule of Benefits. In most jurisdictions, providers other than physicians, such as chiropractors, chiropodists, osteopaths, optometrists, private physiotherapists, private occupational therapists, dentists, audiologists, and pharmacists, bill the WSIB/WCB directly for claims. Out-of-province/territory physicians, opted-out physicians, and private laboratories also bill directly.

When a doctor assesses a client for a workers' compensation matter and also provides a service for an unrelated problem at the same visit, you must submit the unrelated claim separately to the provincial or territorial health plan. There may be restrictions on the type of service you can submit to the public plan. For example, in Ontario, provided that the WSIB claim is for a minor assessment, the other service is claimed using the service code A008, for a mini assessment.

SENDING IN CLAIMS

CLAIMS IN THE HEALTH OFFICE ARE STORED OR FILED ON THE COMPUTER. WHEN YOU WANT to submit the claims, you *batch* them, or prepare them for submission. The process will vary with the software program. Once a batch of files has been prepared for submission, your computer will notify you that the files are ready (Figure 12.6). You then copy the files to a disk or activate the electronic file transfer process.

❽ FEEDBACK FROM THE MINISTRY

ONCE THE CLAIMS PAYMENT AGENCY HAS RECEIVED AND REVIEWED YOUR CLAIMS, IT WILL send out various forms that let you know the status of your claims. These reports come in different forms depending on your method of submission. If you use electronic submission, log on regularly to check for your reports. They are the only notification that you will receive of files, batches, or individual claims that have been rejected. *All downloaded files are kept for a designated time frame, usually five to eight days.* When you transmit files to the Ministry, you will get a transmission receipt.

Unless they are marked for manual review, claims are generally validated electronically. The information submitted will be automatically compared with the guidelines for coverage of service. For example, in jurisdictions where physical examinations are covered once per year, a second examination will be rejected unless the claim is flagged for manual review and supported with documented reasons for the repeat examination.

Electronic submission of claims in most jurisdictions contains the following steps or a combination of them:

- Receipt of a claims file or batch
- Notification if the entire file or components of the file were rejected
- One or more preliminary checks of the file (e.g., may include a pre-edit and an eligibility edit, each checking different components of the claim)

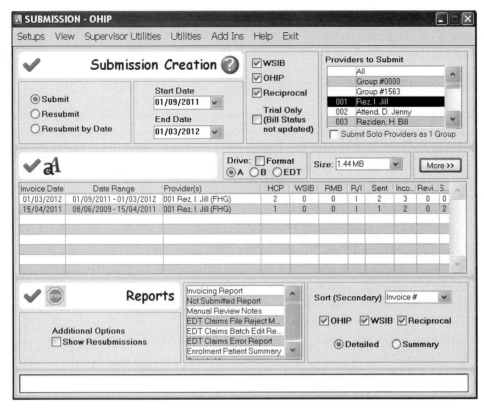

Figure 12.6 Batch of claims for submission to OHIP

Figure courtesy of P & P Data Systems Inc.

- Return of rejected claims so that they can be corrected and resubmitted in the same billing cycle
- Acceptance of corrected claims
- Adjudication—final check on claims—explanatory codes assigned
- Remittance and payment (an RA report listing those claims accepted, partially paid, or ultimately rejected within one billing cycle)

File Reject Message

Systems in all provinces and territories will send a message if all of your files have been rejected. Such messages are uncommon and are usually caused by technical difficulties. You would receive this report a few hours after your claims submission has been received by the Ministry. If an entire file sent on tape or disk is rejected, your local Ministry office will phone you.

Batch Edit Report

This report, offered by some electronic processes, lets you know whether your *claims batch* has been accepted or rejected. If you send files electronically, you should get this report within 24 hours of receipt. If your claims are sent on a weekend, holiday, or at the end of the month, the Ministry will send you this report on the next business day. If you are submitting your claims on disk or magnetic tape and a batch has been rejected, you will be notified by telephone on the next business day.

Claims Error Report

A claims error report lists all the rejected claims from a particular file and gives an error code for each rejection. If you submit electronically, in most jurisdictions you will receive this notification within 48 to 72 hours of submitting a batch of files. If you submit claims on disk or tape, your claims error reports will be on paper and mailed to you. It is not unusual to receive several claims error reports in a month. Rejections (claims errors) occur for a variety of reasons. There may be a problem with the client's health card, the service code given, or the diagnostic code.

Each rejected claim will have an error code to explain the reason for rejection or underpayment. These differ with each jurisdiction, using various combinations of alpha and numeric characters, and are available in your fee schedule. They are usually listed under broad categories, such as eligibility, health number, and errors relating to reciprocal billing. In Ontario, a commonly seen eligibility error code is E5, which indicates that the service date is not within an eligible time frame (e.g., an annual physical or ocular examination within 12 months of the previous one). The code 56 means a claim is under review; 40 indicates that a service is allowed only once per patient. C1 usually accompanies an underpayment and indicates that a claim for a full consultation was allowed only as a repeat limited consultation instead of a full consultation. Note that you may also have overpayments if the fee has increased since your software billing program was updated.

Carefully review all claims that have been rejected or were not paid in full. You must resubmit the corrected claims in order to receive payment. Claims not submitted within a designated time frame (in Ontario, six months) will not be paid. Improper follow-up with each rejected or partially paid claim can add up to thousands of dollars in lost revenue for your provider. Keep a copy of all claims error reports, either on your computer or in hard copy. This will help you with your reconciliation.

Some jurisdictions, if they do not return rejected claims, will allow you to have a submission returned if you discover a problem with incorrect claims that have been submitted. You can correct it and resubmit the claim within the same billing cycle. The onus is on the submitting party to identify errors.

Resubmitting Corrected Claims and Adjudication   You must correct problems noted in error messages and resubmit corrected claims immediately. (As noted above, a huge advantage of ET is that you get your claims error reports more frequently and can respond faster, increasing your chances of being paid within the current billing cycle.)

Payment and Remittance Advice

remittance advice (RA)   a monthly statement of approved claims from the Ministry.

A **remittance advice (RA)** report is a file returned to you once a month from the Ministry listing all submitted claims from the previous billing cycle. It is sometimes also referred to as reconciliation advice. You will receive it on tape, disk, or electronically, depending on how you submitted the claims. Generally, the RA is sent out at the same time as payments; in Ontario, this will usually be about the seventh or eighth of the month if you submit electronically, and between the 12th and 18th if you submit on tape or disk. The RA may be issued to a single provider or to a group that has submitted billings jointly.

The RA is analogous to a bank statement because it includes records of transactions for the previous month. Just as many people reconcile their bank statement by comparing it with entries in their cheque book, you should reconcile the RA by comparing it with your own claim records and investigate any apparent discrepancies. Every claim you submit should correspond with either a line on the RA or a line on a claims error report. Review each one individually (many offices keep a hard copy of both submitted claims and RAs). If there are any **partial claims payments**, you should understand why the amount paid is different from what you claimed.

The RA includes a summary, which categorizes the contents of the report and enables you to determine whether you received what you billed. Rejected claims may be listed as exceptions at the end of the RA. Some software programs will extract rejected claims lines and shift them to another file. This list will include the account number (internal use), the client's name, health card number, date of the service, service code, and a code indicating why the service was underpaid or not paid. (This information is similar to the claims error report except that the latter shows only irregularities.) Payments for WSIB-related services will appear on the RA with "WCB/WSIB" in the payment column.

partial claims payment a payment to a provider of a lesser amount than that claimed; an explanation will be given of why the payment was reduced.

Items Paid in Full   The majority of the items will (hopefully) be claims paid in full (i.e., the amount you billed).

Underpayments   Some items may be *underpayments*; that is, the Ministry has not rejected the claim but has paid less than you claimed. Payment reductions are based on the Ministry's computer analysis, which, in turn, is based on claims policies and regulations. There may be a number of reasons for the reduction, which will be explained by the appropriate codes on the RA. For example, if you claimed a service as an intermediate assessment when (on the basis of the diagnostic code) it should be a minor assessment, you would receive the fee for a minor assessment with an error code explaining the difference. If you were in British Columbia and submitted a service code used for a client over 70 years old, but the client's health information indicated that he was 60 years old, you would likewise be paid a reduced amount and see an error code on your RA. You must review these claims, and you have the option of resubmitting them with an explanation.

Rejected Claims   There may be some rejected claims on the RA report if the error was not picked up during the preliminary batch edit. (Some types of errors can be picked up right away; others are picked up only at the RA level.) Unpaid and partially paid claims that have not been previously corrected and resubmitted after a claims error report will be included, along with a code indicating why the claim was rejected or underpaid. Review each rejection individually. Correct errors and resubmit promptly. Sometimes, you may have to submit supporting documentation or a more detailed explanation. If you do not understand or accept the reason for a rejection or underpayment, use a Remittance Advice Inquiry form. All inquiries should be submitted within one month, and no later than four to six months after the original claim was submitted or the date on which the service was rendered. Submit all inquires relating to the same RA at one time.

If the claim is rejected again, and your provider still believes she is entitled to payment, you can appeal. All jurisdictions have a Medical Eligibility Committee (or equivalent) that examines the facts, interviews the provider, and decides on disputed claims.

Computer-Generated Reports

Computer programs will generate various summaries and highlights of Ministry reports. An example is the rejected billing line report. This report, offered by some software, provides you with rejection details on a line-by-line basis within a reconciliation. At the end of the report is a summary of the number of claim lines rejected, how much was billed, and how much was paid.

Payment of Claims

Of course, the most important return from the Ministry is the monthly payment itself. The provider may receive the payment by cheque or by direct deposit. Arrangements for direct deposit may be made through the providers' registry section at the Ministry office.

Alternative Payment Plans—Primary Care Reform Groups Every jurisdiction has different alternative payment plans that, for the most part, are combined with fee-for-service remuneration. Capitation-based funding is the most widely used. The Ministry pays the physician based on certain demographic and health information specific to each client. You are not required to submit any claims for this payment plan.

In most primary care reform models, physicians are paid bonuses or incentive payments for service goals achieved. Again, you are not responsible for billing the Ministry. You may, however, be responsible for tracking certain client groups regarding services they have received if that service is one the doctor is remunerated for. As mentioned in Chapter 11, these services are primarily preventive in nature, including immunizations, mammograms, flu shots, and Pap smears. You must also be knowledgeable about other new services for which the doctor can claim, such as smoking cessation and diabetic management.

⑨⑩ BILLING FOR SERVICES NOT PUBLICLY INSURED

THE MAJORITY OF A PHYSICIAN'S BILLINGS WILL BE TO SOME FORM OF PUBLIC INSURANCE, most often the provincial or territorial health plan. However, when services are not covered, you will have to collect payment either directly from the client or from a third party.

Services Charged to the Client

A range of services that a client might need or want (listed in Chapter 10) are not covered by provincial and territorial health-care plans. Moreover, sometimes, the client will have to pay for services that would normally be insured because she is not eligible for coverage, perhaps because she is a recent immigrant, because she is a resident of Quebec visiting your province or territory, or because her card is, for one reason or another, invalid. In such cases, you need to collect payment directly from the client.

This will probably be a fairly infrequent, but significant, part of your total billing if you work for a physician. For other providers, such as chiropractors and optometrists, it can be a major part of total revenue. For example, oculo-visual examinations will be covered under certain circumstances, depending on the jurisdiction, but the client will normally pay for the glasses herself. Most companies that offer employee benefits cover eyeglasses, but most optometrists want direct payment, and so the client pays and seeks reimbursement from the insurance company.

In most jurisdictions, the physician must inform the client, or the person responsible for financing the service, of the cost of the service *prior* to rendering the service. This may be accomplished by means of a notice prominently placed in the reception area of the provider's office or a client handout listing all uninsured services the provider offers. However, you should never assume people have read something. In addition to written notices, always discuss payment directly with the client. Be clear. Make sure the client understands what, when, and how he will be paying. This is really the physician's responsibility, but you can provide reinforcement. Also let the client know if there is a way he could get the service covered—for example, if an examination would be covered if he waited a couple of months or if the service is offered free to clients at a hospital.

Note: Recall from Chapter 4 that extra-billing—billing the client more for an insured service than the provincial or territorial plan pays—is illegal. (This does not apply to certain enhanced services for which a co-payment may be made.) You may be held liable for knowingly participating in extra-billing. Be careful not to inadvertently bill a client for any insured service. If you suspect that your provider is extra-billing, speak to your provider to clarify the issue, or seek legal counsel.

Block Fees   Some physicians offer an arrangement in which a client pays a single block fee, for an individual or a family, for a range of uninsured services over a period of time—not less than 3 months and not more than 12 months. Some clients feel more comfortable with a block fee than with having to pay separately for uninsured services. Block fees are particularly appealing to older clients who often need telephone advice or clients on numerous medications who frequently need one renewed.

The College of Physicians and Surgeons in each province and territory has set out rules for the block-fee model. If your provider offers block fees, post these guidelines prominently. Note that block fees are subject to GST or HST (depending on your province/territory).

Transfer of Medical Records   When clients request that their medical records be transferred, they are responsible for the cost. It's surprising how many clients think that a transfer of records involves simply packaging up their original chart. The process should be carefully explained. As well, the client must be *clearly notified in advance that this is an uninsured service* and what the cost will be. A good way to do this is to include the cost of transfer in the consent form that clients must sign. Most doctors base the cost on the number of pages involved. Some will charge a set rate for the first 5 or 10 pages and an additional per-page rate after that. One province recommends a charge of $37.00 for pages 1–5 and $1.50 for subsequent pages. If the doctor spends a considerable amount of time arranging or summarizing the client's chart prior to transfer, she may also charge for the time. If the client's chart is large, it may cost the client less to have the physician review and summarize, transferring only relevant information, than to pay for photocopying everything.

Preparing the chart of a psychiatric client is more detailed. The doctor must be careful about the nature of the information transferred; charges for transfer of this type of information are sometimes higher.

Accepting Payment

Most physicians find that asking for payment at the time the service is rendered is most effective. Many offices keep a petty cash supply on hand and accept only cash. Some offices will also accept personal cheques, certified cheques, debit cards, or credit cards, such as Visa or MasterCard. Note that to accept debit or credit cards, you need prior arrangement with a bank, which involves a fee. You will need a card-swiping device, which may be manual or tied into your computer system and modem. Always record the transaction in a ledger, and issue a dated receipt. Some physicians will agree to bill clients under certain circumstances. Your physician may also be willing to set aside normal policies for financially disadvantaged clients who cannot afford to pay.

Whatever the office's policies, it is important to stick to them. If you make exceptions for clients because "I don't have the correct change" or "I forgot my wallet at home," you will often spend considerable time asking for payment, and in some cases, you will never be paid. One client came into the office to pick up completed insurance forms, which she had been told she would have to pay for. When the AHP asked for $20, the woman looked surprised, hesitated, and said, "I don't have my purse. I can pay you later." She clearly expected to be handed the forms, but the AHP responded brightly, "That's fine, Mrs. Christie. When you have the money, come back and the forms will be waiting." The woman came back less than an hour later with the money.

The more closely you follow a policy of payment at point of service and the more firmly you deal with clients, the fewer outstanding accounts you will have. It may seem harsh, but clients will soon learn that payment is expected. Think about picking up a bag of chips at the local convenience store. Would the clerk let you walk out and come back later to pay?

Tips for Direct Billing

- Always discuss uninsured services with a client before the service is rendered (when the client is booking an appointment, and then again when they arrive at the office).
- Have an office policy either posted or in a handout—it must be detailed and clear.
- Keep your accounts up to date.
- Be consistent with account follow-up, and be organized.

Insurance Coverage

As discussed in Chapter 10, private insurance (often, but not always, as part of an employee benefits package) pays for many services not covered by provincial or territorial plans. Arrangements for payment differ. Most often, the client will pay the provider and then submit receipts to the insurance company for reimbursement. Beyond providing a suitably detailed receipt, you have no involvement with the insurer.

In other cases, the client signs an assignment of benefits, which allows the insurance company to pay the provider directly. In this case, you will need to invoice the insurance company, which will send a cheque directly to the office. Alternatively, the client may ask you to bill the insurance company on her behalf; the insurance company will send a cheque to the client, who endorses it to the provider. These arrangements may be negotiated between the provider and the client and also depend on the policies of the insurance company. Make sure you know your employer's policies. Many providers prefer to bill an insurance company, which will usually pay reliably (if not necessarily quickly). If you are billing on behalf of a client, there is always the risk that the client will forget to endorse and send on the cheque.

Collection

If you send bills, it is inevitable that you will sometimes have outstanding accounts. It is important to have a follow-up policy. Most offices will telephone or mail a bill twice. (Some providers charge interest on outstanding accounts; if so, the rate must be noted on all notices for payment.) After two notices, the account goes either to small claims court or to a collection agency. Before taking that step, it is important to ensure that the client actually received the notices. Sometimes, clients simply forget they owe money, move, and do not receive any reminder until they are contacted by a collection agency. The most reliable approach is to remind the client when he comes into the office or to phone and get the client to confirm that he is aware of the debt.

The small claims court is an option when attempts to collect directly are unsuccessful. However, most jurisdictions require that someone from the office attend court, which is time consuming and may not be cost effective. More physicians are resorting to collection agencies, which charge only if they are successful in collecting.

Third-Party Services

A **third-party service** is generally considered any service carried out at the request of someone other than the client or for the use of someone other than the client. For example, an employer, a camp, or a school may require a physical examination. A health certificate may be a requirement for a pilot's licence or a commercial driver's licence or may be required before entering into a contract for life insurance. An insurance company may need an assessment to settle a claim, or a lawyer may need an assessment to take to court. Services may involve filling out forms or transmitting medical information to the third party and may include a complete physical examination, a system-specific examination, or diagnostic tests. All these services would be billed to the third party or sometimes to the client depending on payment arrangements. Just as with claims to health plans, a bill may include fees for more than one component: for example, for an assessment, a diagnostic test, and a report. Where a third party requires ongoing or subsequent assessments, the physician may bill for additional services. In some circumstances, a service may be covered by a provincial or territorial plan but the related documentation may not. For example, if a physician feels that for the client's health and safety, he should be assessed before returning to work, the health plan would cover the assessment because it is considered medically necessary. However, if the client's employer requires a return-to-work

third-party service a service carried out at the request of someone other than the client or for the explicit use of someone other than the client.

note, that would not be covered; either the employer or, more likely, the client would be responsible for the cost.

Following are some of the common types of third-party services.

Government Forms   The federal government pays for physicians to complete a number of types of forms, including medical reports on applicants for immigration and applicants to the armed forces and reports on disability to qualify for disability payments under the Canadian Pension Plan, the Federal Disability Tax Credit, and similar benefits.

Insurance Forms   Insurance companies generate a vast variety of forms and related services for physicians. Table 12.1 lists some of the more common types; names and specifics may vary. Always make sure you have the client's permission to release any information. This is usually obtained by the insurance company and sent to the physician along with the requested forms. Figures 12.7 and 12.8 show a sample consent form and covering letter.

Medical–Legal Issues   Physicians may become involved in court cases in several ways. A doctor may be served with a subpoena to appear in court to testify in a case involving a regular client or one he saw in an Emergency Department. A physician may also be asked to appear as an "expert witness" in a case involving a client he has never met; he may be asked to further assess the person's medical condition or to give a general opinion. Physician payment in such circumstances is managed by the courts or privately at preset or prearranged amounts. It may be your responsibility to bill for such services. You must be very careful to ensure that proper protocol is followed before releasing any client information. The client must give written consent for the release or discussion of

Table 12.1 Common Types of Insurance Forms	
Attending Physician's Request Statement	Sent out after an applicant for life insurance has completed preliminary information forms. Requests information from the client's chart, including medical history, progress notes, and findings about any noteworthy medical problems.
System of Disease Questionnaire	Requests information about a client's treatment and progress regarding a specific—often a chronic—disease. Usually sent directly from the insurance company.
Insurance Medical Examination	Requires the doctor to complete a general physical examination and related functional inquiry for insurance purposes. The client may bring in this form, or it may be sent by the company.
System-Specific Examination	Asks the doctor to assess a specific system, such as the respiratory or the cardiovascular system, including a functional inquiry. This would be similar to an intermediate medical assessment.
Clarification Report	Usually sent directly to the doctor, this form may be used to settle an insurance claim. Asks for clarification and perhaps an update on previously submitted information and does not usually require the doctor to see the client.

Comprehensive Narrative Report	A more detailed form than the clarification report, used in complicated disability claims. Requests information about specific medical interventions, client progress, and diagnostic test results.
Disability Certificates	May be required by an insurance company or a government agency to certify that a client is injured and cannot work. Requires a physical examination and related functional inquiry. May be sent to the physician or brought in by the client.

any medical information, explicitly specifying to whom it may be released, unless a court order for the release of the information is presented.

Payment   Most third-party services paid for by agencies and insurance companies are paid by cheque or direct deposit. Usually, you do not have to invoice; the company will send a cheque on receipt of the report. Always issue receipts and record transactions in a

---

SLI STABILITY LIFE INSURANCE COMPANY

P.O Box 12345
Edmonton, AB
T3G 5N6
780-564-2929

February 25, 2009

Dear Dr. Linh:

Re: John Doe Contract 2344   **Claim 12344—Member ID 456789**

I am writing about John Doe's claim for long-term disability benefits.

To evaluate Mr. Doe's claim fully, we require his consultation reports from September 30 to December 31, 2008.

We also need you to complete the enclosed Physical Capacities Evaluation form. I have enclosed an authorization form for the release of Mr. Doe's medical information.

I would appreciate receiving the consultation reports and the completed evaluation form no later than April 15, 2009. Please include your correspondence fee with your reply.

Thank you for your assistance in this matter.

Yours truly

JR Benesh

JR Benesh
Disability Adjudications
Stability Life Insurance Company

/jb
encl

Figure 12.7   Covering letter from insurance company requesting medical records and form completion

Figure courtesy of P & P Data Systems Inc.

SLI STABILITY LIFE INSURANCE COMPANY

PO Box 12345
Edmonton, AB
T3G 5N6
780-564-2929

Consent for Release of Information

I authorize the Stability Life Insurance Company to conduct a thorough medical assessment for my condition and:

1. to be allowed to receive, review, and obtain copies of all hospital, medical, X-ray, laboratory, psychological, vocational and other related records related to my medical condition that will assist in completing this assessment and
2. to discuss any relevant information including test results or identifying information with the appropriate health professionals, employer, or related insurance personnel involved in my assessment, disability, and/or rehabilitation process.

I agree to the appropriate photocopying of this information as deemed necessary by those involved in my assessment.

I understand that the main purpose of this referral and gathering of information is to assess my medical condition and determine my entitlement to the appropriate benefits and/or rehabilitation.

DATED THIS 2ND DAY OF JANUARY 2009

At Edmonton, Alberta

SIGNATURE *John Doe*

WITNESS *JR Benesh*

Figure 12.8 Consent form for release of information to insurance company

ledger. In some jurisdictions, a physician may enter into an annual contractual arrangement, similar to a block-fee system, with third parties, jurisdictions such as insurance companies. These payments are subject to GST.

Table 12.2 summarizes the process of billing health-care plans.

Table 12.2 Summary of Health-Care Plan Billing

Methods	• Billing cards (manual, nearly obsolete, and carry a penalty) • Machine-readable input/output • Physical media: ■ Disks (3½″ Mac or IBM) ■ Magnetic tape (used by larger facilities) ■ 380 IBM cartridge • Electronic transfer (ET); sent by modem • Claims will be returned in the same format in which you send them. For example, if you submit claims by magnetic tape, your reports will be sent back by tape.

Timelines	● Claims must be in by the 18th of every month to be guaranteed payment within that cycle. ● If you use ET, you can send in claims up to the end of the month and they will be paid, providing the claims office is not too busy. ● Payment is by the 18th of the next month.
Information Components	Many of these data are entered automatically on some software programs but must be entered manually on cards.
Client's Demographic Data	● Full name ● Address ● Date of birth ● Sex ● Province or territory
Additional Card Information	● Health card number ● Version code, if applicable ● Expiry date (on some systems)
Provider Number	
Payment Program	Most computers default to HCP
Payee	Indicates who is getting the money: P for provider and S for client; opted-out only; rarely used
Accounting Number	Usually computer-generated; optional
Date of Service	
Service Code and/or Procedural Code	
PPU	Price per unit/service
Number of Services	May appear on screen as units
Diagnostic Code Fee	Same as PPU unless service is time based or more than one service is claimed
Facility Number	Used only if the client has been admitted to a hospital or other facility
Referring Number	Used only if the claim is by a specialist; the referring physician's registration number
Admission Date	Used only for a client in hospital

Future Trends

How physicians are paid will continue to change, affecting billing policies and procedures. Primary care reform groups are proving to be effective in giving cost-effective care to individuals. Physicians are showing more interest in payment models other than the fee-for-service, with most saying they prefer blended payment schemes Patient Enrolment Models (PEMs) although popular, have complex billing practices. Because meeting incentive goals for preventive care initiatives generates revenue, the AHP is challenged to maximize client participation. Each year more physicians are moving to computerized office settings. Virtually all offices and clinics are computerized to some degree, particularly for scheduling and billing. Maximizing the use of the computerized environment depends on the administrative staff in the occupational setting as well as the provider. Physicians seem busier than ever, and thus are relying heavily on administrative staff to keep abreast of changes and handle the scheduling and billing components of their practices.

>

Funding to assist with establishing a more electronic environment is not as readily available in some jurisdictions—and it is expensive to implement. This is a deterrent to many doctors. To make EMR/EHR systems effective, all jurisdictions across Canada have committed to collaborating more effectively to develop strategies to ensure that the software systems physicians purchase are compatible. This will require a select number of approved vendors who meet specific standards to choose from when implementing an electronic medical system. This could involve changing the system you are currently using. Consistency must be a priority, especially to ensure the success of a country-wide exchange of health information.

Billing practices will be constantly changing over the foreseeable future in all provinces and territories—not just the software systems, but also the modes of payment, what services are covered, to what extent, and what codes are used. This is an ongoing challenge. The codes and rules the AHP learns today may no longer be in use tomorrow. The ministries of all jurisdictions send out memos of any billing changes—but still, keeping up is not easy. All jurisdictions are encouraging EDT as the favoured method of billing.

SUMMARY

1. Claims submission is one of your major responsibilities. Claims submission is a complex process that has been simplified by the use of specially designed computer software. You need a solid understanding of codes. Focus on accuracy, because errors can result in rejected claims.

2. Claims may be submitted on tape or disk or by electronic transfer (ET). Some jurisdictions will still accept submission on billing cards but penalize the few providers who still use them. ET is becoming the most widely used method because it is the most efficient. It also improves cash flow by allowing faster response to submissions and payment of submissions later in the billing period.

3. When registering a client, it is important to verify client information. Health card validation reduces claims rejection and facilitates prompt claims payment.

4. A variety of software programs are available to facilitate claims preparation. Common modules include registration, billing day sheets, and billing modules. Software can integrate clients' personal and medical information with billing records.

5. A claim must include certain information: physician registration number, client demographic data, payment program, service date, service code, diagnostic code (usually), number of services, price per unit, and fee. Claims may be flagged for independent consideration, and explanations can be added in a manual review field.

6. With the exception of certain excluded services, reciprocal medical billing is handled like a regular claim, except that the payment program is RMB. In Ontario, as well as some other jurisdictions, the Ministry of Health acts as the payment agency for most workers' compensation claims. Be sure to identify the payment program as WCB (or WSIB).

7. Reports from the Ministry in response to claims submissions are supplied in the same format in which the claims are submitted. These reports include remittance advice reports, claims error reports, and, for ET, file reject messages and batch edit reports.

8. Review claims error reports and resubmit claims. Review the next RA form to see whether resubmitted claims have been paid. If a claim is rejected again, submit an RA inquiry.

9. A range of services are not covered by provincial or territorial health-care plans and are chargeable directly to clients. Clients must be told before the service is provided how much it will cost. Some physicians offer block or annual fees rather than charging for individual services. Most physicians ask for payment at the time of service. Firmness prevents problems with outstanding accounts.

10. Third-party services are those done at the request of someone other than the client. Third parties include government agencies, employers, schools, and insurance companies. Insurance companies often require examinations, medical information, and a variety of forms to be filled out. Doctors may also be asked to testify in court.

Key Terms

electronic transfer (ET) 368

machine-readable input (MRI) 368

partial claims payment 383

remittance advice (RA) 382

third-party service 387

Review Questions

1. Outline, in sequence, the steps of the client registration process.
2. List three methods of submitting health insurance claims.
3. What are the main advantages of electronic data transfer?
4. What is the purpose of the accounting number used in claims submission?
5. List and explain the payment programs used in claims submission.
6. What is the manual review field on a billing screen used for?
7. State the difference between a batch edit report and a file edit report.
8. Describe the purpose and content of a remittance advice report.
9. What should you do when you receive a claims error report?
10. Explain each of the headings in the following screen sample:

Item Code	PPU	Units	Type	Date	Diag. Code	MR	Amount	Status

Application Exercises

1. Compare the advantages and disadvantages of electronic claims submission versus submission on disk or tape.
2. Research electronic claims submission in your province or territory. Identify the files generated by this electronic billing system. Compare them with those described in this chapter, considering name, purpose, and content. Are claims submission deadlines the same as those discussed in this chapter?

3. For each of the following scenarios, fill in all the applicable fields in the chart representing the billing screen. Current amounts can be obtained from your jurisdiction's health plan billing schedule website.

a. Ivy comes in to have her ears syringed. She is on warfarin and requires a dose adjustment based on her last INR of 5.

b. Mia comes in for some family planning advice. She is worried about the risks of becoming pregnant. The doctor spends time counselling Mia about genetic risk factors. Mia also has a Pap smear while she is there.

c. Craig comes in complaining of vague symptoms of diarrhea and epigastric discomfort. The doctor does a urinalysis in the office and a fairly thorough examination but cannot reach a conclusive diagnosis.

d. Dr. Shymloski has seen Peter several times for a complaint of chest tightness. He sends Peter to Dr. Jamison, an internist, for a consultation. First he does an ECG in the office. You work for Dr. Shymloski.

e. Complete the chart for the scenario in Part d. This time you work for Dr. Jamison.

f. Dr. Oran made a house call for Mrs. Erickson at 2130 hours. Her diagnosis was congestive heart failure.

g. Regina was assessed for complications of her diabetes, and her insulin regimen was regulated. Home care was ordered to assess and apply a dressing to her foot.

h. At 0100, the doctor delivered Tina Smalley's baby. It was a spontaneous delivery with no complications.

i. The doctor is unable to make a diagnosis for Meena and has put on the chart that she has a collection of vague symptoms.

j. Lana's diagnosis was a plantar wart. The doctor removed the wart using a chemical substance.

k. Harnek is in hospital. Dr. Yu visits him as the MRP on day 1, day 2, and day 3.

l. Hassan visits the office with requiring a form for admission to a long-term care facility to be completed by the doctor.

m. Marcie, who is 6 months old, requires the routine vaccinations.

Item Code	PPU	Units	Type	Date	Diag. Code	MR	Amount	Status Acct#	Err.
a.									
b.									
c.									
d.									
e.									
f.									
g.									
h.									
i.									
j.									
k.									
l.									
m.									

4. Dr. Hui is a busy family practitioner. You discover that he sometimes adds codes for procedures he has not performed and bills for special calls/house calls when you know he has not made these visits. You owe your employer faithfulness according to ethical principles. What would you do? What are your options?

Websites of Interest

British Columbia Health Care
www.health.gov.bc.ca/msp/

BC Medical Services Commission Payment Schedule
www.health.gov.bc.ca/msp/infoprac/physbilling/payschedule/index.html

WorkSafeBC *Physician Reference Guide*
http://www.worksafebc.com/health_care_providers/Assets/PDF/physician_reference_guide.pdf
Physician reference guide for existing and new fee codes for WorkSafeBC

Alberta Schedule of Medical Benefits
www.health.alberta.ca/professionals/SOMB.htm

Saskatchewan Payment Schedule for Insured Services
http://www.health.gov.sk.ca/payment-schedule-oct2011

Ontario Schedule of Benefits
www.health.gov.on.ca/english/providers/program/ohip/sob/physserv/physserv_mn.html

Newfoundland and Labrador Medical Payment Schedule
http://www.health.gov.nl.ca/health/mcp/providers/full_mcp_payment_schedule.pdf

ICD-9 Diagnostic Codes
http://icd9.chrisendres.com/index.php
This site allows you to enter a diagnosis and find the code, or enter a code and find the diagnosis.

Blue Cross information for billing for RCMP officers
https://www.medavie.bluecross.ca/cs/ContentServer?c=ContentPage_P&pagename=MedavieCorporate%2FContentPage_P%2FOneColumnFull&cid=1187208933232

Chapter 13
Health Information Management

Learning Objectives

On completing this chapter, you will be able to:

1. Apply the general principles of health information management to electronic medical records and traditional charts.
2. Differentiate between the electronic medical record and the electronic health record.
3. Explain the advantages of computerized record keeping.
4. Explain the concept, acquisition, and use of an electronic medical records system.
5. List the components of an electronic medical record.
6. Summarize the phases of the health record life cycle.
7. Choose the most appropriate filing method for a particular health office environment.
8. Discuss the importance of security, privacy, and confidentiality of health records and explain how to preserve them.

Health information management is a field in its own right. Many colleges and universities across Canada offer undergraduate and graduate diplomas and degrees in Health Information Management and Health Informatics. A national organization, the Canadian Health Information Management Association (CHIMA), has nearly 4000 members who are largely responsible for client records at both micro and macro levels in private offices, clinics, and all health-care facilities across the country. CHIMA members have the designation Canadian Health Information Manager (CHIM). They manage health records from the time the information is retrieved until the point at which the information is disposed of, in paper or electronic format. Of equal importance is the security of the health information under their management—these individuals are acutely aware of provincial, federal, and agency confidentiality guidelines and ensure they are adhered to. These professionals, with their extensive knowledge of health information, are key players in the continued transition from paper-based record keeping to an electronic format.

This chapter will focus on the management of health information primarily in the electronic format, in a doctor's office—a task less onerous than managing health information in a large facility but one requiring specialized knowledge nonetheless. Most health facilities, medical offices, and clinics across Canada are still in transition to an electronic environment, particularly with the electronic medical chart.

❶ CONVERTING AN OFFICE TO EMR

MANY OFFICES, EVEN THOSE THAT ARE USING e**Charts**, RETAIN THE CLIENT'S "old" **pChart**. Converting pCharts to eCharts is very time consuming. For a practice with 3000 clients, it may take the better part of a year to summarize data from an pChart and scan the necessary information into the client's eChart. Some doctors like to keep paper copies of documents and reports in the client's pChart even after they have been added to the eChart. This is a duplication of work for the administrative health professional (AHP)—scanning and filing into the eChart, then turning around and filing the documents into the pChart. If this is the office routine, try to convince your employer to dispense with storing paper documents.

eChart electronic chart
pChart paper chart

Despite the transition to electronic medical records (EMRs), paper charts, at least in part, will be around for a number of years. If nothing else, they will act as a reservoir for health information not uploaded into an EMR. As well, in many cases, paper charts must be kept for a period for legal purposes.

THE TERMS

FIRST IT IS NECESSARY TO CLARIFY THE MEANING OF SOME OF THE TERMS AND PHRASES associated with handling health information and identify key players involved in the creation, use, and storing of electronic health information.

eHealth is a general term used to describe electronic health information—its creation, use, and management. The electronic health record is a significant part of eHealth initiatives supported by the federal government.

The Canada Health Infoway is a federally funded organization with a mandate to facilitate the national implementation of electronic health records. The organization works collaboratively with all levels of government, regional authorities, health facilities, and a variety of health professionals. The Canada Health Infoway provides a forum where stakeholders can share ideas, information, and successes about implementing and using health records systems. Good ideas can provide a foundation for moving forward with some initiatives; unsuccessful projects can be shelved or modified.

Under the Canada Health Infoway, electronic health information systems and electronic health records projects are approved, funded, and implemented. Examples of these include electronic access to diagnostic imaging, and drug and laboratory information.

The electronic medical record and the electronic health record are part of this process.

Health information is defined as any information pertaining to someone's physical or mental health, condition, or infirmity, whether given orally or recorded in any manner, that is created or received directly or indirectly by a health professional or health organization. It includes services rendered, treatments and treatment plans, health teaching and education, and payment for services. Personal information and demographic data gathered to provide medical services are also considered health information. Although this definition of health information is widely accepted and comprehensive, the definition varies and is interpreted differently by individuals and organizations.

The definition of health information management is equally diverse, meaning different things to different people. Responsibilities related to health information management include the physical management of information systems—ranging from computers to modems and printers. It includes the design and programming of related software. Any person or organization responsible for managing health information is a **health information custodian**.

❷ THE HEALTH RECORD

IN GENERAL TERMS, A HEALTH RECORD IS ANY DOCUMENTATION RELATING TO A health-care client. The term *record* is used for a single document, such as a doctor's note on an assessment or a lab report; it also refers to a collection of documents, such as a client's chart. Records may be paper based or electronic. Whether in a private practice or in a hospital, a record must be kept of every aspect of the client's interaction with a health professional and/or a health facility. This includes the client's presenting problem, assessment, treatment, and outcome. Health-care providers usually create health records, although other professional staff may also capture clinical and non-clinical information. Traditionally, we view a **health record** as a paper-based collection of information, and a chart as a file folder containing this information.

The current trend is managing this information electronically. Electronic management of health records has produced the terms *electronic medical record* and *electronic health record*, each with different characteristics.

A physician in private practice is ultimately responsible for health records; in a hospital, the administration is legally responsible and delegates responsibility to Health Information Services—which is the more current title for what was previously called the Medical Records Department. Standards for documentation are set by professional colleges, by legislation, and by health organizations. This includes *all* activities relating to the care and treatment of a client as well as the names of those rendering the care.

Detailed, accurate health records are essential to high-quality health care. A large component of this is continuity of care—knowing the client's medical history, problems, medications and treatments. If 75-year-old Fred, who lives in Vancouver, was seen by a doctor in Calgary or in the ER in a hospital in Burnaby, his medical records would be

health information any information pertaining to someone's physical or mental health, condition or infirmity, whether given orally or recorded in any manner, that is created or received directly or indirectly by a health professional or health organization.

health information custodian a person, persons, or organization who has the responsibility for safekeeping and controlling personal health information in connection with the powers and duties performed.

health record any documentation relating to a health-care client. The term record is used for a single document, such as a doctor's note on an assessment or a lab report; it also refers to a collection of documents, such as a client's chart.

available to the treating physician, enabling the physician to make informed decisions based on Fred's medical history.

The health record is also used

- for medical–legal purposes,
- as the source information for billing,
- for funding initiatives,
- for mandatory reporting to various governmental bodies,
- as a quality monitoring tool,
- as a program evaluation tool,
- for teaching,
- for research, and
- for hospital, regional, and provincial or territorial health services planning.

The Electronic Medical Record (EMR)

An **electronic medical record (EMR)** is a legal health record in digital format. It contains the client's health information collected by one or a group of providers in one location—a medical practice, hospital, or clinic. *It is a subset of the electronic health record (EHR)—in other words, part of a larger record.*

The Electronic Health Record (EHR)

An **electronic health record (EHR)** is an accumulation of essential information from an individual's electronic medical records that is accessed electronically at different points of service for purposes of client care. The EHR follows the client and is available whenever and wherever he needs care. *The EHR is a compilation of EMRs.*

In the office setting, software that creates, maintains, and stores electronic medical records information is different from software that supports the electronic health record. The EHR system is much broader, and the software supports connectivity to a variety of caregivers to allow for the sharing of a client's medical information. It may include demographic information, cumulative profile, progress notes, pharmacy records, laboratory information, and diagnostic reports. Probably the greatest electronic challenge facing health care is how to effectively network various health facilities within a community, let alone on a national level, so that the EHR is both viable and useful.

Electronic Medical Records Systems

An **electronic medical records system** is a total medical office system—hardware and software—with the capabilities of replacing all components of a paper chart and supporting its use in an electronic format.

Because EMR programs are new and complex, most still have their share of glitches. This is frustrating and expensive for offices that have converted to EMR systems. I have seen medical groups buy and discard entire systems because they did not meet with their expectations or had too many operational glitches and/or inadequate vendor support.

A software program that supports EMR is, in most cases, an extension of the scheduling and billing software. In other words, the software components are created, integrated,

electronic medical record (EMR) a legal health record in digital format. It contains the client's health information collected by one or a group of providers in one location. It is a subset of the electronic health record (EHR).

electronic health record (EHR) an accumulation of essential information from an individual's electronic medical records that is accessed electronically at different points of service for purposes of client care.

electronic medical records systems a total medical office system, including both hardware and software, with the capability of replacing all components of a paper chart (health record) electronically.

and sold as one system. Some venders do have separate EMR systems and scheduling/billing systems that have the connectivity to work together. For example, you could purchase an office scheduling system from The Scheduling Expert and buy an EMR system from Records to Go, thus running two separate systems together. Currently, it is recommended that a provider purchase a system that has both scheduling and EMR units built into one system. A single system seems to have fewer problems.

In terms of storing information, venders will offer two options. A "local solution" stores the health information on-site in your office or clinic. With a local solution, it is the responsibility of the staff and/or the physician to back up the health information and keep it secure.

The other option is a "central solution," where information is hosted remotely by an application service provider (ASP). The provider retrieves and stores all of the health information for its customers in an off-site location. The vendor ensures that the information is backed up regularly and kept secure. It is also the vendor's responsibility to archive electronic files that are no longer of use.

All EMR systems must offer the following functions:

- An audit trail[1]
- The ability to allow providers to sign off on entries and prescriptions using electronic signatures
- The means to regularly save and back up data
- Effective protocols for information recovery

Creation of an EMR The health record, regardless of its storage medium, has a predictable cycle—retrieval of information, storage and management of the information, and archiving the information when it is no longer useful. Components of a paper medical chart, as well as its life cycle, are discussed in more detail later in this chapter.

To create a complete EMR in a doctor's office, the basic information you require includes a client's demographic information, medical history (PH), social and family history, functional inquiry (FI), history of present illness (HPI), diagnosis (Dx), and problem list, medication list, and allergies, if any.

To demonstrate this, consider Mr. Smith and his first appointment with Dr. Ryder, a family physician. Mr. Smith calls Sarah, the receptionist, at the office one Monday morning to make his initial appointment. Sarah asks Mr. Smith the reason he wants to see the doctor. It is for an annual physical, but he also states he has a sore back. With this information, Sarah is able to determine the urgency of the visit as well as the length of time Mr. Smith will need to spend with the doctor. Sarah asks Mr. Smith to bring a summary of his medical history from his previous doctor when he arrives for his appointment the following Tuesday. Sarah records the appointment information in Dr. Ryder's electronic scheduler; this action marks the initial retrieval and documentation of Mr. Smith's health information.

---

[1] An audit trail is necessary to track all activity within the EMR computer system. Unauthorized entry attempts can be tracked, as can the activities of all users, holding them accountable for any irresponsible/illegal breach of security policies. As well, all data entered can be tracked and retrieved. A computer system can have several types of audit trails.

When Mr. Smith arrives the next Tuesday, Sarah obtains his demographic information to initiate a computer database. As well, she needs his health number and other insurance information for billing purposes. The demographic portion of the Mr. Smith's EMR is now complete.

The next step is to obtain Mr. Smith's health history. In a health office, this may be your responsibility or the nurse's—probably by interviewing the client. Alternatively, the questionnaire may be completed by Mr. Smith himself, and scanned and attached to his EMR. In this example, the nurse, Alia, retrieves the information from Mr. Smith by direct questioning, and enters it into the computer as he answers the questions. This information is filed in his EMR under patient or client history, and becomes part of his health information documents.

On his software, Dr. Ryder has chosen a template specifically designed for physical examinations. The template contains fields for all required elements of a complete physical examination (CPX). The doctor completes a thorough investigation of Mr. Smith's problems and a physical examination, addressing all of the elements discussed above. He specifically asks Mr. Smith about the sore back (HPI). Dr. Ryder determines that Mr. Smith has muscle strain but prescribes no treatment. Mr. Smith's physical reveals some osteoarthritis of his lower limbs and mild hypertension. This information is added to Mr. Smith's EMR. His vital signs are taken and become part of a *flow sheet* that will track and graph future vital signs. His past medical records show that he is a borderline diabetic controlled by diet. The visit itself becomes part of Mr. Smith's *encounter record*. Medications Mr. Smith is on are added to his *medication profile*—in this case, "calcium 500 mg tid" and "Actonel 5 mg od."

His *problem list* now contains the diagnosis of back strain, essential hypertension, osteoarthritis, and type II diabetes. Mr. Smith is allergic to penicillin. This is added to the *allergy alert* portion of his EMR. The doctor orders a CBC, FBS, cholesterol and triglyceride levels, and electrolytes. He also orders an X-ray of Mr. Smith's lumbar spine and lower extremities. When the lab sends back these test results, you will add them to the *lab and diagnostic tests* portion of his EMR. They may be sent electronically or as hard copy.

In the coming week, Alia loads all of the essential information from Mr. Smith's transferred health information, thus completing his EMR. You now have a basic electronic chart with the first physician encounter documented and entered directly into the computer.

Managing an EMR System

The paperless office is a myth. However, properly managed, there can be a significant reduction in paper use. The freed-up space available after paper charts are destroyed or evacuated from the office itself is, in itself, an advantage.

Rapid Access to Information   Accessing information in electronic format is easy and efficient. Dr. Ryder's office calls requesting the reports from Mr. Smith's recent diagnostic imaging. It takes seconds to load the chart, locate the images, and send them electronically to Dr. Ryder's office (provided the office had the connectivity capabilities to exchange with other providers). Consider a client calling your office to find out about lab results. Instead of first locating and then shuffling through a paper chart to find the lab section, you simply key in the client's name, electronically open the chart, click on the lab section, and view the latest results.

Documenting Client Information   When Mr. Smith arrives for his next appointment, the AHP or the nurse can obtain the client's vital signs and chief complaint and enter them into the appropriate field in the encounter window in his chart. You can also add alert notes or highlight recently returned lab tests that you want to bring to the doctor's attention. This can all be done from any work station, including the computer in the front office. The doctor can immediately view this entry from a wireless tablet or a computer and be prepared with the required information before entering the examination room.

Follow-Up Tests and Appointments   After completing his assessments, the doctor can enter any lab or diagnostic requests and transfer them to you. You can follow up and be ready with any required information by the time the client is dressed and out of the examination room. The doctor can also send a message requesting any follow-up appointments, which you can immediately schedule.

In most regions, at least some labs provide their results electronically, eliminating the necessity for you to scan the results into the system and store them on the client's EMR.

❸❹ ELECTRONIC HEALTH INFORMATION IN THE DOCTOR'S OFFICE

CONVERSION TO EMR IS EXPENSIVE AND TIME CONSUMING. AS WELL, MANY DOCTORS are not fully comfortable with the use of this technology. They find security in the paper chart—the ability to see it, hold it, and record on it. The information is there and always retrievable, even if the computer system is down. Slowly but surely, however, medical offices are converting to the EMR. Because you are part of this progression, it is helpful to understand the process.

Data Entry on the Electronic Medical Record

Clinical records are usually classified as either *open text* or fully structured. Open text allows the provider to document much as he did on the paper chart. The provider records his findings on a blank page. He can use templates to keep the charting orderly and reduce repetitive entries; for example, there is a template for SOAP charting (subjective, objective, assessment, and plan). One disadvantage of open text is that it holds information as it is entered and does not lend itself to summarizing client health information into categories. For example, you could not pull all clients' blood work together, or send blood pressures into separate flow sheets or summary databases.

Fully structured is the other extreme, and is highly regimented. It requires that client information be entered into defined data fields. It is, perhaps, more time consuming in terms of determining what to put where and in entering infinite detail that many doctors feel is unnecessary. However, this design does lend itself to effortlessly assimilating material into easily accessible summaries.

Most users prefer a mix of the open, or free, text format and the fully structured. For example, it may be more effective to use open text to record the client's chief complaint and history of present illness and related documentation, and use the structured format to record lab data, medications, and vital signs.

Every software system will be somewhat different. For example, the names of the parts of the EMR may vary, available templates will be different, and the appearance of the screens will be different.

Security and the EMR

Each medical practice must identify in writing the level of access by any authorized person using the EMR system. The usual rules for protecting any computerized information apply—protecting the screen from unauthorized viewers, using and updating passwords regularly, and never allowing anyone else to use your password. Passwords should be hard to guess and should contain a combination of alphanumeric characters. Some practices also incorporate **fobs** or authentication tokens, thus implementing a two-step ID process. As well, it is necessary to have audit logging to record the actions of all users.

fob a small security device that can be added to a computer for access purposes. It displays a randomly generated access code that changes every few seconds.

If a provider has computers in an examination room or other areas where a client (or anyone else) has access, it must be electronically "locked down" to prevent unauthorized access.

Because offices using EMR and EHR systems are connected to the internet, it is essential to have an effective firewall. This will provide protection against illegal attempts to access your computer system. Antivirus software is also a must. Moreover, strategies to deal with system failures and lost data are imperative. As previously mentioned, with a local solution, you are responsible for backing up and securing system data. Imagine having to reconstruct all of your clients' medical records! You would have to rescan all of the data from the old paper charts and (somehow) try to find sources for information you have lost. Much of it would be irretrievable.

Back-up systems store encrypted copies of medical records; backups should be performed daily. The information should be stored on a disk or portable hard drive off the premises in case of a fire, theft, or other disaster.

Use of Portable Computers and Devices

Many offices have a combination of desktop and laptop or other portable devices. If the office has a wireless system, ensure that the system is appropriately encrypted. If the office staff and/or physicians use laptops containing health information at home, it is essential to follow through with security procedures. Never leave the computer unattended unless it is locked down or turned off. It's easy to be a little more relaxed in the home environment. However, it's better to be safe than sorry. Following security protocol is also a sensible habit to develop—with no exceptions.

Acquisition of New Computers

When a health office acquires new computers, the information on the existing computer must be professionally destroyed to ensure that the information is permanently removed. Most vendors will provide this service. Moreover, physician groups usually have a team of IT experts capable of removing this information.

Implications for the Staff

Training   Any vendor who sells an EMR system should be responsible for training the users. If you are involved in starting up an EMR system, this training is essential and usually requires several sessions. It is expensive and frequently not included in the purchase price of the system. Your employer will cover the cost.

The sessions can be conducted on site (in the office) or off-site. If the vendor is selling the system to a group of doctors (e.g., a primary care reform group), there will be a significant number of individuals to train—staff and providers. An off-site venue allows the vendor to rent a facility where trainers can set up multiple computer stations to accommodate everyone. Usually once training is completed, the trainers will make appointments for further on-site and hands-on instruction.

Transition from Paper Charts to EMR Format Medical offices that convert to electronic medical records must make a decision about what process they will use to move information from paper charts to electronic format. Special attention must be made to address the security of the information to ensure its safety and confidentiality. The office may decide to scan all or parts of the paper chart as PDFs, or start entering health information from the first day of their EMR implementation. Rules governing how long paper charts must be kept depend on the conversion process. If a client's entire chart is uploaded, the paper version is redundant. However, most Colleges of Physicians and Surgeons across Canada recommend keeping the paper version for at least six months. If chart content is summarized and scanned or preloaded, the client's paper chart must be kept in accordance with provincial or territorial regulations. This is indefinitely if the person remains an active client/patient. Doctors must ensure that all clinical information is available (electronic, paper, or a combination) for the duration of the legal chart retention period. Charts that can be destroyed should be shredded. Companies that specialize in paper shredding will come on site to do this. It is advisable that office staff supervise the process.

Converting pCharts to eCharts and Purging The process of converting pCharts to eCharts is time consuming and tedious, and requires that informed decisions be made about what to keep and what to eliminate. The process requires someone (usually the doctor) to go through each page in the chart and extract all essential information for uploading to the client's "new" EMR. In a general practice, some charts will be several centimetres thick, particularly if they have not been regularly **purged**. It is both unnecessary and impractical to consider scanning an entire chart. Most pCharts contain duplicate, old, and superfluous information. Usually, only vital information from a client's chart is scanned (e.g., important elements of the client's history, lab and diagnostic reports, medications, and latest medical profile). Elements of the client's chart that are lengthy can be reviewed and summarized by the physician and uploaded into the eChart (e.g., OR and consultation reports, interviews/discussions, and old histories).

As an AHP, your responsibilities will likely include preloading the chart: entering demographic information and creating the basic EMR. Once the EMR has been created, you can begin scanning the client's medical information (as provided by the physician) into the chart, and filing it in the appropriate locations within the chart. There may be situations wherein an AHP is asked to assume more responsibilities with respect to purging a pChart, for example, reviewing lab reports and discarding older ones, or updating a medication list. Purging a chart also involves getting rid of information in the chart deemed no longer needed. These records are confidential and must be destroyed according to protocol (shredding is the usual method).

Once the EMR system itself is functional, some doctors and AHPs find it easiest to start uploading a client's new electronic chart when she comes into the office. At that point, her old chart is summarized and either scanned or preloaded. The process of converting a practice of perhaps 2000 clients takes an enormous amount of time. On average, the task takes a year or more, depending on the resources and time assigned to the process.

purge (of file) review and reorganize to remove outdated information that is no longer actively needed to provide care to the client.

❺ THE CLIENT'S CHART

ALTHOUGH A SINGLE DOCUMENT IS SOMETIMES CALLED A CHART, GENERALLY A CHART refers to a folder containing all the records relating to a client's care with a provider or facility. As previously mentioned, the electronic counterpart of this is the electronic medical record.

A client's paper chart, like the EMR, originates when the client first seeks care with the provider. The creation of an EMR was outlined in the example of Mr. Smith's encounter with Dr. Ryder. In terms of creating a paper chart, it can be prepared in advance of the first appointment. The appropriate folder may be selected and the client's name (or numeric identifier) added. As well, a blank form for recording client encounters, a blank cumulative patient profile, and a history and physical form can be added. Having some generic charts made up ahead saves time. The minute the client has her first contact with the health-care provider, the provider must begin keeping records, and the empty folder becomes a client chart. The paper chart will continue as long as the client comes to the provider and/or until the provider converts the chart to EMR format.

Components of a Chart

The format, design, and organization of a client's medical chart will differ with each provider and each agency, but there are common elements. In the electronic setting, the format of the EMR will vary with the type and design of the software.

1. The chart must contain the client's name, address, birth date, and health card number. In the electronic environment, this is part of the client's database and can be electronically transferred to any electronic documents.

2. The chart must be kept neat, accurate, and complete. With a manual chart, keeping it neat entails purging the chart regularly—discarding duplicate information (e.g., lab results) and irrelevant documents. With the EMR, this is done by deleting extraneous information. (Make sure none of the information is legally required for audit purposes.) An advantage to the EMR is legibility of entries. As well, documentation is entered into required fields; thus, good organization is a product of the software.

3. Each encounter and service rendered must be entered into the chart with the appropriate date.

4. Each recorded encounter must contain the relevant history obtained, details of the medical examination rendered, documentation of any investigations ordered by the doctor, and results of those investigations, when available. All advice given to a client and the particulars of any referral must also be entered on the encounter record.

5. The chart must be safely and properly stored.

6. The charts must be kept confidential in accordance with provincial or territorial legal guidelines. Governing bodies of health-care providers also have guidelines.

Even though the content and organization of the client's chart in a doctor's office will vary, most charts contain the same types of records:

History (Interview) Sheet   This is a questionnaire that the client is asked to fill out, usually on the first visit to the provider's office (see Chapter 9). Usually, someone (the doctor, the nurse, or the AHP) will help the client fill out the sheet or review it with him.

Cumulative Patient Profile (CPP) The paper chart version of a cumulative profile, shown in Figure 13.1, starts with the answers to the history questionnaire and is updated periodically to provide a cumulative view of the client's history and current health status. It is often kept at the very front or back of the chart. The CPP may require special attention from a non-physician provider, who likely sees the client less frequently. Figure 13.2a is an example of an electronic CPP for Melissa Sweet. It profiles almost every component of her health history. Figure 13.2b concentrates on her health problems over the previous five visits and her drug allergies/reactions profile.

History and Cumulative Profile

Home Phone

ID# or File #

OHIP Number Version

Present Marital Status						Sex		Date of Birth		
S	M	Sep.	D	W	Other	M	F	D	M	Y

2. PERSONAL AND FAMILY (e.g., occupation, life events, habits) Dates	DATA

3. PAST HISTORY (e.g., past serious illnesses, operations) RISK FACTORS (e.g., genetics/familial diseases)	Dates

4. ALLERGIES/DRUG REACTIONS	Dates

5. DATES OF: ↓ Initial Visit	General Assessment →		
	Summarized Record on CPP →		

Codes /Nos.	6. ONGOING HEALTH CONDITIONS (e.g., problems, diagnoses, dates of onset)	Date Recorded	Date /Co

Codes /Nos.	7. LONG-TERM TREATMENT REG. (e.g., medications, dosage/frequency)	Date Started	Date Discont.

8. CONSULTANTS

Figure 13.1 Patient cumulative profile, paper chart (CPP)

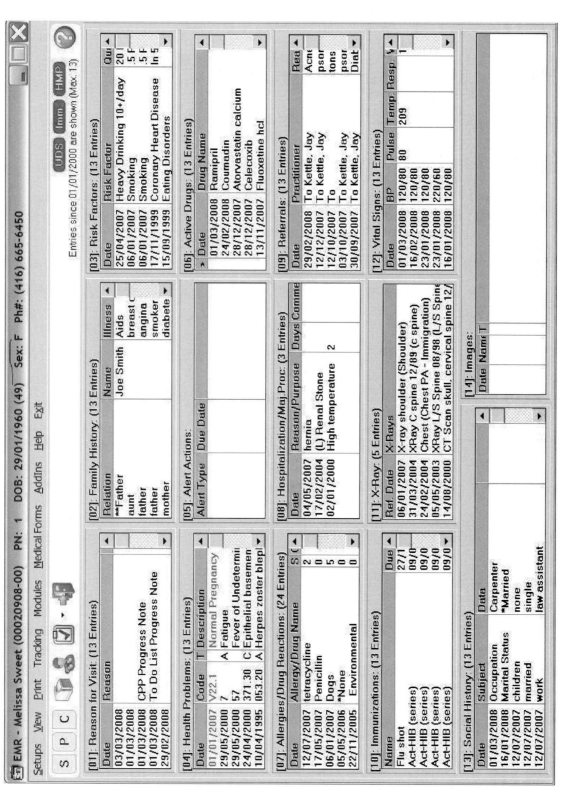

Figure 13.2a CPP from an EMR showing the client's entire health history

Figure courtesy of P & P Data Systems Inc.

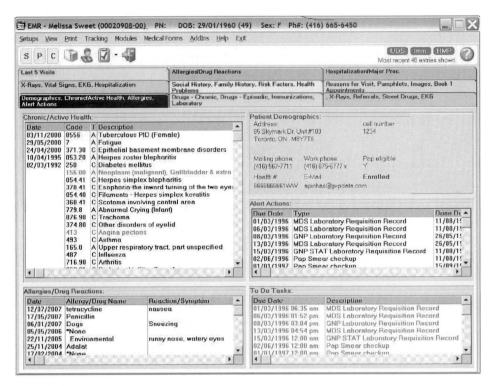

Figure 13.2b CPP from an EMR showing problems related to the previous five visits and the client's allergies and drug reaction profile

Figure courtesy of P & P Data Systems Inc.

List of Allergies The client's allergies will appear on the history sheet but should also be listed in a prominent place at the front of the chart, either on the outside or the inside cover. It is helpful to note allergies in red. Some practices list allergies on each progress sheet as well. With the EMR, these allergies can be noted as an "Alert" on the computer system, popping up as soon as you swipe the client's health card or access his EMR. Depending on the database, some systems will automatically notify the provider if he writes a prescription electronically that the client is allergic to.

Encounter Record This documentation occurs each time the client has an encounter with the health-care provider. With paper charts, the doctor must either take time between seeing clients to complete documentation, or trust his memory and document later in the day. Charting encounters at the end of the day can result in errors or lapses in memory. "Let's see—was Mr. Smith here about a sore back, or was that Mr. Slithers?" In the EMR environment, the physician can document as he completes his assessments, using a PC in the examination room or a portable device, often as he is interacting with the client. However, some clients complain that the doctor spends more time entering data than talking with them.

In a doctor's office, the physician is the primary user of an encounter record. Nurses and other staff members (if trained to do so) may make entries related to telephone calls, test results telephoned to the office, and appointments (e.g., repetitive broken appointments or no-shows). If you notice that documentation is absent from the encounter record of a client the provider has seen, flag it, leave a note, or ask the doctor personally.

In a paper chart, the most current progress sheets should be at the front of the stack. Add a blank sheet to the chart when the current one is approximately two-thirds full. In an EMR setting, the order of encounter entry is up to the provider's preference.

In EMR format, the encounter screen is entered by clicking on an icon—sometimes simply called "patient visit." Once on the screen, you can choose among several preset templates, such as one for a complete physical examination, another for a prenatal visit, or one for a regular encounter. You can also select a documentation template; for example, SOAP charting is commonly used for client visits.

- **S** means subjective and refers to anything the client says to describe his problem: "I feel weak and tired. I have a headache."
- **O** stands for objective and is what the examiner sees. Perhaps the client is flushed, or bent over with pain, or has a swollen hand.
- **A** refers to the examiner's assessment. It is what he elicits from the examination, and his diagnosis.
- **P** is the examiner's plan for the client. He might put the client on an antibiotic or pain medication, or send him to a dietitian, for example.

Figure 13.3 and Figure 13.4 illustrate an EMR template using SOAP charting. Figure 13.3 is a blank template; Figure 13.4 is the same template illustrated as it relates to a well-baby visit.

Physical Assessment   The physical assessment sheet may be formally prepared, as shown in Figure 13.5, or just noted on the progress notes. The doctor should take full notes every time the client has a full examination, whether annual or symptom-driven. Figure 13.6a and Figure 13.6b show a complete physical assessment using an EMR.

Lab Sheets   As discussed in Chapter 6, you will get reports from clients' diagnostic tests, as well as hematology, microbiology, and biopsy results. Some lab requisitions are used for several types of lab tests, which reduces the number of reports on a chart. If you receive results online, print out a hard copy to keep in the file. Some lab reports are cumulative, including earlier test results. If so, discard earlier reports that merely duplicate the same test results. Keep test results together, with the most current on top.

Some labs have the capability to send results electronically; others still fax or send reports by courier. In some jurisdictions, electronic results are sometimes received piecemeal at different times. This makes them time consuming to read and summarize for the EMR. If results come in paper format, you have the option of scanning the reports for electronic storage, or simply adding them to the computer. If the latter, be very sure that you accurately transcribe the results. When you are rushed, mistakes are easy to make—an incorrectly placed decimal point or transposed numbers can result in serious errors.

Operative Reports   Any surgical procedure will generate a report. Keep these and related reports together, the most current on the top.

Consultation Reports/Letters   Consultation reports include initial contact letters, reports on assessment, and progress or follow-up reports. Keep these in the chart along with a copy of any letters sent to the client. Many of these reports are faxed, and may have to be scanned into an EMR for electronic storage.

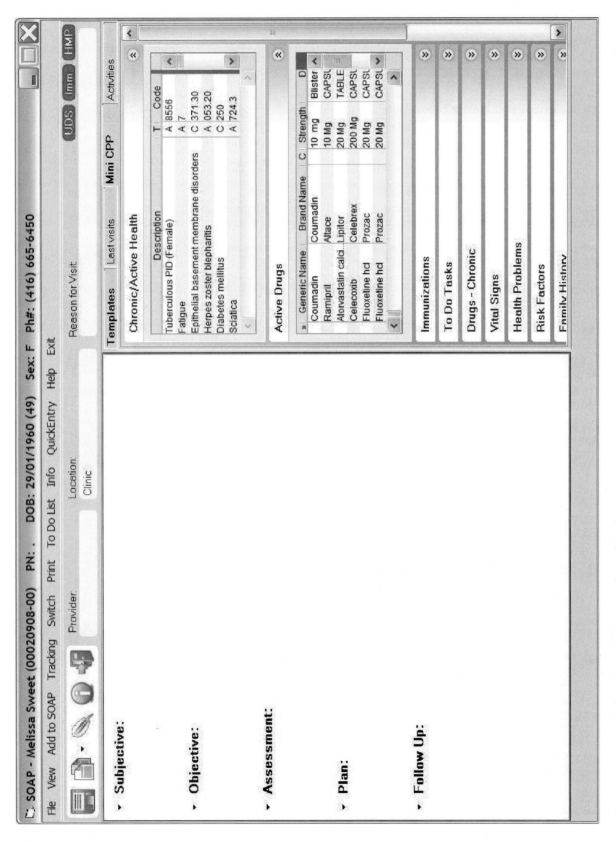

Figure 13.3 EMR showing SOAP template, blank

Figure courtesy of P & P Data Systems Inc.

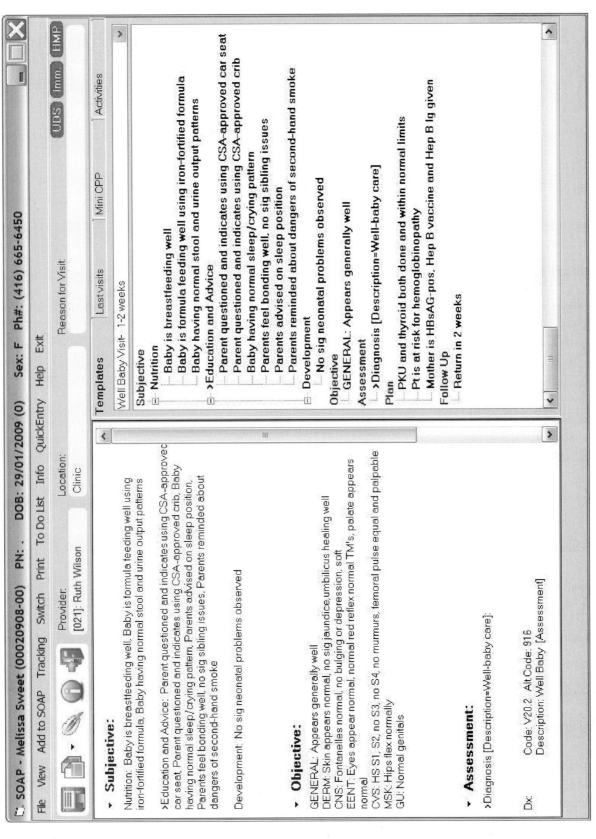

Figure 13.4 EMR SOAP template with data added

Figure courtesy of P & P Data Systems Inc.

DR. D THOMPSON
FAMILY MEDICINE
IMMUNIZATION & PHYSICAL EXAMINATION RECORD

Name: _____   Date of Birth: _____

PHYSICAL EXAMINATION

N-Normal   / Please state defects

Height Weight	Vision O.D. 20/ O.S. 20/	
Eyes	W/ Correction: O.D. 20/ O.S. 20/	
E	Right Left	
Abdomen		
Extremities		
Cardiovascular		
Gastrointestinal	Genitals	
Respiratory		
Nervous System		
Genitourinary	Reproductive	
Nutrition	Skin	
Posture		
Thyroid	Other Glands	
Tonsils	Adenoids	
Allergies Specify:		

Comments

Examination Date: _____   **Physician's Signature:** _____

Figure 13.5   Physical assessment form—paper

Courtesy of Dr. Douglas Thompson

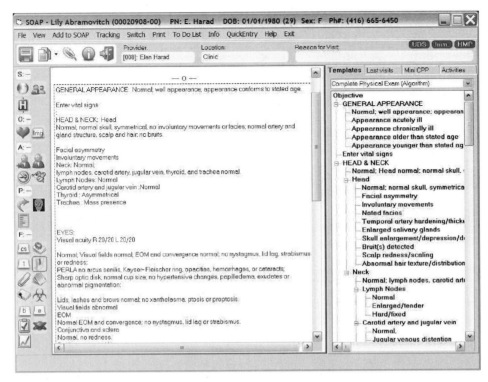

Figure 13.6a Physical assessment form (page 1)—EMR

Figure courtesy of P & P Data Systems Inc.

Miscellaneous   All children's charts should include growth charts. These, along with prenatal or antenatal records and labour and delivery records, are frequently filed after the progress notes. Electronically the data appear on a flow sheet as well as on the encounter record. In most provinces and territories, the EMR contains flow sheets that focus on a specific condition, perhaps related lab values and treatments. An example of a diabetic flow sheet from an EMR is illustrated in Figure 13.7. This diabetic management flow sheet tracks the client's diabetic education, glucose self-monitoring, diet, physical activity, and blood work. This sheet would likely become part of Melissa's EHR as well. If she was, for example, in an ER kilometres from home in a diabetic coma, the doctors could electronically access this sheet and make informed treatment choices for her.

⑥ LIFE CYCLE OF A RECORD

THE LIFE CYCLE OF A HEALTH RECORD IS THE SAME IN BOTH THE HOSPITAL AND THE office/clinic environment. In the hospital setting, the various components of the records cycle are more complex and included in this discussion.

Creation

A client's record originates when he registers for health services from a particular provider. Much like the case of Mr. Smith discussed earlier, the initial retrieval of information marks the initiation of the health record. Specific data include the name, address,

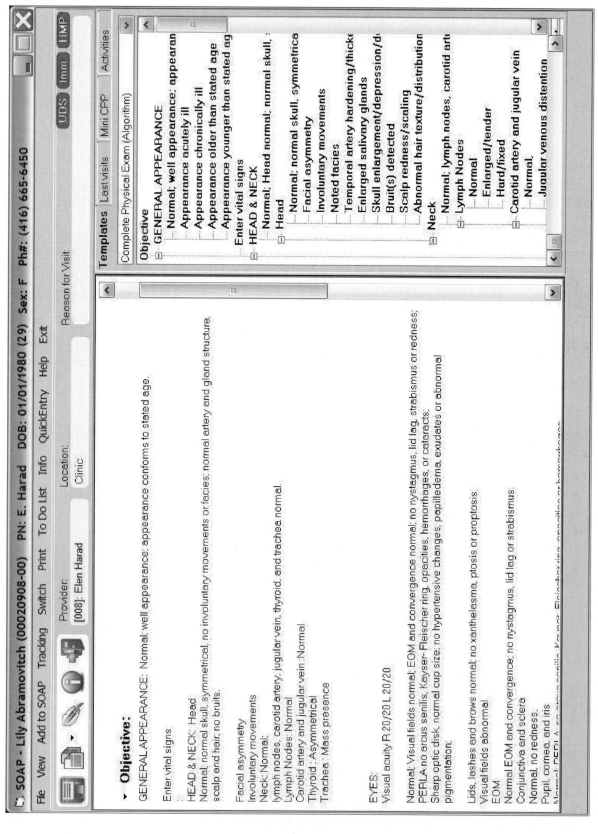

Figure 13.6b Physical assessment form (page 2)—EMR

Figure courtesy of P & P Data Systems Inc.

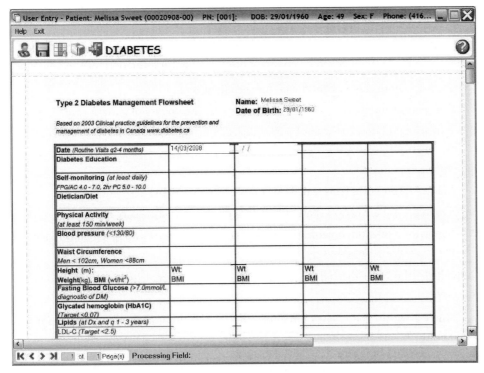

Figure 13.7   Diabetes flow sheet from an EMR

Figure courtesy of P & P Data Systems Inc.

telephone number, date of birth, health insurance number, next of kin, insurance information, and employer information. (See Chapters 11 and 12.) Besides generating a paper chart or EMR, the registration process creates a record in the Master Patient Index (MPI), a database of all clients registered with the practice or facility. The creation of a record includes assigning an identifier, which may be the client's name or a number. Though hospitals create a new chart (electronic or paper) each time the client is admitted, a doctor's office keeps a cumulative chart (electronic or paper), starting with the first encounter. Hospitals across Canada are at various levels of computerization; thus charts are, for the most part, a combination of electronic and paper data. In many hospitals, the medication administration records and doctors' orders remain as hard copies.

Maintenance

Records are maintained on the basis of their value, which may be historical, operational, legal, or fiscal. Although the health record is a legal document, its value is primarily operational and historical as it relates to the individual client. Maintenance includes organizing records through some kind of filing and/or indexing system so that they are accessible.

Provision

Because of the sensitive nature of health records, distribution of and access to the information are strictly controlled. Policies will generally dictate who may have access to a patient record, for what purpose, and for how long.

Although the hospital is responsible for protecting client information, there are situations where health information may be shared or released. A client, by virtue of his admission to the facility, gives implied consent for use of his personal health information for a variety of purposes. The hospital can use or disclose client information for the following:

- Provision of necessary health care for the client
- Risk management purposes aimed at improving the quality of patient care
- Financial purposes (payment for services, submitting claims to the provincial or territorial health plan)
- Research purposes
- Marketing purposes (this usually requires express consent)
- Teaching and education (particularly in a teaching or university hospital)
- Supplying a religious organization with the client's name unless specifically requested not to do so by the client

Individuals who have the right to access the client's personal information include the following:

- Anyone within the client's circle of care—at the hospital to which the client was admitted—and other organizations providing care to the client
- The Ministry of Health if such information is required
- The related chief public health officer or a similar designated authority as established under federal law

Unlawful Access
In the computerized environment, particularly in hospitals, individuals with access to electronic records systems sometimes purposely and inappropriately view health information belonging to others. In other words, they are not part of a client's circle of care and have no business looking at their charts. Hospital IT systems can track such occurrences, and perpetrators may be suspended or fired. Unlawful access is a serious offence because it violates the law as well as the moral and ethical principles of the health professions.

Paper charts, likewise, are vulnerable to someone walking in and looking at the information. I have seen individuals working for insurance companies or law firms attempt to access a client's chart. Question anyone you do not recognize who is doing this.

Lock Boxes
In a physician's office, the term *lock boxes* refers to segments of information within a client's chart that the client has specifically asked the doctor to keep confidential—between him and the physician. That means that others involved in the client's circle of care are denied access to this information. If, during the course of the client's care, the physician feels that this information should be revealed, she must first seek the client's permission. The client has the right to refuse. However, if the physician determines that not sharing this information may result in harm to the client, she can refuse to continue treating the client (unless the situation is an emergency). The only exception is information that must be disclosed according to provincial or territorial law.

Outguiding
Outguiding applies primarily to paper records. In a manual environment, it is frustrating not to find a file when you need it. Clients' charts are more likely to go missing in a hospital, but it can happen in a busy group practice or doctor's office.

outguiding system or charge-out system a system for keeping track of paper health records taken from their normal location.

Paper charts should never be removed from the premises, and only authorized persons should be allowed access to them.

If you work in an environment where more than one or two individuals may be using a file, make sure that you keep track of who has it and where. In a small private practice, this can be done informally; there are only so many places a file could be, and it is easy to check the appointment schedule and look on the physician's desk.

With computerized records, this is not a problem. In larger facilities, the greatest frustration related to accessing electronic chart information is finding a free computer.

Delivery In private practices, records are kept in a secure location and generally do not move out of the office. In a hospital, usually, records are released from Health Information Services only to other areas within the hospital for client-care purposes; all other requests for access to the record require the authorized requestor to view the record in Health Information Services.

In a paper-based environment, records are generally delivered in hard copy to the intended individual. In an electronic environment, physical control of the *paper* record is replaced by controlling access to the *electronic* health record through the use of user names and passwords or some biometric mechanism to uniquely identify the user. In large facilities, users have different levels of access or privileges; for example, patient accounting may display only insurance and billing information. Because electronic records remove the gatekeeper function associated with accessing paper records, access to the EHR must be monitored through the use of audit trails that show what was viewed, by whom, and when.

Disposition

In the hospital environment, as long as a client is alive and has the potential to seek treatment, a health record remains active and therefore should not be destroyed. However, it is not possible to maintain comprehensive health records from birth to death, especially if the record is paper based. Large physical files simply become too unwieldy, and even large facilities have limited space.

Files must periodically be purged to remove extraneous and duplicate information. Even in an electronic environment, making all components of a patient record immediately available at all times is not an efficient use of resources. At some point, electronic records should be transferred to archival media (see later section on archiving).

Transferring Medical Records It is the client's responsibility, not the doctor's, to seek transfer of copies of his chart. If a client requests that you transfer his medical records, keep the originals, and transfer a copy of the records to the requested destination. Even when the transfer is at the client's request, you or the physician must receive a signed consent from the client before the information is transferred. The provider may charge for the costs involved. (See Chapter 12.) The client must be made aware of any costs involved. Take special care to ensure confidentiality of the information when photocopying or downloading. Keep the pages in order, and count them to ensure that you do not misplace any. With a paper chart, return the pages to the original chart, and file the chart appropriately. If the client has left the practice, file it with your inactive charts. In the case of an EMR, the electronic file can be added to an inactive file vault on an alternative hard drive or other storage device. Give the material for transfer to the client in a sealed envelope or send it directly to the new provider by a secure method.

Physician Moves and Retirement   If a doctor moves, dies, or retires, charts must be stored properly and kept accessible to clients. If a doctor relocates or retires but maintains her licence, she is responsible for the records for a minimum of 10 years and must ensure client access, often through a designated custodian. This might be a company whose business it is to store medical charts. If a doctor dies, retires, or gives up her medical licence, she (or her estate) is obligated to keep the charts for only two to six years. The records may be transferred to another provider at the same address and phone number, or clients may be notified that they must, within a specified period (two to six years) collect their medical records or request that they be transferred to another doctor. A physician who is unsure about his obligations in a particular situation should contact the Physician Advisory Service of his College or the Canadian Medical Protective Association (CMPA). Likewise, most provincial and territorial Colleges of Physicians and Surgeons have an information line for clients concerned about their medical information.

COMPUTERIZED VERSUS TRADITIONAL SYSTEMS IN A DOCTOR'S OFFICE

ALTHOUGH MANY FACILITIES ARE MOVING TO COMPUTERIZED FILES, MANY STILL maintain traditional filing systems. This is primarily because converting to an electronic system takes time, and many doctors do not intend to include everything in a client's chart in their EMR. For that reason, traditional charts must be kept until they can legally be disposed of. One of the major disadvantages to storing files the traditional way is lack of space. Many physicians' offices in Canada are faced with increased client loads without a corresponding increase in space to keep their files.

❼ FILING SYSTEMS

IF YOU KEEP PAPER HEALTH RECORDS, YOU WILL NEED SOME WAY TO IDENTIFY AND locate them.

Identification Systems

Whether records are paper or electronic, each client is assigned a unique identifier, which may simply be her name or may be a number assigned by a person or computer system. In any case, it acts as a reference and differentiates that client from others in the system. Usually, the identifier is assigned when a client first seeks services from a provider or facility, is associated with the chart, and remains the same as long as the client continues with the provider or facility. A small practice may choose to use the client's name (last name, first initial, second initial) as the identifier. In a family practice, where more than one member of a family may carry the same last and first names, another variable, such as date of birth (DOB), may be incorporated into the identifier.

Larger offices and hospitals generally use a numbering system. The numbering system may be based on some piece of client-specific data, such as birth date. Or, it may be a serial number assigned to the next new patient, either from a manual log, known as the Master Number Control, or computer generated. In a family practice, often the identification system ties the family members to the same number; the whole family's records may be filed as a unit or may be kept next to each other.

Organization of Files   In physical filing systems, files are usually organized on the basis of the identifier. Most practices that use traditional paper-based charts use fairly straightforward filing systems. To those familiar with a highly sophisticated health information environment, some of these methods may seem somewhat archaic. However, they do work, and they are relatively commonplace. The methods used for chart identification and retrieval reflect those choices discussed earlier.

Alphabetical   Alphabetical filing is one of the oldest and most straightforward systems. Alphabetical filing systems do not require an index. They are considered direct access systems because you need only have the client's name to file or find the record. However, they require the user to be a reasonably good speller.

Using this system, last names are used first, followed by the first name, and then the second name, if applicable. Names are filed by the first different letter. For example, Reid comes before Sachs; Sachs comes before Smith; Smith comes before Smyth; Smyth comes before Smythe. Use legal names, not nicknames or short forms; thus, Robert Smith would come after Richard Smith even if Robert is usually called Bob.

Alphabetical order works well if there is no opportunity of misspelling a client's name. However, even if the client has been registered with the correct spelling and the record is correctly filed, looking for the name under a misspelling may make it hard to find the record.

To overcome problems with misspelling, some organizations use a filing technique known as *phonetic* or *soundex* filing. This method groups similar-sounding consonants together and removes all vowels. Although this has largely gone out of vogue in paper-based systems because it is complex and not easily learned, computer-based registration systems use algorithms to search for names phonetically. Some systems group all names beginning with Mc and Mac together at the beginning (or at the end) of the M section.

In a family practice, if members of a family have different surnames, charts may be cross-referenced.

Numeric   Numeric filing systems are effective with records that are filed and retrieved by number. Unfortunately, filing systems that are organized by a strict numeric sequence almost always require an index or pointer to the record location. If client records are asked for by name, you would need an index that would give the number for each name. For this reason, numeric systems that require an index are sometimes called *indirect access systems*.

There are two methods of filing numbered records: consecutive numeric and terminal digit.

Consecutive Numeric   This system files consecutively numbered files or documents in a strict sequential order (i.e., 101, 102, 103, etc.). As an example, medical records 123455, 123456, and 123457 would all be filed side by side. This system is normally used for records that are pre-numbered, such as cheques, invoices, vouchers, and purchase orders. This method of filing requires very little training.

Terminal Digit   Terminal-digit filing is a variation of straight numeric and was developed to overcome congestion in large filing systems when the most active records are being filed in consecutive order. (This is not usually a concern in an office; these systems are mostly used in large facilities.) Basing the filing sequence on the last few digits of the number disperses the files throughout the system, thus allowing easier access. Terminal digit is particularly valuable when dealing with a long number string. This system segments a number into component parts. As an example, number 123456 could be broken into three segments: 12-34-56. Reading the segments right to left, 56 is the terminal digit, 34 is the secondary digit, and 12 is the primary digit. In this example, the total filing area would be partitioned into 100 filing sections (00–99). Each section would be partitioned into 100 areas, and each area would have room for 100 records. Record 12-34-56 would be filed in section 56, area 34, and would be record 12. Records 11-34-55 and 13-34-57 would be filed immediately before and after record 12-34-56. Middle-digit and primary-digit filing are variations of the terminal-digit sequencing.

Colour Coding   Some practices combine either the alphabetical or numeric method of filing with colour coding. The file folders themselves can be different colours, or you can buy coloured tabs to add to neutral-coloured file folders. Each letter in the alphabet, or each number, may have a specific colour. In a busy office with a large number of charts, colour coding can prevent misfiling (because a misplaced file will stand out) and make it faster to find a chart.

Centralized versus Decentralized Storage

Record storage may be centralized or decentralized. Private practices use a centralized system: all records are stored in one location until they are purged. Hospitals may use centralized, decentralized, or a combination thereof, depending on the facilities' policies, size, geographic proximity to treatment areas, record sensitivity, and staff availability.

Centralized   Centralized filing systems designate one location in which to house all records. In a hospital, this is usually Health Information Services. All health information on a particular patient is stored in one physical chart and is located in one department.

Decentralized   Decentralized filing systems allow parts of the patient record to reside in areas outside Health Information Services, although the locations of these parts of the record are available through the MPI. Records that would not be needed for all visits may be stored in specific clinics, such as ophthalmology, audiology, and dental clinics. This can be convenient if the hospital is spread over more than one site. Particularly sensitive records, such as those relating to therapeutic abortion or AIDS, may also be kept in the treatment areas to keep them out of general circulation.

Filing Paper Charts

Regardless of the method of organizing files, most agencies and providers place clients' health information in charts or individual file folders. These are cardboard folders that come in a variety of colours, thicknesses, and finishes. The two most popular sizes are standard and legal. Most facilities use shelves or filing cabinets to store patient files. You are unlikely to be asked to create and manage a new paper filing system so learning to access, file, and manage existing systems will be required. In most offices, essential components of the client's chart are scanned into a computer and stored electronically. For new documents (consultation letters, laboratory and diagnostic reports) received in paper format, you would scan them into the computer, ensuring they are filed accurately with the right client's electronic chart. Paper charts are still kept by many providers and only referred to if information not contained in the electronic chart is required.

Filing Office Forms

Even offices that keep client records on computer will have some papers to file. For example, every office has a number of blank forms and documents, some of which are used more frequently than others. The most efficient method of filing these is by subject. Variations on this method exist, some very creative. Some systems incorporate alphabetical or alphanumeric sorting and colour coding. For subject filing, it is a good idea to have a broad subject category followed by more specific categories. For example: Insurance forms, WSIB forms, and government-related insurance forms (e.g., disability forms). Familiarize yourself with the ones commonly used in your office. Many lab forms will be online. Common ones you may be required to complete are for ultrasound, MRI, stools for occult blood, hematology, and biochemistry.

COMPUTERIZED RECORD KEEPING

COMPUTER RECORD-KEEPING SYSTEMS MUST MEET CERTAIN CRITERIA:

- The system must provide a visual display of the recorded information.
- The system must provide a means of access to the record of each client by the client's name and, if applicable, the health number.
- The system must be capable of printing recorded information promptly.
- The system must be able to visually display and print the recorded information for each client in chronological order.
- The system must have an audit trail that records the date and time of each entry of data for each client, must indicate any changes made in the recorded information, and must preserve the original content of the recorded information when changed or updated and be capable of being printed separately from the recorded information of each client.
- The system must provide for security by including a password that provides reasonable protection against unauthorized access.
- The system must automatically back up files and allow the recovery of backed-up files or otherwise provide reasonable protection against loss of, damage to, and inaccessibility of information.[2]

You will usually be responsible for maintaining the files accurately and ensuring that the information is relevant and current. As with paper-based charts, this involves periodically reviewing and deleting obsolete, repetitive, or outdated information.

ARCHIVING

FOR A NUMBER OF REASONS, FILES OR CHARTS MAY BE **ARCHIVED**, OR REMOVED FROM current or active use to an inactive status. Charts are *closed* when clients leave the practice for any reason or die. When a client leaves the practice with your knowledge, you would send a copy of the client's files to the new doctor. Charts are considered *inactive*

archive to remove a file from active status and store it in a secondary location or on a secondary medium.

---

[2] Adapted from *The Law and Electronic Medical Records—Ontario Regulation 114/94*, Sections 20 and 21. Copyright © Queen's Printer for Ontario, 2000.

when a provider has not seen a client for a certain period of time but is not sure whether the client has actually left the practice. The length of this period depends on the type of practice. Some specialists may see a client only once a year, or only once in a lifetime. Some consider a client who has not returned within one to three years inactive.

Some providers use inactive files to revitalize their client base. A chiropractor or a dentist, for example, might have the office staff call clients from the inactive list to ask how they are doing; if they are having problems, the staff may suggest that they come in for a reassessment.

All these charts must be stored for a designated length of time. In Ontario, legislation requires that hospitals maintain client records for 10 years after the date of last contact or, in the case of a child, 10 years after the client turns 18. Generally, hospitals view this as a minimum requirement and set their own retention schedules.

In Canada no provincial/territorial or federal privacy legislation states how long health information must be kept. However, the federal government's *Personal Information Protection and Electronic Documents Act* (PIPEDA) does state that organizations must develop their own minimum and maximum retention periods. Legislation at provincial/ territorial and federal levels does hold that personal information is to be destroyed when it is no longer required for functional or legal reasons. Keeping personal and health information longer than required can be done legally only if there is justifiable cause.

Physicians across Canada must turn to their provincial or territorial colleges and medical associations for retention guidelines. The CMPA also has retention recommendations. It is important to note that keeping medical records must also be in compliance with provincial and territorial statutory requirements. Guidelines on the retention of health information are only guidelines and not legally binding. Some jurisdictions do have legislation for physicians relating to retention. From the date of the last entry, physicians in Quebec must keep the information for a minimum of five years (data relating to genetic testing for 10 years); in Ontario, 10 years; and in British Columbia, 6 years. Other jurisdictions do not specify.

Provincial or territorial college guidelines and the CMPA recommend keeping a client's health information for at least 10 years for all jurisdictions. The CMPA also recommends keeping telephone logs and appointment books and scheduling files for 10 years. The statute of limitations in each jurisdiction affects how long records are kept. In Ontario, the limit is 15 years; thus most practitioners and health organizations keep health information for at least that long.

Records of minors must be kept for 10 years after the age of majority. For clients who have disabilities, or when there is an untoward outcome, it may be prudent to keep records for even longer and, in some cases, indefinitely.

Paper Charts

Health offices using manual filing systems usually store files in their original forms in designated storage areas. Inactive and closed files must be stored securely and kept in proper condition. In the case of paper files, space can be a problem. Paper files are sometimes stored off-site in a secondary location. This may be a specialized company or simply a room in the basement. Depending on the location of the storage area, it may be inconvenient to retrieve data. But for an office with paper records, limited space, and no microfilm reader, there may be no other choice. The archive space should be locked, and distribution of keys controlled. Properly stored paper files should stay in excellent physical condition for many years. They must be filed in such a way that they can be retrieved quickly, if needed. The may be filed by the same system used for active files. Some practices store files by year or by range of years (e.g., 1997–2001).

Electronic Health Information

Electronic charts are usually moved to another medium for archiving. For example, you might copy files onto a back-up disk and then remove them from your computer's hard drive. Regardless of the medium on which the record is stored, its integrity must be maintained; that is, it must be possible to produce a copy of the original record with all the information intact. The options for alternative storage are summarized below.

Hospitals and other large facilities will have very old chart information stored on microfiche, microfilm, or CD-ROM. You would likely be involved in retrieving information from those formats only if you work in Health Information Management in a hospital.

❽ PRIVACY, SECURITY, AND CONFIDENTIALITY

THE CLIENT HEALTH RECORD IS A HIGHLY SENSITIVE RECORD CONTAINING INTIMATE personal information. Anyone handling health records must take care to keep them secure so that unauthorized individuals do not gain access to them. Unlike most records, health records have dual ownership: the provider or facility owns the records themselves, but the client owns the information. This includes everything contained within the file except correspondence of a medical–legal nature and third-party/independent health examinations. Property owners must develop policies and procedures to ensure that the capture, use, and disclosure of personal health information follow standards of practice and that clients are informed about how their information is being handled.

Charts in a Group Practice

In most group practices, a client usually sees the same physician, who may be considered the most responsible physician (MRP) for that client. Usually, the group agrees that the client's health information belongs to the MRP. If it is not clear who the primary physician is, the group must come to an agreement about chart ownership. It is best to ask the client whom she wishes designated as her primary physician.

Transfer of Medical Information

As discussed in Chapter 5, in most cases, information may not be disclosed to others without the client's express consent. The major exception is exchange of information between a referring physician and a consultant or between a physician and a hospital. It is important that all providers have current, relevant information. This eliminates subjecting clients to repeat testing and often allows treatment plans to be formulated more quickly. These exchanges are usually based on implied, rather than informed, consent. For other transfers of information, the client must sign a medical records release form first.

One exception is that the Ministry of Health may inspect a physician's medical records. A qualified person designated by the Ministry who shows authorization must be allowed access to the charts.

Mandatory Reporting

There are certain circumstances in which medical information must be reported. In Ontario, some statutes that require mandatory reporting are the *Highway Traffic Act*, the *Child and Family Services Act*, the *Health Protection and Promotion Act*, and the *Aeronautics Act*. Physicians must, for example, report certain communicable diseases that are considered a threat to public health, such as sexually transmitted diseases (STDs) and severe acute respiratory syndrome (SARS). Physicians must report suspected physical or sexual abuse of children. In these cases, client permission is not required. The *Regulated Health Professions Act* (RHPA) requires reporting of any misconduct on the part of a health-care provider. It is permissible to give medical information to other professionals involved directly in that client's care.

Minor Clients

There is no minimum age for consent to the disclosure of health information, which can create difficulties for health-care providers. In Ontario, the *Health Care Consent Act* of 1996 recommends that a physician determine the ability of the minor to understand the consequences of the disclosure of health information. If the child is not capable of such understanding, the physician may not disclose without consent of the parent or guardian. There is also, as discussed in Chapter 5, no clear statement of the age at which physicians should no longer reveal health information to parents. Physicians must make similar judgments of the minor's ability to understand the health information and its consequences. In practice, once a minor is old enough to visit the doctor alone, most doctors will not share information with parents without the minor's permission.

Client Access to Charts

Clients have a right to access all information contained in their medical charts. If a client wishes to view her chart, she should be supervised to ensure that no information is changed or extracted, which in some situations could have legal consequences. Alternatively, you can give the client a photocopy, for which you can charge a reasonable fee. A client may be refused permission to view his chart only if the physician deems that the information would be detrimental to the client's physical, mental, or emotional health or to that of a third party. The physician must be able to defend this decision. Some clients who have no family doctor keep a photocopy of their medical chart from the last provider, presenting it to the Emergency Department, for example, when they seek health care. This is quite legal, as the information is theirs.

Charts from Hospitals

An individual can get copies of her hospital records as well. Most hospitals have clear directions about how to do this online. You must submit a written request accompanied by a signed Consent for Disclosure of Health Information form for release of information. However, a family physician, if his name is listed on the patient's chart, can request a copy of the patient's records without consent. If the name is not on the chart, then the consent for disclosure form must be completed by the patient. Most facilities charge a fee for chart acquisition; this covers the work and materials involved in preparing the chart (for example, printing or photocopying from an electronic or a paper chart). In many hospitals, some departments keep their own records, such as clinics, physicians' offices that are located in that facility, and sometimes medical imaging. If a person is unable to sign for a chart, an authorization must be issued by the patient's power of attorney for personal care or legal next of kin to request records.

Privacy of Information in Canada

There are currently two privacy laws in Canada: the *Privacy Act* (implemented in July 1983) and the *Personal Information Protection and Electronic Documents Act* (PIPEDA). The latter was initiated in January 2001 and implemented in three stages, the final of which became law in January 2004.

The *Privacy Act* concerns departments and agencies within the federal government in terms of outlining obligations, rules, and policies related to the collection, disclosure, and use of personal information. It also gives all Canadians the right to both access and control any personal information the government may have about them.

In addition to national legislation, three provinces, Quebec, Alberta, and British Columbia have their own *private sector privacy legislation* that technically replaces PIPEDA. However, if any information issues cross over the borders of any of these provinces, PIPEDA legislation takes precedent. Thus it is vital that anyone or any organizations involved with the cross-border exchange of information in these provinces are thoroughly familiar with both Acts. The flow of information across provincial borders is commonplace given the internet, the national EHR system in progress, and the establishment of businesses in other provinces. Just what privacy legislation applies where can sometimes be confusing.

Four provinces have *health specific* legislation: Saskatchewan's *Health and Information Protection Act* (HIPA), Alberta's *Health Information Act* (HIA), Manitoba's Personal Health Information Act (PHIA), and Ontario's *Personal Health Information Protection Act* (PHIPA). All of these Acts are similar to PIPEDA. They deal specifically with the collection, use, and disclosure of personal *health* information by provincial health-care organizations and other approved individuals and agencies.

PIPEDA

PIPEDA OUTLINES HOW ORGANIZATIONS AND BUSINESSES *WITHIN THE PRIVATE SECTOR* (including all health-care agencies, offices, and organizations) can collect, use, or disclose personal information.

Note that the federal government retains the power to provide an exemption to any organization that has its own privacy laws if those laws are deemed equivalent to the federal law.

Rights Afforded to Clients under PIPEDA

- To know how and why an organization collects, uses, and discloses their personal information
- To expect the organization to collect, use, and disclose their information reasonably and appropriately and not to use it for any purpose other than that for which it was intended and for which consent was given
- To have their information protected by security measures
- To expect the information that is held to be accurate, complete, and current

- To obtain access to their personal information and ask for corrections, as needed
- To hold the organization accountable to the Privacy Commissioner of Canada through a formal complaints process for the rights mentioned above

See the websites listed at the end of the chapter for more details about these rights.

Ten Principles of PIPEDA

1. *Accountability*—each office/facility should have a Privacy Information Officer who is ultimately responsible for the compliance of the organization with the standards spelled out in the act.
2. *Identifying Purposes*—you must inform the clients of the purpose for the collection of their information either before or at the time of the collection.
3. *Consent*—consent must be obtained in order to collect the information.
4. *Limiting Collection of Personal Information*—a clear link must be established between the information that is collected and the reason for doing so.
5. *Limiting Use, Disclosure, and Retention*—you cannot use or disclose any information for purposes other than those for which it was collected; information must be kept only as long as it serves its intended purpose; information must be appropriately stored and destroyed.
6. *Accuracy*—information should be accurate and complete in terms of how it is recorded to facilitate its proper use.
7. *Safeguards*—the organization must take appropriate and practical measures to protect the information from unauthorized access, use, or tampering.
8. *Openness*—information about policies relating to the management of personal information must be readily available to the clients.
9. *Individual Access*—with written request to the Privacy Information Officer, clients shall be given access to their personal information. Clients have the right to review and correct any information the organization has about them. When required, the organization must provide the client with a copy of any personal information requested; if this is not done, the client must be provided with the reasons why access is denied, subject to the exception set out in Section 9 of the Act.
10. *Challenging Compliance*—each organization must have a process in place to handle complaints with respect to the way personal information is collected, used, or disclosed, or the manner in which the organization complies with the legislation.

Personal Information Defined   Personal information includes information that may be considered factual or subjective. The information may be recorded data or data that are orally exchanged about a person who is identified by virtue of the information disclosed. This includes the following information (in any form):

- Personal Descriptors: including name, age, place and date of birth, date of birth, gender, weight, height, eye colour, hair colour, fingerprint
- Identification Numbers: including health-care/card numbers, Social Insurance and social security numbers, any personal passwords/numbers, and credit card numbers
- Ethnicity and race: including colour, national or ethnic origin

- Health Information: including medical records, any physical or mental disabilities— essentially anything relating to health status, practices, or history
- Financial Information: including credit status, loans, purchases, and expenses
- Employment: including employee files, employment history, evaluations, reference interviews, disciplinary actions
- Legal Information: including any recorded interactions with the law, charges, or criminal convictions
- General Data: including perceived reputation, social or marital status, affiliation with political parties, and educational history

Personal information does not include the name, title, business address, or telephone number of an employee of an organization.

Complaints Process   It is imperative that your organization understand, abide by, and implement the rules and regulations set out by PIPEDA. Any client who is concerned that her right to privacy has been violated may submit a complaint to the Privacy Commissioner of Canada, whose responsibility it is to investigate and resolve complaints. Your organization may be subject to review, reprimand, fine, and/or other legal action.

The Consent Form   Each organization must prepare a consent form for all clients to sign. This consent should clearly outline who the Privacy Information Officer is and establish that all health professionals within the organization are cognizant of and will abide by the policies and rules outlined in the Act. The consent form should contain detailed, pertinent, clearly stated information regarding what the organization is doing to comply with the act, the reasons why personal information is collected, and how it will be used.

For example, an organization might state that the information is used for the following:

- To competently assess the client's health-care needs
- To establish a diagnosis
- To devise a plan of treatment and care for the client
- To deliver high-quality, comprehensive care to the client
- To articulate appropriately to other health professionals regarding the diagnosis and implementation of treatment
- To ensure high-quality, comprehensive, follow-up care as necessary
- To initiate and maintain communication with the client, as required, for direct medical and medically related purposes
- To complete all related third-party insurance forms and related information as designated by law or the client's needs
- To comply with legal and regulatory requirements involving the client's chart and health information contained therein in a timely manner according to the provisions set out by the provincial Ministry of Health, the College of Physicians and Surgeons, and the *Regulated Health Professions Act*
- To process credit card payments
- To collect unpaid accounts
- To comply in general with the law

The client must also be advised of the implications of signing a consent form. Text such as the following should be included:

By signing this consent form, you have agreed that you understand the information contained herein. You give permission for the collection, use, and, when appropriate, disclosure of your personal information for the purposes outlined in this document. Your information may be assessed by the Ministry of Health and our regulatory body [for example, the Royal College of Physicians and Surgeons of British Columbia, or the Royal College of Dental Surgeons of Ontario], fulfilling its mandate under the RHPA and for the analysis and/or defence of any legal issue. If any unusual requests are received, we will contact you (the client) for permission to release any information; we will advise you if we feel that the release is inappropriate. At any time you may withdraw your consent for use or disclosure of any and all personal information collected by this organization.

Provincial Health-Related Privacy Acts

As mentioned above, four provinces have their own privacy Acts related specifically to health. The shared perception was that PIPEDA was never designed to address the specifics of Canadian's personal health information. Health information is considered by most to be more sensitive, personal, and sacred in terms of who has access to it. According to most health-related Acts, health information can only be disclosed by and shared with a health custodian (health providers, health facilities, and others authorized by a health facility). Implied consent is considered and is often valid for the provision of certain types of health care. It is important to note that if there are any conflicts between these provincial Acts and PIPEDA, the federal legislation will supersede the provincial legislation unless the provincial Act has been deemed similar enough to PIPEDA. In that case, provincial legislation would apply.

Privacy by Design

Another valuable privacy model, entitled Privacy by Design, was introduced in Ontario in the 1990s. The concept has grown and is used on an international level. Easily applied to health care, Privacy by Design advocates that privacy policies should be an integral part of anything people use, build, or advocate. How many times have you overheard conversations that you were uncomfortable with, in an insurance office or a lawyer's office, or while waiting for your car to be repaired? Or perhaps worse, have you ever sat in a doctor's office or a diagnostic facility and overheard someone's mammogram results, for example? An exercise at the end of this chapter can provide you with an entirely new perspective on how this concept works. It may well serve to make you think twice about sharing personal information—how and with whom, as well as whether you should publicly discuss something intensely private to another person. Application Exercise 5 in this chapter provides a link to a Privacy by Design exercise, as well as its curriculum. This includes PowerPoint presentations that provoke thought and ideas as to what privacy means and how to take steps towards achieving privacy for yourself, others, and your organization.

Forms Management

You will deal with many forms in your work that are used to collect and transmit data. Most of these will come to you preprinted, and you will only need to file them, send them out, and sometimes help clients fill them out. You always need to be aware of what forms you have and when they must be used. A list of forms is helpful.

Sometimes, you may be asked to help develop or revise a form. For example, the physician may want to develop his own history questionnaire. (See Chapter 9.) Good form design helps you collect the information you need. Poorly designed forms can result in missing or erroneous information and can be time consuming and frustrating to deal with. Clarity is paramount. Make sure questions can be easily understood by the intended user and that they are worded so as to elicit unambiguous answers. Test the form before printing and using it.

Future Trends

Electronic Medical (EMR) and Health (EHR) Records in Canada: Where We Are and Where We Are Going

The Canada Health Infoway, funded by the federal government, was created in 2001 to implement a nationwide electronic health records system. The Infoway continues to oversee this process. Initiatives are jointly funded by the federal and provincial/territorial governments. The goal for Canada's Health Infoway is to have a national system with three operative components:

1. point-of-care systems where data can be retrieved,
2. repositories for storing data, and
3. the ability for all systems to work together.

Completion of these goals at the national level is ongoing.

Storing health information requires several databases to hold specific types of health information, including separate client and provider registries, and repositories for diagnostic imaging, laboratory information, and drug information. Still another is required for such client information as immunization records and clinic/hospital visits. Thus, the process is complex, and as with the other components, the level of completion of these databases varies across the country.

Point-of-service EHR systems refer to where a client receives medical services: physician's office, clinics, private and public labs, and diagnostic facilities and hospitals, to mention a few. Connectivity means that the computer systems in every organization, from small to large, must be able to link and exchange health information.

"Point-of-service" means that all health services must be able to properly retrieve and manage their own health information. To this end, the provinces and territories have the flexibility to build and manage their systems according to priorities within each jurisdiction. As a result, policies and programs differ among jurisdictions. In addition, provincial and territorial governments have different approaches, priorities, and timelines regarding the implementation of electronic medical and electronic health records. Some provinces have offered incentives to providers to move forward with conversion initiatives. BC, Alberta, Saskatchewan, Manitoba, Ontario, and Nova Scotia have led the way in developing EMR networks, mostly because the respective governments have provided financial incentives motivating physicians to move in that direction. Nova Scotia, New Brunswick, Prince Edward Island, and Newfound and Labrador have lagged behind, at least in the initial phases, although a number of physicians have embraced EMR technology at their own expense (and it *is* expensive).

A common problem plaguing connectivity in many jurisdictions is finding and sanctioning suitable and affordable vendors to implement and support EMR conversion. The systems implemented must be sustainable and compatible in order to network with other systems (the founding principle of EMR technology). Imagine 40 or 50 different types of computer systems all trying to link with one another and with no common ground to do so. Some jurisdictions have limited the vendors that providers and facilities can use, and their systems must be able to connect. One issue in Quebec is developing appropriate French-language medical software that can connect with related networks.

To encourage facilities, providers, and health services to update and build an electronic health records system, the Canada Health Infoway recently offered them several project-based funding incentives. Those qualifying for funding must meet certain criteria, such as creating an innovative system that will be of use in other jurisdictions.

EMR in Canada is not as widely entrenched across the country as many may think. The fact that a doctor's office or a clinic is basically electronically operated (computers to manage scheduling, EMR databases, prescriptions, and so on) does not mean that they have a workable system of electronic medical records with the capabilities of networking and transferring health information elsewhere. To accomplish this, there must be many more stakeholders working as a team with proper linkage to each other to transfer health information; for example, to hospitals, pharmacies, clinics, laboratories, etc.

According to the Canadian Health Infoway, in 2012 only 37 percent of Canadian doctors in an office were using computer systems to track their clients' health data, 65 percent of Canadian hospitals were using at least one EHR component, and numerous pharmacies were electronically tracking their customers' drugs and allergies, and monitoring their medications for potential and harmful drug interactions. These figures are never static, but it will be several years until sustainable and interoperable health information exchange is a national reality. Impediments to the development of EMR and EHRs are multiple. Achieving EMR technology in rural settings in Canada—for example in Saskatchewan—is problematic. There is a high turnover of physicians who may not want to invest in the technology, connectivity to the internet is difficult—particularly in northern regions—and when it is available, service is slow (uploading, downloading, and sending files). Politics is also thought to impede the process: promises are made, and governments change. Often EMR support is linked to physician deals (bargaining for provincial/territorial contracts); solo practitioners find the prospect of developing an EMR system a huge output in both time and resources (much more than developing the process within a group). Although there are many communities or "pockets" of EMR/EHR technology, they are like islands—and the connectivity is only as good as those using it. To be successful, everyone has to be on board within a community, region, and province/territory.

Online Access to Health Records: A New and Growing Trend

Sunnybrook Health Sciences Centre in Toronto is the first in Canada to offer its patients virtual access to their health records, using an online network called MyChart, and other hospitals are poised to follow suit.

The portal allows patients to create a personal health record, schedule appointments, read educational materials, and give other physicians or family members access to their files. But ideally a system such as MyChart would also interpret test results and postoperative notes for patients, not just lay out the facts. Of course there are benefits as well as concerns about this initiative. Benefits to the person include knowledge of his health status, which many claim empowers individuals and encourages active involvement in one's own health care. A major concern is that individuals will misread information and misinterpret diagnostic findings. It is hoped that down the road the system will provide information interpreting the information contained in the chart in a way that a non-medical individual can understand. A website listed at the end of this chapter will provide you with more information about MyChart.

SUMMARY

1. Record keeping is a vital component of excellent ongoing health care. The health record, or client chart, documents a client's medical history, treatment, and progress and serves both as a reminder to the provider and as communication with other providers.

2. A client's health record, or chart, typically includes a number of forms such as a history sheet, progress notes, lab reports, reports of assessments, and a summary. The chart must be kept current and accurate. All treatments, tests, and diagnoses must be recorded. Check the chart to make sure the doctor has added the necessary information. Purge duplicate copies.

3. Every record goes through a life cycle, including creation, maintenance, provision, and disposition. A medical chart begins with registration when the client first comes to the office or facility and becomes inactive when the client dies or stops coming.

4. Files may be paper based, electronic, or a combination. Charts are commonly identified either by client's name or numerically. The identification forms the basis for the filing system. Whatever system is used, absolute accuracy is essential to prevent loss of information. Shelves, vertical or lateral filing cabinets, and rotary cabinets are options for storing paper files. A small storage space for currently pulled files helps prevent them from going missing.

5. The main barrier to computerizing records is the cost of transferring files. This may be done by scanning. Electronic filing offers many benefits. All of a client's information can be instantly accessible from your desk or the examining room and can be easily integrated with billing software.

6. The disposal of health records is a complex activity bound by legislation. In Ontario, health records must be kept for at least 10 years or, for minors, 10 years after the age of majority. Inactive records may be put in off-site storage (for paper) or on alternative media (for electronic records) but must be secure and retrievable.

7. A client's record contains personal information and must be kept confidential. Only qualified professionals involved in the client's care should access or add to a client's medical record. A client's health information cannot be released to anyone not directly involved in the client's care (for example, a consulting physician) unless the client signs an authorization for transfer of information or there is an official, legal request for access. The principles and policies outlined in PIPEDA governing client information must be adhered to. Note that physicians are required to report certain types of information, such as that relating to reportable diseases or suspected child abuse. Paper files should be locked up; computer files should require a password for access.

Key Terms

archive 421
eChart 397
electronic health record
    (EHR) 399
electronic medical record
    (EMR) 399

electronic medical records
    systems 399
fob 403
health information 398
health information custo-
    dian 398

health record 398
outguiding system or
    charge-out
    system 416
pChart 397
purge 404

Review Questions

1. Discuss why the management of health records is somewhat different from the management of other records, such as financial or corporate records.

2. List 10 uses of the health record and describe each.

3. What is a unique identifier, and why is it important?

4. utline the life cycle of a record, defining each stage.

5. Name and describe three methods of filing paper records.

6. When and how may a health record be destroyed?

7. Describe three methods of archiving records.

8. Discuss the ownership of the health record.

9. Define security, privacy, and confidentiality in relation to the client health record.

10. Who should be given client information, and under what circumstances?

Application Exercises

1. Identify at least six sources where you would find standards for the creation and maintenance of health records. Discuss the impact these guidelines have on the creation and management of health records.

2. Identify five privacy statements published by any facility, organization, or company. Compare those statements with those of the Canadian Standards Association (CSA)—see the website listed at the end of this chapter.

3. Develop sample medical records for a private practice. Obtain samples of blank forms from a practice, if possible, and include a description of each component.

4. Four provinces have health specific privacy legislation: Saskatchewan's *Health and Information Protection Act* (HIPA), Alberta's *Health Information Act* (HIA), Manitoba's *Personal Health Information Act* (PHIA), and Ontario's *Personal Health Information Protection Act* (PHIPA). Divide the class into small groups. Each group will review one of the four provinces' health privacy acts and compare the fundamental principles to PIPEDA. Discuss your findings in class. Consider these questions: Are these various Acts comparable to PIPEDA? If so how? Where do they differ?

5. a. This activity is meant to stimulate thoughts about how to incorporate privacy into the things you do, your environment, and even your workplace. This Privacy by Design activity should be done in small groups to promote discussion and ideas, and facilitate understanding. Before attempting this exercise, review the concepts of what privacy is in this chapter. Privacy by Design is an initiative produced by Canada's Information and Privacy Commissioner. Access the following website: http://www.ipc.on.ca/english/Privacy/Introduction-to-PbD/. Under Educational Resources, click on Privacy by Design Lesson. Complete the activity provided.

   b. You work in a doctor's office. Your office area is not well protected from the reception area with respect to sound. Conversations you have on the telephone and with clients can be heard by everyone waiting to see the doctor. Discuss what steps you could take to change this, or at the very least, minimize having conversations overheard and potentially sensitive information revealed to others.

Websites of Interest

ARMA—The Association of Records Managers and Administrators
http://arma.org/

CHIMA—Canadian Health Information Management Association
https://www.echima.ca/
This site provides information on management of health records and careers in health information.

AHIMA—American Health Information Management
www.ahima.org
This site offers a wide variety of online publications regarding health information issues.

McMaster University Faculty of Health Sciences
www.fhs.mcmaster.ca/recman/index.html
This site provides a working example of a comprehensive records management plan for a teaching health-care organization.

Office of the Privacy Commissioner of Canada
http://www.priv.gc.ca/resource/fs-fi/02_05_d_15_e.asp
Links to privacy legislation across Canada, fact sheets, and information about health privacy legislation.

College of Physician and Surgeons of Ontario
www.cpso.on.ca
This site provides documentation guidelines for physicians.

Information and Privacy Commissioner of Ontario
www.ipc.on.ca
This site provides up-to-date information on privacy issues and legislation.

Canadian Standards Association (CSA)
www.csa.ca
This site provides information and copies of the 10 privacy principles.

Rights under PIPEDA Legislation
http://www.privacysense.net/privacy-rights-pipeda/
This site provides details about a person's rights under PIPEDA.

Privacy Legislation across Canada
http://www.privacysense.net/privacy-legislation/canadian/

Privacy by Design
http://www.ipc.on.ca/english/Privacy/Introduction-to-PbD/
For the exercise and curriculum follow the links under Educational Resources.

MyChart—Sunnybrook Health Sciences Centre
http://sunnybrook.ca/content/?page=mychartlogin_learnmore

EHR 2015: Advancing Canada's Next Generation of Health Care
https://www2.infoway-inforoute.ca/Documents/Vision_2015_Advancing_Canadas_next_generation_of_healthcare[1].pdf
A look at what has been accomplished and goals for 2015.

College of Physicians and Surgeons of Ontario, Policy—Medical Records
http://www.cpso.on.ca/uploadedFiles/policies/policies/policyitems/medical_records.pdf
Everything you need to know about organizing, filing, storing, and destroying medical records.

Getting Your Medical Records
www.cba.org/BC/public_media/health/421.aspx
At this website, you can find information on medical records and requests for information in British Columbia.

Privacy Commissioner of Canada
www.privcom.gc.ca/fs-fi/index_e.asp
At this website, you can find information about PIPEDA.

Part V
Hospital Procedures

Part V of this textbook has been written specifically for programs that include hospital unit administration. Chapter 14 explains the structure and function of various hospital departments and units and the roles and responsibilities of the clinical secretary. You will learn about the variations among hospitals and departments and about the range of job opportunities. Chapter 15 examines the purpose and structure of documents that are common to most hospitals.

Across Canada, most hospitals use a blend of electronic and manual tools to manage the patient-care units. Some are more advanced than others, with the use of electronic charts, doctor's orders, and electronic medication administration records (CMARs). All hospitals rely on paper-based requisitions, chart forms, and other documents at various times and for various purposes; the following chapters will simulate patient-care units in hospitals using a blend of paper-based and manual operations. Even the environments claiming to be paperless are not entirely so. Thus, it is essential to know how to manage paper chart forms and other documents. Transferring these skills to a computer environment is simply adapting to the same information in a different format.

You will learn how to set up and maintain a patient chart, as well as the administrative responsibilities involved in admissions, discharges, and transfers. Chapters 16 to 21 deal with the responsible and complex task of transcribing or processing doctors' orders—a process called order entry. Chapter 16 gives an overview of the process of transcription and the elements of a doctor's order and emphasizes the importance of total accuracy. The chapters that follow each deal with orders relating to a particular body system. Taken together, they provide a survey of the types of orders you will deal with in a hospital. Each chapter begins with a summary of the related system, to enhance your understanding of the orders you will be transcribing. If you have taken anatomy and physiology, this will serve as a brief review.

Chapter 14
The Hospital Setting

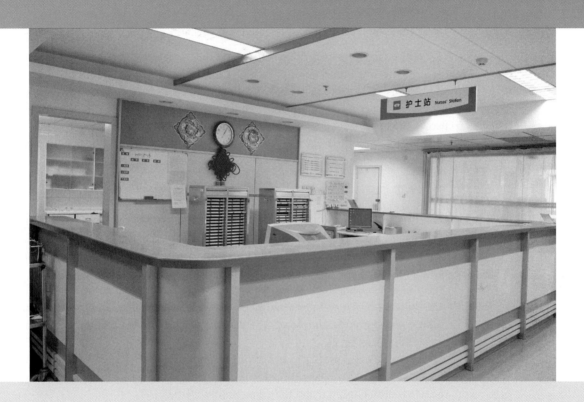

Learning Objectives
On completing this chapter, you will be able to:

1. List the types of health-care facilities.
2. Discuss the concept and purpose of hospital accreditation.
3. Outline the typical organizational structure of a hospital.
4. Summarize the types of hospital restructuring taking place in Canada.
5. List the departments found in hospitals and discuss the purpose of each.
6. List the responsibilities of the various types of health professionals in the hospital setting.
7. Identify the responsibilities of the clinical secretary.
8. Describe the components of a patient-care unit.
9. Summarize the functions of computers in hospitals.
10. Apply the principles of confidentiality in the hospital environment.
11. Discuss hospital security.

A hospital is a health-care facility that is licensed by the province or territory to provide a range of health-care services on both inpatient and outpatient bases. Hospitals' basic functions include

- providing expert medical, surgical, or psychiatric diagnosis and care;

- preventing disease and promoting health;

- meeting the needs of their communities (with input from district health organizations); and

- conducting health-related research and education.

This chapter outlines the structure and functions of a hospital, the various hospital departments, and the responsibilities of a clinical secretary. Health office professionals in hospitals and clinics may also be called ward clerks or health unit coordinators, but clinical secretary is one of the more common terms, and it will be used throughout this part of the book.

The responsibilities are tremendous, the pace in most areas is fast, and stress is part of the job, yet working in the hospital environment is both exciting and rewarding.

❶ TYPES OF HEALTH-CARE FACILITIES

MOST HEALTH-CARE FACILITIES IN CANADA ARE PUBLICLY OPERATED AND FUNDED BY THE provincial/territorial or federal government, although some private, for-profit facilities do exist. "Private" does not necessarily mean that patients pay for services. The province or territory may pay private facilities a fee to provide medically necessary services. Patients receiving insured services present their health cards, and doctors performing these services bill the provincial/territorial plan, just as they would in a public hospital. These facilities may also offer uninsured or enhanced services, which patients would pay for (as discussed in Chapter 10).

Recently, most provinces and territories have delegated funding and funding decisions for hospitals to regional health authorities. Decisions made are more reflective of the needs of the hospital and the community together.

Another initiative that is appearing for building, renovating, and expanding hospitals is the "P3" approach. This refers to a public–private partnership. This is a contractual arrangement wherein a blend of private and public money is used to both build and manage hospitals. The private provider is obliged to deliver a specified level of services, under specified terms, in exchange for public financing. In British Columbia, for example, an acute-care hospital in Abbotsford (under The Fraser Health Authority) is a P3 arrangement, as is an Academic Ambulatory Care Centre at Vancouver General Hospital. The Alberta government has allowed the construction of private surgical facilities through the passing of Bill 11, the *Health Protection Act*. These facilities provide selected services that include overnight stays. This is managed through regional health authorities.

There are several classifications of health-care facilities, some of which are province or territory specific. The most common are

- general or acute-care hospitals (may include specialty hospitals, such as the Hospital for Sick Children in Toronto);

- convalescent hospitals;

- chronic care hospitals;

- nursing homes;
- active treatment/teaching psychiatric hospitals; and
- active treatment facilities for alcohol and drug addiction (rehabilitation hospitals, federal hospitals).

General Hospitals

A general hospital provides the community with a variety of services, 24 hours day, seven days a week, ranging from medical/surgical to obstetric and psychiatric services, both on inpatient and outpatient bases. This type of hospital may also be referred to as an **acute-care** hospital because the majority of hospital beds are designated for those with acute illnesses and conditions. However, they may also have beds designated for chronic care, rehabilitation, palliative care, and respite care. Chronic care beds are usually for short terms, and patients needing long-term care are transferred to a chronic care institute. The kinds and levels of care available vary. Teaching hospitals also provide learning opportunities for medical students.

acute care care for a patient who is acutely ill, that is, very ill but with an illness expected to run a short course (as opposed to a chronic illness). Acute care is provided for patients with a variety of health problems.

Convalescent Hospitals

A convalescent hospital provides recuperative care to individuals who are expected to recover and return to their own homes or to other community placements. A physician and skilled nursing staff are available round the clock.

Chronic Care Facilities

A **chronic care** facility provides long-term inpatient medical care for people with little or no potential for rehabilitation. Patients may have chronic illnesses, such as multiple sclerosis, advanced chronic obstructive pulmonary disease (COPD), or some dementias. Other patients may have severe physical disabilities that require hospital treatment, may have suffered a head or spinal cord injury, or may be past the acute phase of treatment but require ongoing hospital care.

chronic care care for someone with a chronic illness, that is, one that typically progresses slowly but lasts for a long time, often lifelong.

Nursing Homes

Nursing homes provide continuous nursing and medical care for individuals who cannot be maintained at home and who are chronically ill and/or incapacitated. They do not, however, have all the facilities of an acute-care hospital. People in a nursing home depend on the staff for such activities as dressing, walking, bathing, and sometimes feeding. (In contrast, retirement homes are essentially housing choices for individuals capable of living in a reasonably independent manner but that may provide a range of supportive services that either are included in the fee or are purchased separately.) These may be either publicly or privately funded. Patients at a private facility pay the full cost; for public facilities, government subsidies are available to patients who need them. Some provinces and territories offer an income tax break for patients paying for retirement accommodation.

Rehabilitation Hospitals

Rehabilitation hospitals are for people needing professional assistance to restore physical functioning following an illness, an injury, or surgery.

Psychiatric Hospitals

A psychiatric hospital provides diagnosis and intensive and continued clinical therapy for mental illness and mental rehabilitation. (Many general hospitals also offer psychiatric inpatient and outpatient services.)

Drug Addiction/Alcoholic Treatment Centres

These facilities can be publicly or privately funded and offer rehabilitative care for those suffering from drug and/or alcohol addiction. Most facilities have follow-up programs that offer treatment, guidance, and support to patients after discharge.

Federal Hospitals

Federal hospitals are operated throughout Canada by departments of the federal government for the care of special groups of patients. Included are such facilities as military hospitals, veterans' homes, and hospitals for First Nations people.

Hospitals may also be categorized by size and type of service offered. A *primary care* hospital offers basic care, including health promotion and prevention of illness. It is mainly community based. A secondary care hospital offers specialist services. A tertiary care hospital offers highly specialized skills, technology, and support services for patients with acute and chronic illnesses. This type of hospital is usually found in a big city and often takes patients referred from smaller hospitals.

❷ ACCREDITATION OF HEALTH-CARE FACILITIES

Accreditation is the process by which facilities are granted recognition for meeting certain (preset) standards. For hospitals and other health facilities these standards relate to patient care and services. Standards for excellence in health-care facilities across Canada are maintained by a periodic assessment of each facility by *Accreditation Canada*. This organization sets standards of services and care for health establishments as well as by providing a system of external peer reviews for these facilities. Accreditation Canada provides benchmark standards that are recognized nationally and internationally (Accreditation Canada itself is accredited by the International Society for Quality in Health Care). All aspects of health care are scrutinized, from patient care to safety and ethical practices. Although obtaining accreditation is voluntary, most organizations opt for it because it enhances their status as well as improving the services and care they provide. Formal accreditation assessments occur about every three years and give the organization an overview of its strengths and the areas where it can improve. The Canadian Council on Health Services Accreditation (CCHSA) looks at how the organization compares with national standards in the following areas:

- Quality of care
- Community accessibility
- Appropriateness of care (i.e., does the intervention meet the client's needs?)
- Effectiveness of care
- Timeliness

- Continuity of care (i.e., Are patients followed up? Is care modified, if needed? For example, if a patient comes to a diabetic clinic for teaching, does the facility follow through until the patient has met the learning goals?)

- Safety

If the organization meets all of the standards, it becomes an accredited organization, usually for another three years. If a facility falls short, it may be accredited for a year, during which time it is expected to correct the areas in which it was deficient. Losing accreditation not only undermines the facility's reputation but it can also cause it to lose its funding.

The period leading up to accreditation is hectic and stressful in any organization. Most organizations conduct their own review to prepare for the formal assessment. Every component of every service and procedure, both clinical and administrative, is put under a microscope. The goal is to maintain and improve adherence to all standards at all times. This is not entirely realistic. As a clinical secretary, you will be heavily involved in the administrative components of review and evaluation. The work can be overwhelming. The process can be made bearable if everyone involved is organized and efficient, and works as a team.

❸ THE ORGANIZATIONAL STRUCTURE OF A HOSPITAL

EXCEPT FOR THE FEW THAT ARE PRIVATELY RUN, HOSPITALS ARE NON-PROFIT CORPORATIONS that operate under a special section of each province/territory's *Corporations Act*. Rules, regulations, and corporate structures vary by province or territory. Most of these hospitals have formed partnerships with other hospitals/organizations, resulting in centralized management.

As corporations, hospitals are headed by a board of directors. The board of directors is, in theory, elected by its membership. What constitutes the hospital membership varies across Canada. Members may include donors and interested community members. Board members are elected for specific terms; they may be re-elected. Each board will have a nominating committee that accepts nominations of members of the community or invites members to consider standing for election.

The board of directors appoints a chief executive officer (CEO) for their hospital or partnership of hospitals. The CEO is a salaried position, and the CEO is accountable to the board of directors. The CEO is ultimately responsible for the management of the organization, including such things as hiring and operating within a budget set by the board of directors.

The remaining organizational structure of each hospital will be different but will follow similar guidelines. There may be several vice-presidents or vice-chairs reporting to the CEO, chair, or president; in some structures, vice-presidents may report to an executive vice-president. A hospital involved in a **collaborative partnership** usually has a site administrator or a clinical administrator who oversees the daily operation of the hospital. Most hospitals also have a chief of staff who represents the hospital's medical staff. There will be someone who is responsible for each department or group of departments within the organization, such as chief of medicine, chief of surgery, manager of information technology, and director of acute-care services. Titles and exact responsibilities of positions vary among hospitals and may shift rapidly within a hospital. Generally, the position of

collaborative partnership the relationship among hospitals that have entered into an agreement to form a partnership, sharing clinical and administrative responsibilities.

clinical leader or clinical manager has replaced that of the head nurse. This person may be responsible for several nursing units but would have a charge nurse or clinical resource nurse (or several) who takes responsibility for each patient-care unit on each shift. As clinical secretary, you would typically report to the charge nurse or clinical resource nurse. The next person in the chain of command would be the clinical leader or manager.

The Websites of Interest at the end of this chapter provide a couple of examples of hospital organizational charts.

❹ HOSPITAL RESTRUCTURING IN CANADA

OVER THE PAST NUMBER OF YEARS FUNDING CUTS HAVE FORCED COMMUNITIES ACROSS Canada to evaluate what kind of care hospitals provide, where and how they provide it, and how they are managed. Hospitals have been restructured in an attempt to make the best use of limited resources without sacrificing the quality of medical care—although debate continues on whether this has been achieved or is even possible. Hospital restructuring will continue as ministries struggle to find a balance between cost cutting and providing high-quality care. More recently regional health authorities in many jurisdictions have been given the responsibility to oversee governance of health-care issues (including health-care facilities). This is in accordance with the continuing belief that local health authorities/councils can more effectively determine the needs of their own regions.

In most provinces and territories, health-care restructuring resulted from government efficiency studies. Because community-based recommendations were considered, changes have varied from one region to the next. However, across the country, most hospitals have seen beds eliminated, and some hospitals have been closed outright. In search of efficiency, some hospitals have joined collaborative partnerships with a single central administration. **Rationalization of services** has been instituted to avoid duplication. For example, in Kitchener, Ontario, one hospital treats serious cardiac conditions, while another treats cancer. The London Health Sciences Centre now sends pediatric cardiology cases to the Hospital for Sick Children in Toronto. (Hospitals offering specialized services to a wide area are called *regional centres*.) Some hospitals have active Emergency Departments that operate 24 hours a day, while others offer only limited care for certain hours.

Restructuring has also included a plan to meet the needs of an aging population. Although the number of acute-care beds across the country has been reduced, many new chronic care beds have been opened, as well as beds in nursing homes and homes for the aged. Some regions have opened more beds for patients who need a lesser degree of nursing or medical care, called **subacute**, transitional, or **step-down care** (because it is a "step down" from acute hospital care). Ultimately the goal is to care for older Canadians in their homes.

Despite the attempts to cut costs, most regions have had to spend money to modernize aging hospital equipment. Partly to try to avoid readmissions, some hospitals have introduced help lines, staffed by a registered nurse, to answer questions from newly discharged clients. Patients are also encouraged to use government-run telephone advice services, such as Ontario's Telehealth and BC's NurseLine.

Across Canada, restructuring continues to move toward more community-based care, and not just for older Canadians. In general, only very ill people are admitted to hospital, and they stay for a shorter time. Very common now is **day surgery**, in which a patient is admitted in the morning, operated on, and discharged by the end of the day,

rationalization of services centralizing certain services, particularly those that require specialized care, to one hospital in a region.

subacute, transitional, or step-down care medical and nursing care less intensive than traditional acute-care hospital treatment.

day surgery surgery conducted with a hospital stay of less than 24 hours.

if stable. This is made possible partly by a change in attitudes and partly by advances in surgical techniques. Laparoscopic and keyhole surgical techniques are constantly improving expanding the types of procedures that can be done on an outpatient basis. For example, a few years ago, gallbladders were removed by an open cholecystectomy ("open chole," pronounced *collie*), which required a large incision under the right rib cage. Now, surgeons use a visualizing instrument called a **laparoscope** to perform a "lap or closed chole" through a much smaller incision, and patients go home the same day (unless there are complications). Cataract surgery is almost always done on an outpatient basis. Even hysterectomies, under the proper conditions, are done as outpatient surgery. Hospitals are offering more outpatient and ambulatory care services, creating a "hospital without walls" that keeps more patients at home. This approach has been both lauded for giving patients more dignity and independence and criticized for sometimes leaving patients without the care they need and for transferring responsibility to often overburdened family members. Home care in Canada has increasingly become an issue, with more individuals requiring home care because of early discharge from hospitals and with the increasing numbers of older people (many with multiple chronic conditions) requiring home care as well. Home care is underfunded and sometimes disorganized, and there is a shortage of human health resources to manage home care caseloads.

laparoscope   a type of endoscope (a visualizing instrument with a tube and lens) that allows surgeons to visualize internal structures. Using this tool, surgery can be done through incisions often 5 cm in length or smaller.

⑤ HOSPITAL DEPARTMENTS AND SERVICES

HOSPITALS ARE DIVIDED INTO DEPARTMENTS ACCORDING TO THE TYPE OF SERVICES THEY offer: administrative, informational, therapeutic, diagnostic, or supportive. The numbers, functions, and names of hospital departments vary. Larger general hospitals have more services and departments than smaller general hospitals. In a smaller hospital, for example, the Department of Medicine may be responsible for cardiology and internal medicine, which in a larger hospital would be managed as separate departments. Chronic care and rehabilitation facilities do not offer the same range of services as a general hospital. The following descriptions cover the departments typically found in a general hospital.

General Services

Admitting/Patient Registration Department   The Admitting Department is usually the first point of contact for patients coming to hospital for either inpatient or outpatient services. Emergency admissions arrive through the Emergency Department, but, if admitted to hospital, are processed through Admitting. Information is gathered and noted on the admission sheet. The patient is given an identification bracelet in Admitting or the ER or upon arrival at the floor. The Admitting Department tracks all admissions and discharges and directs patient admissions, notifying physicians of bed availability. If beds are limited, Admitting will try to juggle admissions to find suitable accommodation for the client. Often, a patient is admitted to accommodation for which he does not have coverage. The Admitting Department tracks such admissions, moving the patient to the appropriate or insured accommodation as soon as possible.

Some hospital departments and patient-care units handle components of the admission process, but, ultimately, everyone who receives hospital services will be processed in some manner by the Admitting Department. The Admitting Department takes a daily census, checking with all units to record admissions, transfers, and discharges.

The Business Office   This department manages the hospital's business activities, including billing provincial/territorial plans and private insurance companies and collecting from patients for services they are responsible to pay for. Patients are usually asked to go to the Business Office upon discharge to pay any outstanding accounts. The Business Office tracks all financial information for the Finance Department.

Public Relations   The Public Relations Department is responsible for community liaison. It may also be responsible for authorizing any newspaper or magazine articles related to hospital activities. This department tries to generate publicity and community support for fundraising initiatives, which are important to most hospitals.

Human Resources/Employee Services   This department is responsible for recruiting and interviewing new employees and preparing termination agreements for those who leave, voluntarily or otherwise. Human Resources advertises vacant positions internally and externally. Human Resources also manages transfers within the facility and all employee services, such as benefits, leaves of absence, and retirement.

Medical Records/Health Information Services   Health Information Services manages medical transcription and is responsible for all charts and documents generated or used within the hospital. Upon discharge, all patient charts go to this department, where they are reviewed and collated for storage. If parts of the chart are incomplete or missing, someone will contact the appropriate department. When a patient is admitted to hospital, the clinical secretary calls Health Information Services for the client's old records. Anyone wanting to view the chart of a discharged patient must present appropriate authorization.

Purchasing Department   The Purchasing Department is responsible for taking inventory and ensuring that all necessary supplies and equipment are purchased in a timely manner.

Information Services   Information Services is responsible for communication systems within the hospital. This includes computer services. Responsibilities may involve in-service education for new and continuing staff on new technologies and computer procedures and policies.

Auxiliary/Volunteer Services   The services of volunteers are vital to most hospitals. They range from students in a health-care field assisting professionals (see Chapter 1) and junior high school students who visit patients, to people who play key roles in running shops and other fundraising ventures. This department may be headed by a paid manager or coordinator. It is her responsibility to recruit and interview volunteers and check references. Some facilities also require potential volunteers to go through a police background check.

Employee Health Services   This department is responsible for employees' work-related medical needs, including pre-employment medical certificates and immunizations. It also deals with work-related injuries, including needle-stick injuries and exposure to body fluids, and workers' compensation referrals. This department may employ a physician and one or more nurses. In most facilities, the physician is available at designated times throughout the week.

Risk Management/Infection Control   This department oversees infection control policies and procedures within the facility. If there are any infectious outbreaks within the hospital setting, they are investigated by this department for possible breaks in procedure, sources of the infection, and containment solutions. In some facilities, this department oversees any isolation needed.

Pharmacy   Nearly all hospitals have a Pharmacy Department staffed with pharmacists and pharmacy technicians. This department is responsible for all medication used in the hospital. They review doctors' medication orders, supply clients' medications, stock medications, and control narcotics. In the computerized environment, Pharmacy may be responsible for keeping the client's list of medications current and complete. In some hospitals, the chart's computerized medication administration record is the responsibility of the Pharmacy staff.

Nutritional Services   This department provides all patient meals and fills orders for special diets as well as other forms of nutrition. (See Chapters 18 and 19.) It also provides counselling to both inpatients and outpatients upon referral.

Sterile Processing Department (SPD)/Central Supply/Materials Management Department   This department is responsible for sterilizing and distributing sterile equipment, ranging from suture removal trays to operative instruments. In some, but not all, facilities, equipment received from this department has to be requisitioned.

Stores/Materials Management   In some facilities, this department is under the same umbrella as the Central Supply Department or SPD. All equipment and supplies, other than those that must be sterilized, are obtained here. This is where you would call to get most equipment needed on the patient-care unit, ranging from prepackaged sterile dressing trays, catheters, and flashlight batteries to nasogastric suction machines, **emesis basins**, and intravenous supplies.

Environmental Services/Housekeeping   This department is responsible for the cleanliness of the facility, including **terminal cleaning** of rooms.

Laundry   This may be a separate department or may be part of Environmental Services. The Laundry Department is responsible for supplying patient-care units with clean laundry. They have special procedures for dealing with laundry that has been used for patients in isolation or is otherwise contaminated. In many facilities, a certain amount of clean laundry (towels, blankets, sheets, pillowcases, pillows, and so on) is allocated to each patient-care unit, and it may be difficult to get more. Some nurses "hide" clean supplies for the oncoming shift or borrow from other units. The laundry cart may be kept in the clean utility room. Some carts have hamper bags, often colour coded, each for a certain item (fitted sheets, top sheets, gowns, and so on). Individuals from housekeeping collect soiled linen as necessary or at routine intervals. Some departments have laundry chutes. Increasingly, hospitals are sending their laundry to offsite services. Some facilities send out their laundry to independent businesses.

Maintenance/Environmental Engineering   The Maintenance Department ensures that equipment is safe and operational and keeps up with daily repairs to the physical structure, ranging from changing light bulbs to painting. The clinical secretary is

emesis basin (kidney basin or K-basin)   a small basin, usually kidney shaped, used for patients to vomit into or cough up sputum or phlegm into. It is also used to hold solutions for a variety of purposes. It may be ordered sterile or just clean.

terminal cleaning   a thorough wash with a disinfectant solution of all equipment (bed, bedside unit, and so on) used by a patient upon her discharge.

often responsible for passing on messages regarding maintenance issues on the floor. For example, she would call maintenance for any repairs on the patient-care unit. This could be a malfunctioning call bell in a client's room or an electrical outlet at the nurses' station. In some facilities, this department will check any electrical appliances brought in by patients to ensure that they meet the facility's safety standards.

Patient-care Units—Medical

A patient-care unit is a dedicated area for inpatient accommodation, usually an entire floor where services of a similar type are rendered. Each patient-care unit functions both independently and interdependently. It has its own staff and its own nurses' station and looks after its own patient care, communication, and administrative needs. However, it also collaborates with other services both inside and outside the hospital.

Patients are admitted to medical units for diagnosis of, non-surgical treatment of, and recovery from an array of diseases and conditions. The range of medical units reflects a hospital's designation and size. Small to mid-sized hospitals may have a single *general medical unit* serving patients with conditions ranging from heart disease to diabetes. A large regional hospital includes specialized patient-care units.

Nephrology   This unit cares for patients with diseases and disorders relating to the kidney. Often, patients with such conditions are admitted to General Medicine or, if surgical intervention is required, to the Urology or General Surgery unit.

Cardiology and Telemetry   This unit treats medical conditions relating to the heart and vascular system. Telemetry, which involves cardiac monitoring, may be a separate unit or may be part of the Cardiology unit. It is explained in more detail in Chapter 20.

Neurology   This unit provides any non-surgical treatment of diseases relating specifically to the neurological system, such as Parkinson's disease and multiple sclerosis.

palliative care   care for a person with a terminal illness who is in hospital to die, to have the condition stabilized, or for pain control.

Palliative Care   A **palliative care** unit looks after patients who have terminal illnesses. They may be admitted for stabilization or pain management during more acute episodes of their illness. They may be admitted when they are dying. The staff on these units are trained not only to look after the client's emotional and physical needs but also to provide guidance and support to the client's family and loved ones.

Psychiatry/Mental Health Services   This unit, sometimes simply called "Psych," involves the care of individuals with mental or emotional conditions. Many facilities have both inpatient and outpatient Psychiatry units, which may constitute a separate hospital department. Outpatient units offer care, treatment, and support for those who live in the community. Patients who are unable to manage in the community are treated in the inpatient units.

Oncology/Systemic Therapy   This unit treats individuals with cancer. Some communities have specialized hospitals dealing only with cancer. Some patients undergo surgery to remove cancerous tumours. Many receive postoperative treatment, including medication (chemotherapy) and/or radiation. Chemotherapy may be intravenous, oral, or a combination of both. Depending on the type of cancer, the treatment, and the response, therapy may be inpatient or outpatient. Intensive chemotherapy, such as that given for some types of leukemia, may make the patient sick and weak and impair the immune system. Such patients are kept in the hospital until they have recovered some strength. They may be kept in reverse isolation, meaning that extra precautions are taken to protect them from infection.

Rehabilitation   Patients are transferred to "Rehab" to recover function after a stroke, trauma, or surgery. They are often discharged to continue rehabilitation as outpatients.

Pediatrics   This unit treats children, typically up to age 16 years, although the age limit may vary. Some hospitals, such as the Hospital for Sick Children in Toronto, care only for children. A children's hospital will have units specialized for the type of illness, intensity of care needed, and the age of the child.

Gynecology   This unit looks after patients (sometimes surgical as well as medical) with complaints related to the female reproductive system. Some Gynecology units offer pre- and post-abortion counselling and support groups and have community services related to infertility.

Integrated Mother/Child Services   Many facilities now have integrated services combining labour, delivery, and recovery from childbirth. This unit is often grouped together and called "Mat–Child." The mother would be admitted to one room, called the LDR (Labour, Delivery, Recovery) room, where she would labour, have the baby, and recover. Often, there is accommodation for family members or significant others who wish to stay and support the mother. The baby stays with the mother unless there are complications necessitating specialized care. The unit may offer parenting classes and breast-feeding clinics.

If the mother requires an abdominal delivery (caesarean section), she may have to be transferred to the "section room," which is usually on the same floor.

Some hospitals are designated as regional obstetrical or pediatric centres, offering different levels of newborn/infant care. A centre offering full intensive care services is designated a level II care centre.

Patient-care Units—Surgical

Surgical units are also patient-care units, like medical units, but they look after patients preparing for or recovering from surgery. In a large hospital, units are specialized by type of surgery. These units do not include the operating rooms where the actual surgery is done.

General Surgery   General Surgery would be a unit more likely found in a small or mid-sized hospital. Patients come to recover from a variety of relatively simple operations on different organs and systems: gallbladder, gastrointestinal, appendix, bladder, and so on.

Cardiac Surgery   Cardiac surgery units deal with surgery to the heart and vascular system, such as bypass surgery.

Orthopedic Surgery   This unit cares for patients who have had surgical procedures related to the musculoskeletal system, such as hip or knee replacements or spinal surgery.

Thoracic Surgery   This unit deals with surgery of the chest and the respiratory system, such as the removal of a lung section, a lung transplantation, or treatment for a collapsed lung (pneumothorax).

Neurosurgery This unit cares for patients who have had surgery on the brain, spinal cord, and other parts of the nervous system. For example, individuals with brain tumours or **subdural hematomas** would be cared for here.

subdural hematoma a blood clot under the dura mater, the fibrous membrane forming the outer envelope of the brain and spinal cord, usually resulting from trauma to the head.

Gynecological Surgery This unit cares for patients who undergo surgical procedures relating to the female reproductive system. It may be combined with the Medical Gynecology unit. Patients who have had a stillbirth or spontaneous abortion are often transferred to this unit if they must remain in hospital so that they are spared the agony of watching mothers with newborn babies.

GI/Endoscopy This unit cares for patients who have had gastrointestinal (GI) surgery (anything to do with the digestive tract), such as bowel resection, stomach surgery for ulcers, or a colostomy. **Endoscopy** is often an outpatient procedure. Some hospitals designate one large room or a ward to which patients for endoscopy procedures are admitted and discharged. The ward may be a section of the GI unit.

endoscopy examination of a canal, such as the colon, with an endoscope: a thin tube with lenses to allow visualization.

Ophthalmology This unit specializes in procedures related to the eye. Some surgery may be done on an outpatient basis.

Pediatric Surgery This unit is for children who have had surgical procedures. Larger hospitals may have more specialized units, such as pediatric neurosurgery, although more specialized procedures may be performed at designated children's hospitals.

Plastic Surgery Plastic surgery is usually managed on an outpatient basis. Unless the surgery is medically necessary, the cost is borne by the client. Some procedures, such as breast reduction, involve overnight stay, while reconstructive surgery after a car accident or burns usually involves a longer stay.

Vascular Surgery This unit serves patients who have had surgery for an aneurysm or reconstructive vascular surgery.

Urology This unit deals with the care and recovery of patients who have had any surgery done on the urinary system.

Intensive Care Units

critically ill experiencing life-threatening problems; in medical crisis.

Patients who are **critically ill** (whether or not they have received surgery) and who require specialized, intensive treatment and nursing care are cared for in an Intensive Care Unit (ICU). These units can also be specialized, for example, a *Neonatal Intensive Care Unit* (NICU), which cares for newborns, or a *Coronary Care Unit* (CCU), which cares for those with cardiovascular problems. CCU might also refer to a Constant Care Unit which mimics the ICU, for the most part.

Emergency Departments

Emergency Departments, in theory, are for individuals who need urgent care for serious conditions, such as victims of motor vehicle accidents and other traumas or those experiencing uncontrolled bleeding or symptoms of stroke or heart attack.

Outpatient Clinics

Hospitals often have outpatient clinics in such areas as diabetes, psychiatry, orthopedics, and oncology.

Diagnostic and Therapeutic Services

Some departments offer diagnostic services alone, and others offer both diagnostic and treatment services. Most of these departments offer services to both inpatients and outpatients and to the community at large. Physicians order inpatient services and refer outpatients to the clinic.

Renal Dialysis   This unit has a special machine that filters waste from the blood of patients who have advanced kidney disease or whose kidneys are nonfunctional. Smaller hospitals that have a renal dialysis unit may have it managed by a neighbouring larger centre.

Cardiology Services   Health professionals, such as cardiologists and cardiology technologists, provide a range of diagnostic testing to diagnose structural abnormalities of the heart and other factors that may impair its function.

Respiratory Services   Medical staff, along with respiratory technologists and technicians, provide diagnostic procedures, including pulmonary function tests, and therapeutic interventions. Cardiology services and respiratory services may be combined in a single Cardiopulmonary Services unit.

Diagnostic Imaging   In this department, radiologists, medical radiation and nuclear technologists, and **ultrasonographers** offer imaging services, such as ultrasonography, magnetic resonance imaging (MRI), computed tomography (CT), nuclear medicine, fluoroscopy, mammography, and vascular/interventional radiology.

ultrasonographer   a technician who operates an ultrasound machine.

Laboratory Services   In this department, pathologists and other physician specialists, medical laboratory technologists, microbiologists, and phlebotomists deliver a range of laboratory services to inpatients and outpatients in such areas as chemistry (or biochemistry), hematology and blood bank, microbiology (which may include bacteriology, virology, and mycology), and pathology (which may include histology and cytology).

Physiotherapy   The Physiotherapy Department works with patients after illness, surgery, and/or trauma to facilitate rehabilitation and recovery. Patients include those with functional disabilities, such as back and joint problems, cancer, heart attacks, stroke, and those requiring postoperative rehabilitation.

Speech Therapy   The speech therapist works with patients needing corrective or rehabilitative treatment for speech disorders. These include speech impediments, such as stuttering and lisps. Other patients include people who are deaf or hearing impaired and stroke victims.

Occupational Therapy   Therapists here will determine what interests and skills patients have and try to get them involved in recreational activities. Often, they work with Physiotherapy to recommend activities that will be physically therapeutic as well as recreational.

Social Services

This department works with patients to help them re-establish themselves or a family member in the community after an illness or surgery. This service may be ordered by the physician or requested by the nurse, the client, or family members. The social worker draws on community resources to meet the client's needs. If the patient cannot return home, a social worker will work with the patient and family to find an alternative solution, such as placement in a long-term care facility. Social workers also provide patients with support and counselling.

❻ THE PROFESSIONAL STAFF

(SEE CHAPTER 4 FOR MORE DETAIL ON SOME OF THE PROFESSIONS LISTED BELOW.)

If you work in a hospital, you will interact with many different health-care professionals. Each type of facility will have a somewhat different mix. For example, a nursing home will have proportionally fewer registered nurses (RNs) than a hospital and more registered practical nurses (RPNs) and personal support workers.

It is important to know who these professionals are and how they contribute to the health team. In reading the following section, keep in mind that titles and job descriptions vary with facility and location and are constantly shifting as facilities try to improve efficiency while following trends in political correctness.

Physicians

As discussed in Chapter 4, some physicians are salaried and on staff full-time at hospitals, especially teaching hospitals. Emergentologists may work only at a hospital; they may be salaried or bill fee-for-service. Many doctors, including general practitioners and specialists, such as internists and cardiologists, have private practices outside the hospital; they attend their own patients in hospital. Surgeons may be salaried to work in a hospital but also have private practices. Anaesthetists work almost exclusively in hospitals but usually bill fee-for-service.

Health-care providers, such as physicians and midwives, must apply to a hospital for admitting privileges before they can admit patients to that facility and actively participate in the client's treatment. In a process called **credentialling**, their qualifications are first carefully examined by a committee composed of members of the medical staff and perhaps someone from the hospital administration. The provider must then follow the facility's policies and regulations and may have admitting privileges revoked if she fails to meet standards of conduct, practice, and care.

credentialling a process whereby a peer group judges an individual's qualifications to perform certain services.

Unit Manager or Clinical Leader

In the traditional hospital structure, each hospital unit was typically managed by a head nurse. The head nurse almost always worked on the day shift. She did not routinely provide patient care but oversaw all activities that took place on the floor and acted as the primary contact for physicians. She would accompany doctors on their rounds to visit clients, often writing down the physicians' orders. She was a fount of information on each client's condition and treatment plan. She also reviewed all clients' medications for the day and checked the charts for any missed orders. Unless absent from the patient-care unit, the head nurse transcribed all doctors' orders. She completed a staffing schedule for each day and assigned a charge nurse for each shift. Other nurses on the floor would take direction from the charge nurse.

Today, a nurse does not usually accompany the physician on rounds. Instead of instructing a nurse, the doctor writes down the orders or enters them directly into the computer at the bedside using a portable device (discussed in Chapter 16) and informs the client's nurse about anything critical. Each patient-care unit still has a person who is ultimately responsible for the unit, as well as someone on each shift who takes a lead role. Nursing staff and the clinical secretary first turn to this shift leader if they have problems and then to the unit manager.

The person responsible for the unit may be called a *manager* or *clinical leader*. This person may or may not be a nurse. She may be responsible for several floors or units, usually related ones; for example, she may be manager of Surgical and Emergency Services or of Inpatient Medical Services. This person is still usually the ultimate reporting authority for the clinical secretary.

The Clinical Resource Nurse

The person who coordinates and manages a unit for a shift is still sometimes called a charge nurse but is more often called a clinical resource nurse; other titles also exist. This person is always a nurse but may be on a full-time or part-time basis. One person may be permanently assigned to a shift, or several people with the same title may rotate through shifts. This is the person you will work most closely with, who will check your processed doctors' orders, and to whom you will take any problems that arise during the course of your shift.

Professional Nurses

There are a number of categories of nursing professionals: the RN/BScN and RPN/LPN, each with their own scope of practice. Each unit will have different nursing requirements. Some units, such as the Intensive Care Unit (ICU), use only RNs. Some hospitals hire only RNs for specific units. However, the majority of hospital units are staffed by RPNs/LPNs and sometimes health-care aides or personal support workers (PSWs). Some units use team nursing. A team may consist of any blend of professional nurses.

Registered Nurses   The College of Nurses in each province and territory clearly outlines nursing responsibilities of each level of nurse. A registered nurse (RN) may be a graduate of a diploma or a degree program, usually of three or four years. (Ontario, as have most jurisdictions, has phased out diploma programs in favour of BScN degrees.) Some provinces have accelerated degree programs graduating students with BScN in less than the usual four years. After graduation and before writing provincial or territorial examinations, the nurse is known as a graduate nurse. Upon successful completion of provincial or territorial examinations, he becomes a registered nurse. Qualifications are specific to the province or territory; an RN who moves from Ontario to British Columbia or Newfoundland and Labrador will have to recertify by taking that province's exams. In some facilities, RNs are the only nurses who may dispense medications; they maintain responsibility for the drug cart. RNs are also the only nurses who can carry out highly complex delegated responsibilities, such as giving intravenous medications, looking after acutely ill clients, monitoring patient-controlled analgesic pumps, doing complex dressings, and inserting nasogastric tubes. The role of the RPN/LPN is expanding at a rapid rate as it assumes more and more of the responsibilities formerly done by the RN.

Registered psychiatric nurses provide professional nursing and mental health nursing services in mental health-care facilities and in the community. Educated predominately in BC, Alberta, Saskatchewan, and Manitoba, registered psychiatric nurses receive post-secondary education at either the baccalaureate or diploma level.

Registered/Licensed Practical Nurses   The registered practical nurse (RPN/LPN) is a graduate of a college program that varies from one-and-a-half to two years in length. Licensed practical nurses form the second-largest body of regulated nursing professionals in the country. The scope of practice of the RPN is more limited than that of the RN, although it has expanded greatly in recent years. For example, now RPNs do not normally give out medications in acute-care settings, or in nursing homes or chronic care hospitals.

Nurse practitioners are assuming increasingly complex roles within and outside of hospitals (see Chapter 4 for more detail). In most jurisdictions, nurse practitioners can write orders on inpatients. They function as part of a medical or surgical team, and work closely with the attending physician(s). NPs are also employed in many Emergency Rooms in hospitals, doing primary assessments and triaging patients appropriately. In most provinces only midwives, dentists, and physicians may admit or discharge patients from hospital. But that policy is changing—some jurisdictions are approving legislation allowing nurse practitioners to admit and discharge patients as well. Such a law was passed in Ontario in 2012.

Personal Support Workers

This position used to be called a health-care aide, but the term *personal support worker* (PSW) is becoming more popular in some regions. Some agencies still train PSWs on the job, but most are graduates of a three- to six-month certificate program at a community college or equivalent. Although some PSWs work as team members with nurses in hospitals, they are more likely to work in nursing homes, long-term care facilities, and community agencies.

Orderlies   Some hospitals employ orderlies (usually male) to carry out such duties as transporting clients. They may be trained to bathe patients and perform such tasks as male catheterization, especially when there is no male nurse available and a patient is uncomfortable with being treated by a woman. Orderlies may be trained on the job.

Housekeeping Staff

Housekeeping staff are often assigned to specific units, although they may rotate. Their duties include cleaning and disinfecting vacated beds and bedside accessories. You may be responsible for notifying housekeeping (often electronically) when a patient has been discharged so that they can clean the room. It is important to communicate clearly with the housekeeping staff to ensure efficient use of hospital beds. Some clinical secretaries keep an updated list of discharges on the floor for housekeeping staff to refer to (often a book kept at the desk in the nurses' station). There may be times when a bed is urgently needed, but a discharged patient is still occupying it. If the patient is able, he may be asked to wait in the reception area so that the bed can be prepared for the new admission.

Most hospitals request that discharged patients leave by a certain time, often 1100. Do your best to encourage the patient to leave on time to allow for the room to be prepared. Often, elective (nonemergency) admissions are asked to come in around 1500.

Pharmacists

Many patient-care units have an assigned pharmacist and/or pharmacy assistant. Pharmacists are university graduates, often entering into pharmacy with an undergraduate degree in the sciences. (See Chapter 7.) Among other things, the pharmacist manages the stocking of medications, often for more than one floor. This is largely done in conjunction with modernized electronic innovations wherein replenishing medications is mediated by a pharmacy robot or other centralized mechanisms.

Physiotherapists

Physiotherapists are university graduates, often with an undergraduate degree in kinesiology and a Master's in physiotherapy. If you process an order for physiotherapy, you would phone or email the Physiotherapy Department. If a patient is ambulatory, she will probably go to the Physiotherapy Department; if not, the physiotherapist will come to the client. Note the appointment time on the Kardex or patient intervention screen. Keep a list of the client's activities to avoid scheduling conflicts and ensure that the patient is ready. For example, if Jovana (who relies on the nurses to help her get bathed and up in the morning) has an 0830 appointment with the physiotherapist, make a note so that the nurse can plan to get her ready on time. Many physiotherapists work in hospitals, but also practice independently in most jurisdictions.

Respiratory Therapists

A respiratory therapist (RT) may be a graduate of a three- or four-year college program or may have a Master's degree. Some universities provide students with the option to receive a bachelor of health sciences (BHS) in conjunction with an RT diploma. These health professionals may be found in neonatal nurseries, operating rooms, intensive care units, general wards and in the ER. They work with patients of all ages and with a variety of conditions, including those with breathing issues and heart/lung problems. RTs provide inhalation treatments, set up and monitor oxygen therapy, manage patients on respirators or using spirometers, obtain blood gases, and monitor clients' respiratory progress. There is usually an RT on every shift, and one will respond to a cardiac or a respiratory arrest. Nurses will initiate oxygen therapy if an RT is unavailable.

Laboratory Technologists and Technicians

Medical laboratory technologists, as discussed in Chapter 6, are graduates of a postsecondary program and perform a vast array of laboratory tests ordered by the doctor, with the help of laboratory technicians and sometimes phlebotomists.

Dietitians

Registered dietitians are university graduates, usually from a four-year program. They may be helped by dietary assistants. You will work with dietitians and dietary assistants when arranging dietary counselling, processing nutritional orders, or cancelling or delaying a client's meal because of tests.

❼ RESPONSIBILITIES OF THE CLINICAL SECRETARY

THE **CLINICAL SECRETARY** IS OFTEN DESCRIBED AS THE HUB IN THE WHEEL THAT KEEPS THE patient-care unit operational. Consider the following comments by nurses:

"If our clinical secretary calls in sick, I get a sinking feeling in my stomach. We can't really manage without her."

"Our clinical secretary holds our floor together."

"The clinical secretary on our unit is the best thing that ever happened to us. She is competent, organized, and keeps everything on track and running smoothly."

"We simply would not be able to manage without our clinical secretary. I sometimes wonder how she keeps up with the doctors' orders and also keeps our unit so organized."

The scope of responsibilities and duties discussed here is general. Exactly how you carry out these duties will depend on the type of patient-care unit, the facility's policies and organization, and how computerized the hospital is.

Clerical/Secretarial Responsibilities

If you work on a patient-care unit, you will likely

- manage the administrative components of admission, discharge, and transfer;
- prepare and update identity bracelets, bed labels, and so on;
- orient new admissions to the unit;
- distribute patient mail;
- transcribe orders accurately and promptly (see Chapter 16);
- notify nurses of stat orders and changes in clients' care;
- keep charts up to date and prepare forms;
- label charts with patient information and doctor's name;
- ensure that requisitions for blood work, specimens, and X-rays are completed and recorded;
- ensure that lab results are recorded and directed appropriately;
- update unit forms and policy and procedure manuals;
- maintain staffing schedules;

- enter data for patient-care hours/workload analysis;
- schedule replacement staff (for example, if someone calls in sick for the next shift you may need to call nurses from a list until you find someone willing to come in);
- keep notices and posted schedules current (may include a list of what rooms patients are in, admissions and discharges for the day, surgical schedule);
- communicate work requests to volunteers;
- manage inventory and order supplies;
- clean and organize the desk area;
- process diet changes for clients;
- orient new staff to the unit's communication systems (e.g., telephone, call bells, computer);

- check that equipment in the nursing station is in working order; and
- prepare in advance documents needed for admissions (e.g., nursing history, waiver for valuables kept by client).

Communication Responsibilities

In any hospital unit, you will play a vital role as the central point for incoming and outgoing communication. On a patient-care unit, you are likely to

- answer the telephone, direct calls, and take messages;
- page and locate physicians and other members of the health-care team;
- notify staff and physicians of admissions, transfers, discharges, and deaths;
- keep co-workers informed, perhaps by writing messages in a unit communications book;
- respond to and direct intercom calls from patients (call bells);
- screen and direct visitors and health professionals;
- act as an information and education resource for clients;
- make calls to physicians, other hospital departments, and community agencies;
- book appointments and tests for clients;
- direct and send reports, faxes, and photocopies; and
- find replacements for staff members who call in sick.

Communicating effectively in the hospital requires the same skills as for a health office. (See Chapter 8.) Interacting with patients and families can be a special challenge. Hospital patients may have altered communication patterns because they are at various stages of accepting their illness and are missing the familiarity of their homes. Family and friends, too, may be worried and stressed by altered role functions. You need to apply your knowledge of altered role function and sick role behaviour (discussed in Chapter 2) to interact adaptively.

You will also need to deal effectively with physicians, nurses, and many other health-care professionals. This can be challenging, too, especially when you are new. You will be working with every type of personality and with people who are often under stress. An overworked nurse or a surgeon about to perform difficult or critical surgery after the end of his normal shift may be too distracted or tense to remember courtesy. This is when you especially need to call on the communication and interpersonal skills discussed in Chapter 1. Physicians can be your best friends or your worst enemies, depending on how their day is going. You may also feel the brunt of negativism or frustration from the nursing staff. In a hospital, there are (wrongly or rightly) hierarchies. Each profession guards its scope of practice, and power struggles are frequent; sometimes you may be caught in the middle.

Some will treat you as a "gofer," although this attitude is much less prevalent than a few years ago. You have a demanding and responsible position. Be polite, but be firm when you need to be. There is always a way to respond courteously while maintaining control of your own activities. For example:

Dr. Green: "Mary, get me Mr. Reynolds' file. I don't see it on the desk."

(Mary, on the phone taking lab results, holds up her hand and nods to Dr. Green.)

"I'll be a minute, Dr. Green. It might be by the computer over there."

Mary is polite. She acknowledges that she has heard Dr. Green. At the same time, she is going to finish the task at hand. She lets Dr. Green know that she will help her when she can but offers a suggestion, which might prompt Dr. Green to look a little further herself. Review Chapter 8 for more tips on communicating effectively.

Cross-Coverage

cross-coverage moving from one area to another, or covering two units.

In many hospitals, you may be expected to manage two or three patient-care units at different times, each involving different administrative tasks. This is called **cross-coverage** and is one of the reasons your job is so challenging. For example, if another clinical secretary calls in sick, or if another unit is busy and yours is not, you may be asked to move to another unit for part of the day. Because each unit involves different tasks and requires different areas of knowledge, you must be flexible and able to take in a large body of information. You may even be asked to cover both units at once. This double responsibility calls on you to hold many threads in your mind and to set priorities. You need to draw on all your organizational skills. Because hospital staff are dealing with ill clients, you may have to respond to instructions given quickly and in stressful situations. This can be especially difficult if you are on a unit you are not entirely familiar with. Try to keep yourself focused on the task at hand, and set priorities.

Scope of Practice

Scope of practice (discussed in Chapter 1) refers to the boundaries of a person's responsibilities. All professionals have a scope of practice—determined by regulation, by a professional governing body, or by the facility—and it is important to stay within these boundaries. An RPN would not take out someone's appendix, a PSW would not add medication to an IV, and a chiropractor would not excise a skin lesion. These limits assure the public that the person looking after them is qualified.

In some areas, a properly trained clinical secretary may take a client's vital signs. Your employer should assess your skills to make sure you are competent to perform the procedure. If you do take vital signs, remember that you are *not* diagnosing; you are simply completing a technical procedure.

You are *not* qualified to give patient care. If a patient asks you to help her get up to the bathroom or to get her a medication, you must refuse because this is not within your scope of practice. You would, however, find the appropriate person to carry out the task.

In most facilities, the clinical secretary is not permitted to take telephone orders from a physician. (However, in most facilities you are permitted to take the results of lab tests.) Sometimes, a physician can be persistent, demanding, and abrupt if you ask him to wait until you find a nurse. Do not give in; politely put him on hold and find the appropriate person.

When you are new, be aware of your learning curve. Do not attempt to do something unless you are certain that you will do it correctly. If you are in a training position, ask the nursing staff or your predecessor. Be positive and confident, but do not be afraid to clearly state your limitations.

Choosing the Right Area for You

One advantage of working in a hospital is the wide selection of areas in which you can work. Your job description will vary somewhat from one department to another, and the required skills and temperament vary even more. To work in the Emergency Department, you must enjoy a fast, demanding pace and be very organized and able to multitask. ER is a stressful environment, but what is stress to one person is a challenge to another. The work in a palliative care unit is usually less fast paced but requires compassion and the ability to deal with grief and death. If you thrive on patient contact and interpersonal communication, you may find working in Health Information Services unsatisfying. However, if you prefer administrative responsibilities, enjoy detail, and pride yourself on your unwavering accuracy, Health Information Services might be your ideal job. Medical and surgical units, particularly in large teaching hospitals, are challenging environments and, like the ER, require someone who can multitask, who works well under pressure, and who has excellent communication skills.

❽ THE ANATOMY OF A PATIENT-CARE UNIT

ALTHOUGH THE LAYOUT MAY VARY, THE NURSES' STATION IS THE FOCUS OR HUB OF A patient-care unit, and the patient rooms and service rooms revolve around it. A common floor layout is a rectangle with the nurses' station in the middle and rooms up and down each side and at both ends. The central nurses' station keeps nurses as close to all patients as possible, saving steps and allowing them to respond to patient needs quickly in an emergency.

The Nurses' Station

The nurses' station (also called the *nursing station*) is the "head office" of the unit; administration and communication are managed here. The clients' charts (even skeleton charts usually still present in the computerized environment), computers, Kardex (if used), telephones, fax, intercom controls, and stationery are all found here. This, though not your private office, is where you will do most of your work. A wide variety of other staff will also be using the station, and so it is important to keep it organized and uncluttered. One clinical secretary says, "If you have a messy area, then you don't know where things are in case of an emergency. I feel overwhelmed if my area is not organized." The nurses' station also functions as a reception area. Visitors will stop here seeking direction or advice or wanting to speak to a health-care professional.

Equipment and Materials at the Nurses' Station   Generally, you keep track of the equipment at the nurses' station and make arrangements for needed repairs and replacements. Doctors and nurses will often ask you where to find various items.

Mobile Phones   It has become common practice for nurses on a patient-care unit to carry mobile phones. It may be your responsibility to keep them charged and organized and distribute them to oncoming staff. It is important to know who has which phone.

Stethoscopes   **Stethoscopes**, used to listen to the heart and take blood pressure, are usually found hanging on a hook or in a drawer. They are used not only by physicians but also by nurses, respiratory therapists, and physiotherapists. Though many health professionals have their own stethoscopes, some still rely on the supply at the nurses' station. Label stethoscopes clearly (e.g., "3 south") as they are expensive and may easily be taken by mistake and end up in another unit or a doctor's office.

stethoscope   a device that amplifies sound, used by doctors and other health-care professionals to listen to the heart and to take blood pressure.

Blood Pressure Cuffs and Sphygmomanometers   Each floor will have a designated number of blood pressure cuffs and **sphygmomanometers**, kept at the nurses' station. They are used mostly by nurses but also by doctors. They may be the portable type, kept in a soft zippered case, or a larger unit with the sphygmomanometer itself on wheels. Many units have wall sphygmomanometers beside the beds but will also keep a few portable ones. You should have a specific place to keep them so that they are accessible but less likely to be dropped or bumped. These kits do not disappear as readily as stethoscopes, but you should still label them, especially the smaller ones in the cases. Some units account for their blood pressure equipment at the end of each shift. It is the nurses' responsibility to let you know if one is broken. You would then fill out a repair requisition and send the item to Maintenance.

Ophthalmoscope/Otoscope Kit   **Ophthalmoscopes** and **otoscopes** are used primarily by doctors for eye and ear examinations, respectively. Usually, both come together in a small hard case. They have batteries, which are usually rechargeable. You may be responsible for charging the batteries at night or when the devices are not in use and making sure that extra batteries and bulbs are available. This equipment should be checked at the beginning of each shift. There is nothing more frustrating for a physician than having to interrupt an examination to go looking for working equipment.

Flashlights   There are usually several flashlights kept in the unit. Because corridor lights are kept low and many patients would be disturbed by a room light, nurses use flashlights to make their rounds at night. (They usually make rounds at least every half hour to check on patients and make sure that, for example, an IV is in place and flowing). Nurses also use a flashlight for patients with head injuries—the light is shone into the eye to assess the pupil's response to light. An abnormal response may indicate increased pressure in the skull. Doctors may use the flashlights to examine a client's eyes or throat. You may be responsible for making sure the flashlights are in good working order and that spare batteries are available.

Percussion Hammer/Tuning Fork   Doctors, and sometimes nurses, use these in physical examinations. The percussion hammer is used to check reflexes (such as the knee-jerk) as a check of neurological functioning, and the tuning fork is used to check hearing.

Tongue Depressors   These are disposable items. They may be kept on the supply cart in the clean utility or treatment room, but it is a good idea to also keep a small supply at the nurses' station, within easy reach when a physician wants one.

Stationery Supplies   You will be responsible for keeping the nurses' station stocked with basic office supplies—pens and pencils, paperclips, staplers, highlighters, erasers, rulers, and the like. You will have to order these and may have to work within a budget. Keep supplies that you use daily in an organized manner in a convenient spot. Keep a notepad by each telephone. With pens and pencils, you have to find a balance between having too few available and too many. Doctors and nurses will often have their own pens but will sometimes need one from the nurses' station. However, if you have plenty lying around, they will disappear. You may want to keep a few on the desk and some tucked away.

The Treatment Room

This is a room where physicians, nurses, and other health professionals can perform examinations and minor procedures without having to take the patient out of the unit. In a pediatric unit, the treatment room might be used to start an IV or do a biopsy. In Gynecology, it might be used to do pelvic examinations and/or a Pap smear. Not all floors have a treatment room.

Equipment frequently used for examinations in your unit should be kept available in this room. If you know that a particular examination is going to take place, check to be sure that the equipment needed is on hand. You may find it in the clean utility room. For example, if a doctor is going to do a Pap smear, make sure a range of speculums is available in the treatment room. It is disruptive for the patient and the doctor to have to stop and call for equipment.

Clean Utility Room

This is a room for storing frequently used supplies, such as **dressing trays**, various types of bandages and dressing supplies, catheters, intravenous bags and tubing, nasogastric tubes, and emesis basins (also called kidney basins or K-basins). The list varies with the type of unit; a surgical unit, for example, would need more dressing trays and **suture removal** trays than would a medical unit. You may be responsible for taking inventory, checking supplies against a master list, and reordering. These supplies are usually kept on a large cart with several shelves, covered over with a zippered plastic sheet. In some facilities, supply staff exchange the cart at night for a fully stocked one. The clean utility room may also be used by the nurses to set up trays for nursing procedures, such as suture removal, putting in a catheter, or inserting a nasogastric tube.

dressing tray a specially prepared sterile tray containing the basic equipment to change a dressing on a wound or surgical incision. It contains a K-basin, 4 × 4 gauze dressings, a galley cup (a small metal or glass cup about the size of a shot glass used for cleansing solutions), and usually two sets of disposable forceps.

suture removal tray a specially prepared sterile tray similar to the dressing tray, but containing suture removal scissors or clip removers. Some facilities use a dressing tray, and nurses add a disposable suture removal blade or prepackaged clip removers.

The Dirty Utility Room

This is an area for used equipment and supplies, such as dressing trays, bedpans, and basins. Reusable equipment, such as a nasogastric suction machine, may be rinsed or cleaned here and prepared for return to Central Supply or the Sterile Processing Department (SPD). Disposable equipment, such as soiled catheters, nasogastric tubes, IV bags and tubing, and items soiled with body fluids, are disposed of according to Standard Precautions (see Chapter 5) and agency guidelines. Dirty linen may be kept here until picked up for laundry. It is not uncommon to find extra IV poles, wheelchairs, and so on, in this room. This room may also contain a bedpan hopper: an automatic unit for disposal of waste and sanitization of bedpans. (Bedpans will still need to be sterilized before they are given to other clients.) Many patient-care units, however, have two or three separate hopper rooms.

Medication Room

Usually, the medication room is near the nursing station. This is an area where medicines are kept. Often, you will find supplies of stock medications and IV solutions to which medicines have been added by Pharmacy. Most medication rooms also have a refrigerator for storing certain medications.

Many hospitals use a medication cart ("med cart"). The design of the cart varies. There may be a series of small drawers, one for each bed in the unit. Each drawer will contain a single client's medication and will be appropriately labelled (e.g., "Gareth Harley, 301, bed 1"; "Mohammed al-Malek, 301, bed 2"; "Suzette Laronde, 302, bed 1"; and so on). The medication cart should be kept locked when not in use. Narcotics and controlled drugs must always be under a double lock; many carts contain a locked drawer for these medications. If you ever see the medication cart unlocked and unattended, or the medication keys left unattended, notify someone—preferably one of the registered nurses. Most facilities have professionals (usually registered nurses or sometimes a registered practical nurse) designated to carry the keys to the medication carts. How many sets of keys are in circulation depends on the size of the unit, but two or three is typical. One set of keys should always remain on the unit. All too often, however, the nurses carrying the keys are all off the floor at the same time. As Murphy's law predicts, it seems that a patient will call for something for pain the moment the last set of keys leaves the floor. You may have to hunt down a nurse with a set of keys and bring the keys back to the unit or page the nurse to return to the floor.

Storage Room

Not all units have a storage room; some use the dirty utility room for this purpose. When there is a storage room, it is frequently larger than the utility rooms and serves to store such items as wheelchairs, IV poles, gurneys (stretchers), and a larger cart containing a more comprehensive array of supplies than those found in the clean utility room. You might find sterilized bedpans, commodes, and basin sets here as well. If the unit does not have a storage room, these items would be kept in the clean and dirty utility rooms. Sometimes, you will find wheelchairs and gurneys lining the hallways. This obstructs the movement of patients and staff and poses a hazard when people need to move quickly, as in a fire or responding to a cardiac arrest. Try to clear the hall; if no other space is available, put the equipment in an alcove.

Conference Room

Some facilities have a conference room for team conferences, meetings, and patient interviews. Some units would consider this a luxury. If you have such a room, it is an ideal place for nurses to give and take **shift reports**, which often contain highly confidential information. Often, nurses must take reports in the nurses' station, medication room, or other relatively open areas. If you overhear confidential information, politely try to take corrective action. For example, if a door is ajar, quietly go over and close it. If the nurses are taking reports in the nurses' station, ensure that the doors of the rooms around the station are closed. Sound carries, as anyone who has had a bed near the nurses' station can testify.

shift report essential patient information passed on to the next shift of nurses.

Kitchen

Some floors will have a small separate kitchen, or one may be shared by two or more floors. This room usually contains a refrigerator, kettle, dishes (often disposable), and a few food items. Sandwiches, fruit, milk, tea, coffee, and juice may be kept there for patient use, although budget cutbacks often limit the food available. Sometimes, the nurses will put extra sandwiches that have been delivered to the floor in this fridge.

The Dietary Department may send up special snacks that have been ordered for patients (such as a midmorning, afternoon, or bedtime snack for a diabetic) and store them, labelled, in the fridge. Other units might store such special orders in the refrigerator in the medication room.

Dictation Room

This room provides a confidential environment for doctors to dictate progress notes, admission and discharge notes, consultation notes, and operative reports. Nurses may use it to complete charting. It contains dictation equipment and often one or more computer stations. Many doctors dictate notes from home or elsewhere in the hospital. Most have internet access to the hospital's computer system. Some physicians are entering their dictations directly into the computer using voice-recognition software.

Waiting/Reception Room

Most units have a waiting room or reception area. Ambulatory patients may visit friends and relatives in this room. Visitors will wait here for a patient who has not yet returned from surgery or a test. Sometimes, patients like to sit in the reception area for a change of scenery or to watch television.

Most facilities have limits on visiting hours and on the number of visitors a patient may have at a time. Although most patient-care units are somewhat flexible, there are times when these rules must be enforced. If visitors are disturbing the patient in the next bed, you can politely ask them to visit in the reception area. If the patient is not ambulatory, suggest that only two visitors remain in the room at one time and the others wait in the reception area. Many facilities announce the end of visiting hours over the PA system. If visitors ignore this announcement, you might have it repeated. If that fails, you may have to politely remind visitors that visiting hours are over.

Patient Teaching Room

Large hospitals may have a special room for patient teaching, often on an outpatient basis. For example, people scheduled for elective surgery may be asked to come in beforehand to get detailed information about what to expect, including discussions of pain control, diet, and ambulation. You may be responsible for booking these sessions.

Housekeeping Supply Room

This is a smaller area where the housekeeping staff store pails, mops, other cleaning supplies and, sometimes, toilet paper and tissues.

Dumbwaiter

A dumbwaiter, or lift, is a mini-elevator for small objects. It is often found in the kitchen or in a location central to all the units using it. It consists of a large box, sometimes with a shelf, accessed through doors that open vertically. There are two buttons, one to summon the lift, and one to send an object away. You cannot send the dumbwaiter to a particular location. If a department is sending something to you, they will notify you that the item is on the lift. You then go to the lift door, press "come," and the lift will appear shortly with the item on it. There may be several articles for other departments; make sure you take only what is meant for your floor. Everything placed on the lift should be clearly labelled. For example, Dietary may call to notify you that the ginger ale you ordered for Mr. Samuels is on the lift. There may be other bottles of ginger ale for patients on other floors; Mr. Samuels' bottle should have his name on it. When you are finished, close the doors or the lift will remain where it is, and other departments will not be able to use it.

Pneumatic Tube System

Some hospitals also have a pneumatic tube system—a series of interconnecting tunnels nestled in between the walls that connect all units and departments. A small cylindrical container, large enough to hold files and forms, travels along this system to a preset destination. An apparatus somewhat resembling a miniature launching pad is located in the nurses' station. There is an "out" channel or port into which you place a tube, and an "in" channel or port where tubes are received. Each floor has a code; you dial the appropriate code on the top side of the cylinder to determine its destination. Although convenient, the pneumatic tube system is notorious for getting plugged. Most agencies allow only paper items in the tubes.

❾❿ COMMUNICATION TOOLS

COMMUNICATION SYSTEMS IN A HOSPITAL ARE COMPLEX, VARIED, AND VITAL. WRITTEN communication is discussed in more detail in Chapters 15 and 16. You will likely use most of the following tools daily.

Telephones

Most nurses' stations have several telephones, each with a different extension. The style and model of telephone will vary; some are more complex than others. Since you will be on the telephone a great deal, you should have one close to your computer.

Mobile phones (wireless phones) are used by the nurses in most health-care facilities. Nurses use this mobile unit to communicate with you, other nurses, and the patients. For example, if a patient activates a call bell, it will go to his nurse's mobile. If that nurse is unable to respond, by default the call will go to another nurse's phone, and then if not answered, to you at the desk. The use of these phones provides patients with a faster response time. As well, the system also reduces the need for audible alerts, leading to quieter floors. This provides the patients with a more restful environment and serves to lower stress levels for patients and nurses alike.

Paging Systems

Paging by PA   The hospital switchboard is your link to the internal communication system. You contact the switchboard by telephone, usually by dialling 0. If you want to page someone within the hospital, call the switchboard operator and ask her to do so, giving your unit number. Usually, she will announce something like, "Would Dr. Majid please call 3 South," or "Dr. Majid, 345 please." Many facilities avoid loudspeaker messages to decrease noise and disturbance. Instead, they use beepers.

Pagers   Some facilities supply designated health professionals with pagers (also called beepers). You should have a list of all relevant pager numbers and use them to contact any of these people. In this case, the PA would be used more discriminately or perhaps only for emergencies, such as a cardiac arrest or fire. Many hospitals provide pagers to individuals waiting for someone in the OR or undergoing testing; for example, a child having a surgical or diagnostic procedure performed. Instead of having to sit and wait in a designated area, the parents (assigned a pager) can move about the hospital, go for coffee perhaps, and be sure that the moment they are needed they will be paged.

Locating Systems   Some hospitals have a locating system that flashes codes. For example, Dr. Thompson's code might be 234, or Dr. Green's 232. If you wanted Dr. Thompson, the number 234 would flash over the system, and he would call Locating to find out who was calling him.

Cell Phones and Portable Phones   As previously mentioned, nurses and other hospital employees now use wireless or mobile phones in the execution of their duties. These phones belong to the unit or department the individual works on/in.

Mobile Devices and the Patient

At this point the use of mobile devices such as cellphones by patients varies across the country. Policies range from unrestricted but responsible use, to no use, to use in specific areas of the hospital such as the cafeteria, lounges, and private offices (e.g. facilities under the umbrella of the Vancouver Coastal Health Authority). There may be limited use allowed in designated areas, such as where there is the potential for the device to interfere with medical equipment. Patient confidentiality is an issue (because of the camera/video option on these phones) and lack of privacy related to personal conversations. Other restrictions include the times of use, and activating the vibrate option instead of the ring.

Wi-Fi

Many facilities have Wi-Fi now, enabling patients to use their iPads, netbooks, or laptop computers to access the internet. This may be restricted to certain patient-care units and/or other areas of the hospital. The Ottawa Hospital makes internet access available throughout the main hospital building, including patient rooms, waiting rooms, the cafeteria, and the main lobby. There are security issues, confidentiality issues (e.g. email), and patient behaviour issues (e.g., whether they are getting enough rest or spending too much time on the computer). The use of Wi-Fi in hospitals varies greatly and policies are constantly changing. What is certain, though, is that Wi-Fi will be available on some scale in most facilities in the near future.

Unit Intercom System Controls

The unit intercom is a system of communicating with clients. There is an intercom beside each bed or on the wall beside each bed. The patient can call by pulling a cord attached to a switch. Usually, a light will go on over the client's room door, and a signal on the intercom control panel at the nurses' station will activate. Some activation points, such as those in bathrooms, have a sustained ring and flashing light, which indicate a possible emergency. If a nurse attends to the client, she will deactivate the signal at the bedside.

Otherwise, you may communicate with the patient over the intercom. If the patient needs a nurse, tell him that you will have one come to the room. Try to find out what the patient needs. Obviously, if it is an emergency, you must let the nurses know that. Otherwise, try to give the patient a time frame. "The nurse will be in to see you in about five minutes." If you simply say that a nurse is coming and she does not appear immediately, the patient is likely to keep calling. Nurses do their best, but with staffing shortages, waits are often unavoidable. If the request is something that you can handle—for example, the patient simply wants someone to turn out the light, close the door, or put the telephone back on the hook—do so, or ask anyone available to do so. If no one is available, at least you know that the matter is not urgent, even if it seems so to the client.

Computers and Information Technology

As with health offices, hospitals are quickly moving to a computerized environment. Hospital computer systems are complex interconnecting networks that have changed the way hospitals communicate both internally and with the community.

Computers are used to:

- interface with multiple sites, pharmacies, and other community agencies;
- communicate with other departments;
- do billing;
- do order entry;
- track, distribute, and monitor the use of medications;
- transfer patients requiring a medical transfer number;
- schedule treatments, procedures, and diagnostic services;
- register inpatients and outpatients (admit and discharge);
- track admissions and discharges, and keep the hospital census;
- do accounting;
- order supplies;
- calculate a hospital's operational expenses;
- track human resources; and
- handle payroll.

Some hospitals are completely computerized; others are in a transitional state, using the computer for accounting, billing, patient registration, and order entry. Many facilities still transcribe medication orders manually onto medication administration records (MAR) but also record them electronically. Alternatively, they may be entered into the computer and the MAR sheets printed out and manually signed. Computerized medication records are often called CMARs. They are prepared by Pharmacy and sent to the floor. However, if a doctor writes an order in the evening or at night, the clinical secretary must transcribe the order manually to the CMAR. In most hospitals, computerization works well in some areas and not so well in others. Smaller rural hospitals are still not completely computerized; others are leaders in innovation.

Computerization has dramatically changed the clinical secretary's job; you need to be highly skilled with computers and adaptable to technological change. Most of your work will be on the computer, ranging from processing doctors' orders (discussed in Chapter 16) to accessing other departments. Usually, you will have your own computer (or at least one you primarily use) and your own password. There may also be one or more additional computers at the nurses' station for other staff. In a highly computerized unit, most health professionals require access to the client's computerized chart for accessing information and entering data.

Some hospitals create their own software; others purchase commercial software designed for hospitals. The latter must still create their own database, customize and test the system, and train staff. This is a complex process that takes a long time. Staff will need several training sessions, practice time, and a chance to apply and integrate their skills. Many health professionals welcome computerization, but some prefer the old methods. If your area is in the process of being computerized, some health professionals will find the transition a challenge. Most hospitals have a specialized Information Technology Department, which provides orientation, staff education, and support. You probably have a help line available, but you can also ease the struggle by helping familiarize staff with the functions they need to know.

Physicians and the Computer System Physicians use the computer system to gather information on their clients. Physicians can view a client's hospital records, including test results, daily progress, and X-rays, from their offices, their homes, or from terminals within the hospital. Some centres provide nurses with small hand-held computers (often called simply "hand-helds") or have bedside computer stations. With either system, a nurse can take a client's vital signs, enter them immediately, and upload them to the client's file within minutes so that the physician has up-to-the-minute information.

Information Technology and the Clinical Secretary You will need to learn the computer functions used in your area. Two of the main modules you are likely to use are order entry (discussed in Chapter 16) and patient registration (discussed in Chapter 15).

You will be assigned a unique password and must sign on each time you use the computer. Once you have signed on, most systems will display a series of options from which you can select—for example, send interfaculty email, register a client, or transcribe orders.

Confidentiality

Security is essential in hospitals. All information should be treated as confidential unless you are authorized to share it.

Computers Confidentiality is increasingly an issue as hospitals shift to computerized patient records. You will have your own password and, in some hospitals, encrypted digital signatures. Guard these closely.

- Never share your password with anyone.
- Make sure you know who is authorized to access and retrieve information and what information they should have access to.
- Never allow an unauthorized person to view a client's health information.
- Question anyone you do not know who attempts to access the computer system. Physical access to computer terminals should be limited.
- Position your computer screens and keyboards so that others cannot see them.

- Program screensavers to come on if the computer is left idle for any period of time, such as more than a minute.

- Always log out when you leave your computer terminal.

- Store disks and printed information out of sight; if the information is redundant, erase disks and shred paper.

- Ensure that all files are properly and securely backed up.

- Make sure you know hospital guidelines outlining what information is confidential.

- If you send files containing confidential information by email, encrypt them.

- Release medical information only in accordance with legal guidelines and agency policies.

Release of Information

Since you handle most incoming calls, you will get calls from individuals inquiring about a client's health status or progress. As discussed in Chapter 2, you must be very careful about giving out such information. Make sure you know your unit's guidelines. You may be allowed to give a basic status update to family members or to a designated family member. You may recognize family members' voices and know what kind of information they are privy to. If only specified individuals are allowed information on a client, the designated caller can use a code to identify herself. If in any doubt, do not give information, even if it seems harmless. Instead, pass the call on to the client's nurse.

The same rules apply to in-person conversations. Any medical information about a patient must remain confidential. Some people may think that sharing good news is harmless, but that is no excuse to breach confidentiality. Consider the following situation:

> A student we will call Jane was working in labour and delivery when a family friend came in and delivered a baby girl. The student went across to the residence to get a book and then went back to the delivery room. As she passed the hall telephone, Rebecca, another student nurse and a mutual friend, shouted out, "Jane, I hear Elisabeth had her baby. What did she have?" "A girl," replied Jane breathlessly as she rushed back to the hospital. Rebecca made a few phone calls. By the time Elisabeth's husband got out of the delivery room and phoned her parents to announce the new arrival, they already knew. He felt robbed of the opportunity of sharing the news first-hand. This was a blatant breach of confidentiality on the part of both student nurses.

Be mindful of confidentiality at all times, and do not release any information without the client's express consent.

⑪ SECURITY

SECURITY IS A CONCERN IN ANY HOSPITAL AND BECOMES MORE COMPLEX IN A LARGER AND busier environment. Since the devastating events of September 11, 2001, and the subsequent anthrax attacks in the United States, facilities across the continent have begun to review their emergency planning. Very few facilities would be truly prepared to cope with a bioterrorist attack. Yet hospitals now consider themselves potential targets and are upgrading disaster plans to deal with types of attack that still seem unthinkable. They should be able to respond promptly and effectively to an internal threat and to meet the needs of the community in the event of a widespread threat or disaster. This includes being adequately stocked with antibiotics, antitoxins, antidotes, and other emergency equipment needed to treat and sustain potential victims. Hospital laboratories in many larger hospitals are moving to improve their technology for prompt identification of potentially infectious substances. Response to potential bioterrorist attacks should be incorporated into the training and drills for hospital staff.

Although the risk of a terrorist attack is low in most Canadian communities, disasters, such as flood, fire, or violence, can strike without warning. Consider the effects of the forest fires that ravaged British Columbia in the summer of 2003. Most communities see hospitals as a critical resource for medical management of any external disaster. Links with other health facilities and community emergency resources are essential if a hospital is to respond efficiently. Every staff member must have a role and be prepared to perform it efficiently. You may be asked to assist in organizing patient evacuation, triaging clients, recording events, or managing the communication centre. You may be on a reserve list to be called in if such a disaster occurs. You may be calling others in should the need arise. You can prepare to do your share in the event of a disaster by knowing your role, attending in-service seminars, and participating in any mock disaster drills.

Security and Emergency Codes

Even without terrorist attacks or community-wide disasters, hospitals by their nature are subject to a daily risk of smaller-scale emergencies. All hospitals use a set of "universal codes" to alert staff to a variety of emergencies. The codes in Table 14.1 are those recommended by the Ontario Hospital Association; other provinces and territories may use different codes, although these are fairly standard. Be sure to become familiar with the emergency code system in any hospital you may work in.

It may be your responsibility to give the emergency signal.

- Know the protocol. Know your role.
- Stay calm; getting upset will only impede your ability to respond.
- Get all the information needed (including the location of the emergency), and make sure it is accurate.
- Promptly notify the appropriate persons.

Table 14.1 Universal Emergency Codes (Ontario and BC)

Code	Emergency
Red	Fire
White	Violent/aggressive patient or physical danger
Green	Evacuation
Orange	External disaster/lockdown, limited access
Brown	Hazardous chemical spill
Blue	Cardiac arrest/adult medical emergency
Pink	Pediatric cardiac arrest or medical emergency
Yellow	Missing patient
Black	Bomb threat/suspicious object
Grey	Critical infrastructure failure/combative person

In many hospitals, you would notify switchboard or the central communications operator. For example, in the event of a cardiac arrest, you may be required to dial switchboard and say, "Code blue in room 342, west three south."

Missing Patients

Sometimes, a patient will go missing—most often a confused or disoriented client. Such a patient is at risk, particularly if she requires urgent or continuous medical care. There are also times when patients will simply walk out for personal reasons, for example, if they are dissatisfied with the medical care they are receiving (or not receiving). As soon as you hear that a patient seems to be missing, initiate a search. If you learn that the patient has left the unit, announce the appropriate code to notify staff. Internal guidelines will spell out how staff are given further information, such as a description of the client. Security will participate in the search inside the hospital and on hospital grounds. If the patient cannot be located promptly, the police will be notified to assist with a broader search.

If a patient threatens to walk out of the hospital, try to locate a nurse or physician to reason with him. If the patient is upset enough to try leaving, there may be no reasoning. If he refuses to wait or to discuss his concerns, ask him to sign a waiver stating that he has left the hospital without permission of the provider and assumes full responsibility for his own health status. Some will sign, and some will refuse. If he refuses, note down the fact and the time of departure.

Identification Tags

Most facilities require all personnel to wear photo ID tags. If someone you do not know comes to your unit without proper identification, introduce yourself, ask if you can help, and ask for his name and professional designation. For all you know, he may be the hospital's chief of staff—but err on the side of caution. If the person seems suspicious, aggressive, or argumentative or refuses to identify himself, get help. Do not confront anyone alone if you feel the situation is potentially volatile or dangerous.

Secure Units

Some areas may be designated secure units. The psychiatric unit may be one and the maternal–child unit another. Just how secure these units are and what type of security they have may vary. Often, they have a camera to show anyone who is approaching. Some units may be locked, and designated staff will have keys. There will be a bell or signal at the door, which the approaching individual will activate. It may be your responsibility to open the door. If you do not recognize the person, ask for identification and the purpose for visiting the unit. There may be individuals who are not welcome in the unit. For example, a new mother may have told staff that she does not want to see her estranged partner. Follow agency protocol when handling such situations. Many units now apply an electronic band to the baby that will sound an alarm if that child is brought close to an exit. See Chapter 15 for more details about newborn security. Intensive care units, although not usually designated secure, will also have restrictions on who may visit and when. Visitors are often required to ring a bell; a nurse or the clinical secretary will answer and determine whether it is in the client's interest to have a visitor at that moment.

SUMMARY

1. Working in a hospital is challenging, at times stressful, but rewarding. To function competently as a clinical secretary, you must have effective organizational, communication, and computer skills and be able to interact adaptively with a wide range of patients and professionals.

2. Health-care facilities include general (primarily acute-care) hospitals, convalescent hospitals, chronic care facilities, nursing homes, rehabilitation hospitals, psychiatric hospitals, and drug addiction/alcohol treatment centres. Accreditation, while not mandatory, enhances status and funding opportunities. Preparing for accreditation is a hectic process.

3. Hospitals are managed by a board of directors, in most cases, elected, and by a salaried CEO. Most hospitals are in partnerships with a central management. Nursing staff include registered nurses, registered practical nurses, and, sometimes, personal support workers. The clinical secretary often reports to the clinical resource nurse (or charge nurse) and ultimately to a clinical leader or unit manager.

4. Almost all departments are interdependent in some manner. Patient-care units, which house the clients, are central. They are usually specialized, in that care is rendered to patients with similar problems—for example, medical, surgical, obstetrical, or pediatric. Other departments provide administrative, technical, diagnostic, and other types of support.

5. Hospital restructuring has included rationalizing services, discharging patients earlier, and replacing acute care with chronic care and "step-down" beds. There is a concerted effort across Canada to develop strategies to enable older Canadians (and others) with multiple and chronic health problems to live at home for as long as possible.

6. As clinical secretary, you will have clerical responsibilities (such as maintaining charts and schedules, ordering supplies, and transcribing orders) and communication responsibilities (such as answering the telephone and keeping co-workers informed). You will coordinate the unit's administrative functions and liaise with other departments. Never disregard the boundaries that define your scope of practice. If a patient needs care, find a nurse.

7. In terms of choosing the work area best suited to you, try to find the department that suits your skills and personality. If you like a fast pace and cope well under pressure, you may be happy working in the Emergency Department; if you find that too stressful but enjoy detail, you may prefer Health Information Services.

8. Hospitals are becoming increasingly computerized, although some hospitals still keep charts and orders manually. You can become the computer expert for your unit. Embrace new technology; don't drag your heels.

9. Keep health information confidential. Never allow an unauthorized person access to patient charts. Never reveal information on the telephone or in person without authorization.

10. Become familiar with your facility's security policies and emergency procedures. Learn the universal codes (or those used in your facility). Do not hesitate to ask for identification if someone you do not know is seeking access to a closed area or to patient records. Most hospitals require photo ID tags. Some units are "secure" and require that visitors and staff identify themselves before entering.

Key Terms

Review Questions

1. Differentiate between an acute-care or general hospital and a nursing home.
2. What is meant by a partnership agreement among hospitals?
3. What are the implications of hospital restructuring in Canada for health office professionals?
4. List the clerical and communication duties of the clinical secretary.
5. What is meant by the phrase *scope of practice?*
6. List the various parts of the patient-care unit and their functions.
7. What are a clinical secretary's responsibilities in regard to equipment often kept at the nurses' station?
8. Identify three actions you could take to keep electronic charts confidential.
9. What would you do if a patient threatened to leave the hospital without permission?
10. What would you do if a patient had a cardiac arrest?

Application Exercises

1. Using the internet, research the job description of the registered nurse, the registered practical nurse, and the personal support worker. List specific activities that each is qualified to carry out. Interview a family member or friend and ask him what he thinks these professionals do. Interview someone in one of these professions. Compare their answers with those other students have collected and with the internet job descriptions.
2. Interview a clinical secretary (or ward clerk). Ask her to describe her responsibilities. Compare them with those discussed in this chapter.
3. Research the community resources in your community that are available to provide support and services to discharged patients requiring home care. Include long-term facilities, admission policies, and the approximate wait time for a bed.
4. With another student, create a set of guidelines for maintaining confidentiality of electronic medical information on a patient-care unit. Draw on research from your school or municipal library and/or the internet.
5. With two or three other students, investigate the use of cellphones in hospitals within your region. Include the facilities policies on bringing computers to the hospital, and the implementation of Wi-Fi.

6. With another student, investigate the accreditation process in facilities within your region: what hospitals are accredited, how often the review process is conducted, and the impact on hospital staff—including the clinical secretary—when a review is initiated. This will require interviewing some staff members and/or clinical secretaries to complete.

7. Choose two hospitals in your area. Compare their emergency code systems to each other, as well as to the chart found in this chapter. Detail the implications of and actions required for each.

Websites of Interest

Sample Organizational Charts
http://www.sickkids.ca/AboutSickKids/who-we-are/Organizational-Charts/index.html
www.qch.on.ca/Content/File/QCH%20Organizational%20Chart-%20March%202007.ppt

Hospital Trends in Canada
https://secure.cihi.ca/free_products/Hospital_Trends_in_Canada_e.pdf
This report from the Canadian Institute for Health Information provides a historical series analysis of statistical and financial data on hospitals in Canada.

Accreditation Canada
http://www.accreditation.ca/
Complete information on the accreditation of health-care facilities in Canada

Questions and Answers about Private Hospitals (Alberta)
http://cupe.ca/HealthCarePrivatization/BE4573

Nursing Homes
www.retirementhomes.com/homes/Nursing_Care/Canada/index.html
This site provides links to nursing homes across Canada. Search by name, city, or province.
http://www.nursinghomeratings.ca/nursing-homes/
This site lists nursing homes and also provides ratings.

Chapter 15
Hospital Documents and Procedures

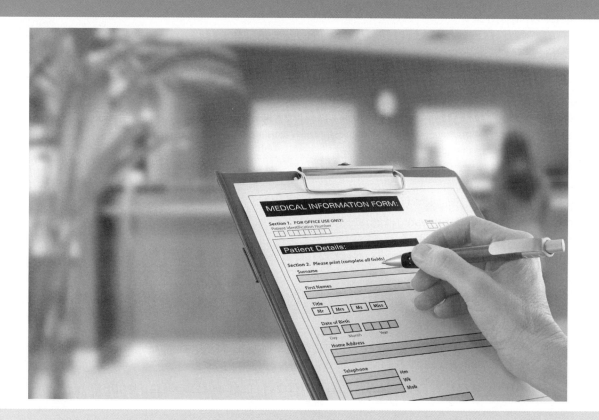

Learning Objectives

On completing this chapter, you will be able to:

1. Discuss the administrative responsibilities related to admitting and discharging a client from hospital.
2. Differentiate among four types of admissions
3. Explain how to admit a patient to hospital
4. Describe how to assemble a medical and surgical chart.
5. Identify the components of a surgical chart
6. Describe the purposes and uses of commonly used chart forms.
7. Discuss a clinical secretary's responsibilities related to preparing a client for surgery.
8. Identify and discuss the purpose of resources commonly kept in patient-care units.

There are several computer applications used in hospitals across Canada. Meditec and MedConnect are two popular ones. Most facilities are computerized to the point where patient registration/admission and the order entry process are electronic. Few facilities are truly paperless, and most, in addition to an electronic chart (**eChart**), still have a binder that contains hard copies of documents that are in the eChart. The binder is referred to as the patient's paper chart (or **pChart**). eCharts hold virtually all of the patient information, with selected documents printed and also kept in the pChart. Although the eChart is efficient and has more advantages, the pChart has some as well—for example, access. When things are busy it is easier to grab the patient's pChart and look up a lab value, for example. In the majority of hospitals, a copy of the patient's admission sheet, the signature sheet, and some lab reports are kept as hard copies. Few hospitals (at this point) have electronic doctors' orders (discussed later). Whatever system you are introduced to, you will use the patient registration and order entry modules frequently. Through the process of order entry you will interface with almost all of the other components of the eChart. You will have the ability to make changes if you make a mistake or the doctor changes an order. You can update information, modify problem lists and "clean up" the main patient care screen (eKardex or Patient Intervention Screen). The procedures and forms discussed in this chapter will provide you with an overview of document usage, content, and format as well as applications to an environment using a mix of computerized and manual practices. Specific features of the electronic order entry system and eChart will be discussed throughout Chapters 16–21.

Echart an electronic chart

Pchart a paper chart

This chapter assumes you will be working in a primarily computerized environment in an acute care hospital as a clinical secretary. Depending on what department you are working in, you will be handling many of the same documents, but perhaps at different stages.

Note: in Chapters 15–21, the use of the term *patient-care unit* instead of *client-care unit* is used to more accurately reflect the language used in the hospital and other health care facilities. The terms *client* or *client-care unit* are almost nonexistent in the occupational setting. The word "patient" more accurately reflects what these areas and individuals admitted to hospital are called.

ADMISSION PROCEDURES

THE CIRCUMSTANCES UNDER WHICH AN INDIVIDUAL IS ADMITTED TO HOSPITAL effects the admission process, how the person adapts to assuming the role of "patient" and to some degree, his recovery. Facilitating the process in a competent, friendly, and professional manner can ease the person's stress level and help to make the hospital experience more positive.

TYPES OF ADMISSIONS

Routine Admissions

Routine hospital admissions are referred to as planned or elective. The patient knows in advance when he is coming to hospital. This type of admission is relatively easy to deal with. Because there is no special rush, the admission sheet, hospital card or ID stickers, ID wrist band, and sometimes the doctor's orders arrive on the floor with the patient. The patient may have already filled out some forms, often a history; she may also have gone through a pre-admission orientation/plan (PAP) and is therefore, likely to be less anxious. Elective admissions are usually for medical or surgical purposes. Often a patient admitted for surgery will be admitted the morning of the surgery. This is called an ASD, or admit same day. These persons would go to a surgical floor from the recovery room.

Most hospitals have preadmission programs for elective admissions that prepare individuals for their hospital stay. This includes what to expect in terms of procedures, treatments, and care as well as familiarizing individuals with hospital policies and routines.

Emergency Admissions

If an individual presenting in the ER is seriously ill or hurt, chances are they will be admitted to hospital. When the physician decides to admit someone, the clinical secretary in the ER must call Admitting to request an appropriate bed (e.g., medical, surgical, pediatric, or obstetrical). Admitting assigns a bed and calls the appropriate patient-care unit to let them know they are receiving an admission. The clinical secretary on the receiving unit notifies the nurses that they are receiving an admission. Once the patient arrives on the unit, she will assemble the client's chart (electronic or paper). A paper copy of the admission sheet, and hospital card or ID stickers are usually sent with the patient. The patient should have his ID band on. There will likely also be a written set of admission orders completed by the emergentologist, possibly on the ER admission sheet. The ER sheet will outline the reason for the admission, a patient assessment, and any procedures or treatments the patient has received. There may be a separate doctor's order sheet. If there are separate doctor's orders, they have probably been written by a consultant who saw the patient in the ER and will be the most responsible physician (MRP). When the patient arrives on the floor, it is important that you look carefully to see if there are any stat or urgent orders to implement as these are common with ER admissions. Also be alert for any returning test results from procedures that may have been ordered while the patient was still in the ER.

Obstetrical Admissions

Most obstetrical (or parent–child) units admit a woman once she is in established labour. Nurses triage based on the woman's status; she may be admitted, sent home, or kept for a while to see if labour becomes clearly established, at which point she will be admitted. If a woman is in early labour, she may be asked to come back when labour has become more active. The actual admission process is the same as any admission except that additional forms are needed for the chart: for example, labour assessments form delivery record, postpartum assessment sheets, and obstetrical flow sheet. In the computerized environment, an obstetrical care plan will be added to the electronic chart. It will contain fields in the patient intervention screen and care plan for the necessary documentation pertinent to through the labour and delivery and postpartum process. The woman must sign a consent form for delivery (which may cover the necessary use of interventions, such as forceps). If a caesarean section is planned, she may need to sign another form. Often the forms needed for frequent documentation in labour and delivery (L&D) are paper based—even in highly computerized environments.

Admitting the Baby   The baby is considered present for admission after it is born. The clinical secretary on the unit must notify the admitting department to "admit" the baby, providing such information as the baby's name, sex, date/time of delivery, type of delivery, weight, mom's full name, room and bed number, and the name of the baby's doctor. This can be accomplished using the computer or by relaying the information by telephone. Admitting will send up a hospital ID bracelet for the baby, generate an admission sheet and a hospital card, or a matrix for ID stickers.

Security on the Maternal-Child Unit

There are secure units in most hospitals, one of which is maternal-child. Parents must have all aspects of unit security explained to them upon admission (this may have been discussed during a preadmit program, but should still be reviewed.). For the protection of the mother and the baby, most maternal–child units are secure units. This is accomplished by the use of an intercom (and sometimes video) system. Individuals visiting must announce their arrival using an intercom placed outside the unit's locked door. The clinical secretary or nurse answers and, if appropriate, remotely unlocks the door to allow the person in.

Many facilities also apply an electronic band to the baby's ankle for added security against potential abduction. The bracelet has a unique ID number and every exit point in the unit is electronically monitored to detect the bracelet. This bracelet will cause an alarm to sound if the baby is brought outside of the secure unit (sometimes it alarms if the baby is carried too close to an exit). It also alarms if someone tries to remove or tamper with the bracelet (other than a member of the health care team).

Outpatient Admissions

Patients who are *not* admitted to hospital overnight, including day surgery clients, are considered in some facilities to be outpatient admissions. They may be admitted to a Medical Day Unit or a Surgical Day Unit. The patient is issued a hospital card or ID stickers—the same as for a routine admission. The basic information required is similar to that required for an inpatient admission. However, the patient's chart (electronic or paper) will contain only forms related to the treatment, service, or procedure the patient is to receive. Most facilities have an outpatient admission sheet.

Insurance and Type of Accommodation

On admission, you must confirm what type of accommodation the patient has coverage for, or requests. A patient who requests accommodation not covered by private or supplemental insurance (noted on the admission sheet) must sign a form assuming financial responsibility for the cost difference between the requested accommodation and provincial or territorial or private coverage. All provincial and territorial health plans provide standard, or ward, coverage, usually four beds to a room. Suppose Janet lives in Newfoundland and requests a private room. She has no insurance other than the Newfoundland and Labrador health plan. You would ask Janet to sign a statement saying that she will pay the difference between ward accommodation (covered by the province) and private accommodation. Now suppose that Janet has a Blue Cross policy covering semiprivate accommodation. She must then assume financial responsibility for the difference between the semiprivate room and the private room.

- The provincial plan covers standard accommodation.
- Blue Cross pays the difference between semiprivate and standard accommodation.
- Janet pays the difference between semiprivate and private accommodation.

Patients are not responsible for the cost of upgraded accommodation if they were not offered the choice. For example, Jeff has only standard accommodation coverage and is admitted to a semiprivate room because that is the only room available. Jeff is *not* charged for the cost of the semiprivate room. As soon as a standard bed becomes available, Jeff should be offered the choice of moving or paying for the added cost of the room from that point on. If he is not offered the choice, he continues to get the semiprivate room at no charge.

Make the choices clear to the patient. Suppose that when Jeff was admitted, the clinical secretary asked him if he wanted a semiprivate room. If he said yes, he would be responsible for the cost of the semiprivate room even if there were no standard beds available. The ethics of doing this are questionable because he was not given full information. He would probably not realize that if he had said no, he could have had the semiprivate room free of charge until a standard bed became available.

ADMISSION PROCEDURES

An individual being admitted to the hospital will usually first go to the Admitting department (also called Patient Registration) or directly on the patient-care unit if it is the policy of that unit to admit its own patients. The ER, Maternal–Child, and Outpatient units are examples of areas that may handle their own admissions.

The Patient Registration Clerk (Clinical Secretary) would: fill out the person's admission database (called an admission or face sheet), prepare a hospital identification (ID) band, prepare and print two or three sheets of ID labels, and direct the patient to the proper unit where admission will be completed (or send him up with a volunteer).

identification (ID) band a plastic bracelet bearing the client's name and hospital number that can be removed only by cutting.

To admit someone, you would use the patient registration module. Select the patient from a central databank which contains a list of all patients who have ever had an encounter with the hospital; if the patient is new, you will enter the information. Most systems will allow you to search for the patient by name, health card number, or hospital number.

For example, suppose Matthew Smith arrives at your unit. Access the registration module and the central name bank. You could start by entering the patient's last name and perhaps the first initial. This would bring up all clients within that name range.

For example:

Smith, Malachi

Smith, Martha

Smith, Matthew

Smith, Matthew

Smith, Michael

Smith, Moira

Smith, Murray

There are *two* Matthew Smiths. Look at the initials, if any, or date of birth. Then, look at the health numbers of both to see which Matthew Smith's chart you need to access.

Most computer programs *colour code* the status of each client. For example, all active inpatients might be blue; discharged clients, yellow; and outpatients, red. Matthew Smith is an inpatient, and so under this system, his name would be highlighted in blue.

Select the correct "Matthew Smith," and press Enter. You can then begin to create a new chart, or access the patient's current chart, or charts from any previous admissions. Each admission or other hospital encounter would be in the databank with a different account number, but in most cases, the same hospital number will be used.

Completing the Admission/Face Sheet

An admission sheet is completed for all individuals who are admitted to hospital. You can populate the admission sheet with the required demographics obtained from the chart for previously admitted individuals. Validate all information. You may be required to print of a copy of the admission sheet to be sent to the floor with the client. Often a hard copy of this document is kept in the client's chart.

On admission, the patient is assigned a computer-generated medical records number (MRN) that appears on the admission sheet, an ID band, and ID labels or a hospital card. The printed admission sheet, and a printed set of ID labels (or hospital card), go to the floor with the patient. Typically, the admitting department assigns the patient bed, although that is sometimes left to the patient-care unit to do.

It is important to note the patient will have only one MRN (**hospital number**) that remains the same for all admissions. The admission sheet will also contain an account file number that is unique to that patient for *that* admission. This number is used by the Finance Department for billing purposes.

hospital number (also called medical records number or MRN): a unique number assigned to each patient admitted to hospital.

Preparing the ID Band

Use of an ID band on every admission is important for basic patient safety. Some facilities use an ID band that is scanned. The band is imprinted with a bar code containing essential patient information. An emerging technology is radio frequency ID (RFID)—which involves implanting a chip on the patient's ID band. The information contained is more detailed and is read using a transponder.

The band may be imprinted with a bar code that can be scanned or composed of printed information encased in a waterproof sleeve that is applied securely to the patient's wrist as part of the admission process (see Fig. 15.1).

```
West, Lorne R.
343 Roan Ave E
Calgary, Alberta 4V5 2R3
403-434-5444            08/11/48
HO 034868 HC# 9243445434
FP. Dr. H deMarco
MRP. Dr. P. Talbot     11/06/09
```

Figure 15.1 Sample of a computer-generated ID sticker used on hospital documents.

Usually the clinical secretary who is actually admitting the patient applies the appropriate ID bands to the patient's wrist (plus an additional colour-coded band if the patient has allergies). If the patient is not wearing an ID band when he arrives on the floor, or if it comes off at any time, call admitting and have it replaced.

Preparing ID Labels   The majority of hospitals have replaced the plastic "hospital card" with ID labels. ID labels are preprinted with essential patient information. They are printed out on 8 x 11 sheets (several to a sheet) and have adhesive backs enabling them to be easily applied to all patient documents (See Fig. 15.1). In the following chapters, I will refer to ID labels instead of imprints of a hospital card for document ID purposes.

Document Identification

Identifying Patient Documents   ID labels must be affixed to all patient documents. In the event that the patient goes to any other hospital department for tests, treatments, or surgery, an extra supply of these ID labels should be kept in the chart that accompanies the patient.

Sometimes, the nurses may want part of a patient's chart (usually medication administration records) before you have finished adding the ID labels. Either immediately label the specific sheets needed or at least make sure that the patient's name and hospital number are handwritten on any documents before giving them to the nurse. *Never* let anyone enter information on a form that is not labelled. Documents are easily mixed up and could end up on the wrong patient's chart. As well, medications could be given to the wrong person, or tests conducted on someone for whom they are not intended.

ASSEMBLING A CHART

IF YOU USE PAPER CHARTS—OR COMPONENTS OF PAPER CHARTS—IT IS A GOOD idea to assemble some in advance and keep them handy. Even the most highly computerized environments invariably keep a stash of pre-assembled skeleton (paper) charts for use during computer downtimes or for certain components of care. Some facilities have what they call a "down box" which you must keep stocked with forms and requisitions needed to function if and when the computer system is not working.

Most facilities keep active components of the patient's information in a binder that is referred to as the patient's chart. A patient-care unit will have a specific place to keep

HPHA
HURON PERTH HEALTHCARE ALLIANCE

STRATFORD GENERAL HOSPITAL
EMERGENCY DEPARTMENT
46 General Hospital Drive,
Stratford, ON N5A 2Y6
Phone: 519.272.8200 Fax: 519.272.8243

CTAS	Patient Name — H #
	DOB — Age — Gender — Visit #
ARRIVAL MODE	Address
AMB.ARRIVAL TIME	City — Postal Code
REFERRED BY	Phone
HISTORY BY	Health Card # — Attending Physician
RECEPT.DATE	Emergency Contact & Relationship — Emerge Contact #
RECEPT. TIME	Family Physician — WSIB ☐ Employer Name & Address
TRIAGE DATE	
TRIAGE TIME	
TRIAGE RN	
REG. DATE	
WT	

CHIEF COMPLAINT

TRIAGE NOTE

T	P	R	BP /	SpO2

TRIAGE REASSESS NOTES

ALLERGIES

MEDICATIONS
☐ Meds ☐ Pt has meds
☐ See attached list/MRF ☐ Meds Unknown
☐ Please call Pharmacy ____________________

SECONDARY NURSE ASSESSMENT

ROOM	TIME	PRIMARY RN

Appearance: Alert Well Drowsy Ill
Colour: WNL Pale Flushed Cyanotic Jaundiced
Behaviour: WNL Anxious Aggressive Withdrawn
Pain: ___/10 ____________________________

Distress: ___/10 ____________________________

PHx: ____________________________

Safety/Confort: Bed Rails Call Bell Warm Blanket
Medical Directive: ____________________________

DIAGNOSTIC TESTS

Hematology	Order Sets	Urine
☐ CBC	☐ ABD	☐ Urine Preg
☐ TB7R(BUN, CREAT, LYTES, GLUC.)	☐ CARDIAC	☐ Urine Dip
☐ LFTs	☐ OD	☐ Urine R&M
☐ AMY	☐ STROKE	☐ Urine C&S
☐ EKG	☐ TRAUMA	
☐ INR	**Imaging**	
☐ PTT		
☐ BHCG		
☐ TROPONIN		
☐ BC x ____		
☐ Ca++, Albumin		
☐ Mg++, PO4		
☐ ________		
☐ ________		
☐ OLD CHARTS		

ORDERS

Ordered At	Ordered By	Order	Admin'd At	Admin'd By

☐ MD Order Sheet Attached

MD Signature: ____________________________

FORM#ER0004M4 12 10 ISBD1 A

Figure 15.2 ER sheet.

Provided courtesy of Stratford General Hospital.

STRATFORD GENERAL HOSPITAL
EMERGENCY DEPARTMENT
46 General Hospital Drive, Stratford, ON N5A 2Y6
Phone: 519.272.8200 Fax: 519.272.8243

HPHA
HURON PERTH
HEALTHCARE
ALLIANCE

Patient Name						H #	
DOB			Age		Gender	Visit #	
Address							
City					Postal Code		
Phone							
Health Card #					Attending Physician		
Emergency Contact & Relationship					Emerge Contact #		

FLUID BALANCE

INTAKE				OUTPUT				INTERVENTIONS		
Time	Oral	IV		Urine	Stool	Emesis		Time		Initials
Total										

☐ Fluid Balance Record Attached

VITAL SIGNS

Time	Temp	Pulse	RR	BP	SpO$_2$	Initials	Time	Temp	Pulse	RR	BP	SpO$_2$	Initials

☐ Vital Signs Record Attachd

Clinical Notes

Time		Initials

☐ Clinical Notes Attached

DEPARTURE

Care Completed/Left ER Time : ____/____ by: ____/_____ Home LWBS LAMA OR Admitted Transferred
Transferred to: _____ Transfer of Accountability given to: _____
Discharge Vital Signs: T:_____ P:_____ BP:____/____ SpO$_2$:_____ Teaching: _____ Initials:_____
Workload (Date/Time/Shift):_____

Name	Signature	Initials	Name	Signature	Initials

ER0004M12

Figure 15.2 (*Continued*)

charts. It may be a "wheel" or large circular structure (like a lazy Susan) that has slots into which the charts fit, or it may be shelves with narrow slots. The charts are labelled and sequenced according to room. A client patient admitted to room 301, bed 1, would have a chart labelled 301-1. Most charts have a sleeve for identifying information: the patient's room (and bed number if not in a private room), first and last names and initial, and the physician's name. Do not write the patient's diagnosis on the chart label. This would be a breach of confidentiality as anyone going by could read it.

When a patient is admitted, take the appropriate binder, label it, and put the chart forms in their appropriate places in the chart. In some hospitals, the various doctors are assigned colours. If Dr. deMarco has red, any clients admitted under her services would have their names written on a red chart insert, with Dr. deMarco's name underneath. If a patient has more than one doctor, use the MRP's name and label colour. For example, suppose Dr. deMarco admitted Lorne West to 301 with a diagnosis of pneumonia on Sunday. On Monday, Dr. deMarco requested a consultation by Dr. Talbot, an internist. If Dr. Talbot assumes care for Lorne for the duration of his hospital stay, Dr. Talbot would become the MRP, and you would have to redo the label. Some patient-care units put the names of both doctors on the label with the MRP's name first. If two specialists are caring for a client, one still assumes the role of the MRP. Sometimes, you have to find out which one is the MRP. This information is important to record so that nurses know which doctor to contact if there are concerns.

You must be familiar with all components of the chart and know what documents need to be added and when. You will be responsible for creating the chart on admission and disassembling it on discharge. In some facilities, you may also be required to review the chart for completeness before it is sent to Health Information Services.

Old Charts

If a patient is re-admitted to hospital, the doctor may request to see her old charts. Paper charts are retrieved from Health Information Services (often still called Medical Records. Retrieved charts are identified using the patient's name and either the DOB or the MRN. Past electronic charts are part of the newly created electronic chart—usually accessible through the patient intervention screen (or stored separately under "history").

This information can be separated into segments—for example, admission demographics, all previous order sets, flow sheets, medications, and a variety of laboratory and radiology reports.

Framework of a Chart

All charts contain many of the same forms. The reason for a patient's admission determines what other documents are required—for example a medical condition such as diabetes, congestive heart failure, a hip replacement, abdominal surgery, or to have a baby. The medical chart is probably the most basic. Documents in paper charts are usually in a specific order: admission sheet, signature sheet, doctor's orders, vital sign sheet, fluid balance sheet (if used), multidisciplinary notes, lab and diagnostic test results, consultation reports, and progress notes. Surgical charts would have documents relating to the surgery at the back of the chart. The same documents are found in the electronic chart. Depending on the system used, you would either click on an identifier or scroll through the various components.

The Basic Medical Chart

Admission Sheet The admission sheet, as illustrated in Figure 15.3, contains a collection of information gathered from the patient upon admission to hospital. It may also be referred to as a face sheet and is generally the first sheet in the patient's chart. Any patient admitted to hospital, regardless of the length of stay, has an admission sheet. This includes outpatients and clients admitted to the Emergency Department who are treated and released. The patient's general information such as name, gender, address, telephone number, and date of birth, family doctor, next of kin, etc. is found here. Note that the admission record is also used for information collected on discharge.

Admitting and Discharge Diagnosis The admission sheet records the patient's admitting (or provisional) diagnosis—the reason for coming to the hospital. This may differ from the diagnosis with which the patient leaves the hospital. There is usually a

Patient ID # _____ Registration Clerk Initials _____	CONESTOGA GENERAL HOSPITAL MOUNT FOREST ON N5A 2Y6	
Surname: Previous Name:	First Name:	Birth Date: _____ YYYY MM DD
Age: Sex: Marital Status:	Previous Admission Date:	Street Address:
City/Town/Village:	Postal Code:	Tel No. Home: Business:
In case of emergency notify:	Relation:	Tel No. Home: Business:
Health Number:	Other Health Insurance: Information (Semiprivate & Private):	
Company Group Name And Address:	Certificate Number:	Group No.
Attending Physician:	Attending Physician:	Family Doctor:
Admitting Diagnosis:	Surgery/Procedure:	
LOS:	Admitted & surgery same day (ASD): Day Surgery:	Inpatient: DS – Short Stay Unit:
Discharge Diagnosis:	Surgical Ambulatory Care: Accommodation: Ward:	Semiprivate: Private:

Figure 15.3 Admission sheet.

space on the admission sheet for the discharge diagnosis, which may be written in by the physician. For example, suppose a patient was admitted with a **provisional diagnosis** of abdominal pain NYD (not yet diagnosed). After investigation, the doctor determined that the patient had ulcerative colitis, which becomes the patient's definitive or actual diagnosis, and entered this as the discharge diagnosis. Alternatively, consider Clair, who was admitted with a provisional diagnosis of ovarian cyst. After investigation, it was determined she had an ectopic pregnancy. The discharge diagnosis would be ectopic pregnancy.

provisional diagnosis a diagnosis subject to change after an actual diagnosis has been established.

Surgical Procedure   Any surgeries the patient has had in hospital will be listed on the admission sheet upon discharge. If there has been more than one surgery, they would be listed in order of occurrence.

Discharge Information: The date and time of the patient's discharge and the length of stay (LOS) are usually noted on the admission sheet. You or a nurse may be responsible for this. *Ensure* that someone has entered this information before the chart is sent to Health Information Services.

Insurance Information   Private insurance companies cover services not included in provincial or territorial plans. It is important for you to know what type of coverage the patient has, particularly if she requests a room other than standard or ward accommodation.

Religion   This is important information if the patient wants contact with someone of her own faith. When the patient is asked about religion, she is usually also asked if she wishes a clergy visit. If the patient later asks to see a member of the clergy (perhaps when she is in critical condition and not communicating clearly), you can look up the chart and know whom to call.

Next of Kin   The next of kin is the person you would contact in case of an emergency. It is usually a spouse, common-law spouse, parent, or other relative but does not have to be. If you need to contact someone on the patient's behalf for any reason, the next of kin is the person to call. If you need to contact someone to make a decision about the patient's medical care when the patient is unable to do so, you must contact the person who has the power of personal care (the aspect of power of attorney relating to health-care decisions) or who has been legally granted the responsibility to do so. This may not be the person listed as next of kin. Ask if it is the same person. If no one has been granted the power of personal care, the decision would rest with the person's closest relative.

Admission Interview/Assessment Form   In most hospitals, nurses complete an interview assessment with each patient. The form is often in questionnaire format. It includes questions asking about a range of things from the person's nutritional, rest, and activity habits to roles and relationships and how they cope with stress. The nurse will also review current medications and ask again about allergies. The purpose of the interview is to provide the care-givers with a holistic overview of the patient so that care can be individualized and the patient's hospital stay made more comfortable. Another important aspect of the interview is to determine any cultural needs the patient may have. The information may be entered electronically or written. In some facilities the patient is given the questionnaire to complete at which point the nurse will review it with the patient. This form is kept either at the front or the back of the chart.

The Patient Care Plan

In the electronic environment, after the admission sheet is completed, a care plan is patched to the chart. To do this, you would do a look-up under a list headed Plan of Care and pick the appropriate care plan. Once you confirm your selection, the computer will tell you that the care plan is being initialized. The care plan corresponds to the reason for the patient's admission (surgical, medical, or obstetrical, for example). Care plans may be very specific, such as for congestive heart failure or a hip replacement surgery. They contain problem lists that can be modified/edited to suit the specific patient.

The electronic care plan generates the patient data screen as well all the required chart documents that become part of that patient's chart, including the patient enquiry screen. In a manual environment the care plan is called the Kardex and is a separate entity from the chart.

Patient Data/Patient Care Inquiry Screen

The patient data screen is automatically available once the care plan has been added and is where any information specific to that patient is kept. It is a view-only screen (much like an index) and is the body of the patient's computerized chart. The screen is populated by data from a variety of other sources. It has an initial look-up menu from which you can select the required data. This includes information and flow sheets from such selections as admission data, health records reports, multidisciplinary notes, vital signs, fluid balance, laboratory and diagnostic reports, and medications.. The user can view data resources within a designated time frame. For example, Dr. Wong wants to see a patient's lab results, pain control flow sheet, and vital signs for the past 24 hours. The pain control flow sheet would show pain assessment, pain control mechanisms used, and how effective they were (all entered by the nurses based on their related interventions and assessments). The equivalent of the data screen in the paper chart would be the dividers in the chart that organize and separate documents contained within.

The Kardex

Although the Kardex is not part of the chart, in a manual environment you would prepare the Kardex prior to entering orders. Some electronic environments keep a Kardex of sorts as well as the patient intervention screen (which is the electronic Kardex). This is discussed in detail in Chapter 16. As you will see, much of the data that results from entering/processing your orders is either recorded on the Kardex or populates the PI screen.

Signature Sheet   Most facilities keep a signature sheet in each patient's chart, or in the medication (MAR) binder. If it is stored in the chart, it is often found behind the admission sheet and in front of the doctor's orders. To save time, instead of writing out their full name, nurses and other health professionals just initial when they record an intervention. For legal and identification purposes, any health professional rendering care to a patient must first write the date, print then sign their full name, and provide a sample of their initials on that patient's signature sheet. This provides a method of tracking initials, thus identifying who gave medications or rendered treatments or patient care. In the electronic document, a PIN or password identifies who is entering data.

Doctor's Orders   The doctor's orders are usually appear at the front of the chart, and are almost always in paper format. Some hospitals have begun converting to electronic documents, but convincing doctors to accept this has been difficult. A major advantage would be that you would not have to cope with trying to decipher a physician's illegible handwriting. Many facilities do have the capability to scan handwritten orders into the system and affix them to the patient's electronic chart. This eliminates any chance of orders being faxed to the wrong place, and provides a permanent record of all orders. The scanned orders are sent to the pharmacy electronically. Scanned orders also act as a quick reference for the nurses in that they do not have to access the paper chart to find them. Where the scanning option is unavailable, the orders are faxed to the pharmacy and then stored in the front of the patient's paper-based chart.

This electronic option streamlines the communication process between the unit and the pharmacy by use of a built-in message board or "smart" board. For example, the pharmacy may question a medication order (perhaps because it is illegible) or ask the nurses to validate a dose. A nurse can message the pharmacy that they are low on the supply of a drug they need for a patient.

Vital Signs Flow Sheet   Used in manual environments, the vital signs record (Figure 15.4) is a graphic illustration of the patient's vital signs, sometimes along with other information, which may include an assessment of the patient's pain scale, oxygen therapy, weight, and height. Vital signs are assessed at designated intervals that are either according to facility protocol or ordered at specific times by the physician.

Vital signs in the electronic environment are entered into the computer by the health professional (usually the nurse) at the point of assessment using a handheld device or the desktop computer in the nursing station. They are automatically graphed onto a flow sheet.

Multidisciplinary Note/Interdisciplinary Notes   These notes are usually located behind the vital signs flow sheet in the paper chart, and sometimes referred to also as clinical notes. By whatever name, these notes are kept mostly by nurses who make entries, usually every shift or as needed, about the patient's care and progress (see Figure 15.5 on page 485). If they are called "nurses' notes," only nurses (strictly speaking) are allowed to make entries. Other professionals, such as physiotherapists, respiratory therapists, or social workers, may keep their own notes or may use the progress notes (see below). If the sheet is called "multidisciplinary notes," these professionals may also make entries in them. Some hospitals use flow sheets or care maps instead of, or as well as, multidisciplinary notes. These are designed to minimize the need for writing and come preprinted with certain milestones to check off to measure a patient's progress. The flow sheet may be devised for a specific unit or for a patient with a specific diagnosis or who is recovering from a certain type of surgery. The notes must be dated and signed after each entry.

Charting Formats   Charting on these notes may follow a variety of formats. **Charting by exception** means that only essential information is charted and may be narrative in nature. Routine care and activities, such as a bath or ambulation, would likely be ticked off on a flow sheet. **DAR charting** refers to Data, Action, and Response. Data is a summary of what the nurse is entering (e.g., Mr. Purves is complaining of incisional pain). Action is the action the nurse took to address the problem (e.g., Mr. Purves was given Demerol 100 mg IM). Response is how the patient responded to

CONESTOGA GENERAL HOSPITAL   Client Data
VITAL SIGNS RECORD

Pulse –Red . Radial × Apex										Respiration –Blue										
Date																				
Time																				
Blood Pressure Indicate with Systolic V Diastolic Λ	260																			
	240																			
	220																			
	210																			
	190																			
	170																			
	160																			
	140																			
	120																			
	110																			
	100																			
	90																			
	80																			
	70																			
	80																			
	70																			
	60																			
	50																			
	40																			
	30																			
	20																			
	10																			
Temp °C Oral/Axilla																				
Pain Scale 0 = No pain 10 = Severe pain																				
Weight																				

Figure 15.4   Vital signs record.

the action and may be charted when a later assessment is made (e.g., Mr. Purves appears much more comfortable and stated his pain was 3 on a scale of 1 to 10). **SOAP charting** is another commonly used format. S stands for subjective assessments or what the patient says ("I am having terrible pain"). O is for objective assessments or what the examiner sees ("The patient is guarding his right side and moving slowly"). A is the assessment ("The patient has not had Demerol for 4 hours, his pain is incisional in nature and a stated 9 on a scale of 1 to 10"). P is for plan, or what the person assessing the client—in

CONESTOGA GENERAL HOSPITAL		
MULTIDISCIPLINARY PROGRESS NOTES		
N UIRSING NM NUCULAR MEDICINE PAL PALATIVE CARE DI DIAGNOSTIC IMAGING SS SOCIAL SERVICES	SS SOCIAL SERVICES CP CONSULTING PHYSICIAN FP FAMILY DOCTOR OT OCCUPATIONAL THERAPY RT RESPIRATORY SERVICES	NP NURSE PRACTITIONER RT DIETITIAN AND FOOD SERVICES PT PHYSIOTHERAPY PS PHARMACY SERVICES SP LANGUAGE PATHOLOGY
DATE/TIME	**RECORD OF INFORMATION**	**ENSURE EACH ENTRY IS SIGNED**

Figure 15.5 Multidisciplinary progress record.

this case the nurse—plans to do about the problem (e.g., the patient was given 100 mg of Demerol IM).

In the electronic environment, the same charting formats might be used but notes are entered directly in to the computer by the health professional, either by way of a handheld device or a desktop computer.

Progress Notes Progress notes are primarily used by physicians, nurse practitioners, and perhaps physician assistants. Typically they contain documentation of the physician's patient assessment including his general well-being and response to treatment while in hospital. The practitioner usually records progress notes each time she sees the client. There may be more than one physician who records in these notes. Each entry must be dated and signed. In a computerized environment, doctors can add notes electronically from any computer linked to the hospital system or remotely from an off-site location (e.g., her office or home).

Other health professionals who participate in the patient's care may use the progress notes or include their own progress notes and other assessment tools in this part of the chart—for example, a respiratory therapist or a physiotherapist.

Reports Reports of any kind in the electronic environment are prepared and attached to the patient's chart electronically. Some facilities that are electronic also print a copy of the report and keep one in the client's paper based chart. In the manual environment a paper copy is either faxed or couriered to the floor and filed at the back of the patient's chart. Consultation and diagnostic reports must be dictated—either using traditional transcription modalities or voice recognition software. With the latter, the report must be edited by a transcriptionist before it is added to the chart. Otherwise it would be processed/typed by a transcriptionist.

Consultation Reports   A consultation report is generated when one physician asks another physician to assess a patient. For example, an internist may ask a cardiologist to see a patient if the patient is having chest pain. The information contained in the consultation report is a result of the specialist's findings.

Diagnostic Reports   A diagnostic report is a summary of the findings resulting from tests that have been done on the patient (such as X-rays, bone scans, mammograms, or an MRI). Diagnostic reports are almost always produced by a radiologist. Diagnostic images are usually available for online viewing by the physician. A pathology report is the analysis of a tissue sample/biopsy as interpreted by a pathologist and would also be filed with reports.

Laboratory reports (discussed extensively in Chapter 6) are customarily generated by the lab department that processed the test, but each lab handles reports differently. The results of all lab tests, including pathology reports from surgery and biopsies may be sent electronically (Figure 15.6 on page 487) or in paper format. If a paper copy is printed, file it in the appropriate section of the patient's chart. In a computerized environment, reports are attached to the electronic chart. However, you need to check to see that results of lab tests are back. The lab will call the floor if the results are abnormal and need prompt attention and physician notification.

Medication Administration Records   In most facilities, the Medication Administration Records (commonly referred to as MARs) are kept in a separate medication binder located on the medication cart. There may be more than one medication binder on a unit depending on the size of the unit. For example rooms 301–312 may have one binder and one med care while rooms 314–328 have another binder and another med cart.

Any medication given to a patient must be recorded and signed for. Several sheets may be used to record medications. This sheet, as well as the format for each, will vary with every facility. As well, pharmacy-prepared cMARs (computerized MARs) will be different from those used in a manual environment.

A separate MAR is used for *standing* or *routine medications*—those given to a patient regularly. There are usually specific sheets to record *single-dose medications*, *patient-controlled analgesia* (discussed in Chapter 17), and *PRN* medications—those given only when needed. Hypoglycemics and anticoagulants may also be recorded on specifically designed MARs, each allowing for the recording of related lab results (blood sugar for the hypoglycemics, APTT and INR for anticoagulants). Whether this is documented on a separate sheet or not is facility specific.

If medication administration procedures are electronic, the pharmacy prepares the cMAR from the doctor's order (scanned, electronic, or faxed) and sends the cMAR to the patient care unit (usually every 24 hours) just after midnight. They are in single-day format, whereas a manual environment may use a MAR that is designed to be used for several days. See Figure 15.7 on page 488 for an example of a single-day cMAR for scheduled medications. Figure 15.7 on page 488 is an example of a MAR that is used for several days

THE SURGICAL CHART

THE SURGICAL CHART IS PREPARED FOR ANY PATIENT COMING INTO HOSPITAL for an operative procedure or an invasive diagnostic procedure requiring anaesthetic. In the electronic environment, a surgical care plan would be patched to the patient's electronic chart on admission. This care plan would contain electronic copies of the forms

CONESTOGA GENERAL HOSPITAL
SCHEDULED MEDICATION ADMINISTRATION RECORD

From Mon 21April/xx 0700h to Tues 22 April/xx @ 0659h	Sevrene Aubert
Allergies: GENTAMYCIN	23 Capilano Dr
Diagnosis	Vancouver B.C.
	#123432333 Dr. G O'Neal

Medication and Directions

Hours	07 08 09 10 11 12 13 14 15 16 17 18 19 20 21 22	23 24 01 02 03 04 05 06
Psyllium Cap 1 cap po tid Swallow one cap at a time 0800 1400 2200		
Initial		
Metronidazole Tab 250 mg 500 mg (2 tabs) po tid with food 0900 1300 1800		
Initial		
Ramipril Cap 10 mg 1 cap po od (hold if SBP > 110)		
Initial		
Amitriptyline Tab 25 mg take 1 tab Po qhs 2200		
Initial		
Initial		
Initial		

Room # 302 Bed # 2	MAR Checked by BT Page # 1	

Figure 15.6 Scheduled single day MAR.

described below. In the manual environment, the required surgical forms would be added by the clinical secretary. Even in electronic environments, many of the surgical forms are required in paper format. The following forms are the ones that you would most frequently have to add to the patient's chart.

STRATFORD GENERAL HOSPITAL				Client Data						

Check here if more than one page ☐

Scheduled Medication Administration Record

Start/ reorder	Stop date	Medication dose, route, frequency	Hour Due						

Figure 15.7 Multi-day MAR for scheduled medications.

Consent Form A consent form may have been filled out in Admitting, or in advance if the surgery is elective. If a form has not been completed, put the patient's ID label on the form, and fill out as much as you can—usually the type of surgery and the date. This information can be obtained from the doctor's orders or the admission sheet. Give it to the nurse to review with the patient and complete. She must have the patient sign it and sign herself as witness.

Pre-anaesthetic Questionnaire The patient should always fill out and sign this questionnaire before any operation or procedure involving anaesthetic. It typically questions clients about factors that may affect the safety of anaesthetic use, including heart, lung, and kidney disease, blood pressure, diabetes, fluid retention, use of tobacco and alcohol, prior experience with anaesthetics, allergies, and current medications. The nurse should review this form with the client. If there are any dubious answers, the anaesthetist may review the information with the client. The anaesthetist usually visits the patient briefly prior to surgery to review the questionnaire and ensure that the patient's questions related to the anaesthetic have been properly answered. The anaesthetist will often write preoperative orders at that time.

History and Physical Assessment You ensure the patient is fit for surgery and/ or to identify any current risk factors the patient must have a history and physical done

RUN DATE 02/03/09				PAGE 1
RUN TIME 1700H	STAT Y	URGENT	ROUTINE	
USER THOMDOUG				

NAME Joe Black	AGE 87	SEX M	MRP Dr. Brown
HOSP # 434543	UNIT 3S	ROOM 302	UNIT # 1234
DOA 02/01/09	STATUS in-patient		

SPECIMEN # 21243	COLLECTED ON	02/03/09	REQ # 543455
	RECEIVED ON	02/03/09	MRP. Dr. Brown
			FAMILY DR. R Fleming OTHER

TEST ORDERED: PTT
RELATED DATA: CLIENT ON ANTICOAGULANTS: Y   N
                        PLEASE DETAIL   heparin drip

TEST	RESULT	FLAG	REFERENCE RANGE
PTT			
> PTT		> 150	29–40 SECONDS

RESULTS CALLED TO UNIT AND TO DR. BROWN

The APTT therapeutic range for clients receiving unfractinated heparin is 52–83 sec

Critical value when not on therapy is   >   100 s
Critical value when on heparin is   >   150 s
****

Figure 15.8 Electronic lab report (APTT).

prior to surgery—usually within two weeks. The report needs to be on the patient's OR chart. If the assessment has not been done or the report is not on the chart, surgery may be delayed or cancelled. This assessment may have been done by the patient's family doctor in his office or by an intern or resident in the hospital. If you can't find the report, there are two actions you can take: 1) Call the family doctor's office to see if it is there. If so, have them fax a copy to you. 2) If the assessment was done in the hospital, it may be that the report was dictated but not edited or transcribed, and thus is sitting in Medical Records. Call them; if it is there, they can prepare the document and send it to the floor.

Pre-Op Check List   The pre-op check list is an inventory of all the essential tasks that must be complete before the patient goes to the OR. This check list is kept on the front of the chart. Check off and initial checks you have made and/or all the tasks you have completed. If an item is not applicable, do not leave it blank; enter N/A and add your initials. If the item is left blank, it may be assumed that a needed step has been missed (see Figs.15.9a and 15.9b).

Anaesthetic Record   This form is used by the anaesthetist during the surgery, and is usually in paper format. You may be required to add the date, patient's age, height and weight (must be actual and not stated weight), the presence of any allergies, and record any preop

STRATFORD GENERAL HOSPITAL
Stratford, Ontario N5A 2Y6

PRE-OP CHECKLIST

Language Spoken: English ☐ Other _____ Nickname/Preferred Name _____

PRE-OP ASSESSMENT

Surgery: _____

Surgery Date: _____Time: _____

Allergies: _____

Mental Status: (Circle as appropriate) altert, confused, agitated, unconscious, relaxed, apprehensive.

        Other: _____

Any change in health history since pre-admit/admission assessment? ☐ Yes ☐ No

PRELIMINARY PRE-OP PREPARATION

Lab Work	NOT APPLICABLE ON	ON CHART	CALL TO OR
1. CBC			
2. Urinalysis			
3. Electrolytes			
4. HCG			
5. Gr & Reserve Serum			
6. C & T# _____ units			
7. Glucose/BUN/Creatinine			
8. FBS @ _____			
9. E.C.G.			
10. Other _____			

Other Documentation	NOT APPLICABLE ON	ON CHART	CALL TO OR
1. Consent			
2. History/Physical			
3. Medical Consult			
4. Surgical Consult			
5. Anaesthetic Consult			
6. Chest X-Ray/Other _____			
7. Pre-op Prep (Type _____)			
8. Pre-Anaesthetic Questionnaire _____			
9. Addressograph			
10. Face Sheet			
11. Arm Band on Patient			
12. Other _____			

NU-069
1993 08

Figure 15.9a Preoperative checklist.

Huron Perth Healthcare Alliance

IMMEDIATE PRE-OP PREPARATION	NOT APPLICABLE	PRESENT	REMOVED
Contact Lenses/Glasses			
Hearing Aid			
Prosthesis (Type)			
Valuables			
Nail Polish			
Make Up			
Medic Alert Tag			
Dental Work			

Type _____ Locked Up ___ Home ___

Caps ___ Loose ___ Dentures ___
Top ___ Bottom ___

Pre-Op Medication

Given . . . .

Held . . . .

Not Ordered . . . .

Signed Off: Order Sheet . . . .

MAR . . . .

Anaesthetic Record . . . .

NPO		No			Yes	@	_____
Voided		No			Yes	@	_____
Catheterized		No			Yes	@	& am't obtained _____ cc

I.V. Therapy		No			Yes	Type	_____ @ _____ cc/hr
Blood Infusing		No			Yes	@	_____ cc/hr
Oxygen		No			Yes	@	_____ litres/min or _____ %

Doctor Please See/Call _____ @ _____

Recovery Room: Lab Work To Be Done   SPECIFY: _____

To OR via	Surgilift	☐ @ _____ hrs.	Initials _____
	Stretcher	☐ @ _____ hrs.	Initials _____
	Crib	☐ @ _____ hrs.	Initials _____
	Walking	☐ @ _____ hrs.	Initials _____
	Carried by Parents	☐ @ _____ hrs.	Initials _____
	Bed	☐ @ _____ hrs.	Initials _____
Received in OR @	_____		Initials _____

Figure 15.9b Preoperative checklist.

Huron Perth Healthcare Alliance

medication that has been ordered (name of drug and dose). The nurse will add what time it was given and sign after she gives it (see Fig. 15.10).

Fluid Balance Sheet   Some clients will have a post-operative order written for intake and output (I&O). In many cases it is automatically assessed. This means that the nurses must keep track of everything that goes into the client—whether through drinking or by IV—and everything that comes out, including urine, vomitus, and drainage from any tube inserted. (For example, a drainage tube called a hemovac is sometimes inserted into a wound after surgery. This would be emptied every shift and the amount of fluid in the tube noted as output.) Clients getting intravenous solutions (discussed further in Chapters 17 and 19) are almost always put on I&O. For example, a post-operative patient is often put on IV until he is drinking well on his own and voiding without difficulty. Even clients without an IV will have their fluid balance assessed until they are voiding properly post-op. In a manual environment, you would therefore add an intake-and-output record to most post-operative charts. Other patients may be on output only. This means that output (urine and so on) must be recorded, but intake does not need to be. As previously noted, in the electronic environment, nurses would enter in and out totals directly into the patient's chart, The entries are collated and visible in a couple of formats; most commonly viewed would be the flow sheet.

In a manual environment, you may be responsible for adding up the numbers at the end of the shift, or every 24 hours, and recording them as a composite value. In computerized settings, fluid balance information is entered onto the patient's chart, and tracked/tallied electronically. Most systems will generate a flow sheet that graphs the patient's intake and output. This is visually much easier for physicians to follow.

Before the patient goes to the OR, add the following to the patient's chart:

- CMARs, (or MARs) transferred from the CMAR binder. Nurses may have transferred these already, but do not rely on them to do so; check that they are there. The anaesthetist must have those sheets to review the patient's most current medication profile.

- Additional patient ID stickers or the hospital card, depending on how documents are identified. If a card is used, there will be a plastic pocket on the front of the chart or just inside the front cover of the binder to hold the card.

When you must add operative sheets in hard copy format, add the patient's ID sticker to each. In many facilities, these records are added to the front of the chart, ahead of the doctor's orders.

RELATED RESPONSIBILITIES

WHEN A PATIENT IS GOING TO THE OR, YOU MAY BE RESPONSIBLE FOR POSTING AN NPO sign in the patient's room or writing NPO on the board beside the patient's bed (precise procedures will vary). Make sure that Nutritional Services cancels the patient's meal trays until further notice. Usually NPO begins at 2200 the night before, although for a surgery late in the day, it may begin at 0600 or 0800 after a light or fluid breakfast. You would change the patient's dietary status to NPO for the morning of the surgery, and change it again when the patient returns to the unit (to whatever is ordered post-operatively).

Stratford General Hospital
ANAESTHESIA RECORD

Page _____ of _____

NAME		CONSENT	DATE	AGE	WT	ROOM NO.	HOSP. NO.

Kg.

PREMEDICATION (DRUG, DOSE, TIME, EFFECT)   ALLERGIES

Sp O_2 (%)
E_T CO_2 (mm/Hg)
AW Press (cm/H_2O)
Time

C 240 — 240
38 220 — 220 38
36 200 — 200 36
34 180 — 180 34
32 160 — 160 32
30 140 — 140 30
120 — 120
100 — 100
80 — 80
60 — 60
40 — 40
20 — 20

N_2O (L/min.)
O_2 (L/min.)

EVENT

SYMBOL BP ⅄   PULSE ●   TEMP ○   SURGERY START   FINISH

INDUCTION AGENTS   DOSAGE
A.
B.
C.
D.
E.
F.
G.

FLUID SUMMARY (IN)
RL
NS
$^2/_3$ - $^1/_3$
P.C.
OTHER

TOTAL

TECHNIQUES
IV:
POSITION:
CIRCUIT: CIRCLE ☐
BAIN ☐ LAERDAL BAG ☐
EYES: ELBOWS:
VENT: CONTROL ☐ SPONT ☐
TV: cc. RR: /min. PEEP:
MONITORS:
EKG ☐   Spirom ☐
Steth   esoph ☐   Oxim ☐
Precord ☐ $E_T CO_2$ ☐
NIBP ☐ O_2 Anal ☐
Temp ☐   Agent Anal ☐
AW Press ☐   Urin Cath ☐
N. Stim ☐
ArtLine ☐
CVP ☐
PA Cath ☐

REMARKS
PREANAESTH   CHECK ☐   SUCTION ☐   SCAVENGER ☐
OTT _____ mm CUFF _____ cc   Easy ☐   Diff ☐   AE Equal ☐

ACCESSORY EQUIPMENT:
IV Fluid Warmer ☐
Warming Blanket ☐
NG Tube ☐

EST FLUIDS (OUT)
BLOOD: _____
URINE: _____
OTHER: _____

OPERATION: TIMES:
ANAEST W/ PT: INDUCTION: FINISH:

SURGEON	ASS'T	ANAESTHETIST'S SIGNATURE		DATE

PRINTED

NU-111 MAY/95

Figure 15.10 Anaesthesia record.
Huron Perth Healthcare Alliance

Current Orders

When a patient goes to the OR, all existing orders are usually considered void until reordered. Generally, medications are put on *hold* until they are reordered. Note this on the patient's cMAR and the Kardex or PI screen. If the meds are the same, the only thing that you need to change is the reorder date (depending of course, on the type of MARs the facility uses). In the computerized environment, new preprinted cMARs would be sent up from the pharmacy.

Orders for Preoperative Preparation

The doctor may not write preoperative orders until the day before the surgery. (See also Chapter 16.) Process any preoperative orders promptly, especially if some of them involve time-sensitive medications, tests, and assessments such as blood work or an ECG. Some preparations are routine, such as the NPO status. For abdominal surgery, bowel prep may be ordered (laxatives and/or enemas). Whether a bowel cleansing routine is given depends on both the surgeon and the procedure.

Premedication   Sometimes medication is ordered for the client preoperatively. There may be instructions to give one hour "preop." In this case, if the surgery is booked at 9 a.m., for example, you would put the time of administration for 0900 and notify the client's nurse. Alternatively, the doctor may order premedication to be given "on call" prior to surgery. In other words, when the OR calls for the client, or someone comes for the client, the medication is given then. You may be required to write the premedication order on the anaesthetic sheet. (See the top of Figure 15.13 below "name.") It is treated as a one-dose-only order or, in some cases, a stat medication.

Scheduled OR Time

Clients booked for surgery, particularly elective surgery, will have a designated time for the surgery assigned by the OR.

A surgical schedule, or OR list, is sent to the floor outlining the surgeries booked for the following day. Usually, this is a master list sent to all surgical units. Because the list is widely circulated, to ensure confidentiality, the list does not give the client's name; only the floor, room, bed number, procedure, and the time are noted. Some facilities will add the clients' names to the list for specific units. For example, the list 3 West gets will display the names of the clients on that unit going to the OR; the names of clients going to the OR from other floors will not be listed. Review the list, highlight any surgeries that pertain to your unit, and post the list in the designated place, usually a bulletin board. You can then prepare the surgical charts on the basis of this list.

These schedules are usually fairly accurate, but there is no guarantee that surgery will take place exactly as scheduled. Emergency surgery or complications with an operation can cause delays. That is why preoperative orders are written to be given one hour or half an hour before surgery. Either you or the nurse can call the OR to see if they are on schedule. In some hospitals, the policy is to assume the OR is on time unless they call the floor to let you know that they are running late.)

On a day surgery unit, clients are admitted on the day of the surgery, usually one to two hours before they are booked for the OR. You would still have an OR list, but unless the client's addressograph card is sent to the unit in advance as part of a **pre-admission**

pre-admission   a process wherein clients who are booked for surgery receive preoperative and postoperative teaching and fill in documents ahead of time.

process, you would have no opportunity to stamp and organize the chart ahead of time. You must prepare it when the client is admitted.

Related Responsibilities

Valuables   Prior to surgery, the nurses will often collect the patient's valuables, such as a wedding ring or a small amount of money, and put them in a sealed envelope to be kept in a locked cupboard in the nurses' station. You may be asked (prior to surgery) to add the patient's ID sticker to the envelope. The nurse and the patient often sign over the sealed envelope. The envelope is recorded in the nurses' notes. After the surgery, nurses should return the valuables. It is helpful to mention this to the nurse as an extra check. For example, you could ask her if she would like you to return the valuables.

Post-op Bed   The patient is usually brought to the OR on a stretcher. Occasionally, the OR will want to transfer the patient directly to his own bed from the OR table, in which case the prepared bed must be brought to the OR. The nurses make what they call a "post-op bed," raised to the height of the gurney and with the linen arranged in a particular way to ease the transfer. The nurses will also set up the room with such things as an IV pole, K-basin, and oxygen. If the OR calls for the bed to be brought to the OR, make sure it is done promptly.

The Patient's Family   Surgery is a trying time for the patient's significant other, family, and friends. Often, they are at a loss as to where to wait, how long to wait, and how to find out about their loved one. You may be their primary contact and source of information. Some facilities provide family member with a pager that allows them to leave for coffee or a bite to eat, or to engage in other activities. When the patient returns to the floor and is ready to be seen, you would page the the family. Otherwise, all facilities provide lounges where family members can wait.

Generally, surgeons tell their patients the anticipated length of the surgery. Still, family members get worried and restless if they feel that the process is taking too long. Delays in the start time of the surgery, unforeseen complications, and time in the recovery room can add to the wait time. You can call the OR or the recovery room to get information on the status of the patient, and a timeline as to when he is expected back on the floor. In some cases, a family member will be given permission to go into the recovery room briefly.

Confidentiality, Security, and Patients' Charts

Even professionals should be looking only at the charts of their own patients. If a physiotherapist or even a doctor comes in and proceeds to look at the chart of a patient she is not taking care of, that is considered unauthorized access unless the patient has given permission. Though you may find it difficult to challenge a doctor, you must question anyone who seems to be seeking unauthorized access. You could approach the person and say something like "I see you are viewing Mrs. Smith's information. Dr. Morgan was in just a few minutes ago. Is there something I can help you with?" The person will usually either explain or stop what he is doing.

Keeping track of actual charts (as opposed to the electronic version) can be difficult in a busy hospital. When a patient is required to leave the floor for a test or an assessment, the chart usually goes with the client. Sometimes, nurses and other health professionals completing assessments will take the charts into a conference room. Doctors may take a chart with them to the patient's room and leave it there unintentionally. Every time the chart leaves the floor, keep a written record of where it has gone: for example, to Diagnostic Imaging. (Review the outguiding systems discussed in Chapter 13.) Check to make sure that the chart comes back when the patient returns to the floor or that the doctor or nurse has returned the chart to its slot. Put charts that are left lying around back in their proper places.

DISCHARGE AND TRANSFER PROCEDURES

Transfers

Sometimes, clients are transferred from one unit to another *within* the facility, usually on a doctor's order, either for medical reasons, such as to receive surgery that the original unit cannot offer, or to provide appropriate accommodation. Remove the chart from the patient's binder (but do not disassemble it), and send it with the patient to the new unit. Make sure all the patient's belongings, medications, hospital card, and MARs go with him. The term *transfer* is sometimes mistakenly used when a patient is being discharged to another facility. For example, a nurse may tell you, "Mrs. Bastone is being transferred from Calgary General to Happy Meadows Nursing Home by ambulance." In actual fact, Mrs. Bastone was admitted for dehydration, was treated, and is now being discharged back to her nursing home residence.

Discharges

discharge any release from a health-care facility by doctor's orders.

transfer the act of moving a patient from one place to another within the same health-care facility.

The term **discharge** applies to any patient who is permanently leaving the hospital, whether for home, a nursing home or retirement home, or to another health-care facility. This is different from a transfer. A **transfer** occurs only when a patient is moved from one place to another within the *same* health-care facility.

Ideally, plans for the patient's discharge begin when the patient is admitted. The length of stay is estimated and the potential needs of the client upon discharge are addressed. Wherever possible, preliminary plans for discharge begin upon a patient's admission.

A patient must have a written doctor's order to be discharged. These orders may be written on the day of discharge or in advance. Often, the physician will come in to do rounds in the morning, decide which patients can go home that day, and write the orders. A discharge order may also be obtained by telephone, but the nurse taking the order must write it on the doctor's orders sheet and sign and date it. The usual discharge time is around 11 a.m. In most jurisdictions, the provincial or territorial plan is charged for another day of hospital stay if the patient is not discharged by noon.

Most health-care facilities will have a discharge protocol detailing what your responsibilities are. Discharging a patient requires teamwork. Doing this efficiently and in a timely manner contributes to effective bed management. Here are some of your responsibilities.

- Confirm that there is a written discharge for the patient.
- Check immediately with the patient about when she expects to go home, and, if necessary, advise the patient of the hospital's policies. The sooner this is done, the better. The patient can make plans, and you can activate discharge procedures in a timely manner. The patient may ask you to call someone to come and get them. If the patient requires an ambulance or the use of medical transport services, plan this well in advance and write down the time they expect to arrive. There will be a protocol to follow for this.

- Assemble any routine discharge information for the patient. This may include follow-up medical appointments, a list of current medications, and discharge teaching material. You should also check to see whether the patient has any medications or valuables in safekeeping; if so, remind the nurses to return them.

- Notify Nutritional Services. In a computerized environment, as soon as the patient's discharge order is processed, Nutritional Services receives notification of the discharge and will automatically cancel the patient's dietary orders. Otherwise, call Nutritional Services as soon as a discharge order is confirmed. If a client is unable to leave before noon, you can have his lunch tray delivered to the floor. If the patient is able to vacate his bed, he can have his lunch sitting in a chair, or in the lounge. If a tray for a discharged patient does come to the floor, the usual policy is to send it back to the kitchen. The nurses may use items on the tray for other patients—for example, a piece of bread, or a cup of coffee. They may even store a sandwich in the unit refrigerator in case someone gets hungry and wants a snack. Under no circumstances should staff members help themselves to the tray. Staff have been reprimanded and even fired for doing this.

- Physical Resources/Housekeeping. A **terminal cleaning** of the bed and other furniture used by the patient is done upon discharge. Items are thoroughly cleaned with a disinfectant solution. For certain rooms (e.g., isolation) the cleaning protocol may be specifically designed. Be sure that housekeeping staff are immediately aware of pending and actual discharges so they can plan their schedules. Although Physical Resources is notified when a discharge is entered into the computer, verbally communicating with the housekeeping staff expedites the process. There will be housekeeping staff assigned to your floor—and they usually check frequently for discharge information. You may want to keep an up-to-date list of discharges on the counter of the nurses' station as a resource for the housekeeping staff.

terminal cleaning the bed and other furniture used by the patient are thoroughly cleaned with a disinfectant solution. For certain isolated rooms, the protocol may be specifically designed.

The Chart and Other Documents

When a patient is discharged, all documents in the paper chart must be dealt with according to facility policies.

- Remove the components of the chart from the binder, and place them in a specific order according to hospital protocol.

- In most hospitals you are required to remove the MAR from the medication binder and add it to the disassembled chart.

- Check that the nurses have completed and signed a discharge summary and initialled all medications they have given on the MAR.

- Make sure the time of discharge has been added to the admission sheet.

- When the client patient has left and all charting is completed, send the chart to Health Information Services. Electronic charts are also filed or stored in Health Information Services, and you must do a similar check for completeness.

- There is a space on the admission sheet, usually marked LOS, for length of stay. You would enter the number of hospital days in that area or field.

- The patient's discharge diagnosis and any surgical procedures are also listed on the admission sheet. Often, the doctor will fill these areas in when he signs the discharge order. If you are not allowed to do this, ask the nurses to complete it. The information is usually on the patient's progress notes. You may be asked to fax the admission sheet and any prescriptions (or the current transfer medication list if there is one) to the family doctor. This contributes to continuity of care by keeping the family doctor informed of where the patient has gone and what medications the patient has been taking.

Unauthorized Departures

If a patient insists on leaving the hospital without a physician's order, ask her to sign a release form stating that she is leaving without permission. This action ensures that she is assuming responsibility for her own health. This is type of departure is referred to as an **AMA** or leaving against medical advice. A patient who insists on leaving is often upset or angry and may refuse to sign the form. Ask a nurse to deal with the situation. If the nurse is not readily available be polite, and try to keep the patient calm. Often giving them undivided attention and just listening to them helps. If the patient leaves before the nurse arrives, you may be asked to chart what occurred. Be clear and concise. Quote directly what you can remember of the conversation. Likewise, the nurses will make the appropriate documentation on the patient's chart. Notify the doctor as soon as possible.

AMA acronym means "against medical advice." This refers to a patient discharging himself from hospital without the physician's approval.

Deaths

When a patient dies, a doctor—or sometimes a nurse—confirms that the patient is deceased. A death certificate must be filled out and signed by a doctor. You man be asked to call the morgue when the body is ready to be removed from the floor. You will need to make sure the death certificate and any other necessary documentation are completed. There may be another form with patient information on it that goes to the morgue with the body. The death certificate itself is placed in an internal envelope and is sent to registration. You may also be asked to contact the coroner as some jurisdictions carry out periodic reviews of hospital deaths.

If you think grieving family members need privacy, direct them to the hospital chapel, if you have one, or to an empty conference or meeting room. Some facilities also post an identifier on the patient's door—such as a butterfly. This indicates that there has been a death and staff know not to randomly enter (e.g., dietary services, housekeeping). In the event of the death of a baby, the mother may be moved off the parent–child unit.

OTHER STANDARD FILES AND RESOURCES
Tracking Controlled Medications

In some facilities, controlled medications may still be tracked manually. When a nurse gives a controlled substance to a patient (morphine, for example), she must record the patient's name, room number, the time, dose, and route it was given either manually or electronically. In manual settings, this information may be recorded in what is called a narcotics control book. Each medication would have its own sheet. Controlled medications are counted at specified intervals to ensure that they have been properly dispensed and that none are missing.

The majority of hospitals now use barcode-enabled solutions that have the capability to receive medication orders, sort, and automatically distribute the medications. Doses are individualized for each patient. Narcotics and other controlled drugs are also dispensed and tracked by the system—thus the need for a narcotic book has been eliminated. Controlled drugs are still counted at regular intervals—for example, weekly. Nurses must scan their index finger and/or enter a password in order to access narcotics (or even the patient's routine medications)

Requisitions

A requisition is simply an order form. Chapter 6 discussed requisitions for laboratory and diagnostic tests. They are most often computer based, but some circumstances warrant the requisition in paper format, thus a supply of various requisitions is kept on the unit. You must add the patient's ID sticker to all paper requisitions.

Community Agency Forms

For many patients, discharge planning involves support from a community agency. Agencies require referral and assessment forms before setting up support. In a paper system, file the blank forms alphabetically by agency. In a computerized environment, the forms are available online.

Teaching Material

Many patient-care units keep preprinted health teaching information of various types. These can also be downloaded from the hospital intranet. These may be given to the client during the hospital stay or upon discharge. An example of this would be postoperative self-care following a hip replacement or physiotherapy instructions.

Lab Book

Some clinical secretaries keep a book to record lab results that are telephoned to the unit. The information must be complete: patient's full name, room number, bed number, doctor, and the lab results. If you are receiving telephoned lab results, also record the name of the person from whom you took the results. *Remember to read back the results for accuracy.* Initial or sign any results you record. It is a good idea to record the time you reported the results and to whom. This information will be useful of there is a question of whether you actually did report the lab results to someone or not. In computerized environments results (including stat or urgent ones) are sent electronically—and may be faxed as well. The lab may phone to say that stat results have been dispatched.

Daily Assignment Schedule

Every facility will have its own method of posting staff assignment schedules. It may be completed on the computer and printed off, available on the desktop, or written on a white board in the nurses' station. Staff assignments include which nurses are looking after which patients, assigned lunch and coffee breaks, and any other specific duties assigned to staff members. (e.g., one nurse may be responsible for giving all the medications and/or doing all the treatments).

If a nurse calls in sick, it may be your responsibility to find a replacement from a staffing list. Be sure to follow proper protocol when calling the nurses. Contacting someone to come in when another nurse is "next" on the list and should have been offered the opportunity can cause problems.

Transportation Services Records

You must also keep a list of transportation services for patients who require assistance moving to another facility. It could be a patient going somewhere upon discharge from the hospital, or a patient being sent to another facility for a test. In some jurisdictions, anyone being transported between facilities requires a special transportation tracking number that is used for tracking purposes. In some jurisdictions, all patients who are transferred to other facilities or discharged to other facilities must have an assigned transport number before they are allowed to leave the hospital. It is to track the patient in the case of an infectious disease. As previously noted, tracking patients and their transfers or discharges is usually done electronically using a tracking system that interfaces with the hospital communicating system (e.g., Meditech).

Critical value a test result that so deviates from normal that it causes concern for the patient's immediate well-being.

If the patient has a **critical value**, usually the lab will call the doctor or nurse in care of that patient on the floor. If you receive a call about an abnormal value, notify the physician or the nurse immediately.

Chart Forms for Special Circumstances A number of other forms may be added to a patient's chart for special circumstances. This can be done electronically by adding a new problem to the patient care plan or PI screen—if not already present. Examples include a respiratory therapy record or a special assessment sheet for patients receiving blood. Patients who have had head injuries and/or related surgery will be placed on **head injury routine**—a special set of checks for neurological functioning, including level of consciousness, pupil dilation, limb movement, ability to open eyes, motor response, and verbal response. These checks produce a rating on the *Glasgow Coma Scale*, a widely accepted means of monitoring changes in the level of consciousness. Results will be recorded on a special neurological observation record form. Patients on intravenous for any reason would have an intake-and-output record and flow sheet activated on the PI screen/care plan. This record may be referred to as the fluid balance sheet—electronically mediated, or in hard copy format.

Head injury routine a special assessment for a patient who has had head trauma or surgery, including checks on neurological functioning, such as verbal response and pupil dilation.

THE CLINICAL SECRETARY'S RESPONSIBILITIES WITH SURGERY

Orders Related to Preoperative Patient Preparation

The anaesthetist will usually order any preoperative medication. These drugs include atropine (to reduce the secretion of salivary and bronchial glands), a sedative, a muscle relaxant, and/or an antinauseant. Some physicians also order ranitidine (Zantac) or metoclopramide preoperatively to deal with gastric reflux problems often associated with surgery (particularly when related to the gastrointestinal system). The latter may be ordered to be taken orally with sips of water despite the fact that the client is NPO. For

elective surgery nonemergency, planned surgery, booked in advance.

some surgeries (e.g., gastrointestinal or orthopedic), IV antibiotics may also be ordered preoperatively.

Discharge Order

Departure Times   Sometimes a patient cannot make arrangements to leave by noon. If the nurses think the patient is able to sit and wait in a general area, formally discharge him and vacate his room so that it can become available for a new admission. Find him a place to sit and rest until his ride arrives, and, if appropriate, arrange for him to get his lunch.

new admission   a client recently admitted to hospital.

It is not uncommon for a doctor to tell the patient that he can go home but forget to tell the nurses or to write the order. The patient may make arrangements to be picked up and arrive at the nursing station to say goodbye only to discover that there is no written order. If a patient tells you that he is going home, check the doctor's order; if there is none, let the nurses know. Depending on protocol, you may have to track down the doctor to confirm that she told the patient he could go home and to get her to prepare an order. Technically, the patient must remain in the hospital until a formal order can be received. In practice, I have never seen a situation where the patient actually had to stay for an extended length of time, but delays in discharge do occur as a result. The doctor or the person responsible for the doctor's practice will usually write the order. However, it is important to check because sometimes the doctor may not have actually told the patient he could leave; it may have been the patient's own idea. If you cannot locate the doctor, ask the nurses to deal with the situation.

Sometimes, a doctor writes an order for a new mother to leave but forgets to write the order for the baby. The baby will have her own chart and cannot be discharged until an order is received. Again, try to contact the doctor; if you cannot locate one, ask the nurses to deal with the situation.

Discharge Information and Belongings

Discharge to Another Health-care Facility   If a patient is to be discharged to another health care facility, find out how she will get there. If she requires an ambulance, order it, preferably at least a day in advance. (Usually, you will have advance notice of such discharges.) Be sure that the nurses know what time the ambulance is coming so that they can have the patient ready. Some communities have alternative transfer services for clients who do not need an ambulance. Arrangements for this type of transportation must also be made in advance.

When discharging a patient to another health care facility, you must call in advance to make arrangements. You will need the following information: patient's name, precise destination, time, and any relevant medical history and needs that will impact the patient during transfer; for example, if the patient requires oxygen, or a wheelchair. You must prepare a copy of their current face sheet, doctor's signed prescription(s) if any, current transfer med list from hospital, the patient's latest blood work, ECG reports (if any), recent x-rays, progress notes, history/physicals reports, and the discharge summary completed by the physician. If the patient has a DNR order it is vital that this information is also included in the patient's package—either a copy of the DNR order or completed form. You would also create this package (or components of it) for when a patient is going out for a test or procedure elsewhere. This ensures that the destination facility has any required information.

Once a transfer or discharge is booked, you will receive a transfer number (MTN) back from the transport agency. This number is important as a transfer cannot occur without one. In many facilities, there is computerized access to the transfer company. You may need a unique password to access this.

MTN medical transfer number a number that is assigned to any patient leaving a hospital. It may be a transfer for either a test or medical appointment elsewhere and the patient returns to the same hospital, or a discharge to another health care facility.

Clients must take with them forms regarding their treatment and medications. Fill out basic information, such as the patient's name, and give the forms to the nurses to complete. You may also need to fill out a form for the ambulance. Keep a list of what documents are required.

Nutritional Services

Physical Resources/Housekeeping

Transfers

In some facilities when a patient is transferred within the hospital, the patient keeps the same hospital number but may be assigned a different account number depending on where he is moved within the facility. Some facilities may have a policy that the patient must be actually discharged if moving to another service within the same hospital; for example, if a patient is moving from a medical unit to a mental health unit, the move could be considered a discharge and not a transfer. If a patient is moving from surgery to ICU, it would a transfer, thus the same account number would be used.

Other Standard Files and Resources

Requisitions   In a computerized environment, requisitions are electronic (unless they are ones that must be signed by the physician such as for an MRI). For example, you would send a request for a CBC to the lab electronically where it would be filed in their system until processed. The lab would print out a label for the specimen and send a report electronically. Whether the requisition is paper or electronic, if an appointment is required, the clinical secretary in the lab would book it and notify the patient-care unit. For stat orders, you would enter the order into your system, and call the lab so they can respond appropriately. In this case, the label (say the order is for a blood specimen) may be printed on the unit. The lab technician would retrieve the label when they come to the unit to get the blood. Orders for specimens collected by nurses (such as urine, sputum, or stool) also require requisitions. In computerized facilities, they may be computer generated and printed right in the nursing unit.

Paper-based requisitions, if used, are often in duplicate, and a copy is kept in the chart. When ordering a test or service electronically, some systems automatically note the order and the date results are expected in the lab section of the PI screen.

http://www.ppcdrugs.com/en/feature-osler4.php

Hospital Resources

The Hospital Intranet   The hospital intranet is a web communications system used within a specific facility. It is made up of an array of resources, infrastructure, and software and is password protected. The intranet contains a wide range of features such as web-based and intranet-enabled medical knowledge resources, and hospital-directed staff education documents. It also provides access to a variety of resource manuals such as hospital policies and procedures (also referred to as a standard operational procedures manual), nursing procedures, nutritional and infection control manuals. Files containing teaching information for patients, online forms, order sets and clinical practice guidelines are also stored on the intranet. It can also provide nurses, physicians and pharmacists with access to online and current pharmaceutical resources. Most intranet systems also contain staffing schedules for nurses and physicians as well as physician on-call schedules. A newer method of scheduling nurses is called self-scheduling. The nurse would log onto the appropriate place on the intranet and enter her desired schedule. Internal job postings would also be contained here. For new employees, the intranet may provide them with forms they must complete and access to certain courses they are required to complete prior to their hospital orientation.

Some of resource/procedure manuals will also be kept on the unit in hard copy. Likewise, you will find a CPS (drug manual), Merck Manual (diagnostic reference), and a copy of the Canadian Medical Directory that will be of more help to other professionals, but you should be familiar with their contents.

Hospital Policy Manual A manual outlines facility policies, such as those related to visiting hours, the work environment, and use of electrical equipment.

Nursing Procedure Manual A resource providing nurses with detailed instructions on such procedures as inserting a nasogastric tube, inserting an indwelling Foley catheter, or monitoring a client on head injury routine.

Future Trends

Hospitals across Canada are in the process of becoming computerized, but the level of computerization varies widely, even within communities. The New Westminster Hospital in Vancouver uses computers differently from St. Paul's Hospital in downtown Vancouver, BC, for example. Over the past few years, however, the electronic environment has become the rule rather than the exception. Electronically prepared and signed doctors' orders as well as completely electronic medication administration records are still emerging in many facilities. Still, even large acute care hospitals operate with a variety of paper-based and electronic functions. This mix of computerized and manual environments requires the clinical secretary to have a wide knowledge base. She must know how to prepare all of the forms and documents in a manual environment and be able to adapt to the same procedures in an electronic setting. It is estimated that it will be more than a decade until all hospitals will be equally computerized. As well, it is recognized that a completely paperless environment is not realistic for

hospitals, and there will continue to be some manual components in the administrative aspects of client care.

As effective as computers are, one cannot assume that systems will always be up and running efficiently. During computer down times, hospital units rely on paper documents—from admitting a patient to processing lab work and orders. A parallel system of paper and electronic methodologies thus is necessary.

The Canada Health Infoway is a national organization whose function is to assist provinces and territories to implement a country-wide EHR system that is compatible and sustainable.

More emphasis is being put on risk management in hospitals and related health facilities. Risk management is an integral element of the operational activities of health care facilities for dealing with areas of actual and potential risk. Most hospitals train their staff in five protocol areas: risk awareness, risk identification, assessment, control, and review. Staff are educated initially upon hiring, and through

>

educational in-service programmes. As well, current information is likely to be contained in the hospital intranet.

It is common to have brief daily meetings with all levels of care providers on the floor to discuss patient care, near misses, and incidents. Risk management software and reporting systems are also common in hospitals now, where all staff members must document near misses and incidents in order to improve patient care as well as reduce the probability of litigation. These incidents include such things as patient falls, needle pricks, medication errors, issues related to improperly transcribed orders, and so on. You must be mindful or the protocol in your facility as well as your specific area of employment—and follow the rules.

SUMMARY

1. Most facilities admit a patient electronically either in Patient Registration or on the unit itself. The patient will arrive with a set of printed ID stickers and sometimes a hard copy of his admission data base. As well, he should be wearing an ID band that was applied in Patient Registration. Any patient admitted to the unit who has had a previous admission to the hospital will have an old chart filed electronically or in paper form. These charts should be available on the floor if requested by the physician.

2. If you use paper charts, pre-assemble some when you have time. When a patient is admitted, add the patient's name and the doctor's name on the binder. Also include the room and bed number (unless in a private room). This will ensure the chart is filed back in the appropriate space.

3. If you use electronic charts, start by searching for the patient's name in the patient registration module. You would then add the appropriate care plan to the patient's electronic chart. Some facilities may require you to add a **workload** tracking option to the chart. After this is done, your next step is to begin the order entry process.

4. The care plan added to the chart is determined by the patient's diagnosis—what he has been admitted for. If the patient is for surgery, a surgical care plan is added; if the admission is for medical purposes (for example, congestive heart failure) a medical care plan is added. The care plan contains all the elements of the paper chart such an admission sheet, admission interview/ history form, multidisciplinary notes, progress notes, and a graphic flow sheet. Many hospitals still have the doctor's orders, medication administration records and signature sheets in paper format. Other reports and documents added are determined by the patient's treatments, assessments and care; for example, diagnostic and lab reports and consultation summaries. Many facilities now scan doctor's orders into the chart where they can be electronically accessed by the pharmacy.

5. Components of a medical and surgical chart differ in that a surgical chart typically includes a consent form, pre-operative questionnaire, history and physical assessment, pre-operative checklist, anaesthesia record, and surgical sheets.

6. You will be responsible for downloading and printing out the list of surgeries scheduled on your unit for the next day. This allows you and the nurses to properly prepare for these patients. Some may already be on the unit; others may be admitted to the unit from Recovery. When a patient goes for surgery, the clinical secretary usually posts an NPO notice, cancels meals, and processes putting medication orders on hold.

7. Patients' charts are confidential. Do not allow unauthorized people—even health-care professionals—to view them. Put away charts left lying around. Keep a written record of charts that leave the unit, and check to make sure they come back.

8. A patient must have a doctor's discharge order to leave. Consult with the patient promptly about when he plans to leave. If the patient cannot leave by the hospital's discharge time, arrange for him to wait somewhere quiet so that the room can be prepared for a new admission. Notify Nutritional Services and Housekeeping of discharges. If paper-based, disassemble the patient's chart according to facility protocol, note the discharge time, and send the chart to Health Information Services. Follow the protocol for closing out the electronic chart of a discharged patient. Being efficient and organized when discharging patients will contribute to efficient bed management in the hospital.

9. If a patient is being discharged to another facility, arrange transportation, and ensure that all records are sent with them. When a patient dies, a death certificate must be issued. A form also accompanies the deceased to the morgue. You can then disassemble or electronically file the chart in the normal way. Provide a quiet space for the grieving family. If a patient insists on leaving without a discharge order, try to get her to sign a release form, and inform the doctor as soon as possible.

10. Other documents kept in a patient-care unit include requisition forms, community agency forms, teaching materials, and a number of resource manuals (if not electronic format).

11. Risk management programs are an important element in the operational protocol of all health care facilities. The aim is to improve patient and staff safety as well as to reduce the risk of litigation against the facility and those who work there. Participation of every staff member is essential to ensure high safety standards for all concerned.

Key Terms

critical value 500	**hospital number** 475	**pre-admission** 494
discharge 496	**identification (ID)**	**provisional diagnosis** 481
eChart 471	**band** 474	**terminal cleaning** 497
elective surgery 500	**new admission** 501	**transfer** 496
head injury routine 500	**pChart** 471	

Review Questions

1. What are the responsibilities of a clinical secretary in a patient-care unit when a new admission arrives?

2. Differentiate between an elective and an emergency admission.

3. What special steps are involved in an obstetrical admission?

4. What is the first step in charting for a new admission in an electronic environment as outlined in this book and in a hospital in your community?

5. What types of information can be found on the admission sheet? State the purpose of each.

6. Compare and contrast the forms contained in the medical and surgical charts in a hospital in your community.

7. What general responsibilities does a clinical secretary have when a patient goes to the OR?

8. Differentiate between a transfer and a discharge.

9. What are the clinical secretary's primary responsibilities related to a patient discharge?

10. What is the purpose of a requisition?

11. Identify the steps hospitals in your area take with respect to identifying and controlling VRE, MRSA, and *C. difficile*.

12. Mrs. Jasper comes to the desk. She has been in a standard room with three loud patients. They are up late at night, talk loudly, and have visitors who disturb her. She angrily demands another room or threatens to go home. She is unwilling to pay for alternative accommodation and no other standard room is available. In a small group discuss how you would handle this, and what your alternatives are.

Application Exercises

1. Using documents supplied by your professor, assemble (a) a medical chart and (b) a surgical chart. Describe the purpose of each chart form.

2. Suppose the cost of ward accommodation is $150 per day. The cost of a semiprivate room is $240 per day. The cost of a private room is $320 per day. State the amount of money that Gina would have to pay for the following:

   ■ Three days' accommodation in a semiprivate room if she has no supplemental insurance

   ■ Three days' accommodation in a private room if she has no supplemental insurance

   ■ Three days' accommodation in a private room if she has semi-private coverage through Blue Cross

3. Sheila is a patient in your patient-care unit. She is upset because she feels that she is not getting the care and attention she deserves. After repeated attempts to contact her doctor, Sheila comes to the nursing station dressed, with her belongings, and crying. She says she is leaving. In small groups, discuss strategies to handle this situation. If Sheila insists on leaving, what steps would you take?

4. Karl has been discharged. He tells you that he cannot possibly leave until mid-afternoon, at which time his daughter can come directly from work to pick him up. Discuss how you might handle this situation.

5. In groups of four or five, visit hospitals in your area and interview a clinical secretary/unit coordinator to find out how computerized their unit is. Include what components of the chart (if any) are paper based, what requisitions are used in paper format, and what type of patient care summary they use (Kardex). Summarize your findings, and present them in class. You may choose to have a group visit different areas within one hospital, such as a medical unit, a maternal–child unit, or ICU.

Websites of Interest

www.ofifc.org/oahai/Acrobatfiles/Hospadmis.pdf
This site offers a summary of hospital admission and discharge processes. It is Ontario based but provides generic information applicable for any jurisdiction.

Chapter 16
Order Entry

FIGURE 2. PATIENT MEDICATION LOG

Learning Objectives

On completing this chapter, you will be able to:

1. Identify the tools required for order entry procedures.
2. Realize the importance of accuracy in order transcription.
3. Differentiate between individualized and standard doctor's orders.
4. Identify the categories of information on the Kardex or PI screen.
5. Process doctors' orders in an efficient and timely manner.
6. Apply the principles of order entry in a computerized environment.

doctors' orders   written or oral directions given by a physician to the nursing staff and other health professionals regarding the care, medications, treatment, and laboratory and diagnostic tests a patient is to receive while in hospital

order entry (order dispensation, order processing)   the process of interpreting, recording, and generating the administrative steps required for doctor's orders to be implemented.

When a person is admitted to hospital, a physician will provide directions to the nursing staff about the person's care and activities. Doctors do this by writing **doctors' orders**.

The administrative steps toward putting those orders into action are called **order entry**. You will also hear staff refer to the process as "transcribing" or "processing" the doctor's orders. This process may take place in a patient-care unit, the Emergency Department, or any area of the hospital where doctors or other qualified health professionals—for example, a nurse practitioner—write orders. (Note that although orders are sometimes generically referred to as "doctor's orders," there is a difference, depending on the health professional writing them.) Order entry is largely the responsibility of the clinical secretary and will be one of your most important responsibilities.

Order entry demands absolute accuracy. Recognize your own limitations; if in any doubt, ask for clarification. The same principles apply to manual and computerized order entry. Although most facilities are using computerized order entry, the ability to process orders manually will remain a necessary skill; there will be times when this is necessary, even in the most highly computerized environment.

Accuracy and knowledge of order entry procedures are only the beginning. To enter orders effectively, you will also need a strong theoretical base in almost all areas of diagnosis, disease, care and treatment, and pharmacology. You must be able to prioritize orders, recognize possible errors, and know the times at which these medications should be administered. You must know how to assign stop dates, which medications require frequent lab assessment (e.g., If a patient is on Heparin—you would order a daily (OD) CBC, and aPTT. If the patient is on Warfarin—you would order daily INR), and when received, results must be reported immediately if abnormal. Otherwise the doctor will assess the results herself prior to assessing the related medication orders. Orders involving nutrition and elimination require a general knowledge of various types of diets and how diet relates to diagnostic tests and procedures. For example, a patient having fasting triglyceride and cholesterol levels done in the morning must not have anything to drink after midnight the night before—although sometimes they are allowed to take medications with sips of water. You need to understand the reasons for parenteral therapy, the medication delivery methods, the equipment needed for particular procedures, and where to obtain it. You must know your hospital's policy on how often to change an IV site and tubing. Orders relating to rest and activity require a knowledge of progressive ambulatory procedures. You need to understand the purpose, procedure, and policies related to diagnostic and laboratory tests to ensure proper booking, patient preparation, and documentation.

You must interact effectively with other hospital departments and know the roles of fellow staff members. For example, if you have an order for stat intravenous medication, you would tell the nurse who is responsible for that patient's care. Becoming expert in this important role will take time and experience. However, solid theoretical knowledge will give you an excellent foundation. This knowledge will make you more accountable, able to assume more responsibilities, and increase your scope of practice within your profession.

TOOLS OF THE TRADE

THE INITIAL DOCTOR'S ORDERS, WHETHER HANDWRITTEN OR COMPUTER GENERATED, represent the beginning of the order entry process. In a completely computerized environment, the computer is your main working tool. In partly computerized facilities, you may need other tools, such as the Kardex (patient intervention record), the medication administration record (MAR), and paper requisitions.

Doctors' Orders

Doctors' orders cover such things as

- type of care,
- tests,
- medications,
- level of activity,
- diet, and
- nursing and therapeutic interventions.

Who Writes Orders? Orders are typically written by the most responsible physician (MRP), sometimes referred to as a hospitalist. In many hospitals, family physicians have relinquished admitting privileges. If a family physician feels that a patient needs hospital care, he refers the patient to the appropriate specialist (also called a consultant); if the patient is admitted to hospital, usually the specialist becomes the patient's MRP if that specialist is providing most of that patient's care. The family doctor usually assumes care for the patient again when he or she is discharged from hospital. When family doctors do admit clients to hospital, they may or may not write orders for the client. If they do, and the patient is also under the care of a specialist, they are giving concurrent care.

In some jurisdictions, other health professionals, including nurse practitioners, pharmacists, and dietitians, are allowed to write certain orders, as well as the physician. Nurse practitioners, who work in the hospital setting, work collaboratively with physicians; they assess certain components of the patient's care and write related orders. When signing the order, the person's designation must be clearly noted.

When more than one practitioner is writing orders on one client, there is a chance that duplicate or contradictory orders may be written. For example, an activity order written by one doctor may state the patient is to remain on strict bed rest, while another may state that the patient can have bathroom privileges. Always clarify such discrepancies. Generally, the MRP's orders will be followed. However, before disregarding or overriding any orders, check patient's nurse first. If she doesn't know, then check with the MRP or the physician who wrote them as he may be able to clarify the situation as well. For example, suppose you have a patient who has been under the care of a specialist, but you have a discharge order from the family physician. You might question the validity of that order. But it might turn out that the specialist has verbally discharged the care of the patient back to the family doctor, who can then write the discharge order. Checking with the appropriate doctor will make this clear. When two or more specialists are caring for a client, they may have to get together to coordinate plans.

Doctor's Orders Sheet If doctor's orders are handwritten, they are usually found in the front of the chart, just behind the admission sheet. The colour of the order sheets vary with the hospital. Some are specially designed or coloured (e.g., pink) to signify that the patient has allergies.

Before you process a doctor's order, ensure that the order sheet contains the patient's identifying information. This may be done by using an addressograph imprint or with an ID label. If you are unable to do this, at the very least write patient's first and last name and hospital number on the order form. The order must also be signed by the physician.

If it was a phone order, the nurse must sign it "per" the physician (e.g., Janet Sumpty RN/ Dr. A. Mahood). The doctor must sign the order sheet herself at the earliest opportunity.

Doctors are notorious for poor handwriting. With practice, you will get used to various handwriting styles and be able to decipher most orders. But even an experienced clinical secretary or nurse can be stumped by a really illegible scrawl. Remember that accuracy must be absolute. If you have any doubt, seek clarification. One incorrect letter in the name of a drug or one misplaced decimal in the dosage could result in a serious (potentially fatal) medication error. Ask the nurses for help; if they cannot make out the order either, or if they are not certain, call the physician who wrote it. It is better to deal with a grumpy physician than with an inaccurate order. Not only do many doctors have poor handwriting, they may also have different short forms to represent a particular test they are ordering. If you don't know what the test is, and cannot find the mnemonic in order entry, ask the nurses around your area to see if they interpret the order. They may know the doctor's "short form" habits. If not the nurses, another unit to which the physician admits patients might be able to help. Even the lab might know. Minimize the calls you make to the doctor; on the other hand, if calling the doctor is the only way to clear something up, you may have to call.

Scanned and Faxed Doctor's Order Forms

As soon as a doctor's order is written it is sent to Pharmacy. This can be accomplished in one of two ways: by faxing the order directly to Pharmacy or by scanning the written order into the computer. Once patched to the patient's chart, Pharmacy has access to it and then has a record of all medications and relevant IV solutions (those that contain medications), which they use to dispense medications appropriately to the floor and/or to list the patient's medications on the patient's chart (visible through the patient inquiry module). In many hospitals the pharmacy prepares the medication administration records during hours of operation. This is done every 24 hours. Each 24-hour cycle will reflect new and/or altered orders ordered by the doctor the previous day. When Pharmacy is unavailable to do this, you or the nurse will manually transcribe the orders onto the CMAR. Note that the form shown on page 511 has three sections for orders. The doctor can record three different sets of orders or, if the order is lengthy, simply take as much space as necessary. (Different sets of orders would be made out at different times; the doctor signs off on a set of orders when completed. He cannot add to that set later because it will already have been processed.)

Preprinted or Standard Orders

In some circumstances, physicians use pre-printed doctor's orders, sometimes called *standard orders*. They are primarily used for routine procedures and for preoperative and postoperative orders for common surgeries. The orders on the forms are drafted by the physicians using them. An individual physician may have his own order forms, or a group of surgeons might use a standard order form. You

DUPLICATE DOCTOR'S ORDER FORM

STRATFORD GENERAL HOSPITAL

DETACH DUPLICATE STRIPS AND SEND TO PHARMACY

AGE _____ WT. _____ (kg)

DATE	TIME	PHYSICIANS - PRINTED NAME	SIGNATURE

PLEASE CHECK IF PATIENT
IS A NEW ADMISSION ☐

WT. _____ (kg)

DATE	TIME	PHYSICIANS - PRINTED NAME	SIGNATURE

WT. _____ (kg)

DATE	TIME	PHYSICIANS - PRINTED NAME	SIGNATURE

Figure 16.1 Doctor's order form.

Huron Perth Healthcare Alliance

would add the appropriate standard order form to the patient's chart pre- and postoperatively as indicated. The physician would tick off the orders he wants implemented and date and sign the order sheet. As well, there is additional space for the physician to write client-specific orders. Figure 16.2 on page 513 shows preprinted preoperative (before the surgery) orders for a colon resection. The lab and diagnostic tests appear first, followed by hydration orders, then activity orders, routine preop prep, and diet orders.

Major Surgery   Figure 16.3 on page 514 shows preprinted *postoperative* (after the surgery) orders for major surgery. Note that options are arranged into a few basic groupings based on the patient's typical needs: a choice of analgesics and routes for the immediate postoperative pain; orders for a PCA pump, followed by a less potent analgesic; something for nausea (numerous routes), which is common postoperatively; a laxative or an enema to stimulate the peristaltic action of the bowels following surgery; a diet graduated according to the needs of the client; the option of a catheter into the bladder, in case the patient has problems urinating after the surgery. There is also provision for ordering intravenous therapy to sustain the patient until he can drink adequately and to provide a route for intravenous medication, if needed. In each category, the physician chooses the option he considers most appropriate. There is space allotted for any additional orders the physician might deem necessary.

Pre-admission Orders and Preparation   Pre-admission orders are those completed prior to the patient's admission to hospital. They apply to clients who come in for procedures and are discharged the same day (day surgery) and to clients admitted the morning of their surgery but who will be staying one night or more (admit same-day or ASD clients).

Your role would be to ensure that the orders have been carried out. These orders typically include blood work, urine testing, and perhaps an ECG. A preoperative examination would have to be completed, and the patient may or may not have had a consultation with a specialist. All reports must be on the patient's chart (electronic or paper). As well, the patient may have been asked to carry out certain procedures at home. These may include an enema or a laxative and remaining NPO after a certain time, usually 2200 hours. This is important because an anaesthetic may cause the patient to vomit any food in the stomach and aspirate. Figure 16.4 on page 515 is an example of preprinted day and ASD orders.

Electronic Doctor's Orders   A few hospitals use electronic doctor's orders, as shown in Figure 16.5 on page 516. The physician enters the orders directly into the computer, using a password and a specialized computer-based signature. Although many facilities are preparing to implement electronic doctors orders, physicians write them by hand in the majority of hospitals.

Requisitions

In a noncomputerized environment, you will want to have requisition forms handy while transcribing orders (see Chapters 6 and 15). Paper requisitions are seldom, if ever, used in the computerized environment. Instead, you would select the appropriate laboratory department, enter the type of test, the date and time the test is to be done, the urgency, who will obtain the test, and any necessary clinical information. Figure 16.6 on page 517 illustrates an electronic requisition for an abdominal ultrasound. File or send the request,

CONESTOGA GENERAL HOSPITAL

Diagnosis   **Client ID**

Allergies (IF NONE INDICATE THIS)

PREOPERATIVE DOCTORS ORDERS: COLON RESECTION
Cross out orders not indicated; Check appropriate box for active orders

Lab and Diagnostic Tests
☐ CBC, electrolytes, serum albumin
☐ FBS, HbAlc (if client diabetic)
☐ Cross and Type for 4 units of packed cells
☐ ECG if client over 45 or has pre-existing heart condition
☐ Chest Xray PA & Lateral if patient over 40
☐ Abdominal CT

Hydration

☐ Start IV NS @ 100cc/hr on the morning of surgery.
☐ 5%D.W @ 100cc/hr the morning of surgery
☐ Give 300cc bolus when OR calls for client.

Activity
☐ As previously odered
☐ Other

Preparation
☐ Routine Bowel prep routine 8 hours prior to surgery
☐ Bowel prep hs day before surgery

Nutrition
☐ DAT until bowel prep
☐ FF
☐ CF
☐ NPO 8 hrs prior to surgery

Other
☐ Actual height and weight on Anaesthetic sheet (not stated)

Physician Signature_____   Printed Name _____

Figure 16.2   Preprinted preoperative orders for a colon resection.

CONESTOGA GENERAL HOSPITAL

MAJOR SURGERY: Client ID
ALLERGIES _____ **None** ____
Analgesics
___Acetaminophen 325 (Tylenol, plain) tab 1-2 q 3-4 h prn po max 4 g/day
___Naproxen (Naprosyn) 250 mg po tid with food
___Meperidine (Demerol) ____mg I.M. q ___h prn x ____ post-op days.
___Tylenol #3 tab 1-2 po q 4-6 h prn x _____ post-op days
_____

PCA OPIOD
__**Morphine 2 mg/ml**
__**Hydromorphine 0.4 mg/mL**
__**Fentanyl 25 mcg/mL**
PCA dose: _____mg/mcg (circle one)
PCS dose/Bolus dose: range 0-____mg/mcg (circle one)
Delay Interval: _____minutes
If pain still not controlled, increase PCA dose by ____ mg/mcg increments q1h until pain is controlled or maximum dose specified in PCA dose range is reached.

_____

Antiemetic:
___Dimenhydrinate inj 50 mg/mL 25-50mg (0.5 – 1mL) IV q6h prn (for IV dilute in 50mL IV fluid and give over 30 minutes).
___Dimenhydrinate (Gravol) 50-100 mg I.M. or po. q _____h prn
___Prochlorperazine (Stemetil) 10 mg I.M. q ___h prn if Gravol ineffective
Other: _____
Laxative:
___Magnolax 30 mL po bid 2nd post -op day prn
___Fleet enema 3rd post op day prn
___Other: _____
Lab:
___CBC first post op day
Diet
___if n/g tube present, CF to DAT after removed.
___Transitional diet starting when bowel sounds present.

Catheter: Parenteral Therapy
___Foley ____remove 1st post-op day   2/3 & 1/3 @_____cc/hr
         ____Other   N/S @_____cc /hr
                                         D/C when drinking well
                                         Other _____
If patient unable to void in 6 hrs post surgery or after catheter removal insert Foley. If output *greater* than 350 cc leave catheter in to straight drainage until further notice

Activity
___ ambulate post op night as able
___ ambulate first post op day.
Other
___Family doctor notified

Additional Orders

Physician's Signature_____
Date _____

Figure 16.3   Preprinted postoperative orders for major surgery.

CONESTOGA GENERAL HOSPITAL

PREADMISSION ORDERS: **Client Data**

__ DAY SURGERY
__ ASD

PREADMISSION ORDERS
Detach Part 11 and Send to Pharmacy
OBTAIN CONSENT FOR _____
                              (Name of Procedure)

LABORATORY TESTS   **PREOPERATIVE CONSULTATION REQUIRED**

____Code: A: CBC   CARDIORESPIRATORY SERVICES
____Code B: CBC DIFF, BUN, Creatine   ___Arterial Blood Gases
   Electrolytes, Random Glucose   ___Capillary Blood Gases
____APTT/INR   ___Oximetry ___Spirometry

____Electrolytes (for all patients on diuretics)   ____Abbreviated Pulmonary Function Tests

____Code U = CBC & DIFF, BUN   HOME CARE __ CCAC __ Other
   Creatinine, Electrolytes, Random Glucose   Specify _____
Urinalysis, Urine Culture and Sensitive   _____
                                          _____
____Code Z = No blood work needed   _____
                                          _____
____HCG (required for all gynecological patients   _____
   Under 50 years of age)   _____
                                          _____.
____Urine Culture & Sensitivity
                                          _____Anesthesiologist Consultation
____Group and Reserve Serum
                                          Social Services
____Cross Match & Type for _____Units   Specify:_____
                                          _____
____ECG (Required for all patients age 40 and up)
                                          Other_____
                                          _____
Other Laboratory Tests:

_____
_____
_____.

DIAGNOSTIC IMAGING: **HOSPITAL USE ONLY**
___Chest X-ray
___Other_____   OR Booking_____
                                                        date/time
Other Orders_____   Clinic Appointment:_____
_____.   Date/time

Figure 16.4   Preprinted pre-admission orders for ASD and day surgery.

CONESTOGA GENERAL HOSPITAL

Aurora Systems Ltd

NAME	Bell, James	AGE	87	SEX	M	MRP	Dr. Thompson
HOSP #	434543	UNIT	3S	ROOM	322	UNIT #	1234
DOAdm	02/01/09	STATUS	in-patient				

| E/O | A/O | C/O | Look Up | INSERT DOCTORS ORDERS | ↓ |

AAT
Clear fluids
Pre and post-op routine bowel orders
Fleet now and repeat at 0600
IV D5/NS with KCL 20 meq/L @ 100cc/hr
Metoprolol 25 mg po bid
Felodipine 5 mg po od
Simvastatin 40 mg po od
Gabapentin 100 mg pot id
Trazadone 100 mg po tabs 2 hs
Aoplicone 7.5 mg po qhsprn
Furosemide 80 mg po gid
B12 2 tabs po od

Dr. D. Thompson.   02/02/09

Figure 16.5 Electronic doctor's orders.

which will be received electronically in the appropriate department. When entering requests for lab of diagnostic tests, you will not always need to free text.

The Patient-Care Record

Many orders—especially those related to assessments, treatments and direct patient care—are recorded on a patient data profile screen/document, or on a computerized patient care plan. Numerous hospitals call this the *patient intervention record/screen* (*PI screen*)—described in Chapter 15. In a manual environment, that document is often called a Kardex (the most common proprietary name). Figure 16.7 on page 518 illustrates an example of an electronic PI screen. The status column is activated by the clinical secretary. "A" means that the intervention is active, and "C" indicates the intervention is complete and/or no longer monitored. Note the similarity of the information contained on the electronic form (Figure 16.7) to that on the paper-based patient data summary (Figures 16.8a and 16.8b on pages 519 and 520)—essentially only the format differs.

Patient Inquiry Screen/Patient Care Summary Screen   The patient care inquiry or PCI screen was described in Chapter 15, and partners with the electronic Kardex or PI screen. Remember that this "master" screen will allow you (and any other authorized user) to look up any recent or past patient data that has been put into place. You can view medications the patient has/or is currently on, lab and diagnostic tests ordered and the results. You can find out if blood products ordered are ready for the patient (e.g., whole blood, packed cells, platelets). As well, you will fine X-ray reports, ultrasound summaries, patient history, consultations, and discharge summaries—basically everything concerning that patient.

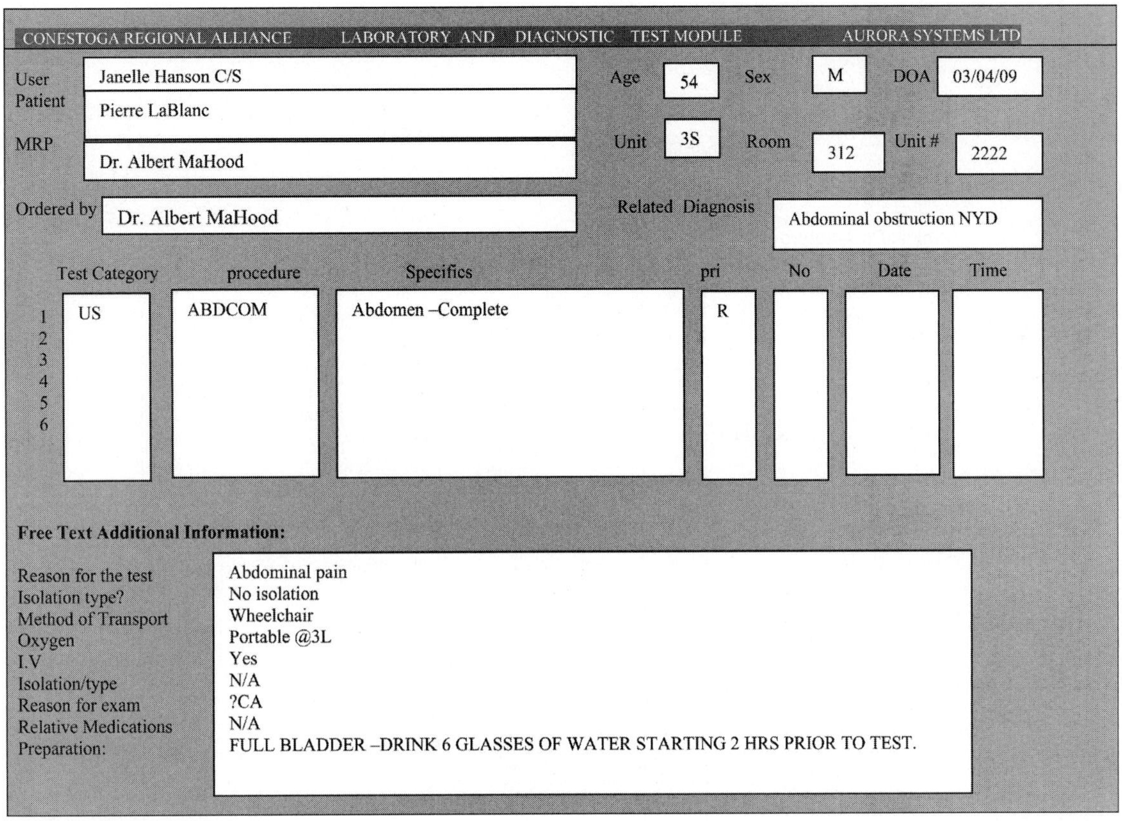

Figure 16.6 Electronic requisition for an abdominal ultrasound.

Many facilities informally call the electronic patient care summary record an "electronic Kardex" or a PI screen interchangeably because it fulfills the same function. The Kardex or PI screen is a centralized source of information that begins with admission and addresses almost every component of the patient's treatment and care while in the hospital. Nurses may print parts of it out at the beginning of their shift and carry it as a guide to treatment. Throughout the following chapters, I will refer to the **Kardex** or **PI screen** and the patient or patient data profile (the latter is what it is called in many hospitals). Keep in mind that your facility may call this summary document by a different name. Many examples in this part of the textbook are illustrated with a Kardex-type format. You will quite likely be using some electronic equivalent; the important thing to note is the *information* captured. Just what is added to the **Kardex** or **PI screen (or electronic health record)** depends on facility guidelines. In electronic environments, the PI screen is usually populated with lists of options for each intervention category. You simply highlight or extract the intervention option the physician has ordered so that the specific order is noted as relevant or active on the PI screen (e.g., bed rest, IV orders, or a dressing change). (Note the "A"—indicating the option is active—under the status column in Figure 16.7.) Computerized systems have vast databases and look-up files from which to choose—ranging from IV solutions and medications to diets. Compare the information contained in Figures 16.8a and 16.8b on pages 519 and 520 with the related document used in a facility in your area.

Kardex commonly used proprietary name for a paper-based patient care document or health record.

patient intervention screen (PI screen) or electronic health record a computer-based client-care document containing the same information as a Kardex. This is an electronic version of a traditional Kardex.

Interventions

Clinical Parameters	Status	Freq
Vital Signs, monitor	A	QS
* ward routine		
I&O, monitor	A	Q4H
Oxygen Saturation, monitor	A	Q8H
* O2 to keep O2S > 92%		
Weight, daily	A	QD
* weight before breakfast		

Treatments	Status	Freq
Oxygen Therapy	A	PRN
* to keep O2S > 92%		
Catheter, foley	A	PRN
Catheter, removal	A	PRN
Catheter, reinsert	A	PRN
Catheter, in&out	A	PRN

Specimens	Status	
Urine, to be obtained	A	
* C&S and R&M		
Sputum, to be obtained	A	
* C&S		
Stool, specimen	C	
* for Occult Blood X 3		

Activity	Status	
Activity, as tolerated	A	
Up, with one assist	C	
Up, with no assist	A	
Shower, independent	A	QD
Hygiene, independent	A	QD
Diet, as at home	A	
* Regular		
Feed, self	A	

Assessments	Status	Freq
Gastrointestinal assess	A	QD
Cardiovascular assess	A	QD
Respiratory assess	A	QD
Physiotherapy assess	A	QD
Occupational Therapy assess	A	QD
Social Work assess	A	once
Nutritional assess	A	once
*poor appetite		
Wound, site 1	A	QD
*left leg ulcer		
Wound, site 2	A	BID
*left heel ulcer		

Medications	Status	Freq
Medications, IV	A	QS
Medications, IM/SC	A	QS
IV Heparin	A	QS
IV Vancomycin	C	

Discharge	Status	
Discharge, home	A	
Discharge, respite care	A	
Discharge, teaching	A	

Patient ____ **Age** ____ **HO Number** ____
Attending MD ____ **Sex** ____ **Start Date** ____
DIAGNOSIS ____ **Room** ____ **Service** ____

Figure 16.7 Example of an electronic patient intervention screen.

Date	TEACHING AND EMOTIONAL SUPPORT	Date	PROCEDURES/TREATMENTS /DIRECT CARE
	□ Routine: □ pr- op □ post-op □ other		□ FP Glucose Times
	□ Extra teaching		**Tubes/drains**
	□ Emotional support : □ routine □ extra (explain below)		□ Hemovac Remove (ed) on
	□ Family conference/teaching		□ Abd Penrose Drain □ Shorten □ Out
	Other		□ Sump Pump
			□ NG (Levine) Tube
	NUTRITION		□ Gomco Suction to low intermittent
	□ NPO		
	□ Diet :		**SAFETY MANAGEMENT**
	Feeding Tube		□ Side rails □ X1 □ X2
	□ Intermittent □ Continuous		□ Call bell
	Solution: □ mealtimes □ HS		□ Night rounds –special consideration
	Other		□ Restraints □ type
	LEVELS FOR ACTIVIES OF DAILY LIVING		Other
	General Assistance Level:		**HYGIENE**
	□ Independent □ Assist X1 □ X2		□ Shower □ Bath
	□ **Toileting:** □ Self Assist X1 □ X2		□ Mouth Care □ Foot Care
	Bath: □ Self □ Assist □ by nurse		Other:
	Diet □ Self □ Assist □ by nurse		
	CLINICAL PARAMETERS		**ELIMINATION –bowel**
	□ No vital signs □ Vital signs □ Temp only BID		□ BR □ Commode □ bedpan only
	□ Q shift □ bid □ *tid* □ *other*		□ Ostomy Care □ Nurse □ Patient
	□ *Print v/s flow sheet q shift*		
	Weight q am ac breakfast : □ qd □ q2d □ Other :		□Enema □ Suppository
	Glasgow Coma Scale □ Yes □ No		
	□ *Print flow sheet q shift*		Other
	Blood Glucose Monitoring □ Yes □ No		**ELIMINATION -Urinary**
	Intake/Output □ Yes □ No		□ Catheter: Insert/Remove
	□ *Print I & O flow sheet q shift*		□ Foley -#
	Lab Values For Regular Monitoring		□ 3-way
	□ Blood sugar □ INR □APTT		□ Suprapubic
	Other		□ Condom cath
	INTRAVENOUS MONITORING (circle solution)		□ Irrigation:
	□ 2/3 & 1/3; □ N/S; □ 5% D/W; □ 0 .45NaCl		□ Strain all urine
	Primary Line Other		**REST AND ACTIVITY**
	1 @ cc/hr		□Turn q2h □ Other
	□ 2/3 & 1/3; □ N/S; □ 5% D/W; □ 0 .45NaCl		□ ROM □ Active □ Passive □ Assist
	Other		□ Skin Care □ decubitus ulcer
	2. @ cc/hr		Rx
	Secondary Line with meds *note times* of med administration		□ pressure mattress □ sheep skin
	1.		Other
	2.		□ **ISOLATION** **Date Started:**
	□ Tubing & site change q 72 hrs. date		Type
			Reason
	□ Dates Change Site: Location		**Date last Hospitalized**
	□ PRN Adaptor –site □ Change Site: Location		**Location:**
	□ **Flush- (minimum once/shift)**		VRE swab + - □ C Difficille + -
	Times:		VRSA swab + - □ MRSA + -
	□ **IV** □ **PRN adaptor d/c** **Date**		□ Infection control notified Date:

NAME   **ROOM #**   **HOSPITAL #**

PROVISIONAL DIAGNOSIS	SECONDARY DIAGNOSIS (other problems)	DISCHARGE DIAGNOSIS
MRP/Hospitalist	FAMILY DOCTOR	NURSE PRACTITIONER

Figure 16.8a   Kardex or patient data profile (page 1).

					Done

CONESTOGA GENERAL HOSPITAL –PATIENT DATA PROFILE

PG 2
ALLERGIES: □ No Allergies

Date	PROCEDURES/DIRECT CARE ORDERS	Date	<u>ROUTINE</u> AND <u>DAILY</u> TESTS		Done
	OXYGENATION		**LAB**		
	□ Yes □ No				
	□ Mask □ N/P				
	Litres-		**DIAGNOSTIC TESTS**		
	□ Oximetry				
	□ Chest Assessment				
	□ Spirometer-				
	□ Aerosol Rx				
	□ Trach cannulae care		**Blood Transfusions ordered/given**		
	□ DB&C □Physio/Nurse		1		
			2		
	SUCTIONING		**3**		
	Type				
	Frequency		**STAT Blood Work & Tests**		
	POST OPERATIVE ASSESSMENTS/CARE				
	Dressing Change/Check				
	Location: Frequency:		**Swabs and Cultures**		
	□ Simple				
	□ Complex:				
	□ Abdominal Assessment:		**CONSULTATIONS (reason/date seen/to be seen)**		
	□ Clip/suture removal □ cast		□ Physician(s)		
	Comments:		□ Pastoral Care		
	□ Pain Management		□ Home Care Liaison Nurse		
	□ CSM (circulation/sensation, movement)		□ Social Worker		
	Other		□ Physio		
	Discharge Planning		□ Dietary		
	□ Destination		□ OT		
	□ Transportation □ Transport #		**Other**		
	Medications		**Level of Nursing Care:**		
	□ Teaching □ Prescription		□ #1nurseX 1 hr		
	□ Ability to fill □ Ability to pay		□ #1nurse X1-4 hr		
	Follow -UP		□ #2 nurseX1h		
	□ Patient aware		□ Constant care □ Private room ordered		
	Notification of Discharge		**Advance Directives**		
	□ Patient □ Caregiver		□ code □ No code		
	□ Family Doctor □ Consultants		□ Details		
	Community Supports		**Organ donation** □ yes □ No		
	□ Home Care □ home care support worker				
	□ Mental Health □ Equipment		**MESSAGES/Other Orders:**		
	□ Oxygen □ Home IV antibiotics				
	□ *Wait-Listed for Facility Date:*				
	Facility 1.				
	2.				
NAME ROOM #		HOSPITAL NUMBER			

Figure 16.8b Kardex or patient data profile (page 2).

The precise *format* of the Kardex will vary not only with the facility but with different services within a facility—variations tailored to meet the unit's need. A postpartum Kardex, for example, contains, in addition to such standard items as diet and medication, information related to breastfeeding and mother–baby interaction, while a surgical

Kardex reports assessment of the patient's incision, pain control, and fluid intake. Some facilities use a set of preprinted patient data profile sheets organized according to room number and kept in a binder as their Kardex. Other facilities keep sheets in a rectangular plastic or metal holder filled with graduated plastic inserts, one for each room and bed number. You will notice that there are variations in the Kardex or patient summary examples used in the following chapters. Most patient-care units that use hard copies of patient summary sheets have two or three Kardexes or binders, each containing information on a designated number of clients, often divided into groups according to rooms. This facilitates access for the nursing staff assigned to specific nursing teams. A team typically cares for a section of patients grouped by room number. For example, rooms 301–312 are assigned to three nurses, and rooms 314–325 are assigned to three other nurses. The ratio of nurses assigned to a group of patients depends on how sick the patients are and how much care they require.

Figures 16.8a and 16.8b show an example of a paper-based Kardex or patient data profile. The rest of this section expands on the categories shown in this figure.

Teaching and Emotional Support

Teaching needs vary with the patient and the situation. It may relate to various areas of self care, or pre- and postoperative expectations. You would automatically check off routine postoperative teaching for all surgery clients. Preop teaching is done to prepare the patient for what to expect postoperatively. This teaching usually includes information on pain control, the importance of early ambulation, deep breathing and coughing exercises to keep the lungs clear, dietary information and so on. If the patient comes in on the morning of the surgery, preop teaching will likely have been done already. When you are admitting the person, it is a good idea to ask the patient if this teaching has occurred. If not, be sure to tell his nurse.

Emotional support is highlighted or noted only if the patient needs extra emotional support. The nursing staff often fills out this area, as they are best able to assess emotional needs. Extra emotional support would be needed, for example, if the patient was facing a limited recovery or a terminal illness; sometimes family tragedy coincides with the person's hospitalization; sometimes the person's coping mechanisms are such that increased emotional support is required in what others consider to be routine situations.

In electronic environments, this will be altered as necessary directly on the computer.

Nutrition

Diet is ordered, at least initially, by the doctor but may change with tests, surgery, and the patient's condition. You are responsible for making routine changes, such as cancelling breakfast or ordering a special diet in preparation for a test. Many facilities mention NPO status under this heading, as well as alternative feeding methods, such as tubes. Often clients who are NPO also have a nasogastric tube connected to a machine called a Gomco suction machine, which may or may not be listed here. In some hospitals, the diet may be ordered or altered by a dietitian (e.g., for a diabetic client).

Activities of Daily Living

Some patient-care summaries list activities of daily living (ADL); some do not. When the heading is present, it calls for a statement about whether the patient needs help with basic activities, such as bathing, eating, and elimination. This may affect the amount of teaching and emotional support the patient requires.

Activity

This is most often ordered by the doctor and reveals the level or type of activity the patient is allowed and/or capable of, and the amount of help the person needs (e.g., activity as tolerated [AAT], complete bed rest [CBR]). A patient weighing 115 kg

(250 pounds) with limited weight-bearing capacity would likely require two nurses to get him up to a chair, whereas the same person who could bear weight may only need one nurse. In both situations, if the person were to walk the length of the hall, two nurses might be advisable until it became apparent the patient was strong enough to manage independently or for one nurse to handle.

Clinical Parameters   Many computerized facilities group anything that has values attached to it under a heading called "Clinical Parameters." This can be confusing, as some of the interventions may also appear in other sections of the patient data profile/Kardex or the PI screen. An example would be a procedure or an intervention that also has a value (e.g., finger-prick glucose or a drain wherein the output is measured). Both of these have values, but also involve nursing intervention and are procedures. Typically included under clinical parameters are vital signs, lab values, parenteral therapy, intake and output, and the patient's height/weight. In Figure 16.8a, the Glasgow Coma Scale is also included. This is a standardized measurement scale used to assess levels of consciousness.

Vital Signs   Vital signs usually include temperature, pulse, respiration, and blood pressure. Most hospital units will have a standard protocol for how often to take vital signs; for example, surgical units take vital signs frequently during the immediate postoperative period, reducing to *q* shift (once every shift) once the patient is stable. The doctor may order more or less frequent assessment. If a patient's condition worsens, the nurses may also decide to take vital signs more often. This would be a nursing order; it would not be written on the doctor's orders but would be entered on the patient care summary record/PI screen. Sometimes the patient's temperature is taken only once or twice a day despite the fact that the pulse, respirations, and BP are done more frequently.

Intake and Output   Intake and output are automatically activated for any patient on parenteral therapy, but a doctor may order it for others as well. The nurses enter the values directly into the computer. The values are then automatically tallied and/or graphed onto a computerized flow sheet. If the environment is manual, the nurses usually take care of entering the values, which are typically totalled every eight hours even if the nurses are doing 12-hour shifts. This is to facilitate closer monitoring of the person's intake and output status. In the manual environment you must ensure that a paper intake and output sheet is on the patient's chart.

Lab Values   Any lab values relating to tests done on a regular basis are kept here. This usually includes blood sugar results and INR or aPTT results. INR results are used for clients on warfarin, and aPTT values for clients on heparin (see Chapter 6 for details). Newer drugs called low macular weight heparins do not require routine blood work (discussed later).

Parenteral/IV Therapy   Monitoring of parenteral therapy or IVs is carefully followed and is the nurse's responsibility. You may be required to keep track of dates when the IV site is to be changed, as well as the IV tubing. Facilities will differ in how often this is to be done. PRN adaptors (also called saline locks) are noted here also—and the times the site is to be flushed. If the adaptors are not flushed at least q shift, they could become clogged.

Procedures, Treatments, and Direct Care   This section lists any entities involving nursing assessment and/or care. In the patient-care summary (Figure 16.8a), the first item in this category is a finger prick blood sugar test. This requires a nursing intervention but also produces a value—so this intervention could also appear under clinical parameters. Tubes and drains appear here because they require assessment as well as measurement and other nursing actions—for example, monitoring and removal.

Safety Management   Safety management entails recording those things the nurses must do to ensure the patient's safety during the hospital stay. This includes the use of side rails, the call bell (e.g., some clients may be unable to use it because of a disability or their condition, necessitating another means for the patient to call the nurse), night rounds (routine checks, but which may be needed more frequently by some clients), and the use of restraints (e.g., wrist, waist, ankle). The patient may be restrained in a geriatric chair (commonly called a Geri Chair). This is like a combination recliner and wheelchair in that it has wheels and a built-in safety belt and tray.

Safety management sometimes includes the use of either physical or chemical restraints—but only in extreme situations. The doctor must order such restraints. It has been proven in many cases that the use of physical restraints increases a patient's anxiety and restlessness and can lead to profound injury. Chemical restraints reduce a patient's cognition and level of both consciousness and awareness, which carries its own set of consequences.

Hygiene   Hygiene identifies specific needs of the client. Some may be allowed to shower, others to take a bath; some may need special mouth care, others foot care (e.g., a diabetic person). Clients unable to ambulate require a bath at the bedside. Clients who are incapable of self care require the nurse to attend to their bath and other hygiene needs. Hygiene also appears under levels of activity, notifying the nurse how much help the patient needs.

Elimination   This section clarifies the needs of the patient regarding use of the bathroom or alternatively, the commode or bedpan. If the patient has an ostomy, knowing this will allow the nurse to prepare for this type of care. You would also note if the patient is to have an enema or not, and add the date if one is given (e.g., 3rd day postoperatively). In this section, you would identify whether the patient has a catheter or not, what type, when it is to be removed, and any other related orders.

Rest and Activity   The *Rest and Activity* section is where you would note the order for the specifics of ambulation (e.g., up as tolerated) or particulars for patients with unique needs for ambulation, skin care, and related treatments.

Isolation Isolation refers to the process of keeping the patient away from the rest of the hospital population either to prevent the spread of an infection he has or to keep him from acquiring an infection from someone else (called reverse isolation), because of a weakened immune system. You would also note here if the patient is VRSA-, MRSA-, VRE- or C. *difficile*-positive and whether Infection Control has been notified. In most hospitals, all new admissions must be tested for some or all of these infectious diseases. If positive, patients are either separated by closed curtains or put into a private room or into isolation.

Diagnosis   The patient's *admitting diagnosis* is written here. It may change during the hospital stay as investigations are completed. The diagnosis might include *a primary diagnosis*—the reason the patient was admitted—and a secondary diagnosis—a condition that was present but not the main reason for admission.

A *differential diagnosis* is an inclusion of other possibilities. For example, Alice might be admitted with a provisional diagnosis of possible appendicitis, meaning the doctor thinks she probably has appendicitis. However, ectopic pregnancy and a ruptured ovarian cyst present with some similar clinical signs, and until further investigations have been completed, the doctor cannot rule these out; they are differential diagnoses. If Alice also had a bladder infection on admission, her secondary diagnosis would be cystitis.

Respiratory Care   This Kardex groups all assessments and treatments related to respiration together, including nursing assessments, treatments rendered by the RRT and physiotherapy. These might also be summarized under Treatments, Assessments, or Procedures. Suctioning orders would be noted also. Details of each assessment are discussed later.

Postoperative Assessments/Care   Any specific needs related to the patient after surgery are highlighted here, such as if the patient has a surgical wound that needs to be assessed and how often; it includes recording when clips or sutures, if present, must be removed. Some facilities also record issues related to pain management here. CMS stands for circulation, sensation, and movement. This assessment is required for a person with compromised circulation. This may be due to a vascular condition, the presence of restrictive bandaging, or a cast.

Transfer/Discharge Planning   Add to this section any formal plans regarding the patient's transfer or discharge, including estimated discharge dates and any community support that the patient might need. You would note here if the patient was transferred within the hospital (e.g., from Intensive Care to a surgical unit). If a patient is moved to another facility, some jurisdictions require a tracking number be issued to keep track of the patient in the event of the outbreak of an infectious disease.

Discharge planning is an important component of care that must be considered the moment the patient is admitted. Immediate discharge planning is part of most bed management programmes. For many patients, this requires contacting a community agency such as the CCAC in Ontario. Services you may network with include home care nursing, rehabilitation, home support, palliative care, adult day programs, and meal programs, as well as assisted living, residential care services, and hospice care.

A well-planned and -managed discharge plan not only shortens the patient's hospital stay but also makes the transition home or to another facility easier for the client.

Lab and Diagnostic Tests   Some facilities also record specific lab tests that have been ordered for the patient on the Kardex (stat, those repeated at specific intervals, and atypical ones). They would be tracked on the computer under the heading of lab tests, or laboratory and diagnostic tests—listed by the date they were ordered. As well, results are entered into the computer by the lab or diagnostic imaging and are thus available to the physician. It may be that only ones that are routinely ordered are added (e.g., FBS and 2h p.c. BS q2 days), or tests that take a while to collect (e.g., sputum for C&S [culture and sensitivity]) or stool for OB (occult blood).

Consultations   Various consultations may be requested for the hospitalized person. This may relate to assessment and care during the patient's hospital stay or to ongoing care upon discharge. *Physician* consultations occur when the MRP determines that further investigation is needed by someone from another specialty. *Pastoral care* provides spiritual support in the face of grave illness or simply at the request of the client. A *home care liaison nurse* in some jurisdictions plans the patient's care after discharge from hospitals.

A *social worker* may be needed to help the patient and his family cope with hospitalization or make plans after discharge, particularly if it involves a move to another facility, such as a nursing home.

If *physiotherapy* has been ordered, it would be noted here. A patient recovering from knee replacement surgery would have physiotherapy ordered to maximize knee function and help with walking. *Occupational therapy* may also be required to help the person achieve maximum psychosocial and physical function. *Dietary* consultations may be ordered for the hospitalized patient or upon discharge to ensure that the patient is able to cope with changes that may have occurred in his dietary needs.

Level of Nursing Care   Facilities that track patient-care hours use this information to assist with collating care hours required by the patient. In most hospitals this is now done electronically and may or may not be document driven. Hospitals that are financed according to other principles do not concern themselves with this.

Advance Directives   If the patient has advance directives, they are noted here. It is vital that *all staff* are aware of the patient's wishes regarding resuscitation and what life-saving measures are to be implemented or withheld.

Surgery   If the patient has surgery, add the type and date here postoperatively.

ORDER ENTRY: THE PROCESS

ORDER ENTRY FOLLOWS A FAIRLY STRAIGHTFORWARD PROCESS; HOWEVER, EACH ORDER WILL be dealt with somewhat differently.

1. Identify Orders to be Processed

The *first* step is to be aware of a newly written order. This is fairly easy when you expect orders, such as when a patient has just been admitted to hospital or just returned from the operating room. It is harder, at times, to catch unexpected orders. Make sure also to check for any diet changes or any new daily blood work that has been added. You would want to write the latter on your daily blood work board (if kept) and add the next day's blood work in Order Entry; for example, T+1 = today plus 1 = tomorrow.

At any point during a patient's hospital stay, a physician may write a new order, amend an order, or discontinue orders, such as treatments and medication. Doctors usually write orders when they come to the floor to see the client. This occurs most often during rounds, in the morning or late afternoon, but may be at any time—particularly when there are interns and residents as well as the specialist caring for the patient. To notify the staff that an order has been written, hospitals usually ask doctors to **flag** charts containing new orders. Facilities have different flagging systems; one of the more common is to stick a coloured marker in the chart (Figure 16.9). Some facilities use an indicator, often red, on the back of the chart.

Check the charts frequently for flags. However, do not count on physicians to flag their orders; sometimes they forget. Routinely check doctors' order sheets in all charts for newly written orders. A good time to do this is at the start of each shift and again around the middle of the shift, or after a group of doctors has left the unit. If it gets busy, for example, a physician will sometimes put a chart back in the wrong slot—or put it back without signing off an order. Every chart must be checked at least once a shift, preferably more frequently to ensure that orders are signed and processed.

flag   (of a chart) to draw attention to a new entry by sticking a coloured marker in, placing a coloured sticker on the back, or using some other device to visually draw attention.

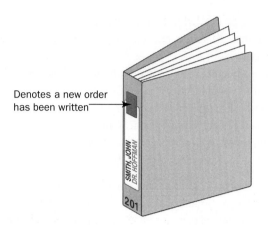

Denotes a new order
has been written

Figure 16.9 Chart flagged for new order.

When you review a newly written order, make sure that the order sheet is identified, dated, and signed by the doctor or, if taken by telephone, by the nurse per the physician (e.g., Nancy Yang/Dr. P. Rosenberg).

2. Review the Orders for Anything Urgent

Next, look over the order for anything that is urgent or stat. If you have more than one set that needs to be processed, quickly review each set, prioritize and complete all of the stat orders in each set of orders in an organized manner.

Stat orders may include medications, intravenous therapy, blood work, and diagnostic tests. Identify or highlight these orders and process them immediately, or place a mark beside the order, not through it. (Note that some facilities do not recommend using a highlighter as it interferes with legibility when they are copied or faxed.) Because stat orders are so frequently medication orders, it is helpful to highlight all of the medication orders (perhaps in yellow, or put a yellow mark beside the medication) after you first look over the sheet. This clearly displays any medication orders and ensures that they have been given the appropriate attention. If the orders involve a change to a medication the patient is already on, go back and highlight the earlier orders in blue (or make a blue mark beside the order) so that a physician or nurse can quickly see the connection if they want to check back. (Do that for all changes in medication orders—stat or otherwise.) In some electronic environments, MARs printed by the pharmacy will have an order number on them that you can use for identification purposes.

Follow through with all the necessary steps connected to a stat order promptly. For example, if you have a stat medication or IV order, you would notify the nurse immediately so that she can implement the order. If it is a stat X-ray, you would have to call Diagnostic Imaging to arrange to do it. If it is stat blood work, you would have to call the lab, or page the technician to come and take the blood (e.g., "This is 7 south calling. We have a stat CBC for Mr. Reaves in room 703").

Have the requisition and label for the blood work ready when the lab technician comes. Electronic orders offer the option of printing a label for the blood work and/or a requisition on the patient-care unit; then, when the technician comes to take the blood, for example, the tube label and requisition are already available. For nonurgent orders, that option is not chosen; the technician would print the label and requisition in the lab when he routinely downloads orders, and bring it to the floor with him.

3. Process the Orders

After you have dealt with anything urgent, organize your time to enter the rest of the orders. Again, if you have several sets of orders to process, deal with the highest priorities first (stat orders aside). For example, if a patient is soon going to the OR, those orders would need prompt attention. If a patient is waiting to go home, and the discharge order has just been written, you should also attend to the patient's discharge order; if a patient is in pain and the nurse is waiting for you to process an analgesic order, that would also require immediate attention. An order for routine blood work, or a change in a patient's activity order, would not be an immediate priority.

If all are equal in terms or priority, draw up your own plan. Some clinical secretaries prefer to deal with shorter orders first, others like to get the longer ones, such as new admissions and postop orders, out of the way first. It is a good idea to complete your medication orders, if any, first. However, the important thing is to be organized. There will rarely be a time when you are not disturbed by the telephone, intercom, or questions from staff or visitors. Many new graduates say that this is one of the greatest hurdles to overcome—multitasking, remaining organized, and completing tasks. It will take patience and concentration to remain focused on what you are doing as well as carrying out your other responsibilities.

Process each order individually. *Think each order through methodically.* Simply entering it into an electronic database or physically processing it is only one step. For each order, ask yourself what else needs to be done. (Is there someone to call? Should I tell the nurse? Are there implications for the client? Is there something about this order that doesn't seem correct—perhaps a medication dose or the patient has an allergy to that family of medications?)

After you finish the medication orders, you might then proceed to IV orders, lab and diagnostic tests, and then to orders relating to nursing care. The actual steps of processing are similar, but naturally, each type of order processed will have variations. For example:

- Copy medications orders to the MAR.

- Enter nursing-related orders, such as assessments, activity and rest, nutrition, elimination and comfort measures, to the Kardex or PI screen.

- If you are in an electronic environment, lab orders are entered as such. Fill out the required information electronically and file it to the appropriate department in the lab. If it is a stat order, call the lab, and print the requisition on the unit. In a manual environment fill out a paper requisition, and send it to the lab per facility protocol (fax, pneumatic tube, or manual transport). (If a person picks up and delivers requisitions, the facility will have an "out box" where completed requisitions are kept; they are picked up and delivered at designated intervals.) As with electronically filed orders, follow up stat orders with a phone call.

- Take the necessary steps to implement referral orders for after-care discharge (e.g., home care, community nursing, outpatient physiotherapy). You will usually have to phone, fax, or email and may also need to prepare a written requisition.

4. Identify the Orders as Completed

On the doctor's order form, *note each order when you finish processing* it to keep track and avoid duplication and omission. Remember that each facility, and sometimes each person, has a *unique set of symbols* that are used to indicate an order has been entered and is thus complete, but the following codes are used in this book.

Electronic

- MAR or MS (for "med sheet") beside a medication order indicates that it has been transferred to the MAR record.

- O/E ("order entered") may be used for any other orders to indicate they have been processed. It means the file has been sent to the appropriate department (Lab, Physiotherapy, Dietary) or noted on the PI screen (or the equivalent).

Manual and Combined Environments

- MAR or MS (med sheet) indicates that a medication order has been copied to the MAR—the same as in the electronic environment.

- R indicates that a requisition has been completed for lab orders (a paper requisition has been completed). Note that you will also do this if there is a paper requisition required for an action in the computerized environment. If the information is also copied to the Kardex, use K as well.

- K (copied to the Kardex) means nursing-related orders or direct client-care orders (e.g., ambulation, insert a catheter, start oxygen) have been copied to the Kardex.

5. Check Your Work

Recheck your orders sequentially, carefully, and thoroughly.

6. Have Your Orders Checked by the Nurse

Unless you have been authorized to complete the orders without checking, have the designated person, usually the charge nurse, check your orders before you sign off. This step takes a bit more time but is well worth it for your peace of mind and, ultimately, the patient's safety. If an error occurs and you did not have the orders validated, you may be held legally responsible. For example, in most facilities, if there is a proper communication system in place between the RN and the clinical secretary, the CS can be held accountable for the "transcription" component of the job. If there is a med error because the RN didn't verify the order, the CS will be considered responsible for the transcription error. In other words, it is the clinical secretary's responsibility to ensure that all the proper checks are completed.

7. Sign Off

Before signing off, check once more to ensure that the patient's name on the orders and the name on the MAR match. Mark the orders completed, as per facility guidelines, usually by signing your name or initial in with the date and time of completion. You must also have the designated nurse check your orders and initial or sign as well, to indicate they have been reviewed.

8. Fax or Scan the Order to Pharmacy

Fax the order to Pharmacy and note on the order that it has been faxed or scanned into the chart and sent. Note that in some facilities the policy is to fax the orders to Pharmacy before they are completed and signed off—this facilitates prompt preparation of the medications ordered; there may be a little box to check off beside the order indicating that you have faxed it to Pharmacy or scanned the order. If the pharmacy department is appropriately computerized, scanned orders will appear on their "smart screen." They show the patient's name and room number and are prioritized on the screen (which is constantly monitored in that department).

9. Return the Chart to Its Proper Place

Once an order has been completed, it is important to return the chart to its proper place. This keeps the desk area tidy and prevents charts from being misplaced or lost. If the chart was flagged for order identification, remove the flag.

TRANSCRIBING MEDICATION ORDERS

THE ATTENDING PHYSICIAN, NURSE PRACTITIONER, OR CONSULTANT MUST ORDER ALL medications given in hospital. Even medications that a person takes routinely at home must be ordered if they are to be continued while in hospital. *No* medication—not even Aspirin—should be given to a patient or taken by a patient if it is not ordered. If clients come with medications, they are asked to send them home with someone. Failing that, the nurse should take the medications and store them until the patient is discharged. It's a good idea to mark somewhere on the patient's chart that there are meds in safe keeping to ensure that they are given back to the patient upon transfer or discharge. Keeping the medications is done, at least in part, to prevent unauthorized self-medication. The physician must have an accurate record of what medications the patient is taking. If a patient self-medicates, there is always a potential for adverse drug interactions with prescribed medications, overdose, or interference with lab tests. For example, Raja was getting Tylenol 3 from the nurses for arthritic pain but found it was not keeping it under control. She had some Percocet in her purse. She took two, resulting in an overdose. Salimu was on anticoagulants; he had a headache and, not wanting to bother the nurses, took four ASAs from the bottle tucked away in his bedside drawer. This affected his blood tests because ASA has anticoagulant properties and potentiates the action of anticoagulants.

Any medication that is ordered in the hospital must be copied onto the appropriate form, usually the MAR. This is done by the clinical secretary, nurse, or by Pharmacy, depending on the circumstances. A profile of the patient's current, amended, and discontinued medications is usually kept on the patient's electronic chart. Some manual environments hand copy all of the medications onto the Kardex. If a medication is changed or discontinued, the clinical secretary draws a neat line through the medication but never erases it.

Medication Administration Records

The format of medication administration records varies with each facility. The design may depend on facility preference, whether the MARs are computer generated, or their purpose (e.g., stat and single-dose medications, scheduled or PRN medications, discussed in detail below). They may even differ in design from one floor to another—surgical, medical, or obstetrical services.

In the computerized environment, medication administration records are typically prepared by the Pharmacy Department. These are often called computerized medication administration records, or CMARs. Computerized MARs are, in most hospitals, generated every 24 hours. The completed MARs are either kept in the MAR binder on the medication cart (med cart), or returned to the patient's chart. There is a MAR for scheduled (regularly taken medications) and another one for PRN meds. Some facilities also have separate MARs for recording anticoagulants and hypoglycemics. Figure 16.10 is an example of a computer-generated single-day MAR for scheduled medications.

In facilities where MARs are manually prepared, the MAR will have enough spaces for five to seven days. See Figure 16.11 for an illustration. The nurses just sign beside the hour they give the medication under the appropriate date. For example, if the nurse, Amy, gives psyllium to a patient at 0800 on January 20th, she would initial the space beside 0800.

Categories of Medication

For purposes of recording, most facilities divide medications into the following categories:

Routine or Scheduled Medication Orders   These usually must be taken as specific times every day: od, bid, tid, qid, or qhs. (See Chapter 7, Table 7.2.) A medication taken every other day or once a week would also be in this category as long as it is taken on a regular schedule. Some scheduled medications are taken for a designated time, others indefinitely. Antibiotics, for example, are usually taken for 7 to 10 days. Some, such as thyroid medication, heart medication, or blood pressure medication (antihypertensives), may be taken throughout the hospital stay as the patient may be on them for life. Others,

CONESTOGA GENERAL HOSPITAL
SCHEDULED MEDICATION ADMINISTRATION RECORD

From Mon 20 April/xx 0700h to Tues 21 April/xx @ 0659h

Allergies: GENTAMYCIN

Diagnosis

Severne Aubert
23 Capilano Dr
Vancouver B.C.
#123432333 Dr. G. O'Neal

Medication and Directions		07 08 09 10 11 12 13 14 15 16 17 18 19 20 21 22 23 24	01 02 03 04 05 06
Hours			
Psyllium Cap 1 cap po tid Swallow one cap at a time 0800 1400 2200		Start Jan 20/xx	
	Initial		
Metronidazole Tab 250 mg 500 mg (2 tabs) po tid with food 0900 1300 1800		Start Jan 20/xx	
	Initial		
Ramipril Cap 10 mg I cap po od (hold if SBP < 110)* 1000		Start Jan 20/xx	
	Initial		
Amitriptyline Tab 25 mg take 1 tab po qhs 2200		Start Jan 20/xx	
	Initial		
	Initial		
	Initial		

Room # 302 Bed# 2   MAR Checked by *BT*   Page # 1

Figure 16.10 Computerized single-day MAR for scheduled medications.

such as anti-inflammatories, are taken until a patient's condition has stabilized or reversed itself.

PRN Medications   This category of medications includes any taken only as needed, usually to relieve a symptom (also called a clinical sign). For example, Genna may take acetaminophen or ASA when she has a headache, dimenhydrinate or dramamine (Gravol) when she experiences nausea, or lorazepam (Ativan) when she feels anxious. In the hospital setting, the decision that the medication is needed is usually made by the patient or collaboratively by the nurse and the client. A maximum frequency will be given; for example, q4h PRN means that the drug may be taken as needed, every four hours. See Figure 16.15 on page 505 for an example of PRN orders.

Stat Medication Orders   Stat medication orders may include antiseizure medications, analgesics, antibiotics, steroids, or anxiolytics, among others. The common element is that the need for the medication is urgent. For example, if a patient suddenly developed very high blood pressure, the doctor would order an antihypertensive or a diuretic stat, perhaps by injection or IV to speed up the effect. In response to a migraine headache, a doctor will sometimes order an analgesic stat. In response to an epileptic seizure, a doctor might order an anticonvulsant stat. If Gertrude has a bladder infection, once a urine specimen is obtained, the doctor often orders an antibiotic with the first dose given stat.

CONESTOGA GENERAL HOSPITAL

Severne Aubert
23 Capilano Rd.,
Vancouver B.C.
#123432333   Dr. G. O'Neal

Check here if more than one page ☐

Scheduled Medication Administration Record

Start /reorder	Stop date	Medication dose, route, frequency	Hour Due	Jan 20	21	22	23	24	25	26
Jan 20/xx		*Psyllium 1 cap po tid*	0800							
			1400							
			2200							
Jan 20/xx		*Metronidazole 250 mg. —*	0800							
		Caps 11 tid with food.	1200							
			1700							
Jan 20/xx		*Ramipril 10 mg po od*	1000							
		Hold if sbp < 110								
Jan 20/xx		*Amitriptyline 25 mg po qhs*	2200							

Figure 16.11   Scheduled MAR for a manual environment.

Stat medications are either recorded on a specific form for stat medications, or on the scheduled MAR and clearly identified as stat. This can be done by underlining it, highlighting it, or writing it in red. You must always notify the patient's nurse of a stat order.

Single-Dose Medications   For a variety of reasons, the doctor may order only one dose of a medication. Often preoperative medications are single-dose medications. Rhogam for an Rh-negative mom who had an Rh-positive baby is also a single dose. As with stat medications, single-dose medications are either recorded on a specific form for single-dose medications or on the scheduled MAR and identified as one dose only. As with stat meds, this can be done by underlining it, highlighting it, or writing it in red.

A doctor will sometimes write an order for a scheduled medication late in the day that would normally start the next morning. If he wants one dose given that evening, he will write instructions to that effect. This is not considered a single dose medication. (See Figure 16.12, Lasix and enalapril, for an example.)

The Process of Transcribing Medication Orders

This section will work through an example of a straightforward set of doctor's orders. You will follow Mary, a clinical secretary, as she processes orders for Mr. Dietz.

CONESTOGA GENERAL HOSPITAL DOCTORS ORDER SHEET *Please fax to Pharmacy & note date/time*			
	cbc		**Dietz, Henry** **123 Duncan St.** **Vancouver B.C.** **DOB 22 09 47 071608** **Dr. G. Hanson**
	Electrolytes		
	Urine for C&S		
	Valium 5 mg po hs		
	Lasix 20 mg od Give first dose tonight		
	Demerol 100 mg IM stat		
	HCT 12.5 mg od		
	Enalapril 5 mg BID Give first dose tonight		
	Eltroxin 0.1 mg od		
	Demerol 50-75 mg IM q4h PRN		
	Gravol 50 mg q4h PRN		
date *Jan 2/XX*	time *2000*	Physician's printed name Dr. G. Hanson	Signature *Dr. G. Hanson*

Figure 16.12 Initial doctor's orders for Mr. Dietz.

The Protocol In this scenario (Conestoga General Hospital), computerized MARs are generated every 24 hours, arriving on the patient-care unit each morning at 0700 hours and used until 0659 the next morning at which time a MAR for the next day is produced. CMARs for new admissions are generated until 1900 hours, after which they are prepared manually by the nurse or clinical secretary. Changes to existing MARs of inpatients are done manually but will be incorporated into the CMARs generated the next morning. In this hospital, stat orders are transcribed onto the scheduled medication administration record.

For this explanatory exercise, all of the medications are to start on the day on which the orders are written, January 03/xx. Note that in this section we will deal only with orders related to medication.

Mr. Dietz has been admitted to Mary's medical patient-care unit from the Emergency Department with a provisional diagnosis of abdominal pain NYD (not yet diagnosed). Because he comes to Mary's floor after 1900 hours (Pharmacy is closed), Mary manually processes the medication orders that are required for Mr. Dietz between admission and 0659 the next morning. Mr. Dietz has been asking for something for his pain.

Step 1: Check Orders The nurse who brought Mr. Dietz to the unit hands Mary orders written by Dr. Hanson in Emergency, who is Mr. Dietz's MRP (Figure 16.12). Mary quickly checks for the date and the doctor's signature. She notes that there are no allergies.

<table>
<tr><td colspan="3" align="center">CONESTOGA GENERAL HOSPITAL
DOCTORS ORDER SHEET</td><td></td></tr>
<tr><td colspan="3">Please fax to Pharmacy & note date/time</td><td></td></tr>
<tr><td></td><td colspan="2">cbc</td><td rowspan="2">Dietz, Henry
123 Duncan St.
Vancouver B.C.
DOB 22 09 47   071608
Dr. G. Hanson</td></tr>
<tr><td></td><td colspan="2">Electrolytes</td></tr>
<tr><td></td><td colspan="2">Urine for C&S</td><td rowspan="11">Note that Mary has identified the meds using checkmarks—the stat med she has chosen to use asterisk to set it apart as needing to be attended to immediately.

As Mary later writes the meds onto the MARs, she symbolized the process by writing MAR in the left column. This is a double check to remind Mary that that medication has been processed. Some facilities use a highlighter, but it has been found to cause visibility problems when the sheet is faxed.</td></tr>
<tr><td>MAR</td><td colspan="2">Valium 5 mg po hs prn √</td></tr>
<tr><td>MAR</td><td colspan="2">Lasix 20 mg od   Give first dose tonight √</td></tr>
<tr><td>MAR</td><td colspan="2">Demerol 100 mg IM stat   ✱✱✱ Nurse notified @ 2010</td></tr>
<tr><td></td><td colspan="2">HCT 12.5 mg od √</td></tr>
<tr><td>MAR</td><td colspan="2">Enalapril 5 mg BID   Give first dose tonight √</td></tr>
<tr><td></td><td colspan="2">Eltroxin 0.1 mg od √</td></tr>
<tr><td>MAR</td><td colspan="2">Demerol 50-75 mg IM q4h prn √</td></tr>
<tr><td>MAR</td><td colspan="2">Gravol 50 mg q4h prn √</td></tr>
<tr><td>:</td><td colspan="2">Because only the Valium, Lasix, Demerol, Enalapril and Gravol are required that evening, she leaves the other drugs for Pharmacy to print off on the CMAR the next morning.</td></tr>
<tr><td>date
Jan 2 / XX</td><td>time
2000</td><td>Physician's printed name
Dr. G. Hanson</td><td>Signature
Dr. G. Hanson</td></tr>
</table>

Figure 16.13 The same doctor's orders for Mr. Dietz, with medications highlighted and transcription symbols added, signifying that the medications have been processed.

Step 2: Identifying and Prioritizing Medication Orders

- Mary glances over the order sheet looking for any stat orders. (See Figure 16.13 on page 534.) She places a check mark beside the medication orders to or make them stand out; finding a stat order for Demerol (which Dr. Hanson has written in response to Mr. Dietz's requests for something immediate for pain), she highlights that with an asterisk and processes that order first.

- Mary notifies the registered nurse of the stat order.

- Mary prints out a blank MAR for scheduled medications and adds Mr. Dietz's ID label (as shown in Figure 16.14a on page 535). She then writes in the order for the Demerol (including the dose and route and the fact that it is a stat order) and underlines it. Mary has also added "stat order given at" so the nurse has to enter the time and initial it once she has given the medication. Mary gives the MAR directly to the nurse.

The nurse takes the MAR record, prepares the medication, gives Mr. Dietz the Demerol, initials the MAR, and gives it back to Mary. In some hospitals, as further

| CONESTOGA GENERAL HOSPITAL | | | | | | | | | | | | | | | | | | | |
| SCHEDULED MEDICATION ADMINISTRATION RECORD | | | | | | | | | | | | | | | | | | | | |

CONESTOGA GENERAL HOSPITAL
SCHEDULED MEDICATION ADMINISTRATION RECORD

From *Jan 2/XX 2000 to: Jan 3/XX @ 0659h*

Dietz, Henry
124 Duncan St.
Vancouver B.C.
DOB 22/09/47
#123432333
Dr. G. Hanson

Allergies: **No Allergies** *None*
Adverse Reactions
Diagnosis
Circle time med given and initial below.

Medication and Directions																									
Hours	07	08	09	10	11	12	13	14	15	16	17	18	19	20	21	22	23	24		01	02	03	04	05	06
Demerol 75 mg. IM stat	*Stat order given at:*																								
Initial																									
	07	08	09	10	11	12	13	14	15	16	17	18	19	20	21	22	23	24		01	02	03	04	05	06
Initial																									
	07	08	09	10	11	12	13	14	15	16	17	18	19	20	21	22	23	24		01	02	03	04	05	06
Initial																									

Figure 16.14a   Mary has transcribed the stat order for Demerol onto a MAR (the same format is used by Pharmacy for CMARs).

verification, a nurse who gives a stat medication also initials or signs the doctor's written order for the medication, along with the date and the word "given." The nurse must have the MAR with her in order to prepare the medication—she uses it as a guide, ensuring she has followed the five rights for giving medications: the right patient, the right drug, the right dose, the right route, and the right time.

■ As her next step, on the doctor's order (Figure 16.13), Mary writes that the nurse has been notified and the time. Mary also writes "MAR" on the order form beside Demerol, meaning transcribed to the med sheet. Mary has now completed the steps for dealing with a stat medication.

Step 3: Completing the Medication Orders   Having completed the stat order, Mary decides to finish processing the medication orders.

Processing Scheduled Medications

Mary has already added Mr. Dietz's ID label the scheduled MAR. The scheduled meds that must be given that evening are the Lasix and the enalapril. (See Figure 16.12 detailing where the doctor ordered a dose for both of those medications to be given that evening.)

■ Mary carefully copies the medications onto the scheduled MAR she has printed off under the stat order for the Demerol. She includes the start date for each medication.

■ She enters the dose, route, and frequency, making sure the information is transcribed accurately.

■ She adds the times at which the medications should be given (most hospitals have a list of the most common medications and when they should be given—for example, with meals, without meals, first thing in the morning).

CONESTOGA GENERAL HOSPITAL
SCHEDULED MEDICATION ADMINISTRATION RECORD

From Jan 2/XX 2000 to: Jan 3 /XX @ 0659h
Allergies: No Allergies *None*
Adverse Reactions
Diagnosis
Circle time med given and initial below.

Dietz, Henry
124 Duncan St.
Vancouver B.C.
DOB 22/09/47
#123432333
Dr. G. Hanson

Medication and Directions		
Hours	07 08 09 10 11 12 13 14 15 16 17 18 19 20 21 22 23 24	01 02 03 04 05 06
Demerol 75 mg, IM stat	*Stat order given at: 2115 RM* Note: the nurse has given the Demerol and added the time and her initials, and given the MAR back to Mary to complete the med orders you see below	
Initial		
Lasix 20 mg po bid *0800 1800*	07 08 09 10 11 12 13 14 15 16 17 18 19 20 21 22 23 24 *Start date: Jan 2/XX* *Give first dose tonight* Note: The nurse will give the Lasix and the enalapril that evening as per the doctors order. The next day, the nurses will resume giving the meds at the times outlined on this MAR	01 02 03 04 05 06 The orders for these 2 meds are not considered stat *or* one dose only
Initial		
Enalapril 5 mg po bid *1000 1800*	07 08 09 10 11 12 13 14 15 16 17 18 19 20 21 22 23 24 *Start date: Jan 2/XX* *Give first dose tonight*	01 02 03 04 05 06
Initial		
	07 08 09 10 11 12 13 14 15 16 17 18 19 20 21 22 23 24	01 02 03 04 05 06
Initial		
	07 08 09 10 11 12 13 14 15 16 17 18 19 20 21 22 23 24	01 02 03 04 05 06
Initial		

Room # Bed#	MAR Checked by *VT*	Page #

Figure 16.14b Scheduled med orders to be given that evening are manually prepared by Mary.

■ She does not include a stop date as none was indicated and these medications are not subject to automatic stop dates. Mary has also written in the doctor's instructions— all medications must be transcribed exactly as the doctor writes them, including explanations and/or specific instructions. (See Table 16.1 for a detailed explanation of the components of a MAR.) Figure 16.14b on page 536 shows those orders added to the MAR.

Processing PRN Medications

Mary must now transcribe the PRN orders. She prints off a PRN MAR. They all must be processed manually because Mr. Dietz may want any one of them during the remainder of the evening or night. His valium can be given at bedtime, and it is likely he will need more Demerol. The Gravol is often given with Demerol to counteract nausea that is sometimes a side effect of the Demerol. Remember that a computer-generated MAR will be sent to the floor at 0700 the next morning. In manual environments, the PRN medication administration record will likely be designed for use over several days.

■ As with the scheduled medications, Mary carefully copies the PRN medications onto Mr. Dietz's MAR. She includes the date on which the medication is started.

Table 16.1 Components of Transcribed Medication Orders (as shown in Figures 16.12 and 16.13)

Name	The name of the drug as the physician ordered it.
Dose	The amount of the drug the patient is to receive (e.g., Lasix 20 mg).
Frequency	How often the medication is to be given (e.g., Lasix od or daily).
Route	How the medication is to be given. Mostly ordered po here. Demerol and Gravol were ordered IM.
Times	She adds the times at which the medications must be given. (There is usually a hospital protocol outlining the times each medication or group of medications is to be given.) On the CMARs you will note that Pharmacy adds the times, as shown in Figure 16.16 on page 507.
Start Order	The start date is the date on which the order should be implemented. If the doctor does not specify otherwise, the start date is the same as the date on which the order was written (Jan. 2, in this case). The start date is written out for each medication. Some MAR formats have two columns for written medication—one for the start date, and one for the stop date.
Stop Date	Automatic stop order policies are meant as a safeguard for patients to prevent prolonged use of specified medications. The stop date is not always filled out. All controlled drugs have automatic stop dates. The controlled drugs, such as Demerol and morphine, will have automatic stop dates hours. This will vary with each facility but the automatic date usually ranges from 48 to 72 hours. As well, doctors can order a stop date—for example if the automatic stop date for morphine is 72 hours, the doctor can extend that time frame as noted in this order: "hydromorphine 0.5—1 mg po q2h prn 7 days for pain."
	Antibiotics often have automatic stop dates of seven days unless otherwise stated. Most facilities review all medications each month. Clients rarely stay that long in an acute-care hospital, but long-term care or nursing facilities often use a standard one-month stop date.
	Computerized systems have posed some problems with automatic stop dates in that some medications have been automatically stopped when the physician wanted them continued.

■ She enters the dose, route, and frequency, making sure to enter numbers accurately.

■ Mary also adds the automatic stop date beside the Demerol (remember, at this hospital all narcotic medications have an automatic stop date of 72 hours). The valium and Gravol do not have automatic stop dates. (In some hospitals, valium would have an automatic stop date of 30 days, but it is highly unlikely that Mr. Dietz will be in the hospital that long, so the stop date is left blank.)

■ Mary adds the transcription symbol "MAR" beside each medication on the doctor's order as she process it, signifying that she has copied the medication to the medication administration record. This is illustrated in Figure 16.13.

All narcotic analgesics have automatic stop dates unless otherwise specified by the doctor. Mary's hospital uses a stop date of 72 hours for Demerol, so Mary counts forward three days from the start date and puts a stop date of January 5. If a patient still needs the drug after the stop date, the nurses will ask the clinical secretary to ask the doctor for a renewal or reorder. In a noncomputerized environment, you could leave a note on the patient's chart or call the doctor. In a computerized environment, there is usually a "bulletin board" or "message board" somewhere in the patient's electronic chart where you would write the request. The physician should check this message board regularly. As with the scheduled medications, a CMAR would be prepared by

CONESTOGA GENERAL HOSPITAL
PRN MEDICATION ADMINISTRATION RECORD

From *Jan 2/XX 2000h to: Jan 3/XX @ 0659h*
Allergies: No Allergies   *None*
Adverse Reactions
Diagnosis
Circle time med given and initial below.

Dietz, Henry
124 Duncan St.
Vancouver B.C.
DOB 22/09/47
#123432333
Dr. G. Hanson

PRN Medication and Directions																							
Hours	07	08	09	10	11	12	13	14	15	16	17	18	19	20	21	22	23	24	01	02	03	04 05 06

Valium 5 mg. po hs prn

Start January 2/XX

Initial

Demerol 50–100 mg IM
Q3–4 h prn

Start January 2/XX
d/c January 5/XX @ 2000h

Initial

Gravol 50 mg IM or po
q3–4 h prn
Disc/renewal January 5/xx

Start January 2/XX

Initial

Room # Bed#	MAR Checked by *VT*	Page # 1

Figure 16.15   The PRN MAR Mary prepared from orders shown in Figure 16.13.

Pharmacy and sent to the floor before 0700 the next morning. It will be for the 24-hour period, Jan 3/xx 0700–Jan 4/xx 0659, at which time a new CMAR would be generated for the next 24 hours.

Dose Range for PRN Medications   Some PRN medication orders are written with a dose range. In this case, the doctor ordered a range of 50–75 mg of Demerol, meaning the nurse may give the patient either 50 or 75 mg, depending on how severe the patient's pain is. The nurse may make this decision in consultation with the client. A *pain scale* is a helpful assessment tool. The patient is asked to assign a number between (usually between 1 and 10) to the pain he is currently experiencing, with 0 as no pain and 5 (or 10) as the worst pain he has ever experienced. If the patient rates his pain at 3, for example, the discomfort probably doesn't warrant 75 mg of Demerol, but if the patient rates it as a 10, it would.

Frequencies for PRN medications are maximums and provide safety parameters. Q4h means that the medication may be given no more often than every four hours. Some doctors order a range, such as q3–4 hours. The Demerol, for example, could be given every three hours if needed. Often, nurses will give it as much as a half-hour earlier, but no sooner. This is considered appropriate by most facilities.

These orders are now complete. Mary rechecks her orders, has the nurse check her orders, and signs off. She either tears off the back copy and sends it to Pharmacy or faxes the order to Pharmacy (depending on hospital routine). She returns the chart to the appropriate place.

CONESTOGA GENERAL HOSPITAL
SCHEDULED MEDICATION ADMINISTRATION RECORD

From Jan 3/xx 0700 to: Jan 4/xx @ 0659

Allergies: No Allergies *None*

Adverse Reactions

Diagnosis   Abd pain NYD

Circle time med given and initial below.

Dietz, Henry
124 Duncan St.
Vancouver B.C.
DOB 22/09/47
#123432333
Dr. G. Hanson

Medication and Directions																									
Hours	07	08	09	10	11	12	13	14	15	16	17	18	19	20	21	22	23	24		01	02	03	04	05	06
Lasix (furosemide) 20 mg po bid **take on empty stomach** 1000 1600 (ward stock) Initial	Start date: Jan 03/xx Stop date: none given																								
	07	08	09	10	11	12	13	14	15	16	17	18	19	20	21	22	23	24		01	02	03	04	05	06
Enalapril (Vasotec) 5 mg po bid **take with or without food** 1000 1800 Initial	Start date: Jan 03/xx Stop date: none given																								
	07	08	09	10	11	12	13	14	15	16	17	18	19	20	21	22	23	24		01	02	03	04	05	06
Hydrochlorothiazide (HCT) 12.5 mg po od (HydroDIURAL) **take with or without food** 1000 Initial	Start date: Jan 03/xx Stop date: none given																								
Eltroxin 0.1 mg po od (levothyroxin) 1000	07	08	09	10	11	12	13	14	15	16	17	18	19	20	21	22	23	24		01	02	03	04	05	06
	Start date: Jan 03/xx Stop date: none given																								
(ward stock) Initial																									
	07	08	09	10	11	12	13	14	15	16	17	18	19	20	21	22	23	24		01	02	03	04	05	06
Initial																									

Figure 16.16 CMAR showing medications from Dr. Hanson's orders (Figure 16.12) printed for a 24-hour period starting Jan. 3.

Discontinuing Existing Orders

Usually only a physician (or a nurse practitioner) can discontinue an order. Orders are discontinued if there is an automatic stop date and the doctor doesn't renew it (e.g., narcotics), after the last dose when a designated time frame is identified (e.g., pen G 500 units po qid 7 days), or because the doctor is changing a dose of a medication or discontinuing the medication altogether, as shown below. The clinical secretary or nurse must go to the appropriate MAR and write d/c beside the medication and, if appropriate, a time. For example, Dr. Hanson comes in on the morning of January 3 to reassess

Mr. Dietz. He decides that Mr. Dietz doesn't need HCT as a diuretic. (He is also on Lasix, a diuretic sometimes used in combination with HCT.) He also finds that Mr. Dietz has become increasingly anxious and feels that prescribing Valium throughout the day as well as at night may help. Mary finds Mr. Dietz's chart on her desk, flagged to notify her that there was a new order (Figure 16.17a).

■ Mary checks the new order to be sure Mr. Dietz's ID sticker is on it. She ensures that the order is dated and signed by Dr. Hanson. She notes again there are no allergies.

■ The medication orders must be transcribed to Mr. Dietz's scheduled medication administration record, so she gets them out of the medication binder, which is on the medication cart. The MAR she uses is the CMAR that was sent to the floor at 0700 that morning. This replaces the one that Mary manually prepared on the evening of January 2, when Mr. Dietz was admitted.

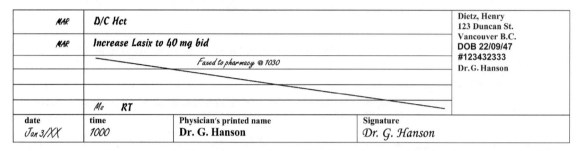

	D/C Hct		Dietz, Henry
	Increase Lasix to 40 mg bid		123 Duncan St. Vancouver B.C. DOB 22/09/47 #123432333 Dr. G. Hanson
date Jan 3/XX	time 1000	Physicians printed name **Dr. G. Hanson**	Signature Dr. G. Hanson

Figure 16.17a Doctor's order sheet showing new orders.

MAR	D/C Hct		Dietz, Henry 123 Duncan St.
MAR	Increase Lasix to 40 mg bid		Vancouver B.C. DOB 22/09/47 #123432333 Dr.G. Hanson
	Faxed to pharmacy @ 1030		
	Ms RT		
date Jan 3/XX	time 1000	Physician's printed name **Dr. G. Hanson**	Signature Dr. G. Hanson

Figure 16.17b Doctor's order sheet showing new orders with transcription codes added by Mary as she processed the orders: discontinues the Hct and increases the Lasix.

■ Mary scans the order, noting medication changes. She immediately notifies Mr. Dietz's medication nurse that his HCT has been discontinued and the dose of his Lasix changed. She also tells her that a new medication, Valium, has been ordered, which the nurse can start immediately. Mary then begins to process the new orders. The first order is to discontinue or stop Mr. Dietz's HCT. To do this, Mary clearly marks d/c on the CMAR record and draws a line across the MAR beside it (Figure 16.18 on page 541). She also writes in the time the HCT was discontinued, which would be effective immediately. If the nurse had already given the 1000 dose of the HCT, the order would, in reality, be effected the next morning. In this case she had not, because Mary had notified the nurse of the medication changes immediately. Mary now repeats her actions for the Lasix, which must be discontinued as well. She adds the new order for Lasix underneath the Eltroxin. Because the nurse had not given the 1000 dose of the Lasix 20 mg the new order can be started at 1000. If the nurse had given the 1000 dose, the new order would start when the next does was due—at 1600 hours. A new CMAR will be sent from Pharmacy the next morning at 0700 that will incorporate the changes Mary manually added to the Jan. 3 CMAR.

Mary adds the transcription symbols as she processes the orders (Figure 16.17b), reviews her orders once transcribed, and has them checked by the nurse. Both Mary and the nurse sign off the order. Mary then faxes the order to Pharmacy, marks the order as faxed, and returns the chart to the holder. She removes the flag from the chart.

Loading Medication Doses

loading dose a medication ordered as a single-order stat medication with a dose that is higher than the usual or routine dose.

A **loading dose** is a higher than the usual dose of a medication given to rapidly increase the level of the medication in the patient's bloodstream. It can be ordered by any route— by mouth, intramuscularly, by subcutaneous injection, or intravenously. If a doctor orders

CONESTOGA GENERAL HOSPITAL
SCHEDULED MEDICATION ADMINISTRATION RECORD

From Jan 3/xx 0700 **to:** Jan 4/xx @ 0659h
Allergies: No Allergies *None*
Adverse Reactions
Diagnosis Abd pain NYD
Circle time med given and initial below.

Dietz, Henry
124 Duncan St.
Vancouver B.C.
DOB 22/09/47
#123432333
Dr. G. Hanson

Medication and Directions	07	08	09	(10)	11	12	13	14	15	16	17	18	19	20	21	22	23	24		01	02	03	04	05	06
Lasix (furosemide) 20 mg po bid **take on empty stomach** 1000 1600 (ward stock) Initial	Start date: Jan 03/xx Stop date: none given *D/C effective 10:10 Jan 3/xx*																								
Enalapril (Vasotec)5 mg po bid **take with or without food** 1000 1800 Initial	Start date: Jan 03/xx Stop date: none given																								
Hydrochlorothiazide (HCT) 12.5 mg po od (HydroDIURAL) **take with or without food** 1000 Initial	Start date: Jan 03/xx Stop date: none given *D/C effective 10:10 Jan 3/xx*																								
Eltroxin 0.1 mg po od (levothyroxin) 1000 (ward stock) Initial	Start date: Jan 03/xx Stop date: none given																								
Lasix 40 mg po bid **new medication* Initial	*Start Jan 3/xx 1000 Hours. Stop date: none noted*																								
Valium 5 mg. po tid *1000 1400 1800* **New medication* Initial	*Start Jan 3 @ 1000 Stop date: none noted*																								

Figure 16.18 CMAR incorporating new orders.

a rapid infusion of an IV fluid—without a medication—it is referred to as a **bolus**. There are numerous types of conditions under which a doctor will order a loading dose of a medication—for example, an antibiotic for a severe infection, a diuretic for congestive heart failure, or a sedative for someone who is extremely agitated.

For an acute infection, such as cystitis or pneumonia, a doctor may order a loading dose of antibiotics (perhaps twice the regular dose) to quickly raise blood levels of the medication and hasten therapeutic effects. For example, Mark Parsons was an inpatient who suddenly developed a high fever because of a newly developed left lower lobe pneumonia. His MRP, Dr. Pinder, ordered 1 g of penicillin stat (a loading dose) and 500 mg four times a day for 10 days (the routine part of the order). See Figure 16.19, where this order is activated and transcribed noting the requested discontinue date.

The stat dose would be recorded either on the MAR under single-dose medications or directly on the scheduled CMAR (depending on the facilities protocol). Stat meds are almost always entered onto the MAR manually because they must be given immediately and there isn't time to have them preprinted in pharmacy. In this case, Mary recorded the routine order for penicillin on the existing CMAR. In some facilities, if the order was faxed to Pharmacy, they could send up a CMAR that would be used for the 1130, 1630, and 2200 doses.

> **bolus** the usually rapid infusion of additional IV fluids in addition to the base amount ordered for the client.

Medications with Special Directions

The doctor may write a medication order with specific directions regarding dose or time of administration (e.g., to be given alternate days or every three days). The CMAR will

CONESTOGA GENERAL HOSPITAL
SCHEDULED MEDICATION ADMINISTRATION RECORD

Dietz, Henry
124 Duncan St.
Vancouver B.C.
DOB 22/09/47
#123432333
Dr. G. Hanson

From *Jan 4 xx 0700 h to: 5 Jan/xx 0659h*
Allergies: No Allergies *None noted*
Adverse Reactions
Diagnosis
Circle time med given and initial below.

Medication and Directions			
Hours	07 08 09 10 11 12 13 14 15 16 17 18 19 20 21 22 23 24		01 02 03 04 05 06
Penicillin 1 g stat	*Stat order given @* Note: The nurse will add the time at which she gives the medication, and initial it. The nest dose will be given at 1100 as Indicated below		
Initial			
	07 08 09 10 11 12 13 14 15 16 17 18 19 20 21 22 23 24		01 02 03 04 05 06
Penicillin 500mg po qid *0600 11:30 16:30 22:00*	*Start Jan 4/xx @ 11:30* *10 / xx after 0600 dose*	*Stop Jan*	**Note:** the nurses will give the 11:30 1630 and 2200 dose using this MAR. The preprinted one will be sent up from Pharmacy the next morning. (Jan 5 @ 0700) Alternatively, in some facilities, if the order is faxed to Pharmacy, they could send up a preprinted MAR to be used for the remainder of that day.
Initial			

Figure 16.19 Order handwritten on an MAR showing a loading dose of penicillin, and underneath, the routine order with a d/c date as noted on the doctor's order sheet.

clearly reflect these orders. If the medication is to be given every two days, it simplifies the process to write on the MAR "q2days (even days)" or "q2days (odd days)," whichever fits the date on which the medication was started.

Anticoagulant Orders

Anticoagulants are medications that prevent blood clots from forming and existing clots from progressing. They may be used to prevent clot formation in the hearts of people with atrial fibrillation or certain types of mechanical heart valves. They are also used **prophylactically** to prevent blood clot formation in some postoperative clients.

prophylactic a measure taken to prevent a problem from developing.

The three anticoagulant medications most commonly used are low macular weight heparin, heparin, and warfarin (Coumadin). Low molecular weight heparin is given subcutaneously and is a newer product used in the primary treatment of such conditions as deep vein thrombosis (DVT). Although an expensive drug, its advantages over heparin include predictable blood levels and a lower chance of untoward bleeding. As well, it interacts less with platelets, eliminating the need to monitor a person's aPTT or an INR. Heparin is given intravenously or subcutaneously and is a fast-acting anticoagulant;examples of these are Fragmin and Lovenox. Warfarin is taken orally. Sometimes clients may be on both heparin and warfarin when they are changing from heparin to an oral anticoagulant; usually the heparin will be continued only until the warfarin reaches therapeutic blood levels. A patient who is on any kind of anticoagulant therapy must be carefully monitored by the physician. Partial thromboplastin time (PTT or aPTT) is used to monitor heparin, and the INR is used to monitor warfarin (see Chapter 6).

Note the difference between anticoagulants and clot-dissolving agents, such as streptokinase and t-PA. The latter are used to limit or reverse damage caused by a clot in an artery to the heart or brain. These must be given soon after the damaging event, such as a

CONESTOGA GENERAL HOSPITAL
MEDICATION ADMINISTRATION RECORD FOR ANTICOAGULANT PROTOCOLS

From 0700 _____ to 0659 _____

New Order _____   Replaces Order _____   Order Verified (initials) _____

Heparin protocol (indicate)
 	
Check APTT and titrate as per protocol
 	
Heparin S.C or I.M.
  Dose_____
 	
  APTT____
	IV Heparin
	Time_____
	  IV Heparin
	Bolus ____units mL
	Rate mL/h____
	Rate units/h_____
	Initials_____
		Time_____
		  IV Heparin
		Bolus _____units mL
		Rate mL/h____
		Rate units/h _____
		Initials_____
			Time_____
			  IV Heparin
			Bolus _____units mL
			Rate mL/h____
			Rate units/h _____
			Initials_____
				Time_____
				  IV Heparin
				Bolus _____units mL
				Rate mL/h____
				Rate units/h_____
				Initials_____

Initials	07 08 09 (10) 11 12 13 14 15 16 17 18 19 20 21 22 23 24			01 02 03 04 05 06
INR _____ Wafarin po od as ordered daily (Coumadin) Dose_____ ordered on_____ By_____ Dose routine_____ Withhold if INR > ___3_____ Notify doctor.	Instructions: Call doctor with INR by 1300hrs for daily orders. WATCH FOR ANY SIGNS OF BLEEDING Transiton period: Warfarin _____ Heparin_____			Client Information

Figure 16.20   MAR designed only for anticoagulants.

stroke, and carry the risk of severe bleeding. They are usually stat orders in the Emergency Department or the Intensive Care Unit.

This medication order involves special instructions. Some facilities use a regular scheduled MAR to record anticoagulants; others use a specially designed MAR (Figure 16.20). This MAR is used for either heparin or warfarin. It has provision for the nurse or the clinical secretary to write in the aPTT or the INR as soon as the results are sent to the floor from the lab. In most cases, the nurse will not give an anticoagulant until the related lab test is known. If the INR or aPTT results are too high, the anticoagulant will be held until the doctor reviews the situation.

In a manual environment using a multiday MAR, transcribing this warfarin order would entail *clearly* marking off the days on which the medication was to be given. This is illustrated in Figure 16.21, which is a MAR for the following order that Dr. Marion has written for Dick Ray: warfarin 2.5 mg q2days. Hold if INR > 3. Figure 16.22 shows the same order on a single-day CMAR.

Warfarin and other anticoagulants are often given at 1400 hours because it allows time for the INR test to be done and the results called back to the patient care unit.

Sliding Scale Orders

Sometimes, a doctor orders a drug with a dosage on a sliding scale—that is, to be adjusted on the basis of test results. Insulin is the most common example. The nurses would take a finger-prick blood sugar reading and adjust the dose of insulin accordingly.

When transcribing this order for Mrs. Carrier, Mary would use the scheduled MAR or a special MAR used for hypoglycemics. She would copy the order exactly as it appears. Either Mary or the nurse is responsible for receiving, reporting, and writing the blood

STRATFORD GENERAL HOSPITAL											
Check here if more than one page □											
Scheduled Medication Administration Record											
Start /reorder	Stop date	Medication dose, route, frequency	Hour Due	Jan 23	24	25	26	27	28	29	30
Jan 23		Warfarin 2.5. mg po od q 2 days			╲		╲		╲		╳
		Hold if INR > 3	1400		╱		╱		╱		
		GIVE ON EVEN DAYS									

Figure 16.21 Warfarin order transcribed on a unit where CMARs are not used.

sugar results from the lab on the MAR. It is up to the nurse to give the appropriate amount of insulin given each time it is administered. An order for insulin on a sliding scale for Mrs. Carrier might look like this:

Give Humulin R 2 units if bs between 10.1 and 12; 4 units if bs between 12.1 and 14, and 6 units if bs between 14.1 and 16. Call if bs is higher than 16.

Another example of a sliding scale order is seen in Figure 16.23. Some facilities put insulin orders—either regular or sliding scale orders—on a special anticoagulant MAR. Almost every facility has a differently designed CMAR or MAR for recording hypoglycemic medications.

Medication Orders Related to Lab Values

Instead of writing a sliding scale order, the doctor might, if the patient has been reasonably well stabilized on a medication, write the order with a static value of insulin to be given (e.g., Regular Insulin 5 U qam). However, she may ask to be called with lab test results and

CONESTOGA GENERAL HOSPITAL SCHEDULED MEDICATION ADMINISTRATION RECORD	Rick Day
From **Jan 23 /xx** 0700 to: Jan 24 /xx @ 0659h Allergies: Sulpha Drugs No Allergies Adverse Reactions Diagnosis Circle time med given and initial below.	2944 Blake St. Calgary, Alberta DOB 22/09/47 #123432333 Dr. G. Merion

Medication and Directions		
Hours	07 08 09 10 11 12 13 **14** 15 16 17 18 19 20 21 22 23 24	01 02 03 04 05 06
Warfarin (Coumadin) 2.5 mg po od **Give odd days only @ 1400hours** <u>**Watch for any signs of bleeding.**</u> <u>**Do not give if INR is above 3.**</u>		
Initial		
	07 08 09 10 11 12 13 14 15 16 17 18 19 20 21 22 23 24	01 02 03 04 05 06
Initial		

Figure 16.22 Warfarin transcribed on a CMAR.

			Dietz, Henry
	Blood sugars 24h during the day		123 Duncan St.
	Regular insulin 3 u if bs > 15 and 10 u if > 20		Vancouver B.C.
	Novolin 30/70 u qam and 5 u ac supper		DOB 22/09/47
			#123432333
			Dr. D. Sung

date	time	Physician's printed name	Signature
Jan 3/XX	1000	Dr. D. Sung	Dr. D. Sung

Figure 16.23 Doctor's order for insulin on a sliding scale.

alter the order, if needed, on the basis of the results. Similarly, when clients receive certain medications, such as digoxin and gentamicin, serum levels of the drug must be monitored to ensure that they stay within the therapeutic range.

Often, the lab will telephone the doctor directly with abnormal results or call the floor and ask you to notify the doctor—this is particularly so if the results are very abnormal. Whether the lab results are available online or paper based, abnormal results will be highlighted or otherwise identified. However, do not rely on someone else to identify problems. Look at lab results yourself, do your best to be aware of abnormal results, and report them promptly to the nurse and/or doctor.

Alternatively, in the electronic environment, the lab may just send the critical or abnormal lab results to the unit electronically and have them printed on the unit.

Computerized Physician Order Entry

Some facilities have introduced a virtually paperless order system called computerized physician order entry (CPOE). The doctor enters her orders directly into the computer, and they are processed on the computer. The clinical secretary is still responsible for ensuring that the orders have been transferred to the department responsible, notifying the appropriate person or department of orders requiring immediate attention.

Such systems are programmed to immediately check all medication orders against the patient's current information to identify potential mistakes or problems, such as allergies. Some hospitals have mobile computerized medication carts. The nurses can access the patient's medication profile and retrieve the required medication using an individualized patient code. Using a handheld computer, they then enter onto the patient's medication record the time and date the medication was given.

Although facilities using electronic orders find them satisfactory and much easier to read, such systems are still not common in many parts of the country. Some physicians and facilities are uncomfortable with computer-generated orders, perhaps fearing tampering with orders without the safeguard of handwritten, signed orders. In fact, hospitals that use electronic orders have security measures, including an electronic signature.

MEDICATION ORDERS RELATED TO SURGERY

As discussed previously, preoperative, or "preop," medication orders, if any, are usually written by anaesthetists.

Preoperative medication orders must be dealt with in a timely and organized manner. With so many clients coming in on the day of the surgery, things can get rushed. If you are prepared, things will be less hectic. If you have preoperative clients on your unit, make it a routine to carefully check the charts of any clients going for surgery for orders; make sure none have been left in an unflagged chart. Do this well before the booked OR time; it is fairly common for the OR to call for the patient ahead of time. If you work on a pre-admit unit, you would anticipate that all clients have preop orders to be processed.

Postoperative Medication Orders

When a patient goes for surgery, all previous doctors' orders for inpatients are automatically discontinued or put on hold. After the surgery, orders must be reordered or renewed. Often, doctors write the orders out again particularly if different from the preoperative orders. Sometimes, the doctor will simply order all the orders that were in effect before the surgery. This type of order would simply read "Resume all preop orders." In a computerized environment the, CMAR generated would reflect the previous orders reactivated. If new orders are written, the CMAR would contain the new medication orders. Surgeons will either use preprinted standard postop order sheets (Figure 16.3, preprinted postoperative orders for major surgery) or write the postop orders out entirely by hand on a doctor's order sheet.

Individualized Postoperative Medication Orders

A physician not using a standard order sheet has to write postoperative orders on the routine doctor's order sheet. Each area of care and treatment must be addressed. Figure 16.24 is an individualized postoperative order sheet for Mr. Dietz.

Standard Orders for Major Surgery

Figure 16.3 shows a standard doctor's order form filled out. As previously noted, the doctor selects the specific orders he wants activated for a particular client. All immediate areas of patient care must be addressed. In these orders you will see an order for patient-controlled analgesia (a PCA or "pain pump"). Alternatively, the doctor could simply order a major analgesic to be given IM or IV; this will be followed by an oral painkiller when the patient is able to take oral meds and when the pain is less severe. Antiemetics are almost always ordered; nausea and vomiting are common postoperatively, particularly if the surgery involved manipulation of the bowel. As well, many of the narcotic analgesics have the nasty side effect of nausea and vomiting. Laxatives are ordered to stimulate bowel evacuation, which is also compromised postoperatively by bowel manipulation and/or the effects of the general anaesthetic. Codeine, which is often ordered as a postop analgesic, also causes constipation, necessitating a laxative. If a laxative is ineffective, a back-up order for an enema is usually included. Resumption of diet depends on the type of surgery and the postop recovery pattern of the client. If the patient has a gastric tube, resumption of anything orally occurs only after the tube has been removed and there are bowel sounds present. This is much like hearing your own stomach grumbling when you are hungry—and indicates that the bowel is active and able to process food. Many postoperative clients have a catheter into the bladder following surgery. It is frequently removed on the first postop day, depending on the type and extent of the surgery. If the patient cannot pass urine (void) within several hours after the chatter is removed, the catheter is ordered reinserted. If the patient can't void, the bladder will continue to fill and become distended and possibly atonic. Activity is encouraged as soon as possible after most operations. Despite the lack of enthusiasm on part of the patient, early ambulation has many benefits and facilitates an earlier recovery.

	CONESTOGA GENERAL HOSPITAL **DOCTORS ORDER SHEET** *Please fax to Pharmacy & note date/time*	Dietz, Henry 123 Duncan St. Vancouver B.C DOB 22 09 47 071608 Dr. G. Hanson

	IV 2.3 and 1.3 at 100cc/hr, Add 20 meg of KCL to alternate bags
	Demerol 50–75 mg IM q2–3h prn
	Gravol 50–100 mg IM q3–4h prn
	Dangle tonight–up in the am
	Shorten penrose drain daily starting day 3
	Foley catheter to straight drainage; remove in the am. May
	Recatheterize if unable to avoid within 8 hours
	Vital signs as per post op routine
	N?G tube to low gomco sucetion. Remove when bowel sounds active
	CBC and lites in am.

date *Jan 2/XX*	time *2000*	Physician's printed name Dr. G. Hanson	Signature *Dr. G. Hanson*

Figure 16.24 Individualized postoperative orders.

Patients who are on a variety of medications preoperatively will need them postoperatively as well. If the patient is NPO and/or has an N/G tube, the doctor will order these medications by another route.

Overlapping Orders

Occasionally, an anaesthetist and a surgeon will both write orders for postoperative analgesics for the same client. Do not implement both sets of orders. Check agency policies on how to handle this situation; in most facilities, the orders written last (which will usually be the surgeon's) apply.

Future Trends Order entry in hospitals will continue to become more computer based. Hospitals across Canada are all computerized to some degree, but few are what

Tip

If any other combination of physicians "double order" for the patient or write conflicting orders, sometimes you can sort out with the nurses whose orders to follow. Technically the last written order is the one that should be followed. That may not always make sense—checking and clarifying does.

you would call "paperless." The last elements to become entirely electronic appear to be doctors' orders and medication administration records. The process by which doctors enter orders directly into the client's EHR is called computerized provider order entry, or CPOE. The term *provider* allows for the fact that other health professionals may be licensed to enter orders for a patient. CPOE improves patient safety by alerting the physician of drug-to-drug interactions, and allows for checking medication doses against the patient's physical constraints and medication history. The system can initiate appropriate laboratory monitoring of a drug and make recommendations to alter the course of therapy.

More recently, pharmacies have advanced to the point where they are almost entirely electronic. Orders faxed or scanned to a pharmacy are received and posted to a smart board. Medications are placed in priority sequence. A central robot in pharmacy prepares and sends medications to the floor. Medication carts are computerized. As nurses dispense medications, a pharmacy can "read" when a patient's supply (or stock medications) are low and will automatically prepare a refill. Nurses must scan a finger and have a password to log to use the pharmacy cart.

Effectively carrying out the responsibilities of the clinical secretary requires a high level of skill and increasing levels of responsibility. This includes applying complex computer skills and coordinating both paper-based and computerized documents, understanding mnemonics, knowing how to move around the computerized system swiftly, using look-up tables, and maximizing the efficacy of the system. Keeping abreast of changes and advances in the computerized environment is essential, and improvements are continuous—for example, the recent addition to some systems of "quick orders" or an "order sentence." This is a dialogue box containing common orders from a specific physician along with details and instructions of how to implement the orders.

SUMMARY

1. Order entry means processing doctors' instructions so that they can be implemented. Order entry is one of the clinical secretary's most complex responsibilities, requiring familiarity with agency policies and computer systems and a knowledge of medications, diagnostic tests, and other components of treatment. Equally important are organization, alertness, the ability to set priorities, and attention to detail. Absolute accuracy is essential. Even a misplaced decimal can have serious consequences.

2. Few environments are all paper based. You will primarily be working with a computer and computerized charts. Doctors' orders are stll handwritten in many facilities, however. You will likely still use actual charts for each patient—used to file that patient's paper documents (which ones and how many will vary with each facility, and sometimes the units within one facility). A few paper lab and diagnostic requisitions may still be used. These include requisitions that must be signed by the physician, and those necessary to process orders during computer down time. Paper medication administration records are still the rule rather than the exception. In some environments you may still be required to use a paper Kardex or patient care

summary, which contains essential information on the patient's assessments, care and treatments.

3. The doctor's order sheet may be standard or individualized. A standard or preprinted form lists the most common orders used for a particular situation, such as pre-admission, following major surgery or minor surgery, a heart attack, or postpartum. Handwritten orders are commonly used for daily orders, atypical situations, minor changes, and additions to established orders. All orders must clearly identify the patient and must be signed by the physician and dated.

4. Develop a routine for transcribing medication orders that works for you. Read over the order sheet first and identify any stat and urgent orders. (Some facilities discriminate between stat and urgent; others do not.) Process those first, notify the appropriate nurse of the stat order, and follow up with any other appropriate actions. Always check and recheck the spelling of the drug, the dose, the route, and the frequency. Never guess; if in doubt, ask a nurse or the doctor, or your clinical pharmacist, for clarification. Alternatively, check spelling in a drug manual (CPS). You may have that resource (or others) on the hospital intranet. Never rush. Always be sure that you are transcribing onto the right patient's chart or electronic file. Be especially careful when there are clients with similar names.

5. Pay attention to the start and stop dates as well as to the dose, route, and frequency. This is very important where medications are handled electronically. Always transcribe the order the way it was written. If you are discontinuing a medication, mark it clearly on the appropriate MAR. If a new medication is started, clearly identify the start date. Medications ordered for a specific time frame likewise must have the start and stop dates clearly marked on the MAR. Always notify the nurse of changes in medication orders.

6. Use tracking symbols or codes to keep track of what you have done. These symbols (also called transcription codes) vary with every facility. Sign off when you have finished transcribing an order. Most facilities require a nurse to check your order entry. Think of this as an extra safeguard, not your primary means of catching errors.

7. Fax your orders to the pharmacy as soon as you get them, or scan then into the patient's chart—checking the stat box if there are stat meds. If the pharmacy is computerized for med distribution, this puts the orders in a priority spot on the smart board in pharmacy. Have your orders checked by a nurse after you have completed the order entry process and be sure she signs them off.

8. Medications fall into two major categories: scheduled or routine and PRN, which means "as necessary." Other types of medication orders include stat (immediately); single dose; sliding scale orders, which adjust dosage based on test results; and bolus dose, a higher than normal dose to rapidly raise serum levels of the medication. Times at which routine drugs are to be given are dictated by the drug itself and by agency routines.

9. All orders, in most facilities, are cancelled (or alternatively, put on hold) when a patient goes for surgery. If the doctor orders previous medications restarted, you must look them up and write in new orders for each. Patients are typically ordered an analgesic after surgery and often an antiemetic and a laxative.

Key Terms

Review Questions

1. What are the basic tools necessary to begin transcribing doctor's orders?

2. Where does the process of order entry begin?

3. What elements must be present on the doctor's order sheet before you can begin transcribing the orders?

4. What are standard doctor's orders, and when are they used?

5. Summarize the information recorded in a Kardex or a PI screen.

6. Why are physicians asked to flag charts? What are the clinical secretary's related responsibilities?

7. What must you do when you have finished transcribing a patient's orders?

8. Differentiate among routine or standing medication orders, PRN, stat, and sliding scale medication orders.

9. Why is it important for you to add a patient's medication administration records to the patient's preoperative chart?

Application Exercises

1. Research a hospital or other health-care facility near you. Interview a clinical secretary or someone in Health information Services. Find out what kind of doctor's order forms, medication administration records, and Kardex or health records are used. How many paper forms are used, and how many records are electronic? In what ways do the forms differ from those shown in this chapter? Are there any specific policies about entry that are not described in this chapter?

2. Using the MAR format used by a local hospital, or one supplied by your instructor, transcribe the following orders written by Dr. Smith for Alison Chambers.

    Demerol 75–100 mg IM q3–4h PRN

    Gravol 50 mg IM or PO q4h PRN for nausea

    Magnolax 30 cc bid start day 3 PRN

    Tylenol 3 po q4h PRN

3. Using the same MAR format as in question 2, transcribe the following orders written by Dr. Martello for Alia Hondo. Alia is diabetic and has a urinary tract infection.

    Insulin Novolin 30/70 20 units q am and 7 units ac supper

    Insulin Novolin R 10 units stat

    Insulin by reaction Novolin R 5 units if BS greater than 15 qam

    Finger-prick blood sugar readings qid

    Lasix 20 mg q2days

    Septra DS I tab bid 7 days

4. Working from the postoperative orders in Figure 16.3, check off medications you think your client, Mrs. Vredeveldt, will need postoperatively. Review each category and each order. Choose a major narcotic analgesic and a less potent one. Pick an antiemetic and a laxative. Process these orders onto the appropriate MARs used in a facility in your area.

Websites of Interest

US FDA: Drug Name Confusion

www.fda.gov/fdac/features/2005/405_confusion.html

This site offers advice on clarifying dose designations, abbreviations, and symbols when interpreting and transcribing medication orders.

National Patient Safety Goal: Identify Look-alike/Sound-alike Drugs

www.jointcommission.org/NR/rdonlyres/C92AAB3F-A9BD-431C-8628-11DD2D1D53CC/0/lasa.pdf

You will find information on look-alike/sound-alike drugs that will clarify drug information and help you to avoid mistakes when transcribing medications.

Chapter 17
Orders for Intravenous Therapy

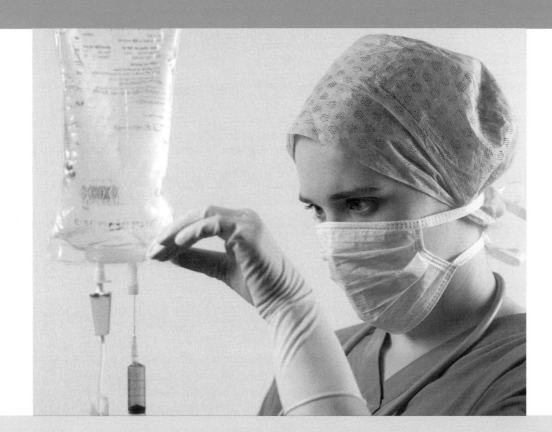

Learning Objectives

On completing this chapter, you will be able to:

1. Explain what homeostasis is and list the main elements responsible for fluid and electrolyte balance in the body.

2. Discuss the indications for and goals of intravenous therapy.

3. Describe the equipment involved in intravenous therapy.

4. Summarize the purpose and advantages of an electronic infusion pump.

5. Explain the advantages of patient-controlled analgesia.

6. Effectively transcribe/enter orders related to intravenous infusion.

7. Effectively transcribe/enter orders related to intravenous medications.

8. Discuss the indications for blood product transfusion.

9. List the more common blood products and state their uses.

Intravenous (IV) therapy is a common hospital treatment and is often critical to the hospitalized patient's recovery. With the current emphasis on home-based care, patients can also be discharged and maintained on parenteral therapy in the home under the supervision of community nurses. Intravenous means "into the vein," when fluids are introduced directly into the body's circulatory system. Intravenous therapy is prescribed for people requiring electrolyte replacement, fluids, calories, vitamins, or other nutritional substances. It is also a route for administering medications, including chemotherapy, and is used for transfusion of blood and blood products.

To accurately transcribe IV orders, you need to understand the purposes and goals of IV therapy, the equipment involved, and the types of solutions ordered by physicians. This chapter will briefly discuss the more common types of intravenous solutions, intravenous medications, and blood products.

Although intravenous solutions themselves are not, strictly speaking, medications, in some facilities they are treated and recorded in much the same manner because they involve introducing something external into the body system. In most facilities, however, IV solutions are tracked and recorded electronically and are not part of the medication administration record. When a medication is delivered by way of an IV solution, the medication, dose, and/or dilution are recorded on the MAR and signed for accordingly by the nurse responsible for the medication's delivery.

> **intravenous (IV)** administered directly into the circulatory system via a vein.

FLUIDS AND ELECTROLYTES

TO FULLY UNDERSTAND THE PURPOSE AND GOALS OF IV THERAPY, YOU NEED A BASIC understanding of the roles that fluids and electrolytes play in maintaining the body's equilibrium.

Electrolyte is a term for salts or ions that dissolve in water and have electrical charges. Salt or sodium (Na), potassium (K), and chloride (Cl) are the three major electrolytes our bodies need to function properly. Imbalances in sodium may be caused by inappropriate fluid loss or retention. Potassium imbalances can cause muscle twitching and an irregular heartbeat. Other electrolytes present are magnesium (Mg), calcium (Ca), and zinc (Zn), bicarbonate (HCO_3), phosphate (PO_3), sulphate (SO_2), as well as minute amounts of other substances, often referred to as trace elements. The human body is mostly water— an estimated 60 percent of an adult's weight comprises fluids—so these electrolytes can be found everywhere. Approximately two thirds of our body fluids are found within body cells (**intracellular**), and the remaining one third is found inside the blood vessels (**intravascular**) and in the spaces between cells (**interstitial** spaces).

Because they are electronically charged, these electrolytes assist in transporting nutrients to and from the cells within the body and play a role in muscle and nerve functions.

Our body depends on a balance, or **homeostasis**, of fluids and electrolytes for normal function and good health.

The body's fluid balance and electrolyte composition are primarily maintained by the respiratory system, the gastrointestinal system, the circulatory and renal systems, and the integumentary system. For example, the kidneys help keep the electrolyte concentrations in the blood properly balanced by decreasing urine output when we are dehydrated. The loss and replacement of body fluids occurs almost continuously. Normally, people lose fluids during the course of the day through breathing and perspiration and through the gastrointestinal system and the kidneys. Generally, we take in fluids at meals and drink when we are

> **intracellular** within the cells of the body.
>
> **intravascular** within blood vessels.
>
> **interstitial** in between the body's cells.
>
> **homeostasis** a balance between the body's internal conditions and the environment.

thirsty. If the weather is hot or we exercise, we usually take extra fluids. The feeling of thirst is a compensatory mechanism triggered when the body feels the need for fluid. Hydration occurs without a thought, and for most of us, our body's fluids and electrolytes remain balanced. When someone is ill, maintaining his body's homeostasis can become more difficult. With illness, our metabolism is altered; dietary and fluid intake may be compromised by nausea and vomiting; we may not feel like eating or drinking; and normal bowel function may be complicated by diarrhea. All of these changes stress our body's ability to maintain homeostasis. Many illnesses can cause an imbalance in the body's fluid and electrolytes. In many cases, these disturbances must be treated promptly, often with intravenous therapy.

Note: Electrolytes are measured in milli-equivalents (mEq) per litre of water, or in milligrams per 100 millilitres.

INDICATIONS FOR IV THERAPY

ANY CONDITION OR CIRCUMSTANCE THAT PREVENTS A PERSON FROM EATING OR DRINKING or from properly absorbing food and fluids or that causes excessive fluid loss will result in the need for fluid and nutritional replacement. If the person is ill and cannot eat or drink adequately, this replacement may be required by alternative methods. Doctors will order IV fluid when the patient

- is unable to take fluids by mouth (injury or trauma to the mouth, throat, or esophagus; tumours; stroke);
- has had an abnormal loss of body fluids, such as from severe vomiting or diarrhea;
- is injured or has a life-threatening condition, such as hemorrhage, and requires immediate life-saving solutions, such as blood or medications (for example, after a heart attack, medications may be given IV for faster effect);
- has had major surgery (an IV line usually provides hydration, nourishment, and sometimes medication, until the person can resume intake of food and fluids by mouth);
- requires medications that can be given only intravenously; and
- requires prophylactic antibiotics while undergoing surgical or invasive diagnostic procedures. Note that some medications can be given intravenously through a PRN adaptor (discussed later), thus the patient doesn't need a continuous IV.

The goals of intravenous therapy reflect the reason the IV therapy is needed:

- To restore the body's acid–base balance
- To restore blood loss caused by hemorrhage
- To stabilize a patient with a bleeding disorder, such as hemophilia
- To correct dehydration by restoring the body's water, electrolytes, and so on
- To provide nutrition when the patient's gastrointestinal tract is resting

IV EQUIPMENT

A DOCTOR'S ORDER IS NECESSARY TO START AN IV. FIRST, THE ORDER IS RECEIVED AND THE required solution selected. Next, the nurse will select the type of IV tubing required, the appropriate device for inserting the IV into the patient's vein, and the site, or spot, on the patient to start the IV.

IV Bag

The IV bag contains the solution itself and is usually a soft pliable container as illustrated in Figure 17.1. (Glass bottles were used for IV solutions until plastic bags were introduced in the early 1970s. Occasionally, glass bottles are still used for medications solutions adversely affected by plastic.) IV bags come in a variety of sizes. The largest routinely used contains 1000 **cc** or mL of fluid. There are 500 cc bags as well. Smaller volumes are also available, from 50 to 250 cc, and are used primarily for medications. IV bags have numbers along the side that indicate the volume of fluid. Nurses reading these markers can see how much solution is remaining in the bag and, therefore, how much has been infused or absorbed into the patient. Nurses will chart the number of cc remaining in the bag as fluid to be absorbed (TBA).

Equipment Used for Starting the IV

IV Access Devices

To start an IV, a needle or IV catheter must be inserted into a patient's vein. Various types are available. The generic name for a catheter is an "intracatheter" or "intracath." This is a plastic IV catheters have several components. A needle with a bevelled tip is used to enter the patient's vein. The catheter itself is made of a synthetic material and can slide over the needle. The needle is withdrawn, leaving the pliable catheter in the vein. When the needle is properly situated in the vein, a small chamber called a flash chamber (located behind the needle) fills with blood. An **Angiocatheter** (patented name) is a common type of IV catheter used, often just called an **antiocath** in the hospital (see Fig. 17.2). The **distal** end of the catheter has an adaptor (also called a connector) to which IV tubing is attached. The IV tubing is attached to the IV bag or solution. The site of insertion is known as the IV site. To stabilize the catheter, the site is usually covered with a pliable transparent film, such as Tegaderm. The transparent film also allows the nurses to assess the IV site for problems. The nurse will write the date of insertion of the IV catheter on the tape.

Butterfly   A butterfly (Figure 17.3) is a device used to start an IV in smaller peripheral veins for short-term IVs and when fragile veins make insertion of a larger intracatheter difficult. The butterfly has two wing-like projections on either side of a small needle. The

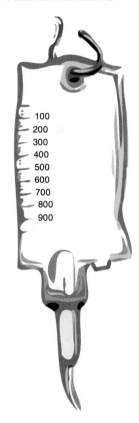

cc   cubic centimetre; 1 cc equals 1 millilitre (1 mL). In hospitals, cc is used more often than mL.

Figure 17.1   The IV bag.

angiocatheter or angiocath a plastic tube, usually attached to the puncturing needle, inserted into a bmn_lood vessel for infusion, injection, or pressure monitoring.

distal   the part farthest from the body

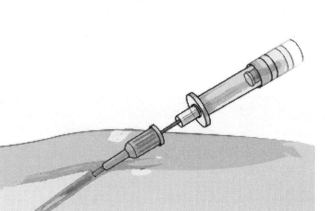

Figure 17.2   An Angiocatheter

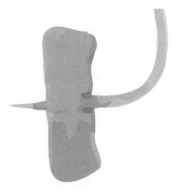

Figure 17.3 A butterfly

flaps are used as handles to guide and insert the needle. The butterfly is easy to insert and can be successfully started in small veins. The disadvantage is that it can easily slip out of a vein and allow the IV solution to seep into the surrounding interstitial tissues.

Central Venous IV   There are a number of devices used to deliver long-term IV therapy, ranging from weeks to years. They are used for chemotherapy, medication, blood or blood products, hyperalimentation, and monitoring central venous pressure. They are also used for patients with poor veins to reduce the trauma of repeated IV starts. Central venous lines increase patient comfort and help reduce anxiety in patients who must have frequent venous access.

Central Venous Access Device/Catheter CVD or CVC   A CVD (also referred to as a central line) is a small, flexible, plastic tube, the tip of which is placed in the superior or inferior vena cava or the right atrium. It is inserted through a central vein—that is, one that lies in the chest cavity or that is linked directly to the right atrium (the right, upper chamber of the heart). The main access veins used are the internal and external jugular and the subclavian veins. Occasionally, the femoral vein (found in the leg) is used. A type of central line called a PICC line (pronounced "pick") is often inserted into the brachial or cephalic vein or others in the arm above the elbow. Although peripheral, these veins are larger and deeper than the ones below the elbow.

Indications and Complications

Inserting a CVD into a patient is more invasive than inserting a peripheral line, and the decision to use one is not taken lightly. It may be done in conjunction with ultrasound by an experienced practitioner. Indications include situations where a peripheral line cannot be establisher, for delivering solutions that are unsafe to deliver using a peripheral line (for example TPN, discussed later in the chapter, some medications used for cardio-vascular purposes, chemotherapeutic agents, or blood products over a long time frame). They are used to place pulmonary artery catheters and heart pacers, and provide access for physicians if frequent blood sampling is required. Complications that can arise from the insertion of a central line include the development of an air embolism, an arrhythmia, an, infection, and perforation of a vessel. Informed consent is required for this procedure, so as the clinical secretary, you would need to prepare this document and fill out as much as you can. The nurse or doctor will obtain and witness the consent.

Types of Central Line Catheters

SPD (central processing department, sometimes referred to as central supply):. This is where items are sterilized for use and where you would call for most equipment used for treatments and patient care.

Peripherally Inserted Central Catheter (PICC Line)   This specialized device (pronounced "pick line") is a long, thin, flexible tube that is inserted in a vein in the arm and then goes through the subclavian vein to the vena cava, a large vein that enters the heart (see Figure 17.4). A chest X-ray is usually taken after the line is inserted to confirm that it is in the right place. An RN can draw blood from the PICC to avoid puncturing a peripheral vein. Many PICC lines have two or more lumina (spaces inside the catheter tube), enabling concurrent treatments. PICC lines are usually held in place by sutures but may sometimes be carefully taped to the skin. The site of insertion is covered with a dressing that must be changed periodically. This may or may not be ordered by the doctor. Some facilities consider changing the dressing a routine part of nursing care. It should, however, be recorded on the Kardex or the care plan.

Tunneled Catheters   Tunneled catheters, such as the Hickman and Broviac cath-eters, are inserted under the skin and "tunnel" some distance before entering the vein. These devices must be inserted surgically and are, therefore, more invasive. The surgeon often inserts this line with the assistance of a type of X-ray called fluoroscopy. As with the PICC line, patients with a tunneled catheter will have a dressing that must be assessed and changed regularly. Most lines require flushing with a heparin solution at specified intervals. These activities must be appropriately noted on the Kardex or patient-care summary. There are also implantable devices that provide this type of intravenous access.

Implanted Ports   An implanted port has similar characteristics to a tunneled cath-eter. It is left entirely under the skin. Required medication is injected *through the skin* into the catheter. Some implanted ports are designed with a small, refillable reservoir to which medications can be added—they are slowly released into the patient's bloodstream. The

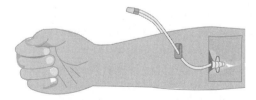

Figure 17.4   An inserted PICC line.

advantage of an implanted port is that it is less restrictive to the patient, out of sight, and requires much less care (as opposed to a daily dressing). Chances of infection are smaller.

The Intravenous Site

The choice of site (the point of insertion) depends on the condition of the patient's veins, how long the IV is needed, and the type of solution ordered. The IV site must be carefully checked by the nurses several times during a shift. They watch for infection or inflammation of the vein and make sure that the solution is infusing properly. Occasionally, the IV goes "interstitial"; that is, the needle or catheter is dislodged from the vein, and the solution begins to seep into the interstitial tissues around the site. If this happens, the IV must be stopped and, if necessary, restarted somewhere else. In most hospitals, the IV site is routinely changed every so often. For example, a hospital may have a policy of changing both the tubing and the site every 72 hours. This policy may be set aside for a patient with poor veins, when finding a new site may be painful and difficult. Any time you transcribe an IV order, you must specify site checks. On a paper record, write down that the site is to be checked. On a computer, the instruction may be added to the electronic record by default; if not, add it manually.

Tubing/Infusion Sets

General Characteristics of IV tubing/drip set
The IV solution is attached to the IV catheter by way of IV tubing—commonly called a drip set or an infusion set. Common components of a drip set include a spiked end that inserts into the IV bag, a drip chamber through which you can see the solution dripping as it drains from the bag, a pinch clamp which the nurses can squeeze to stop the flow, and a regulating clamp that is used to adjust the speed of the infusion (when not connected to an infusion pump). This clamp freely slides up and down the tubing for better flow control if required. In addition, there are two or three access ports which are used to administer intravenous medications or add a second IV line. There may also be a lock adaptor which can attach to the IV catheter, keeping the vein opened but allowing the IV tubing to be removed. One common name for this device is a Luer lock.

Mainline IV Administration Set
A mainline IV set (Figure 17.5) includes a length of tubing (about 2 metres) with a spiked end used to pierce the IV bag port. This allows the solution in the bag to drip into the tubing and upper chamber, located about 15 cm below the insertion port. The IV drops can be visualized in this chamber. These drops are used to calculate the rate of the IV infusion, calculated in **drops per minute (gtt/min)**. A tubing set may be described as a macro drip (which typically delivers about 1cc of fluid for every 10 drops as visualized in the chamber) or a mini drip (which delivers 1cc for every 60 drops), depending on the number of drops per minute. Macro chambers are used do deliver larger volumes of fluid faster. Mini drips are used when fluid is such that smaller volumes of fluids and/or medications are required. The drip chamber is designed to deliver a designated volume/drop. The other end of the tubing has a protected sterile tip that is inserted into the distal port on the intracatheter in the patient's vein. This creates a closed, sterile system for the delivery of the fluid into the vein. Even if the IV is regulated by an electronic pump, the nurses monitor the drops as a safeguard.

Along the length of the tubing are one or two roller clamps, which are used to control the rate of the IV infusion. One roller clamp is usually located higher up on the

drops per minute (gtt/min) measure of the rate of IV infusion.

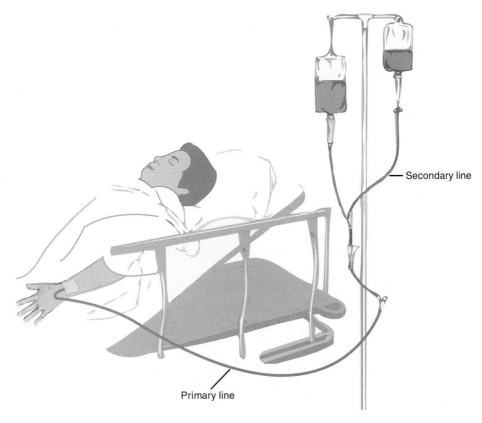

Figure 17.5 Mainline IV set.

tubing near the IV bag. The other, if present, is found at the end of the tubing near the intracatheter.

There are also one or two *ports* (access points) where intravenous medications can be added to the IV, usually found about 5 cm above the site of insertion, and about halfway up the length of tubing. This port is made of rubber. A needle or connector can be inserted; when it is withdrawn, the port will seal itself, maintaining the closed sterile system.

"Y" Tubing Set and Blood Infusion Set   Y tubing has two ports and thus can accommodate two IV bags that allow the infusion of two separate solutions simultaneously. Special Y tubing sets used specifically for blood transfusions have a filter in the drip chamber that filters the infusing blood. Typically one bag is saline and the other the blood or blood product. Y tubing may also be used to deliver medications. Sometimes blood is run with two mainline IV sets that are piggy backed at the level of the angiocatheter. Blood and blood products must *always* be run with normal saline—a good point to remember. Other IV solutions cause the blood to clot.

Medication Administration Sets   When a separate or secondary infusion line is needed, the most popular set-up is a medication administration set or "add-a-line." This is a separate IV tubing set, shorter than a main line set, that is plugged into the main IV line via a port. Using this system may also be referred to as hanging a minibag because the amount of IV solution is usually 250 cc or less (Figure 17.6). Sometimes, a doctor will order a medication to be given IV, and the nurses will automatically deliver it in a

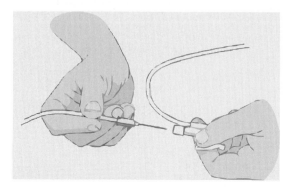

Figure 17.6 Adding a secondary line.

minibag. Occasionally, the doctor will specify that it is to be delivered by an add-a-line or minibag. Special add-a-lines can also be used to deliver blood. As with the Y tubing, this set has a special "blood" filter.

Delivery Systems

Electronic Flow Regulators

Controller   This device controls the intravenous infusion rate by monitoring either the drops per minute (gtt/min) the IV set delivers or the volume of fluid (cc/min or mL/min) delivered. Devices that monitor volume are more popular because the calculations are not affected by the size or viscosity of the drop.

Electronic Infusion Pump   A number of electronic pumps are available, operating on different principles, to deliver intravenous solutions conveniently and accurately (Figure 17.7). These devices exert pressure on the IV tubing, providing accurate delivery

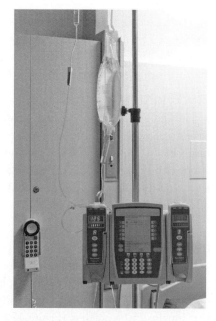

Figure 17.7 An electronic IV infusion pump.

of a programmed volume. They offer read-outs of how much solution has infused and how much remains to be absorbed (TBA). These pumps will sound an alarm if something obstructs the infusion or if the IV bag runs dry. They increase accuracy and decrease the number of times the nurse must check on the infusion. If you hear an IV pump alarm, do not panic. Find a nurse to check it immediately. Alarms can be sensitive and will sometimes go off if a patient merely bends her arm or lies on the tubing. IV pumps may be kept on the floor, or you may need to order them from Central Supply or the Stores.

The Buritrol   A buritrol (shown in Figure 17.8) is a chamber added to an IV line between the bag and the line to control volumes more closely. It is used to ensure safety when the volume of fluid delivered must be carefully monitored, often with children. Some hospitals require buritrols when an IV line is used for a child under a given age or weight.

Gravity-Based Systems

No devices are needed when gravity is used to deliver IV solutions. The bag is on an IV pole, held higher than the IV site. The solution drips into the tubing and into the patient's vein by gravity. The nurses regulate the infusion rate by manually adjusting the roller clamp on the IV tubing to the required gtt/min.

Patient-Controlled Analgesia (PCA)   Patient Controlled Analgesia machines (PCAs) have become the standard of care on post-operative units and elsewhere if significant pain control is required. The pumps are complicated. Nurses are responsible for adding medications, setting the frequency these medications are delivered, and monitoring their overall function. They are rarely used in emergency situations.

Patient-controlled analgesia (PCA) allows the patient to control his own pain by self-administering IV pain medication. It is widely used for postoperative pain. The order may read, "PCA pump for postoperative pain." The pump is attached to the patient's main IV line, sometimes on a portable device, such as an IV pole. It contains a syringe prefilled with a designated amount/dose of medication ordered by the physician. Suppose Dr. Hanson had ordered morphine PCA for Mr. Black. The nurse would program the pump to deliver a specific dose over a specific time frame (e.g., 2 mg every five minutes). Mr. Black would have an activation device that looks much like a call bell. Every time he felt uncomfortable, he would press a little button on the activation device and receive a small amount of morphine intravenously. With this device, Mr. Black does not have to call the nurse when he is in pain and does not have to wait for her to find time to give him an injection. He can get relief almost continuously. Moreover, he is participating in his own care and has a sense of control over his pain. Studies have shown that getting small amounts of analgesic at regular intervals gives better pain control than doses every few hours. In addition, PCA makes patients less anxious, which can itself reduce pain. It is thought that patients require less medication overall by this method than with conventional medications. A patient with a higher tolerance for pain may choose to use even less. The patient cannot exceed the prescribed maximum dose because the pump is programmed to lock out at a certain level. However, a patient who keeps pressing the button after this point has been reached may still experience pain relief through a **placebo effect**. As well, the use of the PCA pump reduces the number of injections a patient receives and saves the nurses time. It has also proven to reduce medication errors resulting from nurses

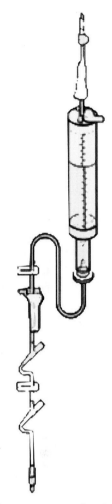

Figure 17.8   A buritrol.

patient controlled analgesia   a mechanism by which a patient can self-administer analgesic intravenously with the assistance of a computerized pump. It allows for the introduction of specific doses at preset intervals into the IV line.

placebo effect   an; improvement in symptoms without active treatment that occurs for psychological reasons when a person thinks he is getting treatment.

administering analgesics every time a patient needs one. Use of this device also provides useful information on an individual patient's pain scale and how much analgesic he needs to control his pain.

There are disadvantages to PCA pumps, but they are few. The pumps can malfunction, although that is infrequent. Malfunction is often related to human error—connecting the pump improperly, incorrect dose programming (e.g., dose too low, lock-out period too long), or an improperly maintained battery. Pumps may not be suitable for some patients with disabilities, resulting in the patient being unable to activate the device to deliver the required analgesic, although pumps are available with alternate delivery modes (other than pressing a button). If a patient falls asleep and is unable to activate delivery of the analgesic, the pain may intensify. This can be overcome by continuous infusion of analgesic in the background—with the bolus being delivered by the patient to curb breakthrough pain.

Continuous Medication Pumps

A number of pumps are designed to deliver continuous medication. They are usually used for pain control, often for chronically or terminally ill patients who may be receiving palliative care. Patients may use these devices in hospital, but they are especially useful in allowing effective pain control that enables some people to remain at home. These pumps deliver specified doses of medications, sometimes from a syringe attached to a port or opening that infuses the medication into the patient. A subcutaneous route is often used.

One such device is a computer-assisted dispatch (CAD) pump. This portable pump is designed for infusions of fewer than 10 cc per day. It can be programmed to provide continuous infusion, to be patient activated, or to deliver doses at specified times. The dose can be altered by the nurse or physician but usually not by the patient.

Heparin/Saline Lock/PRN Adaptor

A **heparin lock** or a **saline lock**, also called a **PRN adapter**, is an intravenous connection device that provides intravenous access (a port) without requiring continuous infusion (or an IV bag of any kind). It sits in the vein and must be flushed at regular to keep it from getting plugged. Some doctors order that it be flushed with a solution containing heparin (Hepalean) to prevent the blood from clotting; this would be called a heparin or hep lock. More commonly, physicians order flushing with normal saline (discussed below); the device is then called a saline lock. Flushing frequency varies; the doctor may write an order to "flush saline lock q4h or q shift." Often, this action is implied and is done automatically, as per agency policy (almost always once every 8-hour shift, although this may not be the case if the lock is regularly used for IV infusion). Otherwise, the clinical secretary must ensure that all related instructions for site change and flushing are added accordingly to either the PI screen or the manual Kardex. If the patient is receiving regular IV medication via a PRN adaptor, it may not need flushing. However, if the adaptor is in place and used infrequently, flushing is a must to keep

heparin (hep) lock (saline lock, PRN adapter) device that provides intravenous access when needed, without continuous infusion. It sits in the vein and must be flushed at specific intervals with saline solution or heparin solution.

Tip

When a "hep" or saline lock is ordered, be sure you follow hospital protocol to alert the nurses when the device must be flushed. This information is usually recorded appropriately on the nursing care plan (PI screen or Kardex). There may be a component to add to the medication administration record, depending on the agencies policies.

the port patent. You can see the spot for recording on a manual Kardex in Figure 17.12. On a PI screen, the instructions for flushing would be marked as "A" for activated.

Indications for ordering a saline lock are mainly to provide IV access to the patient. For example, someone who must have frequent IV medications, or someone who is undergoing a procedure or has a condition where immediate IV access might be required urgently.

Usually, the doctor does not specifically order flushing, as it is considered part of the related routine.

There are several types of these devices on the market. Figure 17.9 illustrates one form of lock. This device can be inserted initially, or an existing IV route can be changed to a heparin or saline lock with the use of an adapter. The doctor might order "Reduce IV to saline lock" or "Reduce IV to hep lock." To implement this order, the nurses would take down the IV tubing and bag and connect an adapter or "lock" to the angiocatheter that sits in the patient's vein.

When transcribing an order for a hep or saline lock, you may be required to record it on the same sheet as other IV medications or just on the Kardex or PI screen. Some facilities put the order to flush a hep lock on the standard MAR, noting the route as IV. On an electronic chart, if the instructions to flush with a specific solution at specific times are not in the look-up table, add the instructions as per order or unit policy.

Intravenous Push (IV Push) Some medications are administered directly into the vein, or into an ongoing IV infusion, using a syringe and needle. This is known as an **IV push (IVP)** or IV bolus. Be careful with the abbreviation IVP, which is also used for intravenous pyelogram, a radiograph of the renal pelvis and ureter done with contrast medium administered intravenously. (Radiograph IVPs are not done as frequently as in the past, giving way to ultrasound.) The context should make clear which is meant. Medications delivered by IV push can be delivered directly into the vein or through a port in the IV tubing.

IV push (IVP) a medication given into the vein or into an ongoing IV infusion, using a syringe and needle.

Suppose Dr. Hanson issues an order for Mr. Black: "Lasix 20 mg IV push stat." Mary records this on the single-dose MAR, noting the route as "IV push." Dr. Hanson then issues another order "Give morphine 2.5 mg IV push now. Repeat in 20 min 2 PRN." This means that Mr. Black is to receive 2.5 mg of morphine through his IV immediately and that the dose can be repeated twice, if needed; each repeat must be 20 minutes apart. You may question the frequency of this order, having seen orders for narcotic analgesics given q3–4h by subcutaneous or intramuscular injection. With the IV route, much smaller doses are administered more frequently. The dose takes effect much more quickly, but it also wears off more quickly. You may see IV orders for morphine or MS Contin to be given every 10 to 15 minutes.

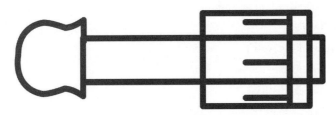

Figure 17.9 A heparin or saline lock.

COMPONENTS OF AN IV ORDER

WHEN TRANSCRIBING AN IV ORDER, ENSURE THAT THE FOLLOWING COMPONENTS ARE included:

- Rate of infusion or flow rate
- Start date
- How long the IV is to be continued and
- Solution ordered

Flow Rate

The rate of flow is how fast the doctor wants the fluid to be infused into the patient's vein. The rate ordered depends on the patient's condition and the purpose of the IV. If the patient is dehydrated, the rate may be fairly fast (e.g., 150 cc/h). If the patient is receiving IV fluid to maintain electrolyte balance and hydration, the rate will be moderate (75cc to 125 cc/h). If the patient is receiving the IV only for medication infusion, the rate may be quite slow (approximately 50 cc/h), noted as to keep the vein open or TKVO. Rates must be carefully monitored; too much fluid too quickly can strain the cardiovascular system and compromise a patient, particularly an older adult or a young child.

The rate of flow is regulated by the use of electronic devices (IV pumps) or manually by the nurses, using a roller clamp on a gravity-fed IV tubing set. The rate is usually ordered as cc/hour. The nurses will convert cc/hour into drops/minute (gtt/min) using a specific formula for the type and/or manufacturer of IV administration set being used. For example, using a Baxter set, 125 cc/h is approximately 21 drops gtt/min; 100 cc/h converts to approximately 17 gtt/min.

Start Date

This is noted because the nurses will use the start date to determine when the IV or the IV tubing has to be changed. The tubing is changed every so often, as is the site for peripheral IVs, with the exception of most central lines. If it is difficult to start an IV on a patient, it may be left in longer than the routine time, sometimes a week or more if no problems occur. The tubing is changed to decrease the chances of infection, and the site is changed to minimize trauma to the vein resulting from prolonged use. The start date should be added to the appropriate places when the order is transcribed, usually on the electronic or traditional Kardex.

When the IV Is To Be Discontinued   An IV may be ordered for a specific period or to deliver a specific amount of solution; in other cases, discontinuation may depend on the patient's condition. For example, the doctor may order an IV until the patient is able to drink sufficiently to provide himself with adequate fluids and nutrition. Orders might be written as follows:

D/C when drinking well

D/C after current bag is absorbed

D/C if IV goes interstitial

D/C when last dose of the medication is through

Carefully note any such instructions on the Kardex or PI screen.

Types of Intravenous Solutions

There are many IV solutions from which a physician can choose to suit the patient's need and condition. They must be transcribed accurately and legibly. The wrong IV solution can harm or even kill a patient. The more common intravenous fluids are discussed below. In choosing what solution to order for a particular patient the doctor will consider the tonicity of the solution as well as any additives, such as potassium or dextrose. Table 17.1 shows some common abbreviations.

Ringer's Lactate Solution   Ringer's lactate (RL) is sometimes called lactated Ringer's (LR). It contains water and electrolytes (sodium, potassium, calcium, and chloride). Lactate is used for milder cases of metabolic acidosis, for dehydration, and for shock states, such as for burn patients who have lost a lot of extracellular fluid. An order for Ringer's lactate may be written in any of the following ways:

> IV lactated Ringer's @ 100 cc/h
>
> Ringer's lactate @ 100 cc/h
>
> RL @ 100 cc/h
>
> LR @ 100 cc/h

2/3 and 1/3   This solution, one of the most frequently ordered, contains 3.3% glucose and 0.3% sodium chloride. The main purpose of this solution is maintaining adequate hydration and normal fluid balance. (It is used for maintenance purposes versus restorative or resuscitative purposes.) It may also be written as "3.3% dextrose and 0.3% NaCl" but you will see it most commonly as "2/3 and 1/3 @ 100 cc/h," for example.

D5W   D5W is also written as 5% D/W (5% DW) and means 5% dextrose in water. This solution is used primarily to replace water loss, such as in a dehydrated patient, and to provide some nutrition (about 200 calories per litre). It does not provide electrolytes.

This solution is frequently used to keep the vein open (TKVO) when the physician wants access to the vein through an IV line but has not ordered a saline lock. To keep the vein open, sometimes the physician will order a certain amount of solution per hour and sometimes not. For example, the doctor might write any of the following:

> D5W TKVO
>
> 5% DW @ 75 cc/h
>
> DW 5% @ 75 cc/h

Table 17.1   Common Abbreviations for Identifying IV Solutions

Abbreviation	Name
RL	Ringer's lactate
2/3 & 1/3	3.3% dextrose in 0.3% NaCL
5% DW	5% Dextrose in water
D5NS	5% dextrose in normal saline
N/S	Normal saline or 0.9% NaCL
D5 1/2NS or .45NS/D5W	5% dextrose in half strength normal saline

Normal Saline Normal saline, which may also be written as 0.9% NaCl, is a solution of pure ordinary salt (made up of sodium and chlorine) in water. It is referred to as *physiological* or *isotonic* because it will not alter normal electrolyte balance. It is used to treat patients who have lost a lot of body fluids, such as from hemorrhage. This solution restores electrolyte balance but does not contain any calories and, unlike dextrose solutions, will not interfere with a diabetic's sugar levels. Normal saline is the only intravenous fluid that may be run with blood. That is, the moment the blood stops flowing, the normal saline will kick in; it is also used to flush the tubing. In most facilities, all IV meds are mixed in normal saline, and normal saline is used for TKVO unless the patient is severely compromised with some such condition as congestive heart failure (CHF) and should not have saline. In that case, the internist may order IV meds in D5W. Aside from being used intravenously, it is also used to flush wounds and eyes because it is not irritating. An order for normal saline might be written in any of the following forms:

0.9% NaCl @ 125 cc/h

N/S @ 125 cc/h

normal saline @ 125 cc/h

5% Dextrose and 0.9 NaCl This solution is also known as D5NS. It is used to treat dehydration and as fluid for daily maintenance of body fluids and nutrition. It is very similar to normal saline.

0.45% NaCl A 0.45% NaCl solution, also ordered as 1/2 NS, has equal proportions of sodium and chloride but has half the sodium chloride of normal saline. It is often used to dilute acid in the blood when a patient is experiencing metabolic acidosis, a condition in which the body is too acidic. It may be a better maintenance fluid if larger amounts have to be administered.

THE PROCESS OF IV ORDER TRANSCRIPTION

Transcribing IV orders follows the same principles as for medications. IV medications are usually delivered in a minibag (a small IV bag containing 100 cc or less of solution) which is piggybacked on the main line through a port. Medication can also be added straight to the larger bag of IV solution itself. In most hospitals, the Pharmacy will premix medications in IV bags as ordered and also stock certain more commonly used mixtures of medications with solutions. A doctor may order more than one solution for a patient and alternate them or otherwise specify just how they are to be infused. Figure 17.10 shows an order for more than one solution and a solution with a medication in it.

This order translates to starting an IV of 2/3 and 1/3 solution, using a 1000 cc bag, to run at 100 cc/h. When this bag is finished, the nurses are to hang a bag of 1000 cc's Ringer's lactate with 20 mEq of potassium chloride added. This is to run at 125 cc/h. When the RL is done, the nurses would put up the 2/3 and 1/3, and keep repeating the pattern.

Mixed Computerized/Manual Environment

In Mary's hospital, as in most computerized/manual environments, IV orders are entered onto the PI screen, often onto a section called Clinical Parameters, Clinical Interventions, or Intravenous Therapy.

CONESTOGA GENERAL HOSPITAL
DOCTOR'S ORDER SHEET

Please fax to Pharmacy & note date/time

				Mr. Black
	100 cc 2.3 & 1/3 @ 125 cc/h alternate with 1000cc RL with 20 meq KCl			
	@ 125 cc/h			

date *April 24*	time	Physician's printed name Dr. G. Hanson	Signature *Dr. G. Hanson*

Figure 17.10 Doctor's orders showing alternating IV solutions.

The only time she manually attends to these orders is when medications are involved that must be physically transcribed onto a c MAR. On April 21 she receives the doctor's order for IV therapy (Figure 17.11) for Mr. Black, an inpatient. She applies the steps outlined in Chapter 16. First, she ensures that the order has been dated, signed, and properly labelled with Mr. Black's identifying information. She notes that Mr. Black has no recorded allergies. She also checks and finds that there is nothing urgent or stat on the order. She prepares to process the order.

- She gets Mr. Black's MAR and goes into Mr. Black's computerized chart.
- She selects "IV therapy" from a look-up menu and accesses the look-up table for IV solutions. A selection of choices appears on the screen.

CONESTOGA GENERAL HOSPITAL
SCHEDULED SINGLE DAY MEDICATION ADMINISTRATION RECORD   Mr. Black
From Mon 21 April/xx 0700h to: Tues 22 April/xx @ 0659h
Allergies:
Adverse Reactions
Diagnosis

Medication and Directions			
Hours	07 08 09 10 11 12 13 14 15 16 17 18 19 20 21 22 23 24		01 02 03 04 05 06
20 meq of KCl/litre of RL +++initial when new bag is started+++ Initial	Start date: April 21/xx Stop date: None specified IV to run at 125 cc/h This IV is alternated with 1/3 and 1/3 running at 100 cc/h		
Ancef 1 g q6h IV × 5 days 0600 1200 1800 2200 +++given in 50cc N/S+++ Initial	Start date: April 21/xx @ 1200h Stop date: April 25 @ 1200h		
  Initial			

Figure 17.11 CMAR showing how IV medications in solution are charted.

- Mary selects the first solution ordered—2/3 and 1/3—and transfers this selection to the appropriate place on Mr. Black's PI screen.

- She repeats the above step, selecting a 1000 cc bag of Ringer's lactate from the drop down menu.

- A prompt appears asking Mary to include any related comments or interventions. If "RL with 20 mEq KCl" appears in the drop-down table, she selects it. Otherwise, she manually adds the 20 meq of KCl that are to be mixed with each litre RL. In almost all facilities medications ordered for larger IV bags (like KCL) or to be given in minibags are prepared in pharmacy and sent to the unit -so nurses are not actually adding medication to IV bags) There may be exceptional circumstances to this. Mary also adds the related nursing care if it is not included by default. It should include a prompt for nursing assessment of the IV site and the frequency with which the IV tubing and the IV catheter should be changed. Mary enters on the PI screen the dates on which these interventions should occur, as well as the specific instructions for alternating bags. Mary completes the order, signs off with the RN and faxes the order to Pharmacy.

- Because the Ringer's lactate contains a medication (20 meq of KCl), Mary must add the medication to a medication administration record—or wait for the CMAR to be sent to the floor from the Pharmacy. Figure 17.11 shows the KCl added to a scheduled CMAR.

- The 2/3 and 1/3 would not go on the CMAR because it doesn't contain a medication. It would be recorded electronically.

The Manual Environment

If Mary were processing the orders manually, she would write the IV solutions and related instructions on the Kardex (Figure 17.12) In this example, Mary has identified the IV solution, and added the rate at which each is to run. She has also written in the instructions to alternate the 2/3 and 1/3 with the RL containing the 20 meq of KCl. Where the kardex asks for the dates for tubing and site changes, Mary has added April 23, 26, and 29. (The tubing and site is changed q72 hours per hospital policy, and the IV was started on April 21. She counts using the day the IV was started as day 1.)

Other	
INTRAVENOUS MONITORING (circle solution)	
Primary lines	
Date: Apr 21 1. □ **2/3 & 1/3;** □ **N/S;** □ **5% D/W;** □ **0 .45NaCl**	
Other: *Ringers lactate with 20 meq of KCl @ 125 cc/h*	
Date: Apr 21 2. X□ **2/3 & 1/3;** □ **N/S;** □ **5% D/W;** □ **0 .45NaCl** *ALTERNATE 1/3 AND 1/3 WITH KOl @ 125 cc/h*	
□ Tubing change (q72h) Dates: *Apr 23/26/29*	
□ Change Site: (q72h) Location *L wrist* Dates: *Apr 23/26/29*	
Other	
Secondary Line with meds note times of med administration	
Date: 1	
Date: 2.	
□ PRN Adaptor □ Change Site: Location	
□ **Flush- (minimum once/shift)**	
Times:	
□ **IV dc** □ **PRN adaptor d/c** **Date**	

Figure 17.12 Portion of a Kardex showing IV order.

There are very few facilities that currently record IV information manually. Those that still do have fluid balance sheets allowing for all IV information to be recorded on them, avoiding the need to put related information anywhere else. This includes when an IV was hung, how much has infused hourly, and any other action involving IV therapy.

Computerized Recording of IV Solutions

Most facilities now record IV solutions only electronically. The clinical secretary would choose the appropriate options for IV management to add to the PI screen. This may appear on the screen as a default under the heading of IV management. The nurses would note on the clinical record, under IV therapy, the amount of IV solution infused and when new bags were hung. The only thing recorded on the hard copy of the MAR would be the medication. As far as other charting is concerned, the nurses would note any irregularities related to the IV on the electronic or paper multidisciplinary/nurse's notes.

When ordering IV medications, the doctor may not specify the solution in which the nurses or pharmacy should dilute the medication or the volume of solution. There are guidelines that clearly outline what medications may be mixed in what solutions and in what volume. Often, the choice will be normal saline or the same solution as the person is getting in the main line, if there is one. If the patient has a saline or heparin lock and is getting only IV infusion with the medication, normal saline or 5% D/W is the usual choice. The nurses would record the solution they infused it in, and the volume would be added to the fluid balance tracking sheet.

Suppose that on April 21, Dr. Hanson also wrote the following order for another patient, Mr. Hiu: "Ancef 1 g IV q6h 5 days." Note that the doctor has specified only the medication, route, dose, and frequency. In this case, Mr. Hiu does not have an actual IV. It is understood, then, that this medication will be delivered in a minibag using an add-a-line through a PRN adaptor. In the computerized environment where the Pharmacy Department prepares the CMARs, they may specify the solution in which the medication is prepared as well as the volume in the information that is printed on the MAR (Figure 17.13). On this CMAR, Pharmacy has specified the type of solution (normal saline) and the volume (100 cc) that the Ancef is mixed in. They have also noted the discontinuation date. For the most part, Pharmacy premixes such medications. There are occasions when the nurse mixes the medications in a minibag on the floor in a solution, following facility/pharmacy guidelines.

CONESTOGA GENERAL HOSPITAL SCHEDULED SINGLE DAY MEDICATION ADMINISTRATION RECORD	Mr. Hiu

From Mon 21 April/xx 0700h to: Tues 22 April/xx @ 0659h
Allergies:
Adverse Reactions
Diagnosis

Medication and Directions			
Hours	07 08 09 10 11 12 13 14 15 16 17 18 19 20 21 22 23 24		01 02 03 04 05 06
Ancef 1 g in 100 cc n/s IV q6h × 5 days Start Apr 21 @ 1200 D/C Apr 26 @ 0600 Initial			
Initial			

Figure 17.13 CMAR recording Ancef for Mr. Hiu.

INTRAVENOUS MONITORING (circle solution)					
Primary lines					
Date:	1. □ 2/3 & 1/3;	□ N/S;	□ 5% D/W;	□ 0.45NaCl	
Other:					
Date: Apr 21	2. X□ 2/3 & 1/3;	□ N/S;	□ 5% D/W;	□ 0.45NaCl	
Other					
Secondary Line with meds *note times of med administration*					
Date: Apr21	1. *Ancef 1 g q6h in 100 cc of N/S 0600 – 1200-1800-2200 h × 5 days last dose 0600 Apr 26/xx*				
Date:	2.				
□ Tubing change (q72h)			Dates:		
□ Change Site: (q72h)		Location	Dates:		
□ PRN Adaptor □ Change Site: (q72h)		*Apr 23/26/29*		Location	*L forearm*
□ Flush- (minimum once/shift)					
Times:					
□ IV □ PRN adaptor d/c		**Date**			

Figure 17.14 Portion of a Kardex showing Ancef delivered in an IV as a secondary line.

An IV medication added to a minibag is considered a scheduled medication and is recorded on the scheduled MAR (shown in Figure 17.13). In the electronic environment, the Ancef in the minibag (also called a secondary line) would be added under the appropriate heading on the PI screen. If using a paper Kardex, the information would be added under the heading of Secondary Line. (See Figure 17.14.) Mary has noted the dates for routine changing of the PRN adaptor. Although the Ancef is to be given for five days, there is no specific order to discontinue the PRN adaptor; hence Mary has left that part of the Kardex blank.

Note that doctors often do prescribe IV antibiotics because this route can overcome many of the drawbacks involving oral agents. The concentration of the antibiotic is more stable and predictable because the medication is not affected by variables in the gastrointestinal tract affecting absorption. As well, IV antibiotics are used for more serious infections that need immediate and aggressive treatment. Some of the more powerful antibiotics are not available as oral agents.

BLOOD TRANSFUSIONS

A physician who wants to order blood replacement for a patient can choose from several blood products, depending on the patient's need and diagnosis and sometimes on the patient's wishes. The patient may refuse to have a blood transfusion for personal or religious reasons. Jehovah's Witnesses, for example, usually refuse to receive any blood or blood products because they believe the Bible prohibits them to from doing so. For the most part, their right to refuse treatment is respected, although there have been cases where the province or territory has overridden the parents' wishes when a physician believes the transfusion is necessary for the child's survival.

Reasons for Blood Transfusion

Doctors most commonly order blood transfusion as prophylaxis for a patient undergoing major surgery, to treat anemia, or to treat blood loss from hemorrhage. Other blood products are administered for various reasons. For example, factor VIII is given to hemophiliacs for clotting, often with other components in the form of a solution called cryoprecipitate.

Prophylaxis   Most surgeons will order blood, usually packed cells (see explanation below) to be available for patients having major surgery in case of excessive blood loss during surgery. Blood will be cross-matched for a patient and held in the lab for her. If she does not need the blood, it will be released and available for another suitable recipient.

Anemia   Anemia is characterized by too few red blood cells in a person's blood. There are a number of causes for this. Severe anemia is usually treated with the infusion of packed cells.

Acute Blood Loss   Any situation in which a person loses an excessive amount of blood (usually by definition over 750 cc) is called a hemorrhage. This causes the body to go into shock. The most effective way to treat massive hemorrhage is by blood replacement.

Preparation

Before receiving a blood transfusion, a patient must be cross-matched and typed (that is, his blood type and Rh factor among other things must be determined) to ensure that he receives compatible blood. Otherwise a serious reaction could occur. The physician will order the type of blood or blood product the patient is to receive.

Types of Blood Products

Whole Blood   If a doctor orders whole blood, it will be ordered as a unit of blood: approximately 520 cc of donated blood. It may be used to treat excessive blood loss resulting from trauma, surgery, or burns. Whole blood is not frequently ordered.

Platelets   Platelets are extracted from whole blood and ordered for someone with thrombocytopenia, or a low blood platelet count. Anyone with low platelets is at risk for bleeding disorders, in particular disseminated intravascular coagulopathy (DIC), a potentially fatal condition characterized by widespread bleeding. Platelets, too, are ordered by the unit.

Fresh Frozen Plasma   Plasma, derived from whole blood, contains all coagulation, or clotting, factors and is given to patients with coagulation defects. One unit is usually approximately 225 cc.

Packed Cells   The most commonly ordered blood product is packed cells: red blood cells separated from whole blood by a process called centrifugation. Packed blood cells may be used to correct anemia when extra volume is not desirable for a patient (e.g., in the case of congestive heart failure). Because it does not contain white blood cells, it poses less risk of minor reactions. A doctor might order "Cross and type for two units of packed cells" or "CT for 2 units of packed cells on cross-match for two units of packed cells."

Albumin   This is a protein extracted from the blood and is often used to expand fluid volume within the blood vessels.

Cryoprecipitate   Cryoprecipitate is part of the fresh frozen plasma that contains a clotting factor called factor VIII. It is most commonly given to hemophiliacs to help control bleeding.

The Blood Transfusion Process and the Clinical Secretary's Responsibilities

Though procedures vary from one hospital to another, the following section outlines the typical process. If the blood is ordered for someone who is going for major surgery, the person will be cross-matched and typed. The selection and amount of blood product ordered will be prepared for the patient and held in the blood bank until used, or until it is clear that the patient will not need it. The blood bank will send a list of the units prepared for the patient. Each unit of blood product will be assigned an identification number. Always note it on the Kardex or PI screen if blood is being held for a patient.

Whether manually or electronically, a requisition is sent to the blood bank, and the blood bank notifies the floor when the blood product is ready. If it is to be given as soon as available, someone from the patient-care unit will go to the lab to pick it up. You may occasionally be asked to do this. If so, you must complete a series of checks with the lab technologist to ensure that you are getting precisely what has been ordered for the patient. Bring the floor's copy of the blood requisition and/or the patient's addressograph card. Check this information against the unit of blood product being sent to the floor and against the ledger in which the same information is recorded. Check the blood product again with the nurses, confirming the patient's name, hospital number, room number, blood type, and the number assigned to the unit of blood product.

In a manual environment, you may need to addressograph a special vital signs graph used for patients receiving transfusions. The nurses check the patient's vital signs frequently to detect any reaction, especially in the first hour when reactions are most likely. In a computerized environment, the nurses would enter the vital signs electronically. Even in computerized environments, vital signs taken frequently are sometimes documented on paper as well.

HYPERALIMENTATION OR TOTAL PARENTERAL NUTRITION

HYPERALIMENTATION OR TOTAL PARENTERAL NUTRITION (TPN) IS THE INTRAVENOUS administration of nutrients to patients who cannot absorb food through their gastrointestinal tract. This is discussed in Chapter 18.

Future Trends

Intravenous therapy will always be an integral part of treatment as required for both medical and surgical patients. However, equipment and IV management techniques are always being improved. For example, the use of heparin has declined in some environments with the increasing use of low-dose heparin products. Pain management is almost always controlled by patient-controlled analgesic devices or "pain pumps" which eliminate the need for frequent injections. Pharmaceutical products for pain control as well as the mode of delivery are constantly being researched. Newer still is the use of regional pain control using an IV pump (like the PCA device) or a disposable elastomeric pump. Local analgesia is delivered to the incisional site.

Modes of recording IV therapy will continue to move to the electronic format and, at some point, be a paperless component of total patient care.

SUMMARY

1. Our health depends on a balance of fluids and electrolytes, known as homeostasis. Healthy people take this balance for granted and maintain it naturally. Our bodies correct imbalances; for example, thirst prompts us to maintain fluid levels. The most common elements in maintaining homeostasis are sodium, potassium, and chloride. These electronically charged ions assist with the transport of nutrients within the body and contribute to muscle and nerve functions. Sick people are especially at risk for fluid and electrolyte imbalances.

2. Intravenous therapy is used to correct electrolyte imbalances, maintain homeostasis, deliver medications, and supply blood products, when needed. It is used to rehydrate patients or maintain hydration and fluid balance in patients who cannot eat or drink because of disease, trauma, or surgery.

3. Infusion can be started with an IV catheter, a butterfly needle, or a central line. These lines are more invasive but are required when a more stable line is needed and patient treatment more complex. A PICC line is one of three types of central lines commonly used. Various types of tubing are available depending on the patient's needs.

4. IV solutions may be delivered by gravity, with the rate controlled by roller clamps, or by various types of pumps. Patient-controlled analgesia (PCA) pumps allow patients to administer their own pain relief as needed (within strict parameters). Small portable pumps, some of which are computer assisted (e.g., CAD), allow patients with terminal or chronic illnesses to manage pain at home.

5. A range of solutions are available; among the more common are D5W (5% dextrose in water), 2/3 and 1/3 (3.3% glucose and 0.3% sodium chloride), normal saline (0.9% NaCl in water), and Ringer's lactate (a solution of sodium, potassium, calcium, and chloride).

6. Intravenous medication is administered in three ways: directly into the vein (an IV push), mixed in the solution in the IV bag, or, most commonly, mixed in a minibag. The minibag is attached to what is an add-a-line or secondary medication administration set.

7. Transcribing IV orders follows the basic steps outlined in Chapter 16. The IV order must include the solution, the rate, and the start date. You would note any related nursing responsibilities or specific criteria, including site assessment and changing the IV and tubing. Orders for the same solution may sometimes be written in several ways. Be sure you understand the order that you are transcribing. Always check the rate carefully as well. Too much fluid, or the incorrect fluid, can be harmful, even fatal. Any medications given are recorded on a MAR. Medications given in minibags are usually recorded as scheduled medications. Those in solution in the main bag may be recorded on the scheduled MAR, or a medication infusion record.

8. Blood and blood products are ordered for anemia or excessive loss of blood and as a precaution for surgery. The most commonly ordered product is packed cells. A patient's blood type and Rh factor must be checked carefully against donor blood to find a match and prevent potentially fatal reactions.

Key Terms

angiocatheter
   (angiocath) 555

cc 555

distal 555

drops per minute
   (gtt/min) 558

patient controlled
   analgesia 561

heparin lock (saline lock,
   PRN adapter) 562

homeostasis 553

interstitial 553

intracellular 553

intravascular 553

intravenous (IV) 553

IV push 563

placebo effect 561

Review Questions

1. List the common elements that control our body's fluid and electrolyte balance, and briefly describe their functions.

2. What are four indications for intravenous therapy?

3. Briefly describe four of the six goals for intravenous therapy outlined in this chapter.

4. What is a medication administration set?

5. Where would you locate an electronic pump, if required?

6. What would you do if you walked into a room and the alarm of electronic pump was sounding?

7. What is the purpose of patient-controlled analgesia, and how does it work?

8. Where are medications added to a minibag usually transcribed?

9. Why is it important to include the flow rate when transcribing IV infusion orders?

10. What information should be transcribed onto the Kardex or PI screen along with the actual IV order?

Application Exercises

1. Interpret the following IV orders, and transcribe them onto the format advised by your professor.

   a. 4000 cc 5% DW over 24 hours

   b. 1000 cc .045% NaCl 3 @ 100 cc/h

   c. 1000 cc 2/3 and 1/3 2 then reduce to TKVO if drinking well.

   d. Infuse 1 unit of packed cells, then reduce IV to saline lock

2. a. Transcribe the following order onto the format advised by your professor.

	Start PICC line @ 125 cc			Long, Tom
	Give 500 cc bolus of N/S then reduce rate to 125 cc/h			978 Victoria St. Stratford ON N5A 2G3 M 29 06 42 099342 744210088 McManus, Dr. N.
Date Apr–07/xx	Time	Physician's Name Printed Dr. McManus	Physician's signature *Dr. N McManus*	

b. Answer the following questions:

      i. Differentiate among a PICC line, a central line, and an intracatheter.

      ii. What is meant by a bolus, and why might it be given in this case?

      iii. How is the gentamicin likely delivered?

      iv. What are some advantages of giving antibiotics intravenously?

3. Jim, who is about to be hospitalized, asks you to describe what an IV is and what he can expect. Draft a brief response. Ask friends or family members who have had an IV; incorporate any helpful information into your draft explanation.

4. Marinna is worried about having a central line inserted and asks you whether it is the same as having a small IV started in her arm. With a partner, draft a brief summary of what a central line is and briefly explain its benefits. Discuss the responsibilities of the clinical secretary related to an order for a central line.

Websites of Interest

Study Table about IV Therapy
www.studystack.com/studytable-26495
Video of someone starting an IV—helps to explain the components of an IV and tubing
http://emprocedures.com/peripheraliv/procedure.htm
http://www.youtube.com/watch?v=xRTTUVNFlgs
Video explaining how medications are added to a saline lock. This site will help you to understand the process and provides a summary of IV therapy indications and complications and an option to test your knowledge base.

Pain Control after Surgery
www.spineuniverse.com/displayarticle.php/article586.html
This site deals with patient-controlled analgesia (PCA)—purposes, advantages, and links to related articles.

Canadian Blood Services
www.bloodservices.ca/
This site has information on blood and blood products.

Chapter 18
Orders Related to Nutrition

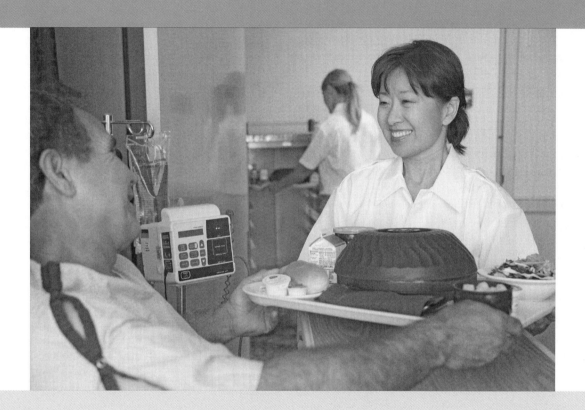

Learning Objectives

On completing this chapter, you will be able to:

1. Discuss the importance of a healthy, balanced diet.
2. Identify five things that affect our metabolism and nutritional needs.
3. Explain the role of the hospital dietitian.
4. Describe various types of diets that may be ordered in the hospital and their purpose.
5. Discuss dietary changes related to laboratory and diagnostic tests.
6. Describe the purpose and progression of postoperative diets.
7. Explain the purpose and types of tube feedings.
8. Summarize various types of tube feedings and related dietary orders.
9. Describe total parenteral nutrition and related dietary orders.

Every person admitted to hospital must have an order for some type of diet. Nutrition is an essential element in the treatment and recovery of all patients. A number of variables affect our dietary intake and nutritional status. These needs are sometimes heightened when we are ill or undergo a surgical procedure and thus must be considered when meeting the nutritional needs of the hospitalized patient. An example is a patient recovering from major surgery—a diet high in protein is essential for tissue repair.

FACTORS AFFECTING NUTRITIONAL NEEDS

Genetics

Our basic body structure is predetermined by genetics and affects our basal **metabolic rate**. Thyroid gland function is also genetically influenced. Low thyroid function slows a person's basal metabolic rate and increased thyroid function increases it.

metabolic rate the amount of energy expended in a given period, or the physical changes that occur in the body that result in heat production.

Age

Metabolic rate usually slows with age, and fewer calories are required. Children, on the other hand, have a much higher metabolic rate and therefore need more calories in proportion to body weight than do adults for ideal growth and development. This is especially so during growth periods, such as during the first two years of life and in adolescence. It is thought that a person's basal metabolic rate starts to slow between the ages of 20 and 22 years.

In hospital, older patients often complain of being served too much, while younger patients ask for more. Dietitians consider a patient's age and weight as well as health status when making up nutritional supplements and special diets.

Gender

Men tend to need more calories than do women, partly because they are, on average, larger and have more muscle mass. Hormones may also play a role in increasing metabolic rate. A diabetic man would usually be prescribed more calories than would a diabetic women. Male hospital patients often eat more than female patients.

Pregnancy

During pregnancy, women must adjust their daily caloric intake to ensure a healthy, well-nourished baby. The woman's **metabolism** increases to meet the energy demands of supporting a pregnancy. Currently, a woman who delivers a baby in hospital spends very little time in the facility. However, when she is there, a diet high in protein and appropriate calories is important. This is especially so if the woman is breastfeeding.

metabolism the physiological and biochemical processes that promote growth and sustain life.

Activity

The more active a person is, the more calories she expends—as those trying to lose weight are usually told. Not only does exercise use energy directly (anywhere from 14 to 40 percent of our total energy is used in activity), but it increases metabolic rates as well. People who are unable to be active because of illness or physical limitations require fewer calories than they otherwise would. Individuals in the hospital are typically inactive and may require fewer calories. Having said that, illness itself, and the process of healing (e.g., from surgery) will increase the body's caloric utilization.

Illness

As previously mentioned, illness will alter a person's caloric needs in various ways. Fever raises the basal metabolic rate, as does trauma, such as surgery. Extra calories, and sometimes extra protein, are also needed to promote tissue repair and recovery.

NUTRITION IN THE HOSPITAL

Canada's Food Guide

Many Canadian hospitals are becoming more conscious about the need to provide patients with food that is not only nutritious, but that offers more variety and tastes good. As with most things, the problem is balancing a budget, shifting expenses, and coming up with innovative ways to accomplish this. A move to using local produce is in motion in many Canadian cities. A website at the end of this chapter details how hospitals are facing these challenges. Canada's Food Guide remains the guiding principle; its website is at the end of this chapter. It includes a link where you can request a free print copy or download a PDF version. It is also available in 10 other languages in addition to English and French. This might be valuable information for patients requesting information about nutritious eating.

The hospital provides all meals and snacks that are ordered by the physician for inpatients, and the cost is covered under the provincial or territorial plan. Hospital schedules reflect traditional meal times. Typically, breakfast arrives between 7 and 8 a.m., lunch between 11:30 a.m. and 12:30 p.m., and supper between 4:00 and 5:00 p.m. Many of a patient's activities, from tests and appointments to medications, revolve around meal times.

Serving Hospital Meals

Patient meals are an integral part of treatment hence the provision and consumption of a balanced diet, essential to aid recovery. A number of food service systems are used to provide meals for patients in the hospital. Most are prepared off-site and brought in at the appropriate times. Special diets, however, are overseen by a team of dieticians.

In a few hospitals, patients' meals are still prepared in the Dietary Department and arrive on trays delivered on cafeteria-style carts. The dietary staff and the nursing staff give out the trays. You may sometimes be asked to help when the unit is short staffed. If you are free, the nurses will always appreciate it if you offer to help distribute trays. Bringing in meal trays sometimes involves "setting up" the patient. The over-bed table may have to be cleared to make room for the tray. Patients may need the head of their bed rolled up and the over-bed table repositioned so they can reach. Some may need to be helped into position. Sometimes, a patient will ask you to arrange the food, cut the meat, pour the tea or coffee, open the milk cartons, or add salt and pepper. More incapacitated patients need to be fed. Feeding patients is not your job; leave it to nurses or family members.

After the trays are delivered, be prepared for complaints from patients about incorrect diets, missing trays, or missing items on trays. Nurses will also let you know if a particular diet has not been changed to match new orders. To save time, check with all the nurses, make a list of required changes, and make a single phone call to Nutritional

Services. If you get an answering machine, leave a message. Nutritional Services will need the patient's name, room number, the type of diet she is on, and then the request. They usually respond promptly. Omitted items and additional food orders may be delivered to the floor or put on the lift if there is one (see Chapter 14). Someone will call to tell you about items on the lift.

Some facilities bring up the food in heated carts; staff ask the patients what they would like, and serve each patient from the cart. This method allows patients their preferences as well as keeping food hotter and all but eliminating the problem of missing trays. Special diets are still prepared as required; however, anyone on a general diet who was missed can be served promptly.

In most facilities, dietary staff will come to the patient-care unit, collect the trays, and take the carts back to the kitchen.

The Dietitian, the Patient, and the Clinical Secretary

All hospitals and other health-care facilities employ a dietitian and often dietary assistants. The dietitian is a knowledgeable and valuable resource for the health-care team.

You will frequently interact with the dietitian to pass on diet orders, including changes because of the patient's condition or scheduled tests. You may also call if the nurses or the physicians request a dietary consultation. Patients who are hospitalized may lose their appetite because they are ill or because the food is different from what they are used to. What people like to eat is affected not only by personal taste but also by cultural factors. Dietitians take on the challenge of designing a diet that takes into account the patient's physical ability to ingest food and nutritional needs, including any special needs caused by illness, while trying to adapt the institutional diet to the person's lifestyle, religion, culture, and personal preferences. They make an effort to accommodate individual needs and wishes within the constraints of the doctor's orders, staff time, and availability of supplies.

You may encounter families that want a specific order requested for the patient. (e.g., the patient would like cereal for breakfast instead of oatmeal). This can usually be done without a doctor's order. If you are uncertain, ask the nurse. In some request cases, you can put in a dietary consult if you are unsure of what is okay for certain patient diets. Sometimes, family will request something simple—e.g., the patient would like apple juice instead of orange juice. You can enter it as a DSN (Dietary Special Needs) for Nutritional Services to keep a note in the patient's file.

TYPES OF DIET ORDERED

Therapeutic Diets

A therapeutic diet is one ordered by a physician as part of a treatment for a disease or clinical condition. It responds to the person's health state and physical ability to tolerate certain foods. Some therapeutic diets are short term; others are long term or for life. Typical diet orders are summarized in Table 18.1 on page 580.

Cardiac   This diet is usually ordered for patients who are admitted with or have preexisting heart disease (e.g., someone who has had a heart attack). There are variations, but the diet is generally low in fat and cholesterol and may restrict sodium (salt) and calories.

Table 18.1 Short Forms for Typical Diet Orders

Usual Order	Explanation	Usual Order	Explanation
NPO	nothing by mouth; place a sign by the patient's bed	Low sodium or low salt	limits sodium intake to less than 3000 mg/day
DAT	diet as tolerated; that is, regular diet: no restriction	Very low sodium	limits sodium intake to 2000 mg/day or less
CF	clear fluids (with no residue)	Soft/surgical soft	low in fibre; some fruits and vegetables not allowed
FF	full fluids		
CF–DAT	start with clear fluids and progress to diet as tolerated	CDA diet 1200 cal	(number of calories may vary) diabetic diet; carbohydrates controlled or
FF–DAT	start with full fluids and progress to diet as tolerated		1200 cal CDA sugary and fatty foods restricted
NAS	no added salt; limits sodium intake to about 3000–4000 mg/day	Cardiac diet	restricts fat, cholesterol, and sometimes salt and calories
		d/c or dc	discontinue

No Added Salt/Na Restricted This diet may be written as NAS, meaning no added salt. Salt should not be added at the table, although sometimes it is allowed in moderation in food preparation. Processed cheeses and cured or smoked meats are avoided, as well as sports drinks, such as Gatorade, and other commercially prepared products with a high sodium content. Desserts, such as sherbet, ice cream, ice milk, yogurt, puddings, and custards are allowed. It is ordered for patients who have problems with **fluid retention** or congestive heart failure (a condition in which the heart does not pump efficiently).

fluid retention an accumulation of fluid in body tissues or body cavities.

Restricted Diets

Restricted diets may limit calories, fat, salt and other substances. A low-fat diet would restrict high fat foods, and allow only low-fat versions of other foods such as yogurt, milk and cheese. Fresh fruits would have no limits.

A variation is the sodium-restricted or low-sodium diet, usually ordered for people with cardiovascular disease, high blood pressure, and kidney problems. Low-sodium is usually considered to be less than 3000 mg per day. How much the doctor wants the patient's sodium restricted depends on the reason for ordering the diet.

metabolic disorder a condition characterized by the body's inability to synthesize or process food into forms the body can use for energy, growth, and development.

Diabetic Diabetes mellitus is a **metabolic disorder** characterized by the inability to properly use glucose. A hormone called insulin, produced by the pancreas, facilitates the entry of glucose from the blood into cells where it can be used. If insulin is absent or insufficient or is inefficiently used, the body cannot properly use glucose, and so it builds up in the bloodstream. Constant high blood sugar levels in the body damage the organs and the vascular system.

Dietary intake is a very important part of controlling a diabetic's blood sugar. Diet control is important for people taking insulin because the dosage needed is affected by diet and exercise. The dietitian plays an important role, especially with a newly diagnosed patient, in education and in establishing and monitoring a diet. Support is important for newly diagnosed diabetics, who usually experience considerable stress; not only have they learned that they have a serious disease, but they must also cope with taking medicine and changing their eating patterns and lifestyle.

A diabetic diet is prepared individually after consultation with the patient and the physician, and it contains a wide range of food choices. It contains a prescribed number of calories and certain proportions of fats, carbohydrates, and proteins. It may be called "1200 cal CDA" or "1400 cal CDA." CDA refers to the Canadian Diabetes Association. Sugary foods should be avoided because they cause the blood sugar to rise very quickly. Excessively fatty foods should also be avoided to reduce heart risk.

Diabetic patients, particularly those with type 1 diabetes (also known as insulin-dependent diabetes mellitus, or IDDM) may receive snacks throughout the day, usually brought by the dietary staff midmorning, mid-afternoon, and at bedtime. They may be placed on a counter in the nurses' station or in the refrigerator in the kitchen. Make sure you know which patients receive snacks and when. Although distributing snacks is not your responsibility, if you see a snack sitting on the counter that you know should be given to a patient, let the nurses know. These snacks are very important to maintain safe blood sugar levels. When insulin is not balanced by food intake, blood sugar drops, and a potentially dangerous insulin reaction can occur. Know the warning sings: irritability, confusion, sleepiness or headaches, shaking, pallor, and sweating. If you suspect a patient is having such a reaction, call the nurse immediately. If the nurse is not available, encourage the patient to eat or drink something containing sugar. Most established diabetics will recognize these signs and know what to do. Newly diagnosed diabetics may not.

Gluten-Free   Celiac disease involves an atrophy of the mucosa (lining) of the upper small intestine. People with this disease cannot properly absorb gluten, a protein found in wheat, rye, barley, oats, triticale, and spelt. If they eat an ordinary diet, they may suffer severe diarrhea and vitamin deficiencies. Individuals diagnosed as celiac must be on a gluten-free diet for the rest of their lives.

Gluten-free versions of common foods, such as bread, pastries, and pasta, are now available in some stores. They are often made with rice flour, which has a short shelf life, and so baked goods are usually sold frozen. Gluten-free all-purpose flour is now available, which can be substituted in some recipes quite successfully. As rice flour tends to be very fine and dry, recipes usually work best if they contain vegetable oil, butter, or eggs.

High-Fibre   Large quantities of fibre stimulate peristaltic action and bowel movements. A high-fibre diet is ordered for patients who have sluggish bowels and constipation. Foods include lean meat, potatoes, vegetables such as spinach or cabbage, and stewed fruit, whole grains, and bran.

Tip

Individuals (celiacs) on gluten-free diets find purchasing gluten-free products expensive. Many do not realize that if the keep all food receipts they can submit them on their income tax returns as a medical expense—worth letting any such patients you may have know in case they do not already.

High-Protein   This diet may be ordered for a patient who needs to gain weight or to repair tissue, such as in the case of someone recovering from major surgery. It emphasizes high-protein foods, such as meat, fish, milk, eggs, legumes, and nuts.

High-Calorie   High-calorie diets are ordered for patients who have had excessive weight loss resulting from illness or who, for other reasons, cannot reach or maintain a healthy weight. As well as ordinary foods high in calories (butter, ice cream, fried foods, and so on), these diets often include special supplements, such as fortified milkshakes (e.g., a product called Ensure).

If someone on your unit is on supplemental feeds, make sure the supplements are refrigerated when they come to the floor, and notify the nurses. Although giving the supplements is the nurses' responsibility, you can help by keeping them informed.

Low-Residue/Surgical Soft   This type of diet, which decreases fibre and cellulose to reduce bowel motility, may be ordered for someone who has had gastrointestinal surgery, who has a partial bowel obstruction, or who has a colostomy or an ileostomy. This diet includes some cheeses, yogurt, eggs, plain pastas, white bread, boiled chicken and turkey, well-cooked beef, and broiled fish. Fruits that are canned, baked, or stewed without skins or seeds (bananas, apple sauce) as well as Cream of Wheat, cornflakes, and rice cereal would be allowed.

Bland   A bland diet may be ordered for someone with long-term or chronic gastritis, peptic ulcers, dyspepsia (upset stomach), or a **hiatus hernia**. This diet contains foods that are easily digested, such as lean tender meats, pasta, potatoes, and canned fruits and vegetables; fried and highly spiced foods are avoided.

> **hiatus hernia**   a condition in which the upper part of the stomach, which is joined to the esophagus or feeding tube, moves up into the chest through a hole (called a hiatus) in the diaphragm.

Regular   A "regular diet" means that the doctor is placing no restrictions on what the patient can eat. It is also ordered as DAT, for "diet as tolerated." With this order, nurses have some flexibility to alter patients' meals and can avoid foods the patients cannot tolerate. Doctors may rely on nurses to alter the diet to suit the patients' needs. A nurse may ask you to order a different diet for a patient, on the basis of nursing assessments.

Ice Chips or Sips Only   This is the first part of a progressive diet and is ordered primarily for patients who have had major surgery. The patient is allowed to suck ice chips or take very small occasional sips of water to moisten the mouth and lips. There is nothing to order for this. Ice is available on most patient-care units as is cold water.

Clear Fluids   A liquid diet minimizes residue and is easier on the digestive system. "Clear fluid" is usually one you can see through; this includes some soups and juices, ginger ale (often given flat), coffee, tea, and plain Jell-O. A clear fluid diet may be ordered for preoperative and postoperative patients or for those who are acutely ill or have acute diarrhea and/or vomiting. It is also ordered prior to certain investigative tests, such as a colonoscopy. A clear fluid diet is not nutritionally adequate in the long run but will keep the patient hydrated until she can tolerate a full fluid or soft diet. Usually, foods are introduced slowly and as tolerated.

Full Fluids   A full-fluid diet offers more choice than a clear fluid diet but is still relatively restrictive. It is ordered for pre- and postoperative patients, patients with stomach problems, and those who cannot tolerate or chew solid foods. If often follows a clear fluid diet and is therefore considered transitional or temporary.

This diet includes all the foods in the clear fluid diet, with the addition of strained soups, milk, and milk products, such as yogurt and ice cream. Fruit and vegetable juices may be taken, as well as eggnog mixtures and custard puddings.

Soft/Mechanical Soft Diet

The mechanical soft diet consists of foods soft in texture, moderately low in fibre, and processed by chopping, grinding or pureeing to be easier to chew. Most milk products, tender meats, mashed potatoes, tender vegetables and fruits and their juices are included in the diet. However, most raw fruits and vegetables, seeds, nuts and dried fruits are excluded.

A soft diet is one that involves little or no chewing and is ordered for patients who have problems chewing or digesting. It may also follow the full-fluid diet as a surgical patient begins to tolerate more foods. It includes liquids, puréed foods, strained cereals, and puddings. Some facilities include eggs and toast.

Puréed   A puréed diet is ordered for patients who cannot chew or who have **dysphagia** (difficulty swallowing). Someone who has had a stroke would be an example. All food is ground to a soft, silky texture. Sometimes, thickeners are added to hot or cold fluids until they are of the desired consistency. Most patients resist a puréed diet; it looks unappealing, and the taste usually is not much better.

dysphagia   difficulty swallowing.

Minced   A minced diet is one in which all food is ground to a fine texture but not as fine as a puréed diet. This diet is used for individuals who can swallow a little but who cannot tolerate larger chunks of food.

Progressive   A progressive diet is a sequence of diets that introduces foods in stages as the patient can tolerate them. It is usually used following major surgery or an illness involving the gastrointestinal tract. It may be ordered as a progressive diet, or the stages may be ordered separately. A progressive diet can start anywhere along the continuum, ranging from sips only through clear fluid, full fluid, and soft, to a regular diet. This diet is discussed in more detail later.

Transitional Diet   A transitional diet is a temporary, limited diet used as an alternative to the progressive diet before and after surgery. This diet may be used for patients before and after abdominal and other types of surgery. Instead of beginning with clear fluids, the patient is immediately introduced to selected solid foods. To reduce indigestible carbohydrates to a minimum, all fruits and vegetables are omitted except strained fruit juice and tomato juice; milk as a beverage is not allowed. Eggs and tender meat are used. Studies have shown that patients tolerate this diet fairly well and receive more nutrients than on a fluid diet. However, some physicians prefer the progressive diet.

TRANSCRIBING DIET ORDERS

IN A PAPER-BASED SYSTEM, A REQUISITION IS NEEDED FOR ANY DIET ORDERED. EITHER CHECK off the required diet from a list on the requisition form, or simply write the type of diet on the requisition. Add the patient's diagnosis and any other relevant information, such as problems with eating, strong food preferences, or food allergies. Stamp the requisition with the addressograph and send it to the Dietary Department. There may or may not be a duplicate copy to retain for the patient's chart. Transcribe the diet order onto the Kardex or PI screen.

PROCEDURES		
MNEMONIC	NAME	ORDER CHECKED
NPO	NOTHING BY MOUTH	
FF	FULL FLUIDS	
CF	CLEAR FLUIDS	
PE	PURÉE	
MN	MINCED	
REG	FULL DIET	
DD	DIABETIC DIET	
GF	GLUTEN-FREE DIET	
LR	LOW RESIDUE	
SS	SURGICAL SOFT	
HP	HIGH PROTEIN	
HF	HIGH FIBRE	
EF	ENTERAL FEEDS	
PAR	PARENTERAL FEEDS	
BRAT	BANANA, RICE, APPLE, TOAST	
T&A	T&A (tonsillectomy and adenoidectomy) DIET— NO RED JELL-O, HOT BEVERAGES	

Figure 18.1 Typical progressive diet after major surgery.

In the computerized environment, select the required diet from a look-up table (Figure 18.1 on page 584). Some software will allow you to access more information about a specific diet, if required. Once selected, the diet appears on another field, along with the patient's identifying information and a field asking for additional information. Enter any relevant information, and enter or file the order. The order will be entered automatically on the PI screen and will also go to Nutritional Services to be processed by the dietitian. If the diet change is for the next meal or some immediate action is required, telephone the dietitian.

Orders for Discharged Patients You need to cancel meals for discharged patients. Find out when the patient plans to leave. As discussed in Chapter 14, patients are encouraged to leave midmorning, so you need to notify Dietary to cancel lunch, using your facility's normal procedure. In some facilities, a formal discharge includes notifying Dietary. In computerized settings, the transcribed discharge order is automatically sent to Dietary, and lunch is usually cancelled automatically. However, if the discharge order comes through late, you need to call Dietary. Also, if a patient has arranged to stay through lunch, you have to call Dietary and ask them to send up the patient's lunch.

DIET ORDERS RELATED TO TESTS AND PROCEDURES

Diagnostic Tests and Hospital Procedures

If the patient is scheduled for a diagnostic test, you often need to ensure that diet has been appropriately altered. The diet preparation will not usually be spelled out in the order for the test; you will be expected to know what tests require diet restrictions and to make sure they are implemented. Before any test requiring an anaesthetic, the patient must remain NPO, usually for 8 to 10 hours. The same holds true for any test that involves visualizing parts of the gastrointestinal tract and for certain blood tests. Other dietary preparations may also apply. Consult the procedure or laboratory manual for clarification. Refer to Chapter 6 for preparatory details regarding the following tests for the hospitalized patient: barium enema, barium swallow, oral glucose tolerance tests, vanillylmandelic acid test (VMA).

Remember that for fasting blood tests for the inpatient, you must post an NPO sign. If a patient is to have a fasting blood sugar or a blood test for cholesterol and triglycerides, he must remain NPO for 8 to 12 hours, except possibly for sips of water with certain medications. Post an NPO sign by the patient's bed the night before. Usually, the blood will be drawn early in the morning just before breakfast arrives, so you may have to hold breakfast briefly but will not usually need to cancel it. Patients who are aware that they are not to eat and are cognitively normal can be trusted to wait but should be reminded. If there is any doubt, the patient should not be given the breakfast tray until after the blood is drawn.

Postoperative Diets

What and how soon the patient is able to eat after surgery will depend on the type and extent of the surgery and the patient's response to the anaesthetic. General anaesthetics cause the gastrointestinal tract to be sluggish and unable to digest food properly; some people recover intestinal motility faster than others. In addition, some people suffer nausea and vomiting. Physicians will consider the patient's response in ordering postoperative diets. Patients who have had surgery on the gastrointestinal tract itself may be NPO for a period of time after the operation and often have nasogastric or **gastric suction.** Patients who have had minor surgery or local anaesthetic are more likely to be able to eat later on the day of surgery but still may require a lighter than normal diet.

When a patient comes back from the OR, the physician typically orders "CF to DAT" (meaning a progressive diet starting with clear fluids and progressing to a regular diet as tolerated) or "Sips to DAT" (meaning starting with ice chips or sips only and progressing to a regular diet). Occasionally, a doctor will just write "as tolerated," leaving the progression of the diet up to the nurses. The nurses will let you know what type of diet to order for the patient or will order it themselves.

Usually, a patient who has just returned from the OR will be given only ice chips or sips of water. If the patient has had major bowel surgery, even ice chips may not be allowed until **bowel sounds are present (BSP).** The postoperative diet would advance then to clear fluids, full fluids, soft, and finally a regular diet. Table 18.2 shows the typical progression. However, the rate of return to a normal diet depends on the patient and the surgery. Some patients may be able to omit certain steps. A patient who has had a minor operation may have clear fluids for the first few hours and then move right on to a soft or regular diet. Some will take longer, especially if the surgery involves the gastrointestinal tract.

Postoperative Orders for Same-Day Admissions   You need to notify the Dietary Department about postoperative diets, but you cannot do so until the patient comes to the patient-care unit and the doctor writes the orders. Some hospitals have a standard protocol; if the patient stays overnight but the surgery is minor, a soft diet might be ordered. For other surgeries, the diet could be clear fluids. If you get orders well ahead of time, you can simply send a manual or electronic requisition, but if you are processing orders close to a meal time and the patient needs a tray, call Dietary. They may not get the requisition or check for new orders in time.

gastric suction   gentle suction applied to a tube placed in the stomach to remove excessive secretions, such as saliva and gastric juices, that tend to accumulate in the stomach after surgery or trauma because the intestine is sluggish. This can prevent or relieve nausea and vomiting.

Table 18.2	Typical Progressive Diet after Major Surgery (not involving the GI tract)
Surgical day	NPO or ice chips or "sips" of water
Day one	Clear fluids . . . maybe full fluids at suppertime
Day two	Full fluids . . . maybe a soft diet at suppertime
Day three	Soft diet to a regular diet

Postoperative Orders for Patients Already in Hospital   Sometimes, surgery is booked for a patient already in hospital. Suppose Mr. Black had been admitted for investigation of abdominal pain. Three days later, his doctor discovered a tumour and decided to operate. As soon as you receive the operative orders and have a confirmed surgery date, cancel the patient's diet, effective after dinner the day before surgery (or otherwise, as ordered). Otherwise, breakfast will appear the next morning for Mr. Black, who is perhaps already in the OR, and the tray will be wasted. (Most facilities have strict rules that unused trays are to be returned untouched. They are not meant to provide snacks for hospital employees or visitors.) If the order comes in just before it needs to be implemented, call Dietary. In the two hours before a meal, they are too busy to check their computers or requisition forms.

TUBE FEEDINGS/ENTERAL FEEDS

An ENTERAL FEED IS ONE THAT IS ADMINISTERED DIRECTLY BY A TUBE INTO THE GASTROintestinal system. Tube feedings bypass a person's swallowing mechanism and carry food directly into the stomach or bowel. They are used for individuals who cannot swallow, such as some stroke victims or people who have had part of their upper gastrointestinal tract removed because of cancer or trauma, and for people who cannot digest food (sometimes called malabsorption syndrome). Tubes may be inserted temporarily or permanently.

Sites of Insertion

Tubes are usually referred to and ordered by site of insertion. Physicians often have preferences.

■   A **nasogastric tube (N-G tube, or Levine tube)** (Figure 18.2) is put through the nose into the stomach. (*Gastric* means "relating to the stomach.") (A tube can also be inserted through the mouth into the stomach. Mouth tubes are rarely used in adults because they are uncomfortable and stimulate the gag reflex. They are more often used with young infants, who have weak gag reflexes and initially breathe only through the nose.) (Note: Levine tubes are also used to decompress the stomach, irrigate the stomach, and treat bleeding.)

■   **Gastrostomy tubes (G-tubes)** are inserted through an incision in the abdomen into the stomach.

■   **Jejunostomy tubes (J-tubes)** are placed through the abdominal wall into the jejunum, or small bowel. This site is chosen when the stomach cannot tolerate food because of such conditions as gastritis (inflammation of the stomach), pancreatitis (inflammation of the pancreas), or gastroesophageal reflux.

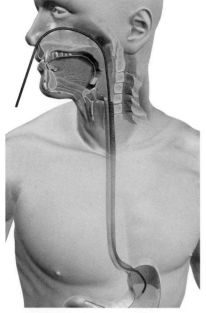

Figure 18.2 Levine tube.

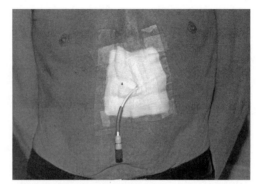

Figure 18.3 PEG tube.

- Tubes can be inserted into the duodenum, but this is not common.

- **A percutaneous endoscopic gastrostomy tube (PEG tube or catheter)** (see Figure 18.3) is inserted through a puncture through the skin and subcutaneous tissues of the abdomen and stomach using an endoscope (a flexible instrument used to visualize organs). This catheter or tube has a bulb that is inflated once inside the stomach or jejunum and keeps the tube from falling out.

- There are a number of skin-level devices available to facilitate gastric feedings. The **Bard button** is one of the most common. These buttons are surgically placed into the stomach through the abdominal wall. The Bard button is made of pliable silicone, with a mushroom-shaped dome at one end and a flat rectangular flap with a safety plug on the abdominal side. Only the flap with the safety plug attached is visible on the skin surface of the abdomen. An anti-reflux valve helps prevent gastric leakage through the tube. Special feeding tubes are necessary to connect the button to a feeding bag or syringe. The MIC key is also made of pliable silicone, with a contoured disc on the abdominal surface and an anti-reflux valve, and requires a special feeding set to connect to a feeding bag or syringe.

percutaneous endoscopic gastrostomy tube (PEG tube, PEG catheter) a feeding tube inserted via endoscopy into the stomach or jejunum.

Bard button (MIC device) a feeding device placed permanently in the stomach to facilitate supplemental feedings.

Tube Sizes

Feeding tubes are measured by *bore*, or diameter, in units called French (Fr.), after the inventor of the feeding tube. A small-bore tube might be 6 to 8 Fr.; a large-bore tube might 10 to 14 Fr. The smaller tubes are more difficult to insert and tend to become clogged easily.

Orders might read as follows:

- Insert a 10 Fr. nasogastric tube.

- Insert a #14 Levine tube.

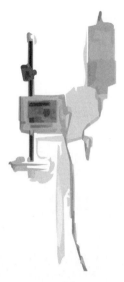

Figure 18.4   Continuous feeding via an electronic pump.

Types of Feeds Ordered

Enteral feeds can be given in two ways: continuous or periodic intervals.

Continuous Feeds   If these are ordered, usually the nurses will infuse the solution in small quantities measured every hour. To control volume, an electronic pump is sometimes used to administer the feed, as shown in Figure 18.4 on page xxx. Continuous feeds are usually better tolerated but are restrictive: the patient cannot easily move around because there is always solution dripping through the tube.

Periodic Feeds   The nurse will administer a certain volume of the prescribed solution every few hours, following a schedule usually drawn up by the dietitian: for example, 100 cc of Ensure @ 0730, 1130, 1630, and 1800.

Enteral Solutions

In many facilities, formulas will be made up for the patient on the basis of standard recipes. These might include blended mixtures of meats, vegetables, and fruits with added nutrients. Therapeutic diets can be accommodated: the formula can be made lactose free, gluten free, and salt free and can be tailored to the appropriate number of calories, carbohydrates, and fat. Even a vegetarian diet can be formulated for tube feeding.

Premixed commercial formulations tailored to different needs are also available. Doctors may order them specifically, or hospitals may use them to save time. Common ones include the following:

- Osmolite
- Jevity
- Ensure
- Ensure Plus
- Compleat B
- Enrich
- Travasorb

Medication may also be crushed and added to the feeding tube. Continuous feeds often help diabetics achieve better blood sugar control because both carbohydrates and insulin can be supplied at a constant rate. Diabetics will need adjustments to their insulin.

TPN FEEDS

TOTAL PARENTERAL NUTRITION (TPN) IS A COMPLETE FORM OF NUTRITION, CONTAINING protein, sugar, fat, and added vitamins and minerals combined to meet the patient's individual nutritional needs. A peripheral vein may be used for short periods, but a central venous line is most suitable for long-term feeding. TPN is indicated for patients who

- are severely malnourished and being prepared for surgery (a malnourished person will not recover as quickly from surgery);
- are receiving radiation therapy or chemotherapy and are malnourished or unable to eat;
- have had major surgery, severe burns, or multiple fractures and are unable to take or absorb nutrients with oral or enteral feeding;
- are in a prolonged coma;
- have severe anorexia;
- have severe inflammation of the bowel, such as ulcerative colitis; or
- are terminally ill and unable to eat.

Accompanying Blood Work

TPN orders are interpreted and handled by Nutritional Services. Most hospitals have a standard order form for TPN. When a TPN diet is ordered, blood work will be ordered at the same time to provide the physician and dietitian with baseline values from which to monitor the patient's state and determine nutritional needs. The doctor might order specific blood work, or, in some facilities, you would automatically order a standard set of tests by a blanket term, such as "TPN baseline." This blood work might include the tests shown in Table 18.3.

Progressive or Transitional Diet and TPN

A physician may order a progressive feeding schedule for a patient that starts with TPN, then moves to enteral feeds, and then to oral food intake. As with any progressive diet, the rate of progress depends on the patient's condition; patients may sometimes have to take a step back to an earlier stage.

Table 18.3 Blood Tests Typically Ordered with TPN	
Glucose	Albumin, INR
BUN	Triglyceride, PTT
Creatinine	Bilirubin total
Electrolytes	AST
Calcium	Phosphorus

SUMMARY

1. Everyone needs a healthy balanced diet. Our caloric needs are determined by our basal metabolic rate, which is affected by age, gender, activity, health state, and the environment.

2. The Department of Nutritional Services is responsible for meals and diet planning. It is staffed by dietitians and dietary assistants. A dietitian tailors diets to suit a patient's needs, consults with doctors and patients, and is an excellent resource for the health-care team. Dietary staff and nurses serve meals; you may sometimes be asked to help. If you have complaints about errors in meals supplied, check with all nurses before phoning for new items.

3. Therapeutic diets include cardiac, no added salt/sodium-restricted, diabetic, gluten-free, high-fibre, high-protein, high-calorie, low-residue, and bland diets. Most are individualized. Those on insulin also receive two or three snacks during the day; help the nurses make sure patients get their snacks.

4. In a paper-based environment, fill out a diet requisition. In a computer-based system, the order will go to Dietary automatically. If an order comes in shortly before a meal is needed or a meal must be cancelled, phone Dietary to make sure they know about it. Likewise, if a patient is suddenly discharged and will leave before the next meal, call to cancel.

5. Diets must be adapted before many diagnostic tests. Make sure to order the adjustments needed. Some tests require restrictions or supplements up to two days in advance. Many tests require an NPO period; cancel or delay the patient's breakfast the day of the test, and put an NPO note at the patient's bedside.

6. After major surgery, the patient is typically on a progressive diet, starting with ice chips and water sips alone or with clear fluids, and progressing by stages to full fluids, soft, and finally regular diet. The doctor will order the diet depending on the patient and the type of surgery, and the nurses will assess when the patient is ready to move to the next stage. Cancel the patient's usual diet on the day of surgery, and transcribe the postoperative orders. If orders come through just before surgery, call Dietary.

7. Tube feedings, also known as enteral feeds, administer nutrients through a tube that is placed into the patient's stomach or intestine. This is done when a patient cannot swallow or cannot digest. Tube feedings are ordered by site and size of tubing. Solutions may be premixed and commercial or prepared by the hospital and can include a full range of foods or be adapted for therapeutic purposes. These feeds can be delivered at set intervals or continuously.

8. Total parenteral nutrition (TPN) involves the infusion of amino acids, glucose, fats, vitamins, minerals, and trace elements through an IV line. TPN is used for severely malnourished patients or those who cannot receive nutrition through the gastro-intestinal route. TPN orders will be accompanied by a routine set of blood tests.

Key Terms

Bard button (MIC device) 587
bowel sounds present 585

dysphagia 583
enteral feed 586
fluid retention 580

gastric suction 585
gastrostomy tube (G-tube) 586

Review Questions

1. What factors alter a person's basal metabolic rate?

2. What is a responsibility of the clinical secretary after trays have been given out to patients?

3. In point form, list the responsibilities of a hospital dietitian.

4. State the difference between a regular diet and a therapeutic diet.

5. Why are diabetic patients given snacks?

6. List the stages of the progressive diet, and describe each.

7. Differentiate between a progressive diet and a transitional diet.

8. What is an enteral feed?

9. Identify five types of feeding tubes, and give an example of how each might be ordered.

10. What is the purpose of total parenteral nutrition?

Application Exercises

1. Choose one of the diets listed in this chapter. Research the conditions for which the diet is ordered and the rationale for the diet. Write up your findings in an essay two to three pages long, and share your findings with the class.

2. Compare and contrast the advantages, disadvantages, and indications for enteral feeds and TPN.

3. With one of two classmates and using information from Canada's Food Guide (link at the end of the chapter), create meals for yourself for a period of one week. Consider individual food preferences as well as affordability, local food, and good nutrition.

4. In small groups, choose a special diet and follow it for a week—for example, a celiac or a diabetic diet, or a restricted-calorie or low-fat diet, or a heart-healthy diet. Prepare your meals in accordance to diet requirements. Record how it feels to be restricted to the diet you choose, and the frustrations. At the end of the week, discuss your experiences in class.

Websites of Interest

Canadian Celiac Association
www.celiac.ca/EnglishCCA/ccaenglish.html
http://www.foodserviceworld.com/foodservice-and-hospitality-mag/feature-articles/3507-hospital-makeover.html
Food Service and Hospitality: A makeover for food services in Canadian Hospitals. Click on links under "Diet" in the left-hand column.
http://www.hc-sc.gc.ca/fn-an/food-guide-aliment/index-eng.php
Canada's Food Guide, plus a link where you can click and order your own copy

Canadian Diabetes Association
www.diabetes.ca/Section_About/nutritionindex.asp
Click on "nutrition" in the left-hand column.

Canadian Heart and Stroke Association

ww1.heartandstroke.ca/Page.asp?PageID=388

Click on "Healthy Living" in the left-hand column and follow the links for information about cardiac diets.

Canada's Food Guide

www.hc-sc.gc.ca/fn-an/food-guide-aliment/order-commander/index-eng.php

You can download a PDF copy for reference.

Soft and mechanical soft diet information

www.gicare.com/pated/edtgs35.htm

Clear fluid diet

www.springboard4health.com/notebook/diet_clear_liquid.html

This site has Information on a clear fluid diet with a sample of what the patient would order.

Life After Surgery

www.misgroup.ca/postop.html

The site has links to examples of a full fluid, puréed, and regular diet.

Chapter 19

Orders Related to Digestion and Excretion

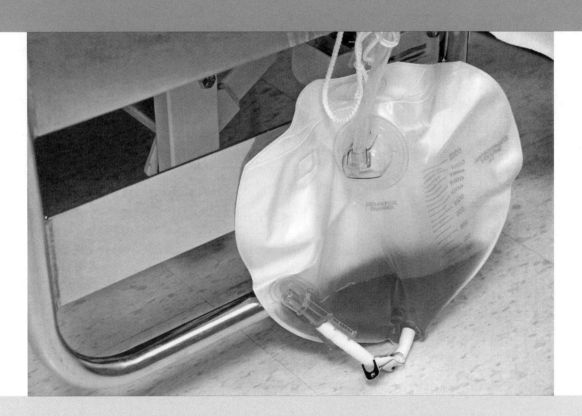

Learning Objectives

On completing this chapter, you will be able to:

1. Summarize the functions of the gastrointestinal system.
2. Briefly discuss the use of enemas and suppositories.
3. Explain the procedures involved with colostomy and ileostomy.
4. Describe nasogastric suction, considering purpose and related procedures.
5. Summarize the function of the genitourinary system.
6. Discuss urinary catheters, considering types and purpose.
7. Understand and correctly transcribe orders relating to the gastrointestinal and genitourinary systems.

❶ THE GASTROINTESTINAL TRACT

Review the anatomy and physiology of the digestive and urinary systems to understand some of the related orders and interventions discussed in this chapter. There is a helpful website listed at the end of the chapter that provides related information.

Altered gastrointestinal (GI) function often indicates the onset of an illness. A variety of tests are used to diagnose related diseases. Surgical procedures, anaesthetics, and other traumatic or invasive events, as well as disease processes and infections, alter gastrointestinal function. Assessment of the GI tract is a routine part of a nurse's assessment of a patient. The depth, frequency, and specificity of these assessments will vary with the patient's condition, diagnosis, treatment, and health state. Associated structures, including the liver, pancreas, and gallbladder, are often tested as well.

A number of conditions will disrupt the normal functioning of the GI system. These range from the flu to **gastritis**, **diverticulitis**, Crohn's disease, ulcerative colitis, ulcers, celiac disease, cancer, and surgery. Following surgery of any type, the GI tract is very sluggish, usually as a result of the anaesthetic. Of course, surgery on the GI tract itself exacerbates this effect. Manipulating the bowel further alters the return to normal function. It is important that the patient's GI tract have some degree of motility or function before she begins to eat or drink in significant amounts, or the food will not be properly processed. Following surgery, the nurses and the doctors need to monitor the return of peristaltic action and adjust the patient's diet accordingly.

gastritis inflammation of the stomach.

diverticulitis inflammation of a sac-like bulge that may develop in the wall of the large intestine.

GASTROINTESTINAL ASSESSMENTS

Most hospitalized patients will have assessments carried out daily—some routine and others specific to the disorders they have or are being assessed for. Assessments do not always relate directly to the reason for hospitalization. For example, if a patient admitted to hospital for a knee replacement had **ulcerative colitis**, irritable bowel syndrome, or an ulcer, part of the nurses' daily assessments would include the GI tract to monitor the these conditions. A person admitted with myocardial infarction who also had a colostomy would be monitored for bowel function.

ulcerative colitis inflammation and ulceration of the innermost lining of the colon (the large intestine).

Bowel Function

Nurses routinely monitor patients' bowel elimination patterns, usually when taking the patients' vital signs (temperature, pulse, and respiration—TPR) at the beginning of the day. Even people who normally have regular bowel movements may be thrown off schedule by hospitalization. Their normal pattern may be affected by emotional strain, different food, and the loss of normal activity. Having to use a bedpan or a commode may contribute to constipation because of difficult positioning and discomfort, as well as lack of privacy.

In the computerized environment, nurses enter information on bowel habits directly into the patient's electronic chart—often on the vital signs graphic flow record. In the noncomputerized environment, they record the information elsewhere, perhaps in a small book or on the paper-based TPR graphic sheet. The nurse doing the morning TPRs usually asks the patient how many bowel movements she has had in the past 24 hours. If the patient goes more than a day or two without a bowel movement, she would likely be given a laxative.

Auscultation for Bowel Sounds

Nurses and doctors can assess bowel activity by **auscultating** for bowel sounds—that is, listening to a patient's abdomen with a stethoscope. Most postoperative patients will have abdominal assessments done q shift until **peristalsis** has returned. A physician's routine postop orders may or may not include abdominal assessment; they are usually included automatically as a routine postop assessment. You would activate abdominal assessments on the computerized chart for any patient having surgery, or add it to the manual Kardex under nursing assessments. You may see a related order directing when the patient can resume a progressive diet that reads "clear fluids until bsp" (or something similar). BSP means "bowel sounds present." It means the person's diet can progress to the next level when return of peristaltic action is evident.

auscultate listen to the sounds made by a body structure as a diagnostic method.

peristalsis wavelike movements of the gastrointestinal tract that propel food and other contents along.

❷ GASTROINTESTINAL TREATMENTS

Enemas

An **enema** is the introduction of fluid to the lower bowel for the purpose of cleansing the bowel or to stimulate bowel function. Many patients have difficulty independently establishing bowel function after an operation. Almost routinely, doctors will order enemas approximately 72 hours postoperatively to stimulate bowel function if the patient is unable to have a bowel movement even with the aid of a laxative. Enemas are also sometimes used instead of or along with a laxative to prepare for bowel surgery and certain diagnostic tests (such as a colonoscopy or barium enema) for which an empty bowel is necessary. Doctors can order several types of enemas.

enema the introduction of liquid into the rectum for cleansing the bowel and for stimulating evacuation of the bowels.

Fleet Enema   A Fleet enema contains a balanced solution in a disposable container that is instilled into the lower bowel. Fleet enemas are small, effective, and convenient. A variety of solutions are used, each with a specific action. The solution may contain bisacodyl or sodium phosphate, both of which are bowel stimulants. The solutions are hypertonic and draw water into the bowel, softening fecal material. Many standard postoperative orders contain an order for a Fleet enema. An order might read, "Fleet enema PRN on 3rd postoperative day." PRN would refer to whether or not the patient has had a bowel movement.

Tap Water Enema   A tap water enema (TWE), also referred to as a large volume enema, shown in Figure 19.1, is more "heavy duty" than some of the others. It involves instilling 500 to 1000 cc of tap water into the lower bowel, sometimes higher than the

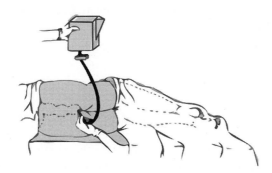

Figure 19.1   Tap water enema

sigmoid colon. Kits used can either be disposable or reusable. A tap water enema is used as an intervention for constipation and for a bowel prep for diagnostic procedures or bowel surgery. A tap water enema can be quite uncomfortable for the patient, causing cramping.

Small Volume Enema

This is the same procedure as that used for a tap water enema, but a smaller volume of fluid is introduced (around 100 cc). It is suitable for evacuating the lower bowel, and is primarily used for constipation.

If a doctor wants a very thorough cleansing of the bowel, she might order enemas until the returns are clear. This means that the nurses would repeat the enema until the liquid expelled from the rectum is clear, with no stool. This is very uncomfortable and can be energy draining, especially for an old or very ill person.

An enema order might be worded in one of the following ways:

Fleet enema 3rd postop day PRN

TWE 2nd postop day

TWE until clear

Oil Retention Enema

This enema instils approximately 100 cc of a mixture with an oil base into the bowel. It is used in constipated patients and is effective in softening hard stool that may be sitting in the lower bowel.

Transcribing Enema Orders

Orders for enemas are added either electronically to the PI screen (or simply activated if already listed) under Nursing Interventions (or the equivalent) or manually to the Kardex under the appropriate heading.

Layouts for Kardexes or patient care summaries vary. If the doctor has ordered an enema to be given on a certain day, it is important to add that date beside where you either recorded or activated that intervention. For example, if the doctor ordered, "Fleet enema 3rd postop day PRN," and the surgery took place on February 16, you would add February 19 as the day on which the enema was to be given. This makes it easier for the nurses to keep track of when to give the enema. The day of surgery is always counted as Day 0, so February 17 is Day 1 (the first day postop), and February 19 is Day 3. On a PI screen, this order would be under such a heading as Procedures or Nursing Interventions.

Suppositories

Rectal suppositories may be ordered to facilitate bowel evacuation. They may soften the stool in the rectum, promote rectal distension by releasing gas, or stimulate nerves in the rectal mucosa, thus promoting evacuation of the bowel. Suppositories are also used as a route to administer medication; medications commonly administered this way include ASA, dimenhydrinate (Gravol), or Indocid.

Transcribing Suppository Orders

A suppository may be ordered as, for example:

glycerin supp. PRN

or

Gravol suppository 50 mg for nausea q4h PRN

Transcribe the order exactly as it is written. If the suppository is a medication, a specific dose *must* be noted. In most facilities, suppositories (other than glycerin) are considered a medication and recorded on the appropriate MAR or CMAR.

❸❹ ORDERS RELATING TO GI SURGERY AND PROCEDURES

IF A PATIENT HAS HAD GASTROINTESTINAL SURGERY, THE NURSES MONITOR THE STATUS and progress of gastrointestinal function closely, including the return of normal motility and normal elimination patterns. The following are some of the more common gastrointestinal surgeries you will deal with if you are working on a surgical unit.

Bowel Resection, Colostomy, and Ileostomy

A **bowel resection** and anastomosis (may also be called end-to-end anastomosis) involves removing a section of the bowel and connecting the healthy ends together again. This can occur anywhere along the large or small bowel. If the bowel cannot be reconnected to the rectal portion because it is diseased, a **colostomy** or an **ileostomy** will be created. This is a procedure wherein the end of the bowel is brought out to the abdomen and a **stoma**, or artificial opening, is created, through which feces are excreted (Figure 19.2). A colostomy involves the colon or large bowel; an ileostomy involves the ileum or distal small bowel. Conditions that necessitate a colostomy or ileostomy include cancer, ulcerative colitis, and Crohn's disease. In the case of a colostomy, the fecal matter has been largely processed, and a formed stool is produced; in the case of an ileostomy, fluid has not been absorbed, and the result is an almost continuous drainage of loose fecal matter.

Colostomy and Ileostomy Supplies A wide range of equipment is used for patients who have colostomies or ileostomies. Disposable or reusable bags, shown in Figure 19.3, collect the waste. They are attached with "wafers," devices that fit around the stoma, or opening. The wafers have an adhesive back and stick to the abdomen, forming a seal around the stoma. The ostomy bag attaches to the wafer, also forming a seal. Doctor's orders do not usually refer to ostomy supplies, but a nurse may ask you to order them.

bowel resection (anastomosis or end-to-end anastomosis)   surgery wherein a section of bowel is removed, and the remaining bowel is reconnected.

colostomy   a surgical procedure that creates an artificial opening from the colon to the surface of the abdomen, through which feces are excreted.

ileostomy   a surgical procedure that creates an artificial opening from the ileum to the surface of abdomen, through which feces are excreted.

stoma   an artificial opening; in this case, one from the bowel through the abdominal wall.

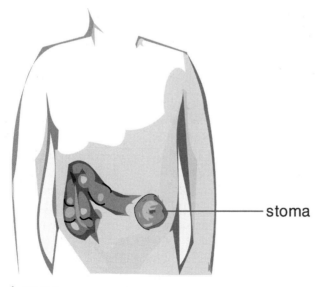

Figure 19.2   A stoma

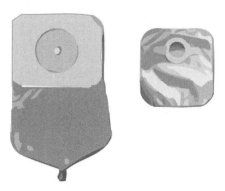

Figure 19.3　Ostomy bag and wafer

Bowel Irrigations　Bowel irrigation may be ordered if a patient with a colostomy is having difficulty passing stool. It is based on the same principle as an enema or an evacuation suppository. Fluid is introduced into the bowel through an irrigation tube placed into the stoma. Bowel irrigation trays or kits are available from Central Supply or Stores.

Nasogastric Suction

Nasogastric suction involves inserting a tube through the nose into the stomach and using an electric suction device to gently remove solids, liquids, or gases from the stomach or small intestine. It may be short term or long term.

Following surgery on the GI tract or related organs (e.g., removal of the gallbladder through a large incision), nasogastric suction is frequently necessary to rest the bowel and/or allow it to heal. It may also be ordered to relieve excessive nausea and vomiting, as occurs in some pregnant women, to obtain a sample of gastric contents for testing, or to empty the stomach prior to gastric surgery. Suction may also be ordered as conservative treatment to decompress the stomach or small intestine when a **bowel obstruction** is suspected.

bowel obstruction　a blockage in the intestines that prevents their contents from moving forward.

Various suction machines are available, most of them portable ones brought to the patient's room. A popular device is the Gomco machine (illustrated in Figure 19.4), an electric pump that gives intermittent suction by varying the air pressure. Red and green lights flash as the pressure changes, indicating that the suction is working. There is also a switch for high and low suction. The high setting is rarely used. If the doctor's order does not specify, low suction is assumed.

The gastric material is collected in a drainage bottle, which must be monitored and emptied appropriately. Nurses must record all drainages. Some facilities leave space for this at the bottom of the vital signs graph. Others record the data as output under Tubes and Drains on a fluid balance sheet. In the electronic environment, nurses usually enter it on an electronic fluid balance document.

If a Gomco suction or any other type of suction unit is required, you may be responsible for ordering it from Central Supply. Nasogastric (Levine) tubes are usually kept in the clean utility room. If none of the correct size is available, the nurses may ask you to order one from Central Supply/Stores (or the equivalent). If they need it immediately, phone and arrange to pick it up or have it sent up. The lift or dumbwaiter could be used for this purpose. As discussed in Chapter 18, nasogastric (Levine) tubes come in a variety

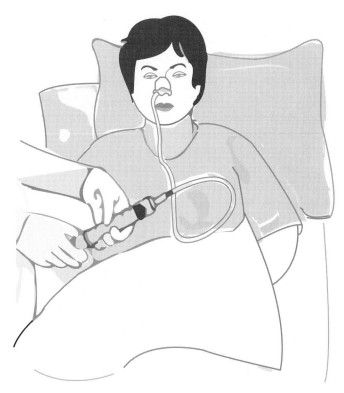

Figure 19.4 Patient with a nasogastric tube

of sizes. The most common sizes used for nasogastric suction in adults are 16 or 19 Fr. The physician may not order a specific size, leaving it up to the nurses' judgment. When you phone Central Supply, specify the type and size of tube you need.

Another type of tube, a sump tube, may be used for gastric lavage.

Suction Orders Doctors ordering suction may be specific about type or may leave details to be assumed. A doctor may order "Insert nasogastric tube to Gomco suction." Using suction with an NG tube is almost without exception low, intermittent suction, so the doctor may simply order "Gomco suction." Or, he may not even specify the type, but just order "NG suction."

In this case, you would assume that he wants whatever type of suction is most commonly used in your facility. If the nurses are unclear about the type of suction or pattern of suction wanted, they can ask the doctor for clarification.

As with other intervention orders, suction orders are appropriately transcribed to the Kardex or added or activated on the electronic PI screen.

Most often following surgery, the NG tube is inserted in the OR, in which case there may be no related insertion orders. The order may say "NG suction to straight drainage," indicating that it is already in place. This would be transcribed in the same manner onto the electronic or traditional Kardex along with any assessments. Orders to remove an NG tube are often included in the postop orders (e.g., "remove NG tube when drainage less than 100 cc/shift"). This means that when the fluid from the GI tract in the Gomco suction container is less than 100 cc in an eight-hour shift, the nurses can remove the tube and discontinue the suction. Alternatively, the doctor will assess the patient daily and order the suction removed when he deems it appropriate.

Trays for NG Tube Irrigation If an NG tube becomes plugged, it must be rinsed or irrigated with normal saline to clear the obstruction. The nurse detaches the NG tube from the tube leading to the suction machine and, with a large syringe, instils a measured amount of saline or water into the tube leading into the patient's stomach. The nurse either withdraws the fluid with the syringe or simply reconnects the NG tube to the suction machine; the fluid then drains into the large bottle at the other end of the suction tubing. The nurses may keep a tray at the patient's bedside containing the apparatus needed to irrigate or flush the tubing. They may ask you to order an irrigation tray. It is important to specify the type of irrigation tray needed; a bladder irrigation tray, for example, is quite different from an NG irrigation tray.

❺ THE GENITOURINARY SYSTEM

Genitourinary (GU) function is monitored in patients admitted with genitourinary complaints or diagnoses and in surgical patients, especially those who have had a general anaesthetic. Patients who have had surgery on the GU system itself will be given closer attention. Failure to eliminate body waste adequately results in a number of problems. Fluid retention could affect the heart and circulatory system or cause a build-up of toxic wastes in the person's body. It also causes edema—swelling of body parts, such as the legs and ankles, because of retained fluid.

An overfull bladder can become so overstretched that it becomes *hypotonic*, meaning it loses its tone or strength. Conversely, someone who excretes more than she takes in will become dehydrated. If there are any concerns, a physician will order monitoring of intake and output (I&O). As discussed in Chapter 17, this is usually automatic when a person has an IV. In the computerized environment, the nurses enter the information into the computer, and the daily values are automatically calculated. In the noncomputerized environment, an intake and output sheet (also called a fluid balance sheet) is used and the data must be added up at the end of each eight-hour nursing shift.

GENITOURINARY CONDITIONS

The following are the most common GU conditions for which you may process orders if you are working on a medical, surgical, or urology unit.

Urinary Tract Infection (UTI)

Bacterial infections of the urinary tract are common and involve a number of pathogens, including intestinal *Escherichia coli*. Infections can occur anywhere in the urinary tract, including the kidneys, but most occur in the lower tract. Especially common is cystitis, an infection of the bladder. Kidney infections may be treated aggressively with intravenous antibiotics. For urinary tract infections, often, a doctor will order a midstream urine (MSU)—usually stat, and, when he gets the results, will start the patient on an antibiotic. If the patient is in great discomfort, the doctor may prescribe the antibiotic before getting the results, making an educated guess; when the results come back, he will change the medication if the results show that the causative organism is resistant to the antibiotic

		Daryl Dark
	MSU stat; then start Amoxil 1 g stat and 500 mg po qid	123 Duncan St. Stratford ON N5A 2G3
	Push fluids	M 22 09 47 071608
	Strain all urine	3238494232
date *Jan 2/xx*	time *1000*	Physician's printed name Dr. G. Hanson	Signature *Dr. G. Hanson*	Dr. G. Hanson

Figure 19.5 Doctor's orders for a patient with a UTI and suspected kidney stone

he prescribed for the patient. If the patient is already on an antibiotic, it is important to state which one on the lab requisition form. Antibiotics commonly used to treat UTIs include co-trimoxazole (Bactrim, Septra), nitrofurantoin (Macrodantin, Furadantin), and amoxicillin (Amoxil). The doctor may also order "push fluids" (meaning encourage the patient to drink a lot) to flush the kidneys. See Figure 19.5 for typical orders.

Kidney Stones

A person may or may not be admitted to hospital with **kidney stones or calculi**. Patients with this condition are more often diagnosed and treated on an outpatient basis. If the person is hospitalized, it may be because of contributing factors or because the person is too frail to be treated as an outpatient.

Kidney stones result from the build-up of crystallized salts and minerals, such as calcium, in the urinary tract. Stones, also called calculi, can also form after an infection. If large enough to block the kidney or ureter, they can cause severe pain in the middle and lower back, radiating around into the abdomen and groin. Although the process can be quite painful, the stones usually pass through the urinary tract on their own. In some cases, they may need to be removed surgically. Patients admitted with a diagnosis of suspected kidney stones may have an order written to strain all of the urine to see if the stones have been passed—which may also be confirmed by X-ray, ultrasound, or by the pain subsiding. Transcribe this order onto the Intervention or Assessments section of the Kardex or PI screen. The patient is given a filter to strain all his urine for the presence of kidney stones. A commonly used filter resembles a large cone-shaped coffee filter. These filters are obtained from Central Supply.

kidney stones or calculi hard objects built up from salts and minerals in the urinary tract.

Cancer of the Bladder

Nearly all cancers of the bladder start in the layer of cells that form the lining of the bladder. Different types of cancer can behave in very different ways. For example, it may occur as a small, wart-like growth on the inside of the bladder, which can be removed in a simple operation and is unlikely to recur. Sometimes, it can form a large growth in the muscle wall of the bladder, which requires more aggressive treatment. This may include systemic chemotherapy, surgery, or any combination thereof.

Cystectomy   If a tumour is too large to be removed using a **cystoscope** to visualize it, it may be necessary to remove all or part of the bladder, an operation called a **cystectomy**. A new storage place for urine will need to be created. If part of the bladder is removed, the operation is called a partial cystectomy. Patients who have had a partial cystectomy can void as usual, but their bladder will obviously be smaller and thus able to hold less urine than previously.

cystoscope   a long, thin, flexible instrument with a light at the end used to examine the bladder. It is inserted through the urethra and threaded up into the bladder.

cystectomy   surgical removal of the urinary bladder.

Urostomy   The most common way of providing a new storage place for urine is to form a *urostomy*, or the creation of an artificial opening. This involves using a segment of the small bowel, joining the two ureters to one end of it, and bringing the other end out to the abdomen, creating an artificial opening. An ileal conduit is created when a piece of bowel (ileum) creates a channel to drain the urine from the ureters to the new opening, or stoma, on the abdominal surface. The urine drains into a bag in a process similar to that used for colostomies and ileostomies. Sometimes, a sac to store the urine is created using part of the bowel. This sac is drained periodically with a catheter so that the person does not have to wear a drainage bag.

6️⃣7️⃣ URINARY CATHETERS

CATHETERIZATION IS ONE OF THE MOST COMMON INTERVENTIONS ORDERED FOR THE patient who has problems passing or retaining urine. Catheterization is the insertion of a flexible tube into the bladder. This is done under sterile conditions and drains the urine that is in the bladder. It can be put in and left for a designated period of time or inserted and removed as soon as the bladder has been drained. The majority of patients who have a catheter will either have their fluid intake and output measured (ordered as "I&O" or "strict I&O") or just their urinary output measured (ordered as "output only").

Reasons for Catheterization

Catheterization is used to

- empty the bladder in case of urinary retention,
- obtain a sterile urine specimen,
- manage extreme urinary incontinence, as a last resort,
- rest the bladder following surgery on genitourinary structures, and
- manage urinary function postoperatively.

Urinary Retention   A patient may be unable to pass urine for a number of reasons, including disease, trauma resulting from surgery on the bladder or related structures, or lack of sensation and muscle tone from the anaesthetic used in surgery.

Obtaining a Sterile Urine Specimen   If a sterile urine specimen cannot be obtained by other means or if it is very important that the specimen is absolutely sterile, the physician may order a catheter to obtain a specimen directly from the bladder.

incontinence   inability to control urine elimination (urinary incontinence) or bowel function (referred to as "incontinent of bowel").

Managing Urinary Incontinence   In some circumstances, **incontinence** is managed by inserting a catheter. Urinary incontinence may result from trauma to the bladder

---

Tip

If you are asked to take a urine specimen for culture and sensitivity to the lab, do so immediately. Or, if you see one sitting at the desk, check to see if someone is looking after transporting it to the lab, or refrigerate it. If the specimen sits around, it will grow bacteria and potentially invalidate the results of the culture.

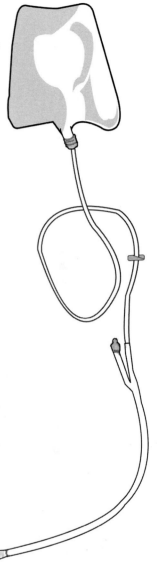

or the urethra, altered states of consciousness, or nerve damage caused by stroke, paralysis, or disease. Some patients can learn to insert a catheter several times a day to empty their own bladders. Infection is always a concern any time a catheter is inserted but seems to be less of an issue when patients self-catheterize at home.

Postoperative Management   A general anaesthetic may suppress the sensation or urge to urinate or affect the tone of the bladder muscle. Postoperative orders generally address bladder function. (See Chapter 16.) To avoid bladder distension, most physicians want the patient catheterized if she is unable to void within eight hours postoperatively. Even if the patient is not taking fluids, she may be receiving continuous fluids by IV, which can quickly fill the bladder.

Types of Catheters

There are a variety of catheters on the market, each with a purpose. They come in a range of sizes, rated according to the same French scale used for nasogastric tubes. The higher the number, the larger is the catheter. Typical adult sizes are 14 or 16 Fr.

Indwelling or Retention Catheter   An **indwelling** catheter or retention catheter is one that is inserted and kept in place for a period of time. It is attached to a disposable drainage tube and bag, forming a closed, sterile system. The most commonly used is the Foley catheter (named after the physician who invented the catheter), which has two lumina, or channels. One channel is for urine; the other is used for inflating a small balloon that sits in the bladder and keeps the tube from falling out. Once the catheter is inserted into the bladder, the balloon is inflated by using a syringe to inject air, sterile water, or normal saline through a small resealable port at the distal end of the second channel of the catheter. The collection tube attached to the catheter has a clamp on it that can be closed off to prevent the urine from draining from the bladder into the bag (see Figure 19.6).

Figure 19.6   Urine drainage bag and tube attached to the Foley catheter

indwelling   left in place.

nonretention or **straight catheter**   one inserted to drain urine and then removed.

Nonretention or Straight Catheter   A **nonretention** or **straight catheter** (also called a *red rubber catheter* to describe a common type) is inserted into the bladder to drain the urine and then removed. It is suitable for specimen collection. It does not have an inflatable bulb.

Suprapubic Catheters   Suprapubic catheters are inserted under general or local anaesthesia through an incision made in the lower abdominal wall and into the bladder. There is a balloon inflated to keep the catheter in place, as with an indwelling Foley catheter. Suprapubic catheters pose less danger of infection than those inserted through the urethra and allow the patient more mobility.

Three-Way Catheters   When bladder irrigation (discussed below) is needed, it is done with a three-way catheter, which has the two channels of a Foley catheter, plus a third leading to a sterile irrigation solution.

Cudet Catheter   When a nurse cannot insert a Foley catheter, especially in men, the doctor may order a Cudet catheter. This device has a curve on the tip that facilitates passage through the urethra, under the prostate, and into the bladder.

Condom Catheters   When for some reason inserting a catheter through a man's urethra is contraindicated, a condom catheter may be used. This is an external device much like a condom that fits over the penis. It has a drainage tube attached to a closed urine drainage system.

Transcribing Catheter Orders

Orders for catheterization might be worded in any of the following ways:

> Catheterize if unable to void 8 h postop
>
> Catheterize PRN postoperatively
>
> Indwelling Foley catheter if unable to void
>
> Indwelling Foley to straight drainage if unable to void

Note that only in the first example does the doctor specify when to catheterize. Often, doctors leave the timing to the nurses. They will assess the patient for bladder distension and discomfort and also keep in mind the eight-hour norm. The last two examples specify an indwelling Foley catheter. The first two do not specify, but it is assumed that the catheter is indwelling. If the doctor wants a straight catheter, he will specify so. "To straight drainage," specified in the final example, means that the drainage system is left attached so that the bladder drains continually. This, too, would be assumed if not specified.

After surgery, trauma, or long-term catheter use, people may have trouble regaining bladder tone and, thus, completely emptying the bladder. To stimulate normal bladder function and retrain the bladder, the doctor may order that the catheter be clamped for a period and then opened.

Catheter orders are transcribed to the Kardex or PI screen, under Elimination or under Tubes and Drains.

Some patients come back from the OR with an indwelling catheter already in place, particularly if they have had major surgery or bladder surgery. In this case, the doctor's orders would address when to remove the catheter. Orders might read: "Remove catheter on 3rd postop day" or "On 2nd postop day start clamping and unclamping catheter q4h."

Transcribe the order to the Kardex or PI screen, probably under Elimination. Transcribe the order as it is written. If the order states a particular day for the removal of the catheter, calculate when that would be, and insert the date.

Residual Urine

Residual urine is urine left in the bladder after voiding. Sometimes, especially after bladder surgery, the bladder does not empty completely, which can lead to infection. To find out how much urine is left in the bladder, the physician will order catheterization after the patient has voided. If the residual urine exceeds a certain volume (typically 50 or 100 cc), the physician might order the catheter to be reinserted and left in place. A physician becomes concerned if the amount of urine remaining in the bladder is more than 50 to 100 cc. An order might read: "On the 4th postop day catheterize for residual urine. If more than 50 cc, leave catheter in to straight drainage." This order would be transcribed to the Kardex or PI screen.

Bladder Irrigation

Postoperative Following surgery on the bladder, prostate, or urethra, it may be necessary to remove blood and debris by irrigating or flushing the bladder with a sterile solution, usually normal saline. After surgery on the bladder or, for men, on the prostate gland, a certain amount of bleeding occurs in the bladder and related structures. Blood clots often plug the catheter, preventing the urine from draining. Irrigating or flushing the catheter tubing restores drainage. Continuous bladder irrigation (CBI) may be ordered; this is a closed, sterile system, usually using a three-way catheter. When a three-way catheter is required, it is almost always inserted in the operating room. Irrigation may also be ordered in one of the following ways: "Irrigate bladder PRN to keep free from clots" or "Irrigate bladder PRN." This order would be transcribed onto the Kardex or PI screen under Elimination or Additional Nursing Care.

For Treatments Sometimes, a physician orders bladder irrigation with a specific solution, such as an antiseptic solution to treat a bladder infection or a chemotherapeutic medication to treat a bladder tumour. A catheter is inserted into the bladder, and the irrigating solution is introduced through the catheter. For this type of irrigation, a two-way Foley catheter is often used. The doctor's order identifies the frequency of the irrigation and the type, amount, and strength of the solution. This may be done over several hours and the catheter removed until the next treatment, or the catheter may be left in place.

❼ ORDERS FOR URINE TESTING

Midstream Urine

Various types of urine specimens may be ordered, the most common being a midstream specimen, also ordered as an MSU or a clean-catch specimen. (See Chapter 6.)

It is important to note that you may be asked to take this to the laboratory's Microbiology Department. A midstream sample must be refrigerated for sterility; if you take a specimen to the lab after hours, leave it in the refrigerator, *not on a counter*. Specimens for routine and micro (R&M) do not require refrigeration.

Timed Urine Specimens

As discussed in Chapter 6, most 24-hour urine collections must be added to a bottle with a special solution in it, an opaque bottle, or refrigerated (or a combination thereof). Call the lab to make sure the correct bottle is on the floor for the patient to begin the collection. Ensure that the bottle(s) are properly labelled and kept according to test requirements.

New diagnostic tests which are less invasive are constantly being investigated. For example, on the horizon is a sero-logic (blood) test for diagnosing celiac disease. At this point, taking a biopsy of the stomach lining (endoscopic biopsy) has been the main method of establishing a diagnosis of celiac disease. The role of endoscopic biopsies is under evaluation because of the availability of high specificity in antibody tests, provided that there is also a clear clinical response to a gluten-free diet. But until more trials have been done, tissue testing (a biopsy) is still recommended.

SUMMARY

1. The elimination pattern of every hospitalized patient is assessed daily, usually when nurses take vital signs. In the computerized environment, this information is entered directly into a hand-held computer and transferred to the patient's chart. In a non-computerized facility, this information is recorded in a vital signs book. You will be responsible for keeping the vital signs book current and may be responsible for adding vital signs and bowel assessments to the patient's chart.

2. An abdominal assessment involves listening for bowel sounds, which indicate the ability of the GI system to process and eliminate food. This assessment must be noted on the Kardex or PI screen.

3. Enemas are routinely ordered PRN for patients who have had major surgery. The order is transcribed onto the Kardex. The most commonly ordered enema is the Fleet enema. Suppositories are also given to assist with bowel evacuation or as a route to administer medication. These are added to the Kardex and/or the appropriate MAR record.

4. Patients who have diseases of the GI tract, including advanced inflammatory bowel disease or cancer, may have to have a section of the bowel removed; they may then need a colostomy or an ileostomy, which creates an artificial opening through the abdomen as an alternative means of evacuating the bowel. A bowel irrigation is sometimes necessary if constipation occurs.

5. Nasogastric suction is used for several reasons, including resting the bowel after surgery. This is most often accomplished by inserting a tube through the patient's nose into the stomach. The tube is attached to a drainage system and a suction machine. Orders relating to nasogastric suction are transcribed to the Kardex or PI screen.

6. Urinary function is monitored for patients with urinary tract complaints and patients who have had surgery. Fluid retention can strain the heart, lead to infection, or cause the bladder to lose tone.

7. A midstream urine will often be ordered to check for urinary tract infection. When kidney stones are suspected, doctors may order that a patient's urine be strained. Cancer of the bladder can necessitate removing the bladder, thus forming a urostomy, an artificial storage place for urine.

8. Catheterization is often ordered PRN postoperatively; if the patient cannot void within eight hours, the nurses will insert a catheter. Catheters are also ordered to relieve urinary retention, manage incontinence, and obtain a sterile urine sample. An indwelling catheter is left in for some time; a straight catheter is inserted to drain the bladder and then removed.

Key Terms

auscultate 595	**cystoscope** 601	**kidney stones**
bowel obstruction 598	**diverticulitis** 594	**(calculi)** 601
bowel resection (anasto-	**enema** 595	**nonretention (straight)**
mosis or end-to-end	**gastritis** 594	**catheter** 603
anastomosis) 597	**ileostomy** 597	**peristalsis** 595
colostomy 597	**incontinence** 602	**stoma** 597
cystectomy 601	**indwelling** 603	**ulcerative colitis** 594

Review Questions

1. Discuss what is meant by an abdominal assessment.
2. Where on the Kardex would an abdominal assessment be transcribed?
3. What are the responsibilities of the clinical secretary with respect to the vital signs book?
4. What is the purpose of giving an enema postoperatively?
5. Differentiate between a tap water enema and a Fleet enema.
6. Where would you transcribe a suppository ordered as "Gravol supp. 50 mg q4h for nausea?"
7. List five indications for nasogastric suction.
8. Describe the apparatus the nurses need to set up and start nasogastric suction.
9. List five indications for insertion of an indwelling catheter.
10. Differentiate between an indwelling catheter and a straight catheter.

Application Exercises

1. Explain the following orders:
   a. Fleet PRN 3rd day postop
   b. Start NG Gomco suction
   c. Insert #16 Foley to straight drainage
   d. Remove catheter 2nd postoperative day
   e. Obtain residual urine. Leave Foley in if more than 75 cc.
   f. Irrigate bladder PRN to remove clots
2. Transcribe the orders in Exercise 1 using the format outlined by your professor.
3. Research the etiology and most common diagnostic tests and treatments for colon cancer, Crohn's disease, or ulcerative colitis.
4. With another student, develop a teaching handout suitable for a patient who has just had a colostomy or an ileostomy.

5. A patient is admitted for surgery related to cancer of the colon. He has been told that he may have to have a colostomy. With another student or in a small group, research the psychological impact this type of surgery may have on a patient and his or her partner. This will assist you in understanding the stress and emotional impact having a colostomy will have on an individual. You will develop more of an understanding of the empathy and support this person will require post operatively.

Websites of Interest

The GI System
www.le.ac.uk/pa/teach/va/anatomy/case6/frmst6.html
This site provides access to information on the anatomy and physiology of the gastrointestinal and genitourinary systems.

About Colostomy Surgery
www.convatec.ca/enca/cvtca-colstmsuca/cvt-cntsngcol/0/detail/0/1339/1727/colostomy-surgery.html
This site explains how and why a colostomy is created. It includes an action diagram of the different locations a colostomy can be placed.

Bowel Resection
http://www.caet.ca/caet-english/education-ileostomy-guide.htm
This site explains the indications for ileostomy and describes the procedure, recovery process, and possible complications.

Chapter 20

Orders Related to Respiration and Circulation

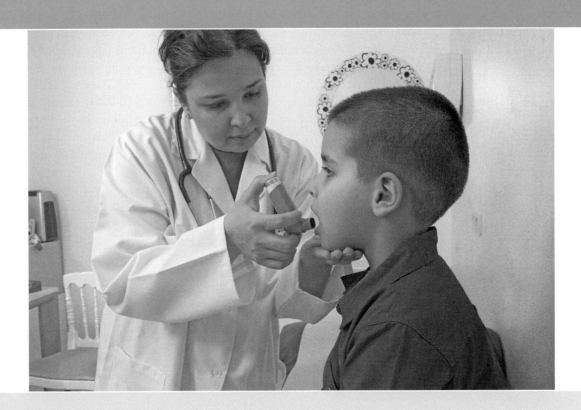

Learning Objectives

On completing this chapter, you will be able to:

1. Describe the role of the respiratory therapist, the physiotherapist, and the nurse in assessments and interventions relating to oxygenation.

2. Discuss the indications for and purpose of nursing assessments the physician may order.

3. Explain what orders are usually written for diagnostic and laboratory tests related to oxygenation.

4. Summarize orders relating to inhalation and oxygen therapies.

5. Describe indications for various types of suctioning.

6. Understand and transcribe orders related to oxygenation.

7. Respond appropriately to a cardiac or respiratory arrest.

Oxygenation is the process of providing the body with adequate amounts of oxygen. Adequate oxygenation depends on proper functioning of a number of entities, including the cardiovascular system and the respiratory system (often referred to as the cardiorespiratory systems). Problems in any body system may affect oxygenation; conversely, inadequate oxygenation will affect every body system. Oxygen to the body is like gas to a car. The blood is like the fuel, and the heart is like the engine. You need all three to be in working order to travel anywhere.

This chapter will familiarize you with conditions common to these systems, and the related interventions for which you will be processing orders if you work on almost any unit in an acute-care hospital. Larger hospitals have specialized units for cardiac and respiratory problems—particularly heart conditions. In many communities across Canada, designated hospitals will have cardiac centres where heart problems are both diagnosed and treated. They will have cardiology patient-care units for patients with less acute conditions or who are well on their way to recovery following cardiac surgery. As well, the facility will have acute-care areas, sometimes called a Coronary Care Unit or CCU (much like an ICU—Intensive Care Unit). Larger facilities may also have a specialized area for patients with respiratory conditions (e.g., a Chest Unit). Medium- and smaller-sized hospitals will care for patients with cardiorespiratory conditions on a medical or surgical unit. Physicians attending to individuals with these conditions are usually cardiologists, internists, or respirologists.

It is recommended that you review the anatomy and physiology of the respiratory and cardiovascular systems; this will help you more clearly understand the related conditions and interventions you will be involved with during the order entry process, as well as other responsibilities that may fall within your scope of practice.

CARDIOVASCULAR CONDITIONS

Common cardiovascular conditions include arteriosclerosis, hypertension, congestive heart failure, and stroke. The majority of hospitalized patients will present with one or more of these conditions. Understanding them will help you recognize related interventions and prioritize your actions.

Arteriosclerosis

arteriosclerosis   hardening of the arteries; reduces blood flow.

atherosclerosis   arteriosclerosis due to deposits of fat in arterial walls.

myocardial infarct (MI, heart attack, or coronary)   damage to the heart caused by a blockage in one of the coronary arteries, cutting off blood supply to a part of the heart.

Arteriosclerosis is commonly referred to as hardening of the arteries. Age, high blood pressure, deposits of calcium, and deposits of fatty plaque in the inner artery walls (**atherosclerosis**) can all narrow the arteries, reducing blood flow and leading to a risk of a blockage in the blood flow. Such a blockage may deprive the heart of oxygen, leading to a **myocardial infarct** (heart attack). Or it may cut off blood flow and, thus, oxygen, to a part of the brain, leading to a stroke.

Myocardial Infarct

A myocardial infarct (or heart attack) occurs when part of the heart muscle is damaged or dies because it is not receiving oxygen. The majority of heart attacks are caused by a blockage in the coronary arteries, most often because of atherosclerosis. Signs of an impending heart attack vary widely. They may include complaints of a crushing chest pain, which may or may not be accompanied by nausea, vomiting, or sweating. The pain may radiate to the jaw and/or left shoulder. Conversely, the patient may experience a sensation similar to that of heartburn and/or a feeling of tightness in the chest and shortness of breath (SOB). All hospital units have a **crash cart**, either on the unit or close by, which contains the essential tools and drugs to treat a heart attack. The cart is checked frequently (each shift in many hospitals) to ensure that it is fully stocked (this may be your responsibility). Someone would be assigned to bring the cart when responding to a call for an arrest.

Cerebral Vascular Accident

A cerebral vascular accident (CVA) is more commonly called a stroke and describes a sudden neurological event caused when a part of the brain is deprived of its blood supply. Strokes can result in temporary or permanent alteration in mental ability, speech, or use of part of the body. They affect the area of the body controlled by the part of the brain where the event occurred.

Hypertension

Hypertension, or **high blood pressure**, means excessive force of blood against the walls of blood vessels as the heart pumps it through the body. Blood pressure is measured in two numbers: the top number, **systolic pressure**, measures the pressure on the vascular walls when the heart is contracting, and the bottom number, **diastolic pressure**, measures the pressure exerted on the vessels when the heart is relaxing. Optimal blood pressure in a healthy young adult is 120/80 or lower; anything over 140/90 is usually classified as hypertension. Hypertension is very common, especially in older people. Obesity, stress, and excessive consumption of salt and fat can be contributing factors, along with genetic predisposition. Hypertension is often called a "silent killer" because the person may have no symptoms for years, until finally the hypertension leads to a heart attack or stroke.

Congestive Heart Failure

Congestive heart failure (CHF) is a condition in which a weakened heart is unable to pump all of the blood away from the lungs each time it beats. Blood pools in the lungs, interfering with breathing.

Atrial Fibrillation

The heart has a conduction system that regulates both the rate and the rhythm of the beat. Normal rhythm is called sinus rhythm. An irregular heartbeat is sometimes referred to as an **arrhythmia**. Although many types of arrhythmia cause no problems, others cause cardiopulmonary difficulties. The most common of these is a condition called **atrial fibrillation** (AF or atrial fib), in which the steady rhythmic contractions of the atrial muscle are replaced by a rapid, irregular twitching, not in synchrony with the ventricular contractions. Blood is not pumped completely out of the atrium, so it may pool and clot, predisposing the person to a pulmonary embolus or a stroke. Treatments include drugs to slow and stabilize the heart, cardioversion (used to restore normal heart rhythm—only done in selected cases), a pacemaker (to regulate the heartbeat), and anticoagulants to prevent stroke.

crash cart a cart carrying the supplies needed for immediate treatment of a heart attack.

cerebral vascular accident (CVA; stroke) damage to the brain that occurs when the blood supply to an area of the brain is diminished or occluded completely.

hypertension or high blood pressure excessive force of the blood against the vessel walls as the heart pumps it through the body.

systolic pressure the pressure on the vascular walls when the heart is contracting.

diastolic pressure the pressure of the vascular walls when the heart is relaxing.

congestive heart failure (CHF) a condition in which a weakened heart is unable to pump all of the blood out of the lungs each time it beats. Blood pools at the bottom of the lungs, interfering with breathing.

arrhythmia loss of normal rhythm of the heartbeat.

atrial fibrillation an abnormality of heart rhythm in which chambers of the heart no longer beat in synchrony, with the atrium beating much faster than the ventricles. The heart rate is fast and irregular.

CONDITIONS THAT AFFECT OXYGENATION

Many conditions affect oxygenation, some of them not directly related to the respiratory system. The most common direct causes of breathing problems are viral or bacterial **pneumonia** (an acute infection of the lungs); **asthma**; chronic lung conditions, such as **emphysema**, a degeneration of the alveolar sacs; and chronic obstructive lung disease (COLD), also known as **chronic obstructive pulmonary disease (COPD)**. Because the cardiovascular system and the respiratory system are interdependent, heart problems also generally affect oxygenation. **Hemorrhage** and surgery can also cause **hypoxia**.

pneumonia   an acute infection of the tissues of the lung.

asthma   a disease that affects the air passages in the lung, causing wheezing and shortness of breath.

emphysema   a lung disease characterized by gradual destruction of the alveoli, which fuse to form larger air spaces. Exchange of oxygen and carbon dioxide through these larger air sacs is inadequate.

chronic obstructive lung disease (COLD) or chronic obstructive pulmonary disease (COPD)   any chronic lung condition in which the flow of expired air is slowed down.

hemorrhage   loss of a large amount of blood (greater than 500 cc for an average adult).

hypoxia   insufficient oxygen in blood or tissue.

❶ HEALTH PROFESSIONALS INVOLVED WITH RESPIRATORY PROBLEMS

Respiratory problems are treated and assessed by a team that includes the physician, the respiratory therapist, the nurse, and the physiotherapist. Although their work may overlap, most facilities use a coordinated team approach to carry out physicians' orders and provide feedback on patients' progress.

Registered Respiratory Therapists (RRT)

RTs are responsible for the cardiorespiratory care of patients of all ages requiring both acute and chronic intervention in their disease. They may initiate, administer, and supervise treatments ordered by the doctor, respond to cardiac arrests, and supervise oxygen therapy devices, such as inhalation devices and respirators. They work closely with the patient, the nurses, the family doctors, and the specialists on both patient-care and specialty units. They also administer and evaluate the results of related tests, for example, the pulmonary function test (PFT) and blood gases. Pulmonary function tests would be booked with Respiratory Services. The requisition can be electronically sent; the department will respond with a date and time. If the individual is going to have the test after discharge, make sure she has the appropriate information and a number to call if she must change the appointment. A website listed at the end of the chapter describes various PFTs the physician may order.

Physiotherapist

Physiotherapists (sometimes referred to simply as "physio," a short form that also describes physiotherapy) provide respiratory assessments and related physiotherapy. When a doctor orders "chest physio," the physiotherapist assesses the patient, devises and helps with deep breathing exercises, and teaches her how to cough effectively to keep her lungs clear.

Nurse

Nursing staff provide ongoing assessment and feedback about a patient's oxygenation status. If an RT or physiotherapist is not available, a nurse can initiate and supervise chest physio or administer oxygen and inhalation treatments.

...

ORDERS RELATED TO OXYGENATION

Chest Physiotherapy

Chest physio is often ordered for patients with a build-up of secretions in the lungs. Techniques vary from routines patients can do on their own to interventions provided by physiotherapists or the nurses.

Deep Breathing and Coughing Exercises

Secretions in the lungs can become thick and difficult for the patient to cough up. If the secretions are left sitting in the lungs, they can become infected or exacerbate an already-present infection, further compromising the patient's breathing. Many patients can cough these secretions up by themselves if they are shown the proper technique. Either a physiotherapist or a nurse can teach the patient deep breathing and coughing exercises (DB&C), which should usually be done every two to three hours while awake. Often, a physiotherapist and a nurse work together to ensure that the patient understands the exercises and performs them properly and regularly. A device called a spirometer (discussed later) may help the patient assess how effectively she is breathing and performing the exercises. Doctors often order DB&C for patients with respiratory difficulties.

Chest Physio with Postural Drainage

People with large amounts of mucus or thick secretions or who have weak breathing muscles or ineffective coughs may need more than DB&C to loosen and move the secretions out of the lungs. They may be helped by chest physio accompanied by **postural drainage**, that is, positioning the patient with her head lower than her body so that gravity can help move the secretions. The physiotherapist may also manually loosen stubborn chest secretions by **clapping** (also called **percussion**): using cupped hands to gently but firmly strike affected regions of the chest to move secretions to the bronchi, from where they can be coughed up more easily. She may also stimulate movement of secretions by placing flattened hands over the congested area and using rapid **vibrations**.

postural drainage positioning the patient with the head lower than the body so that gravity can help drain the mucus and secretions.

clapping or percussion using cupped hands to gently but firmly strike affected regions of the chest to move secretions.

vibrations rapid movements of flattened hands over the patient's chest to move secretions.

Orders for Chest Physiotherapy

When doctors order chest physio, orders may be more or less specific, as in the following examples:

Chest physio bid

Encourage DB&C exercises q2h while awake

Postural drainage by physio tid

Routine postop physio by physiotherapist

If the doctor orders simply "chest physio bid," the order implies a request for an assessment and development of an appropriate routine. Send a requisition (paper or electronic) to the Physiotherapy Department. Transcribe these orders to the Kardex or PI screen, either under Respiratory or under Treatments or Interventions.

A doctor might specifically order, for example, "Encourage DB&C exercises q2h while awake." This order can be initiated and supervised by the physiotherapist or the nurse and does not require a requisition. On many surgical units, a physiotherapist routinely visits all postoperative patients, with or without an order, to implement these exercises, either routinely or if they are having trouble breathing. The physiotherapist may complete an initial assessment and run through the exercises with the patient once or twice. The nurses encourage the patient to continue with the exercises and complete chest assessments as per protocol. If sustained contact with the physiotherapist is required, usually an order and a requisition are necessary.

If a doctor orders "postural drainage by physio tid," this would require a requisition because it is more than the routine treatment. An order for tid would probably involve a morning–afternoon–evening routine or a morning–early afternoon–late afternoon routine. Add the times to the Kardex or PI screen; typical times for this order would be 1000, 1400, and 1700; or 1000, 1600, and 2000. Alternatively, the physiotherapist may choose the hours of treatment based on his schedule. It is important, as with any treatments the patient is receiving, to ensure that you do not book other tests that would interfere with this treatment regime (or if you do, that you notify the Physiotherapy Department). If there is no physiotherapist on duty in the evening, the nurses would complete the postural drainage routine.

If the facility does not have physiotherapists to routinely assess postop patients, the nurses would recommend a physio consult if they deemed it necessary. A doctor may also order a consult, perhaps as "Routine postop physio by physiotherapist." The therapist will visit the patient, assess his needs, and implement a specific routine. If a formal request is made, send a requisition to the Physiotherapy Department. Physiotherapy is often part of a patient's discharge planning.

Nursing Assessment

Vital Signs/Respiratory Assessments
Respiratory rate is part of routine vital signs assessment (along with temperature and pulse), normally done at least once or twice a day. (See Chapter 16.) Nurses will also assess other characteristics of the patient's breathing, such as depth and regularity. Vital signs also provide an indication of the cardiac condition. Blood pressure is not always included in routine vital signs in many facilities. For example, vital signs may be ordered qid, and blood pressure only od. Vital signs are usually taken more frequently for postoperative patients until they are stable and for patients with abnormal vital signs, such as an elevated temperature, pulse, or respiratory rate, perhaps accompanied by **dyspnea**. Nurses may increase the frequency of vital signs within policy guidelines if their assessments indicate a problem, or the doctor may order a certain frequency. For example, a doctor may order one of the following:

dyspnea   difficulty breathing.

> V/S QID
>
> V/S and BP QID
>
> V/S q15 min × 4, q1/2h × 6, q1h × 8 and then QID if stable

In the last example, the doctor wants signs checked every 15 minutes for an hour, then every half-hour for three hours, followed by every hour for eight hours. After that, if the vital signs are stable, the nurses can reduce assessment to four times a day.

If the doctor is concerned about a patient's blood pressure or circulation, she may issue more specific orders for blood pressure assessments. For example, "Monitor BP in lying and sitting position, in both arms bid."

The doctor orders blood pressure to be read with the patient in two different positions to see if it changes with position. If so, the patient may be suffering postural hypotension, that is, an abnormally low blood pressure in certain positions. Taking blood pressure in both arms will identify compromised circulation on one side, for example, because of a narrowed artery.

Chest Assessments In a chest assessment, a doctor, respiratory technician, or more usually a nurse, assesses the patient's colour and ease of breathing and auscultates or listens to the patient's lungs through a stethoscope. If breath sounds are diminished or absent, that indicates impeded or diminished air exchange caused by such conditions as pneumonia. Adventitious or extra sounds include **crackles,** or **crepitation**, and **rhonchi** (singular *rhonchus*)**,** or **wheezes.** Crepitation sounds something like air blown through a straw immersed in fluid and usually indicates the presence of fluid in the small airways. Rhonchi can be high pitched or low pitched and are caused by air moving through airways narrowed by swelling or partial obstruction.

crepitation or crackles sounds produced by air passing over airway secretions.

rhonchi or wheezes musical-pitched sounds produced by air passing through narrowed bronchi, heard on auscultation of the lungs.

Chest assessments (CA) are routine for postoperative patients and for those with cardiorespiratory problems. The physician may order a chest assessment at specific intervals or may rely on hospital routines. A respiratory unit might have qid as routine, whereas an orthopedic unit might have bid or od as routine. Postoperative chest assessments range from bid to qid and decrease as the patient recovers. Transcribe the order to the Kardex or PI screen under Oxygenation or Nursing Assessments/Interventions and add the times; for assessments od, you would probably record the time as 1000. No requisition is required.

Diagnostic Tests for Oxygenation

Pulse Oximetry Pulse oximetry is a method used by nurses and respiratory therapists to determine oxygen levels in red blood cells in the arterial blood. A pulse oximeter, shown in Figure 20.1, is a sensor that can be attached to the patient's finger, toe, or sometimes the earlobe. The measurement is reported as arterial blood oxygen saturation (SaO_2 or O_2 Sat). Normal adult SaO_2 values should be at least 95 percent.

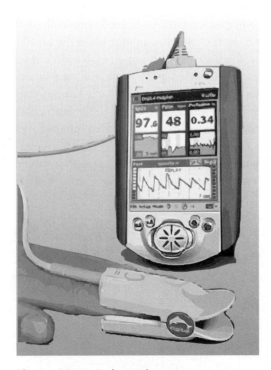

Figure 20.1 Pulse oximeter

Patients are monitored with pulse oximetry after surgery, during surgical and diagnostic procedures, and when there is a concern about oxygenation. Monitoring may be continuous, or oximetry levels may be read at specific times. In orders, oximetry is abbreviated to "ox," and saturation levels to "sats." Thus, doctors may write an order in any of the following ways:

Pulse ox TID

O$_2$ sats bid

Monitor pulse ox for 8 hours

Oximetry qid

Transcribe the orders to the Kardex or PI screen. Some facilities want frequency translated into specific times.

Orders Related to Lung Function Tests

Tests that relate more specifically to the hospitalized patient and order entry procedures are also discussed here—related to the responsibilities of the clinical secretary.

Arterial Blood Gases   An arterial blood gas (ABGs) assessment is done on a patient to determine the amounts of oxygen and carbon dioxide dissolved in the blood. The test also calculates the blood's pH, or acid–base balance. Table 20.1 shows the categories of results and normal ranges. These measures indicate how well the person's blood is being oxygenated and thus their respiratory status. The test helps physicians monitor the effects of oxygen therapy and respirator management.

Blood gases are usually ordered as "ABGs." Usually this is a stat order. The sample must be arterial and is a little more complex to take than a routine blood sample. The physician, respiratory therapist, or specially trained nurse collects the blood. If the order is stat and the patient is on the patient-care unit when the blood is drawn, prepare and keep the requisition on the floor (as with any stat lab order). If using a manual system, label the requisition and set it aside for the nurse, RT, or physician. In a computerized environment, select the option of printing the sample label in the unit instead of in the laboratory. The request will be sent electronically to the lab for their records. Depending on where you are working, you will have to call Respiratory Services if an RT is going to draw the blood. In a larger teaching hospital, you may have to page the appropriate resident or intern. You may have to call the lab to bring the required equipment to draw and store the blood sample.

Table 20.1   Laboratory Results for Arterial Blood Gases

Test	Explanation	Normal Values
O$_2$	Saturation percentage of arterial hemoglobin carrying oxygen	95%–98%
PO$_2$	Partial pressure of oxygen in the blood	80–100 mm Hg
PCO$_2$	Partial pressure of carbon dioxide in the blood	38–42 mm Hg
HCO	Related to the pH of the blood	24–18 mEq/L
Ph	Acid–base measurement of the blood	7.35–7.45

The lab usually phones the results to the patient-care unit, or faxes the results to the floor. As with any lab test, read back the values to ensure accuracy, and verify the patient's name and hospital number. Report the results to the physician immediately, especially if the physician has asked you to do so, if the order is stat, or if the results are not within normal limits. In most cases, the physician will want you to report the results even if normal.

The first order in Figure 20.2 is for arterial blood gases. The nurses will ask you to organize stat blood gases (as above) if the oxygen saturation (also referred to as pulse ox or ox sats) drops below 90 percent. The orders for sputum for cytology and AFB would be entered appropriately onto the PI screen or Kardex. There is no one to call because the nurses (or sometimes the physiotherapist) would obtain the specimens when the patient can give them, print a label, and send the specimen to the lab. You would book the PFT with Respiratory Services, ensuring that the patient was not involved in another procedure. A paper requisition may be required in a noncomputerized environment. For the thoracocentesis, you would tell the nurses, ensure that an extra nurse was available the next morning, and order the equipment from CSR or SPD (Central Supply Room or Sterile Processing Department). You would also check to be sure that the treatment room was free and that a consent for the test was prepared for the patient to sign. Some patient-care units have a schedule for use of the treatment room. If this is the case, mark in the date and time the room will be in use for the procedure.

Spirometry   See Chapter 6 for details about this test. Because respiratory therapists usually perform this test in the Respiratory Department, you would electronically remit an order for spirometry to that department. Note on the requisition how the patient will arrive (e.g., ambulatory, by stretcher, by wheelchair). Note also if the patient has altered cognition. Spirometry requires patient cooperation and may be ineffective if the patient is

	CONESTOGA GENERAL HOSPITAL DOCTOR'S ORDER SHEET			
Please fax to Pharmacy & note date/time				Dietz, Henry
	ABGs stat if pulse ox drops below 90			123 Duncan St.
	Sputum for cytology X 3			Vancouver B.C.
	Sputum for AFB X 3 am spec			DOB 22 09 47 071608
	Book for PFT this week			Dr. M. Label
	Thoracocentesis tomorrow @ 1000 in the treatment room—have tray on floor and			
	nurse available for assist.			
date Jan 6/xx	time	Physician's printed name **Dr. M. Label**	Signature *Dr. M. Label*	

Figure 20.2   Order for blood gases and other tests related to respiratory conditions

too confused. The Respiratory Department will notify you by telephone or electronically of the date and time of the test. Note it on the Kardex.

Sputum Specimens All sputum specimens should consist of mucous secretions, not saliva, from the airways (bronchi), lungs, or throat. Because of this, the nurse or doctor may request chest physio for the patient to assist the patient to cough up the mucus. The physician may order a test to identify cell types, or "sputum for cytology." For this type of test, usually three specimens must be collected and must be coughed up early in the morning. The doctor may write "sputum for cytology 3," as shown in Figure 20.2, or may assume that you know that three specimens are needed. When transcribing this order to the Kardex or PI screen, note that three specimens are to be collected and add "early morning." Write in "1, 2, 3" for the nurses to keep track of the specimens. As they collect each, they cross out the number. The same information can be noted under Comments or Additional Information on an electronic record. See Figure 20.2 for a typical order.

Lung Scan You would book a lung scan with Nuclear Medicine. If the order is stat, call the department for a booking time. As with spirometry, it is important to relay information about the patient's condition, ability to mobilize for the test, and level of cognition. It may be that a nurse has to accompany the patient. Lung CT scans may also be done. Handle the order as described for Spirometry.

Thoracocentesis A thoracocentesis (also called a pleural tap) is a procedure to remove fluid from the space between the lining of the outside of the lungs (pleura) and the wall of the chest. It is done for diagnostic and/or therapeutic purposes. This procedure may be done in the patient's room or in the treatment room if there is one in the patient-care unit. Usually, the physician ordering the test performs it, and so he may set the date and time himself.

This procedure requires the patient's consent. Label a consent form, fill it out as completely as possible, and leave it in the front of the patient's chart for the nurses to have it signed. It is the physician's responsibility to ensure that the patient understands the procedure, but as with many surgical consent forms, the nurses actually obtain the consent and sign as a witness to the consent. If your unit does not stock thoracocentesis trays, the nurses might ask you to order one from Central Supply. No requisition is required. In the order the physician may have asked for a tray and for a nurse, but they will often omit that part. It is up to you to know what is required and have things ready; you would order the tray and notify the nurses so that someone is available to assist with the procedure.

Inhalation and Oxygen Therapies

Incentive Spirometer Incentive spirometers, also known as sustained maximal inspiration devices (Figure 20.3), are often used after surgery to encourage the patient to do deep breathing exercises. (Note that this differs from the spirometry described above as an assessment.) The patient breathes through a mouthpiece into a container that has little balls at the bottom; she is encouraged to inhale deeply to keep the balls floating as long as possible. This allows assessment of how effectively the patient is breathing. Spirometry may also be ordered to diagnose pulmonary disease or to determine the progression or regression of existing diseases, such as pneumonia and emphysema.

Figure 20.3 Incentive spirometer

Inhalation Therapy   The physician may order selected medications to be delivered by a mask to the patient, often to treat asthma. RTs, or sometimes nurses, administer this therapy. Commonly used drugs include salbutamol (Ventolin), ipratropium bromide (Atrovent), and budesonide (Pulmicort). The medication is usually diluted in a measured amount of normal saline before it is added to the aerosol chamber in the mask. Sometimes, the medication can be given using corrugated tubing instead of a mask, especially to children, who usually do not like the mask. Medications are also given by a metered dose inhaler as discussed in Chapter 7. Salbutamol inhalation is frequently ordered as a PRN medication, and both budesonide and ipratropium bromide are ordered as scheduled inhalation treatments. For example, a doctor may order "Atrovent inhalation qid." To transcribe these orders, enter the treatment on the scheduled or PRN medication sheet, notify Respiratory Therapy, and add the treatment to the patient's Kardex or PI screen in the appropriate place (often under Oxygen Therapy).

Oxygen Therapy   Patients who, for any reason, do not have enough oxygen in their blood require supplemental oxygen. The decision to order oxygen for a patient is based on his diagnosis, general condition, cardiopulmonary status, oxygen saturation levels, and blood gases. Patients may also be put on oxygen postoperatively until the anaesthetic wears off and an effective respiratory pattern is re-established.

Oxygen may be dispensed from a cylinder (compressed gas), piped in (wall oxygen), given as liquid oxygen (which uses a small portable tank that must be refilled), or given through an oxygen concentrator. Oxygen may be delivered by face mask or nasal prongs (NP). A face mask fits over the patient's mouth and nose. A variety of masks are available, the simplest of which (shown in Figure 20.4) delivers oxygen concentrations from 40 to 60 percent when set between five and eight litres. When possible, nasal prongs will be used instead. As shown in Figure 20.5, the prongs are small and fit into the nose, connecting to the oxygen tubing fitted around the face. They are less restrictive than an oxygen mask and allow the user to speak and eat comfortably with the oxygen running. They are not suitable, however, for patients who require oxygen concentrations of more than 40 percent or when the patient is a mouth breather. If the oxygen is set at 1 L/min, the patient will get 24 to 25 percent oxygen; if the oxygen is set at 6 L/min, he will get approximately 40 percent. Typically, doctors will order nasal prongs with the oxygen delivery level set for 2–3 L/min.

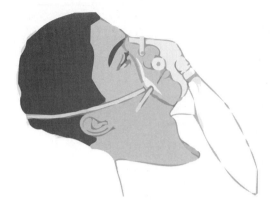 

Figure 20.4 Simple oxygen mask   **Figure 20.5** Nasal prongs

A Venturi mask (also called a high-flow mask) is ordered when the physician is trying to titrate the patient's oxygen levels, when the patient has trouble with nasal prongs, or when more accurate control of the amount delivered is required. This mask, usually disposable, contains a mechanism that draws in room air and mixes it with 100 percent oxygen to a predetermined concentration. The oxygen delivered can be set to levels ranging from 24 to 32 percent.

Unless she is confined to bed, a patient usually uses a combination of stationary and mobile oxygen systems. At the bedside, oxygen is obtained from a wall unit. A variety of portable oxygen tanks on specially designed transporters are available for use within and away from the hospital. More sophisticated units, containing oxygen-conserving devices, weigh only a few pounds and can provide up to eight hours of oxygen. Electric or battery-operated devices (called oxygen concentrators) that concentrate oxygen from the air are also available. The Respiratory Department is responsible for maintaining portable oxygen supplies in the patient-care unit. If oxygen tanks are kept on the floor, they must be stored safely in cool places that do not obstruct traffic.

If a patient on oxygen leaves the unit for any reason, make sure the nurses have assessed her to determine whether she requires a portable oxygen system. In most hospitals, these units are ordered from the Respiratory Therapy Department, although most clinical areas have two or three portable units. Note that if you are asked to move a patient on oxygen in her bed, make sure the oxygen tubing has been disconnected from the wall unit. It's surprising how often the nurses forget to do this, particularly in an emergency.

Safety measures must be observed near oxygen. Oxygen facilitates combustion. People must not smoke, light a match, or do anything that might initiate a spark. Often patients or visitors forget or are unaware of this danger. Although most facilities are smoke free, reminders should still be posted. Oxygen can be ordered continuously or PRN; if the order does not specify, it is assumed to be continuous.

Oxygen is ordered by the physician. In some situations, other health professionals may initiate oxygen therapy and obtain an order later. In ordering oxygen, the physician specifies the amount or concentration of oxygen, the method of delivery, and the number of litres per minute, often two litres. A typical order would be "O_2 per N/P @ 2L." If the patient required more oxygen, the levels may be set higher. The order might read "O_2 by mask @ 2 litres" or "O_2 by Venturi mask @ 35%."

If the records are manual, complete a requisition when you transcribe the order. In a computerized environment, the Respiratory Therapy Department will be notified electronically. In either case, if the order is stat, phone to notify the RT Department. Oxygen may be set up by an RT or a nurse depending on the facility's policy and the time of day. (Some facilities do not have an RT available on the late evening or night shift, and so the nurse assumes this responsibility.)

Humidifier   A humidifier is often used for a patient who is experiencing respiratory difficulties. A humidifier moistens the air, helps keep mucous membranes moist, and loosens secretions in the upper respiratory tract. Most oxygen delivered to a patient is also humidified.

Artificial Airways

Tracheostomy   A **tracheostomy** is the creation of an artificial airway through an incision in the neck into the trachea. A tube is inserted to assist with breathing and to keep the trachea from collapsing.

tracheostomy   an artificial airway through an incision in the trachea.

You are may see orders for the maintenance of a tracheostomy, especially if you work on a specialized respiratory unit. The order might read "Trach care q2h" (or "q4h" or "PRN"). Nurses must keep the airway patent (open) and clean. They will often need to suction the airway and change the dressing around the tracheostomy from time to time. This care is considered a sterile procedure. You may be asked to order a tracheostomy tray or kit for the nurses. This would be obtained from the CSR/SPD. A patient who has a permanent tracheostomy eventually learns how to care for it himself.

Endotracheal Tube   An endotracheal tube is a device that is inserted into the airway of a patient about to receive a general anaesthetic, or as an emergency procedure for someone who cannot breathe independently. It is inserted with an instrument called a laryngoscope. One would be kept on the crash cart in every patient-care unit. Doctors will sometimes write an order to *extubate* a patient, that is, to remove the tube. Extubation typically takes place in an Intensive Care Unit, not on a patient-care unit.

Suctioning   In terms of the respiratory system, suctioning or aspiration means applying negative pressure to remove mucus, phlegm, and other secretions from the airways to make it easier for a person to breathe. Suctioning is used to clear airway obstructions, to remove built-up secretions that may lead to infection, and to keep airways clear for patients on mechanical ventilation. It may also be used to obtain a specimen. It is necessary mostly for patients who are unconscious, have altered consciousness, or are too weak to cough up secretions.

Suctioning requires a catheter, attached tubing, a wall-mounted or portable suction machine, and a drainage bottle. Suction catheters and tubing should be kept in the treatment room on your unit.

Simple suctioning can be done through the nose or the mouth. Suctioning through the mouth is called **oropharyngeal (mouth and throat) suction**. It reaches only the mouth, or the mouth and the back of the throat. Suctioning through the nose is called **nasopharyngeal (nose and throat) suctioning**, and it reaches the back of the mouth and throat. **Deep suctioning**, such as **endotracheal suctioning**, is more complicated and involves going through an endotracheal tube to reach deeper into the breathing passages. This is a strictly sterile procedure.

Suctioning is always ordered PRN. The physician may write "Suction PRN." Sometimes suctioning is ordered after chest physio to remove the loosened secretions. The doctor may also order "Endotracheal suctioning PRN." If the doctor does not specify the route, suctioning is assumed to be via nose or mouth; the nurse or RT will decide which is more appropriate or convenient. The physician may also indicate the type and size of the suction catheter needed. Add suction orders to the Kardex or PI screen under Respiratory or under Additional Nursing Care.

Ventilator You will not encounter an order for a ventilator unless you work in a critical care unit or in long-term care where a person has a ventilator for life. A ventilator is a machine used to support breathing. It is used when a patient is anaesthetized, such as during surgery, or if for some reason he is unable to breathe on his own. Another situation requiring mechanical ventilation is keeping someone in an induced coma (such as Canadian freestyle skier Sara Burke, who died after a tragic accident in January 2012). To receive mechanical ventilation sufficient for life support, the patient must first be intubated. The doctor would write the order for the desired type of mechanical ventilation, and an RRT from Respiratory Services would be responsible for setting it up and maintaining the patient on the ventilator.

❷ CARDIOVASCULAR ASSESSMENTS AND TREATMENTS

Nursing Assessments

In taking vital signs and checking the respiratory status, nurses are conducting a basic cardiac assessment as well. More complex assessments may be ordered.

Peripheral Vascular Assessment Doctors may order peripheral vascular assessment (PVA) for patients admitted with peripheral vascular disease (PVD), including arteriosclerosis, varicose veins, thrombophlebitis, or general evidence of poor circulation. This assessment may also be called a CSM, for *circulation*, *sensation*, and *movement*. Nurses observe the colour and temperature of the skin in the affected area (for example, the legs), ask about the patient's feeling or sensation in the area, note any edema or other abnormalities, and check for peripheral pulse in the affected area. Transcribe this order onto the Kardex or PI screen under Nursing Assessments or Vascular Assessments. No requisition is required.

Although the following tests are discussed in Chapter 6, what is detailed here is relevant data for order entry procedures.

Chest X-Ray

For an inpatient, a chest X-ray would be booked with Diagnostic Services, and the patient would go to that department for the X-ray. A chest X-ray may be ordered as a "portable"

oropharyngeal suctioning suctioning with a catheter through the mouth to reach the mouth only or the mouth and the back of the throat.

nasopharyngeal suctioning suctioning with a catheter through the nose to reach the mouth and throat (pharynx).

deep suctioning introducing the suction catheter into the lower trachea and bronchi.

endotracheal suctioning suctioning through an artificial airway known as a tracheostomy.

for the patient who is unable to leave the floor. This is usual if the patient is very ill and moving him would be detrimental. For a portable X-ray, call the X-ray Department, and keep the requisition on the floor.

Telemetry

Most hospitals have what is called a Telemetry Unit. A patient can be admitted directly to this unit for cardiac monitoring or may be transferred to this unit as a "step down" from the Intensive Care Unit for ongoing assessment. A telemetry monitor—a small box connected to the chest by wires and electrodes, much like a Holter monitor—is used to trace the heart's activity; however, the readout is displayed on a small screen. A nurse continuously monitors the screen for abnormalities. An alarm sounds if the patient's heartbeat slows down or speeds up to preset rates or becomes irregular. When a doctor orders telemetry, arrange for an in-hospital transfer, including transferring any hard copies of the patient's chart, MAR, and any old charts that may be on the floor.

Pacemakers

A pacemaker is a small electronic device that regulates the heartbeat by sending electrical signals to the heart. Pacemakers are used for patients with abnormal heartbeats, which may be irregular or too slow (**bradycardia**). These abnormal beats affect the patient's circulation and decrease oxygenation. The pacemaker is implanted in the hospital on an inpatient or outpatient basis, with the patient sedated. When a physician orders pacemaker insertion, book the procedure with the cardiologist's office. For an inpatient, prepare an OR chart, and initiate preoperative routines, such as cancelling or delaying meals and ensuring that the nurses know that the patient will be NPO the night before the procedure. A consent is required for this procedure.

bradycardia extremely slow heartbeat.

Cardiac Catheterization

This test is booked with and performed in a special unit referred to as a Cardiac Cath Lab. If the hospital does not have this service, the patient will be sent to another facility that does. Book the appointment at the appropriate facility, and then implement the preparation for the patient. In many regions, you must obtain a transportation number for a patient requiring any test at another facility. As well you must send the patient's chart (or printed components of the patient's electronic chart) and any MARs along with him. The patient must be NPO the night before the procedure. The morning of the procedure, a groin prep will be done. A consent is necessary.

Other Tests

The ECG, stress test, Doppler ultrasound, and echocardiogram are all tests that you would book with Cardiopulmonary Services. With the exception of the ECG, the patient goes to the department for the test. An ECG can be ordered stat or routine—they are usually done at the patient's bedside. If it is stat, as usual, print the requisition on the floor and call the lab to have someone come to do it.

Although previously mentioned, remember that when booking any test, ensure the appointment does not conflict with another test the patient is having. Be sure to add in the free text field any relevant information regarding the patient's ability to ambulate, whether he is on oxygen, or has any cognitive impairment. In some cases, a nurse will accompany the patient. If so, be sure that a nurse is available. You may need to call someone in or have someone come from another unit.

Chest CT Scan

A chest computed tomography scan (or chest CT scan) shows much more detail than a standard X-ray and is used when better visualization of the lungs is required, for example, to follow up on questionable abnormal findings on a chest X-ray. This test is booked with Diagnostic Imaging. A website listed at the end of the chapter details this test.

Computerized Tomography Angiogram (CT Angio)

A CT angiogram (combines angiography and a CT scan) usually requires the patient to have a dye injected into the arm prior to the test. Some facilities ask the patient to avoid solid foods for 4 hours prior to the test (clear fluids are allowed). One of the most common reasons for this test is to diagnose a **pulmonary embolism**. This test is booked with Radiology and may be done on an inpatient or outpatient basis.

pulmonary embolism a blockage in one or more of the blood vessels in the lungs. The embolism is usually a blood clot which often originates in the deep veins of the legs.

❼ CARDIOPULMONARY EMERGENCIES

YOU NEED TO BE ALERT TO THE POSSIBILITY OF CARDIAC OR RESPIRATORY ARRESTS AND know what you have to do if one occurs.

On any hospital patient-care unit, there is the possibility that a patient will have an arrest. This can be a respiratory arrest or a cardiac arrest. If a cardiac or respiratory arrest occurs, you must "call the arrest," that is, notify the appropriate people. Know the procedures and codes for cardiac and respiratory arrests. In some facilities, the same code is used for both; other facilities use two different codes. Act quickly, but remain calm. Collect the required information, usually the patient's room and bed numbers—make sure you have the correct numbers. Most facilities have a special emergency number. Go to the nearest telephone and dial the number. Give the information clearly and concisely to the operator. Response will be swift. During the course of resuscitation attempts, you may be asked to keep a record of what is happening—drugs that are given and procedures that are implemented, as well as who does what. You would be given this information by health professionals attending the arrest and asked to record it. (You would not be expected to guess what is happening.) In some cases you may be directed to fetch equipment needed from the crash cart or the treatment room (e.g., an IV solution). Stay out of the way, follow directions, and remain calm. If you are recording information, write neatly, clearly, and stay organized. Record in the order that the information is given to you. If possible, include the time you are given the information—for example, "IV hung at 12:32," "paddles applied at 12:35." As well, you may be asked to record the official time of death when CPR efforts are terminated.

Be aware of any family members who are nearby. If they are present and necessary, guide them to a place where they can wait during resuscitation procedures. Keep them informed; be empathetic and supportive. Comfort for friends and family members at such a time is extremely important and can go a long way to reducing their stress and assisting them to cope with their loss.

SUMMARY

1. The cardiovascular and respiratory systems work independently and interdependently to maintain adequate amounts of oxygen in the blood. Any condition that affects one system will affect the patient's oxygenation and may also affect other systems. Patients who are admitted with respiratory or cardiovascular conditions and postoperative patients will likely be monitored for oxygenation status.

2. Respiratory therapists, physiotherapists, and nurses provide ongoing assessment and care related to respiratory problems.

3. The purpose of chest physio is to assist with the removal of secretions from the lungs. Patients are taught deep breathing and coughing exercises (DB&C). Physiotherapists may manually loosen secretions by clapping or vibrating. Postural drainage uses gravity by positioning the head lower than the body.

4. Respiratory assessment (rate, rhythm, volume, etc.) is done as part of routine vital signs assessment. Chest assessments, completed by nurses, respiratory therapists, and physiotherapists, involve auscultating for abnormal sounds, such as crackles (crepitation) and wheezes (rhonchi). Chest assessment (CA) is routine for postoperative patients and may be ordered with specific frequency.

5. Pulse oximetry uses a small light-sensing device to determine oxygen saturation; it may be ordered as continuous or intermittent. An arterial blood gas assessment (ABGs) measures the levels of oxygen and carbon dioxide in blood and the pH level. It is often ordered stat. For a stat order, keep the requisition on the floor until the sample is taken. Report ABG results promptly. Sputum samples may be taken for culture and sensitivity or cytology. Pulmonary function tests are usually done in the Respiratory Department and require a requisition.

6. Incentive spirometers encourage patients' deep breathing exercises. Inhalation therapy is often used to treat asthma. Oxygen therapy is commonly ordered postoperatively and for patients who do not have enough blood oxygen. Oxygen may be given through nasal prongs (NP) or by face mask. Oxygen orders may be continuous or PRN; they specify concentration, method of delivery, and volume per minute. Observe safety measures around oxygen. Ventilators help patients who cannot adequately breathe independently. They are most frequently seen in intensive care units. A tracheostomy is an artificial opening in the throat through which a tube is inserted to help with breathing.

7. Patients who are unable to cough up secretions by themselves may be suctioned. Suctioning through the nose and mouth reaches the back of the mouth and throat. Deep suctioning involves the bronchi. Endotracheal suctioning goes through an endotracheal or tracheostomy tube and is a strictly sterile procedure.

8. Orders relating to the cardiovascular system often overlap with those relating to respiratory assessments. Vital signs, chest assessments, and chest X-rays relate to both systems. In doing a peripheral vascular assessment (PVA), a nurse checks skin colour and temperature, pulse, and sensation. A chest X-ray is usually ordered as AP and lateral, specifying front, back, and side views. It may be ordered as a portable if the patient cannot move to Diagnostic Imaging. An ECG (or EKG) measures the heart's electrical activity and is one of the most commonly ordered cardiovascular tests. Variations include a stress test and a Holter monitor, which provides continuous monitoring.

9. Pacemakers are inserted to regulate the heartbeat through electrical signals; insertion is an operative procedure.

10. A respiratory arrest or a cardiac arrest is an emergency. You must know your responsibility and how to call the arrest. Act swiftly, make sure you have the correct information, and remain calm.

Key Terms

arrhythmia 611
arteriosclerosis 610
asthma 612
atherosclerosis 610
atrial fibrillation 611
bradycardia 623
cerebral vascular accident (CVA; stroke) 611
chronic obstructive lung disease (COLD) or chronic obstructive pulmonary disease (COPD) 612
clapping (percussion) 613

congestive heart failure (CHF) 611
crash cart 611
crepitation (crackles) 615
deep suctioning 622
diastolic pressure 611
dyspnea 614
emphysema 612
endotracheal suctioning 622
hemorrhage 612
hypertension (high blood pressure) 611
hypoxia 612

myocardial infarct (MI, heart attack, or coronary) 610
nasopharyngeal suctioning 622
oropharyngeal suctioning 622
pneumonia 612
postural drainage 613
pulmonary embolism 624
rhonchi (wheezes) 615
systolic pressure 611
tracheostomy 621
vibrations 613

Review Questions

1. What is the relationship between the cardiovascular and respiratory systems with respect to oxygenation?

2. List the main organs in the cardiovascular and respiratory systems.

3. What roles do respiratory therapists and physiotherapists play in respiratory assessment and care?

4. What is included in a chest assessment, and what is the purpose of this assessment?

5. What is the principle by which pulse oximetry works?

6. Why are blood gases sometimes ordered along with or instead of oximetry?

7. What is unique about an order for sputum for cytology or AFB?

8. Describe the purpose and use of the spirometer on the patient-care unit.

9. What would you do if a patient had a respiratory or cardiac arrest?

Application Exercises

1. Summarize the physiology and function of the respiratory and cardiovascular systems. Use a detailed diagram to illustrate the structure of each.

2. With one or two other students, research three common respiratory conditions and three common cardiovascular conditions. For each, describe the following:

   a. Common assessments used to diagnose and monitor the condition

   b. The etiology of the condition

   c. How it interferes with oxygenation

	V/S quid x 48 then bid		Loton, Walter
	Chest physio quid suction after physio PRN		477 Grange St.
	Sputum for cytology x 3		Acton, ON L7R 2R4
	O₂ by Venturi mask @ 34%		M 17 04 38 034902
	Pulse ox quid. ABGs if sats drop below 92%		2779453775
	EKG in 2 days & chest X-ray PA and lateral stat portable		Dr. R. Bobb
Date Sept 1/xx	Time	Physician's Name Printed Dr. R. Bobb	Physician's signature Dr. R. Bobb

Figure 20.6 Doctor's orders for Walter Loton

3. Review the standard procedures for CPR online. If your program does not require you to have CPR certification, research available resources in your area where these courses can be taken (including cost). Organize a group—maybe the class—to become certified.

4. Mr. Loton is in hospital with CHF and SOB. He is weak and semiconscious.

   a. What is meant by the acronym SOB?

   b. What is meant by the acronym CHF?

   c. Why might Dr. Bobb have ordered suction after the patient had chest physio?

   d. Briefly describe the function and purpose of the Venturi mask.

   e. Why were ABGs ordered based on O₂ sats from oximetry?

   f. What is meant by PA and lateral in the order for the chest X-ray?

   g. Why is a portable X-ray ordered in this case?

   h. Transcribe the orders in Figure 20.6 according to the protocol outlined by your professor.

Websites of Interest

The Respiratory System
http://www.medicalvideos.us/play.php?vid=560
This video shows graphic detail of a tracheostomy being performed. See how much terminology you know here.
http://www.youtube.com/watch?v=HiT621PrrO0
3-D animation of the respiratory system.

The Cardiovascular System, animated
www.innerbody.com/image/cardov.html
www.biologyinmotion.com/cardio/

Abnormal Breath Sounds
www.rnceus.com/resp/respabn.html

Spirometry Video
http://oac.med.jhmi.edu/res_phys/Encyclopedia/Spirometry/Spirometry.HTML

Pulmonary Function Tests
http://www.childrenscolorado.org/conditions/lung/treatments/PF_lab.aspx#lung_volumes

Chest CT
http://www.radiologyinfo.org/en/info.cfm?pg=chestct
http://medmovie.com/mmdatabase/MediaPlayer.aspx?ClientID=65&TopicID=0
This website of the American Heart Association shows a variety of videos related to heart tests, pathophysiology, and heart function.

Chapter 21
Orders Related to Rest and Activity

Learning Objectives

On completing this chapter, you will be able to:

1. Discuss the criteria used to assess rest and activity orders.
2. Understand the common rest and activity orders ordered by the physician.
3. Describe the various positions a patient can assume.
4. Transcribe rest and activity orders correctly.
5. Identify the equipment used that relates to rest and activity.

In the past, individuals were kept in bed for long periods of time during when they were ill or recovering from surgery or childbirth. Advancement in surgical techniques and changes in philosophy have shifted the focus to activity. Doctors now realize that bed rest and limited activity have harmful effects on most body systems. The respiratory system is compromised because of ineffective breathing patterns, including decreased ability to cough and breathe deeply. Secretions can pool in the alveoli, harbouring bacteria and leading to **hypostatic pneumonia**. The circulatory system is compromised and blood clots or thrombus can result. The muscular system loses tone and strength. The integumentary system is affected. Some people develop pressure sores, especially older patients or those with compromised skin integrity.

Therefore, patients are encouraged to be as active as possible as soon as they can. People with hip replacements are now **weight bearing** within a couple of days of surgery. Some people who have had back surgery are ambulating the next day. Women are up as early as an hour after giving birth.

However, as important as activity is for maintaining health, rest is also required to help the body heal from disease, trauma, or surgery. The goal is to find a balance that provides the optimal level of activity for each patient. Physiotherapy helps patients maintain and improve their ability to be active.

hypostatic pneumonia pneumonia developing as a result of decreased air exchange combined with an inability to drain pooled bronchial secretions.

weight bearing putting body weight on the lower limbs.

❶ CRITERIA USED IN ACTIVITY ORDERS

When a person is admitted to hospital, the physician will provide a specific order related to activity level. To determine the optimal activity level, physicians consider several factors.

Physical Energy

Activity orders must be realistic and take into account the patient's strength, endurance, and desire to be active. Disease and surgery can undermine a person's physical energy. Age also plays a role. Usually, a 21-year-old will have more energy than an 80-year-old, even in the face of illness. Requiring patients to do too much is as harmful as allowing them to do too little. It can be difficult to find the balance. Sometimes, after surgery, patients just do not want to move because of pain and weakness.

Physical Capabilities

Often, physical disabilities limit the extent and type of activity a patient is capable of, especially in the hospital. Space is limited and unfamiliar, and the patient may not have the same assistive devices she has at home. A patient may ambulate with assistance at home; however, with limited staff, the same kind of assistance may not be available in hospital. However, patients should be encouraged to be as independent as they can safely and comfortably be. The doctor may order an assessment by a physiotherapist, who will provide appropriate assistive devices and a modified activity routine. The physiotherapist may come two or three times a day to get the patient up and walking.

The Nature of the Illness

Some illnesses can best be treated with a period of rest; others require activity. For example, with an unstable heart condition, activity increases the heart's workload and can lead to further problems, such as angina. A patient with such a condition may be required to rest initially and then gradually increase activity. In contrast, the sooner a stroke victim begins an active rehabilitation program, the better it will be for her.

Consciousness and Cognition

Altered consciousness can range from being unconscious to simply being confused or disoriented. It may result from a number of conditions, including a stroke, head injury, terminal illness, or sedation.

Patients who are unconscious or semiconscious are obviously unable to ambulate. They will be on bed rest and dependent on staff to meet all of their needs.

Patients who have had narcotic analgesics may know where they are and where they want to go but lack the neuromuscular integrity to do so safely. Often, patients who have had sedation experience some altered cognition and, perhaps, confusion. For example, a postoperative patient may know where the bathroom is and think he can manage on his own but may misjudge his abilities and end up falling. Nurses may leave the side rails on the bed up for patients who have been sedated. Leaving side rails up is controversial. On the one hand, it may stop a patient from getting up; on the other hand, a patient who is determined to get up (often becoming increasingly agitated by any barriers) may climb over the side rails and be at increased risk of injury.

Patients often ring a bell and ask for help going to the bathroom, getting out of bed, or getting back into bed. You may be tempted to help them if the nurses are busy. However, this is considered nursing care and is generally not within your scope of practice. Without the proper training and experience, your help may result in injury. Reassure the patient that you will find a nurse.

Any alteration in a person's ability to think clearly will affect the level of activity that can be safely allowed. Patients who have dementia or Alzheimer's disease may be able to walk and move independently but have little idea how to interact with the environment. People with severe cognitive impairment may be cared for in a "secure" or locked unit to prevent them from wandering off and getting lost or injured. A doctor's order might read "Not to leave the floor unless accompanied by a nurse or family member."

Surgery

Many patients recovering from major surgery will have their level of activity restricted initially. The seriousness and type of operation naturally affects how much and when the patient can ambulate. Most patients do get out of bed the first postoperative day. Even patients with numerous tubes, intravenous lines, and heart monitors can be helped to get up. Heart transplant recipients are often up and walking within a couple of days.

Many patients dread getting up the first couple of times after an operation. Getting a patient up, particularly for the first time, can be as difficult for the nurse as it is for the patient! Patients often do not appreciate the need to become active—or do not care—and view the nurse as not having any compassion. To deal with pain, nurses often give the patient an analgesic half an hour before getting them up or remind patients with a patient-controlled analgesia (PCA) pump to self-medicate. Regardless, some patients flatly refuse to get out of bed. Nurses will often contract with the patient to work up to ambulation. For example, the patient agrees to sit on the side of the bed for the first time, the next time to move to the chair, the next time to walk to the door of the room, and so on.

Sometimes, the doctor will intervene, telling the patient that remaining in bed is not an option. He may write an order, such as "encourage ambulation" or "patient must ambulate at least qid."

❷❸❹ ACTIVITY ORDERS

THERE ARE A VARIETY OF ACTIVITY ORDERS GEARED TO THE CAPABILITIES OF THE INDIVIDUAL patient. These orders are usually transcribed onto the Kardex or PI screen. They do not require a requisition unless someone other than the nurses—a physiotherapist, for example—is needed.

Any time a patient leaves the unit for a test or an appointment, notify anyone who will be working with the patient of any limitations in mobility or independence. Requisitions for tests that involve moving the patient will ask for this information. On a computerized requisition, it may be a mandatory field.

Complete Bed Rest

Complete bed rest (CBR) means that the patient must stay in bed at all times. The patient must eat, eliminate, and wash in bed; the bed must be changed with the patient in it. (This is called making an occupied bed.) Unconscious and semiconscious patients are on CBR by necessity; otherwise, doctors order CBR for more than a brief period only when absolutely necessary because of the risks to the cardiovascular, respiratory, musculoskeletal, and integumentary systems.

Orders for complete bed rest might be written in one of the following ways:

CBR

Bed rest

Strict CBR

When the doctor orders CBR, nurses may sometimes decide that it is less stressful to allow the patient to get up to use the bathroom or commode than to struggle with a bedpan. When the doctor orders "strict CBR," it means that the patient must not get out of bed for anything. Transcribe this order as written to maintain this emphasis.

Patients on CBR require certain extra nursing care to minimize its harmful effects.

Turning   Even the gentle pressure of a mattress, when applied to the same spot for a prolonged period, can cause tissue hypoxia and breakdown, especially on bony prominences, such as the hip bone, tail bone, and elbows. This pressure can cause decubitus ulcers (pressure sores or bedsores). The elderly, very thin people, and those with thin, dry skin are at increased risk. To alleviate pressure, patients unable to move about in bed themselves must be turned regularly. Realistically, nurses rarely have time to turn a patient more than once every two to four hours.

The physician may order "Turn q2–4h and PRN" or "turn q2h," or "turn q1h." Transcribe this order onto the Kardex or PI screen under Nursing Measures or Comfort Measures. If the doctor does not specify, nurses may make their own orders to turn a patient. The nurse will usually note the decision on the Kardex or enter it onto the PI screen under Nursing Care or Nursing Interventions.

Physiotherapy   Patients who are relatively or completely inactive must maintain mobility of all body parts to avoid muscle wasting, progressive muscle weakness, and contractures (permanent contraction). Physiotherapy is ordered to maintain muscle and joint functions or to regain lost mobility caused by disease, trauma, or surgery. Exercise may be classified as active (done by the patient independently), assisted (done by the patient with help), or passive (done by someone else, such as a physiotherapist, a nurse, or a trained family member). The physician may order **range of motion (ROM)** exercises: moving limbs through normal movements to take each joint through its complete range of positions.

range of motion (ROM) exercises   a set of exercises that puts joints through their full range of positions.

Bed Rest with Bathroom Privileges

"Bed rest with bathroom privileges" ("BR with BRP") means that the patient is allowed up only to go to the bathroom. Sometimes, even when getting up to go to the bathroom involves some discomfort or physical problem, it is less stressful than struggling with a bedpan or urinal. Most people find using these devices unpleasant. Some may be unable to defecate, both because of the psychological barrier and because of the awkward position, which does not allow gravity to help with the bowel movement. Bed rest with bathroom privileges is often a helpful compromise.

Bed Rest with Commode Privileges

When the doctor wants to allow an anatomically sound position for elimination but does not want the patient to walk, he may write this order, allowing the patient to get up only to use a commode. A commode is like a small chair with arms (Figure 21.1). Part of the seat is cut out and a bedpan fitted underneath. The commode can be brought right to the bedside.

Up in Chair

This order indicates that the patient may be out of bed and in a chair but may not ambulate freely around the room or out in the halls. The doctor may specify a frequency: "Up in chair bid" (or tid or qid). Sometimes a regular chair is used, and sometimes a special chair called a Geri-Chair—a large, reclining chair with footrest—is used, especially for

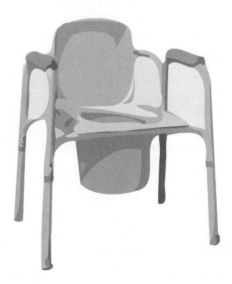

Figure 21.1   A commode

older adult patients and those with chronic medical problems. The patient allowed up in the chair is usually also allowed bathroom privileges unless otherwise stated.

Up with Assist

"Up with assist" means the patient may get up with someone helping him. "Up with one assist" means one person must help; "Up with two assists" means two people must help, one taking each arm. This may be ordered as "assist × 1" or "assist × 2."

Activity as Tolerated/Up Ad Lib

"Activity as tolerated" (AAT) or "up ad lib" means that there are no formal limits on the patient's activity. She may be as active as she can manage. This does not necessarily mean that the patient will be fully active. It means that the nurses should help the patient to be as active as appropriate for her physical abilities and energy needs. A postoperative patient, for example, will likely start with bed rest and progress to sitting in a chair, taking a short walk with a nurse's help, and ultimately to ambulating independently. Most people do walk on their first postoperative day. Sometimes, the doctor will order "Ambulate 1st postoperative day."

Occasionally, the surgeon will order that the patient "dangle" on the evening of the OR day. The nurses help the patient sit on the edge of the bed with her feet dangling over the side. Next, the patient may be able to sit in a chair briefly.

Restraints

Restraints include any physical or chemical means to prevent a patient, against his will, from moving or from moving a specific body part. Physical restraints include wrist and ankle restraints, mitts, and an abdominal or chest belt. In most facilities, a written doctor's order is needed for restraints. Orders for restraints may state "may use restraints PRN." Transcribe the order onto the Kardex or PI screen.

Restraints should be applied only to patients who endanger themselves or others, such as confused patients who may wander off and risk personal injury or who are interfering with medical treatment. Restraints may keep a patient in bed or in a chair. Sometimes, the wrists or upper torso are restrained to keep a patient from pulling at a dressing or pulling out an intravenous line or GI tube.

Whatever the reason, the use of restraints remains controversial. Their use can have serious legal implications for all involved. Their use must be ordered by a physician, and even then ethical, moral, and legal issues may arise. While they may, on occasion,

Tip

A patient may ask you for assistance out of bed, back to bed, or to the washroom. Do not attempt to help any patient ambulate, ever. This is a nursing responsibility. You cannot determine a patient's ability to support himself. Assisting without the proper techniques and knowledge can result in injury to the patient or to yourself. What you can do is find a nurse to help the patient as quickly as possible.

be deemed by some to be necessary, restraints usually make patients more restless and combative and are very disturbing for family members. The patient may be struggling, crying, shouting, begging, pleading, or bargaining with anyone who will listen to have the restraints removed. Even confused people seem to recognize that they are being held captive and hate it. Family members and friends may not understand the need for restraints and resent their use. They may protest:

"How could you do such a thing? Aunt Mary isn't dangerous. Take those off."

"Why have you got Dad tied into that chair? You are treating him like a common criminal."

"What kind of people are you? This is unacceptable. Take those off now."

You cannot deal with such issues. Remain calm and be empathetic. Imagine how you would feel if your mother or brother were tied into a chair and struggling to get out. Tell the family member that you will get the nurse so that they can discuss the matter.

Chemical restraints involve the use of sedation to immobilize a patient or to keep him quiet and sedated. Patients who are continually aggressive and combative are often kept sedated. The use of chemical restraints is also controversial.

❺ EQUIPMENT RELATED TO REST AND ACTIVITY

A NUMBER OF DEVICES RELATED TO REST AND ACTIVITY ARE USED. MOST OF THESE ARE ordered from Central Supply. Some may be kept in the patient-care unit.

Special Mattresses

To alleviate the effects of constant pressure, a doctor or nurse may order an alternating-pressure mattress (also called a ripple mattress or air mattress). This mattress is electric; a device applies alternating air pressure to various parts of the mattress. Another option is an egg-crate mattress, named for the varied heights of the surface. As the patient shifts in bed, a spot on the body will rest sometimes on a bump and sometimes on a hollow, producing variable pressure. Although not as effective as a ripple mattress, an egg-crate mattress does help and can be purchased for home use.

Sometimes, a sheepskin is also ordered—a pad made from the wool-pile of tanned and shorn sheepskin or lambskin. The high-density wool fibres provide a cushion that distributes the patient's weight and relieves pressure. The sheepskin also absorbs moisture. It must be changed and laundered frequently. Elbow and heel protectors made out of sheepskin are also available in most hospitals. They reduce reddening and chafing of the skin and help to prevent skin breakdown.

Anti-embolic Stockings

embolism obstruction of a blood vessel by a blood clot, an air bubble, or foreign matter.

Anti-embolism or pressure stockings (also called TED stockings for a common brand name) use elastic support to augment circulation in the legs, thus helping prevent **embolisms** and blood clots. They may be full length or calf length. They may be ordered for patients who are on bed rest, have poor circulation in the legs, or are at risk of developing clots. You may be responsible for ordering stockings from Stores or Central Supply by phone or computer. Although the stockings come only in small, medium, and large sizes, Supply usually wants the diameters of the calf and thigh and the length of the leg from groin to ankle. The nurse takes these measurements before giving you the order. Some physicians routinely use stockings for postoperative patients. In this case, the nurses usually have them available for the patient when he returns to the floor postoperatively. Some facilities have all the patients wear the stockings preoperatively.

Foot Boards

These are boards that fit at the bottom of the bed. The patient pushes her feet against them in exercising or to stay sitting up in bed. They also help to keep the patient from sliding down in the hospital bed.

Bed Cradles

A bed cradle is a hoop that fits over the bottom part of the bed to keep the covers off the patient's legs. This may be ordered for a patient with sensitive skin or one who has had leg trauma or surgery, such as for varicose veins.

Trapeze Bar

The trapeze bar is ordered for patients who need something to grab onto to assist with exercising, positioning themselves in bed, and getting in and out of bed. This is often used for patients who have had orthopedic surgery.

Abduction Pillow

A long, wedge-shaped, firm pillow, called an abduction pillow or wedge pillow, is used primarily immediately after hip surgery to keep the legs apart.

Side Rails

All hospital beds should have side rails. Some beds have one long side rail and others have two on each side, one that starts at the top and goes to the midpoint in the bed and the second starting at the midpoint and going close to the bottom. Side rails are used to help patients position themselves. They are also kept up when a patient has been sedated or is confused or unconscious.

Sometimes, the doctor will order "Keep side rails up." Often, patients feel claustrophobic if both side rails are up. Keeping one side rail up may be adequate. Sometimes, a physician will specify "Side rails up × 1." Usually, the nurses make that decision and decide on any other necessary safety measures. The nurses may write their own "nursing orders" and add them to the patient-care plan.

Hoyer Lift

A Hoyer lift is a device used to get patients who are too heavy to get up any other way out of the bed and perhaps into a chair. It operates with a series of supports and levers operated by a hydraulic pump. The Hoyer lift is found primarily in long-term care, rehab, and chronic care settings, but sometimes in acute-care settings as well.

Assistive Mobility Devices

A variety of assistive devices increase mobility. The most common assistive devices are canes, walkers, and wheelchairs. Some patients bring their assistive devices to the hospital with them, preferring to use the familiar devices they are comfortable with rather than rely on unfamiliar hospital supplies. Ensure that any devices that belong to patients are clearly labelled with their names. Keep them in a safe place—in the patients' rooms if there is space. Sometimes, other patients—or even nurses—borrow privately owned devices, thinking "Mr. Bowman won't mind." Patients *do* mind. Never suggest that a nurse might be able to use someone's personal property.

Most hospitals have a few wheelchairs available for patients to use. They are usually standard ones that fold up in the middle for easy storage. Even fairly mobile patients are often transported to other units in a wheelchair for speed and safety. In some hospitals, it remains the policy to discharge patients in a wheelchair regardless of their level of mobility. Patients who normally use wheelchairs may bring their own to the hospital. Motorized wheelchairs are not usually brought into the hospital but may be seen in a rehabilitation unit if space allows.

Patients who use wheelchairs routinely do so for a variety of reasons, including loss of limbs, weak leg muscles, spinal or brain injury or disease (including paralysis), and arthritis. For some, the use of a wheelchair is temporary; for others it may be permanent. Some people use wheelchairs only for longer distances and are able to walk short distances independently or with the use of other devices. Wheelchairs can become a routine part of a person's lifestyle; although people may think of someone as confined to a wheelchair, users often value the greater mobility and independence the wheelchair offers them. Do not assume that wheelchair users are necessarily particularly sick; certainly do not assume that they have mental limitations. Treat them with respect, as you would treat anyone, in and out of hospital. Wheelchairs should be kept in a designated place on the unit, and never left out where they can be a fire hazard or impede traffic flow on the unit.

ACTIVITIES OF DAILY LIVING

Think about the activities that you carry out as part of your daily routine. You probably take for granted

- getting up in the morning;
- going to the bathroom;
- brushing your teeth;
- washing your face, showering, or having a bath;
- eating your breakfast, lunch, and supper; and
- getting ready for bed.

Activities of daily living (ADL) are those activities performed every day as a routine part of self-care: eating, dressing, getting up, grooming, toileting, and bathing. Being able to complete ADL independently is important psychologically, affording the patient a sense of dignity and privacy. Nurses make every effort to help patients complete their own ADL or to do as much as possible on their own.

Following surgery, most patients rely on the nurses for much of this care but quickly progress to accomplishing much of their ADL independently. Patients with advanced disease states or conditions that interfere with muscle strength, coordination, or cognition need varying degrees of assistance. Some will need only a little help in reaching or need a steadying hand; others cannot participate at all. Quadriplegics may be reliant on health professionals but are fully aware of the tasks and their degree of dependence. They should be allowed to direct their own activities when possible.

Patients' ADL status may be classified as "independent" (or "self"), "self with assistance," or "by nurse." Doctors do not usually provide this information, but it must be noted on the health record. If you have the information, enter it on the Kardex or PI screen in the ADL section. If not, the nurses will add it after they have assessed the patient.

Future Trends

More and more, the effects of immobility are recognized as being detrimental to a person's recovery from almost any malady. Post-surgical patients are being mobilized earlier and earlier. In particular it is increasingly recognized that in the elderly a host of complications can be reduced or avoided by even small increments in activity level. Orders for ambulation may well be more open—for a patient to ambulate as soon as able—as opposed to bed rest orders. Primary care givers (nurses, physiotherapists) will have a greater involvement in making decisions regarding rest and activity. Patients will be pressed into ambulating earlier with, of course, appropriate pain management. Community resources will also retain a focus on keeping individuals as mobile as possible.

The benefits of exercise are widening to include psychological wellness, the reduction of stress, and preservation of memory.

The Canadian government continues to advertise the benefits of general exercise. One thrust is to encourage Canadians to walk half an hour a day, instead of an hour, because it is deemed more realistic. Often people will not exercise at all if the recommendations are too hefty—so it is hoped that recommending a more manageable routine will activate more people. Participaction Canada recognizes the increasing problem of inactivity as part of the growing trend of obesity and diabetes in children. Thus part of the Participaction campaign is to encourage lifestyle changes in children and teens.

SUMMARY

1. Each patient admitted to hospital must have an activity order written by a physician. It is important to find a balance between activity and rest. Activity levels are individualized to the patient's condition and capabilities. Usually, these orders are only noted on the Kardex or PI screen. A requisition is needed only if staff other than nurses (e.g., physiotherapists) are involved.

2. The use of restraints is controversial. They must be ordered by a physician. They may be physical (e.g., wrist restraints) or chemical (sedatives). If family members are upset by restraints, be empathetic and refer them to the nurse.

3. Any time a patient leaves the unit for an appointment or test, make sure anyone working with the patient is aware of her mobility and ability to cooperate. This information is required on requisitions for tests conducted off the unit.

4. Common activity orders include complete bed rest (CBR); bed rest with bathroom privileges ("BR with BRP"); and activity as tolerated (AAT or "up ad lib"). An order may specify that a patient needs help getting up ("assist 1" or "assist 2").

5. To prevent bedsores, patients who cannot move about in bed must be turned or repositioned, usually every two to four hours.

6. Devices to support rest and activity include special mattresses to vary pressure, anti-embolic stockings, foot boards, bed cradles, trapeze bars, abduction pillows, side rails, and lifts.

7. Activities of daily living include eating, dressing, getting up, performing hygiene, grooming, toileting, and bathing. Patients' ADL status may be "independent," "self with assist," or "by nurse." Because taking care of their own basic needs preserves dignity and privacy, patients should be helped to do as much as they can.

Key Terms

embolism 634
hypostatic pneumonia 629

range of motion (ROM)
exercises 632

weight bearing 629

Review Questions

1. What is the philosophy behind encouraging the patient to be as active as possible as soon as possible?

2. What criteria does the physician consider when ordering a patient's level of activity?

3. When is a requisition needed for activity orders?

4. Where are activity orders usually transcribed?

5. Why do nurses turn immobile patients?

6. Why is the use of restraints controversial?

7. Explain the purpose of anti-embolic stockings. Where would you order them from? What measurements would you need?

8. What is a Geri-Chair?

9. What is a Hoyer lift used for?

10. What information must you note when requisitioning a test off the unit? Why?

Application Exercises

1. Define each of the following rest and activity orders, and explain when it would be given. Using the format of the Kardex shown in Figure 21.2 or one supplied by your professor, transcribe each order appropriately:

   a. AAT

   b. BR with BRP

   c. Up assist 1

   d. Commode privileges

   e. Strict bed rest

   f. Turn q2h

   g. Nurse in prone position

TEACHING/EMOTIONAL SUPPORT	ELIMINATION	Order Date		Order Date	X-RAYS	
Pre/postop	BR					
Extra teaching	Catheter:					
Emotional support						
	Hygiene:					
	Self					
Vital signs	Assisted				LAB	
Q shift ×1 (routine)	Complete					
A shift ×2						
Q2-4 hrs					X-rays	
Post-op ×48 hrs	Other direct care:					
	Ht/Wt					
Activity	Urine testing					
Self	Finger prick BS					
Assisted ×1						

Figure 21.2 Kardex for Exercise 1

h. Up with physio

i. ROM qid by physio

j. May be up in Geri-Chair PRN

2. Fred, 72 years old, has been hospitalized and is new on your unit. You go down to discuss his menu choices with him. Fred looks desperate as you enter the room. He pleads with you to help him get up to the bathroom, and to put his side rails down. He claims it has been over an hour since he called for the nurse and he can't wait any longer. He looks fit and appears oriented. With another student, discuss what you would do. List reasons why you might want to help him, and reasons why not. Discuss the risks involved both for yourself and for Fred. How can you maintain his dignity and show compassion, yet stay within your scope of practice? Are there extenuating circumstances under which assisting him to the bathroom would be acceptable?

3. Janice comes to the floor to find her elderly mother in a Geri-Chair with a chest restraint and arm restraints on. She has an IV. Janice is furious and lashes out at you, asking how the staff could sanction such inhumane and cruel behaviour. She claims her mom is a little confused but does not deserve this. The patient is anxious and crying at this point, asking to be untied. There is no nurse in sight. The daughter moves to take off the restraints. With a classmate, review this situation and discuss how you would deal with it, and what you might say to the daughter.

4. Mrs. James arrives at the patient-care unit to find her mother, Mrs. Anderson, sitting in the hall in a Geri-Chair. She is held in the chair with an abdominal restraint, and her wrists are tied to the arms of the chair. Her hair is messy. She has her hose rolled down to below her knees and no shoes on. She is crying and saying, "Get me out. Oh God, get me out! Look what they are doing to me. I want to go home. Please let me go." Mrs. James stands for a moment looking at her mother. She bursts into tears and turns to the nursing station where you are sitting. "How could you? How could you? Look at her! Do you people have no compassion?" Her voice is rising. You look around and see no nurses. How would you handle this situation?

Websites of Interest

Explanation of Decubitus Ulcers or Pressure Sores
http://www.apparelyzed.com/pressuresores.html
Excellent explanation of pressure sores, emphasizing the importance of written orders for prevention and care of them.

Walkers
http://www.youtube.com/watch?v=OH5fRCAi5gc
Explanation of the types and uses of walkers.

Restraints
www.cno.org/docs/prac/41043_Restraints.pdf

How to Use a Hoyer Lift
http://www.thiscaringhome.org/spec_concerns/vid_7_usingahoyerlift.php
This video will give you an appreciation of how time-consuming it is to get a patient up using a Hoyer lift, as well as how careful the nurses have to be to ensure patient safety.

Glossary

absorption the process by which a medication is taken into to the body, broken down, and transformed into a form that the body can use.

active infection an infection in which signs and symptoms are present.

acute care care for a client who is acutely ill, that is, very ill but with an illness expected to run a short course (as opposed to a chronic illness). Acute care is provided for clients with a variety of health problems.

acute infection an infection that is time limited.

aerobic bacteria bacteria that require oxygen to grow.

affinity, cluster, categorization, or analogous scheduling scheduling similar appointments together, for example, scheduling physical examinations on a certain day.

allied health care any duty or profession that supports primary health-care professionals, such as physicians, in delivering health-care services.

alternative health care or complementary health care nontraditional methods and practices, based on a natural approach, including chiropractic, acupuncture, massage, and aromatherapy.

anaerobic bacteria bacteria that do not require oxygen to grow.

angiocatheter or angiocath a plastic tube, usually attached to the puncturing needle, inserted into a blood vessel for infusion, injection, or pressure monitoring.

antenatal before birth.

antibody a protein specific to a certain antigen that weakens or destroys pathogens.

antigen a pathogen or any other substance that induces an antibody response.

antiseptic a cleansing agent that can be applied to living tissue to destroy pathogens.

archive to remove a file from active status and store it in a secondary location or on a secondary medium.

arrhythmia loss of normal rhythm of the heartbeat.

arteriosclerosis hardening of the arteries; reduces blood flow.

asepsis a state in which pathogens are absent or reduced. There are two principal types of asepsis: medical and surgical.

asthma a disease that affects the air passages in the lung, causing wheezing and shortness of breath.

asymptomatic without clinical signs or symptoms.

atherosclerosis arteriosclerosis because of deposits of fat in arterial walls.

atrial fibrillation an abnormality of heart rhythm in which chambers of the heart no longer beat in synchrony, with the atrium beating much faster than the ventricles. The heart rate is fast and irregular.

attribute an inborn personal quality or characteristic.

auscultate listen to the sounds made by a body structure as a diagnostic method.

autoclave a device using steam for sterilization.

autonomy a person's right to self-determination. In health care it refers to a patient's/client's right to make his own decisions without coercion—decisions for treatment, for example, based on fact and being fully informed of all treatment options.

autopsy the examination of a body to determine the cause of death and/or to identify disease processes.

auxiliary file a temporary filing space for files in current use.

bactericidal killing microorganisms.

bacteriostatic reducing or inhibiting the number of microorganisms.

Bard button (MIC device) a feeding device placed permanently in the stomach to facilitate supplemental feedings.

behaviour a person's discernible responses and actions.

beneficiary a person eligible to receive insurance benefits under specified conditions.

billing code, service code, item code, or fee code a number that identifies the service a provider has performed for an insured client and that determines the fee to be paid by a provincial or territorial health plan.

bolus the usually rapid infusion of additional IV fluids in addition to the base amount ordered for the client.

bowel obstruction a blockage in the intestines that prevents their contents from moving forward.

bowel resection (anastomosis or end-to-end anastomosis) surgery wherein a section of bowel is removed, and the remaining bowel is reconnected.

bowel sounds present (BSP) the audible return of gastrointestinal movement or function, also called peristalsis, often charted as BS X4, meaning it sounds audible in all four abdominal quadrants.

bradycardia extremely slow heartbeat.

bruit a sound, especially an abnormal one, heard on auscultation or by ultrasound.

capitation or population-based funding a funding system that pays a physician a given amount per patient enrolled, regardless of the number of services performed.

cc cubic centimeter; 1 cc equals 1 millilitre (mL). In hospitals, cc is used more often than mL.

cerebral vascular accident (CVA) (stroke) damage to the brain that occurs when the blood supply to an area of the brain is diminished or occluded completely.

chronic care care for someone with a chronic illness, that is, one that typically progresses slowly but lasts for a long time, often lifelong.

chronic infection one that is persistent over a long period, perhaps for life.

chronic obstructive lung disease (COLD) or chronic obstructive pulmonary disease (COPD) any chronic lung condition in which the flow of expired air is slowed down.

clapping or percussion using cupped hands to gently but firmly strike affected regions of the chest to move secretions.

client a person seeking or receiving health care; synonymous with patient, but suggests a more active role.

clinic a facility providing medical care on an outpatient basis. Many clinics have a specialty, such as ongoing care for diabetes or cancer.

clinical secretary (SC) or ward clerk a health office professional working in a hospital; an individual who assumes responsibilities for the secretarial, clerical, communication, and other designated needs of a hospital unit or department.

code of ethics a set of guidelines for ethical conduct.

collaborative partnership the relationship among hospitals that have entered into an agreement to form a partnership, sharing clinical and administrative responsibilities.

colostomy a surgical procedure that creates an artificial opening from the colon to the surface of the abdomen, through which feces are excreted.

combination scheduling or blended scheduling a combination of affinity and random scheduling.

computed tomography (CT) a type of X-ray that produces three-dimensional images of cross-sections of body parts.

congestive heart failure (CHF) a condition in which a weakened heart is unable to pump all of the blood out of the lungs each time it beats. Blood pools at the bottom of the lungs, interfering with breathing.

contagious or communicable disease a disease that is spread from person to person.

contamination the presence of pathogens on an object.

controlled drugs drugs defined by federal law to which special rules apply because they are liable to be abused.

core competency the basic or essential skills that one needs to succeed in a particular profession.

crackles or crepitation sounds produced by air passing over airway secretions.

crash cart a cart carrying the supplies needed for immediate treatment of a heart attack.

credentialling a process whereby a peer group judges an individual's qualifications to perform certain services.

critical value a test result that so deviates from normal that it causes concern for the client's immediate well-being.

critical value one that indicates a life-threatening situation and requires immediate attention.

critically ill experiencing life-threatening problems; in medical crisis.

cross-coverage moving from one area to another, or covering two units.

culture the languages, beliefs, values, norms, behaviours, and even material objects that are passed from one generation to the next.

cystectomy surgical removal of the urinary bladder.

cystoscope a long, thin, flexible instrument with a light at the end used to examine the bladder. It is inserted through the urethra and threaded up into the bladder.

day surgery surgery conducted with a hospital stay of less than 24 hours.

deductible the portion of a benefit that a beneficiary must pay before receiving coverage.

deep suctioning introducing the suction catheter into the lower trachea and bronchi.

deregulated (of a service) removed from a province's or territory's fee schedule so that it is no longer insured under that jurisdiction's health plan.

diastolic pressure the pressure of the vascular walls when the heart is relaxing.

discharge any release from a health-care facility by doctor's orders.

disinfectant a chemical substance that destroys or eliminates specific species of infectious microorganisms. It is not usually effective against bacterial spores.

disinfection a more thorough removal of contaminants than sanitization but less thorough than sterilization.

distal the part furthest from the body.

distribution the process by which metabolites are transported to various parts of the body.

diverticulitis inflammation of a sac-like bulge that may develop in the wall of the large intestine.

doctors' orders written or oral directions given by a physician to the nursing staff and other health professionals regarding the care, medications, treatment, and laboratory and diagnostic tests a client is to receive while in hospital.

double scheduling or double-column booking scheduling two client appointments at the same time, on the assumption that one of the appointments will involve little of the doctor's time.

dressing tray a specially prepared sterile tray containing the basic equipment to change a dressing on a wound or surgical incision. It contains a K-basin, 4 x 4 gauze dressings, a galley cup (a small metal or glass cup about the size of a shot glass used for cleansing solutions), and usually two sets of disposable forceps.

drops per minute (gtt/min) a measure of the rate if IV infusion.

duty a moral obligation.

dysphagia difficulty swallowing.

dyspnea difficulty breathing.

elective surgery nonemergency, planned surgery, booked in advance.

elective surgery surgery that is necessary but not an emergency and can therefore be booked in advance. Examples of elective surgery include removal of a tumour, a hip replacement, or a hysterectomy. Appendicitis usually necessitates emergency surgery.

electronic health record (EHR) an accumulation of essential information from an individual's electronic medical records that is accessed electronically at different points of service for purposes of client care.

electronic medical record (EMR) a legal health record in digital format. It contains the client's health information collected by one or a group of providers in one location. It is a subset of the electronic health record (EHR).

electronic medical records systems a total medical office system, including both hardware and software, with the capability of replacing all components of a paper chart (health record) electronically.

electronic transfer (ET) vehicle for the electronic transmission of medical claims from the source computer to the Ministry's mainframe computer.

embolism obstruction of a blood vessel by a blood clot, an air bubble, or foreign matter.

emergentologist a physician specializing in emergency medicine.

emesis basin (kidney basin or K-basin) a small basin, usually kidney shaped, used for clients to vomit into or cough up sputum or phlegm. It is also used to hold solutions for a variety of purposes. It may be ordered sterile or just clean.

emphysema a disease characterized by gradual destruction of the alveoli, which fuse to form larger air spaces. Exchange of oxygen and carbon dioxide through these larger air sacs is inadequate.

endoscopy examination of a canal, such as the colon, with an endoscope: a thin tube with lenses to allow visualization.

endotracheal suctioning suctioning through an artificial airway known as a tracheostomy.

enema the introduction of liquid into the rectum for cleansing the bowel and for stimulating evacuation of the bowels.

enteral feed feeding by tube directly into the gastrointestinal system.

enzyme a protein capable of initiating a chemical reaction that involves the formation or breakage of chemical bonds. When muscle damage or death occurs, enzymes within the muscle cell are released into the circulating blood.

ethics the philosophical study of standards accepted by society that determine what is right and wrong in human behaviour.

ethnic relating to groups of people with a common racial, religious, linguistic, or cultural heritage.

ethnocentrism the tendency to use our own culture's standards as the yardstick to judge everyone; the belief in the superiority of our own group or culture.

exacerbation a period in which a chronic infection shows symptoms.

exacerbation the phase of a chronic disease characterized by a return of clinical signs or symptoms.

externship a cooperative or workplace experience or period of training for a student that is provided by the student's educational facility.

extra billing charging a client more than the amount paid by the provincial or territorial health plan for a medically necessary service.

family physician an MD with a specialty in family medicine who looks after the general medical needs of a varied practice population.

fee for service a system under which a provider is paid for each insured service rendered to an insured client.

fidelity the ethical principle of faithfulness. In health care it refers to carrying out obligations and duties to employers, clients, and peers. It also means keeping commitments.

fixed oils (also called base or carrier oils) oils, extracted primarily from plants, that do not evaporate.

flag (of a chart) to draw attention to a new entry by sticking a coloured marker in, placing a coloured sticker on the back, or using some other device to visually draw attention.

fluid retention an accumulation of fluid in body tissues or body cavities.

fob a small security device that can be added to a computer for access purposes. It displays a randomly generated access code that changes every few seconds.

fundus the top of the uterus. Measuring how high the fundus is in the abdomen provides valuable information about the size of the uterus and the progression of fetal growth.

gastric suction gentle suction applied to a tube placed in the stomach to remove excessive secretions, such as saliva and gastric juices, that tend to accumulate in the stomach after surgery or trauma because the intestine is sluggish. This can prevent or relieve nausea and vomiting.

gastritis inflammation of the stomach.

gastrostomy tube (G-tube) a feeding tube inserted through an incision in the abdomen into the stomach.

global budget any arrangement in which a facility or provider receives a fixed amount of money for medical services, regardless of patient volume, length of stay, or services rendered.

head injury routine a special assessment for a client who has had head trauma or surgery, including checks on neurological functioning, such as verbal response and pupil dilation.

health information custodian a person, persons, or organization who has the responsibility for safekeeping and controlling personal health information in connection with the powers and duties performed.

health information any information pertaining to someone's physical or mental health, condition or infirmity, whether given orally or recorded in any manner, that is created or received directly or indirectly by a health professional or health organization.

health office professional (HOP) a graduate from an accredited health office administration program who assumes administrative, communication, and/or clinical responsibilities in a health-care setting. Depending on the occupational setting, this graduate may be assigned such job titles as *medical secretary* or *medical office assistant*. In the hospital setting, titles include *nursing coordinator, communications coordinator, communications clerk, ward clerk,* and *clinical secretary.* Dental offices use the titles *dental practice receptionist, dental health office manager, dental treatment coordinator,* and *dental administrative assistant.* Such terms as *clinical secretary* may be used in this book if relevant to the specific occupational setting being discussed.

health record any documentation relating to a health-care client. The term *record* is used for a single document, such as a doctor's note on an assessment or a lab report; it also refers to a collection of documents, such as a client's chart.

health according to one definition, "a relative state in which one is able to function well physically, mentally, socially, and spiritually in order to express the full range of one's unique potentialities within the environment in which one is living."

hemorrhage loss of a large amount of blood (greater than 500 cc for an average adult).

heparin an anticoagulant (blood thinner) given to people who are at risk for developing blood clots.

heparin (hep) lock (saline lock, PRN adapter) a device that provides intravenous access when needed, without continuous infusion. It sits at the vein and must be flushed at specific intervals with saline solution or heparin solution.

hiatus hernia a condition in which the upper part of the stomach, which is joined to the esophagus or feeding tube, moves up into the chest through a hole (called a hiatus) in the diaphragm.

homeostasis a balance between the body's internal conditions and the environment.

hospital number a unique number assigned to each client admitted to hospital.

hypertension or high blood pressure excessive force of the blood against the vessel walls as the heart pumps it through the body.

hypostatic pneumonia pneumonia developing as a result of decreased air exchange combined with an inability to drain pooled bronchial secretions.

hypoxia insufficient oxygen in blood or tissue.

identification (ID) band a plastic bracelet bearing the client's name and hospital number that can be removed only by cutting.

ileostomy a surgical procedure that creates an artificial opening from the ileum to the surface of abdomen, through which feces are excreted.

immunity an individual's ability to fight off disease.

immunoglobulin a serum that contains antibodies that can help protect an exposed person from contracting the disease.

incontinence inability to control urine elimination (urinary incontinence) or bowel function (referred to as "incontinent of bowel").

indwelling left in place.

infection a disease process that results from the entry and spread of a microorganism.

insured health-care services medically necessary hospital, physician, and surgical-dental services provided to insured persons.

interstitial in between the body's cells.

intracellular within the cells of the body.

intravascular within blood vessels.

intravenous (IV) administered directly into the circulatory system via a vein.

ischemia a local lack of red blood cells because of mechanical obstruction of the blood supply, usually caused by arterial narrowing.

IV push (IVP) a medication given into the vein or an ongoing IV infusion, using a syringe and a needle.

jejunostomy tube (J-tube) a feeding tube placed through the abdominal wall into the small bowel.

Kardex commonly used proprietary name for a paper-based client care document or health record.

kidney stones or calculi hard objects built up from salts and minerals in the urinary tract.

laparoscope a type of endoscope (a visualizing instrument with a tube and lens) that allows surgeons to visualize internal structures. Using this tool, surgery can be done through incisions often 5 cm in length or smaller.

latent infection one in which the symptoms disappear and recur, while the disease-causing agent remains in the body.

licensure a legal document, obtained after passing written and clinical examinations, that is required for health-care practitioners in regulated fields.

loading dose a medication ordered as a single-order stat medication with a dose that is higher than the usual or routine dose.

local infection an infection that is confined to a specific region of the body, for example, a finger.

locum tenens (locum) a doctor temporarily taking over another doctor's practice.

machine-readable input (MRI) any information that can be read by a computer.

magnetic resonance imaging (MRI) a diagnostic tool that uses a magnetic field to produce images of body structures and organs.

mammography a specialized X-ray of the breast.

managed care a set of strategies, procedures, and policies designed to control the use of health-care services, sometimes by organizing doctors, hospitals, and other providers into groups in order to improve the quality and cost-effectiveness of health care.

medical assistant (U.S.) a person who is trained to assist a physician with various clinical tests, examinations, and procedures.

medical office assistant (Canada) a person who handles primarily administrative but also some clinical duties in a health office.

medically necessary referring to those services or supplies that are essential to the care and treatment of an illness or injury and that could not have been omitted without adversely affecting the client's medical condition or the quality of the health care rendered under generally accepted professional standards of medical practice at the time and place incurred.

metabolic disorder a condition characterized by the body's inability to synthesize or process food into forms the body can use for energy, growth, and development.

metabolic rate the amount of energy expended in a given period, or the physical changes that occur in the body that result in heat production.

metabolism the physiological and biochemical processes that promote growth and sustain life.

metabolism the process of breaking down a drug or other substance into metabolites used by the body.

microorganism an organism so small that it can only be seen under a microscope.

midstream urine specimen (MSU) also called clean catch urine specimen; a urine specimen collected after cleansing oneself and discarding the first part of the urine stream in order to avoid contamination; used for culture and sensitivity tests.

morals what a person believes to be right and wrong pertaining to how to act, treat others, and get along in an organized society.

myocardial infarct (MI, heart attack, or coronary) damage to the heart caused by a blockage in one of the coronary arteries, cutting off blood supply to a part of the heart.

nasogastric tube (N-G tube or Levine tube) a feeding tube put through the nose into the stomach.

nasopharyngeal suctioning suctioning with a catheter through the nose to reach the mouth and throat (pharynx).

new admission a client recently admitted to hospital.

nonpathogenic not causing disease.

nonretention or straight catheter one inserted to drain urine and then removed.

nosocomial infection a hospital-related infection; one that is not present or incubating when a patient is admitted to a hospital or a health-care facility.

ophthalmic relating to the eye.

ophthalmoscope a device used to examine the eyes.

opportunistic infection an infection that does not ordinarily cause disease but does so under certain circumstances, for example, in compromised immune systems; so called because it takes advantage of an "opportunity."

opted-in (of a physician) billing the provincial or territorial plan for health services rendered.

opted-out (of a physician) billing clients for services rendered; clients pay the fee to the doctor and submit a claim to the health plan. Very few physicians chose to opt out. This may change, however, if private health care becomes more prevalent and clients can buy private insurance for medically necessary services.

order entry (order dispensation, order processing) the process of interpreting, recording, and generating the administrative steps required for doctor's orders to be implemented.

oropharyngeal suctioning suctioning with a catheter through the mouth to reach the mouth only or the mouth and the back of the throat.

orphan patient a client who does not have a family physician and must get medical services from clinics and emergency departments.

otic via the ear.

otitis media infection of the middle ear.

otoscope a device used to examine the ears.

outguiding system or charge-out system a system for keeping track of paper health records taken from their normal location.

palliative care care for a person with a terminal illness who is in hospital to die, to have the condition stabilized, or for pain control.

parenteral by injection or intravenous administration.

partial claims payment a payment to a provider of a lesser amount than that claimed; an explanation will be given of why the payment was reduced.

pathogen a microorganism that causes disease.

patient intervention screen (PI screen) or electronic health record a computer-based client-care document containing the same information as a Kardex. This is an electronic version of a traditional Kardex.

percutaneous endoscopic gastrostomy tube (PEG tube, PEG catheter) a feeding tube inserted via endoscopy into the stomach or jejunum.

peristalsis wavelike movements of the gastrointestinal tract that propel food and other contents along.

pharmacology a biological science and academic discipline that deals with the properties, uses, and action of drugs and chemicals in living beings.

physician registration number or billing number a unique number assigned by the Ministry of Health to every provider eligible to bill a provincial or territorial health plan, and required for billing.

placebo effect an improvement in symptoms without active treatment that occurs for psychological reasons when a person thinks he is getting treatment.

pneumonia an acute infection of the tissues of the lung.

postexposure prophylaxis (PEP) treatment after exposure to a pathogen, aimed at preventing infection.

postpartum after delivery.

postural drainage positioning the client with the head lower than the body so that gravity can help drain the mucus and secretions.

pre-admission a process wherein clients who are booked for surgery receive preoperative and postoperative teaching and fill in documents ahead of time.

preceptor a mentor who guides and supervises a student throughout a workplace experience.

primary care reform groups, or primary care groups (PCGs) a variety of structurally similar groups of physicians and/or other health professionals working collaboratively under an organizational framework to deliver primary health services. The health professionals may or may not be in one physical location.

primary health care (1) integrated health care by a provider who addresses the majority of a client's health concerns; (2) treatment administered during the first medical contact for a health concern.

prophylactic a measure taken to prevent a problem from developing.

provider any person or group of persons who delivers a health-care service.

provincial or territorial billing the process whereby a health-care provider submits a claim to a province or territory for insured health services rendered.

provisional diagnosis a diagnosis subject to change after an actual diagnosis has been established.

provisional diagnosis a tentative diagnosis made before a procedure is done, which may be confirmed or changed by findings.

purge (of file) review and reorganize to remove outdated or irrelevant information.

quality assurance any systematic process of checking to see whether a product or service is meeting specified requirements. In health care, it is a systematic assessment to ensure that services are of the highest possible quality using existing resources.

quarantine isolating or separating a client, client-care unit, or facility.

range of motion (ROM) exercises a set of exercises that puts joints through their full range of positions.

rationalization of services centralizing certain services, particularly those that require specialized care, to one hospital in a region.

recurrent infection a distinct episode of an infection after recovery from the initial infection; may involve the same pathogens or different ones.

reference range the normal range; the values expected for a particular test.

regulated profession one legally restricted to practitioners with a specific professional qualification and/or provincial or territorial registration.

relapse the re-emergence of an initial infection after it appears to have subsided but has not been cured.

remission a period in which a chronic infection shows no symptoms.

remission the phase of a chronic disease characterized by a relief or absence of clinical signs or symptoms.

remittance advice (RA) a monthly statement of approved claims from the Ministry.

rhonchi or wheezes musical-pitched sounds produced by air passing through narrowed bronchi, heard on auscultation of the lungs.

right a moral, legal, cultural, or traditional claim.

role a position in life that carries expectations of responsibilities and of appropriate behaviour.

rostering establishing a list of clients who agree to participate in a primary health network according to the rules of the province or territory.

sanitization removal of gross contaminants and some microorganisms from instruments, skin, and so on; the lowest level of medical hygiene.

sanitizer a substance that significantly reduces the bacterial population in an inanimate environment but does not destroy all bacteria or other microorganisms.

scope of practice working within the parameters of duties and responsibilities outlined by one's professional training and skill set.

serum the fluid portion of the blood. Often used in phrases describing levels of blood components, as in serum creatinine.

sharp any instrument with a sharp edge or point, such as a scalpel, scissors, or a needle.

shift report essential client information passed on to the next shift of nurses.

sick role a particular social role that an ill person adopts, which involves giving up normal responsibilities and accepting care. May sometimes involve uncharacteristically passive behaviour.

specialist a physician who holds a certificate from the Royal College of Physicians and Surgeons and who has completed postgraduate studies in a particular specialty field.

sphygmomanometer a device used to take blood pressure.

stat (short for Latin statim) immediately.

sterilant a substance that destroys or eliminates all forms of microbial life in an inanimate environment.

sterile technique methods to avoid contamination of sterile materials.

sterile completely free of pathogens.

sterilization the process of destroying all microorganisms, including bacterial endospores and viruses. This is the highest level of cleanliness.

stethoscope a device that amplifies sound, used by doctors and other health-care professionals to listen to the heart and to take blood pressure.

stoma an artificial opening, in this case, one from the bowel through the abdominal wall.

stream scheduling or fixed-interval scheduling allotting a specific, unique time slot for each client appointment; the most common method of scheduling.

subacute, transitional, or step-down care medical and nursing care less intensive than traditional acute-care hospital treatment.

subculture the values and practices of a group that distinguish it from the larger culture.

subdural hematoma a blood clot under the dura mater, the fibrous membrane forming the outer envelope of the brain and spinal cord, usually resulting from trauma to the head.

suture removal tray a specially prepared sterile tray similar to the dressing tray, but containing suture removal scissors or clip removers. Some facilities use a dressing tray, and nurses add a disposable suture removal blade or prepackaged clip removers.

systemic infection an infection that has spread to more than one region of the body.

systemic circulating through the bloodstream to produce a general effect on the body.

systolic pressure the pressure on the vascular walls when the heart is contracting.

teratogenic causing abnormalities in the fetus.

terminal cleaning a thorough wash with a disinfectant solution of all equipment (bed, bedside unit, and so on) used by a client upon her discharge.

terminal cleaning the bed and other furniture used by the client are thoroughly cleaned with a specifically selected disinfectant solution.

third-party service a service carried out at the request of someone other than the client or for the explicit use of someone other than the client.

topical applied to the skin or affected area.

tracheostomy an artificial airway through an incision in the trachea.

transcription creating a written copy of a dictated or recorded message.

transfer the act of moving a client from one place to another within the same health-care facility.

triage assessing the seriousness of a client's presenting problem to determine who needs to have medical help first. For example, someone coming to the emergency department with chest pain would be brought in to see the doctor immediately, whereas someone with a sore throat would be considered a non-urgent case and able to wait.

ulcerative colitis inflammation and ulceration of the innermost lining of the colon (the large intestine).

ultrasonographer a technician who operates an ultrasound machine.

ultrasonography a procedure that uses high-frequency sound waves directed at an organ or object to produce a visual image.

values the beliefs a person holds dear and that guide that person's decisions and behaviour or conduct.

vibrations rapid movements of flattened hands over the client's chest to move secretions.

virulence the power of a microbe to produce disease in a particular host.

volatile oils oils, extracted primarily from plants, that evaporate

ward clerk an individual who manages the administrative and communication needs of a client care unit. The title is being replaced with *clinical secretary* or *communications coordinator*.

wave scheduling scheduling several clients for the same block of time, typically an hour.

weight bearing putting body weight on the lower limbs.

wellness a state of physical and emotional well-being, broadly considered.

workload analysis a software component that tracks types of care provided as a basis for billing the provincial or territorial health-care plan.

Photo Credits

Index

enteral feeds, 586, 588–589
enteric-coated medications, 189
environment
    health, 133
    of hospitals, 69
    manual, 566–569
    risk factors, 137
    workplace, 22–23
Environmental Engineering Department,
    443–444
Environmental Services, 443
enzyme, 154
EPs. *See* eligible providers
Equalization, 86
ERCP. *See* endoscopic retrograde
    cholangiopancreatography
e-referrals. *See* electronic referrals
error codes, 366
ERs. *See* emergency rooms
ER sheet, 477*f*–478*f*
erythrocyte sedimentation rate (ESR), 149
Escherichia coli (*E. coli*), 114
Esmail, Nadeem, 57, 102
ESR. *See* erythrocyte sedimentation rate
Essential Research, 256
Established Programs Financing, 83*t*
ET. *See* electronic transfer
ethics, 17
    attitude, 15
    code of, 17
    decision making, 19
    principles, 17–18
ethnic, 64
ethnicity, 64–65
ethnocentrism, 66
exacerbation, 71, 113
examination
    annual, 334, 336–337
    assisting with, 133
    complete, 334
    complete physical, 401
excretion, 192
exercise, 637
exercise ECG, 164
expiration date, 305
explanatory codes, 366
explanatory systems, 71–72
externship, 29, 30
extra-billing, 96, 385
extraordinary life support, 73
eye contact, 77
eye protection, 132

F

face shield, 132

face-to-face communication with clients,
    246–249
facility number, 375
factor VIII, 570, 571
Fair PharmaCare, 298
faithfulness, 18
family
    information about, 238
    of patient, 495
    visit, 280
Family Caregiver Leave, 47
Family Health Clinics, 89
family health groups (FNGs), 90
family health networks (FHNs), 90
family health organizations (FNOs), 90
Family Health Teams, 89
family physicians, 87–88, 101
family practice, 88
    prefixes used in, 357*t*
Family Responsibility Leave, 47
fasting blood sugar (FBS), 153
fatigue, 136
fax machine
    doctors' orders forms, 510
    faxes, receiving and sending, 214–215
    pharmacies, 215
    prescriptions, 215
    prescription requests, 202–203
    reports, 216
    scanning, 216
    specialty appointments, 215
FBS. *See* fasting blood sugar
FDA. See Food and Drug Act
federal government, 85
federal hospitals, 438
fee code, 330
fee-for-service (FFS), 93, 95
    providers eligible to bill, 98–101
    remuneration, 293
fee submitted, 378
FFS. *See* fee-for-service
FHNs. *See* family health networks
file organization, 419
file reject message, 381
filing systems
    alphabetical, 419
    centralized, 420
    colour coding, 420
    consecutive numeric, 419
    decentralized, 420
    file organization, 419
    identification systems, 418–420
    numeric, 419
    office forms, 421
    pCharts, 420

    phonetic, 419
    soundex, 419
    source-oriented, 171
    terminal digit, 419–420
financial security, 56
financing, 85–87
First Nations, 71
fixed-interval scheduling, 274
fixed office hours, 270–271
fixed oils, 179
flag, 526
Flagyl, 115
Fleet enema, 595
flexibility, 14
flow rate, 564
flow sheet, 401
    diabetes, 415*f*
    vital signs, 483
fluids, 553–554
    balance sheet, 492
    clear fluids diet, 582
    full fluids diet, 582–583
    retention, 580
FNGs. *See* family health groups
FNOs. *See* family health organizations
fob, 403
Foley catheter, 603
food
    allergies, 193–194
    boards, 635
    Canada's Food Guide, 578
Food and Drug Act (FDA), 181, 195
forms management, 429
forms submission, 220
fraudulent health cards, 325
Freedom of Information and Privacy Act, 348
fresh frozen plasma, 571
friendly personality, 13
full fluids diet, 582–583
fully structured, 402
funding, population-based, 93
fundus, 337
fungi, 115
    antifungal, 185
future trends
    AHPs, 32
    appointment scheduling, 287–288
    billing, 352, 392
    communication, 255–256
    culture, 77–78
    diagnostic tests, 172–173, 606
    diseases, 137–138
    exercise, 637
    health-care plans, 315
    health-care system, 101–102